Microsoft® Office XP 8-in-1

Joe Habraken

201 West 103rd Street, Indianapolis, Indiana 46290 USA

Microsoft® Office XP 8-in-1

International Standard Book Number: 0-7897-2509-6

Library of Congress Catalog Card Number: 2001087725

Printed in the United States of America

First Printing: June, 2001

04   03   02   01   4   3   2   1

Trademarks

Warning and Disclaimer

Associate Publisher
Greg Wiegand

Acquisitions Editor
Stephanie J. McComb

Development Editor
Todd Brakke

Managing Editor
Thomas F. Hayes

Project Editor
Tonya Simpson

Copy Editor
Barbara Hacha

Indexer
Tim Tate

Proofreader
Maribeth Echard

Technical Editor
Dallas Releford

Team Coordinator
Sharry Lee Gregory

Interior Designer
Gary Adair

Cover Designer
Dan Armstrong

Layout Technician
Ayanna Lacey

Contents

Part II: Outlook   71

Part IV: Excel   397

Part V: Access   501

Part VII: FrontPage

Appendix

About the Author

Joe Habraken is a bestselling author whose publications include *The Complete Idiot's Guide to Microsoft Access 2000*, *Practical Cisco Routers*, and *The Absolute Beginner's Guide to Networking (3rd Edition)*. Joe currently serves as a technical director at Reviewnet, a B2B Web-based company, and he is also a computer-training instructor at the University of New England. Joe has taught networking and computer software courses and seminars throughout the country.

Dedication

With much love to my wonderful wife, Kim. Thank you for all your support and encouragement. You make my life very, very special.

Acknowledgments

Creating books like this takes a real team effort. I would like to thank Stephanie McComb, our acquisitions editor, who worked very hard to assemble the team that made this book a reality and kept us all on track as the book evolved toward completion. I would also like to thank Todd Brakke, who served as the development editor for this book and who came up with many great ideas for improving its content. Also a tip of the hat and a thanks to Dallas G. Releford, who, as the technical editor for the project, did a fantastic job making sure that everything was correct and suggested a number of additions that made the book even more technically sound. Finally, a great big thanks to our project editor, Tonya Simpson, who ran the last leg of the race and made sure the book made it to press on time—what a great team of professionals.

Tell Us What You Think!

As the reader of this book, *you* are our most important critic and commentator. We value your opinion and want to know what we're doing right, what we could do better, what areas you'd like to see us publish in, and any other words of wisdom you're willing to pass our way.

As an associate publisher for Que, I welcome your comments. You can fax, e-mail, or write me directly to let me know what you did or didn't like about this book—as well as what we can do to make our books stronger.

Please note that I cannot help you with technical problems related to the topic of this book, and that due to the high volume of mail I receive, I might not be able to reply to every message.

When you write, please be sure to include this book's title and author as well as your name and phone or fax number. I will carefully review your comments and share them with the author and editors who worked on the book.

Fax: 317-581-4666

E-Mail: feedback@quepublishing.com

Mail: Greg Wiegand
           Que
           201 West 103rd Street
           Indianapolis, IN 46290 USA

Introduction

Congratulations! You are about to harness the incredible features and tools of the latest version of Microsoft Office. Office XP provides you with all the applications that you need to do everything from creating letters to balancing your sales books, to managing your contacts, to creating great presentations and Web pages. It's all here: word processing, spreadsheets, databases, personal information management, Web site creation, and much, much more. This book is designed to get you up and running quickly on all the Office applications, such as Word, Excel, Access, PowerPoint, and Outlook, and to make it easy for you to use their basic features and a number of their advanced features.

Microsoft Office XP provides you with all the familiar Office applications and provides you with many new enhancements that make it easier for you to create your various Office documents. Microsoft Office XP includes the following applications:

- **Word**—A versatile word-processing application that enables you to create every possible type of document from simple letters to newsletters to reports that include charts and tables.

- **Excel**—A powerful spreadsheet program that enables you to create simple worksheets or specialty worksheets such as invoices and financial statements. Excel provides all the tools and formulas for doing simple math or special statistical and financial calculations.

- **PowerPoint**—An easy-to-use presentation application that enables you to create eye-catching and impressive slide shows that can be shown from your computer monitor or other video output device. PowerPoint also enables you to print presentation outlines and speakers' notes for your presentations.

- **Access**—A relational database application that is extremely powerful, yet very straightforward to use. Access provides several database wizards that help you create your own databases quickly and efficiently.

- **Outlook**—A personal information manager that will help you keep organized. Outlook not only helps you manage your contacts, appointments, and tasks, it also serves as your e-mail and fax client.

- **FrontPage**—A Web design tool that provides wizards to create several kinds of Web sites. You can quickly create a personal, business, or other type of Web site using FrontPage, and you can include graphics and navigational tools, such as hyperlinks.

Using This Book

Microsoft Office XP 8-in-1 is designed to help you learn the six applications in the Office XP suite. All the most important and useful tasks are covered in this book, and the short, concise lessons make it easy for you to learn a particular feature quickly.

This book is organized into eight parts. The first part covers new features found in the Microsoft Office XP applications such as smart tags and the Speech feature and also provides you with information on common Office features such as the Help system. Part I of the book also contains lessons that teach you how to share information among your Office applications and send e-mails and faxes directly from the various applications.

Each of the subsequent sections (Parts II–VII) covers a particular Office application: Outlook, Word, Excel, Access, PowerPoint, and FrontPage. A special bonus section (Part VIII) provides you with information on how to use Internet Explorer to get the most out of the World Wide Web and get a good look at any HTML creations you make using Office XP.

An appendix is also included in the book that walks you through the Office XP installation process. This should get you started on the right foot as you set out to learn and use the different Office applications.

Conventions Used in This Book

Each lesson in this book includes step-by-step instructions for performing specific tasks. To help you as you work through these steps and to help you move through the lessons easily, additional information is included and identified by the following icons:

 Term   New or unfamiliar terms are defined to help you as you work through the various steps in the lesson.

TIP   **Tip**   Read these tips for ideas that cut corners and confusion.

 Caution   This icon identifies areas where new users often run into trouble; these hints offer practical solutions to those problems.

CAUTION

In addition to the icons discussed, the following conventions are also used:

Text you should type	Information you need to type appears in **bold monospace type**.
Items you select	Commands, options, and icons you are to select and keys you are to press appear in **bold type**.

Office XP Introduction and Shared Features

What's New in Office XP?

In this lesson, you learn about the new features provided by the Office XP application suite.

Introducing Microsoft Office XP

Microsoft Office XP is the latest version of the popular Office application suite. Microsoft Office XP includes Outlook, Word, Excel, Access, PowerPoint, and FrontPage. These different application tools enable you to tackle a large variety of business and personal tasks on the computer.

Microsoft Office XP offers a number of new enhancements to the Office suite. This lesson serves as a quick overview of some of these new features. Coverage of these features as they relate to specific applications in Office XP, such as Word or PowerPoint, are covered in the part of the book that is dedicated to that particular application.

Introducing Voice Dictation and Voice Commands

One of the most exciting new features in Office XP is voice dictation and voice-activated commands. If your computer is outfitted with a sound card, speakers, and a microphone (or a microphone with an earphone headset), you can dictate information into your Microsoft applications, such as Word and Excel. You also can use voice commands to activate the menu system in that application. The voice feature also has the capability to read text back to you over your speakers or headset.

Voice commands, voice dictation, and setting up the Speech feature are discussed in more detail in Lesson 4, "Using the Office Speech Feature."

Smart Tags Provide Quick Options

Another new enhancement that Microsoft Office XP provides is the smart tag. A smart tag is a special shortcut menu that provides you with additional options related to a particular feature. There are paste smart tags, AutoCorrect smart tags, and smart tags for dates, times, and addresses that you place in your Office documents.

Document   A document is any file you create or use in an Office application. These files include Word documents, Excel workbooks, and PowerPoint presentations.

For example, in the case of date and addresses smart tags, if you are typing a letter to a new contact, you can quickly add the address information that you place in the Word document into the Outlook Contacts list. The different Office XP applications, such as Microsoft Word, automatically detect date, time, and address information and provide you with the appropriate smart tag.

Figure 1.1 shows a smart tag that has been placed on an address that has been entered into a letter. You can tell whether information has been "smart tagged" because it is underlined with a dotted red line. When you place your mouse on a smart tag, you can click to open a menu of options.

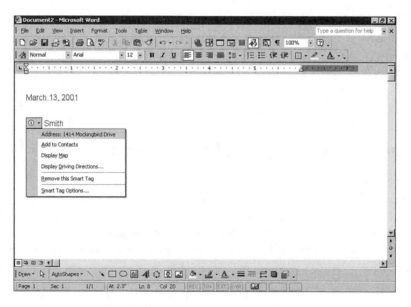

Figure 1.1 Smart tags provide you with quick access to additional options.

Notice in Figure 1.1 that, in addition to the name "Smith" having a smart tag, Word has underscored the date with a dotted red line, indicating the presence of a smart tag.

When you paste information into an Office application, you will find that a paste smart tag appears at the bottom of the pasted item. This enables you to access options related to your paste job, such as whether the information pasted should maintain its original formatting or be formatted the same as text or numbers that are in the same part of the document where you pasted the new information.

Smart tags are discussed throughout this book as you encounter them in the various Office applications.

Introducing the Office Task Panes

One of the biggest changes to the Office environment in Microsoft Office XP is the introduction of the Office task pane. The task pane is a special pane that appears on the right side of a particular application window. It is used in each Office application to house a number of features that were formerly controlled using dialog boxes.

For example, there are task panes for using the Office Clipboard and the Clip Gallery. Figure 1.2 shows the Insert Clip Art task pane in the Microsoft Excel Application window. You learn more about the task panes in Lesson 3, "Using Office Task Panes," of this part of the book.

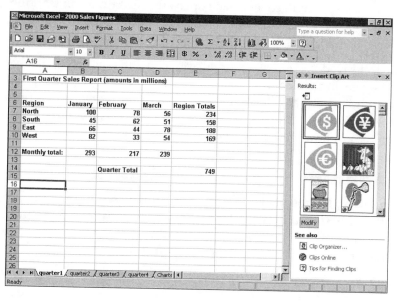

Figure 1.2 Office task panes provide easy access to a number of Office application features.

Using the Ask a Question Box

Many Office users who have used previous versions of Microsoft Office will be pleased to find that the Office Assistant is hidden by default in Office XP. In fact, the help system can be quickly accessed using a new feature called the Ask a Question box.

This box is located in the upper-right corner of all the Office application windows. To access the Help system for a particular topic, you type a question into the Ask a Question box and then press **Enter**. A list of topics appears in a shortcut menu below the Ask a Question box that enables you to quickly jump to a particular topic. You learn more about the Ask a Question box in Lesson 5, "Getting Help in Microsoft Office," of this part of the book.

Using Document Recovery

Another new Office XP feature relates to document recovery when your computer crashes. When an Office application locks up and closes or when your entire computer crashes, a special Recovery pane opens the next time you start the application. This Recovery pane lists all the documents that were open in a particular application when the crash occurred.

Only the last saved version of a particular document, workbook, database, or presentation opens in the Recovery pane, but you can quickly reopen it in the particular application by clicking the document's name. The Recovery pane is meant to get you back up and working on a particular document as soon as you restart your system and open the application that you were working with.

Understanding Product Activation

After you install Microsoft Office XP (which is discussed in Appendix A, "Installing Microsoft Office XP") and start one of the Office applications, a product activation window opens, as shown in Figure 1.3. You can activate Microsoft Office XP on only one computer; trying to activate it on subsequent computers will fail.

Activating your copy of Microsoft Office XP is crucial. If the product is not activated, it runs only for a limited number of times before it becomes deactivated and unusable. This new feature is an effort by Microsoft to stop software piracy related to Microsoft Office. You can activate Microsoft Office XP using the Internet or by phone. Just follow the prompts for activation after you install Microsoft Office XP from the Office CD.

Figure 1.3 Activation is required for you to use your copy of Office XP.

Using Common Office Features

In this lesson, you learn how to use common Office features such as menus, toolbars, and dialog boxes.

Starting Office Applications

The Microsoft Office applications can be quickly started from the Windows Start menu. Desktop icons can also be quickly created for an Office application to provide quick access to that application.

To start an Office application from the Start menu, follow these steps:

1. From the Windows desktop, click **Start**, and then point at **Programs**. The Programs menu appears (see Figure 2.1).

2. To open a particular Office application, click that application's icon on the menu. The program window for that application appears.

Figure 2.1   Use the Start menu to start your Office applications.

Starting an Application by Choosing a Document Template

You can also start a particular Office application by choosing the type of Office document that you are going to create. This is done using the Start menu.

1. From the Windows desktop, click **Start**, **New Office Document**. The New Office Document dialog box appears (see Figure 2.2).

Figure 2.2   The New Office Document dialog box can be used to quickly start a new document in any Office application.

2. All the Office application templates are available on the different tabs of the New Office Document dialog box. You can create blank documents or special documents from the templates that are provided (specific templates are discussed in more detail in the various parts of this book as they relate to a particular Office application). Select a particular template in the dialog box.

3. Click **OK**. The application that uses that particular template opens (such as Word if you select the Blank Document icon), and the new document appears in the application window.

Creating Desktop Icons

You can also create shortcut icons for your Office applications on the Windows desktop. When you install Microsoft Office, a desktop icon is automatically created for Outlook (you can open Outlook by double-clicking this icon).

To create desktop icons for Office applications, follow these steps:

1. From the Windows desktop, click **Start** and then point at **Programs**.

2. Right-click the Office application icon that you want to use to create the desktop icon.

13

3. Select **Copy** from the shortcut menu that appears (see Figure 2.3).

Figure 2.3   Create desktop icons using the Copy command.

4. Click anywhere on the desktop to close the Start menu.

5. Right-click the Windows desktop and select **Paste Shortcut** from the shortcut menu that appears.

A desktop icon for the selected application appears on the Windows desktop. You can double-click the icon to start the specific application. You can also use the steps discussed in this section to create shortcut icons for your other programs (including non-Office applications), as needed.

Using the Menu System

The menu bar that you find in the Office applications gives you access to all the commands and features a particular application provides. These specific menu systems are found below the title bar and are activated by selecting a particular menu choice. The menu then opens, providing you with a set of command choices.

The Office XP applications use a personalized menu system that was first introduced in Microsoft Office 2000 (the previous version of Office). It enables you to quickly access the commands you use most often. When you first choose a particular menu, you find a short list of menu commands. As you use commands, the Office application adds them to the menu list.

To access a particular menu, follow these steps:

1. Select the menu by clicking its title. The most recently used commands appear; hover the mouse pointer for just a moment and all the commands on a particular menu appear.

2. Select the command on the menu that invokes a particular feature.

You will find that several of the commands found on the menu are followed by an ellipsis (...). These commands, when selected, open a dialog box or a task pane. Dialog boxes require you to provide the application with additional information before the particular feature or command can be used (more information on working with dialog boxes appears later in this lesson).

Some of the menus also contain a submenu or a cascading menu that you can use to make your choices. The menu commands that produce a submenu are indicated by an arrow to the right of the menu choice. If a submenu is present, you point at the command (marked with the arrow) on the main menu to open the submenu.

 TIP   **Activating Menus with the Keyboard**   You can also activate a particular menu by holding down the **Alt** key and then pressing the keyboard key that matches the underscored letter, also called a hotkey, in the menu's name. For example, to activate the File menu in Office applications, press **Alt+F**.

If you would rather have access to all the menu commands (rather than just those you've used recently), you can turn off the personalized menu system. To do this, follow these steps in any Office application:

1. Click the **Tools** menu, and then click **Customize**.

2. In the Customize dialog box, click the **Options** tab.

3. To show all the commands on the menus (without delay), click the **Always Show Full Menus** check box.

4. Click **OK** to close the dialog box.

Using Shortcut Menus

A fast way to access commands that are related to a particular item on an Office document, such as selected text or a picture, is to right-click that item. This opens a shortcut menu that contains commands related to the particular item you are working with.

For example, if you select a chart on an Excel worksheet, right-clicking the chart (see Figure 2.4) opens a shortcut menu with commands such as Cut, Copy, and Paste.

Figure 2.4 Shortcut menus provide quick access to application commands.

You will learn about shortcut menus as you work with the Office applications in the various parts of this book.

As you learned in Lesson 1, some items in your Office application documents are also marked with smart tags. Pointing at an item underscored with a dotted red line allows you to access the smart tag menu and access options related to that document item, such as a pasted item.

Working with Toolbars

Toolbars provide you with a very quick and straightforward way of accessing commands and features in the Office applications. When you first start one of the Office applications, you typically see the Standard and Formatting toolbars sharing one row, as shown in Figure 2.5.

To access a particular command using a toolbar button, click the button. Depending on the command, you see an immediate result in your document (such as the removal of selected text when you click the **Cut** button), or a dialog box appears, requesting additional information from you.

Figure 2.5   Toolbars, such as the Standard and Formatting toolbars in this PowerPoint window, provide quick access to an application's features and commands.

TIP   **Finding a Toolbar Button's Purpose**   You can place the mouse pointer on any toolbar button to view a description of that tool's function.

Other toolbars, such as the Drawing toolbar and toolbars that are specific to a particular Office application, open when you access a particular application. You can also open them manually by right-clicking any visible toolbar and then selecting the toolbar you want to use from the list that is provided. You can also use this method to close a toolbar you no longer need.

Missing Toolbar Buttons?   If the Standard and Formatting toolbars have been configured to share one row, you might not be able to see every button on the toolbars. To find a hidden button, click the **More Buttons** button on either toolbar.

CAUTION

In Lesson 6, "Customizing Your Office Applications," you learn how to customize common Office features, including how to make the Standard and Formatting toolbars into the two separate toolbars that users of Office 97 are probably used to.

Understanding Dialog Boxes

When you are working with the various commands and features found in Office applications, you will invariably come across dialog boxes. Dialog boxes are used when an Office application needs more information from you before it can complete a particular command or take advantage of a special feature. Dialog boxes always appear when you select a menu command that is followed by an ellipsis. Dialog boxes also appear when you invoke this same command using the appropriate toolbar button.

Figure 2.6 shows the Word Font dialog box. This dialog box enables you to make selections using check boxes and drop-down lists. Other dialog boxes use option buttons, spinner boxes, and other methods of enabling you to quickly make selections in a particular box.

Figure 2.6   Dialog boxes are used to allow you to make your choices related to a particular feature.

In most cases, when you complete your selections in a dialog box, you click the **OK** button to close the box and complete the command, which was originally started with a menu choice or a toolbar button.

Using Office Task Panes

In this lesson, you learn how to use Office XP's task panes.

Understanding the Task Pane

A major change to the Office XP application environment is the introduction of task panes. A task pane is a multipurpose windowpane that appears on the right side of the window of an Office application. A task pane basically takes the place of dialog boxes that were used to navigate certain application features, such as opening a new file or inserting clip art into an application document. The list that follows describes the global task panes that you will find in all the Office applications:

- **New File Task Pane**—Enables you to start a new file in a particular application (for example, in Word it is called the New Document task pane; in Excel it is called the New Workbook task pane). It also provides access to various document templates and the capability to open recently used files.

- **Office Clipboard Task Pane**—Enables Enables you to view items that you copy and cut to the Office Clipboard. You can manage up to 24 items on the Clipboard and paste them within an application or between applications.

- **Insert Clip Art Task Pane**—Enables you to search the Office Clip Gallery and insert clip art into your Office application documents.

- **Search Task Pane**—Enables you to search for files from any of the Office applications.

 TIP　**Outlook and Access**　Outlook does not use task panes, and Access uses them only in a very limited way. The New File task pane is used in Access to create new database files. Access also uses the Search task pane to search for files on your computer.

You look at the Search, Clip Art, and Clipboard task panes in more detail later in the lesson.

Task panes also house features that handle specific purposes in each of the Office applications. For example, in PowerPoint, the Slide Layout task pane (shown in Figure 3.1) is used to select a design format for a new or existing PowerPoint presentation slide. You learn about the different task panes in the Office applications as you use them in the different parts of this book.

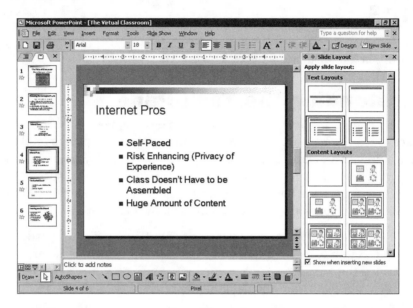

Figure 3.1   The task pane provides specific features in the different Office applications.

When you are working in an Office application, such as Word or Excel, you can open a task pane and switch between the different task pane features offered in that particular application. To open a task pane, follow these steps:

1. In the Office application window, select the **View** menu and select **Task Pane**. The New File task pane appears on the right side of the application window (the New File task pane is the default task pane for the Office applications).

2. To switch to a particular task pane that is available in the current Office application, click the task pane's drop-down arrow (see Figure 3.2).

3. Click the task pane on the menu that you want to use.

You will find that the task pane also pops up when you select specific features in an application. For example, in Word, when you select **Format** and then **Styles and Formatting**, the Styles and Formatting task pane appears in the Word window.

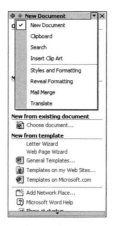

Figure 3.2   Use the task pane's menu to switch to a particular task pane in an application.

The Search Task Pane

The Search task pane enables you to locate files stored on your computer or company network without leaving the Office application that you currently have open. To use the Search task pane, follow these steps:

1. From an Office application window, select the **File** menu and then select **Search** to open the Search task pane (see Figure 3.3).

Figure 3.3   Use the Search task pane to locate files on your computer or network.

2. Type the keyword or keywords that you want to use for the search into the Search text box.

3. To specify the locations that should be searched, click the **Selected Locations** drop-down box. You can expand any of the locations listed, such as My Computer, by clicking the plus (+) symbol to the left of the location. This enables you to view folders and subfolders at that location. Use the check boxes to the left of each location to specify whether that location should be searched.

4. To specify the types of files that are located during the search, click the **Selected File Types** drop-down list. Select or deselect the check boxes for particular Office applications (such as Word or Excel) to specify the types of files that should be included in the search.

5. When you are ready to run the search, click the **Search** button.

The files that meet your search criteria appear in the Search task pane. To open one of the files (in the application that it was created in), click the filename.

 TIP   **Run an Advanced Search**   You can also click the Advanced Search link in the Search task pane to run an advanced search. The Advanced Search task pane enables you to create a search that uses conditional statements and allows you to search by file type, the date that the file was last modified, and a number of other parameters.

Other Standard Task Panes

The other two standard task panes that you will probably use a lot are the Insert Clip Art and Office Clipboard task panes. Although using these task panes is covered within the context of specific Office applications in the parts of this book, you can take a brief look at both of them in the following sections.

The Insert Clip Art Task Pane

How you find and insert clip art in the Office applications has been made much easier by the introduction of the Insert Clip Art task pane. This task pane enables you to quickly search for clip art using a keyword search. Clip art that matches your search parameters is then immediately listed in the Clip Art task pane as thumbnails.

To use the Insert Clip Art task pane, follow these steps:

1. In an Office application such as Word or PowerPoint, select **Insert**, point at **Picture**, and then select **Clip Art**. The Insert Clip Art task pane appears (see Figure 3.4).

Figure 3.4 Search for clip art by keywords using the Insert Clip Art task pane.

2. In the task pane's Search Text box, type keywords that Office can use to find your clip art images.

3. Use the **Search In** drop-down box to specify the collections you want to include in the clip art search. Selected collections are marked with a check mark in their check box that you can toggle on and off with a simple click of the mouse.

4. Use the Results Should Be drop-down box to specify the type of files that should be included in the search. You can select or deselect file types such as Clip Art, Movies, and Sounds.

5. When you have finished setting your search parameters, click the **Search** button. When the search is complete, the clip art that meets your search criteria appears in the task pane.

6. In the Image list, locate the image that you want to place into your Office document. Then, click the image. The application inserts clip art into your document.

Using the Office Clipboard

Microsoft Office XP provides a new version of the Office Clipboard that enables you to accumulate a list of 24 copied or cut items. This makes it very easy to paste items within an Office document, between Office documents in an Office application, or to copy, cut, and paste items among your different Office applications.

To use the Office Clipboard, follow these steps:

1. In an Office application, select **Edit** and then select **Office Clipboard**. The Office Clipboard task pane opens.

2. As you cut or copy items from your various Office applications, the items are placed on the Office Clipboard, as shown in Figure 3.5.

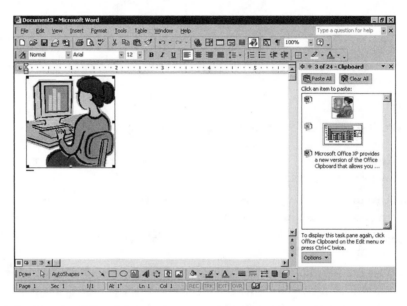

Figure 3.5 Use the Office Clipboard to copy, cut, and paste multiple items in your Office applications.

3. To paste an item from the Clipboard, place the insertion point in your Office document at the place where you want to insert the item, and then click the item on the Office Clipboard task pane.

You can remove items from the Office Clipboard at any time by placing the mouse on the item. A drop-down arrow appears; click the drop-down arrow and select **Delete** from the shortcut menu that appears. You can clear the entire Clipboard by clicking the **Clear All** button at the top of the task pane.

Using the Office Speech Feature

In this lesson, you learn how to train and use the Office Speech feature.

Training the Speech Feature

Microsoft Office XP provides a brand-new feature called the Speech feature. This feature enables you to enter information into an application by using a microphone. It also enables you to access an application's menu system using voice commands.

Before you can really take advantage of the Speech feature, you must provide it with some training so that it can more easily recognize your speech patterns and intonation. After the Speech feature is trained, you can effectively use it to dictate text entries or access various application commands without a keyboard or mouse.

CAUTION

Requirements for Getting the Most Out of the Speech Feature   To make the Speech feature useful, you will need a fairly high-quality microphone. Microsoft suggests a microphone/headset combination. The Speech feature also requires a more powerful computer than the other Office XP applications typically need. Whereas Office XP needs only 32MB of RAM (memory) on a computer using Windows 98/Me (64MB for Windows 2000), Microsoft suggests using a computer with 128MB of RAM and a Pentium II (or later) processor running at a minimum of 400MHz. A computer that meets or exceeds these higher standards should be capable of getting the most out of the Speech feature.

The first time you start the Speech feature in an Office application, you are required to configure and train the feature. Follow these steps to get the Speech feature up and running:

1. In an Office application window such as Word or Excel, select the **Tools** menu and select **Speech**. The Welcome to Office Speech Recognition dialog box appears. To begin the process of setting up your microphone and training the Speech feature, click the **Next** button.

2. The first screen of the Microphone Wizard appears. It asks you to make sure that your microphone and speakers are connected to your computer. If you have a headset microphone, this screen shows you how to adjust the microphone for use. Click **Next** to continue.

3. The next wizard screen asks you to read a short text passage so that your microphone volume level can be adjusted (see Figure 4.1). When you have finished reading the text, click **Next** to continue.

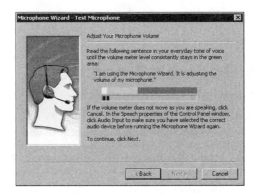

Figure 4.1   The Microphone Wizard adjusts the volume of your microphone.

4. On the next screen, you are told that if you have a headset microphone, you can click **Finish** and proceed to the speech recognition training. If you have a different type of microphone, you are asked to read another text passage. The text is then played back to you. This is to determine whether the microphone is placed at an appropriate distance from your mouth; when you get a satisfactory playback, click **Finish**.

When you finish working with the Microphone Wizard, the Voice Training Wizard appears. This wizard collects samples of your speech and, in essence, educates the Speech feature as to how you speak.

To complete the voice training process, follow these steps:

1. After reading the information on the opening screen, click **Next** to begin the voice training process.

2. On the next screen, you are asked to provide your gender and age (see Figure 4.2). After specifying the correct information, click **Next**.

3. On the next wizard screen, you are provided an overview of how the voice training will proceed. You are also provided with directions for how to pause the training session. Click **Next**.

Figure 4.2 Supply the voice trainer with your gender and age.

4. The next wizard screen reminds you to adjust your microphone. You are also reminded that you need a quiet room when training the Speech feature. When you are ready to begin training the speech recognition feature, click **Next**.

5. On the next screen, you are asked to read some text. As the wizard recognizes each word, the word is highlighted. After finishing with this screen, continue by clicking **Next**.

6. You are asked to read text on several subsequent screens. Words are selected as the wizard recognizes them (see Figure 4.3).

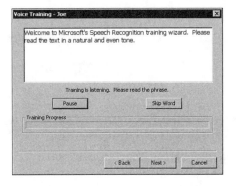

Figure 4.3 Read the text provided by each of the wizard screens.

7. When you complete the training screens, your profile is updated. Click **Finish** on the wizard's final screen.

You are now ready to use the Speech feature. The next two sections discuss using the Voice Dictation and Voice Command features.

The Speech Feature Works Better Over Time   Be advised that the voice feature's performance improves as you use it. As you learn to pronounce your words more carefully, the Speech feature tunes itself to your speech patterns. You might need to do additional training sessions to fine-tune the Speech feature.

CAUTION

Using Voice Dictation

When you are ready to start dictating text into an Office application such as Word, put on your headset microphone or place your standalone microphone in the proper position that you determined when you used the Microphone Wizard. When you're ready to go, select the **Tools** menu and then select **Speech**. The Language bar appears, as shown in Figure 4.4. If necessary, click the **Dictation** button on the toolbar (if the Dictation button is not already activated or depressed).

Figure 4.4   Dictating text into the Office application.

After you enable the Dictation button, you can begin dictating your text into the Office document. Figure 4.4 shows text being dictated into a Word document. When you want to put a line break into the text, say "new line." Punctuation is placed in the document by saying the name of a particular punctuation mark, such as "period" or "comma."

CAUTION

How Do I Insert the Word "Comma" Rather Than the Punctuation Mark?
Because certain keywords, such as "period" or "comma," are used to insert punctuation during dictation, you must spell these words out if you want to include them in the text. To do this, say "spelling mode," and then spell out the word, such as c-o-m-m-a. As soon as you dictate an entire word, the spelling mode is ended.

When you have finished dictating into the document, click the **Microphone** button on the Language bar (the second Microphone button from the left; the first is used to select the current speech driver, which you can leave as the default). When you click the **Microphone** button, the Language bar collapses, hiding the **Dictation** and the **Voice Command** buttons. You can also stop Dictation mode by saying "microphone."

You can minimize the Language bar by clicking the **Minimize** button on the right end of the bar. This sends the Language bar to the Windows System Tray (it appears as a small square icon marked EN, if you are using the English version of Office).

With the Language bar minimized in the System Tray, you can quickly open it when you need it. Click the **Language Bar** icon in the System Tray, and then select **Show the Language Bar** (which is the only choice provided when you click on the Language Bar icon).

Using the Dictation feature correctly requires that you know how to get the Speech feature to place the correct text or characters into an Office document. For more help with the dictation feature, consult the Microsoft Office Help system from any Office application.

Using Voice Commands

Another tool the Speech feature provides is voice commands. You can open and select menus in an application and even navigate dialog boxes using voice commands.

To use voice commands, open the Language bar (click **Tools**, **Speech**). Click the **Microphone** icon, if necessary, to expand the Language bar. Then, click the **Voice Command** icon on the bar (or say "voice command").

To open a particular menu such as the Format menu, say "format." Then, to open a particular submenu such as Font, say "font." In the case of these voice commands, the Font dialog box opens.

You can then navigate a particular dialog box using voice commands. In the Font dialog box, for example, to change the size of the font, say "size"; this activates the Size box that controls font size. Then, say the size of the font, such as "14." You can also activate other font attributes in the dialog box in this manner. Say the name of the area of the dialog box you want to use, and then say the name of the feature you want to turn on or select.

When you have finished working with a particular dialog box, say "OK," (or "Cancel" or "Apply," as needed) and the dialog box closes and provides you with the features you selected in the dialog box. When you have finished using voice commands, say "microphone," or click the **Microphone** icon on the Language bar.

Believe it or not, you can also activate buttons on the various toolbars using voice commands. For example, you could turn on bold by saying "bold." The Bold button on the Formatting toolbar becomes active. To turn bold off, say "bold" again.

A Final Word About the Speech Feature

The Speech feature actually provides a number of possibilities for using voice dictation and voice commands. You will probably want to practice on some documents that aren't all that important as you become familiar with the different features provided.

If you find that you aren't getting very good results with either voice dictation or voice commands, you can do some additional training for the Speech feature. On the Language bar, click the **Tools** icon and then select **Training** from the shortcut menu that appears (see Figure 4.5). Do the additional training exercises supplied by the wizard.

Figure 4.5   Use the Language bar's Tools button to select the Training feature.

Getting Help in Microsoft Office

In this lesson, you learn how to access and use the Help system in Microsoft Office.

Help: What's Available?

Microsoft Office supplies a Help system that makes it easy for you to look up information on application commands and features as you work in a particular Office application. Because every person is different, the Office Help system can be accessed in several ways. You can

- Ask a question in the Ask a Question box.
- Ask the Office Assistant for help.
- Get help on a particular element you see onscreen with the What's This? tool.
- Use the Contents, Answer Wizard, and Index tabs in the Help window to get help.
- Access the Office on the Web feature to view Web pages containing help information (if you are connected to the Internet).

Using the Ask a Question Box

The Ask a Question box is a new way to access the Office Help system that Microsoft Office XP provides. It is also the easiest way to quickly get help. An Ask a Question box resides at the top right of every Office application.

For example, if you are working in Excel and would like to get some help with Excel functions (functions are discussed in Lesson 5, "Performing Calculations with Functions," of the Excel part of this book), type **functions** into the Ask a Question box. Then press the **Enter** key. A shortcut menu appears below the Ask a Question box, as shown in Figure 5.1.

To access one of the Help topics supplied on the shortcut menu, click that particular topic. The Help window opens with topical matches for that keyword or phrase displayed.

Figure 5.1   The Ask a Question box provides a list of Help topics that you can quickly access.

In the case of the "functions" question used in this figure (which was really just a keyword; you can type more complete questions into the box, such as **How do I format numbers?**), the Help window opens and displays a list of the Excel functions by category (see Figure 5.2).

Figure 5.2   The Ask a Question box provides a quick way to access the Help window.

In the Help window, you can use the links provided to navigate the Help system. You can also use the Contents, Answer Wizard, and Index tabs to find additional information or look for new information in the Help window. You learn more about these different Help window tabs later in this lesson.

Using the Office Assistant

Another way to get help in an Office Application is to use the Office Assistant. The Office Assistant supplies the same type of access to the Help system as the Ask a Question box. You ask the Office Assistant a question, and it supplies you with a list of possible answers that provide links to various Help topics. The next two sections discuss how to use the Office Assistant.

Turning the Office Assistant On and Off

By default, the Office Assistant is off. To show the Office Assistant in your application window, select the **Help** menu and then select **Show the Office Assistant**.

You can also quickly hide the Office Assistant if you no longer want it in your application window. Right-click the Office Assistant and select **Hide**. If you want to get rid of the Office Assistant completely so it isn't activated when you select the Help feature, right-click the Office Assistant and select **Options**. Clear the **Use the Office Assistant** check box, and then click **OK**. You can always get the Office Assistant back by selecting **Help, Show Office Assistant**.

Asking the Office Assistant a Question

When you click the Office Assistant, a balloon appears above it, as shown in Figure 5.3. Type a question into the text box. For example, you might type **How do I print?** for help printing your work. Click the **Search** button.

Figure 5.3   Ask the Office Assistant a question to get help.

The Office Assistant provides some topics that reference Help topics in the Help system. Click the option that best describes what you're trying to do. The Help window appears, containing more detailed information. Use the Help window to get the exact information that you need.

Although not everyone likes the Office Assistant because having it enabled means that it is always sitting in your application window, it can be useful at times. For example, when you access particular features in an application, the Office Assistant can automatically provide you with context-sensitive help on that particular feature. If you are brand new to Microsoft Office, you might want to use the Office Assistant to help you learn the various features that the Office applications provide.

 TIP **Select Your Own Office Assistant** Several different Office Assistants are available in Microsoft Office. To select your favorite, click the Office Assistant and select the **Options** button. On the Office Assistant dialog box that appears, select the **Gallery** tab. Click the **Next** button repeatedly to see the different Office Assistants that are available. When you locate the assistant you want to use, click **OK**.

Using the Help Window

You can also forgo either the Type a Question box or the Office Assistant and get your help directly from the Help window. To directly access the Help window, select **Help** and then the help command for the application you are using, such as **Microsoft Word Help.** You can also press the **F1** key to make the Help window appear.

The Help window provides two panes. The pane on the left provides three tabs: Contents, Answer Wizard, and Index. The right pane of the Help window provides either help subject matter or links to different Help topics. It functions a great deal like a Web browser window. You click a link to a particular body of information and that information appears in the right pane.

The first thing that you should do is maximize the Help window by clicking its **Maximize** button. This makes it easier to locate and read the information that the Help system provides (see Figure 5.4).

When you first open the Help window, a group of links in the right pane provides you with access to new features for the current application and other links, such as a link to Microsoft's Office Web site. Next, take a look at how you can take advantage of different ways to find information in the Help window: the Contents tab, the Answer Wizard tab, and the Index tab.

 TIP **View the Help Window Tabs** If you don't see the different tabs in the Help window, click the **Show** button on the Help window toolbar.

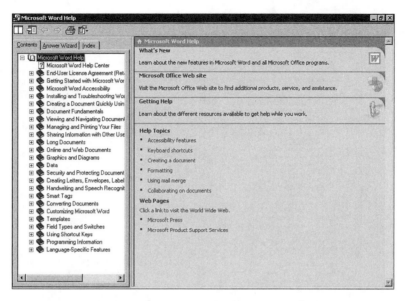

Figure 5.4 The Help window provides access to all the help information provided for a particular application.

Using the Contents Tab

The Contents tab of the Help system is a series of books you can open. Each book has one or more Help topics in it, which appear as pages or chapters. To select a Help topic from the Contents tab, follow these steps:

1. In the Help window, click the **Contents** tab on the left side of the Help window.

2. Find the book that describes, in broad terms, the subject for which you need help.

3. Double-click the book, and a list of Help topics appears below the book, as shown in Figure 5.5.

4. Click one of the pages (the pages contain a question mark) under a Help topic to display it in the right pane of the Help window.

5. When you finish reading a topic, select another topic on the Contents tab or click the Help window's **Close** (**X**) button to exit Help.

Figure 5.5   Use the Contents tab to browse through the various Help topics.

Using the Answer Wizard

Another way to get help in the Help window is to use the Answer Wizard. The Answer Wizard works the same as the Ask a Question box or the Office Assistant; you ask the wizard questions and it supplies you with a list of topics that relate to your question. You click one of the choices provided to view help in the Help window.

To get help using the Answer Wizard, follow these steps:

1. Click the **Answer Wizard** tab in the Help window.
2. Type your question into the What Would You Like to Do? box. For example, you might type the question, **How do I format text?**
3. After typing your question, click the **Search** button. A list of topics appears in the Select Topic to Display box. Select a particular topic, and its information appears in the right pane of the Help window, as shown in Figure 5.6.

TIP   **Print Help**   If you want to print information provided in the Help window, click the **Print** icon on the Help toolbar.

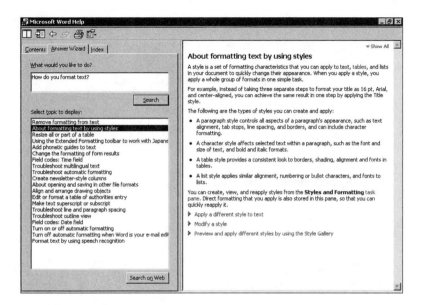

Figure 5.6   Search for help in the Help window using the Answer Wizard tab.

Using the Index

The Index is an alphabetical listing of every Help topic available. It's like an index in a book.

Follow these steps to use the index:

1. In the Help window, click the **Index** tab.

2. Type the first few letters of the topic for which you are looking. The Or Choose Keywords box jumps quickly to a keyword that contains the characters you have typed.

3. Double-click the appropriate keyword in the keywords box. Topics for that keyword appear in the Choose a Topic box.

4. Click a topic to view help in the right pane of the Help window (see Figure 5.7).

TIP   **Navigation Help Topics**   You can move from topic to topic in the right pane of the Help window by clicking the various links that are provided there. Some topics are collapsed. Click the triangle next to the topic to expand the topic and view the help provided.

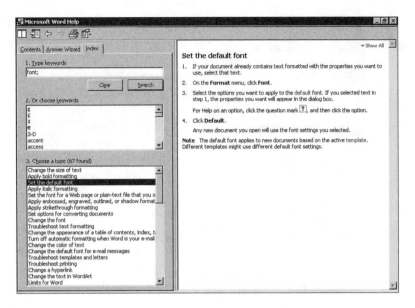

Figure 5.7   Use the Index tab to get help in the Help window.

Getting Help with Screen Elements

If you wonder about the function of a particular button or tool on the screen, wonder no more. Just follow these steps to learn about this part of Help:

1. Select **Help** and then **What's This?** or press **Shift+F1**. The mouse pointer changes to an arrow with a question mark.

2. Click the screen element for which you want help. A box appears explaining the element.

TIP   **Take Advantage of ScreenTips**   Another Help feature provided by the Office applications is the ScreenTip. All the buttons on the different toolbars provided by your Office applications have a ScreenTip. Other buttons or tools in an Office application window can also provide ScreenTips. Place the mouse on a particular button or icon, and the name of the item (which often helps you determine its function) appears in a ScreenTip.

Customizing Your Office Applications

In this lesson, you learn how to customize your Office applications.

Navigating Options Settings

Office applications provide you with a great deal of control over the desktop environment that you work in. You can control options such as how the application window looks for a particular Office application and where the application should store files, by default, when you save them.

Every one of the Office applications has an Options dialog box that provides access to different settings that you can customize. Next, you take a look at how you open and navigate the Options dialog box in an Office application. Then, you look at several of the applications and some of the key options they offer that you might want to customize.

Customizing Office Applications   You might want to work with the Office applications described in this book before you change a lot of options for the applications. A good way for you to do this is to explore the other parts of this book and then return to this lesson when you are ready to customize some of the options in the Office applications you use most.

CAUTION

To open and navigate the Options dialog box in an Office application, follow these steps:

1. In an Office application (such as Word), select **Tools, Options**. The Options dialog box for that application appears (see Figure 6.1).

2. To switch between the different options, click the appropriate tab on the Options dialog box. Each tab controls a subset of the options available in that application.

3. To change settings on the various tabs, use the check boxes, drop-down lists, or spinner boxes to make your selections for various features.

4. When you have finished customizing the various options in the Option dialog box, click **OK**. You are returned to the application window.

Figure 6.1   The Options dialog box in an application enables you to customize various settings.

You will find that you can set a large number of options in the Options dialog box for each Office application. This doesn't mean that you have to change them all (if you're not sure what you're doing, in many cases you shouldn't change them). Next, take a look at some of the common settings that you might want to change in your Office applications; you'll look at Word, Excel, PowerPoint, and Access individually in the sections that follow.

TIP   **Customizing Outlook**   Because Outlook is customized differently than the other Office applications, see Lesson 20, "Customizing Outlook," in Part II of this book.

Setting Options in Word

When you work in Word, you are probably going to create letters and envelopes for mailings. One of the options related to Word that you will want to set up is your user information. This way, the return address on any letters and envelopes you create with Word are inserted automatically into certain documents.

Another set of options that you might want to customize in Word are the options related to the Spelling and Grammar Checker. For example, you might want to customize the types of things that are automatically flagged by the Spelling and Grammar Checker when you run these features in Word.

To customize some of the Word options, follow these steps:

1. In Word, select **Tools** and then select **Options** to open the Options dialog box.

2. Click the **User Information** tab on the Options dialog box (see Figure 6.2).

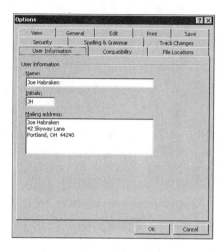

Figure 6.2   Provide your name and address on the User Information tab.

3. If necessary, type your name into the Name box on the User Information tab. Type your address into the Mailing Address box. That takes care of the User Information tab.

4. To set options related to the Spelling and Grammar features, click the **Spelling & Grammar** tab (see Figure 6.3).

5. Check boxes are provided that allow you to check spelling as you type or to hide any typing errors in the document (by default, typing errors are flagged as you type with a red underscore). You can also determine whether you want the Spelling feature to ignore uppercase words, words with numbers, and Internet and file addresses. Select or deselect check boxes as needed.

6. Use the Grammar box on the Spelling & Grammar tab to set options such as Check Grammar As You Type. You can also set whether the grammar in the document is checked whenever you run the Spelling and Grammar Checker (select **Check Grammar with Spelling**).

7. When you have finished setting options on the two Options dialog box tabs discussed in these steps, click **OK** to close the Options dialog box. If you don't want any of your changes to take effect, click **Cancel**.

Figure 6.3   Set Spelling and Grammar options on the Spelling & Grammar tab.

Setting Options in Excel

When you work with Excel, you work with numbers and calculations. As you learn in Part IV of this book, Excel is a number cruncher. It is built to do math and provide you with correct results when it does calculations.

Two of the options that you might want to adjust related to Excel specify when it recalculates all the formulas in an Excel workbook and the rules that it uses to check for errors in an Excel worksheet.

Follow these steps:

1. In Excel, select **Tools** and then select **Options**. The Options dialog box opens.

2. Click the **Calculation** tab on the Options dialog box (see Figure 6.4).

3. When you work with very large worksheets and worksheets that are linked to other Excel Workbook files, your worksheet is recalculated every time you change or add data on the worksheet. If you have a computer with marginal processing power and memory, this process can take a while. You can turn off the automatic recalculation feature on the Calculations tab by clicking the **Manual** option button. If you do this, you must press **F9** to make Excel recalculate the sheet.

4. You might want to look at another set of options on the **Error Checking** tab (click it). This tab contains a list of errors that Excel can automatically check for as you work on your worksheet (see Figure 6.5).

Figure 6.4 Set options related to calculations on the Calculation tab.

Figure 6.5 Error checking helps make sure that your worksheet data is entered correctly.

5. To set a default color for errors found in a worksheet, click the **Error Indicator Color** drop-down box and select a color from the color palette (because the Spelling Checker and smart tags use red, don't pick red).

6. You probably want to leave the error rules listed all in force. However, notice in Figure 6.5 that the Formulas Referring to Empty Cells check box is not selected. This is because you typically enter formulas into worksheets even before data is entered. After creating a worksheet, you might want to select this option, especially if you are working on a large, complex worksheet. This will make sure that you get all the data into the appropriate cells, or Excel will start sending error messages your way.

7. When you have finished setting these options, click **OK** to close the Options dialog box (or **Cancel** to discard changes).

Setting Options in PowerPoint

After you work in PowerPoint for a while, you might find that you want to specify a view to be the default view when you open presentations that you have created. Another option you might want to set is the default location where presentations that you save are placed.

Follow these steps to change these PowerPoint options:

1. In PowerPoint, select **Tools** and then select **Options** to open the Options dialog box.

2. Click the **View** tab on the Options dialog box (see Figure 6.6).

Figure 6.6 Set the default view that will be used when you open a saved presentation.

3. Click the **Open All Documents Using This View** drop-down list and select a view that you want to use whenever you open a saved presentation. The views range from **Normal-Outline, Notes, and Slide** to **Slide Sorter**.

4. Another option you might want to set is the default folder that is used when you first save a presentation. Click the **Save** tab on the Options dialog box.

5. In the Default File Location box, type the path that you want to use.

6. When you have finished changing your settings, click **OK** (or **Cancel** to reject any changes made).

Setting Special Options in Access

When you work in Access, you spend a lot of time in the Datasheet view, adding and manipulating records in a database table. Although forms can be used to handle some of the data entry and editing chores (as discussed in Part V of this book), you still will work a great deal with table datasheets. Therefore, you might want to customize the Datasheet view to make it easier to work with and provide an environment that is a little easier on your eyes.

Follow these steps to customize Access options:

1. In Access, select **Tools** and then select **Options**. The Options dialog box opens.
2. Click the **Datasheet** tab on the Options dialog box (see Figure 6.7).

Figure 6.7 You can edit the datasheet colors and other settings on the Datasheet tab.

3. Use the Font drop-down box to select a color for the font used in the Datasheet view.
4. The Background and Gridlines drop-down boxes can be used to adjust the colors of these items to complement the Font color you select.
5. If you want to change the Default Cell Effect, select either the **Raised** or **Sunken** option buttons.
6. You can also specify a wider default column width for your datasheets in the Default Column Width box.
7. When you have finished making your changes, click **OK** (or **Cancel** to discard any changes made).

Customizing Toolbars

You might find as you use your Office applications that you would like to customize your toolbars. This enables you to add or remove buttons from the toolbars so that they provide you with quick access to the commands and features you use the most often.

For example, suppose you would like to add or remove buttons from a particular toolbar, such as the Formatting toolbar (which is common to a number of Office applications). Follow these steps:

1. In any application (such as Word), place the mouse on a toolbar's drop-down arrow (it is on the far right of the toolbar). Click the drop-down arrow to open a shortcut menu.

2. On the toolbar shortcut menu, point at **Add or Remove Buttons**, and then point at the toolbar's name on the pop-up menu that appears. A list of all the buttons available for that toolbar appears (see Figure 6.8). The buttons that are being used on the toolbar have a check mark to the left of them.

Figure 6.8 You can add or remove buttons from a toolbar.

3. Click a button to deselect it (remove it) or click one of the unselected buttons listed to add it.

4. Repeat step 4 until you have customized the buttons shown on the toolbar. Then, click anywhere in the application window to close the Button drop-down list.

 TIP　**Resetting a Toolbar**　If you want to reset a toolbar and start from scratch with the default buttons, open the Button drop-down list for a particular toolbar and then click **Reset Toolbar** at the very bottom of the Button drop-down list.

Another setting related to toolbars that you might want to adjust is for the Standard and Formatting toolbars in your Office applications, which are set up, by default, to share one line. This limits the number of buttons that can be shown on either of the toolbars at any one time. To place each of these toolbars on its own line, follow these steps:

1. In any application (such as Word or Excel), select the **Tools** menu and then select **Customize**.

2. The Customize dialog box opens. Click the **Options** tab, if necessary.

3. On the Options tab, click the **Show Standard and Formatting Toolbars on Two Rows** check box.

4. Then click **Close**.

 TIP **Get Toolbars in Two Rows Quickly** You can also quickly place the Standard and Formatting toolbars on two rows by clicking the **Toolbar Options** button on the Standard toolbar (when the toolbars are in a single row) and selecting **Show Buttons on Two Rows**.

Sharing Information Among Office Applications

In this lesson, you learn how to share data among the different Office applications.

Sharing Data

After you become familiar with the various applications in Microsoft Office XP, you will find that you can take information that resides in different applications and pull that information together into a report or a presentation. Before you embark on creating complex documents containing information from different Office applications, you should become familiar with the features and capabilities of the different Office applications as they are discussed in the various sections of this book.

Therefore, you might want to save this lesson for a time when you are comfortable with the individual applications in Microsoft Office XP. In the next section, which discusses object linking and embedding (OLE), you can begin to look at sharing information among applications.

What Is Object Linking and Embedding (OLE)?

OLE (pronounced "oh-LAY") stands for object linking and embedding. It is a Windows feature that enables the Windows applications that employ it to share information directly, without any conversion of the data.

For example, you might create a quarterly report in Microsoft Word that contains an Excel chart. The Excel data in the chart changes each quarter. When it comes time to generate the next quarterly report, you could find the most up-to-date version of the Excel chart and copy and paste it into the report, or you could relax while your OLE link updates the report automatically with the changes made in each supporting document.

What Is Linking?

When you link an *object* to a document or other application file, you are creating a connection between the *source file* and your current document, the *container file*. The object does not reside in the container; it is represented there by a linking code. When you update the object, the update is done in the original source application, and the results of the update are seen in the container. For example, you can link a Microsoft Excel workbook to a Word document. When you activate the workbook with a double-click, its source application is started (Microsoft Excel), and the file is opened in it.

 Object Any snippet of data that you want to link to another document. It can be as small as a single character or as large as a huge report with many graphics.

 Source File The file from which the information to be pasted originated.

 Container File The file that's receiving the object. For example, if you're linking an Excel chart to a Word document, the Word document is the container file.

The great thing about links is that you can have the same object linked to several destinations. When you update the file in its source application, the file is updated in all the places to which it is linked. Because the linked object is not actually made part of the container file, the container file does not increase dramatically in size. When you double-click a linked object to make changes to it, the file is opened in the source application.

What Is Embedding?

Embedding gives you the same results as linking but is a different process. An embedded object does become part of the destination file, increasing the file's size. It is basically a transplanted copy of the original file. Because the embedded file resides in the destination file, updating the original file in the original application does not update the embedded copy; there is no link between the two.

Embedded objects are dynamic, however, which means that they can be manipulated and updated right in the destination application. When you activate an embedded object (double-click it), the *server application* opens right inside the current application. In many cases, the menu system of the server application temporarily replaces that of the current application, so in essence, you are running the server application from inside the application that holds the embedded object.

Server Application   The native application for the object that's being linked or embedded. For example, if you embed an Excel worksheet into a Word document, Excel is the server application.

A good example of this is an Excel workbook (such as sales figures for your company) embedded in an Outlook appointment. Double-click the embedded image, and the Outlook menus and toolbars are temporarily replaced by the Excel menus and toolbars. You edit the object, and when you click outside the object window, the menus and toolbars of your container application are returned to you (we discuss embedding an Excel workbook in Part II, "Outlook" in Lesson 12, "Using the Calendar.")

Choosing Between Linking and Embedding

You might be wondering when it's best to link and when you should embed. This really depends on the type of information that you want to place in a particular file. Objects, such as worksheets built in Excel or reports written in Word, that are dynamic (the information in them is updated constantly) are best linked to your container file. This enables you to update the object in the application you created it in and still have the current results linked to several containers.

Objects, such as scanned photos or video clips of your vacation, which are static and not updated over time, can be embedded into your documents or other application files. This makes the object part of that file. For example, you might place scanned photos into an Access table field, or you might place your company's logo on a particular Excel worksheet.

Linking or Embedding with Paste Special

The easiest way to link or embed is with the Paste Special command on the Edit menu.

When an object is pasted into a document with the regular Paste command, the object is dropped in with no information about its origin. In contrast, when an object is pasted into a document with Paste Special, several pieces of information about the object are stored as part of the container file, including the source file's name and location, the server application, and the location of the object within the source file. This extra information is what makes it possible for the object to be updated whenever the source file is updated.

OLE needs the name of a source file to refer to later in order to link, so you must save your work in the source program before you create a link with OLE. However, if you merely want to embed and not link, you do not need a named source file. The only information OLE needs to edit the object later is the name of the *server application*.

 TIP **Container Application** The application to which you are linking or embedding the object. For example, if you embed an Excel worksheet into a Word document, Word is the container application.

To link or embed with Paste Special, follow these steps:

1. Open the application that contains the object that you want to link or embed (such as Excel, when you want to link an Excel worksheet). Select the item that will serve as the object (for example, click and drag to select the worksheet cells that will serve as the object).

2. To copy the object to the Clipboard, select **Edit, Copy**.

3. Open the application that is to receive the linked or embedded object and open the specific container file (the file in which you want to paste the object). Place the insertion point where you want to place the object.

4. Select **Edit** and then **Paste Special**, and the Paste Special dialog box appears. The one for Word appears in Figure 7.1; they are similar in all Office applications.

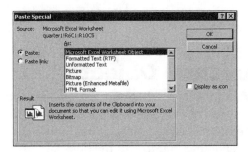

Figure 7.1 The Paste Special dialog box is used to link or embed a copied object.

5. In the dialog box, select the object that you want to place into the current application (in this case, it is the Microsoft Excel Worksheet Object).

6. Choose **Paste** or **Paste Link**, depending on the type of connection you want:

   • **Paste**—Pastes the contents of the Windows Clipboard into the document at the location of the insertion point. The link is not maintained, but you can double-click the pasted material to edit it. (This is embedding.)

- **Paste Link**—This option is available if the contents of the Clipboard can be linked back to its source file. With this option selected, a link is created between the source file and the container file. If you have not saved the source file, the Paste Link option is not available.

7. (Optional) If you want to display the pasted object as an icon instead of as the data itself, select the **Display As Icon** check box. This option is available only if you have selected **Paste Link**. This is useful for pasting sounds and media clips because you can double-click the icon that represents the file if you want to play it later. It also negates a very large picture file from opening in the application you are working with and stressing out your computer's memory.

8. Click **OK**. The object is embedded or linked into the container file, depending on the options you chose.

When deciding which options to select in the Paste Special dialog box, pay close attention to the notes that appear in the Result area. These notes tell you what happens if you choose **OK** with the present set of options.

 TIP **Linking or Embedding an Entire File**   You can also link or embed an entire file into another application document. Select **Insert**, **Object**. Then, use the Create from File tab on the Object dialog box to locate the file that you want to link or embed in the current document. Use the **Link to File** check box in the dialog box to link the file rather than embed it.

Editing Embedded Objects

Editing an embedded object is where the greatest advantage of embedding comes into play. You do not have to remember the name and location of the source file that you used to create the embedded object. You double-click the object and the source application starts, enabling you to edit the object.

Follow these steps to edit an embedded object:

1. Open the document containing the embedded object you want to edit.

2. Double-click the object. The server application of the embedded object starts.

3. Edit the object using the server application's toolbars and commands, which will take the place of the toolbars and menus found in your current application (see Figure 7.2).

4. Click outside the object on the container document to return to your container application.

Figure 7.2   Embedded objects can be edited using the server application's toolbars and menus.

Editing Linked Objects

After you have created a linked object, you might want to edit and update the information in the object. At this stage, you realize the full benefit of an OLE link because you can edit the object one time, and it is updated in every document to which it is linked.

You can edit a linked object in two ways. The first is to start at the source file, using the server application to make changes to the object. The second is to start at the container file and let the link information lead you to the correct source file and server application. With the second method, you do not have to remember the name of the source file or even which server application created it. In the next sections, you learn how to edit objects using these two methods.

Editing from the Source File

To edit a linked object starting from the source file, follow these steps:

1. Start the server application, and then open the source file that contains the object you want to edit.

2. Edit and make changes to the object.

3. Save the document and close the server application.

4. Switch to (or start) the client application and open the container file. The changes should automatically be reflected in the container file.

Editing from the Container File

Editing from the container file is quick and easy because you do not have to find and open the server application manually. To edit a linked object from the container file, follow these steps:

1. From the container file, double-click the linked object you want to update. The server application starts and displays the source file. If double-clicking the object does not start the server application, select the **Edit** menu and then select **Links** to open the Links dialog box. Select the link you want to edit and click the **Open Source** button. The server application starts and displays the source file.

2. Edit the object in the source file, making as many changes as necessary.

3. In the server application, choose **File** and then **Save**.

4. In the server application, choose **File** and then **Exit**. You're returned to the container file, which reflects the changes you made to the linked object.

Breaking Links

If at some point, you decide that you want a linked object in your document to remain fixed and no longer be updated by its source file, you can break (or cancel) the link. This does not delete or alter the object; it merely removes the background information that directly ties the object to its source file. The object becomes like any other object that was placed using the Windows Copy and Paste operations.

To break or cancel a linked object, follow these steps:

1. Open the container file that contains the object whose link you want to break.

2. Select **Edit** and then **Links** (or **Link Options** in some applications). The Links dialog box appears, showing linked object information (see Figure 7.3).

3. Select the link name of the object you want to break.

4. Click **Break Link** (or **Delete** in some applications). A warning box might appear cautioning that you are breaking a link. Click **OK** or **Yes** to confirm your choice.

Figure 7.3 You can control the links of objects that have been linked to a particular document.

Using Smart Tags to Share Data with Outlook

Microsoft Outlook is your personal information manager, as you will learn in Part II of this book. You use it to keep track of your contacts and their addresses and e-mail information. Office XP supplies smart tags to help you keep your Outlook Contacts list up to date.

Smart tags are a very quick way to share information that you place in documents, worksheets, or presentations with Microsoft Outlook.

Smart tags, as discussed in Lesson 1, are a new feature found in Microsoft Office XP. They make it easy for you to take name and address information and even dates that you place in an Office document and immediately share that information with Outlook.

For example, you might be writing a letter in Word to a particular client. Word will mark the client's address information in the heading of the letter with a smart tag. You can use the smart tag to link up with Outlook and place the client's information in your Contacts list.

You will find that dates, times, and addresses are automatically tagged with smart tags. You can tell whether an item has been tagged because it is underscored with a dotted red line. Figure 7.4 shows a smart tag that has been placed on an address in a business letter.

To use a smart tag, such as an address smart tag, to place information in Outlook, follow these steps:

1. Place the mouse on an item, such as an address, that has been "smart tagged." A Smart Tag icon appears (refer to Figure 7.4).

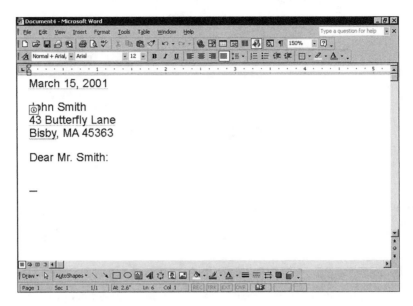

Figure 7.4   Use smart tags to share information in a document with Outlook.

2. Click the **Smart Tag** icon. To add the address to your Outlook Contacts list, click **Add to Contacts** on the menu that appears.

3. An Outlook Contact window opens. The address is automatically pasted into the Address box (see Figure 7.5).

Figure 7.5   Smart tags can paste information into an Outlook Contact window.

4. Enter the other information regarding the contact into the window as needed. Then click **Save and Close**. You are returned to the application that you were originally working in.

You can also use smart tags on dates to create meetings or appointments in Outlook. The procedure is similar to the steps outlined in this section to create a new contact.

Using Office Web Integration Features

In this lesson, you learn how to use various Web features in your Office applications.

Adding Hyperlinks to Office Documents

Microsoft Office provides several features that allow you to integrate features that you typically associate with the World Wide Web into the Office documents that you create. Office documents can be saved in the HTML format and then incorporated into Web pages. Hyperlinks can be placed into Office documents, including Excel workbooks and even Access tables. A *hyperlink* is a text entry or a graphic that, when clicked, takes the user to a Web page on the World Wide Web, to a file on your hard disk, or to a file on a local network.

Hyperlinks are basically pointers that enable you to quickly access Web content or another file when the hyperlink is clicked. Hyperlinks can also take the form of an e-mail address and can be used to quickly fire off an e-mail message when the link is selected.

Adding a hyperlink to an Office document follows pretty much the same procedure in all the Office applications. In fact, the Insert Hyperlink dialog box is identical in Excel, Word, PowerPoint, FrontPage, and Access.

Next, take a look at adding a hyperlink to an Excel worksheet. To add a hyperlink, follow these steps:

1. Select the text or graphic you want to use for the hyperlink (in Excel, select a cell; in Access, click in a Table field).
2. Select the **Insert** menu and then select **Hyperlink**. The Insert Hyperlink dialog box appears, as shown in Figure 8.1.
3. Type the address of the Web page to be used by the hyperlink into the Address box at the bottom of the dialog box.

Figure 8.1 Insert a hyperlink into an Office document, such as an Excel worksheet.

4. If you would like to select the address of the Web page from a list of Web sites that you have recently browsed with Internet Explorer, click the **Browsed Pages** button in the dialog box. Click a link in the list that appears. It will be placed into the Address box.

5. If the link is to an e-mail address rather than to a Web page or file on your computer, click the **E-Mail Address** icon on the left of the dialog box.

6. A list of recently used e-mail addresses that you can select from appears in the dialog box, or you can type the e-mail address into the **E-Mail Address** box, as shown in Figure 8.2.

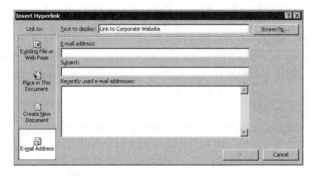

Figure 8.2 Hyperlinks to e-mail addresses can also be inserted using the Insert Hyperlink dialog box.

7. To display a ScreenTip when the mouse pointer rests on the hyperlink, click the **ScreenTip** button; in the dialog box that appears, enter the description you want to display. Click **OK**.

8. Click **OK** to close the Insert Hyperlink dialog box. The text or graphic that was selected becomes a hyperlink. Text hyperlinks appear in a blue font and are underlined.

Figure 8.3 shows a text hyperlink on the words, "Link to First Quarter Summary Web page," that has been added to an Excel worksheet. The link could be used to quickly access a Web page that has information related to the worksheet shown in the figure.

Figure 8.3 Hyperlinks provide quick access to Web pages and files.

When you move the mouse pointer over this link, it changes to a hand. Next to the hand, you can see the address of the link. Click the link and you jump to the appropriate worksheet, Web page, file, or e-mail program. The text of the link changes to purple to indicate that you have used the link.

TIP   **Creating Hyperlinks to Documents on Your Computer**   To insert a hyperlink for a document on your computer, use the Look In box in the Insert Hyperlink dialog box to find the drive that the file resides on, and then open the appropriate folder to locate the file. Select the file in the dialog box to create the link.

Saving Office Documents As Web Pages

You can save any of your Office documents, such as Word documents, Excel worksheets, and PowerPoint presentations as HTML documents. After you save an Office document in the HTML format, you can view the document in the Internet Explorer Web browser. You can also include your Web-ready Office documents in Web sites that you create using FrontPage (creating Web sites using FrontPage is discussed in Part VII of this book).

 HTML Short for Hypertext Markup Language, HTML is the language in which data is presented on the World Wide Web. Office uses the term "Web Page" to define the format type in which you save an Office document for the Web. You are actually converting the document to HTML format.

Saving Office documents as Web pages is similar no matter whether you are using Word, Excel, or PowerPoint. The Save As Web Page command on the File menu is used to save an Office document in the HTML format. Access is the exception, however, and Access objects, such as tables, are made into Web pages using the Export command on the Access File menu.

Before you save a Word document, Excel worksheet, or a PowerPoint presentation as a Web page, you might want to preview the document as it would appear in a Web browser. For example, suppose you have a PowerPoint presentation and you would like to see how it would look on the Web.

Select the **File** menu and then select **Web Page Preview**. It might take a moment as your file is prepared; after it is, Internet Explorer opens and your Office document appears in the browser window. Figure 8.4 shows a PowerPoint presentation in the Internet Explorer window. Notice that links to all the slides in the presentation have been automatically created for the Web version of the presentation.

Figure 8.4 You can preview an Office document as a Web page.

After you preview your Office document as a Web page, if things look good, you can quickly save it as a Web page in the HTML format. Next, take a look at saving a PowerPoint presentation as a Web page to get the overall feel for converting any Office document to the HTML format (the procedure is similar in Word and Excel). Follow these steps:

1. Choose the **File** menu and then choose **Save As Web Page**. The Save As dialog box appears (see Figure 8.5).

Figure 8.5 Office documents can be saved as Web pages.

2. In the **File Name** text box, enter a filename for the Web page document or go with the default name provided (it will be the current name of the file). Notice that in the Save As Type box, the file type is Web Page.

3. If you want to change the page title for the presentation, click the **Change Title** button. Type a new title and then click **OK**.

4. Click **Save**. Your Office document (in this case, a presentation) is saved.

TIP   **PowerPoint Enables You to Select the Slides for the Web Page**   In the case of PowerPoint, you can select the slides in the presentation that you actually want to include in the Web page document that you are creating. Click the **Publish** button and select the slides you want to include in the HTML document. You can also specify in the Publish dialog box which Web browsers (such as Internet Explorer or Netscape Navigator) that the PowerPoint Web page should support.

When you save an Office document, such as a Word document or PowerPoint presentation, as a Web page, you will find that several files are created, not a single HTML file. Any graphics, objects, or other special elements in the document are saved as separate files in the appropriate format for the Web.

For example, in the case of PowerPoint, if the presentation file were named Broadway.ppt, the home page would be named Broadway.htm. Then, it creates a folder named *Presentation Name* Files (for example, Broadway Files) that contains all the other HTML, graphics, and other files needed to display the complete presentation. If you are transferring the HTML presentation to another PC (which is very likely, if you are going to make it available on the World Wide Web), you must transfer not only the lone HTML home page, but also the entire associated folder.

Adding an FTP Site to Your Save In Box

After you save an Office document as a Web page or create a Web page using Microsoft Word (discussed in Lesson 21, "Creating Web Pages in Word," in Part III of this book), you may need to load that file onto a Web server. Although FrontPage makes it very easy to publish Web sites to the Internet (which is discussed in Lesson 8 in Part VII of this book), you can save the Web pages that you create in the other Office applications directly to a Web server that also functions as an FTP site.

  FTP   An FTP (File Transfer Protocol) site is a special computer connected to the Internet (or intranet) that handles only file transfers (file uploads and downloads).

You can save your workbook to an FTP site on the Internet (or a company intranet), provided you have the permission to do so. The first step is to add the FTP site to the Save As dialog box:

1. Open the **Save In** list and select **Add/Modify FTP Locations**. The Add/Modify FTP Locations dialog box appears, as shown in Figure 8.6.

Figure 8.6   Saving to an FTP site can get files onto the Web or a company's intranet.

2. In the **Name of FTP Site** text box, enter the site's address, such as **ftp.microsoft.com**.

3. Select **Log On As**, either **Anonymous** or **User**, and enter a password, if necessary.

4. Click **OK**.

5. After the site has been added to the Save As dialog box, you can select it from the FTP Locations folder in the Save In list.

Faxing and E-Mailing in Office XP

In this lesson, you learn how to fax and e-mail documents from Word.

Understanding E-Mails and Faxes in Office

The capability to send e-mail and faxes directly from your Office applications enables you to quickly take the information on your screen and either fax it or e-mail it to a recipient. When you send an e-mail message directly from an Office application client, such as Word, Excel, Access, FrontPage, or PowerPoint, you are actually using your default e-mail client, such as Outlook, to send the message. The Office document that you have open in the application window is sent within the e-mail message (except in the case of Access and PowerPoint, where it is sent as an attachment).

The capability to fax a document from within an Office application is an extension of your computer's printing services. Any fax service installed on your computer (your computer must also be outfitted with a fax modem) can be used to "print" an Office document to the fax service, which faxes the document over your phone line to its final destination.

Word makes the process of sending a fax easy and provides a Fax Wizard to walk you through the steps. The other Office applications send faxes the same as they would print a document; you use the Print command and a couple of manipulations in the Print dialog box that are discussed later in this lesson. The next sections take a look at faxing Office documents, starting with the Word Fax Wizard and then looking at faxing from the other Office applications by using the Print dialog box.

Using the Word Fax Wizard

The Word Fax Wizard walks you through the steps of preparing your Word document. It also helps you select the fax service that you will use to fax the document.

To use the Word Fax Wizard, follow these steps:

1. Select **File**, point to **Send To**, and then select **Fax Recipient** from the cascading menu. The Word Fax Wizard starts (see Figure 9.1).

Figure 9.1 The Fax Wizard walks you through the process of sending the current document as a fax.

2. The Fax Wizard walks you through the process of sending the current document as a fax. Click **Next** to continue the process.

3. On the next wizard screen, a series of option buttons enables you to select whether to send the current document, send a cover sheet with the document, or send just a cover sheet with a note. Choose the appropriate option buttons (see Figure 9.2) and click **Next** to continue.

Figure 9.2 You can select whether to send the current document with a cover sheet or just send a cover sheet with a note.

4. On the next screen, you select your fax service. Microsoft Fax is the default. If you use a different fax program on your computer, select the **A Different Fax Program Which Is Installed on This System** option button, and then select your fax program from the **Fax Service** drop-down list. Then, click **Next** to continue.

5. On the next screen, enter the recipient and the fax number into the appropriate boxes. If you have the recipient listed in your e-mail program's address book, click the **Address Book** button and select the person from the Address Book list. Depending on the e-mail package you are using, it may include an address book feature that enables you to enter information on clients and friends, including their e-mail addresses, home addresses, and even their fax and phone numbers. If a fax number is listed in the address book (as it is in Microsoft Outlook), all you have to do is select the recipients from the address book for your Word fax, and the fax numbers are entered for you automatically. When you have finished entering the recipient information for the fax, click **Next** to continue.

6. On this screen, select the type of layout you want to use for your fax cover page. Select the option button for either **Professional**, **Contemporary**, or **Elegant**. When you select each option button, a preview of the layout appears on the screen. When you have selected your cover sheet layout, click **Next** to continue.

7. On the next screen, input the information regarding who the fax is from (such as your name, fax number, and so on). When you have entered this information, click **Next**.

8. On the final screen of the Fax Wizard, you are given advice on what to do if the fax doesn't send. Click **Finish**.

The cover sheet that you designed for the fax is displayed in the Word window. Fill in any information that is required, and then click the **Send Fax Now** button. Your fax is sent using the fax service you selected.

Sending Faxes from Other Office Applications

You can also send faxes directly from other Office applications. You "print" the document to the fax service installed on your computer.

Follow these steps to send a fax from an Office application such as Excel or Access:

1. Select **File** and then select **Print** to open the Print dialog box.

2. In the Name box in the Print dialog box, select the fax service that you have installed on your computer (see Figure 9.3).

3. Click **OK**. Depending on the fax service you are using on your computer, a dialog box or wizard specific to the fax service opens. For example, if you have the Windows fax service installed on your computer, the Send Fax Wizard opens. You would then click **Next** to advance past the opening screen provided by the wizard.

Figure 9.3   Select your fax service as the printer in the Print dialog box.

4. Use the dialog box or wizard that your fax service has provided to enter the fax recipient's name and fax phone number. Figure 9.4 shows the Send Fax Wizard screen that is used to enter the information needed to send the fax. Then, click **Next** or advance to the next step of the process using your particular fax service.

Figure 9.4   Use the wizard or dialog box provided by your fax service to enter the recipient's name and fax number.

5. Complete the other tasks that your fax service requires, such as selecting a cover page and entering text for the cover page. Then send the fax. When you use the Send Fax Wizard, as shown in the figures in this section, you have the capability to add a cover page to the fax and schedule when the fax is sent. Clicking **Finish** sends the fax using the Send Fax Wizard.

Sending E-Mails from Office Applications

If you have an e-mail client (software for sending and receiving e-mail) on your computer, such as Microsoft Outlook, you can send Office documents in e-mails. You can send a Word document, an Excel worksheet, or even an entire PowerPoint presentation with an e-mail message.

E-Mail Client The e-mail program installed on your computer that you use to send and receive e-mail.

The process for sending e-mail from the different Office applications is the same for Word, Excel, PowerPoint, and Access. You use the Send To command on the File menu. Microsoft FrontPage also enables you to send e-mail Web pages from FrontPage, but you use the Send command on the FrontPage file menu.

When you send Word, Excel, or FrontPage documents as e-mail, they are actually placed in the body of the e-mail message. In the case of PowerPoint and Access, the file you currently have open in the application is sent with the e-mail message as an attachment.

Next, look at how you can use the e-mail feature in an Office application. This example uses Word.

Follow these steps:

1. Select **File** and then point at **Send To**. Select **Mail Recipient** from the cascading menu that appears. An E-Mail pane appears at the top of your Office document (see Figure 9.5).

2. Type the e-mail address of the recipient into the To box, or click the **To** icon and select an e-mail address from an address book, such as your Outlook Contacts list.

3. When you are ready to send the e-mail, click the **Send a Copy** button at the top of the e-mail address pane.

Your e-mail is sent and the E-Mail pane is removed from the top of your Office document window.

Sending Office Documents As Attachments If you are sending e-mail to other users who do not have Microsoft Outlook or Outlook Express as their e-mail clients, you might want to send your office documents as attachments. To do this, select **File**, **Send To**, and then **Mail Recipient (As Attachment)**. They can then open the attachment in the appropriate Office application.

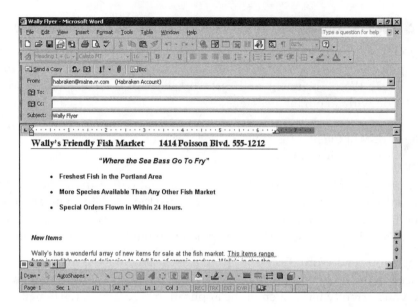

Figure 9.5 The E-Mail pane enables you to specify the recipient of your Office document e-mail.

One thing to remember when you are e-mailing documents directly from Office applications is that you must be connected to the Internet or your company's network to actually send the mail. If you use a dial-up connection to access the Internet (and Internet e-mail), either connect to the Internet before sending the e-mail from the Office application or configure your e-mail client, such as Outlook, to automatically connect to the Internet when you send messages. For information on configuring Outlook as your e-mail client, see Lesson 20, "Customizing Outlook," in Part II of this book.

Outlook

Getting Started in Outlook

In this lesson, you learn how to start and exit Outlook, identify parts of the Outlook window, and use the mouse to get around the program.

Starting Outlook

You start Outlook from the Windows desktop. After starting the program, you can leave it open, or you can minimize it to free up the desktop for other applications. Either way, you can access it at any time during your day.

CAUTION

Outlook and System Performance   If you leave Outlook open on your desktop, it still requires a certain amount of your system resources. This means that if you normally run multiple applications, such as Word and Excel, you might see some loss of performance as you work. If this becomes a problem, close Outlook (or any program not being used) to free up your system's memory. Adding memory to your system, of course, also is an alternative for increasing performance. The suggested amount of memory for running Office XP is 64MB for Windows 98, Me, and Windows NT. For Windows 2000, 128MB is suggested.

To start Microsoft Outlook, follow these steps:

1. From the Windows desktop, click the **Start** button, choose **Programs**, and then select **Microsoft Outlook**.

TIP   **Shortcuts to Launching Outlook**   You can also double-click the **Outlook** shortcut icon on the desktop to start Outlook, or you can click the **Outlook** icon on the Quick Launch toolbar on the Windows taskbar (next to the Start button).

2. If your PC is set up for multiple users, the Choose Profile dialog box appears; click **OK** to accept the default profile or choose your profile and open Microsoft Outlook. Figure 1.1 shows the Outlook screen that appears.

Profile   The profile includes information about you and your e-mail accounts and is
created automatically when you install Outlook (the e-mail accounts are added to
the profile when Outlook is set up for the first time, as discussed in Lesson 2,
"Understanding the Outlook E-Mail Configurations"). Multiple profiles become
an issue only if you share your computer with other users.

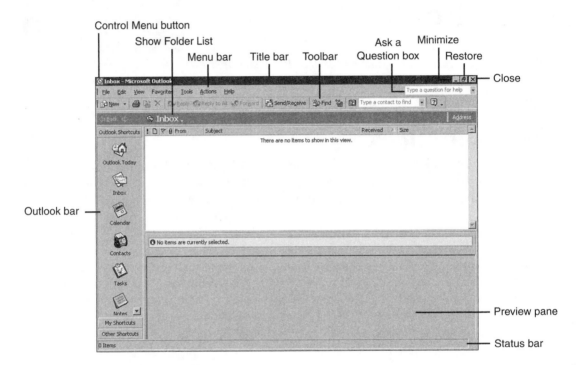

Figure 1.1 The Outlook window includes all the icons and items you need to access its
various features.

In situations where you connect to the Internet using a modem dial-up connection,
the Connection Wizard attempts to make a dial-in connection as Outlook opens.
This enables Outlook to check your e-mail server.

The First Time You Start Outlook   The very first time you start Outlook on a computer that has not had a previous version of the software installed, you will be
required to configure the e-mail accounts that you use. Setting up your e-mail
accounts is discussed in Lesson 2, "Understanding the Outlook E-Mail
Configurations."

Understanding the Outlook Window

The Outlook window includes items you can use to navigate in and operate the program. If you do not see some of the items listed in Figure 1.1 on your screen, open the **View** menu and select the command for the appropriate element (such as **Toolbars, Status Bar, Folder List,** or **Outlook Bar**). A check mark in front of an item means the item is currently showing. If you find the Preview pane distracting when you first open the Outlook window, click the **View** menu and click **Preview Pane** to close the Preview pane.

Table 1.1 describes the elements you see in the opening screen.

Table 1.1 Elements of the Outlook Window

Element	Description
Title bar	Includes the name of the application and current folder, plus the Minimize, Maximize, and Close buttons.
Control Menu button	Opens the Control menu, which provides such commands as Move, Size, Minimize, and Close.
Minimize button	Reduces the Outlook window to a button on the taskbar; to restore the window to its original size, click the button on the taskbar.
Maximize button	Enlarges the Outlook window to cover the Windows desktop. When the window is maximized, the Maximize button changes to a Restore button you can click to return the window to its previous size.
Close (x) button	Closes the Outlook program window.
Menu bar	Contains menus of commands you can use to perform tasks in the program.
Toolbar	Includes icons that serve as shortcuts for common commands, such as creating a new message or printing a message.
Show Folder List	Displays the current folder. Click this to display a list of personal folders you can open.
Outlook bar	Displays icons representing folders: Inbox, Calendar, Contacts, and so on. Click an icon to change to the folder it names. The Outlook Shortcuts, My Shortcuts, and Other Shortcuts buttons on the bar list specific groups of folders (for example, the My Shortcuts button lists icons related to your e-mail, such as the Drafts, Outbox, and Sent items).
Status bar	Displays information about the items currently shown in the Information Viewer.
Preview pane	Displays a preview of the currently selected item in your Outlook Inbox or other selected folder.
Ask a Question box	This box allows you to quickly ask the Outlook Help system a question. It also allows you to forgo using the Office Assistant to access the Help system.

Finding a Toolbar Button's Purpose You can place the mouse pointer on any toolbar button to view a description of that tool's function.

Using the Mouse in Outlook

Like most Windows-based programs, you can use the mouse in Outlook to select items, open e-mail and folders, move items, and so on. In general, clicking selects an item, and double-clicking selects it and performs some action on it (for example, displaying its contents). In addition to clicking and double-clicking, there are some special mouse actions you can use in Outlook:

- **Drag**—To move an object to another position on the screen (to transfer a mail message to another folder, for example), you can drag the object with the mouse. To drag an object to a new location onscreen, point to the object and press and hold down the left mouse button. Move the mouse pointer to the new location and then release the mouse button.

- **Right-click**—You can display a shortcut menu by clicking the right mouse button when pointing to an item. For example, you can right-click a folder in the Outlook bar or a piece of e-mail. A shortcut menu appears, which usually contains common commands relating to that particular item.

- **Multiselect**—You can act on multiple items at once by selecting them before issuing a command. To select multiple contiguous items, hold down the **Shift** key and click the first and last items you want to select. To select noncontiguous items (those that are not adjacent to each other), hold down the **Ctrl** key and click each item.

If you have a mouse, such as the Microsoft IntelliMouse, that includes a scroll wheel, you can use it in Outlook. Turn the wheel toward you to move down through any list in Outlook, such as your Contacts list, or move the wheel up to scroll up in a list.

TIP **Keyboard Shortcuts** You can use the keyboard to move around Outlook and to access many, but not all, of its features. For example, to open a menu with the keyboard, press the **Alt** key and then press the underlined letter in the menu name (press **Alt+F** to open the File menu, for instance).

Working Offline

In cases where you use a modem connection to access your e-mail server, you can close the connection while still working in Outlook. This allows you to free up your phone line or, if you pay for your connection based on the time you are connected, save on connection time. Working offline in Outlook does not affect any Outlook features or capabilities. E-mail that you create while working offline is held in the Outbox until you reconnect to your Internet connection.

To work offline, select the **File** menu and then select **Work Offline**. If you are prompted to confirm the closing of your dial-in connection, click **Yes**.

Exiting Outlook

When you are finished working in Outlook, you can exit the application in a couple of ways. You can use the File menu: select **File**, **Exit**. Or you can close Outlook by clicking the Outlook window's **Close** (x) button. In cases where you are connected to the Internet using a dial-up connection, you are prompted as to whether you want to log off your connection. If you want to close the dial-up connection, select **Log Off** in the message box.

Understanding the Outlook E-Mail Configurations

In this lesson, you learn how to set up Outlook for different types of electronic mail.

Types of Outlook E-Mail Configurations

The type or flavor of e-mail that you use in Outlook depends on who provides your e-mail account. Outlook contains support for the three most common providers of e-mail service:

- **ISP**—When you sign up for an Internet service provider (ISP), the company usually provides you with at least one e-mail account.
- **Exchange**—In networked environments (most offices, for example), an e-mail server such as Microsoft Exchange may control delivery of e-mail.
- **Web**—Outlook also provides you with the capability to connect to Web-based e-mail services, such as Microsoft's Hotmail or Yahoo!'s Yahoo! mail.

Because Outlook serves not only as your e-mail client, but also as your personal information manager (allowing you to build a contacts list and keep track of your appointments and tasks), it is designed to operate either in a standalone environment or in a corporate service environment. As a standalone application, your contacts, appointments, and tasks are stored locally on your computer and you access your e-mail through the Internet. However, in a corporate environment, your calendar and tasks folders are kept on a corporate communication server (typically Microsoft Exchange Server) where your information can be shared with other users.

E-Mail Client   Software that is configured on a user's computer to connect to e-mail services on a company's network or on the Internet.

Making Your E-Mail Choice

The first time you start Outlook (double-click its desktop icon), you must communicate to Outlook the type of e-mail account that you use on your computer. Outlook assists you in this task by launching the Outlook Startup Wizard. Click **Next** to move past the opening screen. The E-Mail Accounts screen appears as shown in Figure 2.1.

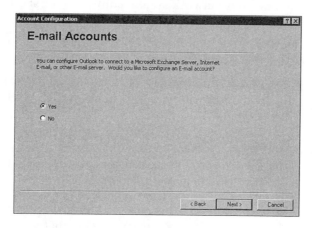

Figure 2.1   The Outlook Startup Wizard helps you set up your e-mail accounts.

To configure an e-mail account for use in Outlook, make sure that the **Yes** option button is selected, and then click **Next** to continue. The next screen presents a selection of different e-mail servers, as shown in Figure 2.2.

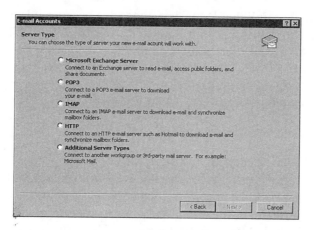

Figure 2.2   Outlook can function as an e-mail client for several e-mail types.

How your e-mail functions depends on which option you select to configure Outlook as a specific e-mail client. The possibilities are

- **Microsoft Exchange Server**—This type of account makes Outlook an Exchange Server client; mail boxes and other resources, such as shared public folders, are managed on the Exchange Server computer. If this is what your Outlook installation requires, your network system administrator should provide these settings for you.

- **POP3**—POP3 is a protocol that most ISPs use, which allows a POP3 e-mail server to function as a mail drop.

  This means that your Internet e-mail is forwarded to the POP3 server and sits there until you connect with your e-mail client (Outlook) and download the mail to your computer.

POP3 (Post Office Protocol Version 3)   A set of software protocols or rules used to download mail to your computer. Your e-mail resides on the POP3 server until you connect and download it to your computer.

- **IMAP**—IMAP is a protocol that allows Outlook to download e-mail from an IMAP mail server. IMAP differs from POP3 in that your e-mail is not removed from the mail server when you connect to the server with your e-mail client (Outlook). Instead, you are provided a list of saved and new messages, which you can then open and read. IMAP is particularly useful when one e-mail account may be accessed by more than one computer, allowing the messages to be available from more than one computer.

  You might think that IMAP is a good idea because it leaves the e-mail on the mail server. However, you can use IMAP only if your ISP or company provides an IMAP mail server. In most cases, ISPs don't want your mail on their server, so they use POP3, which sends the mail to your computer when you connect.

IMAP (Internet Message Access Protocol)   A set of software rules used by an e-mail client to access e-mail messages on a shared mail server as if the messages were stored locally.

- **HTTP**—The Hypertext Transfer Protocol is the protocol and set of rules that enables you to browse Web sites using a Web browser. HTTP e-mail is accessed through a Web site, and your inbox actually resides on a server that is hosted by the provider of the e-mail Web site. Common providers of this type of e-mail include Microsoft (in the case of Hotmail) and Yahoo! (in the case of Yahoo! mail). Normally, such e-mail is accessed from the provider's Web site;

however, Outlook can be configured to act as your e-mail client with HTTP mail providers.

- **Additional Server Types**—This selection allows you to configure Outlook as a mail client for other e-mail server types, such as Microsoft Mail or third-party e-mail server software. It also provides you with the capability to create a special e-mail account that allows you to receive faxes in the Outlook Inbox.

Even though Outlook pretty much demands that you configure an e-mail account during the initial Outlook setup, it doesn't easily provide for the fact that you might want to set up more than one account. However, it is very easy to add additional e-mail accounts as needed, which is discussed later in this lesson. The two most common uses for Outlook are as a Microsoft Exchange Server e-mail client or as an Internet e-mail client using POP3, IMAP, or HTTP. In the following sections, you take a closer look at the configuration steps for setting up your first POP3 or HTTP account. You can then learn how to add additional accounts after Outlook has been initially configured.

 TIP **Importing E-Mail Settings** If you are already using an e-mail client, such as Outlook Express, you can import all the e-mail messages and the settings for your e-mail accounts into Outlook. Outlook actually prompts you to perform this import when you start it for the first time. If you import mail settings, you won't be required to add an e-mail account as outlined in this section. You can use the information in this lesson, however, to add any additional e-mail accounts that you might need.

Internet POP3 E-Mail

If you connect to the Internet using a modem, a DSL router, or a broadband cable modem, your Internet connection is of the type that an Internet service provider (ISP) provides. Most ISPs provide e-mail to their users in the form of a POP3 account. This means that the ISP's e-mail server holds your e-mail until you connect and download your messages to Outlook.

 TERM **ISP (Internet Service Provider)** A commercial, educational, or government institution that provides individuals and companies access to the Internet.

ISPs that provide e-mail service also must have some mechanism for you to send e-mail to other users on the Internet. A computer called an SMTP server handles the sending of e-mail from your computer, over the Internet, to a final destination. That destination is typically the POP3 server that serves as the mail drop for the person to whom you are sending the Internet e-mail.

TERM **SMTP (Simple Mail Transfer Protocol)** A set of rules used to transfer Internet mail; your ISP goes through an SMTP host, or relay, server to get your mail to you.

If you do not use an e-mail account (such as a POP3 account) that your ISP supplies to you, you can still use Outlook for Internet e-mail. In this case, sign up for an HTTP e-mail account on the Web and configure Outlook to use it. Configuring HTTP e-mail is discussed in a moment, but first take a look at the steps required to configure a POP3 e-mail account as Outlook's initial e-mail account.

The first thing Outlook needs you to provide is information related to the POP3 account, such as your username, password, and SMTP and POP3 servers, all of which your ISP must provide. To complete the configuration of your POP3 account, follow these steps:

1. Select the **POP3** button on the E-Mail Accounts screen, and then click **Next** to continue.

2. On the next screen, shown in Figure 2.3, enter your name, your e-mail address, your username, and your password. You also must provide the name of your ISP's POP3 (incoming server) and SMTP server (outgoing server) in the appropriate box. If your ISP uses Secure Password Authentication, which provides a second layer of authentication for their mail servers, click the Log on using Secure Password Authentication (SPA). (If SPA is used, you are provided a second username and password, other than your e-mail username, to log on to the servers; most ISPs do not use SPA.)

Figure 2.3 You must supply all the information listed on the Internet E-Mail Settings (POP3) screen.

3. You can test your new account settings to make sure that they work; be sure you are connected to the Internet, and then click the **Test Account Settings**

button. Outlook tests the user account and the servers listed. A Test Account Settings dialog box appears, as shown in Figure 2.4. To close the dialog box, click **Close**.

Figure 2.4   You can check your Internet e-mail settings after entering the appropriate information.

4. When you have completed your POP3 configuration settings (and tested them), click the **Next** button.

5. A final screen appears, letting you know that you have provided all the necessary information. Click **Finish** to end the process and open the Outlook Inbox.

TIP   **Configuring for IMAP**   The steps to configure an IMAP account are the same as those listed to configure the POP3 Internet e-mail account. The only differences are that you select IMAP on the initial setup screen and then make sure that the IMAP server name is provided on the configuration screen rather than the POP3 server name.

HTTP E-Mail Accounts

Although most people use either an Exchange Server (configured by a system administrator) or a POP3 account as their primary e-mail account, Web-based HTTP accounts, such as Microsoft Hotmail, are convenient for checking personal e-mail from any computer. Typically, you must log on to the appropriate Web site and provide a username and password to access your HTTP e-mail account. Although this offers a degree of flexibility that is appealing to many users, others are often put off because, in the past, this has prevented them from checking their e-mail using Outlook.

Fortunately, Outlook now has the capability to access HTTP e-mail accounts directly from Outlook. Before you can configure the HTTP account, however, you must sign up for an account on the site of HTTP mail service provider that you want to use. Assuming that you have an active account, follow these steps to configure an HTTP e-mail account:

1. Rather than selecting POP3, as you did in the previous section, select the **HTTP** option button on the E-Mail Accounts dialog box (shown previously in Figure 2.2). Click **Next** to continue.

2. On the next screen, shown in Figure 2.5, enter your name, your e-mail address, your username, and your password (supplied by your mail provider). If you use an HTTP provider other than Hotmail, select **Other** in the HTTP Mail Service Provider dialog box, and then provide the URL of your HTTP service (you are providing the Web page address of the service).

Figure 2.5   You must supply all the information listed on the HTTP E-Mail Settings screen.

3. Click **Next** after entering all the necessary information. On the final screen that appears, click **Finish**.

You are then returned to the Outlook window. When you add an HTTP account, such as a Hotmail account, to Outlook, a second set of folders appears in the Outlook folder listings, including Deleted Items, Inbox, Outbox, and Sent Items. Figure 2.6 shows this new set of folders.

Because a second set of folders is created, you can access the HTTP account from Outlook, but you manage received, sent, or deleted mail in their own set of folders. Mail received on any other accounts you might have, such as a POP3 account, are still located in your main Outlook Inbox.

Figure 2.6 The HTTP mail folders, such as Hotmail, appear on the Outlook Folders list.

Adding Other Types of E-Mail Accounts

As previously mentioned, Outlook is typically used as an e-mail client for either Exchange Server environments or for Internet e-mail where an ISP supplies either a POP3, an IMAP, or an HTTP e-mail account. However, many users find that they have more than one type of account at their disposal. Very often, users get one or more accounts through their ISP, but also sign up for an HTTP account that they can have easy access to from multiple locations (these HTTP accounts are usually free).

TIP **Configuring Exchange Server E-Mail Accounts** If you are using Outlook on a corporate network that uses an Exchange Server as the e-mail server, your account will typically be set up on your computer by the network administrator. The name of the Exchange Server and your network user name are required to complete the configuration. If you use Outlook on a corporate network, consult your network administrator for help in configuring Outlook. Using Outlook for e-mail on an Exchange Server network enables several e-mail features that are not available when you use Outlook for Internet e-mail, such as a POP3 account. On a network, you can redirect replies, set message expirations, and even grant privileges to other users who can then monitor your e-mail, calendar, contacts, and tasks.

You can use the following steps to add e-mail accounts to the Outlook settings after you have already made your initial configuration, as discussed in the previous sections of this lesson. Remember, you can add any type of e-mail account to Outlook after the fact.

In the Outlook window:

1. Select **Tools**, **E-Mail Accounts**. The E-Mail Accounts dialog box opens, as shown in Figure 2.7.

Figure 2.7   E-mail accounts are added using the E-Mail Accounts dialog box.

2. Select the **Add a New E-Mail Account** option button, and click **Next** to continue.

3. The Server Type screen opens with a list of the different types of e-mail accounts (this is the same screen provided during the initial e-mail configuration for Outlook, shown in Figure 2.2).

4. Select the type of e-mail account you want to add to the Outlook configuration, and then click the **Next** button.

The information needed to configure a particular e-mail type is requested on the next screen, as previously discussed in this lesson.

Deleting E-Mail Accounts

As you've seen in this lesson, configuring Outlook with different types of e-mail accounts is a pretty straightforward process. You might also find, on occasion, that you want to delete an e-mail account from the Outlook configuration. To do so, follow these steps:

1. Select **Tools**, **E-Mail Accounts**. In the E-Mail Accounts dialog box, select the **View or Change Existing E-Mail Accounts** option button, and then click **Next**.

2. The E-Mail Accounts dialog box appears as shown in Figure 2.8. To delete an account, select the account, and then click the **Remove** button.

Figure 2.8 E-mail accounts are managed in the E-Mail Accounts dialog box.

3. You are asked to confirm the deletion of the account. Click **Yes** to continue.

You can also use the E-Mail Accounts dialog box to edit the settings for any of the e-mail accounts that you have created. Select the appropriate account, and then select the **Change** button. A dialog box for that specific account opens as shown in Figure 2.9, and you can change settings as required.

Figure 2.9 E-mail accounts settings can be edited using their settings dialog box.

In some cases, you might need to configure special settings for an e-mail account, such as how your computer connects to the Internet when you are using a particular e-mail account. Select the **More Settings** button on the e-mail accounts settings dialog box. The E-Mail Settings dialog box appears for the e-mail account (see Figure 2.10).

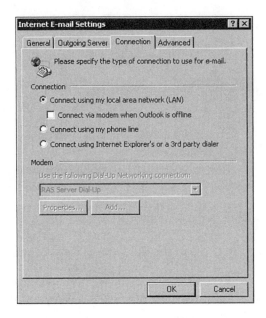

Figure 2.10 Special settings related to an e-mail account can be reached by clicking the More Settings button.

The E-Mail Settings dialog box has a series of tabs that differ depending on the type of e-mail account you are editing. In most cases (unless your ISP has provided you with special settings information), the only settings you will want to adjust are on the Connection tab, which allows you to specify how Outlook connects to the Internet when you are checking this particular account for e-mail.

After completing the addition of any special settings to the E-Mail Settings dialog box, click **OK** to close it. You are returned to the dialog box for the e-mail account. Click **Next** to return to the E-Mail Accounts dialog box, and then click **Finish** to return to Outlook.

Using Outlook's Tools

In this lesson, you learn how to change views in Outlook, how to use the Outlook bar, and how to use the Folder list.

Using the Outlook Bar

Each Outlook organizational tool has its own folder. You have a folder for e-mail (Inbox), a folder for the calendar (Calendar), and so on. The Outlook bar is a tool you can use to quickly change folders in Outlook. The icons in the Outlook bar represent all the folders available to you and provide shortcuts to getting to the contents of those folders. Figure 3.1 shows the Outlook bar and other areas of the Outlook window.

Three shortcut groups are located within the Outlook bar: Outlook Shortcuts, My Shortcuts, and Other Shortcuts. Each group contains related folders in which you can work.

- **Outlook Shortcuts**—This group contains folders for working with the different organizational tools in Outlook, such as Inbox, Calendar, Tasks, and so on.

- **My Shortcuts**—This group contains folders for organizing and managing e-mail you compose and send, such as the Outbox and the Sent Items folder. This group also provides access to the Journal (which keeps track of Office documents that you open and e-mail that you send) and an icon that takes you online to the Outlook Update Web page.

- **Other Shortcuts**—This group contains folders on your computer, such as My Computer, My Documents, and Favorites, which is a list of your favorite Web sites. You can use each of these folders to work with files and folders outside Outlook.

To switch from one group to another, click the **Outlook Shortcuts**, **My Shortcuts**, or **Other Shortcuts** button on the Outlook bar. The Outlook shortcuts group is displayed by default, providing you with quick access to tools such as your Inbox, Calendar, and Contacts list.

Figure 3.1 Use the Outlook bar to view various items in your work.

The Outlook Shortcuts Folders

The Outlook Shortcuts group's folder icons in the Outlook bar enable you to access your work in Outlook. That includes your e-mail messages, appointments, contact list, and so on. Table 3.1 describes each of the folders within the Outlook Shortcuts group.

Table 3.1 Outlook Shortcuts Group Folders

Folder	Description
Outlook Today	Although not really a folder, the Outlook Today icon on the Outlook bar provides a summary of Calendar events, tasks, and new messages for the current day (today).
Inbox	Includes messages you've sent and received by e-mail and fax.
Calendar	Contains your appointments, events, scheduled meetings, and so on.
Contacts	Lists names and addresses of the people with whom you communicate.
Tasks	Includes any tasks you have on your to-do list.

Table 3.1   Continued

Folder	Description
Notes	Lists notes you write to yourself or others.
Deleted Items	Includes any items you've deleted from other folders.

The My Shortcuts Folders

The My Shortcuts group folders provide a method of organizing your incoming and outgoing e-mail messages (see Figure 3.2). Table 3.2 describes each folder in the Mail group.

Table 3.2   My Shortcuts Folders

Folder	Description
Draft	Contains messages you have started but not sent.
Sent Items	Stores all messages you've sent.
Outbox	Contains messages to be sent.
Journal	Keeps track of your activities in Outlook, such as the logging of e-mail sent to specific contacts. The Journal also can keep track of your activities in other Office applications, such as Word or Excel.

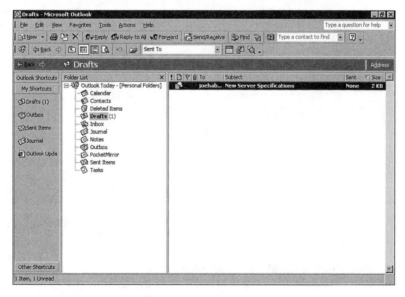

Figure 3.2   The My Shortcuts folder icons give you access to your e-mail and fax messages that have been saved as drafts, that have been sent, or that are waiting to be sent.

I See Other Folders in My Groups   You can add additional folders and folder icons very easily to Outlook. If you find folders other than the ones described here, folders have probably been added to your particular installation of Outlook.

CAUTION

The Other Shortcuts Folders

The Other Shortcuts group contains folders that are on your computer but not within Outlook: My Computer, My Documents, and Favorites. You can access a document or information in any of those areas so that you can attach it to a message, add notes to it, or otherwise use it in Outlook.

For example, with My Computer, you can view the contents of both hard and floppy disks, CD-ROM drives, and so on (see Figure 3.3). Double-click a drive in the window to view its folders and files. Double-click a folder to view its contents as well. Then, you can attach files to messages or otherwise use the files on your hard drive with the Outlook features.

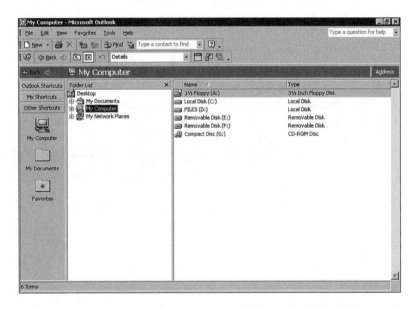

Figure 3.3   View your entire system through the My Computer folder in Outlook.

TIP   **Moving Up a Level**   Use the **Back** button on the Advanced toolbar (right-click the Outlook toolbar and select **Advanced** on the shortcut menu) to return to a folder or drive after you've double-clicked to expand it and view its contents.

Using the Folder List

Outlook provides another method of viewing the folders within Outlook and your system: the Folder List. The Folder List displays the folders within any of the three groups (Outlook Shortcuts, My Shortcuts, or Other Shortcuts). From the list, you can select the folder you want to view.

To use the Folder List, first select the group (such as Outlook Shortcuts or Other Shortcuts) that contains the folders you want to view, and then select a particular folder (using the appropriate shortcut) from the Outlook bar to display the list (see Figure 3.4).

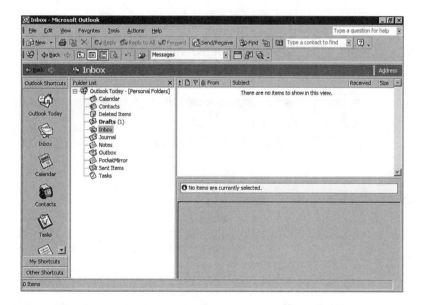

Figure 3.4 The Folder List shows all folders in the group you selected.

TIP **Pinning Down the Folder List** When you open the Folder List button on a particular folder's name, the Folder List floats on top of the current folder window. Click the **Push Pin** button in the upper-right corner of the Folder List to pin down the list in the Outlook window. If you want to close the Folder List, click its **Close** (X) button.

Choose any folder from the list, and the Information Viewer changes to reflect your selection. If you want to display another folder in the Information screen, click the folder to display its contents.

Changing Views

In Outlook, you are provided with different views that enable you to look at the information in your various folders from a particular perspective. Each view presents the information in a different format and organizational structure.

The easiest way to select the different views provided for each of your Outlook folders is to use a Current View drop-down box that is present on the Advanced toolbar for each folder type (Inbox, Calendar, Contacts, and so on). To open the Advanced toolbar (it doesn't matter which Outlook folder you currently have selected), follow these steps:

1. Point to the Standard toolbar for an Outlook folder (such as the Inbox) and click the right mouse button.

2. A shortcut menu appears, as shown in Figure 3.5. Click **Advanced**. The Advanced toolbar appears.

Figure 3.5   Right-click the Standard toolbar to access the Outlook Advanced toolbar.

3. If you find later that you would like to close the Advanced toolbar, repeat steps 1 and 2 to remove the check mark next to Advanced on the shortcut menu that appears.

TIP   **You Must Open the Advanced Toolbar Only Once**   After you've opened the Advanced toolbar for a folder, such as the Calendar or Inbox, it will be available for all the other Outlook folders.

Each folder, such as the Inbox, Calendar, Contacts, and so on, has a different set of buttons on the Standard and Advanced toolbars. This is because the commands and features that you access on a toolbar are particular to the folder that you currently have selected.

After you have the Advanced toolbar open, you can change the current view of any folder by clicking the **Current View** drop-down box, as shown in Figure 3.6. Each Current View box contains views that are appropriate for the currently selected folder on the Outlook bar.

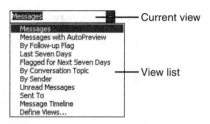

Figure 3.6   Select a view to change the format of the information.

As you can see in Figure 3.6, you can change your view of the Inbox so that you can see the following:

- **Messages**—All messages
- **Messages with AutoPreview**—Messages and their first three lines of text
- **By Follow-Up Flag**—Messages that have been tagged with a follow-up flag
- **Last Seven Days**—Messages from the last seven days
- **Flagged for Next Seven Days**—Messages tagged with a flag for the next seven days
- **By Conversation Topic**—Messages organized by topic
- **By Sender**—Messages organized by sender
- **Unread Messages**—Unread messages only
- **Sent To**—Messages by recipient
- **Message Timeline**—Messages arranged in a timeline

Similarly, the Calendar folder, which is arranged in the Day/Week/Month view type by default, enables you to view your appointments and events by Active Appointments, Day/Week/Month with AutoPreview, Events, Recurring Appointments, and several other view types.

You can also change the view type for any of your folders by selecting the **View** menu and then pointing at **Current View**. The View list appears at the top of the Current View submenu.

As you work your way through the Outlook part of this book, you'll see examples of some of the different view types as they are used when you are working in Outlook. When you change folders in Outlook, take a quick look at the available views in the Current View drop-down list.

Creating Custom Views

In addition to Outlook's many presupplied views, you can also create custom views of the information in your Outlook folders. To create a custom view for one of your Outlook folders, follow these steps:

1. Click the **View** menu and then point at **Current View**. Select **Define Views** (near the bottom of the Current View submenu). A Define Views dialog box for the currently selected folder opens.

2. Click the **New** button in the Define Views box. The Create a New View dialog box appears, as shown in Figure 3.7.

Figure 3.7   You can create custom views for your Outlook folders.

3. Enter a name for your new view and select a view type from the list in the Type of View box.

You can select different view types for a custom view:

- **Table**—Presents items in a grid of sorts in rows and columns. Use this view type to view mail messages, tasks, and details about any item.

- **Timeline**—Displays items as icons arranged in chronological order from left to right on a time scale. Use this to view journal entries and other items in this type of view.

- **Card**—Presents items such as cards in a card file. Use this to view contacts.

- **Day/Week/Month**—Displays items in a calendar view in blocks of time. Use this type for meetings and scheduled tasks.

- **Icon**—Provides graphical icons to represent tasks, notes, calendars, and so on.

TIP **Using the Create a New View Option Buttons** If you work on a network where Outlook folders are shared on an Exchange Server, you can create your new view so that you see only the information in the view. Alternatively, you can share the view with other users that access the information. The default option in the Create a New View dialog box is **This folder, visible to everyone**. To reserve the custom view for yourself, click the **This folder, visible only to me** option button. If you want to use the new view for all your mail folders, click the **All Mail and Post folders** option button.

4. After you've selected the type of view you want to create, click the **OK** button. A View Settings dialog box appears based on your selection. In this box, you determine which fields you want to have in the view and the fonts and other view settings you want to use.

5. After you've selected the fields and view settings, click **Apply View**. The items in the current folder appear in the new view.

Fields A specific type of information that you want to appear in your custom view. For a custom Inbox view using the Timeline view type, the fields include Received (when the message was received), Created (when the message was created), and Sent (when the message was sent).

Your newly created view appears on the Current View list on the Advanced toolbar. You can select it by clicking the list's drop-down arrow and then clicking the custom view's name.

Should I Design My Own Views? Designing your own views can be complicated. Outlook provides several views for each folder on the Outlook bar. You might want to explore all these possibilities before you begin to create your own views.

CAUTION

Using Outlook Today

Outlook Today is a great way to get a snapshot view of your day. This feature provides a window that lists all your messages, appointments, and tasks associated with the current day.

To open the Outlook Today window, click the **Go** menu and select **Outlook Today**. Icons for your Calendar, Messages, and Tasks appear in the Outlook Today window, as shown in Figure 3.8. Items for the current day are listed below the icons.

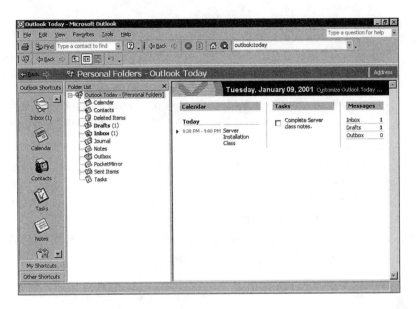

Figure 3.8 Outlook Today provides a list of all the items associated with the current day.

You can click any of the listed items (a particular appointment or task) to open the appropriate folder and view the details associated with the items. You can even update the items.

The Outlook Today Standard toolbar also provides a Type a Contact to Find box that you can use to quickly find people in your Contacts folder. Type a name into the Type a Contact to Find box (on the left of the Standard toolbar) and then press **Enter**. A Contact window appears for the person. You can edit the person's information or close the Contact box by clicking the **Close** button.

After you have viewed the items in the Outlook Today window, you can return to any of your folders by clicking their icons on the Outlook bar. Outlook Today is an excellent way to get a handle on what your day has in store for you.

Creating Mail

In this lesson, you learn how to compose a message, format text, check your spelling, and send e-mail. You also learn how to use different e-mail formats such as plain text and HTML.

Composing a Message

You can send an e-mail message to anyone for whom you have an e-mail address, whether that address is in your list of contacts or scribbled on a Post-it note. In addition to sending a message to one or more recipients, in Outlook you can forward or copy messages to individuals in your Contacts list. You can even e-mail groups of people who are listed in your various distribution lists.

 TIP   **Compose Your Messages Offline**   If you connect to an Internet service provider and don't want to waste precious connect time while you compose e-mail messages, you can create new messages in Outlook without being connected to the Internet. New messages you send are placed in your Outbox until you connect to the Internet and actually send them on to their final destination. When you are connected to the Internet, all you have to do is click the **Send/Receive** button on the Standard toolbar (or **Tools**, **Send/Receive**, **Send All**) to send any messages held in the Outbox.

To open a new e-mail message while in the Outlook Inbox, select **File**, point at **New**, and then select **Mail Message** in the Outlook Inbox window (you can also click the **New** button on the Standard toolbar). A new message window appears (see Figure 4.1).

E-mail addresses can be placed in the To box of a message that you want to send (a message you create from scratch or an existing message that you are forwarding) in several ways. You can

- Use your Outlook Contacts list.
- Use your Outlook Address Book.
- Type in an e-mail address that you don't currently have in any of your lists.

In the case of e-mail messages that you reply to, the e-mail address of the person who sent you the message is automatically placed in the To box, making it ready to be sent.

Figure 4.1   Compose a new message in the Untitled Message window.

Having e-mail addresses listed in either your Contacts list or the Outlook Address Book is the easiest way to add an e-mail address to a list. It also helps you keep organized, and that is probably one of the reasons why you're using Outlook in the first place. You will also find that having e-mail addresses readily available in an Outlook list makes it easier to send carbon copies (duplicate e-mails) or blind carbon copies of messages when you are composing a particular message.

   Blind Carbon Copy   A blind carbon copy (Bcc) of a message is a copy sent to someone in secret; the other recipients have no way of knowing that you are sending the message to someone as a blind carbon copy.

You can find more information on using Outlook's Personal Address Book in Lesson 10, "Using the Outlook Address Books." Lesson 11, "Creating a Contacts List," shows you how to use contacts.

To address a new e-mail message, follow these steps:

1. In the message window, click the **To** button to display the Select Names dialog box. Names that have been entered in your Contacts list appear on the left side of the dialog box. If you want to switch to a different list, such as the Outlook Address Book, click the drop-down list on the upper-right corner of the dialog box and make a new selection.

If the e-mail address you want isn't in your Contacts list, instead of clicking the **To** button, type the e-mail address directly into the To text box (if you do this, you can then skip steps 3 through 7).

2. From the list of addresses that appears on the left of the dialog box, choose the name of the intended recipient and select the **To** button (or you can double-click the name). Outlook copies the name to the Message Recipients list. You can also add any distribution lists to the To box that appear in your address list. To send a carbon copy or blind carbon copy to a recipient, use the **Cc** or **Bcc** buttons.

Figure 4.2 shows a message that is addressed to an individual whose address was contained in the Contacts list and also to a group of people who are listed in a distribution list (you can enter as many addresses as you want).

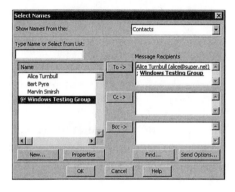

Figure 4.2   Add e-mail addresses or distribution list names quickly with the Select Names dialog box.

3. Click **OK** to return to the message window. Click in the Subject box and type the subject of your message.

4. Click in the text area, and then enter the text of the message. You do not have to press the Enter key at the end of a line; Outlook automatically wraps the text at the end of a line for you. You can use the Delete and Backspace keys to edit the text you enter.

 5. When you finish typing the message, you can send the message, or you can format the message or check the spelling as detailed later in this lesson. To send the message, click the **Send** button on the message's Standard toolbar.

No Address   If you try to send a message without entering an address, Outlook displays a message that at least one e-mail address must be in the To box. Type in an address or select an address from your Contacts list or Address Book.

CAUTION

Formatting Text

You can enhance the format of the text in your message to make it more attractive, to make it easier to read, or to add emphasis. Any formatting you do transfers to the recipient with the message if the recipient has Outlook or another e-mail client that can work with HTML or Rich Text Format messages. However, if the recipient doesn't have an e-mail client that can handle these special message formats, formatting might not transfer and the message will be received in plain text.

HTML   Hypertext Markup Language is used to design Web pages for the World Wide Web. Outlook can send messages in this format, providing you with several text formatting options. Graphics can even be pasted into an HTML message.

Rich Text Format   A special e-mail format developed by Microsoft for use with Microsoft mail systems. Outlook can send and receive messages in Rich Text Format. This enables you to send and receive messages with special formatting, such as bold, italic, various fonts, and other special characters and graphics.

You format text in two ways. You can format the text after you type it by selecting it and then choosing a font, size, or other attribute; or you can select the font, size, or other attribute to toggle it on, and then enter the text, which will be formatted as you type.

To format the text in your message, first make sure the Formatting toolbar is showing. On the menu system provided by the message window, select **View**, and then select **Toolbars** and click **Formatting**. Figure 4.3 shows a message with the Formatting toolbar displayed. Formatting options have also been applied to the text in the message. Table 4.1 explains the buttons found on the Formatting toolbar.

CAUTION

The Formatting Toolbar Buttons Don't Work   Only messages sent in HTML or Rich Text Format can be formatted. Plain-text messages don't supply you with any formatting options. So, even if the Formatting toolbar appears at the top of a plain-text message, the formatting options will not be available. Selecting the message type (such as HTML or plain text) is discussed in the section "Selecting the E-Mail Message Format," found later in this lesson.

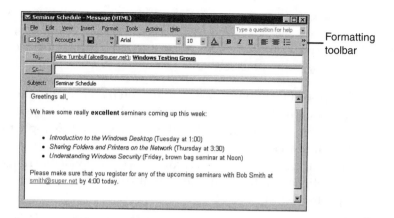

Formatting
toolbar

Figure 4.3   Use the Formatting toolbar to modify your message text.

Table 4.1   Formatting Toolbar Buttons

Button	Name
A	Font Color
B	Bold
I	Italic
U	Underline
≣	Align Left
≣	Center
≣	Align Right
≔	Bullets
≔	Numbering
≔	Decrease Indent
≔	Increase Indent
—	Insert Horizontal Line

CAUTION

My Toolbars Look Completely Different! If you are using Microsoft Word as your e-mail editor, the toolbars that are present in the new message window reflect those you have selected in your Word installation. The Word and Outlook toolbars have many of the same buttons.

1. To apply a new font to selected text, on the Formatting toolbar, click the down arrow in the **Font** box. Scroll through the font list, if necessary, to view all fonts on the system, and then click the font you want to apply to the text. You can also apply a style to selected text in the message. On the Formatting toolbar, click the **Style** drop-down arrow. The styles available range from a set of predefined heading styles to special styles such as Numbered list and Bulleted list.

2. Assign a size by clicking the down arrow beside the **Font Size** drop-down list and choosing the size; alternatively, you can type a size into the Font Size text box.

3. To choose a color, click the **Color** button and select a color from the palette box that appears.

4. Choose a type style to apply to text by clicking the **Bold**, **Italic**, and/or **Underline** buttons on the Formatting toolbar.

5. Choose an alignment by selecting the **Align Left**, **Center**, or **Align Right** button from the Formatting toolbar.

6. Add bullets to a list by clicking the **Bullets** button on the Formatting toolbar. If you prefer a numbered list, click the **Numbering** button.

7. Create text indents or remove indents in half-inch increments by clicking the **Increase Indent** or **Decrease Indent** buttons. (Each time you click the Indent button, the indent changes by one-half inch.)

8. If you want to divide the text in the message using a horizontal line, place the insertion point at the appropriate place in the text and then click the **Add Horizontal Line** button.

TIP

Yuck, No Thanks! If you assign formatting to your text and don't particularly like it, click **Edit** and select **Undo** to remove the last formatting that you assigned.

Selecting the E-Mail Message Format

The default message format in Outlook is HTML. If you send most of your messages to individuals who don't have mail clients that can read the HTML format, you might want to change the default to plain text. On corporate networks, you might find an advantage to using the Rich Text Format as the default text format for your messages. This file format was developed for the Exchange Server mail environment used on most business networks.

The default format is set in the Outlook Options dialog box on the Mail Format tab. Fortunately, Outlook makes it very easy for you to switch the format of a mail message while you are composing the message. First, take a look at how to set the default mail type, and then look at how to change the message format while composing the message.

To set the default message format:

1. Click **Tools, Options**. The Options dialog box appears.

2. Click the **Mail Format** tab (see Figure 4.4).

TIP **Include Hyperlinks** If you use the HTML or Rich Text Format message formats, you can include hyperlinks in your e-mails. Hyperlinks are Web addresses and e-mail addresses that can be accessed by clicking them in the message. Just type the Web address or e-mail address, and the hyperlink is created automatically in the message.

Figure 4.4 You can send your messages in HTML, Rich Text Format, or plain-text format.

3. To select the message format, click the **Compose in This Message Format** drop-down box. Select **HTML**, **Rich Text**, or **Plain Text**. If you want to use Microsoft Word as your e-mail editor, click the **Use Microsoft Word to Edit E-Mail Messages** check box.

TIP **Using HTML Stationery** If you use the HTML format for your messages, you can also select to use a particular stationery on the Mail Format tab. Stationery types can be previewed using the **Stationery Picker** button. Be advised that HTML stationery will slow down the loading of e-mail messages on the recipient's computer, and not everyone will have a mail client that can view the stationery. You probably should use the stationery only for personal messages to friends and family members who also use Outlook as their e-mail client.

Changing Message Format On–the-Fly

You can also change the format of a mail message that you've already started to work on. This enables you to format your message either in HTML or plain text, as needed.

With a new mail message open in the Outlook window, follow these steps:

1. In the mail message window, select the **Format** menu.

2. Near the bottom of the Format menu, the default message format, such as HTML, will have a check mark to the left of it. To change the format to another option, such as **Plain Text**, click the format type.

3. When you switch from HTML or Rich Text Format to plain text, a message box opens. This message lets you know that you will lose any formatting or graphics that have been placed in the message. Click **OK** to close the message box.

TIP **Text-Only Format Works for Everyone** If you send most of your messages to recipients who do not use Outlook or another e-mail client that can take advantage of HTML-formatted messages, you might want to set your default message type to Text Only. This sends all your messages in plain text that can be read by all e-mail clients.

Checking Spelling

Because you don't want to look like you wedged a crayon in your brain during your childhood years, and you generally want to maintain your professional image, you should check the spelling in your mail messages before you send them. Outlook includes a spelling checker you can use for that purpose. If you are using Word as your e-mail editor, you will use the Word Spelling and Grammar features. (Using Word as your e-mail editor also allows you to check for grammar errors.) These features are discussed in Lesson 4 of the Word section of this book, "Using Proofreading Tools."

To check the spelling in a message, follow these steps:

1. In a message window, choose **Tools**, and then select **Spelling** or press **F7**. If the spelling checker finds a word whose spelling it questions, it displays the Spelling dialog box (shown in Figure 4.5). (If no words are misspelled, a dialog box appears saying that the spelling check is complete; choose **OK** to close the dialog box.)

Figure 4.5 Check your spelling before sending a message.

2. Your response to the word Outlook questions in the Spelling dialog box will vary. If you recognize that Outlook has correctly flagged a misspelled word, choose one of the following:

   - **Suggestions**—Select the correct spelling in this text box, and it automatically appears in the Change To text box.

   - **Change**—Click this button to change this particular occurrence of the word in question to the spelling in the Change To text box.

   - **Change All**—Click this button to change the word in question to the spelling listed in the Change To text box every time the spelling checker finds the word in this message.

   If Outlook checks a word that you know is already spelled correctly (such as a proper name), choose one of the following:

   - **Not in Dictionary**—Enter the correct spelling into this text box.

   - **Ignore**—Click this button to continue the spelling check without changing this occurrence of the selected word.

   - **Ignore All**—Click this button to continue the spelling check without changing any occurrence of the word in question throughout this message.

   - **Add**—Click this button to add the current spelling of the word in question to the dictionary so that Outlook will not question future occurrences of this spelling.

- **Undo Last**—Click this button to undo your last spelling change and return to that word.

3. Continue until the spelling check is complete (or click **Cancel** to quit the spelling check).

4. Outlook displays a message box telling you that the spell check is complete. Click **OK** to close the dialog box.

 TIP **Set Your Spelling Options** Click the **Options** button in the Spelling dialog box to set options that tell Outlook to do such things as ignore words with numbers, ignore original message text in forwarded messages or replies, always check spelling before sending, and so on.

Add a Signature

You can further personalize your e-mails by adding a signature to the message. A signature can be as simple as just your name, or the signature can include your phone number or extension or other information. Some people even add a favorite quote to their signature. If you use HTML as your message format, you can even include signature files that contain graphics. Plain-text signatures (for use with plain-text messages) will consist only of text characters.

First, take a look at how you can create a signature. Then you can take a look at how you apply it to a message.

Creating a Signature

1. Choose **Tools, Options** to open the Options dialog box, and then select the **Mail Format** tab.

2. Click the **Signatures** button at the bottom of the dialog box. The Create Signature dialog box opens.

3. Click the **New** button; the Create a New Signature dialog box opens as shown in Figure 4.6.

4. Type a name for your new signature, and then click **Next**.

5. The Edit Signature dialog box appears. Enter the text you want included in the signature. You can use the Paragraph or Font buttons to add formatting to the text in the signature.

6. When you have finished creating your signature, click the **Finish** button. Click **Close** to close the Create Signatures dialog box, and then click **OK** to close the Options dialog box.

Figure 4.6 Outlook walks you through the steps of creating a signature.

TIP **You Can Edit Signatures** To edit a signature, select the signature in the Create Signatures dialog box and then click **Edit**.

Inserting the Signature

After you've created a signature or signatures, you can quickly add it to any message by placing the insertion point where you want to place the signature, choosing **Insert**, and then choosing **Signature**; all the signatures that you have created appear on the menu. Select the signature from the list you want to use in the message you are currently composing.

You can also preview the signatures before inserting them; choose **Insert**, **Signature**, and then select **More** from the cascading menu. The Select a Signature dialog box opens. Select any of your signatures to view a preview of the signature. When you find the signature you want to use, click **OK**.

Sending Mail

You probably know that after you add recipient addresses, compose your message, format the text, spell check the message, and insert a signature in the e-mail, you are ready to send the message. But you can use a couple of ways to actually send the message on its way.

The fastest way to send the message using the mouse is to click the **Send** button on the Message toolbar. If you prefer, press **Ctrl+Enter**. In either case, your message is heading out to its destination. If you are working offline, the message is placed in the Outbox until you connect to the Internet and send and receive your messages.

Recalling a Message

If you use Outlook as an e-mail client in a Microsoft Exchange Server environment, you can actually recall or replace e-mail messages that you have sent. But you can recall or replace only messages that have not been opened by the recipient or moved to another folder by a recipient.

If the Folder List is not visible, click the **View** menu, and then click **Folder List**.

1. Click the **My Shortcuts** button on the Outlook bar, and then select the **Sent Items** folder.

2. Double-click to open the message that you want to recall.

3. In the message window, click the **Actions** menu, and then click **Recall This Message**. The Recall This Message dialog box opens as shown in Figure 4.7.

Figure 4.7   Messages that have not been read can be recalled or replaced.

4. To recall the message, click the **Delete Unread Copies of This Message** option button, and then click **OK**. A notice appears in the message window informing you that you attempted to recall this message on a particular date and at a particular time.

5. If you want to replace the message with a new message, click the **Delete Unread Copies and Replace with New Message** option button. When you click **OK**, a new message window opens with a copy of the message you want to recall in it. Just change the message text or address and then send the message.

6. You eventually receive a notification in your Inbox (as new mail) notifying you whether the recall was successful.

Working with Received Mail

In this lesson, you learn how to read your mail, save an attachment, answer mail, and close a message.

Reading Mail

When you log on to Outlook, your Inbox folder appears, and any new messages you've received are downloaded from your ISP's (or your company's) mail server. If you use Internet mail and a dial-up connection (in contrast to DSL or cable modem connections, which are always connected), a dial-up connection must be made before Outlook can check the mail server for new mail.

No matter what the connection situation, after you download any new e-mail to your computer, the new mail appears in the Outlook Inbox (see Figure 5.1). If you watch closely when you connect to your network or Internet service provider, a downloading mail icon appears in the lower right of the Outlook window, showing you that new mail is being received.

As you can see in Figure 5.1, the Inbox provides important information about each message. For example, one message has been labeled as high priority and one message has an attachment. Messages that have already been replied to are marked with a curved reply arrow. You'll learn about file attachments in Lesson 7, "Attaching Files and Items to a Message," and mail priorities in Lesson 9, "Setting Mail Options," of the Outlook section.

Additional information about a particular message, such as the actual reply date, is contained at the top of the Preview pane when that particular message is selected. At the bottom of the Outlook status bar (on the left), information such as how many items are in the Inbox and how many message are unread is also provided.

To read a message, you can select it, and its contents appear in the Outlook Preview pane. You can also open a message in its own window; double-click a mail message to open it. Figure 5.2 shows an open message.

High priority
Read and replied to message
Message with attachment
Unread message

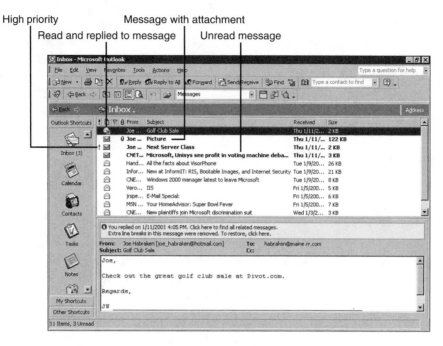

Figure 5.1 The Inbox provides information related to your received messages: the sender, the subject, the date received, and priority and attachment icons.

Previous Item button

Next Item button

Figure 5.2 The message window displays the message and tools for responding to the message or moving to the previous or next message in the Inbox.

To read the next or previous mail message in the Inbox when you have opened a mail message, click either the **Previous Item** or the **Next Item** button on the message window toolbar. To access more view choices, select the **View** menu, and then point at **Previous** or **Next**; submenu choices are provided for each of these choices that allow you to jump to another item, an unread item, or to a message that has been assigned a particular priority or that has been flagged.

Item Outlook uses the word *item* to describe a mail message, an attached file, an appointment or meeting, a task, and so on. Item is a generic term in Outlook that describes the currently selected element.

After you open a message in the Inbox, it is marked as read (notice that the envelope that represents the message is opened). You can also mark messages as read or unread by selecting **Edit** and then selecting either **Mark As Read** or **Mark As Unread**. Additionally, you can mark all the messages in the Inbox as read by choosing **Edit, Mark All As Read**. You might want to mark mail messages as read so you don't read them again; you might want to mark important mail as unread so you'll be sure to open it and read it again.

TIP

No Mail? Maybe Outlook is not configured to check for mail automatically. To force Outlook to look for mail, click the **Send and Receive** button on the toolbar, or choose **Tools**, point at **Send/Receive**, and then select **Send/Receive All**. Any new messages are placed in the Inbox.

Saving an Attachment

You often receive messages that have files or other items attached to them, such as graphical images. In the Inbox list of messages, an attachment is represented by a paper clip icon beside the message. Save any attachments sent to you so that you can open, modify, print, or otherwise use the attached document or image. Messages can contain multiple attachments.

CAUTION

What About Viruses? Unfortunately, there is a chance that an attachment to a message can be a virus or other malicious software. Computer viruses can really wreak havoc on your computer system. When you receive an e-mail message from someone you don't know and that message has an attachment, the best thing to do is delete the message without opening it or the attachment. Because viruses can read your address book and send themselves to the people it contains, even e-mail from known parties bears at least some scrutiny. If you save an attachment to your computer, you might want to check the file with an antivirus program before you actually open the file. Be especially cautious if the file that you receive as an attachment has an .exe or .vba extension. These extensions, which virus creators commonly use to get you to unleash a virus on your own computer, mark that the attachment is an actual program.

To save an attachment, follow these steps:

1. Open the message containing an attachment by double-clicking the message. The attachment appears as an icon below the subject area of the message (see Figure 5.3).

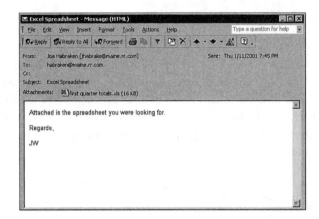

Figure 5.3 An icon represents the attached file.

2. (Optional) You can open the attachment from within the message by double-clicking the attachment icon. A message appears, as shown in Figure 5.4, warning you that attachments can contain viruses. To open the file, click the **Open It** option button and then click **OK**. The attachment will be opened in the application in which it was created (such as Word or Excel). When you have finished looking at the attachment, you can return to the e-mail message by closing the open application.

   If you choose **Save the File to Disk**, a Save Attachment dialog box appears, allowing you to save the file to your hard drive.

3. You probably noticed in the Opening Mail Attachment message box that you also had the option to save the attachment (see Figure 5.4). There is another way to save your attachments, and it actually makes it easier when you have to save multiple attachments attached to the same e-mail message. In the message window, select **File, Save Attachments**. The Save Attachment dialog box appears (see Figure 5.5).

Figure 5.4   You can open or save an attachment by double-clicking its icon.

Figure 5.5   Save the attachment to a convenient folder.

4. Choose the folder in which you want to save the attachment or attachments and click **Save**. The dialog box closes and returns to the message window. You can change the name of the file in the File Name box, if you want. After you save the attachment, you can open the attachment, which is now like any other saved file on your computer, at any time from the application in which it was created.

TIP   **Use the Right Mouse Button**   You can also quickly save an attachment by right-clicking the attachment icon. On the shortcut menu that appears, click **Save As**, and then save the attachment to an appropriate folder.

Answering Mail

You might want to reply to a message after you read it. The message window enables you to answer a message immediately, or at a later time if you prefer. To reply to any given message, follow these steps:

115

1. Select the message in the Inbox window, and then click the **Reply** button on the Inbox toolbar.

If you have the message open, click the **Reply** button in the message window. The Reply message window appears, with the original message in the message text area and the sender of the message already filled in for you (see Figure 5.6).

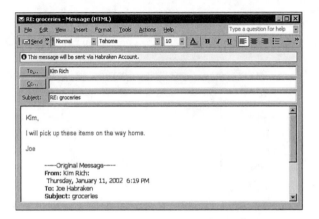

Figure 5.6   You can reply to a message quickly and easily.

 TIP   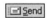 **Reply to All**   If you receive a message that has also been sent to others—as either a message or a carbon copy (Cc)—you can click the **Reply to All** button to send your reply to each person who received the message.

2. The insertion point is automatically placed above the message text that you are replying to. Enter your reply text.

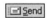 **3.** When you finish your reply, click the **Send** button. Outlook sends the message.

The next time you open a message to which you've replied, there is a reminder at the top of the message window telling you the date and time you sent your reply. Don't forget that the purple arrow next to a message in the Inbox window shows that the message has been replied to.

Printing Mail

You can print mail messages, either directly from the Inbox when they have been selected or from a message window when you have opened a particular message. To print an unopened message, select the message in the message list of the Inbox or other folder and choose **File, Print**. The Print dialog box opens; click **OK** to send the message to the printer. If the message is already open, you can follow these steps:

1. Open the message in Outlook.

2. Choose **File** and then select **Print**, or press **Ctrl+P** to view the Print dialog box.

3. In the Print dialog box, click **OK** to print one copy of the entire message using the printer's default settings. See Lesson 17, "Printing in Outlook," in this section of the book for detailed information about configuring pages and changing printer options.

  Toolbar Shortcut   Click the **Print** button on the toolbar to print an unopened or opened message using the default print settings.

When you finish reading or printing a message, click the **Close** button on the message window.

Managing Mail

In this lesson, you learn how to delete and undelete messages, forward messages, and create folders. You also learn how to move messages to these folders.

Deleting Mail

Although you might want to store certain important messages and perhaps even create folders to store them in, which is discussed in Lesson 8, "Saving Drafts and Organizing Messages," you'll definitely want to delete much of the mail that you receive after reading it. You can easily delete messages in Outlook when you're finished reading and sending replies to them.

X The easiest way to delete a selected message is to click the **Delete** button on the Outlook toolbar. If the message is open, just click the **Delete** button on the message window toolbar instead.

If you want to delete several messages in the Inbox, just select the messages using the mouse. To select several contiguous messages, click the first message, and then hold down the **Shift** key when you click the last message in the series. To select noncontiguous messages, hold down the **Ctrl** key and click each message. When you have all the messages selected that you want to delete, click the **Delete** button (or you can select the **Edit** menu and then select **Delete**).

Undeleting Items

If you change your mind and want to get back items you've deleted, you can usually retrieve them from the Deleted Items folder. By default, when you delete an item, it doesn't disappear from your computer; it merely moves to the Deleted Items folder. Items stay in the Deleted Items folder until you delete them from that folder—at which point they are unrecoverable. Typically, when you exit Outlook, the Deleted Items folder is emptied automatically. To retrieve a deleted item from the Deleted Items folder, follow these steps:

1. Click the scroll-down arrow on the Outlook bar to locate the Deleted Items folder.
2. Click the **Deleted Items** icon in the Outlook bar to open the folder.

3. Select the items you want to retrieve; you can then drag them back to the Inbox by dragging them and dropping them onto the Inbox icon in the Outlook bar. Or if you don't like dragging messages, select the files you want to move from the Deleted Items folder, and then select **Edit, Move to Folder**. The Move Items dialog box appears as shown in Figure 6.1.

Figure 6.1 Deleted messages can be moved out of the Deleted Items folder back into the Inbox.

4. Select the folder you want to move the items into (such as the Inbox) and then click the **OK** button.

 TIP **Use Undo Immediately** If you want to undelete a message or messages that you just deleted, select the **Edit** menu, and then select **Undo Delete**.

Emptying the Deleted Items Folder

If you're sure you want to delete the items in the Deleted Items folder, empty the contents of the folder. To delete items in the Deleted Items folder, follow these steps:

1. On the Outlook bar, choose the **Outlook Shortcuts**, and then select the **Deleted Items** folder. All deleted items in that folder appear in the message list, as shown in Figure 6.2.

2. To permanently delete an item or items, select it (or them) in the Deleted Items folder.

 3. Click the **Delete** button, or choose **Edit** and then select **Delete**. Outlook displays a confirmation dialog box asking whether you're sure you want to permanently delete the message. Choose **Yes** to delete the selected item.

4. To switch back to the Inbox or another folder, select the folder from either the Outlook bar or the Folder List.

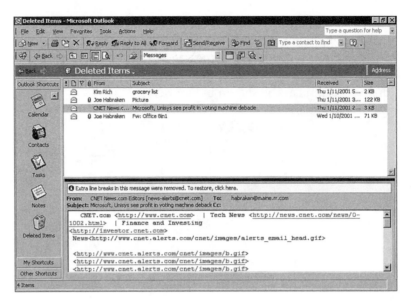

Figure 6.2   Deleted messages remain in the Deleted Items folder until you permanently delete them.

 TIP   **Automatic Permanent Delete**   You can set Outlook to permanently delete the contents of the Deleted Items folder every time you exit the program. To do so, in the Outlook window choose **Tools**, and then click **Options**. Select the **Other** tab of the Options dialog box and click the **Empty the Deleted Items Folder upon Exiting** check box. Then click **OK**.

Forwarding Mail

You can forward mail that you receive to a co-worker or anyone else with an e-mail address. When you forward a message, you can also add comments to the messages if you so desire.

 TERM   **Forward Mail**   When you forward mail, you send a copy of a message you have received to another person; you can add your own comments to the forwarded mail, if you want.

You can forward an open message or a message selected in the message list in the Inbox in the same way. To forward mail, follow these steps:

 1. Select or open the message you want to forward. Then click the **Forward** button. The FW Message window appears (see Figure 6.3).

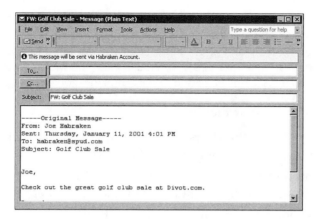

Figure 6.3 When you forward a message, the original message appears at the bottom of the message window.

2. In the To text box, enter the addresses of the people to whom you want to forward the mail. If you want to choose an address or addresses from a list, click the **To** button to display the Select Names dialog box, and then select the address or addresses from your Contacts list.

3. (Optional) In the Cc text box, enter the addresses of anyone to whom you want to forward copies of the message.

4. In the message area of the window, enter any message you want to send with the forwarded text.

 TIP **Attachments Are Forwarded, Too** If the message that you forward contains attached files, the attachments are also forwarded.

 5. When you are ready to send the message, click the **Send** button.

Creating Folders

Although Outlook provides you with an Inbox, an Outbox, a Sent Items folder, and a Deleted Items folder, you might find it advantageous to create your own folders. This provides you with alternative places to store items and can make finding them in the future easier (rather than just having all your messages languish in the Inbox). Folders can also be used to store items other than messages, so you could even create subfolders for your Contacts folder or Calendar.

TIP **Folders Aren't the Only Way to Get Organized** Although the creation of folders can help you organize messages and other items that you want to store in Outlook, another tool called the Organizer has been designed to help you move, delete, and even color code received e-mail messages. You will take a look at the Organizer in Lesson 8, "Saving Drafts and Organizing Messages."

To create a folder, follow these steps:

1. Click the **Folder List** drop-down button, and then click the **Folder List pin** to "pin it down" to the Outlook window.

2. To create a folder in the Folder List, right-click the folder, such as the Inbox, that will serve as the parent folder for the new folder.

3. On the shortcut menu that appears (see Figure 6.4), select New Folder. The Create New Folder dialog box appears.

Figure 6.4 Folders can be created anywhere in the Folder List.

TIP **Create Folders from the File Menu** You can also open the Create New Folder dialog box from the File menu. Just select **File**, point at **New**, and then select **Folder**.

4. In the Create New Folder dialog box, type a name for the folder into the Name box.

5. Use the icons in the New Folder dialog box main pane area to select the type of folder that you want to create. For example, if you want to hold mail messages in the folder, select the **Mail and Post** icon (see Figure 6.5).

Figure 6.5   Folders can be created to hold mail messages, contacts, and even calendar appointments.

6. Select the **Location** drop-down list to select the location for the new folder. If you want to nest the new folder in an existing folder, such as the Inbox, select that folder on the list. If you want to create the new folder as a first-level folder, select **Personal Folders**.

7. When you have finished making your entries and selections in the New Folder dialog box, click **OK** to create the folder.

8. You are asked whether you want to add a shortcut icon for the new folder to the Outlook bar. If you want to create the icon, click **Yes**.

The new folder appears on the Outlook bar and in the Folder List.

TIP   **Add an Outlook Bar Shortcut for a Folder**   Even if you choose not to add a shortcut for the folder to the Outlook bar when you create the folder, you can add it later. Right-click any folder you've created in the Folder List and select **Add to Outlook Bar** from the shortcut menu that appears.

I Want to Delete a Folder   If you add a folder and then decide you don't want it, right-click the folder in the Folder List and select **Delete** from the shortcut menu. You then must verify the deletion; click **Yes**.

CAUTION

Moving Items to Another Folder

You can move items from one folder in Outlook to another; for example, you can create a folder to store all messages pertaining to a specific account or just make a folder that holds personal messages instead of business-related messages. You can easily move any messages to a new folder and then open them later to read them or to reply to them.

To move an item to another folder, follow these steps:

1. From the Inbox or any Outlook folder, select the message or messages you want to move.

2. Select **Edit, Move to Folder**. The Move Items dialog box appears (see Figure 6.6).

Figure 6.6   Choose the folder in which you want to store the message or messages.

3. In the Move Items dialog box, select the folder to which you want to move the message or messages.

4. Click **OK**. The message or messages are moved to the destination folder.

 TIP   **Quickly Move Items**   You can quickly move any message or other Outlook item by dragging it from the open folder in which it resides to any folder icon in the Outlook bar.

Attaching Files and Items to a Message

In this lesson, you learn how to attach a file and Outlook items to an e-mail message.

Attaching a File

You can attach any type of file to an Outlook message, which makes for a convenient way of sending your files to your co-workers or sending pictures to family members across the country who use Internet e-mail. You can send Word documents, Excel spreadsheets, a family photo (taken from a digital camera or scanned from a photograph), or any other file you have on your hard drive.

When you attach a file, it appears as an icon in an attachment box that resides in the message window right below the Subject box, as shown in Figure 7.1. A button to the left of the attached file can be used to quickly access the Insert File dialog box if you want to change the attached file or add additional attachments before sending the message.

Figure 7.1 Attached files appear as an icon in the Attach box.

You can also open or view any files that you attach to your e-mail messages (before or after you send them) by double-clicking the file. Next, you take a look at attaching and viewing attachments, such as files created in other applications and picture files. Then, you can take a look at attaching an Outlook item such as a contact or appointment to an e-mail message.

 TIP **E-Mail Attachments and E-Mail Clients**   Depending on the e-mail client they are using, the way recipients of your file attachments retrieve them will vary. For example, some e-mail packages do not show the attachment as an icon, but save the attachment directly to a specific folder on the recipient's computer after the e-mail message is downloaded.

To attach a file to a message, follow these steps:

 1. In the new message window, choose **Insert** and then select **File,** or click the **Insert File** button on the toolbar. The Insert File dialog box appears (see Figure 7.2).

Figure 7.2   Select the file you want to attach to a message.

2. From the **Look In** drop-down list, choose the drive and folder that contain the file you want to attach.

3. Select the file you want to attach.

4. Click **OK** to insert the file into the message.

An Attach box appears below the Subject box on the message, and an icon and the filename are inserted.

TIP **Large Files Take Time** Sending an extremely large file can take a great deal of time, depending on your connection speed. Some ISPs, such as America Online, set a limit for attachment file size for sent or received attachments. Using tools that reduce the size of files—applications such as WinZip or Microsoft Compressed Folders—you can compress larger files. However, the recipient of a message in which you have included a "zipped" attachment needs the appropriate tool, such as WinZip, to uncompress the attached file.

Attaching Outlook Items

In addition to attaching files from other programs, you can also attach an Outlook item to a message. An Outlook item can be any item saved in one of your personal folders, including an appointment, a contact, a note, and so on. You can attach an Outlook item in the same manner you attach a file.

Follow these steps to attach an Outlook item:

1. In the message window, choose **Insert, Item**. The Insert Item dialog box appears (see Figure 7.3).

Figure 7.3 Select items from any folder in Outlook, such as a contact's information from the Contacts folder.

2. From the **Look In** list, choose the folder containing the item you want to include in the message.

3. Select from the items that appear in the **Items** list when you have the appropriate folder selected. To select multiple adjacent items, hold down the **Shift** key and click the first and last desired items; to select multiple nonadjacent items, hold down the **Ctrl** key and click the items.

4. In the Insert As area, choose from the following option buttons:

- **Text Only**—Inserts the file as text into the message, such as the contact's information or the text in an e-mail message.

- **Attachment**—Attaches the e-mail message or Contact record as an attachment to the current e-mail message.

- **Shortcut**—If you are using Outlook in a networked environment where Exchange Server is used and all your folders, such as Contacts, are stored on the network, you can attach shortcuts to your e-mail message. Then, another user on the network can double-click the shortcut to access its information.

5. Click **OK**, and Outlook inserts the selected items into your message (either as an attachment or as inserted text).

Figure 7.4 shows an attached contact record in an Outlook e-mail message. When the e-mail recipient receives the message, he or she can access the contact information by double-clicking the attachment icon. The recipient can then save the contact information to their Contacts folder.

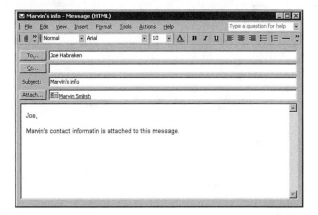

Figure 7.4   Select an item from any folder in Outlook, such as a contact's information, and attach it to your e-mail message.

 TIP   **It Doesn't Work Without Outlook**   If recipients don't have Outlook on their computers, they will not be able to view the attached item, such as an Outlook contact record. If you know that a recipient doesn't have Outlook, insert the contact information into the message as text using the Text Only option in the Insert Item dialog box.

Saving Drafts and Organizing Messages

In this lesson, you learn how to save a draft, view messages that you've sent, and manage messages by creating rules using the Outlook Organizer.

Saving a Draft

Suppose you start a message but you are called away or need to do something else before you can finish it. You don't have to lose the message by canceling, forcing you to start over again later; you can save the message in the Drafts folder and then open it later to complete it.

To save a draft, open and begin composing a new message. Then, follow these steps:

1. In the message window, click the **Close** button. A dialog box appears, asking whether you want to save changes, as shown in Figure 8.1.

Figure 8.1   Click **Yes** to save the message in the Drafts folder for later completion.

2. Click **Yes**. Outlook places the current message into the Drafts Folder.

To open the message and continue working on it at another time, follow these steps:

1. Click the **Drafts** folder icon in the My Shortcuts group on the Outlook bar, or choose **Drafts** from the Folder List.

2. Double-click the message to open it. At the top of the Message tab, you'll see a reminder that reads: This Message Has Not Been Sent.

3. Continue your work on the message. If you need to store it again before you're finished, click the **Close** button and answer **Yes** to the message box that asks you to save the file. Alternatively, you can choose to save changes that you have made to the message by clicking the **Save** button on the message toolbar and then closing the message. The message remains in the Drafts folder until you move or send it.

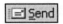 **4.** When you've actually completed the entire message and are ready to send it, click the **Send** button to send the message.

 TIP   **Create an Outlook Bar Icon for Drafts**   If you would like to place a Drafts folder icon on the Outlook bar when you are in the Outlook Shortcuts group, open the Folder List, pin the Folder List down (click on the push pin that appears when you open the Folders list), and then right-click the **Drafts** folder. On the shortcut menu that appears, select **Add to Outlook Bar**. An icon appears on the Outlook bar for the Drafts folder.

Viewing Sent Items and Changing Defaults

By default, Outlook saves a copy of all e-mail messages that you send. It keeps these copies in the Sent Items folder, which can be opened using the Sent Items icon found in the My Shortcuts group on the Outlook bar. You can view a list of sent items at any time, and you can open any message in that list to review its contents.

Viewing Sent Items

To view sent items, follow these steps:

1. In the Outlook bar, choose the **My Shortcuts** group.

 TIP   **Save Time Using the Folder List**   You can select the Sent Items folder from the Folder List instead of using the icon in the My Shortcuts group.

2. On the Outlook bar, click the **Sent Items** icon; Outlook displays a list of the contents of that folder. Figure 8.2 shows the Sent Items list. All messages you send remain in the Sent Items folder until you delete or move them.

3. (Optional) To view a sent item, select it to view its contents in the Preview pane, or double-click it to open it. When you have finished viewing its contents, click the **Close (X)** button.

 TIP   **Open the Preview Pane**   If you don't see the Preview pane when you are working in the Sent Items folder, select the **View** menu, and then select **Preview Pane**.

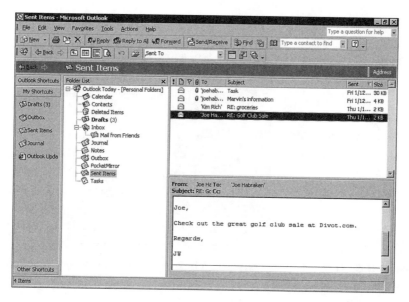

Figure 8.2   You can open any sent message by double-clicking it.

Changing Sent E-Mail Defaults

You can control whether Outlook saves copies of your sent messages (this is also true for unsent messages that are, by default, saved to the Drafts folder). Follow these steps:

1. Select **Tools**, **Options**, and the Options dialog box appears.
2. Select the **Preferences** tab on the Options dialog box.
3. Click the **E-Mail Options** button. The E-Mail Options dialog box appears (see Figure 8.3). This dialog box provides a series of check boxes that you can use to toggle several e-mail–related features on and off; to make sure that saved copies of messages are placed in the Sent Items folder, click the **Save Copies of Messages in Sent Items Folder** check box. To have e-mail that is not sent automatically saved in the Outbox, click the **Automatically Save Unsent Messages** check box.

The E-Mail Options tab also gives you control over several other features related to the management of your e-mail. More mail option settings are discussed in the next lesson.

Figure 8.3 The E-Mail Options dialog box gives you control over various features related to sending and saving unsent e-mail messages.

Using the Organize Tool

You have already learned how to create folders and move e-mail messages to folders to help keep your Outlook information organized (look back at Lesson 7, "Attaching Files and Items to a Message," for more info). Outlook also provides an easy-to-use tool, called the Organize tool, that can help you move, delete, or color code received and sent mail. The Organize tool can even help you deal with annoying junk e-mail that you receive. The Organize feature is able to read the e-mail address of the sender of a particular message and use it to find all the messages in the Inbox that this person has sent. The Organize feature can also use other criteria, such as key-words, to help organize e-mail that you receive. It can actually be configured to delete certain junk mail as soon as you receive it.

The Organize tool provides the Move Message and Create a Rule commands for getting messages out of a particular folder, such as the Inbox, and placing these items into a different folder. Each of these avenues for moving messages to a particular Outlook folder has its own set of commands in the Organize pane.

Moving Messages with the Organizer

Suppose that you decide to move a message or messages from a particular person to a new location in Outlook. You can use the Move Message command and place the items into a different folder. However, if you receive additional messages from this individual at a later time, you would have to again manually move the messages to the new location. Wouldn't it be easier to have Outlook move these messages automatically?

To automatically manage future messages from an individual, you can use the Create a Rule command. This creates a rule that moves new messages from an individual to the new location automatically. That way, you can find all the messages from a particular person in the same place when you need them.

 Rules   Rules are a set of conditions (such as a particular e-mail address or message content) that you identify to move, delete, or manage incoming e-mail messages.

 Rules and Attachments   The rules you create to organize your messages can look at the sender, receiver, message subject, and message text. Attachments to a message are not governed by the rules that you create, so the content of file attachments to a message do not govern how they are handled by the Organize tool or rules.

To use the Organize tool to manage messages from a particular sender, follow these steps:

1. In your Inbox, select a message that you want to work with.

 2. Click the **Tools** menu and then click **Organize**, or click the **Organize** button on the toolbar. The Organize window appears (see Figure 8.4).

The Organize tool helps you manage and organize your messages using these methods:

- **Using Folders**—This method is used to move or delete messages; they can be moved to a folder that you create or moved to the Deleted Items folder.
- **Using Colors**—This option enables you to color code messages according to the rule you create.
- **Using Views**—This option uses the rule to categorize messages by their view (Flagged, By Sender, and so on).
- **Junk E-Mail**—An option is also provided that helps you deal with junk e-mail.

To manually move the currently selected message in your Inbox, follow these steps:

1. Click **Using Folders**. The e-mail address of the person who sent you the selected e-mail appears in the From box.

2. In the Move Message Selected Below To box, click the drop-down arrow and select the Outlook folder to which you would like to move the message.

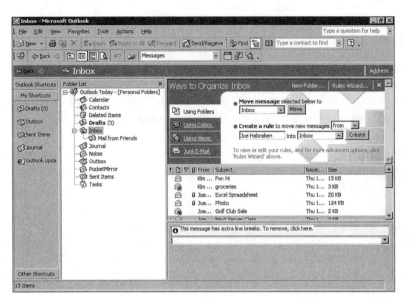

Figure 8.4   The Organize tool helps you manage messages using folders, colors, and views.

3. Click the **Move** button and the message is moved to the new location.

4. If you want to move other messages, select the message in the Message list and repeat steps 2 and 3.

As already mentioned, you can manage any new messages you receive from a particular individual by creating a rule that automatically moves these new messages to a folder of your choice. To create a new rule for the sender of the currently selected message in your Inbox, follow these steps:

1. Click **Using Folders**. The e-mail address of the person who sent you the selected e-mail appears in the From box.

2. In the Create a Rule to Move New Messages drop-down box, make sure **From** is selected.

3. In the **Into** box, click the drop-down arrow and select the name of the folder to which you want to move the messages. If you want to move the messages to a folder that is not listed on the drop-down list, click **Other Folder**. The Select Folder list dialog box appears. Double-click the folder that you want to use.

4. When you have selected the folder that the messages are placed in by the rule, click **Create**.

A message box appears in the Organize window (see Figure 8.5).

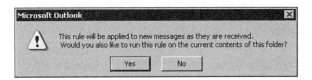

Figure 8.5   The new rule can act on existing messages or just new messages.

To run the rule on messages already in the folder (they will be moved by the rule), click **Yes**. If you want the rule to act only on new messages received, click **No**.

That's all there is to creating the new rule. Now, whenever you receive a message from that particular person, the message will be moved to the new location as soon as you receive the message.

Using Organizer to Manage Junk E-Mail

When you browse the World Wide Web, you will often come across Web sites that ask you to register with the site using your e-mail address. This is very common with Web sites that provide special content or allow you to enter various contests. After you provide a site with your e-mail address, chances are that they will sell your e-mail address to other Web sites and companies (it's not unlike having your home address placed on a mailing list). This means that it doesn't take very long before you begin to receive junk e-mail messages in Outlook.

The Organize tool also provides you with an automatic strategy for dealing with annoying junk mail. Click **Junk E-Mail** in the Organize window (see Figure 8.6). The Organize tool enables you to either color code junk mail and adult-content e-mail or move these kinds of e-mail to a folder of your choice. In most situations, junk e-mail and other unwanted e-mail can be moved directly to the Deleted Items folder, and the items can then be easily discarded. Outlook automatically identifies these types of mail messages as you receive them by using a list of keywords as identifiers.

To color code junk messages or adult-content messages, make sure the Automatically drop-down box for each junk-mail type (junk messages or adult content) contains the choice **Color**. Then, use the appropriate color drop-down box to select the color you want to use to code these messages as they are received. After you have selected the color, click the **Turn On** button to begin color coding all new messages that are identified as junk mail or adult-content mail by Outlook.

To send junk messages or adult-content messages directly to a specific folder (such as Deleted Items), select **Move** in the Automatically drop-down box for either type of message. In the Messages To drop-down box for either message type, select **Junk Mail** or **Deleted Items** to send mail messages directly to either of these folders. You can also send these messages directly to an alternative folder of your choice by clicking **Other Folder**. After you have selected the folder you want to send these messages to, click the **Turn On** button. Messages that Outlook identifies as junk mail or adult content are sent directly to the folder you specified.

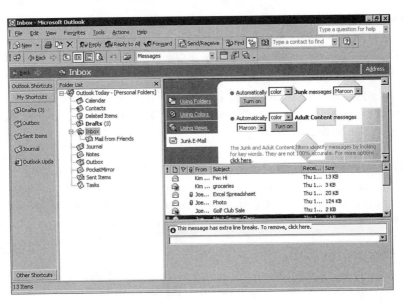

Figure 8.6 The Organize tool's Junk E-Mail manager can help you deal with incoming junk mail.

You can also click the **For More Options Click Here** selection at the bottom of the Organize pane to access additional options related to junk mail and adult content. Links are provided so that you can access the list of e-mail addresses that you have identified as sources of junk mail or adult content. Any e-mail address on these lists is used to identify incoming e-mail that should be color coded or moved to a specific folder by the Organize tool. After you have completed your selections in the Organize window, click its **Close** button.

You can quickly add e-mail addresses to the Junk E-Mail or Adult Content list by right-clicking any message in your Inbox. A shortcut menu appears; point at Junk E-Mail on the menu, and then select either **Add to Junk Senders List** or **Add to Adult Content Senders List** from the cascading menu that opens. This adds this e-mail to the list, marking it as a source of junk mail or adult-content messages.

Creating Advanced Rules with the Wizard

If the Organize tool isn't able to manage your e-mail to the degree you desire, you can create more advanced rules for managing messages using the Outlook Rules Wizard. The Rules Wizard enables you to create pretty sophisticated rules using simple sentences.

To open the Rules Wizard, follow these steps:

1. Click **Tools, Rules Wizard**. The Rules Wizard dialog box appears (see Figure 8.7).

All the rules previously created using the Organize tool appear in the Rules Description box. You can copy, modify, rename, or delete a rule in this dialog box. You can also change a rule's priority by selecting a rule and then moving it up or down using the Move Up or Move Down buttons.

Figure 8.7   The Rules Wizard helps you create rules for managing mail messages.

2. To create a new rule, click the **New** button. The Rules Wizard walks you through the rule-creation process. The first screen asks you to choose either to create the rule from an existing template or create a new, blank rule. Step 3 describes creating a rule from scratch (although both possibilities offer similar options from the wizard).

3. Click the **Start from a Blank Rule** option button. Now you can select the type of rule you want to create, such as **Check Messages When They Arrive** (see Figure 8.8), and then click **Next**.

Figure 8.8 In the Rules Wizard, you select the type of rule you want to create.

4. Select the type of rule you want to create, and then click **Next**.

5. The next screen asks you to select conditions that are to be used by the new rule (see Figure 8.9). These conditions range from messages sent directly to you, to e-mail addresses that you have placed on your junk e-mail list. Use the check boxes provided to select the condition or conditions for your new rule. Click **Next** to continue.

Figure 8.9 You select the conditions that are to be used by the rule.

TIP   **Conditions That Require Input from You**   Some conditions such as From People or Distribution List or Specific Words require that you provide a list of people for the condition to use or certain words. Conditions requiring additional information have an underlined selection for you to click.

6. The next screen asks you to decide what the rule should do to a message that meets the rules criteria. Several choices are provided, such as Move It to the Specified Folder or Delete It (see Figure 8.10). Make your selections in the check boxes provided. Click **Next** to continue.

Figure 8.10   You determine the type of action you want Outlook to take when it finds a message that meets the rule's criteria.

7. The next screen provides you with the opportunity to add any exceptions to the rule. These exceptions can include Except If Sent Only to Me or Except Where My Name Is in the To Box. You add the exceptions by clicking the check box next to a particular exception. You can select multiple exceptions or choose to have no exceptions to the rules. Then, click **Next** to continue.

8. The Rules Wizard's final screen asks you to type a name for your new rule. After you've done that, click **Finish**. The new rule appears in the Rules Wizard dialog box. You can create more new rules or click **OK** to close the dialog box.

 TIP   **Delete "Bad" Rules**   If you find that a rule or rules that you have created are actually doing things to messages that you hadn't planned, you can delete the rules. Rules created with the Organize tool can also be deleted in this manner. Open the Rules Wizard (click **Tools**, then **Rules Wizard**). In the Rules Wizard dialog box, select rules that you want to delete and then select **Delete**. They will be removed from the rule list.

When you use the Rules Wizard for the first time, you may want to create a simple rule or two that handle messages that you do not consider extremely important. A poorly designed rule could delete important messages that you receive. A good general rule is to use the Organize tool first and let it create simple rules, and if you need more advanced message-management help, use the Rules Wizard.

Setting Mail Options

In this lesson, you learn how to set options for messages related to message priority and the delivery of messages. You also learn how to work with message flags.

Working with Message Options

Outlook provides options that enable you to mark any message with certain options that emphasize a certain aspect of the message's importance. You can use Priority status so that the recipient knows you need a quick response. Using a sensitivity rating makes it so that not just anyone can change your message after it is sent. With other options you can enable the recipients of your message to vote on an issue by including voting buttons in your message and having the replies sent to a specific location.

You also can set delivery options. For example, you can schedule the delivery of a message for a specified delivery time or date if you don't want to send it right now.

Recognizing Priority Flags Not all e-mail packages recognize the priority flags that you place on messages you send. These priority flags work ideally in a network situation, where Outlook is the e-mail client for all users. Microsoft's Outlook Express e-mail client also has the capability to recognize priority flags that you use on sent messages.

CAUTION

To set message options, open a new e-mail and click the **Options** button on the toolbar (or select **View, Options**). As you can see in Figure 9.1, the Message Options dialog box is separated into four areas. The next four sections discuss each group of options in detail.

Message Settings

In the Message Settings area, set any of the following options for your message:

- Click the **Importance** drop-down arrow and choose a priority level of **Low**, **Normal**, or **High** from the list. (Alternatively, you could click the **Importance High** or **Importance Low** button on the message's toolbar when you compose the message.) When importance isn't specified, the message is given Normal importance.

Figure 9.1   Use the Message Options dialog box to govern how your message is sent.

- Click the **Sensitivity** drop-down arrow and choose one of the following options:

    - **Normal**—Use this option to indicate that the message contents are standard or customary.

    - **Personal**—Use this option to suggest that the message contents are of a personal nature.

    - **Private**—Use this option to prevent the message from being edited (text changes, copy, paste, and so on) after you send it.

    - **Confidential**—Use this option to indicate that the message contents are restricted or private. Confidential messages can be edited by the recipient. Marking the message Confidential is only to suggest how the recipient should handle the contents of the message.

 TIP   **Mark All Messages As Private**   You can mark all your new messages as private automatically. Choose **Tools**, **Options**. On the **Preferences** tab, click the **E-Mail Options** button. In the E-Mail Options dialog box, click the **Advanced E-Mail Options** button. Use the **Sensitivity** drop-down box at the bottom of the Advanced E-Mail Options dialog box to set the default sensitivity for all your new e-mail messages.

Outlook also supplies you with options related to the security settings for a message. You can choose to encrypt the contents of your message or add a digital signature to the message.

To set the security option for the message, click the **Security Settings** button. This opens the Security Properties dialog box, as shown in Figure 9.2.

Figure 9.2   You can set security options for a message, such as encryption and the use of a digital signature.

If you want to encrypt the message, click the **Encrypt Message Contents and Attachments** check box. If you want, you can also add a digital signature to the message that verifies you are the sender; click the **Add Digital Signature to This Message** check box.

Encryption   Messages are coded so that they remain secure until the recipient opens them.

Digital Signature   A digital ID that is electronically stamped on messages that you send. This allows recipients of the message to verify that the message is truly sent by you.

Before you can use either the encryption or the digital-signature features, you must obtain a digital ID, which is also often called a certificate. Digital IDs are issued by an independent certifying authority. Microsoft's certifying authority of choice is VeriSign Digital ID. For a fee, you can obtain, download, and install your digital ID from VeriSign by following the steps on their Web page at
`http://digitalid.verisign.com/`.

Most e-mail traffic doesn't really require encryption or the use of digital signatures. You will have to determine for yourself whether your e-mails require extra security precautions such as encryption and digital signatures.

Voting and Tracking Options

The Voting and Tracking Options enable you to control special features such as voting buttons (these allow recipients of the message to reply with a click of the mouse), which supply you with the means to track the receipt of your message. The delivery and read notification options allow you to receive notification that the recipient of the message has received the message or opened and read it, respectively.

- Select the **Use Voting Buttons** check box to add the default choices (Approve and Reject) to your message. You can also add Yes and No choices or Yes, No, and Maybe choices using the drop-down list to the right of the Use Voting Buttons check box. If you want to provide other choices, enter your own text into the text box (using semicolons to break up your choices). When you send a message with voting buttons to several people, you can view a summary of all the voting results by clicking the voting summary message on any of the e-mail responses.

- Select **Request a Delivery Receipt for This Message** to receive an e-mail notification that the intended recipient has received the message.

- Select **Request a Read Receipt for This Message** to receive e-mail confirmation that the recipient has opened the message.

Delivery Options

In addition to voting and tracking options, you can set certain delivery options, such as having replies sent to individuals you select. You can also choose a folder where a copy of the message is saved, or schedule the time of the delivery. In the Delivery Options area of the Message Options dialog box, choose any of the following check boxes:

- Normally, a reply to an e-mail message returns to the e-mail address of the sender. Sometimes, especially if you have multiple e-mail accounts, you might want replies to your message to go to a different e-mail address than the one you're sending from. Choose the **Have Replies Sent To** check box and specify in the text box the e-mail address to which you want the replies sent (see Figure 9.3). You can use the **Select Names** button to view your Contacts or Outlook Address Book and choose an e-mail address or addresses from the selected list.

- Select the **Save Sent Message To** check box to save your message to a folder other than the Sent Items folder. The Sent Items folder is specified by default, but you can choose to save the sent message to any folder in Outlook. Use the **Browse** button and the resulting Select Folder dialog box to specify a particular folder.

Figure 9.3 You can specify that responses to a message be sent to specific e-mail addresses (including or excluding your own).

- Select the **Do Not Deliver Before** option to specify a delivery date. Click the down arrow in the text box beside the option to display a calendar on which you can select the day. This option enables you to send out e-mail even when you are not at your computer (or in the office). The message will be held in your Outbox folder until the specified time. If you are using Internet e-mail, your computer and Outlook must be up and running for the e-mail to be sent. In a corporate environment where Exchange Server is used, the e-mail is stored on the mail server and is sent automatically on the delivery date.

- Select the **Expires After** check box to include a day, date, and time of expiration. You can click the down arrow in the text box to display a calendar from which you can choose a date, or you can enter the date and time yourself. Messages marked to expire are made unavailable after the expiration date. This means the message is basically recalled from any computer where the message has not been read (this feature works only in networked environments using Microsoft Exchange Server).

The delivery options are really great in cases where someone other than you needs to keep track of the responses related to an e-mail message that you sent or in cases where you don't want to immediately deliver a message using the Do Not Deliver Before option. Using the Expire option means that people who have been on vacation won't have to read old messages that you have sent; they will no longer be available because of the expiration date.

Assigning Contacts and Categories to a Message

The Message Options dialog box also enables you to link a contact or contacts to a message. Linking a contact (or contacts) to a message allows you to view the message on that contact's Activities tab (when you are viewing the contact's actual record in the Contacts folder). The use of the Activities tab on a contact's record is discussed in Outlook Lesson 11, "Creating a Contacts List."

CAUTION

Do Contact Links and Categories Appear on Sent Messages? When you link contacts and categories to messages, you are actually just applying organizational tags to the e-mails. You can then view all the e-mail sent to a particular contact in the Contacts folder or sort sent e-mail by a particular category. The recipient of e-mail that you have tagged in this manner does not know that you created the link.

To assign a contact link to the message, click the **Contacts** button in the Message Options dialog box. The Select Contacts dialog box opens, showing all your contacts. Double-click a contact to add it to the Contacts box on the Message Options dialog box. Now the sent message is linked to a particular contact or contacts and can be accessed for later consideration when you are working with that contact or contacts in the Contacts folder.

Another option that Outlook provides for organizing sent messages is the use of categories. You can assign your messages to different categories, such as Business, Goals, Hot Contacts, Phone Calls, and so on. You set the category for a message in the Categories dialog box.

TERM

Categories Categories offer a way of organizing messages to make them easier to find, sort, print, and manage. To find all the items in one category, choose **Tools**, **Find Items**. Click the **More Choices** tab, choose **Categories**, and check the category for which you're searching.

To assign a category, follow these steps:

1. In the Message Options dialog box, click the **Categories** button. The Categories dialog box appears (see Figure 9.4).

2. To assign an existing category, select the category or categories that best suit your message from the Available Categories list. To assign a new category, enter a new category into the **Item(s) Belong to These Categories** text box, and then click the **Add to List** button.

3. Click **OK** to close the Categories dialog box and return to the Message Options dialog box.

Figure 9.4   Organize your messages with categories.

 TIP   **Create Your Own Categories**   If you want to create a new category to assign to your e-mail messages, click the **Master Category List** button on the Categories dialog box. The Master Category List dialog box appears. Type the name of the new category in the New category box, and then click **Add** (repeat as necessary). To return to the Categories dialog box, click **OK**. Your new categories appear in the Categories dialog box.

When you have set all the options for the current message, click the **Close** button to close the Message Options box and return to the message window.

The whole point of tagging sent messages with categories is so that you can view messages by category when you open the Sent Items folder. For example, you might want to quickly check the messages that have been tagged with the Competition category. Changing the view of a particular folder, such as the Sent Items folder, is handled using the View menu.

1. Use the Folder List to open the Sent Items folder.

2. To view the messages by category, select the **View** menu, point at **Current View**, and then select **Customize Current View**. The View Summary dialog box opens.

3. Click the **Group By** button on the View Summary dialog box. The Group By dialog box opens as shown in Figure 9.5.

4. Click the **Group Items By** drop-down list and select **Categories**, and then click **OK** to close the dialog box.

5. Click **OK** to close the View Summary dialog box.

6. When you return to the Sent Items folder, a list of the categories that you have assigned to your sent messages appear. To view the messages listed under a particular category, click the **plus (+)** symbol to the left of a particular category.

147

Figure 9.5   View your messages by category.

Now My View Is All Messed Up!   To remove the custom view, repeat steps 2–5; in step 4 select **None** in the Group By drop-down box. This returns your view of the folder to the default view.

CAUTION

Using Message Flags

Another tool for tagging messages is a message flag. A message flag enables you to mark a message as important, either as a reminder for yourself or as a signal to the message's recipient. When you send a message flag, a red flag icon appears in the recipient's message list, and Outlook adds text at the top of the message telling which type of flag you are sending. In addition, you can add a due date to the flag, and that date appears at the top of the message.

The following list outlines the types of flags you can send in Outlook:

Call	No Response Necessary
Do Not Forward	Read
Follow Up	Reply
For Your Information	Reply to All
Forward	Review

Using these various flags is like sticking a brief note on the message that provides you with a clue as to what type of follow-up might be required by a particular message. To use a message flag, follow these steps:

1. Open a new message or existing message that you want to flag. In the message window, click **Actions** and then select **Follow Up**. The Flag for Follow Up dialog box appears (see Figure 9.6).

Figure 9.6 Flag a message to show its importance or as a reminder for your follow-up.

2. Click the **Flag To** drop-down arrow and choose the flag type you want to add to the message.

3. Click the **Due By** drop-down arrow and use the calendar that appears to enter a date into the text box. Use the **Time** drop-down box to set a specific time. Assigning a due date and time makes you act on the message as dictated by the flag by a particular date.

4. Click **OK** to return to the message window.

Figure 9.7 shows the Inbox with some flagged messages.

Figure 9.7 Flagged messages "pop out" of a particular folder, reminding you to deal with them.

Marking messages with the Follow Up flag is a great way to remind yourself that you need to attend to a particular issue. Flagging messages for your e-mail recipients helps them prioritize responses, so you receive the needed reply within a particular time frame.

When you double-click a flagged message and open it in a message window (see Figure 9.8), the flag type appears at the top of the message, just above the From box.

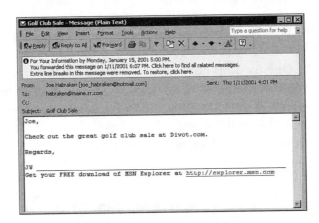

Figure 9.8 To view the type of flag attached, open the message.

Viewing the flag type on the message provides you with a quick reminder as to what your next action should be regarding the particular message.

Using the Outlook Address Books

In this lesson, you learn about different Outlook address books and how to import lists to Outlook from other applications.

Understanding the Outlook Address Books

Outlook has the capability to access different stores or lists of information that can provide you with people's e-mail addresses and other contact information, such as phone numbers and addresses. The address books that you can access include the Personal Address Book your Contacts list, and other directory lists that are provided by other e-mail systems and communication servers. For example, in a corporate network, a Microsoft Exchange Server can provide you with a Global Address list that is shared by all users on the Exchange network. The e-mail address of any users on the network are then easily found in one resource.

 The Contacts List   You might notice contacts in the list of address books; this list contains entries you create in your Contacts list. For more information about the Contacts list, see Lesson 11, "Creating a Contacts List."

Where your e-mail addresses and other contact information are stored depends on whether you are using Outlook on a corporate network that uses Active Directory, a network that uses Exchange Server, or as a standalone product where you use an Internet e-mail account. However, no matter where your contact information is kept, Outlook makes it easy for you to access your different address books using the Address Book feature.

Using the Address Book

The Address Book is basically a launch pad that allows you to access information lists (they are all considered address books) that contain e-mail addresses and other contact information. Because you create your own Contacts list, you always have this resource available, even if you aren't connected to a special network server and you access your e-mail by connecting to the Internet. You can find more information about building your Contacts list in Lesson 11, "Creating a Contacts List." Outlook also has the capability to access Web-based address directories such as Bigfoot and InfoSpace, which are both Web directories that can help you find people's e-mail addresses.

 You can open the Address Book feature by clicking the **To** button or **Cc** button on a new message or by clicking the **Address Book** icon on the Outlook toolbar. After the Address Book dialog box is open, as shown in Figure 10.1, you can use the **Show Names from the** drop-down list to select the specific address book (such as your Personal Address Book or Contacts list) that you want to view.

Figure 10.1   The Address Book enables you to access any of your address books.

Finding Records in an Address Book

The Address Book dialog box also makes it easy for you to search through a particular address book for a particular person. In the Type Name box, begin to type the name of a contact you want to find in the list; as soon as you type enough of the contact's name for Outlook to find that particular contact, it will be highlighted in the list provided.

In cases where you want to search for a record or records by a particular character string (such as all records in the address book that have the last name of Smith), the Address Book provides you with a Find dialog box.

Click the **Find Items** button on the Address Book toolbar. The Find dialog box appears as shown in Figure 10.2.

Type your search string into the Find Names Containing box. Then, click **OK** to run the search. The search results appear in the Address Book dialog box. Only the records that match your search parameters appear in the list.

Figure 10.2 You can search a particular address book by keywords or text strings using the Find dialog box.

Adding Records to an Address Book

You can also add records to any of the address books that you have access to. For example, you can add records to your Personal Address book or to your Contacts list directly in the Address Book window. Keep in mind that in a corporate environment, your network administrator likely controls some address books, such as the Global Address Book. This means that you won't be able to add information to these address books; you can use them only as resources to find information such as e-mail addresses.

To add a record to an address book that you do control:

1. In the Address Book dialog box, make sure that you have the address book selected that you want to add the new record to.

2. Click the **New Entry** button on the Address Book toolbar. The New Entry dialog box appears (see Figure 10.3).

Figure 10.3 You can add new records to address books using the New Entry dialog box.

3. Use the **Put This Entry in the** drop-down box at the bottom of the New Entry dialog box to make sure that your new record ends up in the correct address book. To add a new record (a new contact, for example), click **New Contact** and then click **OK**.

Distribution List   A distribution list allows you to create a record that includes the e-mail addresses for several people. This makes it easy to send e-mails to a group of people. You can create distribution lists in the New Entry dialog box. You will learn how to create distribution lists in the next lesson.

4. A blank record appears for your new entry. Enter the appropriate information for the new record, such as the person's name, e-mail address, and so on into the appropriate text boxes. When you have finished entering the information, click **OK** to save the new entry. In the case of new contacts added to the Contacts list, click the **Save and Close** button.

The blank records that open for your new entries will look slightly different, depending on the address book in which you are creating the new record. In the case of new contacts (which is discussed in the next chapter), you can enter information for the new entry that includes the person's address, phone number, fax number, and even a Web page address. Some address books may allow you to enter only the name and e-mail address of the person.

TIP   **Create a New Message from the Address Book Dialog Box**   If you opened the Address Book using the **Address Book** icon on the Outlook toolbar (or selected **Tools**, **Address Book**), you can open a new message for any of the contacts listed in one of the address books. Select the particular person, and then click the **New Message** icon on the Address Book icon. A new message opens addressed to that particular person.

Importing Address Books and Contact Lists

If you are migrating from another personal information manager or e-mail client and want to import your address book or Contacts list, Outlook contains different conversion filters for this purpose. Outlook even provides you with an Import/Export Wizard that walks you through the steps of importing address lists and address books from these other software packages.

To start the Outlook Import/Export Wizard, follow these steps:

1. Click **File**, and then select **Import and Export**. The Outlook Import and Export Wizard opens (see Figure 10.4).

Figure 10.4 The Import and Export Wizard walks you through the process of importing your old address books or information from other applications.

2. On the first wizard screen, you can choose to import e-mail and contacts information from another e-mail client, such as Outlook Express or Netscape, by selecting **Import Internet Mail and Addresses**. Then, click **Next**.

3. On the next screen, select the e-mail client, such as Outlook Express, that holds the information that you will import to Outlook (remember that this feature imports e-mail messages and address information from the e-mail client to Outlook). Then, click **Next**.

4. The next wizard screen asks you to select the Outlook address book that will hold the imported information. Select the **Personal Address Book** option button or the **Outlook Contacts Folder** option button to specify the destination for the imported records. Additional option buttons on this screen allow you to specify how duplicate records are handled; select one of the following:

- Replace duplicates with items imported; this option replaces any records currently in the address book with duplicates from the imported file.

- Allow duplicates to be created; any duplicates currently in the address book are not overwritten during the import and duplicate records are placed in the address book.

- Do not import duplicate items; any duplicate items found in the address book that is being imported are not imported into Outlook.

5. After making your selections, click **Finish**.

The e-mail messages and the e-mail address records are imported into the Outlook address book that you chose. A message appears letting you know how many records were imported. The address records are placed in the address book that you chose. Imported e-mail is placed in the appropriate Outlook folder, such as your Inbox and Sent Items folders.

TIP **Importing Information from Database Programs** If you want to import address records or other information from programs such as Microsoft Access or Lotus Notes, select the Import from another program or file option on the initial Import and Export Wizard screen. You are then walked through the steps of selecting the program and file that holds the data that you want to import. You will have the option of selecting the Outlook Contacts list or another address book, such as the Personal Address Book, to hold the information after it is imported.

Exporting Outlook Address Records

There might be occasions where you would like to take the records in one of your Outlook address books such as the Contacts list and export this information to another software package. For example, you may want to place all the records in your Contacts list in an Access database file (this is particularly useful in cases where you might be using Outlook to hold information about your customers or clients). Outlook records can be exported using the Import and Export Wizard.

Follow these steps:

1. Click **File**, and then select **Import and Export**. The Outlook Import and Export Wizard opens.

2. Select **Export to a File**, and then click **Next**.

3. On the next screen, you are provided with a list of file types that you can use for your export file (see Figure 10.5). Select a file type such as Microsoft Access, and then click **Next**.

Figure 10.5 The Import and Export Wizard walks you through the process of importing your old address books or information from other applications.

4. On the next screen, you are provided with a list of file types that you can use for your export file (see Figure 10.5). Select a file type such as Microsoft Access, and then click **Next**.

5. On the next screen, you are asked to select the Outlook folder that contains the information that you will export. Select the appropriate folder such as **Contacts**. Then, click **Next**.

6. On the next screen, type a name for the file in the Save Exported File As: box. If you want to specify a specific location on your computer for the file to be saved in, use the **Browse** button to open the Browse dialog box. When you have returned to the wizard (click **OK** to close the Browse dialog box), click **Next**.

7. The next screen lists the folder that will be exported. Click **Finish**. The export file is created.

After the information has been exported to the new file (it is actually copied to the new file; your Contacts list remains intact in Outlook), you can open the file using the destination application. For example, if you created an Access database using the export feature, you can open the file created using Microsoft Access.

Creating a Contacts List

In this lesson, you learn how to create and view a Contacts list and how to send mail to someone on your Contacts list. You also learn how to create a distribution list.

Creating a New Contact

You use the Contacts folder to create, store, and access your Contacts list. You can enter any or all of the following information about each contact:

- Name
- Job title
- Company name
- Address (street, city, state, ZIP code, and country)
- Phone (business, home, business fax, mobile)
- E-mail address
- Web page address
- Comments, notes, or descriptions
- Categories

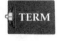 **Contact** In Outlook, a contact is any person or company for which you've entered a name, address, phone number, or other information. You can communicate with a contact in Outlook by sending an e-mail message, scheduling a meeting, sending a letter, and so on.

You also can edit the information at any time, add new contacts, or delete contacts from the list. To open the Contacts folder and create a new contact, follow these steps:

1. To open the Contacts folder, click the **Contacts** shortcut on the Outlook bar. The Contacts folder opens.

 2. To create a new contact, select **Actions** and then choose **New Contact**, or click the **New Contact** button on the Standard toolbar. The Contact dialog box appears, with the General tab displayed (see Figure 11.1).

Figure 11.1 You can enter as much or as little information about each contact as you need.

3. Enter the contact's name into the Full Name text box. If you want to add more detailed information for the name, click the **Full Name** button to display the Check Full Name dialog box, and then enter the contact's title and full name (including first, middle, and last names) and any suffix you want to include. Click **OK** to close the Check Full Name dialog box and return to the Contact dialog box.

4. Press the **Tab** key to navigate from one field in this dialog box to the next. After the name field, the insert point moves down to the contact's job title and then the company name. This information is optional.

5. In the **File As** drop-down box, enter or select the method by which you want to file your contact's names. You can choose **Last Name First** or **First Name First**, or you can enter your own filing system, such as by company or state.

TIP **Keep It Simple** The default filing method for contacts is last name first, which makes it easy to quickly find the contact when you need it.

6. Enter the address into the Address box and choose whether the address is **Business**, **Home**, or **Other**. Alternatively, you can click the **Address** button to enter the street, city, state, ZIP code, and country in specified areas instead of all within the text block. You can add a second address (the Home address, for example) if you want. Address information is optional.

7. In the **Phone** drop-down lists, choose the type of phone number—Business, Callback, Car, Home Fax, ISDN, Pager, and so on—and then enter the number. You can enter up to 19 numbers into each of the four drop-down boxes in the Phone area of the dialog box.

8. You can enter up to three e-mail addresses into the **E-Mail** text box. The box below the e-mail address allows you to enter how the e-mail address appears when you send a message to a person (for example, smith@mail.com could appear as Bob Smith); in the **Web Page Address** text box, enter the address for the company or contact's URL on the World Wide Web.

If you have more than one e-mail address for a contact, the first number or address in the list serves as the default. For example, when e-mailing a contact, the first e-mail address in the list is placed in the To box on the new message. If you want to use a different e-mail address for the contact, double-click the contact's name in the Message To box and select one of the other e-mail addresses in the contact's Properties box. When you want to call a contact for whom you have multiple numbers, a drop-down list appears in the New Call dialog box that enables you to choose the appropriate number.

 URL (Uniform Resource Locator)   The address for a Web page on the World Wide Web. A typical URL is written `http://www.companyname.com`, such as `http://www.mcp.com`.

9. In the comment text box, enter any descriptions, comments, or other pertinent information. Then, select or enter a category to classify the contact.

10. After you have finished entering the new contact information, click the **Save and Close** button to return to the Contacts folder. You can also save the new contact by opening the **File** menu and choosing one of the following commands:

- **Save**—Saves the record and closes the Contact dialog box.
- **Save and New**—Saves the record and clears the Contact dialog box so that you can enter a new contact.

 Other Tabs in the Contacts Window   Most of the information that you need to enter for a contact is contained on the General tab. You can also add additional information, such as the person's nickname or spouse's name, on the Details tab. The Certificates tab allows you to specify a certificate to use to send encrypted e-mail to this particular contact (Certificates are discussed in Lesson 9, "Setting Mail Options," of the Outlook section).

You can edit the information for a contact at any time by double-clicking the contact's name in the Contacts list; this displays the contact's information window. Alternatively, you can work on the fields in a record directly in the Contacts list window. Click within the information listed below a contact's name (such as the phone number or address) to position the insertion point in the text and then delete or enter text. Press **Enter** to complete the modifications you've made and move to the next contact in the list.

Viewing the Contacts List

By default, you see the contacts in an Address Cards view (Address Cards appear in the Current View list on the Outlook Advanced toolbar). The information you see displays the contact's name and other data, such as addresses and phone numbers. The contact's company name, job title, and comments, however, are not displayed by default. Figure 11.2 shows the Contacts list in the default Address Cards view.

Figure 11.2   View your contacts in Address Cards view.

You can use the horizontal scrollbar to view more contacts, or you can click a letter in the index (on the right side of the screen) to display contacts beginning with that letter in the first column of the list.

You can change how you view the contacts in the list by choosing one of these options from the Current View drop-down list on the Standard toolbar:

- **Address Cards**—Displays full name, addresses, and phone numbers of the contacts, depending on the amount of information you've entered, in a card format.

161

- **Detailed Address Cards**—Displays full name, job title, company, addresses, phone numbers, e-mail addresses, categories, and comments in a card format.

- **Phone List**—Displays full name, job title, company, File As name, department, phone numbers, and categories in a table, organizing each entry horizontally in rows and columns.

- **By Category**—Displays contacts in rows by categories. The information displayed is the same as what's displayed in a phone list.

- **By Company**—Displays contacts in rows, grouped by their company. The information displayed is the same as what's displayed in a phone list.

- **By Location**—Displays contacts grouped by country. The information displayed is the same as what's displayed in a phone list.

- **By Follow-Up Flag**—Displays contacts grouped by follow-up flags. The view also displays the due date for the follow-up that you specified when you marked the contact with a flag (flags are discussed in Lesson 8, "Saving Drafts and Organizing Messages," and can be assigned to Contacts the same as they are assigned to e-mail messages).

Viewing a Contacts Activities Tab

Although the Contacts folder provides different views for perusing the actual contacts in the Contacts list, these views really don't give you any indication of the messages that you have sent to a particular contact or the tasks that you might have assigned to a particular contact (assigning a task to a contact is covered later in this lesson).

You can view all the activities related to a particular contact on the contact's Activities tab. With the Contacts folder open, follow these steps:

1. Double-click a contact in the Contacts folder to open the contact.

2. Click the **Activities** tab on the contact's window. All the activities, such as sent and received e-mails and any assigned tasks, appear in the Activities pane (see Figure 11.3).

3. To see a subset of the Activities list, click the **Show** drop-down box. You can choose to view only E-Mail, Notes, or Upcoming Tasks/Appointments related to that particular contact (any items that you delete in the Activities list are removed from the list and the folder that contained them).

4. You open any of the items on the Activities list by double-clicking that item. Close an opened item by clicking its **Close (X)** button.

5. When you have finished viewing the activities related to a particular contact, you can close the contact's window.

Figure 11.3 You can view all the activities related to a particular contact.

Using Distribution Lists

If you find that you are sending e-mail messages or assigning tasks to multiple recipients, you might want to create a distribution list. A distribution list enables you to group several contacts. Then, to send an e-mail to all the contacts in the distribution list, you address the e-mail with the name of the distribution list.

The distribution lists that you create are listed in your Contacts folder. You can open an existing distribution list by double-clicking it. You can then add or delete members of the list.

To create a distribution list, follow these steps:

1. Select the **Actions** menu, and then select **New Distribution List**, or you can right-click an empty space of the Contacts folder and select **New Distribution List** from the shortcut menu that appears. The Distribution List window appears (see Figure 11.4).
2. To enter a name for the distribution list, type the name into the Name box.
3. To add contacts to the distribution list, click the **Select Members** button, which opens the Select Members dialog box. Use the **Show Names from the** drop-down list to select the address book, such as the Contacts list, that you want to use to add names to the distribution list.
4. Select a contact to add to the distribution list, and then click the **Members** button to add the contact to the list (see Figure 11.5).

Figure 11.4   You can add contacts to a distribution list for mass e-mail mailings.

Figure 11.5   Add your contacts to the list from any of your address books.

5. To select multiple contacts at once, hold down the **Ctrl** key, click the mouse on each contact, and then click the **Members** button.

6. When you have finished adding the contacts to the distribution list, click the **OK** button on the Select Members dialog box. You are returned to the Distribution List window.

7. To save the distribution list, click the **Save and Close** button on the list's toolbar.

After you have saved the distribution list, it appears as a contact listing in your Contacts folder. You can use the distribution list's name in the To box of an e-mail message to send the message to all the contacts listed in the distribution list.

If you find that you want to remove names from a distribution list, open the distribution list from the Contacts folder. In the Distribution List window, select the name or names you want to remove from the list. Then, click the **Remove** button. Make sure that you save the changes that you have made to the distribution list.

 TIP **Add People to the Distribution List Who Are Not Current Contacts** If you want to add names and associated e-mail addresses for people who are not in an address book to a distribution list, click the **Add New** button in the Distribution List window. The Add New dialog box allows you to enter a name and e-mail address for a new member of the distribution list.

Communicating with a Contact

You can send messages to any of your contacts, arrange meetings, assign tasks, or even send a letter to a contact from within Outlook (this also includes any distribution lists that you have created in the Contacts folder). To communicate with a contact, make sure you're in the Contacts folder. You do not need to open the specific contact's information window to perform any of the following procedures.

Sending Messages

To send a message to a contact, you must make sure you've entered an e-mail address in the General tab of the Contact dialog box for that particular contact. If Outlook cannot locate the e-mail address, it displays a message dialog box letting you know.

To send a message from the Contacts folder, select the contact, select **Actions**, and then select **New Message to Contact** (or you can right-click the contact or the distribution list and select **New Message to Contact** from the shortcut menu that appears).

In the Untitled - Message dialog box, enter the subject and message and set any options you want. When you're ready to send the message, click the **Send** button.

Scheduling a Meeting with a Contact

To schedule a meeting with a contact (or with contacts contained in a distribution list), you must first select the contact or distribution list (as with sending mail messages, the contacts involved must have an e-mail address). After you've selected the contact or list, select **Actions**, and then select **New Meeting Request to Contact** to open the Untitled - Meeting dialog box.

Enter the subject, location, time, date, and other information you need to schedule the meeting, and then notify the contact by sending an invitation (invitations are sent automatically during the process of creating the meeting). For more information about scheduling meetings, see Lesson 13, "Planning a Meeting," in the Outlook section of this book.

Assigning a Task to a Contact

As with mail messages and meetings, a contact must have an e-mail address to assign that individual a task. To assign a task to a contact, select the contact (tasks cannot be assigned to distribution lists), select **Actions**, and then select **New Task for Contact**. The Task dialog box appears. Enter the subject, due date, status, and other information, and then send the task to the contact, just click the Send Task button on the task's toolbar. For detailed information about assigning tasks, see Lesson 14, "Creating a Task List."

Sending a Letter to a Contact

If you want to create a hard copy letter and send it using "snail mail" (meaning sending it using the postal system), Outlook can help you create the letter based on the information in a particular Contact's record. Outlook uses the Microsoft Word Letter Wizard to help you create a letter to send to a contact. Within the Word Letter Wizard, you follow directions as they appear onscreen to complete the text of the letter.

To send a letter to the contact, select the contact in the Contacts folder and choose **Actions**, and then select **New Letter to Contact**. Word opens the Letter Wizard onscreen. The Letter Wizard helps you format and complete the letter (see Figure 11.6). Just follow the onscreen directions to create the letter.

Figure 11.6   Use Word's Letter Wizard to create a letter to a contact.

Calling a Contact

Another obvious way to communicate with a contact is over the telephone. For Outlook to dial the phone number for you, you must have a modem hooked to your computer that can dial out for you. With the right equipment, Outlook makes it easy for you to make a phone call to a contact by dialing the phone number for you.

For Outlook to manage your calls, you must have a modem hooked to your computer that can dial out for you. If you're in a networked environment that has access to a network modem pool, you can also dial out using your computer. The line you dial out on, however, must also be accessible by your telephone.

To initiate a phone call to a contact, select the contact in the Contact list and follow these steps:

1. Select **Actions**, point at **Call Contact**, and then select the appropriate phone number from the cascading menu that appears (all the phone numbers for the selected contact appear, including business, home, and fax). You can also click the **Dial** button on the Standard toolbar and select the appropriate phone number from the drop-down list. In both cases, the New Call dialog box appears (see Figure 11.7).

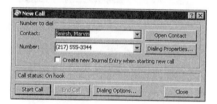

Figure 11.7   You can quickly initiate a telephone call to a contact using the Actions menu or the Dial button.

2. Click the **Start Call** button to allow Outlook to dial the contact's phone number using your modem.

3. The Call Status dialog box appears. Pick up your phone and click the **Talk** button in the Call Status dialog box. This engages the phone and you can speak to your contact when they answer your call.

Viewing a Map of a Contact's Address

A useful feature Outlook offers is the capability to view an area map based on the address of a particular contact (requires an active Internet connection). This can be incredibly useful when you aren't sure where a particular contact is located.

To view a map of a contact's address, double-click the contact in the Contact list. The contact's record opens in the Contact dialog box.

Click the **Display Map of Address** button on the Contacts toolbar. Microsoft Internet Explorer opens to the Microsoft Expedia Web site and displays a map based on the contact's address, as shown in Figure 11.8.

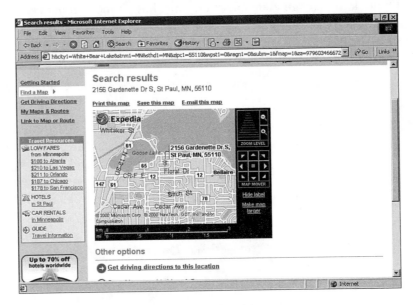

Figure 11.8   You can view a map of a contact's address.

You can zoom in and out on the map, and you can print a hard copy. When you are finished viewing the map and want to return to Outlook, simply close the Internet Explorer window.

Using the Calendar

In this lesson, you learn how to navigate the Calendar, create appointments, and save appointments. You also learn how to insert an Office object, such as an Excel workbook, in an appointment.

Navigating the Calendar

You can use Outlook's Calendar to schedule appointments and create a task list. If necessary, Outlook can also remind you of appointments and daily or weekly tasks. You can schedule appointments months in advance, move appointments, cancel appointments, and so on. The Calendar makes it very easy to identify the days on which you have appointments.

To open the Outlook Calendar, click the **Calendar** icon in the Outlook bar, or select the **Calendar** folder from the Folder List. Figure 12.1 shows the Calendar in Outlook.

Outlook provides multiple ways for you to move around in the Calendar and view specific dates:

- Scroll through the Schedule pane to view the time of an appointment.
- In the Monthly Calendar pane, click the left and right arrows next to the names of the months to go backward and forward one month at a time. Click a date to display that day's information in the Schedule pane.

 TIP **Changing Calendar Views** You can change to different views of the Calendar by clicking the **Current View** drop-down arrow on the Advanced toolbar. Views including Active Appointments, Recurring Appointments, and By Category are available.

- In the monthly calendar pane, click a particular date on one of the months shown to display that date in the schedule pane.
- To view a different month in the Monthly Calendar pane, click the current month in the Monthly Calendar pane and select the name of the month from the shortcut list. Or you can use the **Back** or **Forward** arrows to the left and right of the shown months (respectively) to go back or forward on the calendar.
- To view a week or multiple days in the Schedule pane, select them in the Monthly Calendar pane.

Today's date   Monthly Calendar pane

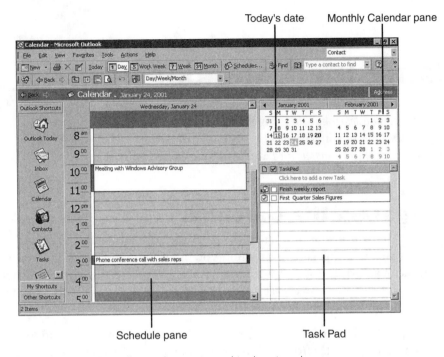

Schedule pane   Task Pad

Figure 12.1   You can view all appointments and tasks at a glance.

- To add a task to the Task Pad, click where you see **Click Here to Add a New Task** on the Task Pad.
- Use the scrollbars for the Task Pad to view additional tasks, if necessary.

TIP **Change the Date Quickly**   To quickly go to today's date or to a specific date without searching through the Monthly Calendar pane, right-click in the Schedule pane and choose either **Today** or **Go to Date**.

Creating an Appointment

You can create an appointment on any day in the Outlook Calendar. When you create an appointment, you can add the subject, location, starting time, category, and even an alarm to remind you ahead of time.

Follow these steps to create an appointment:

1. In the Monthly Calendar pane, select the month and the date for which you want to create an appointment.

2. In the Schedule pane, double-click next to the time at which the appointment is scheduled to begin. The Untitled - Appointment dialog box appears, with the Appointment tab displayed (see Figure 12.2).

Figure 12.2 Enter all the details you need when scheduling an appointment.

3. Enter the subject of the appointment in the **Subject** text box (you can use a person's name, a topic, or other information).

4. In the **Location** text box, enter the meeting place or other text that will help you identify the meeting when you see it in your calendar.

5. Enter dates and times in the **Start Time** and **End Time** boxes (or click the drop-down arrows and select the dates and times).

TIP   **Autodate It!**   You can use Outlook's Autodate feature: Enter a text phrase such as **next Friday** into the Start time or End time box, and then press **Enter**; Outlook figures out the date for you and places it into the appropriate box.

6. If you want your PC to let you know when you're due for the appointment, select the **Reminder** check box and enter the amount of time before the appointment occurs that you want to be notified. If you want to set an audio alarm, click the **Alarm Bell** button and browse your hard drive to select a specific sound file for Outlook to play as your reminder.

7. From the **Show Time As** drop-down list, you can select how the appointment time block should be marked on the calendar. The default is Busy. But you can also block out the specified time as Free, Tentative, or Out of Office. The drop-down list uses different colors and patterns to specify each of the different appointment types.

8. In the large text box near the bottom of the Appointment tab, enter any text that you want to include, such as text to identify the appointment, reminders for materials to take, and so on.

9. Click the **Categories** button and assign a category (or categories) to the appointment.

10. Click the **Save and Close** button to return to the Calendar.

The Scheduling tab enables you to schedule a meeting with co-workers and enter the meeting on your calendar. See Lesson 13, "Planning a Meeting," for more information.

Scheduling a Recurring Appointment

Suppose you have an appointment that comes around every week or month or that otherwise occurs on a regular basis. Instead of scheduling every individual occurrence of the appointment, you can schedule that appointment in your calendar as a recurring appointment.

To schedule a recurring appointment, follow these steps:

1. In the Calendar folder, choose the **Actions** menu, and then **New Recurring Appointment**. The Appointment dialog box appears, and then the Appointment Recurrence dialog box appears on top of the Appointment dialog box (as shown in Figure 12.3).

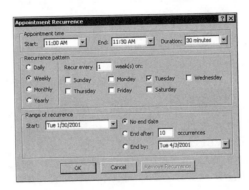

Figure 12.3 Schedule a recurring appointment once, and Outlook fills in the appointment for you throughout the Calendar.

2. In the Appointment Time area, enter the **Start** and **End** times for the appointment. Outlook calculates the duration of the appointment for you.

3. In the Recurrence Pattern area, indicate the frequency of the appointment: **Daily, Weekly, Monthly,** or **Yearly.** After you select one of these options, the rest of the Recurrence Pattern area changes to provide you with appropriate options, such as days of the week for a weekly recurring appointment or day-of-the-month options for a monthly recurring appointment.

4. Enter the day and month, as well as any other options in the Recurrence Pattern area that are specific to your selection in step 3.

5. In the Range of Recurrence area, enter appropriate time limits according to the following guidelines:

- **Start**—Choose the date on which the recurring appointments begin.
- **No End Date**—Choose this option if the recurring appointments are not on a limited schedule.
- **End After**—Choose this option and enter the number of appointments if there is a specific limit to the recurring appointments.
- **End By**—Choose this option and enter an ending date to limit the number of recurring appointments.

6. Click **OK** to close the Appointment Recurrence dialog box. The Appointment dialog box appears.

7. Fill in the Appointment dialog box using the steps in the "Creating an Appointment" section already discussed in this lesson. When you finish providing all the details for the recurring appointment, click the **Save and Close** button to return to the Calendar.

The recurring appointment appears in your calendar on the specified date and time. A recurring appointment contains a circular double-arrow icon to indicate that it is recurring.

 TIP **Make Any Appointment Recurring** If you have already started creating an appointment and then would like to make it recurring, click the **Recurrence** button on the appointment's toolbar. The Appointment Recurrence dialog box opens.

Planning Events

In the Outlook Calendar, an *event* is any activity that lasts at least 24 hours, such as a trade show or a conference. You can plan an event in the Calendar program to block off larger time slots than you would for normal appointments. In addition, you can schedule recurring events (such as a monthly seminar you attend that lasts all day).

To schedule an event, choose **Actions**, and then select **New All Day Event**. The Event dialog box appears (see Figure 12.4; it looks similar to the New Appointment dialog box).

Figure 12.4   You can block out an entire day on the Calendar by scheduling an All Day Event.

Fill in the **Subject, Location, Start Time**, and **End Time** text boxes. Make sure the **All Day Event** check box is checked (that's the only difference between an event and an appointment). Click the **Save and Close** button to return to the Outlook Calendar. The appointment appears in gray at the beginning of the day for which you scheduled the event.

To schedule a recurring event, open a New All Day Event window and fill in the information as described earlier. To make the event recurring, click the **Recurrence** button in the Event window. The Event Recurrence dialog box opens; fill in the appropriate information and click **OK** (this dialog box is similar to the one for recurring appointments). Complete the information in the Event window, and then click the **Save and Close** button.

To edit an event or a recurring event, double-click the event in your calendar. Like a mail message or appointment, Outlook opens the event window so that you can change times, dates, or other details of the event.

Inserting an Object

Outlook has the capability to insert an object, such as an Excel workbook or a file from any other Office application, into any Outlook item such as an appointment. For example, you might have an appointment to discuss some tax issues with your accountant and you have an Excel worksheet that details some of the information you want to go over. You can insert the Excel workbook right into the appointment. This makes it easy for you to view the data before you attend your appointment or even print the information.

You can insert an existing object into an appointment, or you can create an object within a message using the source application. For example, you could place an existing Excel workbook in an existing appointment.

To attach an existing object to an appointment in the Calendar, follow these steps:

1. Click the **Calendar** icon in the Outlook bar. Select **File**, **New**, **Appointment**. The new appointment will appear in the Outlook workspace. Position the insertion point in the appointment text box. This is where you will insert the Excel object.

2. In the appointment window, select **Insert**; then select **Object**. The Insert Object dialog box appears.

3. Choose the **Create from File** option (see Figure 12.5).

Figure 12.5 Insert an object, such as an Excel worksheet, into an Outlook task.

4. In the **File** text box, enter the path and the name of the file you want to insert. (You can use the **Browse** button and the resulting dialog box to search for the file, if necessary.)

5. Click **OK**. Outlook inserts the object into the Outlook item. The workbook or other inserted object actually resides inside a frame.

To edit an object, double-click within the frame, and the source application opens from within Outlook. Note that you'll still see your Outlook item and Outlook toolbars; however, you'll also see tools associated with the object's source application, which you can use to edit the object.

Figure 12.6 shows an Excel spreadsheet object within an Outlook appointment. Notice that the Excel toolbar and icons appear at the top of the Outlook window because an Excel object requires Excel's capabilities for editing.

Figure 12.6   You can edit the object from within your Outlook appointment.

You can resize the object to suit your needs. First, select it, and a frame appears with eight small black boxes (called *handles*) on the corners and along the sides. To resize the object, position the mouse pointer over one of the black handles; the mouse pointer becomes a two-headed arrow. Click and drag the handle to resize the object.

When you change data in an embedded object, such as an Excel worksheet, remember to save the changes. Just click the **Save** button on the Excel toolbar (or the toolbar of the application that you are using to create the object). If you have resized an object in an item or inserted an object, remember to save the Outlook item (select **File**, then **Save**).

Objects can also be inserted in tasks and meetings. Inserting objects enables you to have information related to a particular appointment, task, or meeting right at your fingertips.

Planning a Meeting

In this lesson, you learn how to schedule a meeting, enter attendees for a planned meeting, set the meeting date and time, and invite others to the meeting.

Scheduling a Meeting

Outlook enables you to plan the time and date of a meeting, identify the subject and location of the meeting, invite others to attend the meeting, and identify resources that will be needed for the meeting. You use the Calendar folder to plan and schedule meetings.

Meeting   In Outlook, a meeting is an appointment to which you invite people and plan for the inclusion of certain resources.

Resources   Any equipment you use in your meeting, such as a computer, a slide projector, or even the room itself.

To plan a meeting, follow these steps:

1. Click the icon for the Calendar folder on the Outlook bar. Then, in the Month pane, select the date on which you want to hold the meeting. To open a new meeting, select **Actions** and select **Plan a Meeting**. The Plan a Meeting dialog box appears (see Figure 13.1).

2. To enter the names of the attendees, click in the **All Attendees** list where it reads Type Attendee Name Here. You can type a name into the box and then press **Enter**. Continue adding new names as necessary. Names that you type into the list do not have to coincide with records in your Contacts list, but if you include new names, Outlook will not have an e-mail address for those particular attendees when invitations are sent for the meeting.

3. A better way to invite attendees to your meeting is to click the **Add Others** button and choose the attendees from your Contacts list or other address book. This opens the Select Attendees and Resources dialog box, as shown in Figure 13.2. You can add attendees and any resources needed for the meeting in this dialog box. When you have finished adding attendees and resources, click **OK**.

Attendees list   Green bar is starting time.

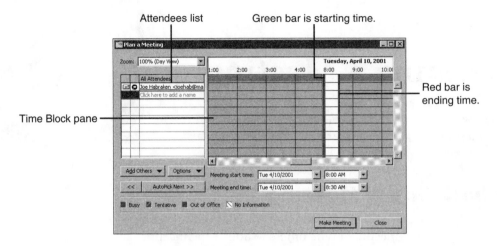

Time Block pane

Red bar is ending time.

Figure 13.1   Choose the date and time of your meeting as well as the attendees.

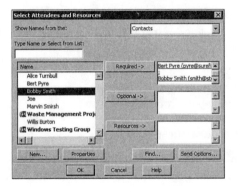

Figure 13.2   Attendees of the meeting and resources that will be needed can be added using the Attendees and Resources dialog box.

 TIP   **A Word About Adding Resources**   The Select Attendees and Resources dialog box enables you to add attendees and resources to a meeting. Because you probably don't list resources, such as overhead projectors, in your Contacts folder, you will have to type the resource names for the meeting as detailed in step 1 of this section (placing them in the Attendees list). In the case of resources, click the e-mail icon that appears to the left of the resource and select **Don't Send Meeting to This Attendee**. This keeps Outlook from trying to e-mail the resource. You can also use this option if you have listed attendees for the meeting who are not contained in your Contact's list.

4. To set a date for the meeting, open the **Meeting Start Time** drop-down list and select the date from the calendar, or just type the date into the text box. The ending date (in the **Meeting End Time** drop-down list) automatically shows the same date you set in the Meeting Start Time date box; you can change the End Time date if you want.

5. To set a start time for the meeting, do one of the following:

- Open the **Meeting Start Time** drop-down list and select the time.
- Type a time into the text box.
- Drag the green bar in the Time Block pane to set the start time.

6. To set an end time for the meeting, do one of the following:

- Open the **Meeting End Time** drop-down list and select the end time.
- Type a time into the text box.
- Drag the red bar in the Time Block pane of the dialog box to change the ending time of the meeting.

After you select the date and time for the meeting, notice that the time grid to the right of each attendee's name shows the currently scheduled appointments that they have on the day of the meeting. The times blocked out in each attendee's grid are based on appointments and meetings in their Outlook Calendar. Outlook is able to check your corporate network and check attendee availability by using their calendars. If you have a conflict between your meeting time and an attendee's appointment, you can adjust the time of your meeting and avoid availability conflicts.

 TIP   **Check the Availability of Internet Colleagues**   On a corporate network that uses Exchange Server, it's easy for Outlook to check other people's calendars to see whether they have a conflict with a meeting that you are planning. If you aren't using Outlook in an Exchange Server environment, you can also avoid scheduling conflicts by having people you invite use Internet e-mail to subscribe to Microsoft's Office Free/Busy Service. Outlook then periodically publishes a person's schedule to the service. All users that have subscribed can check the availability of participants using the service.

For more information about this service, go to `http://www.microsoft.com/office/` on the Web.

7. When you finish planning the meeting, click the **Make Meeting** button. The Meeting window appears, allowing you to refine the meeting details. Details on using this dialog box are described in the next section.

TIP **Use AutoPick to Shift the Meeting Time Frame** You can click the **AutoPick Next** or **AutoPick Back** buttons to shift the meeting time (including the beginning and ending) to a half hour later or earlier, respectively. Each time you click one of the AutoPick buttons, the meeting shifts another half hour.

Working Out Meeting Details

After you plan a meeting, Outlook enables you to send invitations, identify the subject of the meeting, and specify the meeting's location. You enter these details in the Meeting dialog box.

When you schedule a meeting, as described in the previous section, you finish by clicking the **Make Meeting** button in the Plan a Meeting dialog box. When you do that, Outlook displays the Meeting dialog box with the Appointment tab in front (see Figure 13.3).

Figure 13.3 Specify the details related to the meeting in the Appointment tab of the Meeting dialog box.

Follow these steps to specify meeting details for a meeting you've already scheduled:

1. If you did not list the attendees in the Plan a Meeting dialog box, either click in the **To** text box and enter the names of the people that you want to attend the meeting, or click the **To** button to select the attendees from an address book or Contact list.

2. In the **Subject** text box, enter a subject for the meeting.

3. In the **Location** text box, enter a location for the meeting.

4. (Optional) You can change the starting and ending dates and/or times in the Appointment tab. You also can choose the Attendee Availability tab to view the meeting in a format similar to that of the Plan a Meeting dialog box; make any changes to attendees, time, dates, and so on in the Attendee Availability tab.

5. (Optional) Select the **Reminder** check box and enter a time for Outlook to sound an alarm to remind you of the meeting. See Lesson 12, "Using the Calendar," for more information on using the Reminder feature.

6. (Optional) Enter any special text you want to send the attendees in the text box provided beneath the Reminder fields.

7. (Optional) If you plan to hold your meeting online using Microsoft NetMeeting, select the **This Is an Online Meeting Using** check box on the Appointment tab of the Meeting dialog box. Online meetings are scheduled the same as a face-to-face meeting; an online meeting, however, requires that you specify a Directory Server (this drop-down box is enabled when you select the online meeting check box) that will be used to connect the participants. In most cases, online meetings are held using Microsoft NetMeeting.

8. After you have entered all the required information for the new meeting, you can send invitations. However, before you send the invitations, you might want to make sure that the recipients reply to your meeting invitation. Select the **Action** menu and make sure that a selection check mark is next to **Request Responses**. If there isn't, click this selection to place a check mark next to it.

9. Now you can send the invitations; click the **Send** button. The meeting is saved and the Meeting window closes.

Editing Meeting Details and Adding Attendees

You can edit the details of a meeting and change the date and time of the meeting at any time by opening the Meeting window. Opening the Meeting window also allows you to add attendees to the meeting.

Follow these steps:

1. In the Calendar folder, select the meeting date in the Monthly Calendar pane (any date that has scheduled appointments or meetings will be in bold on the Monthly Calendar pane). After you've opened the appropriate day, locate your appointment and double-click it to open it.

2. You can edit any information on the Appointment or Scheduling tabs.

TIP **Any Responses?** Choose the **Tracking** tab of the Meeting window to see whether the people you invited to the meeting have responded to your invitation.

3. You can also add additional attendees to your meeting. On either the Appointment tab or the Scheduling tab of the Meeting dialog box, use the **To** or **Add Others** buttons, respectively, to open the Select Attendees and Resources dialog box.

4. Open the **Show Names from the** drop-down list and choose either **Contacts** or another address book (you can also add a new record to the selected address book by clicking the **New** button; see Lesson 10, "Using the Outlook Address Books," for more information).

5. Select any name in the list on the left side of the dialog box and click the **Required** or **Optional** button to specify attendance requirements.

6. Click the **New** button to add resources to the list; then remember to notify the person who is in charge of those resources of your meeting.

7. Click **OK** to close the dialog box and add the new attendees to your list.

When you have finished editing the meeting and/or adding new attendees, click the **Save and Close** button on the meeting's toolbar. A message box appears as shown in Figure 13.4, asking you whether you want to send the new meeting details to your original and added attendees.

Figure 13.4 Updating meeting details requires that you send new invitations to the meeting participants.

Because changing meeting details means that you also need to inform the attendees of any changes, click **Yes** to send the updated invitations. Attendees will be required to respond to the new invitation if the Request Responses option is selected on the Actions menu.

Creating a Task List

In this lesson, you learn how to enter a task and record statistics about the task. You also learn how to assign tasks to other users.

Entering a Task

You can use the Tasks folder to create and manage tasks that you need to accomplish and don't want to forget about. You can list due dates, the status of a task, task priorities, and even set reminder alarms so your PC can keep you from forgetting a task entered in the list. To open the Tasks folder, click the Task shortcut in the Outlook Bar.

 Task List A task list is a list of things you must do to complete your work, such as plan for a meeting, arrange an event, and so on. Various tasks might include making a phone call, writing a letter, printing a spreadsheet, or making airline reservations.

To enter a task, follow these steps:

 1. In the Tasks folder, click the **New Task** button on the toolbar or double-click any empty space on the Task list. The Untitled - Task dialog box appears (see Figure 14.1).

 TIP **Use the Menu to Start a New Task** To start a new task from the Task folder menu, select **Actions**, **New Task**.

2. On the Task tab, enter the subject of the task into the **Subject** box.

3. Enter a date on which the task should be complete, or click the down arrow to open the **Due Date** drop-down calendar, and then choose a due date.

4. Enter a start date, or click the down arrow to open the **Start Date** drop-down calendar, and then choose a start date.

5. From the Status drop-down list, choose the current status of the project: **Not Started, In Progress, Completed, Waiting on Someone Else,** or **Deferred**.

6. In the Priority drop-down list, choose **Normal, Low,** or **High** priority.

7. In the % Complete text box, type a percentage or use the spinner arrows to enter one.

Figure 14.1   Enter data such as the subject of the task, due dates, and the task's priority.

8. (Optional) To set an alarm to remind you to start the task or complete the task, select the **Reminder** check box and enter a date and a time in the associated text boxes.

9. Enter any comments, descriptions, or other information related to the task in the comments text box located beneath the Reminder fields.

10. Click the **Categories** button and choose a category if you want to assign the task to a particular category, or enter your own category in the text box.

 TIP   **Keeping a Task Private**   If you are using Outlook on a corporate network that uses Exchange Server, your folders are kept on the Exchange Server and, to a certain extent, their contents can be viewed by other users. Select the **Private** check box if you don't want others to see information about a task that you are creating.

11. Click the **Save and Close** button when you're finished.

 TIP   **Create Tasks in the Calendar Folder**   You can also create tasks on the Task Pad of the Calendar folder. Double-click the Task Pad to start a new task.

Creating a Recurring Task

You can also create recurring tasks. For example, you might always have to hand in a weekly report every Friday; so why not schedule a recurring task that always reminds you to get that Friday report completed?

1. Double-click the Task Pad to open a new task window.

2. Enter the subject and other details of the task into the appropriate boxes.

3. To make the task a recurring task, click the **Recurrence** button on the Task toolbar. The Task Recurrence dialog box opens.

4. You can set the recurrence of the task for Daily, Weekly, Monthly, or Yearly. After selecting an appropriate recurrence, such as Weekly, select how often the recurrence of the task occurs (see Figure 14.2).

Figure 14.2   Set the recurrence pattern for a recurring appointment.

5. When you have finished setting the recurrence options, click **OK** to return to the task window.

6. Click **Save and Close** to save the new task. Recurring tasks are labeled in the task folder by a small circular arrow icon (letting you know that the task recurs).

Assigning Tasks to Others

You can also assign tasks to others, such as co-workers or subordinates. Assigned tasks appear in your Task folder; however, the person you assign the task to has control over the task or the changing of the task parameters. To assign a task, follow these steps:

1. Double-click the Task pane to open a new task window.

2. Enter the subject and other details of the task into the appropriate boxes.

 3. Click the **Assign Task** button on the Task toolbar. A To line is added at the top of the task window (see Figure 14.3).

4. Click the **To** button on the task and the Select Task Recipient dialog box opens.

5. Select the appropriate address book, such as your Contacts list, and then assign the task to a person or persons. Click **OK** to close the Recipient dialog box after you have finished assigning the task.

185

Figure 14.3　Use the To button to assign the task to people in your Contacts list.

6. Click **Send** on the Task toolbar to send the task to the recipient or recipients. A message appears saying that, because you no longer own this task (because you have assigned it), no reminder will be assigned to the task (meaning you are not reminded if the task becomes past due). Click **OK** to close the message box.

Outlook sends the new task to the recipient or recipients. The task is actually sent as an e-mail message. When the recipient opens the e-mail message in their Outlook Inbox, two buttons appear at the top of the message, Accept and Decline (see Figure 14.4).

When the **Accept** button is selected, a message box appears (see Figure 14.4). This message box lets the recipient know that a response will be sent to the originator of the task and that the task will be moved to the Task Folder. To clear the message box, click **OK**. Now, when the recipient looks in the Outlook Task folder, they will find the task in the list.

If the task is declined (by clicking the Decline button), a message box appears saying that the task will be moved to the Deleted Items folder and that a message declining the task will be sent to the originator of the task (which in this case was you) and will appear in the originator's Inbox. Because a copy of the task is kept in your Task folder, you can open the task and assign it to another user.

Accept task   Decline task

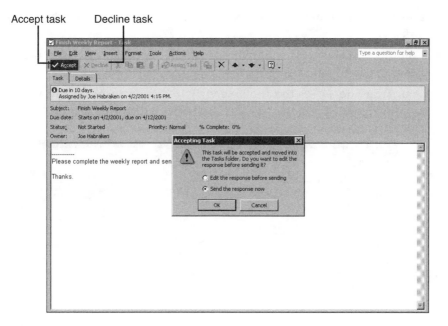

Figure 14.4   When a task recipient accepts the task it is moved to their Task list.

Viewing Tasks

As in any Outlook folder, you can change how you view tasks in the list using the Current View drop-down list in the Standard toolbar. By default, the Tasks folder displays tasks in a Simple List view. Following is a description of the views you can use to display the Tasks folder:

- **Simple List**—Lists the tasks, completed check box, subject, and due date.
- **Detailed List**—Displays the tasks, priority, subject, status, percent complete, and categories.
- **Active Tasks**—Displays the same information as the detailed list but doesn't show any completed tasks.
- **Next Seven Days**—Displays only those tasks you've scheduled for the next seven days, including completed tasks.
- **Overdue Tasks**—Shows a list of tasks that are past due.
- **By Category**—Displays tasks by category; click the button representing the category you want to view.
- **Assignment**—Lists tasks assigned to you by others.

- **By Person Responsible**—Lists tasks grouped by the person who assigned the tasks.

- **Completed Tasks**—Lists only those tasks completed, along with their due dates and completion dates.

- **Task Timeline**—Uses the Timeline view to display tasks by day, week, or month. Figure 14.5 shows the tasks assigned within one week.

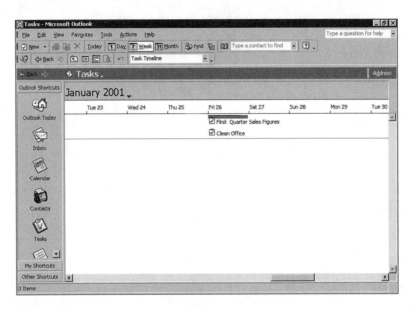

Figure 14.5 You can view your tasks in different views, such as the Task Timeline view.

CAUTION

Save What Settings?   Depending on the changes you make to a view, Outlook might display the Save View Settings dialog box asking whether you want to save the view settings before you switch to a different view. Generally, you'll want to discard the current view settings and leave everything the way you found it.

Managing Tasks

When working with a task list, you can add and delete tasks, mark tasks as completed, and arrange the tasks within the list. You also can perform any of these procedures in most of the task views described in the previous sections. For information about printing a task list, see Lesson 17 in the Outlook section of this book, "Printing in Outlook."

- To edit a task, double-click the task in the list. The Task dialog box appears.

- To mark a task as completed, click the check box in the second column from the left, or right-click the task and choose **Mark Complete** from the shortcut menu. Outlook places a line through the task.

- To delete a task, right-click the task and choose **Delete** from the shortcut menu.

- To assign an existing task to someone else, right-click the task and choose **Assign Task** from the shortcut menu. Fill in the name of the person to whom you want to assign the task (or use the To button to bring up the Select Task Recipient dialog box); after assigning the task, click the **Send** button to send the task to the recipient or recipients.

Recording Statistics About a Task

You can record statistics about a task, such as time spent completing the task, billable time, as well as other information, for your own records or for reference when sharing tasks with your co-workers. This feature is particularly helpful when you assign tasks to others; you can keep track of assigned tasks and find out when they're completed.

To enter statistics about a task, open any task in the task list and click the **Details** tab. Figure 14.6 shows a completed Details tab for a sample task.

Figure 14.6   Fill in the statistics related to the completion of the task for later reference.

The following list describes the text boxes in the Details tab and the types of information you can enter:

- **Date Completed**—Enter the date the task was completed, or click the arrow to display the calendar and choose the date.

- **Total Work**—Enter the amount of time you expect the task to take.

- **Actual Work**—Enter the amount of time it actually took to complete the job. You can then compare the estimated time that you placed in the Total Work box with the actual time that it took (entered in the Actual Work box).

- **Mileage**—Enter the number of miles you traveled to complete the task.

- **Billing Information**—Enter any specific billing information, such as hours billed, resources used, charges for equipment, and so on.

- **Companies**—Enter the names of any companies associated with the contacts or with the project in general. Use semicolons to separate multiple names.

- **Update List**—Automatically lists the people whose task lists are updated when you make a change to your task. This is available only in situations where you are working in a Microsoft Exchange Server environment.

- **Create Unassigned Copy**—Copies the task so that it can be reassigned; use the button to send a task to someone other than an original recipient. This button is available only on tasks that you have assigned to other people.

Tracking Tasks

Outlook also enables you to track tasks that you assigned to others. You can even receive status reports related to a task that you have assigned to another person or persons. To track tasks, follow these steps:

1. On the **Tools** menu, click **Options**; the Options dialog box appears. Click the **Preferences** tab.

2. On the Preferences tab, click the **Task Options** button. The Task Options dialog box opens (see Figure 14.7).

Figure 14.7 Make sure that you set task options so that you receive updated tasks and status reports for assigned tasks.

3. To automatically track the progress of new tasks you assign to others, make sure a check mark appears in the **Keep Updated Copies of Assigned Tasks on My Task List** check box.

4. To automatically receive notification when an assigned task is complete, select the **Send Status Reports When Assigned Tasks Are Completed** check box.

5. After you've made your selections, click **OK** to close the Task Options dialog box, and then click **OK** to close the Options dialog box.

 TIP **Color Your Task List** You can also set color options for overdue and completed tasks on the Task Options dialog box. Click the **Tools** menu, select **Options**, and from the Preferences tab, click the **Task Options** button.

Using the Journal

In this lesson, you learn how to create Journal entries manually and automatically and how to change views in the Journal.

Creating a Journal Entry

You can create a record of various actions so that you can track your work, communications, reports, and so on. In the Journal, you can manually record any activities, items, or tasks you want. For example, you might want to record the results of a telephone conversation.

You also can automatically record e-mail messages, meeting requests, meeting responses, task requests, and task responses. Additionally, you can automatically record activity related to documents created in the other Office applications: Access, Excel, PowerPoint, and Word.

The Journal is especially useful for recording information related to phone calls to and from people in your Contacts list. You can record information about the call and you can also time the conversation and enter its duration (which is very useful information when you need to record billable-hours information for a particular client).

Journal A folder within Outlook that you can use to record interactions, phone calls, message responses, and other activities important to your work.

Turning On the Journal

As already mentioned, you can automatically or manually record items in your Journal. Before you can take advantage of the Journal, however, you must turn it on.

The first time you open the Journal folder (using the icon in the Folder List or the Journal icon in the My Shortcuts list on the Outlook bar), a message appears, asking whether you want to turn the Journal feature on. Click **Yes**. The Journal Options dialog box appears as shown in Figure 15.1.

Figure 15.1 Click the check boxes in the Journal Options dialog box to have actions and events recorded automatically.

In this dialog box, you can specify what type of events you want to have automatically recorded in the Journal. Check boxes are provided to include e-mail messages, meeting requests, and other events that are received from people in your Contacts folder. To specify the items that you want automatically recorded, follow these steps:

1. In the **Automatically Record These Items** list, check those items you want Outlook to automatically record in your Journal. (The items recorded correspond with the people selected in the list of contacts in step 2.)

2. In the **For These Contacts** list, check any contacts you want automatically recorded in the Journal. Outlook records any items selected in step 1 that apply to the selected contacts.

3. In the **Also Record Files From** list, check the applications for which you want to record Journal entries. Outlook records the date and time you create or modify files in the selected programs.

4. When you have completed your selections, click the **OK** button. The Journal opens. It is now ready to automatically record the items that you chose in the Journal Options dialog box.

Suppose that you wanted Excel sessions to be automatically recorded in the Task list. You would make sure that Excel was selected in step 3. Then, whenever you work in Excel, that event is recorded. Figure 15.2 shows a Journal entry for an Excel event.

Figure 15.2 Journal entries for applications, such as Excel, are recorded automatically when you work in that application.

Recording an Entry Manually

You can also record items in the Journal manually using existing items such as e-mail messages. For example, you might add an e-mail message to the Journal that is not normally recorded (because you didn't select messages from that particular contact as something you want automatically recorded in the Journal).

To create a Journal entry manually, follow these steps:

1. In the Inbox folder (or any other folder in Outlook), select the item you want to record in the Journal and drag it onto the Journal folder icon in the Folder List (or drag it onto the Journal icon on the Outlook bar). The Journal Entry dialog box appears (see Figure 15.3).

2. The information in the Subject, Entry Type, Contact, and Company boxes and some other information is entered for you from the selected task, contact, or other selected item. However, you can change any of the statistics you want by entering new information into the following text boxes:

    • **Subject**—Displays the title or name of the Journal item.

    • **Entry Type**—Describes the item based on its point of origin, such as a Word document, a meeting or appointment, and so on.

Figure 15.3 Drag an item onto the Journal icon, and the Journal Entry dialog box opens.

- **Company**—Lists the company or companies associated with the contacts.
- **Start Time**—Displays the date and time of the meeting, appointment, or other item.
- **Start Timer**—Like a stopwatch, the timer records the time that passes until you click the Pause Timer button.
- **Pause Timer**—Stops the timer.
- **Duration**—Enter the amount of time for completing the item.
- **Shortcut box**—Displays a shortcut to the item you originally dragged onto the Journal icon to create a new entry (such as a Calendar appointment, a contact, or a message). You can actually open the item by double-clicking the shortcut icon.
- **Contacts**—Lists the name(s) of any attendees, contacts, or other people involved with the selected item.
- **Categories**—Enter or select a category that you want to assign to the Journal entry.

3. Click **Save and Close** to complete the Journal entry.

If you want to create a new Journal entry, but you don't have a contact, a task, an e-mail, or other item that you want to use to create the entry, you can create a Journal entry from scratch (meaning it is not associated with any existing Outlook item such as an e-mail message). For example, you might want to create a Journal entry that holds information related to a phone call that you have made. Follow these steps:

1. Change to the Journal folder.

2. Choose **Actions**, and then select **New Journal Entry** or double-click any empty portion of the Journal pane. The Journal Entry dialog box appears.

3. Enter the subject for your new journal entry.

4. Select the type of entry you want to make; in this case, the default is already set to Phone Call. Leave the Journal Entry window open on your desktop.

 5. Make your phone call; you can actually have Outlook dial the phone call for you using the **AutoDialer** icon, which can be accessed on the toolbar in the Contacts folder (click the **AutoDialer** icon, and then select **New Call**; use the **Contacts** drop-down list in the New Call dialog box to specify the contact that you want to call, and then click **Start Call**).

6. When your call is answered, click the **Start Timer** button in the Journal Entry window. Type any notes that you want to record during the phone conversation in the entry's text box.

7. When you finish the call, click the **Pause Timer** button. Notice that the duration of the call is entered in the Duration box. To save the Journal entry, click the **Save and Close** button.

Changing Journal Settings

You might find that when you started the Journal for the first time, you didn't configure that many events to be automatically recorded by the Journal. No problem; you can return to the Journal settings and change the options related to the automatic recording items in the Journal.

In the Journal folder, choose **Tools**, **Options**. The Options dialog box appears. Click the **Preferences** tab if necessary, and then click the **Journal Options** button. The Journal Options dialog box appears.

You can also choose to have your Journal entries AutoArchived. Click the **AutoArchive Journal Entries** button, and then choose a folder on your computer where you want to have the Journal Archive file stored (selecting the default folder is your best bet). Then, click **OK** to complete the process (for more information about the AutoArchive feature, see Outlook Lesson 19).

When you have finished making changes to the Journal options, click **OK** to close the Journal Options dialog box. Then, click **OK** to close the Options dialog box.

Viewing Journal Entries

By default, the Journal folder displays information in the Timeline view and By Type, as shown in Figure 15.4. However, you can display the entries in various views, as described in the following list. To select a particular view, click the **Current View** drop-down button on the Advanced toolbar.

Figure 15.4   The default Journal view is the Timeline view.

> **TIP**   **Save Settings?**   As in other views, Outlook might display the Save View Settings dialog box to ask whether you want to save the view settings before you switch to a different view. You're probably getting used to this dialog box by now.

- **By Type**—In Timeline view, this option groups Journal entries by type, such as e-mail messages, meetings, Word documents, and so on. Double-click a type to display its contents, and then position the mouse pointer over an entry to view its contents or name. When you switch to the Journal in the Type view, a Journal Options dialog box appears. This dialog box allows you to specify which e-mail messages will be recorded in the Journal, based on the contact they are received from. This dialog box also allows you to select which application use will also be recorded in the Journal, such as Excel, Word, or Access.

- **By Contact**—In Timeline view, this displays the name of each contact that you selected in the Options dialog box. Double-click any contact's name to view recorded entries.

197

- **By Category**—If you've assigned categories to your Journal entries and other items, you can display your Journal entries by category in the Timeline view.

- **Entry List**—Displays entries in a table with columns labeled Entry Type, Subject, Start, Duration, Contact, and Categories.

- **Last Seven Days**—Displays entries in an entry list but includes only those entries dated within the last seven days.

- **Phone Calls**—Lists all entries that are phone calls.

Using Outlook Notes 16

In this lesson, you learn how to create, sort, and view notes.

Creating Notes

If you've ever used a Post-it note to remind yourself of tasks, ideas, or other brief annotations, Outlook's Notes are for you. Notes are similar to paper sticky notes. You can use Notes to write down reminders, names, phone numbers, directions, or anything else you need to remember. In Outlook, all notes are kept in the Notes folder. You'll have to remember to look at the folder so you can view your notes.

 TIP   **The Long and Short of It**   You can enter pages and pages of text if you want. As you type, the page scrolls for you; use the arrow keys and the Page Up and Page Down keys to move through the note's text. Keep in mind, however, that the purpose of the note is a quick reminder, or information that you will eventually transfer to one of the other Outlook items, such as an appointment or task.

To create a note, click the **Notes** folder on the Outlook bar and then follow these steps:

1. In the Notes folder, choose **Actions**, and then select **New Note** or double-click an empty spot in the Notes pane. A new note appears, ready for you to type your text.

2. Enter the text for your note (see Figure 16.1).

3. When you finish, click the **Close** (x) button to close the note. You can reopen a note and edit the text as you need to.

If you press Enter after entering text in the note, you create a line break and you create a title, of sorts, at the same time. Only the text before the hard return displays when the note is closed. If you do not add a hard return but enter the note text so that it automatically wraps from line to line, the entire note text appears below the note in Icons view.

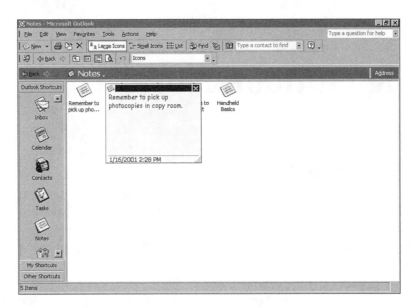

Figure 16.1 A note automatically includes the date and time it was created.

Setting Note Options

You can change the default color and size of your notes. You also can change the default font used for your notes. To set note options, follow these steps:

1. In the Notes folder (or in any of the Outlook folders), choose **Tools**, **Options**. The Options dialog box appears. On the Preferences tab, click **Notes Options**; the Notes Options dialog box appears (see Figure 16.2).

Figure 16.2 You can customize your notes.

2. The Notes Options dialog box enables you to change the color, size, and font for your notes. Using the Color drop-down box, you can change the color to yellow, blue, green, pink, or white. The default is yellow.

3. Open the **Size** drop-down list and choose **Small**, **Medium**, or **Large** for the size of the notes. The default is Medium.

4. To change the font, click the **Font** button. The Font dialog box appears. Change the font, font style, size, color, and other options, and then click **OK**.

Managing Individual Notes

To open an existing note, double-click it in the Notes folder. You can edit the text in an open note the same as you would edit any text. To move a note, drag its title bar. You can delete, forward, or print notes; you can change the color of individual notes; and you can specify categories for your notes. You can also drag the notes to the Windows desktop and arrange them there.

Click an open note's Control Menu button (click the very upper left of the note) to display a menu with the following commands:

- **New Note**—Creates a new note but leaves the first note open.
- **Save As**—Enables you to save the note and its contents.
- **Delete**—Deletes a note and its contents. (You also can delete a note by selecting it in the Notes list and pressing the **Delete** key.)
- **Forward**—Enables you to send the note as an attachment in an e-mail message.
- **Cut, Copy, Paste**—Enables you to select text from the note and cut or copy it to the Clipboard. The Paste command enables you to paste items on the Clipboard at the insertion point in the note.
- **Color**—Choose another color for the individual note.
- **Categories**—Enter or choose a category.
- **Print**—Print the contents of the note.
- **Close**—Closes the note. (You can also click the **Close** (**x**) button in the note's title bar.)

Viewing Notes

The Notes folder provides various views for organizing and viewing your notes. The default view is Icons, but you can change the view using the Current View drop-down list on the Advanced toolbar. Figure 16.3 shows the Notes folder in the default view.

You can choose to display your Notes folder in any of the following views:

- **Icons**—Displays the notes as note icons with the message (or a portion of the message) displayed below the icon.

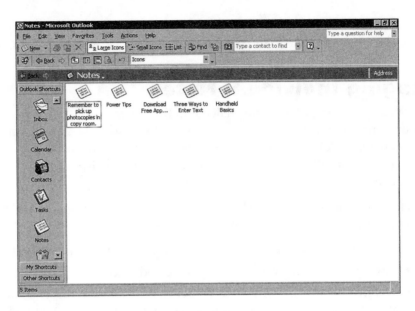

Figure 16.3 This view displays the notes in Icons view.

- **Notes List**—Displays the notes in a list, showing the title and note contents in the Subject column, the creation date and time, and the categories.

- **Last Seven Days**—Displays all notes written in the last seven days, by subject, creation date, and categories.

- **By Category**—Displays the categories; double-click a category to show its contents.

- **By Color**—Displays notes by their color. Double-click a color to display the notes.

Printing in Outlook

In this lesson, you learn how to print items in Outlook, change the page setup, preview an item before printing it, and change printer properties.

Choosing Page Setup

In Outlook, before you print, you choose the print style you want to use. Each folder—the Inbox, Calendar, Contacts, and so on—offers different print styles, and each style displays the data on the page in a different way.

 Page In Outlook, this is the area of the paper that will actually be printed on. You might, for example, print two or four pages on a single sheet of paper.

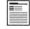 **Print Style** The combination of paper and page settings that control printed output.

You can choose from Outlook's built-in print styles, modify the default print styles, or create your own print styles. These lists show the default print styles available for each folder. To access the print styles for a particular item, select **File**, **Print**. The Inbox, Contacts, and Tasks use the Table style and the Memo style; the Journal and Notes use only the Memo style.

- **Table Style**—Displays data in columns and rows on an 8 1/2×11 sheet, portrait orientation, 1/2-inch margins.

- **Memo Style**—Displays data with a header of information about the message and then straight text on an 8 1/2×11 sheet, portrait orientation, 1/2-inch margins.

The Calendar folder provides the Memo style as well as the following styles:

- **Daily Style**—Displays one day's appointments on one page on an 8 1/2×11 sheet, portrait orientation, 1/2-inch margins.

- **Weekly Style**—Displays one week's appointments per page on an 8 1/2×11 sheet, portrait orientation, 1/2-inch margins.

- **Monthly Style**—Displays one month's appointments per page on an 8 1/2×11 sheet, landscape orientation, 1/2-inch margins.

• **Tri-fold Style**—Displays the daily calendar, task list, and weekly calendar on an 8 1/2×11 sheet, landscape orientation, 1/2-inch margins.

 • **Calendar Details Style**—Shows the currently displayed Calendar items and the body text of each item (such as an appointment) in a list format.

The Contacts folder provides the Memo style as well as the following styles:

 • **Card Style**—Two columns and headings on an 8 1/2×11 sheet, portrait orientation, 1/2-inch margins.

 • **Small Booklet Style**—One-column pages that print the contacts in a format similar to mailing labels by placing multiple contacts on a page. This style can be printed in Portrait or Landscape mode.

 • **Medium Booklet Style**—One column that equals 1/4 of a sheet of paper. Four pages are on one 8 1/2×11 sheet of paper, portrait orientation, with 1/2-inch margins.

 • **Phone Directory Style**—One column, 8 1/2×11 sheet of paper, portrait orientation with 1/2-inch margins.

 Will Page Setup Change My View?   No matter how you set up your pages, it will not affect your view of tasks, calendars, or other Outlook items onscreen. Page setup applies only to a print job.

CAUTION

You can view, modify, and create new page setups in Outlook. To view or edit a page setup, follow these steps:

1. Change to the folder for which you're setting the page.

2. Choose **File** and then point at **Page Setup**. A secondary menu appears that lists the available print types.

3. Select the print type you want to view or edit, and the Page Setup dialog box appears (see Figure 17.1).

4. Click the **Format** tab to view and/or edit the page type, to choose options (in some cases), and to change fonts.

5. Click the **Paper** tab to view and/or edit paper size, page size, margins, and orientation.

6. Click the **Header/Footer** tab to view and/or edit headers for your pages.

Figure 17.1 Customize the print style to suit yourself.

Previewing Before Printing

To make sure an item looks the way you want it to look, you can choose to preview it before printing it. If you do not like the way an item looks in preview, you can change the page setup.

Open the folder that contains the item that you want to print preview. You can then open the item in the Print Preview view in any of the following ways:

- Click the **Print Preview** button in the Page Setup dialog box.
- Choose **File** and then select **Print Preview**.
- Click the **Print Preview** button on the Advanced toolbar.
- Click the **Preview** button in the Print dialog box.

Figure 17.2 shows a calendar and task list in Print Preview. You can change the page setup by clicking the **Page Setup** button; the Page Setup dialog box appears. Click the **Print** button to send the job to the printer. Click the **Close** button to exit Print Preview and return to the Outlook folder.

TIP **Enlarge the View** When the mouse pointer looks like a magnifying glass with a plus sign in it, you can click to enlarge the page. When the mouse pointer looks like a magnifying glass with a minus sign in it, you can click to reduce the view again.

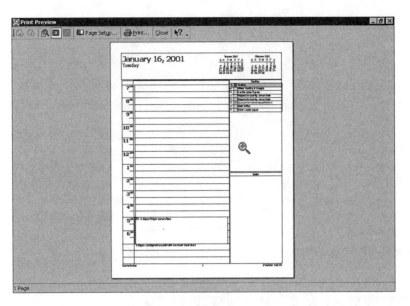

Figure 17.2 Preview the item before printing it.

Printing Items

After you choose the print style and preview an item to make sure it's what you want, you can print the item. You can indicate the number of copies you want to print, select a printer, change the print style or page setup, and set a print range.

When you're ready to print an item, follow these steps:

1. Choose **File**, and then select **Print** or click the **Print** button on the Standard toolbar. The Print dialog box appears, as shown in Figure 17.3.

2. Your default printer appears in the Printer area of the dialog box. If you have a different printer connected to your system that you would like to use, choose a different printer from the **Name** drop-down list.

3. In the Print Style area, choose a print style from the list. You also can edit the page setup (with the **Page Setup** button) or edit or create a new style (with the **Define Styles** button).

4. In the Copies area of the dialog box, choose **All**, **Even**, or **Odd** in **Number of Pages**, and enter the number of copies you want to print. This function is useful if you are going to print on both sides of the paper (this is called manual duplexing). You print the even pages, and then flip the sheets over in your printer and print the odd pages. Click the **Collate Copies** check box if you want Outlook to automatically assemble multiple copies.

Figure 17.3   Set the printing options before printing the item.

5. Set the print range with the options in that area. (The Print Range options vary depending on the type of item you're printing.)

6. Click **OK** to print the item.

Printing Labels and Envelopes

A handy Outlook feature is the capability to print mailing labels and envelopes from your Contacts list. To take advantage of this feature, you also need to have Microsoft Word installed on your computer. Creating form letters, mailing labels or envelopes is called a *mail merge*. Basically, in Word, you create some type of main document (such as mailing labels, envelopes, and so on) that holds field codes that relate to the information you keep on each contact, such as name or address.

To actually start the merge process, open your Contacts folder and select **Tools**, **Mail Merge**. The Mail Merge Contacts dialog box opens (see Figure 17.4) and allows you to specify both the contacts for the merge and the Word document into which the contact information is merged. Using the option buttons at the top of the dialog box, you can specify that all the contacts or selected contacts are included in the mail merge. If you want to have only certain fields included in the mail merge, you can create a custom view of your Contacts folder (discussed in Outlook Lesson 3, "Using Outlook's Tools") before starting the Mail Merge.

After you specify the various options in the Mail Merge Contacts dialog box (see tip that follows) and click **OK**, you are taken to Word, where the mail merge is completed. Lesson 19 in the Word section of this book, "Creating Personalized Mass Mailings," covers mail merges using Word in greater detail.

Figure 17.4 Contact data can be merged with a document in Word for mass mailings.

TIP   **Setting Up a Mail Merge from Outlook**   The Mail Merge Contacts dialog box (refer to Figure 17.4) provides several options for customizing your mail merge using your Outlook Contacts. If you select the **Permanent File** check box, you can specify a filename and have your Contacts list saved as a data document for use in future Word mail merges (you won't have to start the merge from Outlook in the future if you select this option). You can also specify the type of document that Word creates during the mail merge using the Document type drop-down list. You can create form letters, mailing envelopes, and mailing labels.

Setting Printer Properties

Whether you're printing to a printer connected directly to your computer or to a printer on the network, you can set printer properties. The properties you set apply to all print jobs you send to the printer until you change the properties again.

TERM   **Printer Properties**   Configurations specific to a printer connected to your computer or to the network. Printer properties include paper orientation, paper source, graphics settings, fonts, and print quality.

CAUTION   **Access Denied?**   If you cannot change the printer properties to a network printer, it's probably because the network administrator has set the printer's configuration and you're not allowed access to the settings. If you need to change printer properties and cannot access the printer's Properties dialog box, talk to your network administrator.

To set printer properties, open the Print dialog box (by choosing **File, Print**). In the Printer area, select a printer from the Name drop-down list, and then click the **Properties** button. The printers' Properties dialog boxes differ depending on the make and model.

Most likely, you'll be able to set paper size, page orientation, and paper source using options on a Paper tab in the dialog box. In addition, you might see a Graphics tab, in which you can set the resolution, intensity, and graphics mode of your printer. A Fonts tab enables you to set options on TrueType fonts, font cartridges, and so on. You might also find a Device Options tab, in which you can set print quality and other options. For more information about your printer, read the documentation that came with it.

Saving and Finding Outlook Items

In this lesson, you learn how to use the Outlook Save As feature and find items in Outlook.

Using the Outlook Save As Feature

Generally, when you finish adding a new task, appointment, meeting, contact, or other item, Outlook automatically saves that item for you, or you're prompted to save the item yourself. You can also save most items in Outlook in other file formats, such as text or some other format using the Save As command. Saving an item in a different format allows you to open that information in another application.

In fact, any application that supports the file format in which you save your Outlook item could be used to open that new file. For example, you might save an item—a journal entry or an appointment page—as a text file so that you can open the file in Word and include the journal information in a report (virtually every application that manipulates some form of a document is capable of opening text files).

 TIP **Using Save As** When you save an item using the File, Save As command, you can designate a drive, folder, and new filename for that item, as well as a file type.

 TERM **File Type** A file type is the same thing as a file format. When you save a file, you specify a file type that identifies the file as one that can be opened in specific applications. For example, the file extension .doc identifies a file type that you can open in Word, and the extension .txt represents a text-only format that you can open in nearly any word processor or other application.

The following are some of the available file formats:

- **Text Only**—Saves an item in ASCII format (ASCII is a basic coding system that is readable by most applications), which you can use in other applications, such as Word, Notepad, and so on. Save Outlook items in text only when you want to send them to someone who does not have Outlook and text-only format will suffice. Any special formatting in the item is lost when you save in this format. Files saved in other applications in text-only format can also be opened in Outlook.

- **Rich Text Format**—This file format was originally created for the Microsoft Exchange environment so that mail messages could include text formatting. You can use this format in Word, Outlook, or Lotus Notes. This format enables you to save items for use in other applications and maintains the text formatting, such as bold, underline, and other font attributes.

- **HTML**—Hypertext Markup Language is a file format designed for use as World Wide Web pages. It maintains all the font attributes, such as bold or italic, that you have placed in an Outlook item such as a message. All the Office applications can open HTML documents; they also can save files to this format.

- **Outlook Template**—This format enables you to take an Outlook item in the current view (such as a custom view that you have created) and save the item as a template. The template can be used to create custom forms for use in Outlook (this is an advanced feature and is typically used by a network administrator to create custom forms for use on a Microsoft Exchange network).

- **Message Format**—The Message format is embraced by Microsoft e-mail clients such as Outlook and Outlook Express. It can be used to save an e-mail message as a separate file in case you want to have a readily available backup of that particular e-mail message on your computer.

Figure 18.1 shows an e-mail message from Outlook saved as an HTML file and opened in Word. After opening a file such as the e-mail message shown, you can format it, cut or copy items to it, insert objects, print, edit, and otherwise manipulate the file. Because you used Save As to save the message as a new file, the original message is still available in your Outlook Inbox or Sent Items folder (depending on whether the message was received by you or sent by you).

You will find that being able to use the different Office applications together to get projects done can really make your work life easier. Think of Office as a toolkit with different tools. In the "Office XP Introduction and Shared Features" section of this book, Lesson 7, "Sharing Information Among Office Applications," looks at different ways to share information between the members of the Office suite.

 TIP **Getting Data from Other Applications**   Although you can use Save As to quickly save an Outlook Item in a format that can be used in another application, the best way to get external data into Outlook is to use the Import/Export Wizard. This wizard is discussed in Lesson 10, "Using the Outlook Address Books."

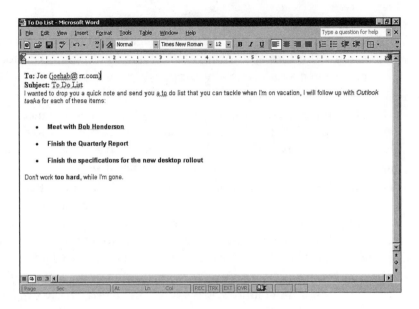

Figure 18.1 Exchanging data between applications makes your work easier.

To save an item using Save As, follow these steps:

1. In the folder containing the item you want to save, choose **File**, **Save As**. The Save As dialog box appears (see Figure 18.2).

Figure 18.2 Save Outlook files in different file formats for easy use in other applications.

CAUTION

Why Is Save As Dimmed? When the Save As command is dimmed, you must first select an item in the current folder—a message, an appointment, a meeting, a task, or a note—before you can save it using Save As.

2. From the **Save In** drop-down list, choose the drive to which you want to save the file. From the folders on that drive, select the one you want to save to. The Folder icons on the left of the dialog box give you quick access to your History, My Documents, Desktop, and Favorites folders.

3. In the **Save As Type** drop-down list, choose a file type. You can save the file in any of the file types discussed earlier in this section (Text, Rich Text, HTML, Outlook Template, or Message Format).

4. After you choose the type, enter a name for the item in the **File Name** text box or accept the default.

5. Click the **Save** button. The file is saved.

Finding Items

Outlook provides a Find feature that you can use to locate items in your various Outlook folders. You can search for messages, files, journal entries, notes, tasks, contacts, appointments, and so on, depending on which folder you are currently in. When you use the Find feature, it opens in its own pane at the top of the current folder window. You type in a key word or phrase, and the Find feature searches all the items in the current folder for your search word or words. When it finds items that match the search phrase, it lists them in the current folder window. Items not matching the search criteria are hidden.

To find an item in an Outlook folder, follow these steps:

 1. Select the folder in which you want to conduct a search for an item. Choose **Tools**, and then select **Find** or click the **Find** button on the Standard toolbar. The Find box appears at the top of the current folder, as shown in Figure 18.3.

2. Type your search criteria in the **Look For** box. To include any subfolders that you have created under the current folder (such as additional e-mail folders under the Inbox), click the **Search In** drop-down list to include these folders.

3. When you are ready to run the search, click **Find Now**.

4. The items that match your search word or phrase appear in the Folder List (if no matches were found, the Folder List appears empty).

5. You can perform a new search by clicking the **Clear** button and repeating steps 2–4. When you have completed your search, you can close the Find pane by clicking its **Close (x)** button.

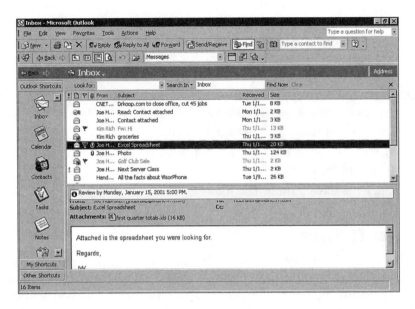

Figure 18.3   Use the Find feature to search for items in the current folder.

Using the Advanced Find Feature

If the Find feature doesn't provide you with enough search muscle, you can use Advanced Find to perform more detailed searches. Using the Advanced Find feature, you can set multiple search criteria such as a category, from, sent to, and subject (when searching for mail messages, additional search criteria exist for each of the other items found in Outlook).

To use the Advanced Find feature, follow these steps:

1. Select **Tools**, and then select **Advanced Find**. The Advanced Find dialog box appears (see Figure 18.4).

2. In the Advanced Find dialog box, set the criteria for your search using the criteria boxes found on the various tabs that appear. For example, the Message Advanced Find dialog box includes tabs for Messages, More Choices, and Advanced. Each tab provides more advanced methods for conducting the search.

3. Set your search conditions on the various tabs. The More Choices tab is the same for each Outlook item and lets you search for items that have not been read or items that have an attachment.

Figure 18.4   The Advanced Find dialog box provides you with more search parameters than the Find feature does.

4. When you've finished setting your criteria, click the **Find Now** button. A box opens at the bottom of the Advanced Find dialog box that lists the items that have met the search criteria. To open an item, double-click it.

Archiving Items

In this lesson, you learn how to use AutoArchive and how to archive files, retrieve archived files, and delete archived files manually.

Using AutoArchive

You can configure Outlook so that mail messages and other items are periodically and automatically archived to file. This feature, AutoArchive, cleans your Inbox for you but saves the specified messages in an archive file. AutoArchiving is similar to the backup procedure many people use to compress and save files on their computers in case they crash.

CAUTION

Be Wary of AutoArchive   The AutoArchive feature is set up by default to run every 14 days. This means that an AutoArchive dialog box will appear, asking you whether you want to archive Outlook items. Until you have had a chance to configure AutoArchive and use the feature as outlined in this lesson, you might want to click **Cancel** and not run the AutoArchive feature at that time.

The point of archiving is to save Outlook items, such as messages, for later reference, but also to remove some of the older items that are floating around your Outlook folders. Items autoarchived by Outlook are compressed and saved in a file. This file can then be transferred to a storage device such as a floppy disk, a rewritable CD, or other removable storage medium (such as an Iomega Zip drive or Imation Superdisk) for safekeeping.

TERM

Archive   To save items to a file that you can open at any time and print, view, or otherwise use. You might, for example, want to archive some of your mail messages to keep for your records instead of leaving those messages in your Inbox. Archived items are removed from the folder and copied to an archive file.

To use AutoArchive, follow these steps:

1. Choose **Tools**, **Options**. The Options dialog box appears.
2. Click the **Other** tab.
3. Click the **AutoArchive** button to display the AutoArchive options (see Figure 19.1).

Figure 19.1 Specify your options for automatically archiving items into an archive file.

4. Choose from the following check box options:

- **Run AutoArchive Every X Days**—Enter a number for how often (in days) you want Outlook to automatically archive items. If you enter **14**, for example, every fourteenth day it automatically archives the contents of your folders into an archive file.

- **Prompt Before AutoArchive Runs**—If you check this, Outlook displays a dialog box each time it is about to perform the AutoArchive; you can click **OK** to continue or **Cancel** to stop the operation.

- **Delete Expired Items (E-Mail Folders Only)**—Check this box to have Outlook delete messages from the Inbox after archiving them.

- **Show Archive Folder in Folder List**—This option makes the archive folder available from the Folder List, making it easier to access archived files. Each folder archived, such as the Inbox or Contacts folder, will appear as subfolders under the Archive folder. This allows you to view the contents in each of the archived folders as you would any other Outlook folder.

5. In the Default Folder Settings for Archiving boxes, use the click arrows to select the number of months, weeks, or days for the age of an item that should be archived. Use the drop-down box to select the unit, such as **Months**, **Weeks**, or **Days**.

6. In the Move Old Items To box, enter a path to where you want to save the file, and name it (if you don't want to use the default).

7. If you want to permanently delete old items rather than archive them, select the **Permanently Delete Old Items** option button.

8. To apply these settings to all folders, click the **Apply These Settings to All Folders Now** button.

9. Click **OK** to close the AutoArchive dialog box. Click **OK** to close the Options dialog box.

If you do not want to apply the AutoArchive options that you set in the AutoArchive dialog box to every Outlook folder, you can set AutoArchive options individually for each folder, such as Tasks, Calendar, and so on. To set an individual folder's AutoArchive options, follow these steps:

1. Right-click the folder in the Outlook bar or the Folder List to display a shortcut menu.

2. Choose **Properties**. The item's Properties dialog box appears.

3. Choose the **AutoArchive** tab. Figure 19.2 shows the Inbox's AutoArchive tab.

Figure 19.2   Set AutoArchive options for individual folders.

4. To set custom archiving options for this folder, select the **Archive This Folder Using These Settings** option button. You can set the age for items to be archived in Months, Weeks, or Days. You can also specify the path to be used for the archiving, or you can choose to have old items deleted rather than archived.

5. If you do not want to archive the items in the current folder, select the **Do Not Archive Items in This Folder** option button.

6. When you have finished setting the archiving options for the folder, click **OK** to close the dialog box.

Archiving Manually

If you are still feeling a little squeamish about using AutoArchive, you can choose to archive folder items manually. This feature allows you to archive only one folder at a time (and any subfolders it might hold), but the process does provide you with complete control over how and when the archives are created. The manual archive can be created using the current AutoArchive settings for a folder (such as the age of items that should be archived), or you can select new age parameters while doing the manual archive.

To manually create an archive, follow these steps:

1. Choose **File** and then select **Archive**. The Archive dialog box appears (see Figure 19.3).

Figure 19.3 Enter settings for manual archiving.

2. Choose one of the following options:

- **Archive All Folders According to Their AutoArchive Settings**—Use this option to manually archive all the Outlook folders using their individual AutoArchive settings. Using this option is no different from running an AutoArchive, except that you are prompting Outlook to archive the folders immediately.

- **Archive This Folder and All Subfolders**—Select this option to archive the selected folder. Using this option requires that you provide an age date for items to be archived, and you can also specify the path for the archive to be created.

3. Enter a date into the Archive Items Older Than text box, or select a date from the drop-down calendar (click the drop-down arrow on the right of the date box).

4. In the Archive File text box, enter a path and filename with which to save the file.

5. If you want to archive items in a folder that has been marked as Do Not AutoArchive in its Properties dialog box, select the **Include Items with "Do Not AutoArchive" Checked** check box.

6. Click **OK** to archive the selected folder.

Retrieving Archived Files

After you create an archive either by using the AutoArchive feature or by manually archiving a folder or folders, an Archive Folders icon is added to the Outlook Folder List as shown in Figure 19.4. To open the Folder List, click the Folder List arrow next to the name of the currently open folder; use the pushpin on the right of the Folder list to place the Folder list in the Outlook window. You can retrieve archived items from the subfolders in this Archive folder and copy or move them back to any of your Outlook folders.

To retrieve an archived file, follow these steps:

1. Open the Outlook Folder List. An Archive Folders icon will have been added to the list immediately after an archive file has been created (see Figure 19.4).

2. Click the **plus symbol** (+) to the left of the Archive Folders icon to expand the folder. Folders that you have automatically or manually archived are present as subfolders. For example, if you archived your Inbox, an Inbox folder is available under the Archive Folders.

3. To view the archived items in a particular folder, select that folder (such as the Inbox or Calendar). The archived items, such as messages, appear in the Contents pane.

4. To move an item or items, select the items in the Contents pane and then drag them to an Outlook folder. For example, you could drag messages from the Archive Inbox folder to your Inbox.

Any or all items can be moved or copied from an archive folder to your Outlook folders such as the Calendar or the Inbox. That you can quickly view the contents of an archived folder makes it easier for you to see how the archive options that you set for AutoArchive or a manual archive have actually archived items in a particular folder.

Archive Folders icon

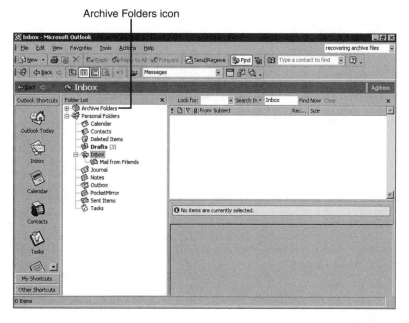

Figure 19.4 Archived items can be copied or moved from Archive Folders to other Outlook folders.

Deleting Archived Files

You can delete the contents of a folder or the folder itself from the Archive Folders container. To delete an item in a folder, select the folder then select the item or items in the Contents pane. Select **Edit**, **Delete** to delete the archived item or items.

You can also delete folders found in the Archive Folders container. Select the folder in the Folder List and then select **Edit**, **Delete**. You are asked to confirm the deletion of archive folders; click **Yes** to delete the folder.

You can also delete entire Outlook archive files from your computer. Do this only if you think you no longer need the archive files or if you want to start fresh with a new archive file. The easiest way to delete a particular archive file is to use the Windows Explorer.

To delete an archived file, follow these steps:

1. Open Windows Explorer and locate the files. Archived files are saved with a .pst or .lst extension in the My Documents folder (by default) or any other folder you designate.

2. Open the folder containing the files and select the archive file(s) you want to delete.

3. Press the **Delete** key, or drag the file(s) to the Recycle Bin.

4. Empty the Recycle Bin by right-clicking it and choosing **Empty Recycle Bin**.

5. Close the Explorer by clicking the **Close** (**x**) button.

Customizing Outlook

In this lesson, you learn how to set e-mail, calendar, and other options in Outlook.

Setting Outlook Options

You can set all of Outlook's options by using the Options dialog box (see Figure 20.1). To open the Options dialog box, select **Tools** and then choose **Options**. The number of tabs on this dialog box depends on whether you are using Outlook:

- On a company network that uses Microsoft Exchange Server for communications services such as e-mail

- At home or on a small network that uses an Internet service provider (ISP) for Internet e-mail

Figure 20.1   The Options dialog box gives you control over the various features of Outlook.

Figure 20.1 shows the Options dialog box provided for an Outlook user who uses a service provider for Internet e-mail. The only additional tab provided to users of Outlook on a Microsoft Exchange Server network is a Delegates tab. The Delegates tab allows users to "delegate" access of their Outlook folders to other users on the

Exchange Server network. This is because all the personal folders of Outlook users connected to an Exchange Server are actually kept on the server (this makes it very easy to share information between users). You should rely on your network's system administrator to manage the settings for this tab.

Each tab on the Options dialog box controls a logical grouping of settings that you control with option buttons, text boxes, or check boxes. Each tab also contains buttons that are used to access additional groupings of more specific settings.

Setting E-Mail Options

E-Mail, Calendar, Tasks, Journal, and Notes options are set on the Preferences tab of the Options dialog box. To open a more specific dialog box related to the features of each of the Outlook item types, click the appropriate button on the Preferences tab (see Figure 20.2).

Figure 20.2 Customize E-Mail, Calendar, Tasks, Journal, and Notes options on the Preferences tab.

To set e-mail options, click the **E-Mail Options** button. The E-Mail Options dialog box appears. This dialog box allows you to set items using check boxes and drop-down menus; buttons also exist for Advanced E-Mail Options and Tracking Options.

In the Message Handling box of the E-Mail Options dialog box, check the boxes of the options you want to activate, such as **Close Original Message on Reply**, **Forward**, and **Save Copies of Messages in Sent Items Folder**.

Two drop-down boxes in the On Replies and Forwards section provide you with options for replying to and forwarding messages. You can choose whether you want to include the original message text with replies and forwards or attach the original message as an attached file.

You can also set Advanced E-Mail options and Tracking options in this dialog box. When you click the **Advanced E-Mail Options** button, the Advanced E-Mail Options dialog box appears (see Figure 20.3). This dialog box allows you to control how unsent messages are handled, what happens when new mail arrives, and the importance level of new messages that you send. When you've finished setting options in this dialog box, click **OK**.

Figure 20.3   Options related to the saving of unsent messages and received messages are set in the Advanced E-Mail Options dialog box.

The **Tracking Options** button in the E-Mail Options dialog box opens the Tracking Options dialog box. In this box, you can set options that notify you when e-mail you send is received and when that e-mail is read. After setting options in this dialog box, click **OK**. Click **OK** again to close the E-Mail Options dialog box.

Setting Calendar Options

Options related to the Outlook Calendar are also accessed from the Preferences tab of the Options dialog box. For example, if you don't work a typical Monday through Friday workweek, you can change your default Calendar settings in the Calendar Options dialog box to reflect this. Suppose your workweek runs from Tuesday through Saturday and your workday is from 4 a.m. to 12 noon. You can make changes to the Calendar so that it reflects your actual workweek. You can also set your time zone and add holidays to your calendar.

To make changes to the Calendar Options, open the Calendar Options dialog box:

1. Click the **Calendar Options** button on the Preferences tab of the Options dialog box (see Figure 20.4). In the Calendar Work Week area, set your starting and ending time (the default is 8 a.m. to 5 p.m.).

Figure 20.4   Calendar options are set in the Calendar Options dialog box.

2. To set the time zone for your area, click the **Time Zone** button, and then choose the zone that describes your location.

3. To add holidays to your calendar, click the **Add Holidays** button. Then, check the box representing your country (U.S. is the default) and click **OK**. Outlook imports the holidays from your selected region to the calendar.

4. When you finish setting the options in this dialog box, return to the Preferences tab by clicking **OK**.

The Preferences tab also allows you to set options for your other Outlook items, such as Tasks, the Journal, and Notes. For information on setting preferences for Tasks, the Journal, or Notes, see Lessons 14, 15, or 16, respectively, in the "Outlook" section of this book.

Setting Mail Setup Options

The Mail Setup tab of the options dialog box allows you to access existing e-mail accounts or create new accounts (see Figure 20.5). This tab also controls other options, such as which e-mail accounts are accessed when you use the Send and Receive command on the Outlook toolbar. An additional set of options related to your Outlook data files, such as your archive files and files that hold your personal folders, can also be accessed on this tab.

Outlook Data File Placement Is Crucial Outlook places your personal folders and archive files based on whether you are working on an Exchange Server network or a PC connected to an Internet service provider. Therefore, you might want to forgo manipulating the names and placement of these files using the Data Files option on the Mail Setup tab. You could potentially cripple Outlook by changing these filenames or locations.

CAUTION

Figure 20.5 The Mail Setup tab provides access to e-mail accounts, send and receive options, and Outlook data files.

To set up a new e-mail account or edit a current e-mail account, click the **E-Mail Accounts** button. The E-Mail Accounts dialog box opens, providing you with options for creating a new e-mail account, editing an existing account, adding a new address book, or editing an existing address book. This dialog box can also be reached from Outlook by selecting **Tools, E-Mail Accounts**. Creating e-mail accounts is covered in detail in Outlook Lesson 2, "Understanding the Outlook E-Mail Configurations." When you have finished creating a new account or editing an existing account, you are returned to the Mail Setup tab.

To set options related to the Outlook Send/Review command, click the **Send/Receive** button on the Mail Setup tab. The Send/Receive Groups dialog box opens. By default, all accounts are included in a All Accounts group and checked for new messages and any messages created using the account are also sent when you use the Send/Receive command (either on the Outlook toolbar or by selecting **Tools,**

Send/Receive, **Send All**). New groups of e-mail accounts can be created using this dialog box (click **New** to create the group). After a new group has been created, you can double-click the group name to see a list of all e-mail accounts. Select the accounts you want to place in the new group.

Setting Mail Format Options

The Mail Format tab on the Options dialog box (see Figure 20.6) allows you to choose your message format, such as HTML, rich text, or plain text. You can also select whether to use Microsoft Word as your e-mail editor. The mail format that you use dictates any special fonts or stationery templates that are available to you (only HTML supports different stationery for your e-mail messages).

Figure 20.6   The Mail Format tab allows you to choose your message format and select Word as your e-mail editor.

To set the format for your messages, use the Compose in This Message Format drop-down list. If you want to use Word as your e-mail editor, click the **Use Microsoft Word to Edit E-Mail Messages** check box.

If you use HTML as the format for your messages, you can select a stationery type. Select stationery using the Use This Stationery by Default drop-down list. If you want to view the stationery, select the Stationery Picker button. In the Stationery Picker dialog box, select a stationery in the Stationery list to view it. When you have finished selecting your stationery, click **OK** to close the Stationery Picker dialog box.

> **TIP** **Applying Your Changes** When you make changes on the tabs of the Options dialog box, you can apply these new options to Outlook by clicking the **Apply** button. The Options dialog box remains open so that you can configure other options.

Other Options Dialog Box Tabs

The Options dialog box also contains additional tabs that control other features associated with Outlook. Each tab is listed here with a description of the settings available:

- The Spelling tab enables you to change settings associated with Outlook's spell checker. You can choose (using check boxes) to have the spell checker always suggest replacements for misspelled words, always check spelling before sending, and ignore words in uppercase. A drop-down box also enables you to pick the language of the dictionary you want to use to spell check your Outlook items.

- The Security tab enables you to set options regarding whether outgoing messages should be encrypted or have digital signatures attached to them. An option also allows you to get a digital ID to use for your outgoing messages. Digital IDs and information on encrypting messages are covered in Outlook Lesson 9, "Setting Mail Options."

- The Other tab enables you to set options such as whether the Deleted Items folder is emptied when you exit Outlook. Other options included on this tab include Advanced Options (accessed by clicking the Advanced Options button), which allow you to specify the folder (such as the Inbox) that is selected when Outlook is opened. The Other tab also provides access to settings related to the AutoArchive feature, which is discussed in Lesson 19, "Archiving Items."

When you have finished all the changes you want to make to the various Outlook options, click **OK** to close the Options dialog box. This returns you to the currently selected Outlook folder (such as the Inbox or Contacts folder).

Word

Working in Word

In this lesson, you learn how to start Microsoft Word and navigate the Word window. You also learn how to use common tools such as menus, toolbars, and dialog boxes.

Starting Word

Microsoft Word is an efficient and full-featured word processor that provides you with all the tools you need to produce a tremendous variety of document types—everything from simple documents, such as memos and outlines, to complex documents, such as newsletters and Internet-ready HTML pages. You create your Word documents in the Word window, which provides easy access to all the tools you need to create all your documents.

Before you can take advantage of Word's proficient document processing features, you must open the Word application window. To start the Word program, follow these steps:

1. From the Windows desktop, click **Start**, **Programs**. The Programs menu appears (see Figure 1.1).

Figure 1.1   Open the Programs menu and click the Word icon to start Word.

2. To start Word, click the **Word** icon. The Word program window appears.

TIP   **Create a Desktop Shortcut**   You can create a shortcut icon for Word on your desktop. Then, you can double-click this icon to start Word. Select the **Start** button, and then point at **Programs**. Right-click the **Word** icon and select **Create Shortcut** from the menu that appears.

Understanding the Word Environment

When you start the Word program, the Word application window opens (see Figure 1.2). You create your documents in the Word window. The Word window also provides items that help you navigate and operate the application itself.

Figure 1.2   Create your documents and access Word's features and commands in the Word window.

TIP   **Control the View**   If your view differs from the view shown in Figure 1.2 (the Normal view), or if you don't see all the Word window elements shown in the figure (particularly the ruler), you can easily change your view. Select **View**, and then choose the menu selection (such as **Normal** or **Ruler**) that matches your view to the figure.

Notice that the largest area of the window is blank; this is where you create your new document. All the other areas—the menu bar, the toolbar, and the status bar—either provide a fast way to access the various commands and features that you use in Word, or they supply you with information concerning your document, such as what page you are on and where the insertion point is currently located in your document.

Table 1.1 describes the elements you see in the Word application window.

Table 1.1   Elements of the Word Window

Element	Description
Title bar	Includes the name of the application and the current document, as well as the Minimize, Maximize, and Close buttons.
Control Menu button	Opens the Control menu, which provides such commands as Restore, Minimize, and Close.
Minimize button	Reduces the Word window to a button on the taskbar; to restore the window to its original size, click the button on the taskbar.
Maximize/Restore button	Enlarges the Word window to cover the Windows desktop. When the window is maximized, the Maximize button changes to a Restore button that you can click to return the window to its previous size.
Close (x) button	Closes the Word program. "x" is the icon for closing any window.
Menu bar	Contains menus of commands you can use to perform tasks in the program, such as Edit, Format, and Tools.
Toolbar	Includes icons that serve as shortcuts for common commands, such as Save, Print, and Spelling.
Status bar	Displays information about the current page number, the document section in which you are located, and the current location of the insertion point (inches, line, and column). The status bar also shows you other information, such as whether you have turned on the Typeover (OVR) mode by pressing the Insert key on the keyboard.
Document window	This is where you type and format your documents.

Table 1.1 Continued

Element	Description
Scrollbars	The horizontal scrollbar is used to scroll your view of the current document in a left-to-right motion. The vertical scrollbar is used to scroll up and down through the current document.
Task pane	The column of information on the right side of the document is the task pane. This is where you can access features such as the Clipboard, styles, and formatting; you can also open another document or mail merge.

Using Menus and Toolbars

Word provides several ways to access the commands and features you use as you create your documents. You can access these commands by using the menus on the menu bar and the buttons on the various toolbars.

You can also access many Word commands using shortcut menus. Right-clicking a particular document element (a word or a paragraph, for example) opens these menus, which contain a list of commands related to the item you are currently working on.

The Word Menu Bar

The Word menu bar gives you access to all the commands and features that Word provides. Like all Windows applications, Word's menus reside below the title bar and are activated by clicking a particular menu choice. The menu then drops open, providing you with a set of command choices.

Word (and the other Office applications) adopted a menu system called personalized menus that enables you to quickly access the commands you use most often. When you first choose a particular menu, you find a short list of Word's most commonly used menu commands. This list of commands will actually be the ones that you have used most recently on that particular menu.

If a menu has a small double arrow at the bottom of its command list, you can click that to gain access to other, less commonly needed, commands. As you use hidden commands, Word adds them to the normal menu list. This means that you are basically building the list of commands available on the menu as you use Word.

This personalized strategy is also employed by the toolbar system. As you use commands, they are added to the toolbar (this personalized toolbar feature is available only when you have the Standard toolbar and the Formatting toolbar on the same

line in an application window). This provides you with customized menus and toolbars that are, in effect, personalized for you.

To access a particular menu, follow these steps:

1. Select the menu by clicking its title (such as **View**), as shown in Figure 1.3. The
   most recently used commands appear; wait just a moment for all the commands on a particular menu to appear (if the commands do not appear, click
   the down arrow at the bottom of the menu).

2. Select the command on the menu that invokes a particular feature (such as
   Header and Footer).

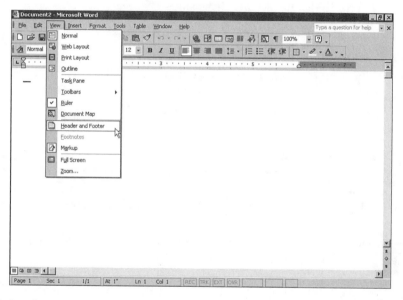

Figure 1.3   Select a particular menu to view, and then point to a Word command.

You will find that many of the commands found on Word's menus are followed by
an ellipsis (…). These commands, when selected, open a dialog box that requires you
to provide Word with additional information before the particular feature or command can be used. More information about understanding dialog boxes is included
later in this lesson.

Some of the menus also contain a submenu or cascading menu from which you
make choices. The menu commands that produce a submenu are indicated by an
arrow to the right of the menu choice. When a submenu is present, you point at the
command (marked with the arrow) on the main menu to open the submenu.

The menu system itself provides a logical grouping of the Word commands and features. For example, commands related to files, such as Open, Save, and Print, are all found on the File menu.

 TIP **Activating Menus with the Keyboard** You can activate a particular menu by holding down the **Alt** key and then pressing the keyboard key that matches the underscored letter in the menu's name. This underscored letter is called the hotkey. For example, to activate the File menu in Word, press **Alt+F**.

If you find that you would rather have access to all the menu commands (rather than accessing only those you've used recently), you can turn off the personalized menu system. To do this, follow these steps:

1. Click the **Tools** menu, and then click **Customize**.
2. In the Customize dialog box, click the **Options** tab.
3. To show all the commands on the menus, click the **Always Show Full Menus** check box.
4. Click **OK** to close the dialog box.

Shortcut Menus

A fast way to access commands related to a particular document element is to select that document object and then right-click. This opens a shortcut menu that contains commands related to the particular object you are working with.

 TERM **Object** Any element found in a document, such as text, a graphic, a hyperlink, or other inserted item.

For example, if you select a line of text in a document, right-clicking the selected text (see Figure 1.4) opens a shortcut menu with commands such as Cut, Copy, and Paste, or it provides you with quick access to formatting commands, such as Font and Paragraph.

Word Toolbars

The Word toolbars provide a very quick and straightforward way to access commands and features. When you first start Word, you are provided with the Standard and Formatting toolbars, which reside as one continuous toolbar found directly below the menu bar.

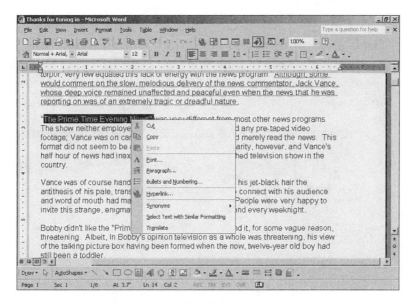

Figure 1.4   You can quickly access Word commands using shortcut menus.

To access a particular command using a toolbar button, click the button. Depending on the command, you see either an immediate result in your document (such as the removal of selected text when you click the **Cut** button) or the appearance of a dialog box requesting additional information from you.

TIP   **Finding a Toolbar Button's Purpose**   You can hover (but do not click) the mouse pointer on any toolbar button to view a description of that tool's function.

Word offers several toolbars; many of them contain buttons for a specific group of tasks. For example, the Drawing toolbar provides buttons that give you access to tools that enable you to draw graphical elements in your documents (such as text boxes, lines, and rectangles).

To place additional toolbars in the Word window, right-click any toolbar currently shown and select from the list that appears. Specific toolbars exist for working with tables, pictures, and the World Wide Web.

You can also easily add or remove buttons from any of the toolbars present in the Word window. Each toolbar is equipped with a Toolbar Options button that you can use to modify the buttons shown on that particular toolbar.

To add or remove buttons from a toolbar, follow these steps:

1. Click the **Toolbar Options** button on any toolbar; a drop-down area appears.

2. Click **Add or Remove Buttons** and then select the name of the toolbar that appears on the pop-up menu. A list of all the buttons for the current toolbar appears, as shown in Figure 1.5.

Figure 1.5   You can easily add or remove buttons from a toolbar using the button list.

3. For a button to appear on the toolbar, a check mark must appear to the left of the button in this list. For buttons without a check mark next to them, clicking this space puts the button on the toolbar. These buttons work as toggle switches; one click adds the check mark, another click removes it.

4. When you have completed your changes to the current toolbar, click outside the button list to close it.

 TIP   **Give the Standard Toolbar More Space**   Another way to provide more space for buttons on the toolbars is to place the Formatting toolbar below the Standard toolbar. Then, both toolbars have the width of the screen on which to display their respective buttons. Select the **Toolbar Options** button on a toolbar, and then select **Show Buttons on Two Rows**.

The Word toolbars provide fast access to the commands you need most often. Buttons exist for all the commands that are available on the Word menu system.

Exiting Word

When you have completed your initial survey of the Word application window or whenever you have completed your work in the program, you will want to exit the software. More than one way exists to close the Word window, which is the same as exiting the program.

You can exit Word by selecting the **File** menu and then **Exit**. Or you can close Word with one click of the mouse by clicking the Word **Close** (**x**) button in the upper-right corner of the application window.

When you close Word, you might be prompted to save any work that you have done in the application window. If you were just experimenting as you read through this lesson, you can click **No**. The current document will not be saved, and the Word application window closes. All the ins and outs of saving your documents are covered in Lesson 2, "Working with Documents."

Working with Documents

In this lesson, you learn how to start a new document and enter text. You also learn how to take advantage of Word document templates and Word document wizards.

Starting a New Document

When you choose to start a new document in Word, you can take three routes. You can

- Create a blank new document using Word's default template
- Create a document using one of Word's many other templates or a custom one you created yourself
- Create a document using one of the Word *wizards*, such as the Fax or Envelope Wizard

The amount of software assistance you get in creating your new document is greatly increased when you choose the template or wizard option.

 Template A blueprint for a document that may already contain certain formatting options and text.

 Wizard A feature that guides you step by step through a particular process in Word, such as creating a new document.

When you create a new document from scratch, you are actually using a template—the Blank Document template. Documents based on the Blank Document template do not contain any premade text (as some of the other templates do), and the formatting contained in the document reflects Word's default settings for margins, fonts, and other document attributes (including any you customized specifically to your needs or preferences). To find more information on default Word settings involving font and document attributes, see Lesson 5, "Changing How Text Looks," and Lesson 9, "Working with Margins, Pages, and Line Spacing," respectively).

As covered in Lesson 1, Word automatically opens a new blank document for you when you start the Word software. You can also open a new document when you are already in the Word application window.

To open a new document, follow these steps:

1. Select **File**, **New**. The task pane opens on the right side of your screen. Under **New from Template**, select **General Templates**, and Word opens the Templates dialog box with a range of templates from which to choose (see Figure 2.1).

Figure 2.1   When you choose **New** on the File menu, the task pane opens and you can choose **General Templates**.

2. Make sure that the General tab is selected in the Templates dialog box, and then double-click the Word **Blank Document** icon. A new document appears in the Word application window.

Although the steps shown here are designed for you to create a new blank document, you could have chosen any of the templates available in the Templates dialog box to create a new document. The fastest way to create a new blank document is to click the **New Blank Document** icon on the Word Standard toolbar.

CAUTION

What Happened to My Previous Document?   If you were already working on a document, the new document will, in effect, open on top of the document you were previously working on. You can get back to the previous document by clicking the appropriately named document icon on the Windows taskbar (if you haven't yet named the first document, it might appear as Document1 on the taskbar). You can also select the **Windows** menu to see a list of currently opened documents. Click any document in the list to switch to it.

TIP

Removing Multiple Document Icons from the Taskbar   If you prefer not to see the open document icons on the taskbar, select the **Tools** menu, select **Options**, and click the **View** tab. Clear the **Windows in Taskbar** check box. You must then use the Windows menu to switch between documents.

Entering Text

After you have opened a new document, you are ready to start entering text. Notice that a blinking vertical element called the *insertion point* appears in the upper-left corner of your new document. This is where new text will be entered.

Begin typing text from the keyboard. The insertion point moves to the right as you type. As soon as you reach the end of the line, the text automatically wraps to the next line for you using word wrap.

When you reach the end of a paragraph in Word, you must press the **Enter** key to manually insert a line break. If you want to view the manually placed line breaks (called paragraph marks) in your document, click the **Show/Hide** button on the Word Standard toolbar.

If the Show/Hide button is not visible on the Word toolbar, click the **Tool Options** button located at the end of the Standard toolbar. From the shortcut menu that appears, select **Add or Remove Buttons** and then **Standard**. A drop-down box of other buttons, including the Show/Hide button, appears. Clicking this button adds it to the Standard toolbar. When you are finished, click outside the drop-down box to return to your document. Now you can turn the Show/Hide option on and off as previously described.

TIP

How Word Views Paragraphs   Word considers any line or series of lines followed by a line break (created when you press the Enter key) a separate paragraph. This concept becomes very important when you deal with paragraph formatting issues, such as line spacing, indents, and paragraph borders.

Using Document Templates

You don't have to base your new documents on a blank template. Instead, you can take advantage of one of the special document templates that Word provides. These templates make it easy for you to create everything from memos to newsletters.

Templates contain special text and document attributes; therefore, the look and layout of the document you create using a template are predetermined by the options contained in the template. This can include margins, fonts, graphics, and other document layout attributes.

To base a new document on a Word template, follow these steps:

1. Select the **File** menu, and then click **New**. The task pane opens in your current document window.

2. Several template category links are available under the **New from Template** heading. These links include categories such as Normal, General Templates, and Templates on Microsoft.com. Select the category link for the type of document you want to create. For example, to create a new memo, click the **General Templates** link. In the Templates dialog box that appears, choose the **Memos** tab (see Figure 2.2). Select your favorite style of memo and click **OK** (or double-click the icon of choice).

Figure 2.2   The document category tabs in the Templates dialog box contain templates for different document types.

3. The new document based on the template appears as shown in Figure 2.3.

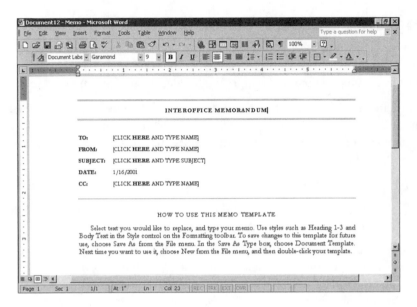

Figure 2.3   The new document contains predetermined text and formatting attributes derived from the template.

Most new documents based on templates already contain text, such as headings, as well as a variety of document layouts and text attributes, such as a particular font. For example, the document based on the Elegant Memo template already contains the layout for a memo, and it automatically enters the current date in the memo for you.

Text can easily be entered into the document using the Click Here and Type boxes that are placed in the document. Just click anywhere on the bracketed box and type the text you want to enter.

Many templates (the Elegant Memo template, for example) contain text that gives you advice on how to use the template. Any of this explanatory text can be selected and removed or replaced with your own text (for more about selecting and editing text, see Lesson 3, "Editing Documents").

Using Word Wizards

If you find that you would like even more help as you create a new document, you can use any of a number of Word document wizards. These wizards actually walk you through the document creation process, and in many cases, they make sure that you enter the appropriate text in the proper place in the new document.

The wizards are found on the same tabs that housed the templates located in the Templates dialog box (reached through the task pane). The wizards can be differentiated from standard templates by a small wizard's wand that appears over a template's icon.

To create a new document using one of the wizards, follow these steps:

1. Select the **File** menu, and then click **New** to open the task pane.

2. Under the **New from Template** heading, select the link for the document category you want to create (many useful templates are under the **General Templates** link). In the Templates dialog box that appears, choose the new document tab of your choice.

3. To start the document creation process using the wizard, double-click the appropriate wizard icon (for example, the Memo Wizard on the Memos tab).

When you double-click the wizard icon, the wizard dialog box opens with an introductory screen and outlines the document creation process for the type of document you want to create. For example, the Memo Wizard shown in Figure 2.4 details the memo creation process on the left side of the wizard dialog box.

Figure 2.4   The various document wizards, such as the Memo Wizard, outline the new creation process and then walk you through the steps of creating the document.

If you find that you need help as you work with a wizard, you can click the **Office Assistant** button on the wizard dialog box. The Office Assistant, which appears as an animated paper clip by default, appears with context-sensitive help related to the wizard screen on which you are currently working. If the button is not available, cancel the wizard, select the **Help** menu, and then **Show the Office Assistant**; then repeat the steps necessary to open the particular document wizard.

To move to the next step in the document creation process, click the **Next** button at the bottom of the wizard screen.

The various document wizards walk you through the entire document creation process. After completing the steps for document creation, click the **Finish** button to close the wizard. A new document appears in the Word window based on the choices you made as you worked with the wizard. Figure 2.5 shows a new document created using the Memo Wizard.

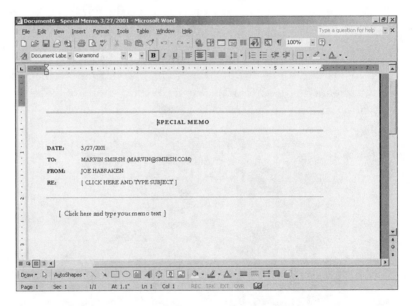

Figure 2.5   The Memo Wizard prompts you to input the appropriate information for a memo and provides the formatting for the new document.

The wizards you use vary in look and feel, depending on the type of document you are trying to create. For example, the Resume Wizard produces a decidedly different product than the Envelope Wizard does. A good rule to follow is to read each wizard screen carefully. Remember that you can always back up a step by clicking the **Back** button if you find that you've made an inappropriate choice (or you can close the unwanted document and start over).

Saving a Document

Whether you create your new document using the Blank Document template, a Word template, or a document wizard, at some point you will want to save the new document. Saving your work is one of the most important aspects of working with any software application. If you don't save your Word documents, you could lose them.

CAUTION

Save and Save Often   You don't want to lose your valuable documents as you create them in Word. Power failures, an accidentally kicked-out power cord, or your computer locking up as you work can all lead to lost work. If you are really absent-minded about periodically saving your work, use the AutoSave feature. Select the **Tools** menu, then **Options**. Click the **Save** tab on the dialog box. Make sure the **Save AutoRecover Info Every** check box is selected. Use the minutes box to set the time interval between autosaves. This feature doesn't replace periodically saving your document using the Save command, but it will help you recover more of your document if there is a problem such as a power failure.

To save a document, follow these steps:

1. Click the **Save** button on the Word toolbar, or select the **File** menu and then **Save**. The first time you save your new document, the Save As dialog box appears.

2. Type a filename into the File Name box. If you want to save the file in a format other than a Word document (.doc), such as a text file (.txt), click the **Save As Type** drop-down arrow and select a different file type.

3. To save the file to a different location (the default location is My Documents), click the **Save In** drop-down arrow. After you select a particular drive, all the folders on that drive appear.

4. Double-click the desired folder in the Save In box to open that folder.

5. After you have specified a name and a location for your new document, select the **Save** button to save the file. Word then returns you to the document window.

As you edit and enhance your new document, you should make a habit of frequently saving any changes that you make. To save changes to a document that has already been saved under a filename, just click the **Save** button.

If you would like to keep a backup of a document (the version as it appeared the last time you saved it) each time you save changes to it, you need to set the backup option.

1. Click the **Tools** command on the toolbar, and then select **Options**.

2. In the Options dialog box, click the **Save** tab and then the **Always Create Backup Copy** check box. Click **OK** to return to the document.

3. Name your file and save it for the first time to an appropriate location.

Now, when you use the Save command to save changes you've made to the document, a backup copy of the file (with the extension .wbk) is also saved. This backup copy is the previous version of the document before you made the changes. Each subsequent saving of the document replaces the backup file with the previous version of the document.

There might be occasions when, rather than using the backup option, you want to save the current document under a new filename or drive location. This can be done using the Save As command. To save your document with a new filename, follow these steps:

1. Select **File**, **Save As**.

2. In the Save As dialog box, type the new filename into the File Name box (make sure that you are saving the document in the desired path).

3. Click **Save**. The file is saved under the new name.

Closing a Document

When you have finished working with a document, you need to save your changes and then close the document. To close a document, select the **File** menu and then select **Close**. You can also close a document by clicking the **Close** (x) button on the right side of the document window. If you are working with multiple documents, closing one of the documents does not close the Word application. If you want to completely end your Word session, select the **File** menu, and then select **Exit**. Before closing a document, Word checks to see whether it has changed since it was last saved. If it has, Word asks whether you want to save these changes before closing. If you don't want to lose any recent changes, click **Yes** to save the document.

Opening a Document

Opening an existing document is a straightforward process. You will find that the Open dialog box shares many of the attributes that you saw in the Save As dialog box.

To open an existing Word file, follow these steps:

1. Select the **File** menu, and then **Open**. The Open dialog box appears.

2. By default, Word begins showing the files and folders in your My Documents folder. If the document you need is located elsewhere on your computer, click the **Look In** drop-down arrow to select the drive on which the file is located, and navigate to the folder containing the document you need.

3. To open the file, click the file, and then click the **Open** button (you can also double-click the file). The file appears in a Word document window.

If you are working with text files or documents that have been saved in a format other than the Word document format (.doc), you must select the file type in the **Files of Type** drop-down box to see them.

Editing Documents

In this lesson, you learn how to do basic text editing in Word, including moving and copying text; you work with the mouse and keyboard to move your document, and you learn how to save existing documents under a new filename.

Adding or Replacing Text and Moving in the Document

After you have completed a draft of your document, you probably will find yourself in a situation where you want to add and delete text in the document as you edit your work. Word makes it very easy for you to add new text and delete text that you don't want. You also will find that, whether you use the mouse or the keyboard to move around in your document as you edit, Word offers a number of special keystrokes and other tricks that make moving within the document a breeze. Figure 3.1 highlights some of these tools and Word screen areas.

Adding New Text

You actually have two possibilities for adding text to the document: *insert* and *type-over*. To insert text into the document and adjust the position of the existing text, place the *I-beam* mouse pointer where you want to insert the new text. Click the mouse to place the insertion point at the chosen position. Make sure that the OVR indicator on the Status bar is not active (it will be gray rather than bolded). This means that you are in the insert mode.

 I-beam   This is the shape that the mouse pointer takes when you place it over any text in a Word document. Use it to place the insertion point at a particular position in a document.

 Insert Mode   The default text mode in Word. New text is added at the insertion point and existing text is pushed forward in the document so that it remains as part of the document.

I-beam: Used to place the
insertion point in the document.

Vertical scrollbar: Scroll up
and down in a document.

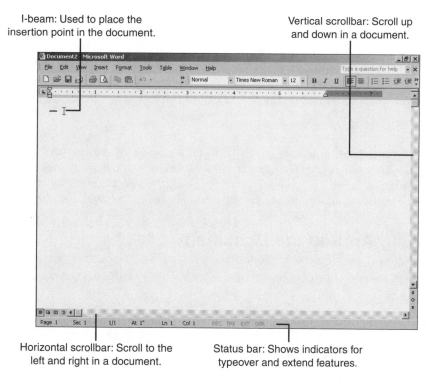

Horizontal scrollbar: Scroll to the
left and right in a document.

Status bar: Shows indicators for
typeover and extend features.

Figure 3.1 A number of different tools and approaches are available for editing and selecting text in Word and moving around in your Word documents.

Type your new text. It is added at the insertion point, and existing text (the text to the right of the inserted text) is pushed forward in the document.

Replacing Text

If you want to add new text to a document and simultaneously delete text to the right of the insertion point, use the mouse to place the insertion point where you want to start typing over the existing text. Press the **Insert** key on the keyboard and add your new text. The added text types over the existing text, deleting it (see Figure 3.2). When you switch to Typeover mode using the **Insert** key, the Word status bar displays the message OVR. This means that you are currently in Typeover mode.

Typeover indicator

Figure 3.2 When you are in Typeover mode, existing text is overwritten by the new text.

Typeover Mode   Press the **Insert** key to enter this mode; new text is added at the insertion point and types over the existing text, deleting it.

If you want to return to Insert mode, press the **Insert** key again (it toggles Word between the Insert and Typeover modes) and the OVR message on the status bar is dimmed (you can also double-click **OVR** on the status bar to toggle this feature on and off).

Undo That Typeover   If you inadvertently type over text in a document because you are in the Typeover mode, click the **Undo** button (it might take several clicks in cases where you have added several words to the document) on the toolbar to return the deleted text to the document (or press **Ctrl+Z**).

CAUTION

Moving Around the Document

Whether you are a mouse aficionado or prefer to stick close to your keyboard, Word provides several shortcuts and tools for moving around a document that you are trying to edit.

When you use the mouse, you can move to a different position in the current page by placing the mouse pointer (the I-beam) over a particular text entry and then clicking. This places the insertion point where you clicked.

You also can use the mouse to move through your document using the vertical and horizontal scrollbars. For example, clicking the up scroll arrow on the vertical scrollbar moves you up through the document. Clicking the down scroll arrow moves you down through the document. If you want to quickly move to a particular page in the document, you can drag the scroll box to a particular place on the vertical scrollbar. As soon as you click on the scrollbox, a page indicator box appears that you can use to keep track of what page you are on as you drag the scroll box up or down on the vertical scrollbar.

The vertical scrollbar also provides Previous Page and Next Page buttons (the double-up arrow and double-down arrow buttons on the bottom of the scrollbar) that can be used to move to the previous page and next page, respectively. Use the mouse to click the appropriate button to move in the direction that you want to go in your document.

The horizontal scrollbar operates much the same as the vertical scrollbar; however, it offers the capability to scroll only to the left and the right of a document page. This is particularly useful when you have zoomed in on a document and want to scrutinize an area of the page in great detail.

You should be aware that clicking the mouse on the vertical scrollbar to change your position in a document allows you to view a different portion of a page or a different part of the document; however, it does not move the insertion point to that position on the page. To actually place the insertion point, you must move to a specific place or position in the document, and then click the mouse I-beam where you want to place the insertion point.

When you're typing or editing text, you might find that the fastest way to move through the document is with the help of the keyboard shortcuts shown in Table 3.1. Keeping your hands on the keyboard, rather than reaching out for the mouse, can be a more efficient way to move in a document while you compose or edit.

 TIP **Scroll Quickly with a Wheel Mouse** You might want to purchase a wheel mouse, such as Microsoft's IntelliMouse, which provides a rolling device on the top of mouse (between the click buttons). With your finger on the wheel device, you can literally "roll" the vertical scrollbar through the document at the pace of your choice—rapidly or slowly.

Table 3.1 Using the Keyboard to Move Through the Document

Key Combination	Movement
Home	Move to the beginning of a line
End	Move to the end of a line
Ctrl+Right arrow	Move one word to the right
Ctrl+Left arrow	Move one word to the left
Ctrl+Up arrow	Move to the previous paragraph
Ctrl+Down arrow	Move to the next paragraph
PgUp	Move up one window
PgDn	Move down one window
Ctrl+PgUp	Move up one page
Ctrl+PgDn	Move down one page
Ctrl+Home	Move to the top of a document
Ctrl+End	Move to the bottom of a document

Selecting Text

Having a good handle on the different methods for selecting text in a document makes it easy for you to take advantage of many features, including deleting, moving, and formatting text. You can select text with either the mouse or the keyboard. Both methods have their own advantages and disadvantages as you work on your documents.

Selecting Text with the Mouse

The mouse is an excellent tool for selecting text in your document during the editing process. You can double-click a word to select it and also use different numbers of mouse clicks (quickly pressing the left mouse button) or the mouse in combination with the Shift key to select sentences, paragraphs, or other blocks of text. You also can hold the left mouse button down and drag it across a block of text that you want to select.

How you use the mouse to select the text depends on whether the mouse pointer is in the document itself or along the left side of the document in the *selection bar*. The selection bar is the whitespace on the left edge of your document window, just in front of your text paragraphs. When you place the mouse in the selection bar, the mouse pointer becomes an arrow (in contrast to placing the mouse in the document where the pointer appears as an I-beam).

Selecting text lines and paragraphs from the selection bar makes it easy for you to quickly select either a single line or the entire document. Table 3.2 shows you how to select different text items using the mouse. Figure 3.3 shows the mouse pointer in the selection bar with a selected sentence.

Table 3.2   Using the Mouse to Quickly Select Text in the Document

Text Selection	Mouse Action
Selects the word	Double-click a word
Selects text block	Click and drag
	Or
	Click at beginning of text, and then hold down Shift key and click at the end of text block
Selects line	Click in selection bar next to line
Selects multiple lines	Click in selection bar and drag down through multiple lines
Selects the sentence	Hold Ctrl and click a sentence
Selects paragraph	Double-click in selection bar next to paragraph
	Or
	Triple-click in the paragraph
Selects entire document	Hold down Ctrl and click in selection bar

You will find these mouse manipulations are particularly useful when you are editing the document. Selected text can be quickly deleted, moved, or copied.

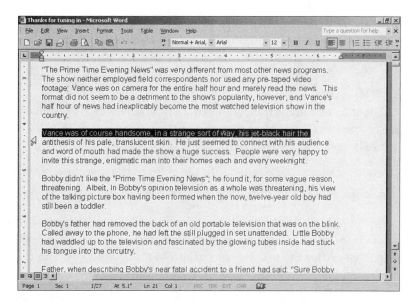

Figure 3.3 Place the mouse pointer in the selection bar to quickly select a line, a paragraph, or other text block.

Selecting Text with the Keyboard

You can also select text using only the keyboard. Press the F8 function key to turn on the extend (or select) feature; the EXT indicator becomes active on the Word status bar (meaning it is no longer "grayed" out).

To select text using the extend feature, use the arrow keys to move over and highlight characters, words, or sentences you want to select. You can quickly select entire words by pressing **F8** and then pressing the spacebar. To select an entire sentence, turn on the extend feature, and then press the period (.) key. Entire paragraphs can be selected using this method by pressing the **Enter** key. To turn off the extend feature, press the **Esc** key.

Finally, you can select text by pressing only the F8 function key. Press **F8** once to turn on the select feature where you want it, press it twice to select a word, three times to highlight an entire sentence, four times to select a paragraph, and five times to select your entire document.

Deleting, Copying, and Moving Text

Another important aspect of editing is being able to delete, move, or copy text in your document. Each of these tasks can be easily accomplished in Word and uses the mouse or the keyboard to select the text that you want to delete, move, or copy. Then, it's just a matter of invoking the correct command to delete, move, or copy the selected text.

Deleting Text

Deleting text can be accomplished in more than one way. The simplest way to remove characters as you type is with the Backspace key or the Delete key. With no selected text

- **Delete**—Deletes the character to the right of the insertion point.
- **Backspace**—Deletes the character to the left of the insertion point.

You will probably find, however, that when you delete text you want to remove more than just one character, so use the keyboard or the mouse to select the text you want to delete. After the text is selected, press the **Delete** key. The text is then removed from the document.

You can also delete text and replace it with new text in one step. After the text is selected, type the new text. It replaces the entire existing, selected text.

CAUTION

Delete and Cut Are Different   When you want to erase a text block forever, use the **Delete** key. When you want to remove text from a particular place in the document but want to have access to it again to place it somewhere else, use the **Cut** command on the **Edit** menu. When you cut an item, it is automatically placed on the Office Clipboard. These steps are covered later in this lesson.

Copying, Cutting, and Pasting Text

Copying or cutting text and then pasting the copied or cut item to a new location is very straightforward. All you have to do is select the text as we have discussed earlier in this lesson and then invoke the appropriate commands. Use the following steps to copy and paste text in your document:

1. Using the mouse or the keyboard, select the text that you want to copy.
2. Select the **Edit** menu, and then select **Copy**, or press **Ctrl+C** to copy the text.
3. Place the insertion point in the document where you want to place a copy of the copied text.
4. Select the **Edit** menu and then select **Paste**, or press **Ctrl+V**. A copy of the text is inserted at the insertion point.

TIP   **Use the Copy, Cut, and Paste Icons**   To quickly access the copy, cut, and paste features, use the Copy, Cut, and Paste icons on the Word toolbar, respectively.

After pasting your selected text, the Paste Smart Tag icon appears just below the text that you have pasted. When you click this icon, it provides a shortcut menu that allows you to keep the formatting that was applied to the source text that you copied, match the formatting supplied by the destination for the text (the paragraph you are placing the text in), or just paste the text into the new location with no formatting at all (which means it will assume the formatting that is provided at the current location).

Smart Tags are a new feature found in Office XP. Figure 3.4 shows pasted text and the Paste Smart Tag provided for the text.

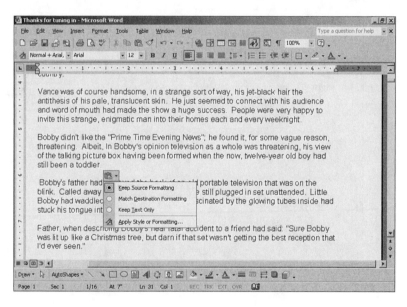

Figure 3.4   The Paste Smart Tag allows you to choose how the text is pasted into the new location.

Cutting text from the document and then pasting it to a new location is every bit as straightforward as using copy and paste. Select the text, and then press Ctrl+X or click the **Cut** button on the Standard toolbar. Click the I-beam to place the insertion point on the document, and then you can then use Ctrl+V or the **Paste** button on the Standard toolbar to place the text in a new location. A Paste Smart Tag will appear below the pasted text as shown in Figure 3.4.

Using the Office Clipboard to Copy and Move Multiple Items

The Office Clipboard feature now resides in the task pane of your Office application windows as discussed in Chapter 3, "Using the Office Task Pane," which is found in Part I of this book. If you want to copy or cut more than one item and then be able to paste them into different places in the document, you must use the Office Clipboard. Follow these steps:

1. To open the Clipboard task pane, select the **Edit** menu and select **Office Clipboard**. The Clipboard appears in the task pane.

2. As shown in Figure 3.5, select and copy each item to the Clipboard.

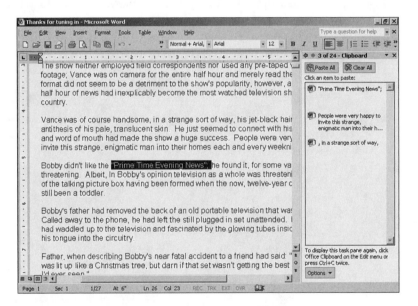

Figure 3.5   The Clipboard can hold up to 24 separate items.

3. After you have copied your items onto the Clipboard, place the insertion point where you want the first item to be pasted. Then, return to the Clipboard and with the mouse, point to your first item and click; Word automatically inserts the item into the document.

4. Repeat step 3 as needed to paste other items from the Clipboard into your document.

If you want to cut and paste (or move) multiple items, you must use the Office Clipboard. Follow these steps:

1. To open the Clipboard, select the **Edit** menu and select **Clipboard**. The Clipboard appears in the task pane.

2. Select and cut each item to the Clipboard.

3. After you have your cut items on the Clipboard, place the insertion point where you want the first item to be pasted. Then, return to the Clipboard and with the mouse, point to your first item and click; it will automatically be inserted into the document.

4. Repeat step 3 as needed to paste other items from the Clipboard into your document.

Using Drag and Drop

One other way to move text is by selecting it and dragging it to a new location. This is called drag and drop. After the text is selected, place the mouse on the text block and hold down the left mouse button. A Move pointer appears, as shown in Figure 3.6.

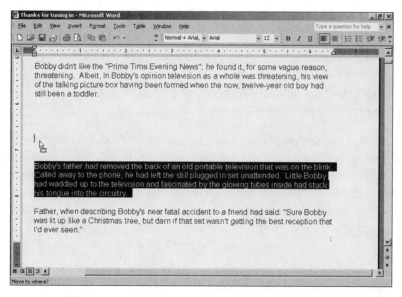

Figure 3.6 Drag a block of selected text to a new location with drag and drop.

Drag the Move pointer to the new location for the text. A dotted insertion point appears in the text. Place this insertion point in the appropriate position and release the mouse button. The text is moved to the new location.

Copying and Moving Text Between Documents

You can copy and move text easily between documents. All you have to do is open the appropriate documents and then use the methods already discussed for copying or moving text. You can even use drag and drop to move information from one document to another.

To copy information from one document to another, follow these steps:

1. Open the document you want to copy information from and the one you want to copy that information to (see Lesson 2, "Working with Documents," for more information on opening documents).

2. Switch to the document that contains the text you want to copy by clicking the document's button on the **Taskbar** or selecting the **Windows** menu and then the name of the document.

3. Select the text you want to copy, select the **Edit** menu, and then select the **Copy** command.

4. Using the instructions in step 3, switch to the document into which you want to paste the text.

5. Select the **Edit** menu, and then select **Paste**. The text is pasted into your document.

You can also use the preceding steps to move text from one document to another by substituting the Cut command for the Copy command. You can also use drag and drop to move text from one document to another. Working with multiple document windows can be tricky. You probably won't want to have more than two documents open if you want to use drag and drop, because you won't have enough space in the Word workspace to scroll through the documents and find the text you want to move or the final resting place for the text in the other document.

To view multiple document windows, open the documents. Select the **Windows** menu and then select **Arrange All**. Each document is placed in a separate window in the Word workspace. The windows might be small if you have several documents open. Locate the text you want to move and select it. Drag it from the current document window to the document window and position where you want to place it.

Using Proofreading Tools

In this lesson, you learn to check your documents for errors such as misspellings and improper grammar. You work with the spell checker and grammar checker and learn how to find synonyms with the thesaurus, how to proof your document as you type, and how to use the AutoCorrect feature.

Proofing As You Type

Word offers several excellent features for helping you to create error-free documents. Each of these features—the spell checker, the grammar checker, and the thesaurus—are explored in this lesson. Word also gives you the option of checking your spelling and grammar automatically as you type. You can also use the AutoCorrect feature to automatically make some proofing changes for you (for more about AutoCorrect, see "Working with AutoCorrect" in this lesson).

Proofing as you type simply means that errors in spelling and grammar can be automatically flagged as you enter text into your document. This enables you to quickly and immediately correct errors as you build your document.

When you proof as you type, spelling errors—words not found in the Word dictionary file or in your custom dictionary file—are flagged with a wavy red underline. Errors in grammar are underlined with a wavy green line. Spelling and grammar errors marked in this way can be corrected immediately, or you can correct them collectively by running the spelling and grammar checking features after you have finished entering all the text. For information on using the Spelling and Grammar Checker on a completed document, see the section "Using the Spelling and Grammar Checker," later in this lesson.

The check-as-you-type features are turned on in Word by default. To change the defaults associated with the automatic spelling and grammar checking features (or to turn them off completely), follow these steps:

1. Select the **Tools** menu, and then choose **Options**. The Options dialog box opens.
2. Make sure the **Spelling and Grammar** tab is selected, as shown in Figure 4.1.

Figure 4.1   You can turn the automatic spelling and grammar checking options on or off in the Options dialog box.

3. To toggle the automatic spelling checker on or off, click the **Check Spelling As You Type** check box in the Spelling area of the dialog box.

4. To toggle the automatic grammar checker on or off, click the **Check Grammar As You Type** check box in the Grammar area of the dialog box (near the bottom).

Several other options are also available in this dialog box that relate to how the Spelling and Grammar features operate when you use them in Word.

- **Hide spelling errors in this document**—This option hides the wavy red lines that flag misspellings in the document.

- **Always suggest corrections**—This option provides a list of suggested corrections for each misspelled word when the spell checker is used.

- **Suggest from main dictionary only**—This option uses only the main dictionary for spell checking the document. Any customized dictionaries that have been created are ignored.

- **Ignore words in UPPERCASE**—This option ignores uppercase words in the document.

- **Ignore words with numbers**—This option ignores combinations of text and numbers in the document.

- **Ignore Internet and file addresses**—This option ignores Web addresses and filenames (such as C:\my documents\joe.doc).

- **Hide grammatical errors in the document**—This option hides the wavy green line that marks potential grammar errors in the document.

- **Check grammar with spelling**—This option is used to check the grammar in the document when you run the spell checker.

- **Show readability statistics**—This option is used to display different readability statistics that show you the readability level and grade level of your text.

After you have finished making your selections in the Options dialog box, click **OK**.

With the check–as-you-type options enabled, suspected misspellings and grammatical errors are flagged with the appropriate colored wavy line.

Correcting Individual Spelling Errors

As mentioned, Word marks all words not found in its dictionary with a wavy red line. Because Word's dictionary isn't entirely complete, you might find that it marks correct words as misspelled. To correct words flagged as misspelled (whether they are or not), follow these steps:

1. Place the mouse pointer on the flagged word and click the right mouse button. A shortcut menu appears, as shown in Figure 4.2.

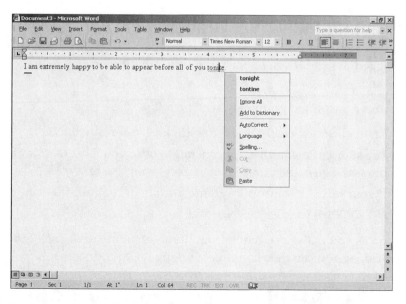

Figure 4.2 Right-click any flagged word to get a list of suggested spellings.

2. Word provides a list of possible correct spellings when it encounters a word not in its dictionary. If the correct spelling for the word you want appears in the list, simply click it, and Word replaces the incorrect spelling with the correct one.

If the flagged word is correctly spelled (and just not in Word's dictionary) or the correct spelling is not in the suggestions list, you have three other options:

- If the word is correct and you don't want it flagged at all in the current document, you can click **Ignore All** and the wavy red line will be removed from all occurrences of the word.
- If the word is correct and you don't want it flagged in this or any other document, you can add the word to the dictionary file; click **Add**.
- If you find that you constantly misspell the word as it currently appears in your document, you can add the word to the AutoCorrect list (discussed later in this chapter). Point to **AutoCorrect**. Suggested spellings will be listed. Select a spelling from the list; the incorrect spelling and the correct spelling are entered into the AutoCorrect list. The word in your document is corrected, and the next time you type the word incorrectly, it is automatically corrected.

Correcting Individual Grammatical Errors

Correcting grammatical errors as you type is similar to correcting spelling errors that are flagged in the document. Suspected grammatical errors are marked with a green wavy line.

To correct a suspected grammatical error, follow these steps:

1. Right-click text blocks marked with the green wavy line.

2. The shortcut menu that appears might offer you a list of grammatically correct phrases. Select the phrase that corrects your text entry.

3. If your text is not incorrect grammatically or requires that you manually make any necessary changes, click **Ignore**.

As soon as you make a selection from the shortcut menu or click **Ignore**, the shortcut menu closes. You can then continue working on your document.

Using the Spelling and Grammar Checker

You might prefer not to correct spelling and grammatical errors as you type. If you're a touch typist, you might not even notice Word has flagged a word or sentence as incorrect. Waiting to correct the document until you have finished composing enables you to concentrate on getting your thoughts down without interruption. Then, you can check the entire document upon completion.

To use the Word Spelling and Grammar feature, follow these steps:

1. Select **Tools, Spelling and Grammar,** or click the **Spelling and Grammar** button on the toolbar. The Spelling and Grammar dialog box appears as shown in Figure 4.3.

Figure 4.3   The Spelling and Grammar dialog box displays the suspected spelling and grammar errors in your document and offers you options for correcting them.

2. Words not found in the dictionary are flagged, and the text in which the word is contained is displayed in the Not in Dictionary box. You can manually correct the highlighted word in the box and then click **Change** to correct the word in the document. The following are other options available for the flagged word:

• Select the appropriate selection for the flagged word from the Suggestion box and click **Change**. If you want to correct all occurrences of the misspelled word (assuming you have consistently and knowingly misspelled it), click **Change All**.

• Ignore the flagged word if it is correctly spelled. Click **Ignore Once** to ignore this occurrence of the word, or click **Ignore All** to ignore all occurrences of the word in the document.

• You can also add the word to the dictionary; just click **Add**.

• If you would rather add the misspelled word and an appropriate correct spelling to the AutoCorrect feature, click **AutoCorrect**; the word is corrected, and future insertions of the word (even in other documents when they're opened) with the incorrect spelling are automatically corrected.

Whichever selection you make, the word is dealt with appropriately and the spelling checker moves on to the next flagged word. Make your selection either to correct or to ignore the word, as previously outlined.

If the Check Grammar check box in the Spelling and Grammar dialog box is selected, Word also checks the grammar in your document.

When the Spelling and Grammar dialog box flags a grammatical error in the document, the suspected error appears in the text box at the top of the Spelling and Grammar dialog box with a heading that describes the type of error. Figure 4.4 shows a sentence fragment that has been caught by the grammar checker.

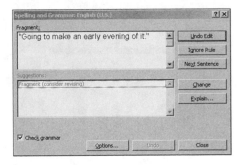

Figure 4.4 The grammar checker flags suspected grammar errors and offers suggestions and possible fixes for the problem.

Suggested corrections, if available, appear in the Suggestions box. In the case of the fragment, the suggestion is to consider revising the fragment. In other cases, more suggestions with actual sentence revisions might appear in this box. If present, select the appropriate revision and click **Change**.

You are also presented with different ignore options for flagged grammatical errors:

- You can choose to ignore the suspected grammatical error by clicking **Ignore**. This ignores only the currently flagged error.

- In some cases, **Ignore All** is also an option. If you click **Ignore All**, the grammar checker ignores all occurrences of this same grammatical error in the rest of the document.

- Word also provides you with the option of ignoring the actual grammar rule that was used to flag the current grammatical error; click **Ignore Rule** to do this throughout the document. This means that any error (not just the current error) that is flagged because of that particular rule (fragment or long sentence, for example) is not flagged as a grammatical error.

Use the Grammar feature to check the entire document using the options discussed in this section. When you reach the end of the document and the Grammar check is complete, a dialog box will appear letting you know that the spelling and grammar check has been completed.

Finding Synonyms Using the Thesaurus

The Word thesaurus provides you with a tool that can be used to find synonyms for the words in your document. Synonyms are words that mean the same thing. Because the thesaurus can generate a list of synonyms for nearly any word in your document, you can avoid the constant use of a particular descriptive adjective (such as "excellent") and actually add some depth to the vocabulary that appears in your document.

 TIP   **The Thesaurus Also Lists Antonyms**   Depending on the word you select to find synonyms, you might find that a list of antonyms—words that mean the opposite—are also provided. Antonyms are marked with (antonym) to the right of the suggested word.

To use the thesaurus, follow these steps:

1. Place the insertion point on the word for which you want to find a synonym.

2. Select the **Tools** menu, point at **Language**, and then select **Thesaurus**. The Thesaurus dialog box appears as shown in Figure 4.5.

Figure 4.5   The Thesaurus dialog box offers a list of synonyms for the selected word.

3. To replace the word with a synonym, select the synonym in the synonym list, and then click **Replace**.

4. You can also choose to see a list of synonyms for any of the words listed in the synonym list. Select the word, and then click **Look Up**. This can provide a greater number of possible words to use when you replace the particular word in your document. Synonyms provided for a word in the synonym list might be less close in meaning, however, to the word in your document.

After you have selected a synonym and clicked **Replace**, the word is replaced in the document and the Thesaurus dialog box closes.

TIP **Right-Click for Synonyms** A quick way to check for a list of synonyms for a word is to right-click that word in your document and then select **Synonyms** from the shortcut menu. A list of synonyms (if available for that word) appears. Select the appropriate word on the list to replace the currently selected word. Words flagged as misspelled or in a sentence marked as a grammar error will not provide a list of synonyms when you right-click them.

Working with AutoCorrect

Some of your misspelled words are automatically corrected as you type. This is done by the AutoCorrect feature that uses a list of common spelling errors and typos to correct entries in your documents. For example, Word has already arranged to have the incorrect spelling of "t-e-h" to be replaced with "the." You can also add your own words to the AutoCorrect feature. For example, if you always spell aardvark as ardvark, you can set up AutoCorrect to correct this spelling error every time you type it.

You've already seen that the Spelling feature provides you with the option of placing misspelled words into the AutoCorrect library. You can also manually enter pairs of words (the incorrect and correct spellings) into the AutoCorrect dialog box.

To place words in the AutoCorrect list, follow these steps:

1. Click the **Tools** menu, and then click **AutoCorrect Options**. The AutoCorrect dialog box appears as shown in Figure 4.6.
2. In the **Replace** box, enter the word as you misspell it. In the **With** box enter the correct spelling of the word.
3. Click **Add** to add the entry to the AutoCorrect list.
4. When you have completed adding entries, click **OK** to close the dialog box.

Now when you misspell the word, Word corrects it for you automatically. You can also use the AutoCorrect dialog box to delete AutoCorrect entries that you do not use (highlight the entry and click **Delete**) or that inadvertently correct items that you want to have in your document (clear the applicable check box).

This feature can also be used to help speed your typing along. For example, suppose that you are writing a technical paper that includes a long organizational name, such as the National Museum of American Art. If you tell the AutoCorrect feature to replace "nmaa" with "National Museum of American Art," it saves you a lot of typing.

Figure 4.6   The AutoCorrect feature enables you to build a list of commonly misspelled words for automatic correction.

TIP   **Override the AutoCorrect Feature**   If you type a text entry that is automatically changed by the AutoCorrect feature but you want it spelled your original way, immediately place your mouse on the corrected text. The AutoCorrect Smart Tag (it has a lightning bolt symbol on it) appears. When you click this Smart Tag's arrow, you can choose to return the word to its original text, among other options.

Changing How Text Looks

In this lesson, you learn basic ways to change the look of your text. You work with fonts and learn how to change font attributes. You also work with text alignment, such as centering and right justification.

Understanding Fonts

When you work in Word, you want to be able to control the look of the text in the documents that you create. The size and appearance of the text is controlled for the most part by the font or fonts you choose to use in the document. Each available font has a particular style or typeface. A variety of fonts exists, with names such as Arial, Courier, Times New Roman, CG Times, Bookman Old Style, and so on; the fonts you can choose depend on the fonts that have been installed on your computer (Windows offers a large number of default fonts; other font families are added when you install Office, and you can purchase software for special lettering and printing projects). Each font has a particular look and feel that makes it unique.

 TIP　**Keep Your Business Documents Standard**　The standard point size for most business documents is 12 point, which is 1/6 of an inch tall. So, when selecting a new font, it's generally a good idea to make sure that you use 12 point for documents such as business letters and memos.

You can change the font or fonts used in a document whenever you have the need, and you can also manipulate the size of the characters and their attributes, including bold, underlining, and italic. You can select a new font before you begin typing your document, or you can select text and change its fonts and text attributes at any time.

Changing Font Attributes

The easiest way to change font attributes is through the use of the buttons provided on the Word Formatting toolbar. Figure 5.1 shows the Word Formatting toolbar with some of the most common font attribute buttons displayed.

Figure 5.1   The Word Formatting toolbar gives you quick access to control the font attributes in your documents.

You can quickly change the font of selected text by clicking the **Font** box and selecting a new font from the list that appears. Other attributes, such as bold, italic, and underline, require that you select the text and then click the appropriate button once to add that attribute to the text. For example, you might want to apply special formatting to a heading so that it stands out from the rest of the text. You can do that by adding bold to the text.

To add bold to text in a document, follow these steps:

1. **Select** the word or other text to be bold.

2. Click the **Bold** button on the Formatting toolbar. The text appears in bold.

3. Click any other part of the document to deselect the text and view the results of your formatting.

You can use this same technique to underline and italicize text in your documents.

> **TIP** **I Don't Have Those Buttons on My Toolbar**   Click the **Toolbar Options** drop-down arrow, point at **Add or Remove Buttons**, and then select the name of the toolbar you want to add the buttons to (such as the Foramtting toolbar). From the drop-down list, select the buttons that you want to add to the Formatting toolbar. If you don't see the Formatting toolbar at all, right-click any of the toolbars and select **Formatting** on the menu that appears.

You can also use the various font buttons to select font attributes for the new text you type into a new document or insert into an existing document. Select the appropriate font attributes on the Formatting toolbar, and then type the text. To turn off a particular attribute, such as bold or italic, click the appropriate button a second time. To change to a new font or size, use the appropriate drop-down box.

When you are typing in a document, you might find that selecting font attributes from the toolbar actually slows you down because you must remove one hand from the keyboard to use the mouse to make your selection. You can also turn on or off a number of the formatting attributes using shortcut keys on the keyboard. Table 5.1 shows some of the common keyboard shortcuts for formatting attributes.

Table 5.1   Font Attribute Shortcut Keys

Attribute	Shortcut Keys
Bold	Ctrl+B
Italic	Ctrl+I
Underline	Ctrl+U
Double underline	Ctrl+Shift+D
Subscript	Ctrl+equal sign (=)
Superscript	Ctrl+Shift+plus sign (+)

To use any of the shortcut key combinations, press the keys shown simultaneously to turn the attribute on, and then repeat the key sequence to turn the attribute off. For example, to turn on bold while you are typing, press the **Ctrl** key and the **B** key at the same time. Press these keys again to turn the bold off.

Working in the Font Dialog Box

Although the Formatting toolbar certainly provides the quickest avenue for controlling various font attributes, such as the font and the font size, you can access several more font attributes in the Font dialog box. The Font dialog box gives you control over common attributes, such as font, font size, bold, and so on, and it also provides you with control over special font attributes, such as superscript, subscript, and strikethrough.

To open the Font dialog box, click the **Format** menu, and then select **Font**. The Font dialog box appears, as shown in Figure 5.2.

As you can see, the Font dialog box enables you to choose from several font attributes. You can control the font, the font style, and other character attributes such as strikethrough, superscript, and shadow.

- To change the font, click the **Font** drop-down box and select the new font by name.
- To change the font style to italic, bold, or bold italic, make the appropriate selection in the **Font Style** box.
- To change the size of the font, select the appropriate size in the **Size** scroll box.
- For underlining, click the **Underline Style** drop-down box and select an underlining style.
- To change the color of the font, click the **Font Color** drop-down box and select a new color.
- To select any special effects, such as strikethrough, superscript, or shadow, select the appropriate check box in the lower half of the dialog box.

Figure 5.2   The Font dialog box provides you with control over several font attributes not found on the Formatting toolbar.

As you make the various selections in the Font dialog box, a sample of what the text will look like appears in the Preview box at the bottom of the dialog box. After you have made all your selections in the Font dialog box, click **OK**.

TIP   **Change the Default Font**   To change the default font that you use for your documents (those created using the current or desired template), select the font attributes in the Font dialog box and then click the **Default** button at the lower left of the dialog box. Click **Yes** when Word asks for a confirmation of the change.

Aligning Text

Another important basic attribute of the text in your documents is how that text is oriented on the page. When you first start typing in a new document, all the text begins at the left margin and moves to the right as you type; this means the text is left-justified using the default align left feature. Left-justified text is characterized by text that is straight or unvarying on the left margin but has a ragged right-edged margin.

Text that serves a special function in a document, such as a heading, would probably stand out better in the document if it is placed differently than the rest of the text. Word makes it easy for you to change the alignment of any text paragraph. Several alignment possibilities are available:

- **Align Left**—The default margin placement for normal text, aligned on the left.
- **Align Right**—Text is aligned at the right margin and text lines show a ragged left edge.
- **Center**—The text is centered between the left and right margins of the page (with both margins having irregular edges).
- **Justify**—The text is spaced irregularly across each line so that both the left and the right margins are straight edged and uniform (often used in printed publications such as the daily newspapers).

CAUTION

Remember How Word Sees a Paragraph   Any text followed by a paragraph mark—created when you press the **Enter** key—is considered a separate paragraph in Word. This means that when you use alignment features, such as those discussed in this section, only the paragraph that currently holds the insertion point will be affected by the alignment command that you select (such as Center). If you need to align multiple lines that are in separate paragraphs, select that text before selecting the alignment command.

Figure 5.3 shows examples of each of the alignment possibilities.

The easiest way to change the alignment of text in the document is to use the alignment buttons on the Formatting toolbar. Also, a button exists in the Paragraph dialog box for each of the alignment possibilities. Table 5.2 shows the buttons and their functions.

Table 5.2   Alignment Icons on the Formatting Toolbar

Button	Justification
	Align left
	Center
	Align right
	Justify (full justification)

These justification buttons can be used to align new text or selected text. Again, if you are typing new text with a particular justification, your selected justification will still be in force even after you press Enter. You must change the justification as needed.

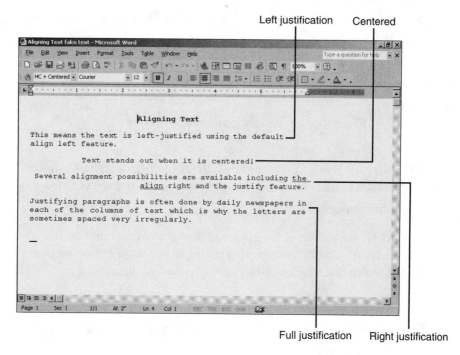

Figure 5.3 You can align the text in your document to suit your particular needs on a document page.

Aligning Text with Click and Type

Word offers a unique and quick way to insert and align text or to insert graphics, tables, and other items in a blank area of a document. Before entering text or another item, place the mouse pointer on a blank line on the page. As you move the mouse pointer from right to left on the blank line, the pointer (or I-beam, in this case) changes shapes as you move it, denoting a particular line alignment. This makes it very easy to center or right align the insertion point before you insert the text or other item.

Click and Type Option Must Be On To use Click and Type, you must also make sure that it (**Enable Click and Type** box) is selected on the **Edit** tab of the Options dialog box (select **Tools**, **Options** to open this dialog box).

CAUTION

To use the Click and Type feature, you must be in the Print Layout or Web Layout view. The feature is not available in the Normal view. To switch to the Print Layout or Web Layout view, select **View**, and then select the appropriate view from the View menu.

Then, to use Click and Type to align your new text, follow these steps:

1. Move the mouse pointer toward the area of the page where you want to place the insertion point. The pointer icon changes to

- Center (the centering pointer appears)

- Right (the align-right pointer appears)

2. After the mouse pointer shows the centering or right-align icon, double-click in the document. The insertion point moves to the selected justification.

3. Type your new text.

After you've typed the centered or right-aligned text and you've pressed **Enter** to create a new line, you can return to left justification by placing the mouse on the left of the line (the align-left icon appears on the mouse pointer) and double-clicking.

Automatically Detecting Formatting Inconsistencies

Word 2002 offers a new feature that marks formatting inconsistencies in your document. This allows you to make sure that the text in your document is formatted as you intended. The Detect Formatting feature keeps track of the formatting in your document and can also be configured to flag any formatting inconsistencies.

To configure the Detect Formatting feature to flag formatting inconsistencies, follow these steps:

1. Select **Tools**, and then select **Options**. The Options dialog box opens.

2. On the Options dialog box, select the **Edit** tab.

3. Under Editing options, select the **Keep track of Formatting** check box, if it is not already selected. Also select the **Mark Formatting Inconsistencies** check box.

4. Click **OK** to close the Options dialog box.

Now, formatting inconsistencies will be marked with a wavy blue line as you type. When you find a word or paragraph that has been flagged with the wavy blue line, right-click the word or paragraph. A shortcut menu appears as shown in Figure 5.4.

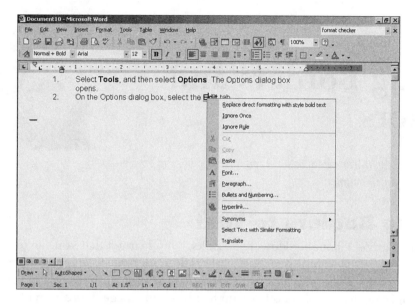

Figure 5.4 You can have formatting inconsistencies flagged in your documents.

Use the menu choices on the shortcut menu to either replace the direct formatting with an available style or ignore the direct formatting occurrence. To ignore this occurrence of the formatting, click **Ignore Once**. If you want all occurrences of the formatting that has been flagged by the Detect Formatting feature to be ignored in the document, click the **Ignore Rule** choice on the shortcut menu.

Be advised that the Detect Formatting feature doesn't always catch formatting errors. For example, if you have most of your text in a 12-point font, some font that you might have inadvertently formatted for 14 point won't necessarily be flagged. Word assumes you might be using the 14 point for a heading or other special text.

The Detect Formatting feature is best at detecting direct formatting changes that you have made to text in a document (such as directly adding bold to text, as shown in Figure 5.4), where other text that has been bolded has been formatted using a "bold" style that you created (styles are covered in Lesson 10, "Working with Styles"). The inconsistency that Word picks up on is that you didn't use the style to bold the item as you had done in the rest of the document.

Using Borders and Colors

In this lesson, you learn how to use borders and colors to emphasize text in your documents.

Adding Borders to Text

In Lesson 5, "Changing How Text Looks," you learned that you can use various font attributes, such as font size, bold, italic, and underline, to emphasize and otherwise denote certain text in your document. You also learned that alignment, such as centering, can be used to set off certain text lines on a page. Word provides you with the capability to add borders to your text and even place a shadow on the edge of a border for greater emphasis.

A border can be placed around any text paragraph (any line followed by a paragraph mark). This means that one line of text or several lines of text can have a border placed around them.

 TIP **¶** **Remember How Word Views a Paragraph** Whenever you type a line or several lines of text and then press Enter, you are placing an end-of-paragraph mark at the end of the text. Word views any line or lines followed by a paragraph mark as a separate paragraph. If you need to view the paragraph marks in your document, click the **Show/Hide** button on the Word Standard toolbar.

To place a border around a text paragraph, follow these steps:

1. Place the insertion point in the paragraph that you want to place the border around. If you want to place a border around multiple paragraphs, select all the paragraphs.
2. Select the **Format** menu, and then **Borders and Shading**. The Borders and Shading dialog box appears, as shown in Figure 6.1.
3. Make sure the **Borders** tab is selected on the dialog box. You are provided with several settings for how the border should appear around the text.

Click here to put a line over the text.

Click here to put a line under the text.

Click here to put a line to the right of the text.

Click here to put a line to the left of the text.

Figure 6.1 The Borders and Shading dialog box enables you to place a border around your text.

4. In the Setting area of the dialog box, select the type of box you want around your text: choose **Box, Shadow, 3-D**, or **Custom** by clicking the appropriate setting sample. The Custom option enables you to create a border that uses different line styles for the various sides of the border.

TIP **Removing a Border from a Paragraph** If you want to remove the border from a paragraph, choose **None** in the Setting area of the Borders and Shading dialog box.

5. Several line styles are available for your border. Click the **Style** scroll box to scroll through the various line styles, and then click the style you want to use.

6. To change the color of the border lines, click the **Color** drop-down arrow and select a color from the color palette that appears.

7. As you select the various parameters for your border (in cases where you have selected Box, Shadow, or 3-D as the border setting), you can view a preview of the border in the Preview box. The Preview box also makes it easy for you to place an incomplete border around a paragraph in cases where you might only want a line above or below the text (refer to Figure 6.1).

8. When you have finished selecting the settings for the border, click the **OK** button. The border appears around the paragraph or paragraphs in the document, as shown in Figure 6.2.

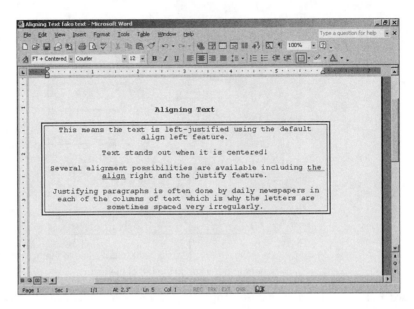

Figure 6.2 A border appears around the selected paragraph after you set the border parameters in the Borders and Shading dialog box.

Borders Around More Than One Paragraph If you select several paragraphs that are using the same style and indents, Word places one border around all the paragraphs. If you want separate borders around the paragraphs, assign a border to them one at a time. For more discussion about indents, see Lesson 7, "Working with Tabs and Indents." You can find more information about styles in Lesson 9, "Working with Margins, Pages, and Line Spacing."

CAUTION

You also can quickly place a border around a paragraph or other selected text by using the Tables and Borders toolbar. Right-click anywhere on one of the currently shown toolbars and select **Tables and Borders** from the toolbar list. The Tables and Borders toolbar appears in the document window. Figure 6.3 shows the Tables and Borders toolbar.

To apply a border to a paragraph, make sure the insertion point is in the paragraph, and then click the **Borders** drop-down button on the Tables and Borders toolbar. From the border list provided, select the type of border you want to place around the text.

Figure 6.3 You can add borders to selected text using the Tables and Borders toolbar.

Placing a Border Around a Page

If you find that you would like to place a border around an entire page or pages in your document, you need to use the Page Border feature.

Follow these steps to place a border around the entire page:

1. Open the Borders and Shading dialog box (click the **Format** menu and select **Borders and Shading**) and click the **Page Border** tab (see Figure 6.4).

Figure 6.4 Borders can be placed around an entire page.

2. Select the **Border** setting and style as you would for a paragraph border.

3. Click the **Apply To** list drop-down arrow and select one of the following:

- **Whole Document**—Places a border around each page in the document.
- **This Section**—Places a border around each page in the current section of the document.

- **This Section-First Page Only**—Places a border around the first page of the current section.

- **This Section-All Except First Page**—Places a border around each page of the current section except the first page of the section.

To put a border around pages in a section, you must place sections in your document. Sections enable you to break a large document into smaller parts that can have radically different formatting attributes. For more about sections and how to create them, see Lesson 20, "Working with Larger Documents."

Section A portion of a document that has been defined as a discrete part. Each section can then have different formatting and even headers and footers defined for the section.

Adding Shading to the Paragraph

You can place a color or a grayscale pattern behind the text in a paragraph or paragraphs. This color or pattern is called shading and can be used with or without a border around the text.

To add shading to text, you must select the text for a particular paragraph—just make sure the insertion point is in the paragraph. After you've designated the text that you want to place the shading behind, follow these steps:

1. Select **Format, Borders and Shading**. The Borders and Shading dialog box appears.

2. Select the **Shading** tab, as shown in Figure 6.5.

Figure 6.5   You can apply shading to a paragraph or selected text.

3. To select a fill color, click one of the colors on the color palette in the **Fill** area.

4. To select a pattern for the fill color, click the **Style** drop-down arrow and select a pattern from the list.

5. Use the **Apply To** drop-down arrow to designate whether the current paragraph or selected text should be shaded.

6. When you have completed your selections, click **OK**.

Your selected text or paragraph will now be shaded.

 TIP   **Take Advantage of More Colors**   If the color you want to use is not shown on the Shading tab, click the **More Colors** button. This opens the Colors dialog box, which provides a huge number of colors on a color palette. You can even click the **Custom** tab on this dialog box and mix your own custom colors.

Changing Font Colors

When using the shading options, you might find that the current text color does not show up that well on the fill color or pattern that you selected. You can quickly change the font color for selected text anywhere in your document.

To change the color of text, follow these steps:

1. Select the text that you want to change to a different font color.

2. Select the **Format** menu and select **Font**. The Font dialog box appears.

3. In the Font dialog box, click the **Font Color** drop-down arrow and select the color you want to use (Word automatically defaults to black-colored fonts because this is typically what you use in business documents that you print).

4. When you have completed your selection, click **OK**.

You might find that you have to play around with the fill color and the font color to get an ideal combination on the page. You might even have to print out a sample page to see whether the colors work well on a printed page. Intensity of color typically varies between color printers. You might also find that by bolding the text that you've placed on top of a fill color, the text becomes more readable.

Working with Tabs and Indents

In this lesson, you learn how to set and use tabs and indents in your documents.

Aligning Text with Tabs

Although the left and right alignment of text in your document is governed by the margins set in the document, there are times when you want to align the text to emphasize a list of items or otherwise offset text from the rest of the items on the page. In Lesson 5, "Changing How Text Looks," you worked with centering and justification as a way to change the alignment of text. Another way to align text in a document is to use tabs. Tabs are set every half inch by default in a new document. Every time you press the Tab key on the keyboard, you offset the text line from the left margin one tab stop.

You can use tab stops to align text lines in columns. Word gives you complete control over where the tab stops are set in your document. Word also provides different tabs that enable you to align text in different ways:

- **Left Tab**—Aligns the beginning of the text line at the tab stop
- **Center Tab**—Centers the text line at the tab stop
- **Right Tab**—Right-aligns the text line at the tab stop
- **Decimal Tab**—Lines up numerical entries at their decimal point

Each of these tab types makes it easy for you to create lists that are offset from other text elements in the document. Your tab stops fall between the left and right margins on each page of the document. Each paragraph in the document can potentially have a different set of tab stops with different kinds of tabs set at the stops.

One way to set tabs in your document is using the Tabs dialog box. Select the **Format** menu, and then select **Tabs**. The Tabs dialog box requires that you specify a tab position in the Tab stop position box (the position you specify is the number of inches from the left margin); use the spinner box arrows to specify the position for the tab or type a position directly in the box.

After the tab stop position is set, click the appropriate Alignment option button to select the type of tab you want to create at the tab stop (see Figure 7.1). If you want to have a leader (a repeating element, such as a dash), fill the empty space to the left of the tab stop and select one of the leader option buttons in the Leader box. After you have specified a position and a tab type (and an optional leader), add the tab by clicking **Set**.

As you create the tabs, they will appear in the Tabs list on the left of the dialog box. If you want to remove a particular tab from the list, select it, and then click the **Clear** button. If you want to clear all the tabs listed (and start over), click the **Clear All** button.

Figure 7.1   You can set and remove tab stops in the Tabs dialog box.

After you have finished setting your tabs, click **OK**. Although you can certainly set all the tabs for a document or section in the Tabs dialog box, it is not necessarily the best place to quickly set the tabs for your documents. It does not really provide you with a visual display of how the tabs will look in the document. However, if you are creating tabs that include leading characters (such as dot leaders often seen in a table of contents) and you want to precisely set the tab positions to previously determined settings, the Tabs dialog box gives you complete control over all the settings.

Setting Tabs on the Ruler

An excellent alternative to setting tabs in the Tabs dialog box is to use the Word Ruler and actually set the tabs on the Ruler itself. This enables you to visually check the position of the tab stops and makes it easy for you to change the type of tab at a particular tab stop and delete unwanted tabs.

To view the Ruler in the Word document window, select **View**, and then **Ruler**. The Ruler appears at the top of your document.

TIP **Quickly View the Ruler** If the Ruler is not displayed in the Word window, place the mouse pointer at the top of your current document, below the toolbars. If you wait for just a moment, the Ruler drops down onto the document. This allows you to view current tab settings. When you remove the mouse, the Ruler folds up.

To set a tab on the Ruler, click the **Tab** button on the far left of the Ruler to select the tab type (Left, Center, Right, or Decimal). Each time you click the Tab button, you are cycled to the next tab type. If you go past the type of tab you want to set, keep clicking until the tab type appears on the Tab button.

After you have the appropriate tab type selected on the Tab button, place the mouse pointer on the ruler where you want to create the tab stop. Click the mouse and the tab is placed on the ruler. It's that simple.

Figure 7.2 shows the Ruler with each of the tab types set. The figure also shows how text aligns at each of the tab types.

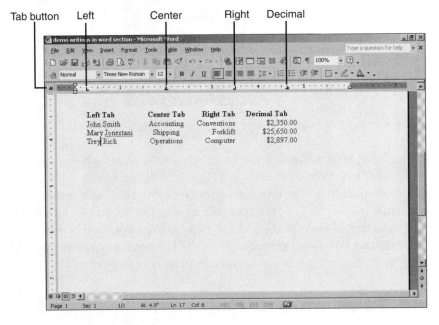

Figure 7.2 Setting tabs on the Ruler allows you to view their position and type.

TIP **Moving or Removing Tabs** If you want to delete a tab on the Ruler, use the mouse to drag the tab off the Ruler. If you need to reposition a particular tab, drag it to a new location on the Ruler.

CAUTION

I Adjust the Tabs but It Works for Only One Line   Remember that Word treats each line followed by a paragraph mark as a separate paragraph. When you adjust the tab positioning on the ruler, it affects only the paragraph containing the insertion point. To adjust the tabs for several paragraphs, select all the lines (or the entire document if you want) and then adjust the tabs on the Ruler.

Working with Indents

Although tabs enable you to align text at various tab stops on the Ruler, you might want to indent or offset lines and paragraphs from the left or right margins. Word provides different indent settings that indent the text at a particular setting on the Ruler.

TERM

Indent   The offset of a particular paragraph or line of text from the left or right margin.

The easiest way to indent a paragraph from the left margin is to use the **Increase Indent** button on the Formatting toolbar. Place the insertion point in the paragraph you want to indent, and then click the **Increase Indent** button on the toolbar. Remember that you can also use the Click and Type feature for left indents (see the previous lesson, "Using Borders and Colors").

Each time you click the button, you are increasing the indent one-half inch. You can also decrease the left indent on a particular paragraph. Click the **Decrease Indent** button on the Formatting toolbar.

Setting Indents on the Ruler

You can also indent a paragraph from both the left and right margins using the Ruler. The Ruler has a left and right indent marker on the far left and far right, respectively (see Figure 7.3).

To indent a paragraph from the left margin, use the mouse to drag the **Left Indent** marker to the appropriate position. Grab the marker at the very bottom, because the top of the marker is the First Line indent marker. These two markers separate if you don't grab both markers together at the bottom. You can also indent a paragraph from the right margin using the Right Indent marker. Slide the marker to the appropriate position on the ruler to create your indent.

Left Indent marker

First Line Indent marker   Right Indent marker

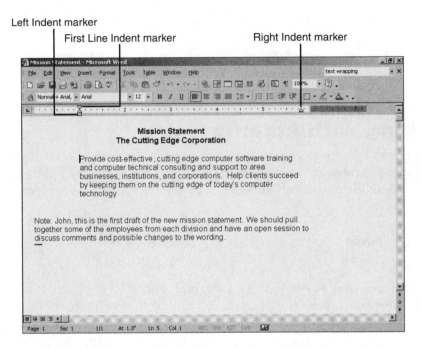

Figure 7.3   The Left Indent and Right Indent markers can be used to indent paragraphs from the left and right margins, respectively.

Creating Hanging Indents

The hanging indent is a special kind of indent. With this type of indent, the text (a single line or multiple lines) that wraps under the first line of the paragraph is indented more than the first line. Hanging indents are created by separating the First Line Indent marker from the Left Indent marker on the ruler.

To create a hanging indent, follow these steps:

1. Place the insertion point in the paragraph that you want to indent.

2. Drag the **Left Indent marker** (drag it by the square bottom of the marker) to the position where you want to indent the second and subsequent lines of the paragraph.

3. Drag the **First Line Indent marker** (drag it by the top of the marker) back to the position where you want the first line to begin.

Figure 7.4 shows a paragraph with a hanging indent. You can increase or decrease the offset between the first line and the rest of the paragraph by dragging either the

First Line Marker or the Left Indent Marker. If you prefer to enter numerical information for your hanging indents, choose the **Indents and Spacing** tab (select **Format** menu and then **Paragraph**) and in the **Special** list under **Indentation**, select **Hanging**. Then, set the amount of space for the hanging indent in the **By** box.

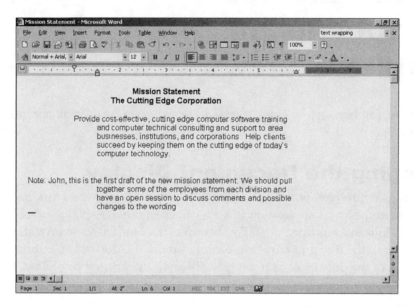

Figure 7.4 Hanging indents enable you to offset the indent on the first line of a paragraph and the remainder of the paragraph.

Examining Your Documents in Different Views

In this lesson, you learn how to examine your document using the different document displays offered in Word.

Changing the Document Display

Word provides you with several viewing possibilities as you work on your documents in the Word application window. Each of these display modes provides a different look at your document. For example, the Normal view provides you with a look at all the font and paragraph formatting in the document, but does not give you a view of the document as it would appear on the printed page. Instead, the Print Layout view supplies this viewpoint.

Using the different document views to your advantage can help you visualize and create great-looking documents in Word. Special views are even supplied for creating outlines and creating Web pages in Word. You take advantage of these different views using the View menu. Table 8.1 shows the various views available to you and describes, in general terms, what they are best used for.

Table 8.1   The Word Views

View	Typical Use
Normal	Use for general word processing tasks.
Web Layout	Use for designing HTML documents and viewing Web pages.
Print Layout	Use for document layout and documents containing graphics and embedded or linked objects.
Outline	Use to view document as an outline.
Full Screen	Use when you want to use the entire screen to view the document and avoid seeing the toolbars and other marginal information.

The Normal View

The Normal view provides you with a view that is perfect for most word processing tasks. It is the default view for Word; to change to the Normal view (from any of the other views), select **View**, and then **Normal**.

 Switch to Normal with a Click You can also change from view to view in Word using the View toolbar in the lower-left corner of the Word window. To go to the Normal view, click the **Normal** icon.

This view displays character and paragraph formatting that you place in the document (see Figure 8.1). Normal view, however, does not display the document headers and footers or show graphics in the document as they will print. Also, items created using the Drawing toolbar are not displayed in the Normal view.

In the Normal view, you see the following:

- Page breaks appear as dashed lines.
- Headers and footers are displayed in a header/footer-editing pane (when **Header and Footer** is selected on the **View** menu). Only the header or footer can be edited at this point.
- Footnotes and endnotes are displayed in a footnote or endnote editing pane (when **Footnotes** is selected on the **View** menu). Only the footnote or endnote can be edited at this point.
- Margins and column borders are not displayed in this view.

Web Layout View

The Web Layout view is perfect for designing *HTML* documents that you want to use as Web pages. The Web Layout view displays your document as it would appear in your Web browser window. To switch to the Web Layout view, select **View**, and then **Web Layout**.

 HTML Hypertext Markup Language—This document format is used for the creation of Web pages for the World Wide Web. The special document format is read using a Web browser or some other application (such as Word) that can display HTML documents.

In the Web Layout view, text is wrapped to fit in the window and graphics are placed as they will appear online. Any backgrounds present on the page are also seen in this view. Figure 8.2 shows a Web page in the Web Layout view.

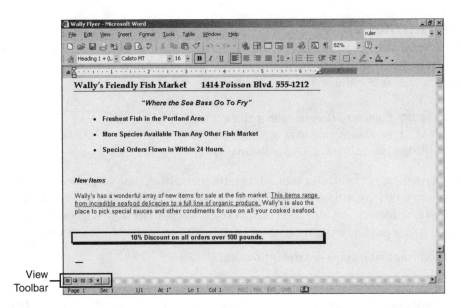

Figure 8.1 The Normal view shows all the formatting in the document but does not show graphics, margins, and other special elements as they will appear on the printed page.

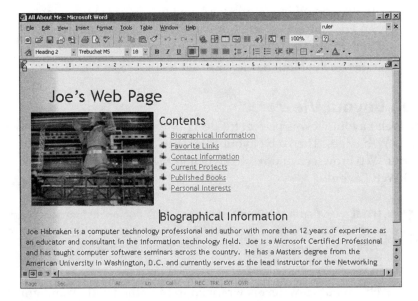

Figure 8.2 The Web Layout view allows you to look at and edit your HTML documents as they will appear in a Web browser.

TIP **Switch to Web Layout View Quickly**   To switch to the Web Layout view, click the **Web Layout** icon on the **View** toolbar.

The Web Layout view is the perfect view for designing your personal Web pages or for viewing Web pages using the Web Page Wizard (for more about Word and the Web, see Lesson 21, "Creating Web Pages in Word").

Print Layout View

The Print Layout view shows your document exactly as it will appear on the printed page. Working in this view allows you to fine-tune your document and work with graphic placement and text formatting as you prepare your document for printing.

To switch to the Print Layout view, select **View, Print Layout**. This view enables you to view headers, footers, footnotes, endnotes, and the margins in your document. Graphics are also positioned and sized as they will appear on the printed page. Figure 8.3 shows the same document that appeared earlier in Figure 8.1. Notice that in the Page Layout view, the margins of the document and (more importantly) a graphic in the document appears.

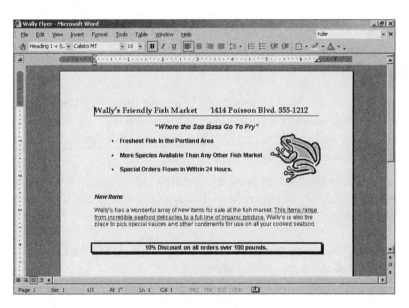

Figure 8.3   The Print Layout view enables you to fine-tune your document for printing.

TIP **Switch to Print Layout View Quickly**   To switch to the Print Layout view, click the **Print Layout** icon on the **View** toolbar.

Outline View

The Outline view allows you to create and edit your document in an outline format. Using the Word built-in heading styles is the key to creating the document in this view (for more about styles, see Lesson 9, "Working with Margins, Pages, and Line Spacing"). Each heading (Heading 1, 2, 3, and so on) is treated as a different level in the outline. For example, a heading assigned the Heading 1 style would be a Level 1 heading in the outline. You can promote and demote headings using the appropriate buttons on the Outline toolbar (a special toolbar that appears when you are in Outline view).

The Outline toolbar also provides an Outline Levels drop-down box that allows you to quickly change the level of the text where the insertion point currently resides. These levels coincide with different styles used by the outline feature. For example, Level 1 is equivalent to the Heading 1 style.

You can also collapse and expand the outline to better organize your document. Collapsing the document to all Level 1 Headings allows you to ignore the body text in the document and concentrate on the overall organization of the document.

TIP **Move a Heading and Associated Text**   You can drag a heading to a new position, and the subheading and body text associated with the heading move to the new position as well. This makes it very easy for you to reorganize the text in your document.

To change to the Outline view, select **View**, and then click **Outline**. You can easily select a heading and the text that is subordinate to it by clicking the hollow plus symbol (+) to the left of the text (see Figure 8.4). After the text is selected, it can be dragged to a new position.

When you have finished creating and editing a document in the Outline view, you can switch to any of the other views (such as the Print Layout view) to see your document in a more typical format.

TIP **Switch to Outline View Quickly**   To switch to the Outline view, click the **Outline** icon on the **View** toolbar.

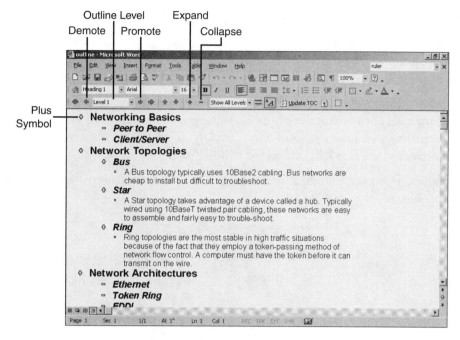

Figure 8.4   The Outline view makes it very easy to organize your document by collapsing and expanding different levels.

Using the Full Screen View

In situations where you want to concentrate on the text and other items in your document, it is great to be able to clear all the visual clutter from the screen (toolbars, scrollbars, and other Word tools) and view only your document. For example, you might be proofreading a particular page and want to place as much of the page's text on the screen as you can. You can switch to a view where your document occupies all the space available on the screen. Select **View**, **Full Screen**.

You can still add or edit the text in your document when you are in the Full Screen view. You can also quickly return to the previous view you were using (such as Normal view or Print Layout view) before you switched to the Full Screen view. Click the **Close Full Screen** box that appears in the document window and you return to the previous view.

Zooming In and Out on Your Document

You can use the Zoom command to zoom in and out on your documents. This allows you to increase the magnification of items on the page, such as small fonts, or allows you to step back (zoom out) from the document to view its general layout.

You can use Zoom in any of the Word views. In Normal, Web Layout, and Outline views, the effect of zooming in or out just changes the magnification of the onscreen elements. When you use Zoom on the Print Layout view, you get a very good look at how the document is laid out on the printed page.

To zoom in or out on your current document, select **View, Zoom**. The Zoom dialog box appears (see Figure 8.5).

Figure 8.5   The Zoom dialog box can be used to change the current zoom level of your document.

A series of option buttons is used to change the zoom setting for the current document. When you click a particular option button (such as the **200%** option button), you see a preview of this magnification in the Preview box.

You can also set a custom zoom level in the **Percent** box. Use the click arrows in the box to increase or decrease the current Zoom percentage. When you have selected the zoom level for the current document, click **OK**.

TIP   **View Multiple Pages on Your Screen**   When you are in the Print Layout view, you can use the Zoom dialog box to view two or more pages at the same time. Click the **Many Pages** option button (when in Zoom option), and then click the **Computer** icon below the option button. Drag over the page boxes to select the number of pages you want to display, and then click **OK**.

You can also quickly change the zoom level in your current document using the Zoom drop-down box on the Word Standard toolbar. Click the drop-down arrow on the **Zoom** box and select the appropriate zoom level. If you want to set a custom zoom level, select the current zoom percentage on the Zoom box, and then type your own value.

Working with the Document Map

The Document Map view is somewhat similar to the Outline view in that it gives you a quick reference to the overall structure of your document. A special pane appears in the document window (on the left) that shows the headings in your document. The Document Map can be used to quickly move from one area of a document to another by clicking the appropriate heading.

To open the Document Map, select **View**, **Document Map**; the map pane appears in the document window (see Figure 8.6). You can change the width of the document map pane by placing the mouse on the border between the pane and your document. The mouse arrow changes to a sizing tool—a double-headed arrow. Drag the sizing tool to create a custom document map width.

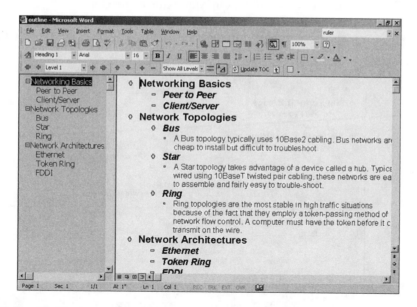

Figure 8.6 The Document Map view makes it easy to jump to a particular part of a document by clicking the appropriate heading.

The document map pane is available in any of the Word views. When you want to close the Document Map, select **View**, and then **Document Map** to deselect it.

Splitting the Document Window

Another useful way to view your documents is to split the current document window into two panes. This allows you to view the same document in both panes, which is particularly useful when you want to view two different parts of the same document.

You can use the two panes to drag and drop information from one part of a document into another. Remember that changes you make in either of the split panes will affect the document.

To split the document screen into two panes, select **Window**, **Split**. A horizontal split appears across the document window. Notice that as you move the mouse in the document window, the split bar moves with it. Place the mouse where you want to split the document window, and then click the left mouse button.

A set of vertical and horizontal scrollbars appears for each pane in the split window (see Figure 8.7). Use the scrollbars in each pane as needed.

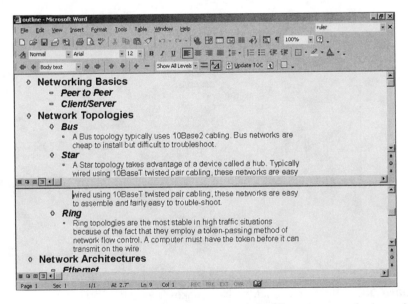

Figure 8.7   You can split the document screen to view different areas of a long document.

When you have finished working in the split document window, select **Window**, and then **Remove Split**. The splitter bar is removed from the document.

 TIP   **Split a Window Using the Splitter Bar**   You can split a document window by manually dragging the splitter bar down into the document window. Place the mouse just above the Up arrow on the vertical scrollbar on the splitter bar. Your mouse becomes a splitter sizing tool. Drag to split the window as needed, and then click the mouse to set the bar.

Working with Margins, Pages, and Line Spacing

In this lesson, you learn how to set margins, insert page breaks into your documents, and control line spacing and line breaks in your documents.

Setting Margins

Margins control the amount of whitespace between your text and the edge of a printed page. Four margins—Left, Right, Top, and Bottom—can be set for your pages. The default margin settings for documents based on the Word Normal template are shown in Table 9.1.

Table 9.1   Default Margin Settings for the Normal Template

Margin	Setting (in Inches)
Left	1.25
Right	1.25
Top	1
Bottom	1

You can change any of the margin settings for your document or a portion of your document at any time. The Page Setup dialog box provides you with access to all these margin settings. You also have control over how your margins affect the layout of multiple pages in a document. For example, you can set up your pages to be laid out in book folio fashion (two pages arranged horizontally on each piece of paper) or two pages per sheet arranged vertically.

To change the margin settings for your document, follow these steps:

1. Select **File**, **Page Setup**. The Page Setup dialog box appears as shown in Figure 9.1.

Figure 9.1 Use the Margins tab of the Page Setup dialog box to set your document margins and arrange them on multiple pages if necessary.

TIP **Margins Can Be Different for Different Parts of the Document** You can set different margin settings for different portions of your document. The easiest way to do this is to divide your document into sections. Each section can then have a different set of margins. For information on creating sections in your documents, see Lesson 20, "Working with Larger Documents."

2. Click the **Margins** tab if necessary. Use the click arrows in the **Top, Bottom, Left,** or **Right** margin boxes to increase or decrease the current setting. Or double-click in any of the boxes and type in a new value.

CAUTION **Maximum and Minimum Margins** Be advised that your printer defines the minimum margins for a page. For example, most inkjet printers limit you to a minimum top and bottom margins of .25" and .5", respectively, and left and right margins of .25". If you set margins less than the minimum, a dialog box appears when you close the Page Setup dialog box, letting you know that your margins are outside the printable area of the page. Click the **Fix** button on this dialog box to set the margins to the minimum for your printer. For maximum margins, Word notifies you via a dialog box if you select margins that overlap or negate any usable space on the page.

3. After you have selected the new margin settings, you can apply the margins to the entire document, to a section of the document (this option is available only if you have more than one section in the document), or to the document from the current page forward in the document. Using the last choice allows you to have different margin settings in the same document without requiring you to divide the document into sections (for more about sections, see Lesson 20). Click the **Apply To** drop-down box and select **Whole Document** (the default setting), **This Point Forward**, or **This Section** (if available).

4. After you have finished selecting your new margin settings and the amount of the document that they will affect, click **OK**.

TIP **Set a Gutter for Bound Documents** If your document will be bound (left or top) or placed into a three-ring notebook, set a value in the Gutter box to provide extra space for the binding or punch holes. Setting the **Mirror Margins** (under multiple pages) ensures that margins on facing pages are similar.

The new margins take effect in your document. The best way to view how these margins will look when you print the document is to switch to the Print Layout view (if you are not already in this view). Select **View**, **Print Layout**. The margins you've selected appear on the top, left, right, and bottom of your document in the Word document window.

When you are in the Print Layout view, you can also adjust the margins in your document using the Ruler. To view the Ruler, select **View**, **Ruler**. The vertical ruler is visible in the Print Layout View only.

In the Print Layout view, horizontal and vertical rulers appear in the document window. The margins appear as shaded areas on the edge of the respective ruler. For example, the left margin is a gray-shaded area on the left side of the horizontal ruler (see Figure 9.2).

TIP **Open the Page Setup Dialog Box Using the Ruler** Double-click any of the margins shown on the vertical or horizontal ruler. This opens the Page Setup dialog box.

To adjust a margin, place the mouse pointer between the gray margin and the white document area on the ruler. A margin-sizing arrow appears. Drag the gray margin to increase or decrease the respective margin. Figure 9.2 shows the margin-sizing arrow on the top margin on the vertical ruler.

Figure 9.2 Drag the respective margin-sizing arrow to increase or decrease a margin.

Controlling Paper Types and Orientation

Other page attributes that you need to control in your documents are the paper size and the page orientation. Word's default settings assume that you will print to paper that is a standard 8.5 by 11 inches. The default page orientation is portrait, meaning that the maximum distance from the left edge to the right edge of the page is 8.5 inches.

You can select different paper sizes, which is particularly important if you want to print to envelopes or a different paper size, such as legal-size paper. You can also change the orientation of your text and images as they appear on a page from portrait to landscape, where the page contents are rotated so that the distance between the left and right edges on a standard sheet of paper would be 11 inches.

Paper size and page orientation are both set in the Page Setup dialog box. Follow these steps to edit the settings for these page attributes:

1. Select **File**, **Page Setup**. The Page Setup dialog box opens.
2. Click the **Paper** tab on the dialog box (see Figure 9.3).

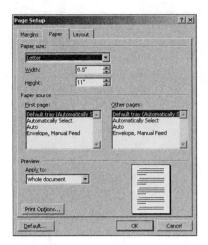

Figure 9.3   The Paper tab of the Page Setup dialog box enables you to set your paper size and source.

3. To select a new paper size, click the **Paper Size** drop-down box and select the paper type. For nonstandard paper sizes, select **Custom Size** in the **Page Size** box, and then type the paper's width into the **Width** box and its height into the **Height** box.

4. To change the orientation of the page to portrait or landscape, select the **Margins** tab and click the **Portrait** or the **Landscape** option button as needed (refer to Figure 9.1).

5. Finally, in the Apply To drop-down box, select **Whole Document** to apply the new settings to the new document or **This Point Forward** to apply the settings to the document from the current page forward.

6. When you complete editing the settings, click **OK**.

Inserting Page Breaks

As you create your document, Word automatically starts a new page when you fill the current page with text or other document items (such as graphics, tables, and so on). However, you can insert your own page breaks in the document as needed. These types of page breaks are often referred to as *hard*, or manual, page breaks.

To insert a page break into your document, follow these steps:

1. Place the insertion point in the document where you want to force a page break.

2. Select **Insert, Break**. The Break dialog box appears.

3. Make sure the Page Break option button is selected, and then click **OK**.

A page break is placed in your document. In the Normal view, the page break appears as a dashed line across the page, with "Page Break" denoted at the center of the line. In the Print Layout view, you can move to the new page by clicking the **Next Page** button on the bottom of the vertical scrollbar.

 TIP **Use the Keyboard to Place a Page Break** You can also place a page break in your document using the keyboard. Hold down the **Ctrl** key, and then press the **Enter** key.

To remove a page break, switch to the Normal view (select **View, Normal**). The page break appears as a dotted line in the document and is denoted as a "page break." Select the page break with a mouse and press **Delete** to remove it.

Changing Line Spacing

Another setting that greatly influences the amount of whitespace on the page is line spacing. When you consider whether you want your text single-spaced or double-spaced, those text attributes are controlled by changing the line spacing.

Line spacing can be set for each paragraph in the document or for selected text. Setting line spacing for a blank document allows you to set a default line spacing for all text paragraphs that will be placed in the document.

To set the line spacing for a new document, a paragraph, or selected text, follow these steps:

1. Select **Format, Paragraph**. The Paragraph dialog box appears (see Figure 9.4).

2. Make sure the **Indents and Spacing** tab on the dialog box is selected.

3. To change the line spacing, click the **Line Spacing** drop-down box and select one of the following choices:

- **Single**—Spacing accommodates the largest font size found on the lines and adds a small amount of whitespace (depending on the font used) between lines.
- **1.5**—The line spacing is 1 and 1/2 times greater than single spacing.
- **Double**—Twice the size of single line spacing.
- **At Least**—(The default setting) line spacing adjusts to accommodate the largest font on the line and special items, such as graphics.

Figure 9.4   The Paragraph dialog box allows you to control the line spacing in your text.

- **Exactly**—All lines are equally spaced, and special font sizes or items such as graphics are not accommodated. These items, if larger than the setting used here, appear cut off in the text. You can still accommodate these items by using the Multiple box described next to shift all the text lines to a higher spacing percentage that accommodates special items.

- **Multiple**—You specify the line spacing by a particular percentage. This feature is used in conjunction with the Exactly option to set a line spacing percentage that accommodates special font sizes or graphics found in the document. For example, if you want to decrease the line spacing by 20%, you enter the number 0.8. To increase the line spacing by 50%, you enter 1.5.

4. The **Line Spacing** option selected in step 3 is influenced by the point size entered in the **At** box (this applies only when you have selected At Least, Exactly, or Multiple). Use the click arrows to increase or decrease the point size of the line spacing, if needed.

TIP   **Set Spacing Before and After a Paragraph**—You can also set special spacing **Before** and **After** a particular paragraph. This is particularly useful for headings or other special text items.

5. When you complete setting the line spacing parameters, click **OK**.

If you find that you don't like the new line spacing settings for a particular paragraph, click the **Undo** button on the Standard toolbar to reverse the changes that you have made.

Working with Styles

In this lesson, you learn how to create text and paragraph styles. You also learn how to edit your styles and take advantage of the styles in the Style Gallery.

Understanding Styles

Word styles provide an excellent way to manage the character and paragraph formatting in a document. A *style* is a grouping of formatting attributes identified by a style name. You can create styles for text that contain character-formatting attributes such as bold, italic, or a particular font size; these types of styles are called *character styles*. You can also create styles for paragraphs that include paragraph attributes, such as alignment information, indents, and line spacing; this type of style is called a *paragraph style*.

You view the style names in the Styles and Formatting task pane (see Figure 10.1). To open the Styles and Formatting task pane, select the **Format** command, and then click **Styles and Formatting**.

Figure 10.1 The Styles and Formatting task pane is the starting place for creating, editing, and managing the styles and formatting in your documents.

TIP **Select Styles and Formatting at the Touch of a Button** The easiest way to access the Styles and Formatting task pane is to use the **Styles and Formatting** button on the Formatting toolbar.

Word includes several built-in styles, such as the headings, that you can take advantage of in your documents. Styles are particularly useful because if you use them to format text or paragraphs in the document, you can change the attributes saved in the style at any time. These changes immediately take effect on all the text that has been assigned that style.

Updating the look of text or the layout of paragraphs by editing a style allows you to quickly edit the look of text in your document. Using styles also provides you with a way to make certain categories of text, such as headings or figure captions, look uniform throughout the document without having to assign each of them character or paragraph attributes individually.

CAUTION **Paragraph Styles Versus Text Styles** Paragraph styles (the more commonly used option) assign both character and paragraph attributes to the paragraph containing the insertion point. Text styles affect only the word or words you select before you apply the style.

Creating Text Styles

Creating text styles is extremely easy. Select the text you want to emphasize with special character formatting and assign it all the character attributes (font type, bold, underline, italic, and so on) that you want to include in the style. You may assign the attributes using either the Font dialog box (by selecting **Format**, **Font**) or the appropriate buttons on the Formatting toolbar. Fonts are covered in Lesson 5, "Changing How Text Looks."

Make sure that the desired text is selected, and then follow these steps to create the style:

1. Select the **Styles and Formatting** task pane and then **New Style**; the New Style dialog box appears.

2. Click the **Style Type** drop-down box and select **Character** for the style type.

3. Look in the Formatting of Selected Text area of the Styles and Formatting task pane. Here you can see the text attributes that you have assigned to your selected text. Note that the new style is based on the current style (the default paragraph style or the normal style) plus your added attributes.

4. Type a name for your new style into the Name box.

5. Click **OK** to conclude the style creation process. You are returned to the Styles and Formatting task pane. Notice that your new style now appears in the Pick Formatting to Apply list in the task pane.

You can now assign the new character style to text in your document as needed. Simply select the text to which you want to assign this unique style, and then select the **Styles and Formatting** task pane. Select your unique style from the list provided. The style is applied to the selected text.

 TIP **View All the Text Assigned a Particular Style** If you would like to select all the different text items that you assigned a particular style, select the style in the Styles and Formatting task pane, and then click the Select All button.

Creating Paragraph Styles

Creating paragraph styles is similar to creating text styles. Apply to a paragraph the formatting that you want to include in the style (you can use alignment settings, indents, and all the paragraph attributes that you are familiar with). Make sure that the insertion point is in the paragraph, and then follow these steps to create the style:

1. Select the **Styles and Formatting** task pane, and then **New Style**; the New Style dialog box appears.

2. Click the **Style Type** drop-down box and select **Paragraph** for the style type.

3. Type a unique name into the **Name** box for the style.

4. Click **OK** to return to the Styles and Formatting task pane. The style is now available on the Style list. You can now apply the style to any paragraph in the document by placing the insertion point in the paragraph.

Editing Styles

You can also edit or modify the attributes found in any of your styles or the default styles in the document. You edit styles using the Styles and Formatting task pane. Remember that when you edit a style, all the text to which the style was applied reflects the new text and paragraph attributes of your edited style.

To edit a style, follow these steps:

1. Select the **Styles and Formatting** task pane.

2. Under **Pick Formatting to Apply**, select the style you want to edit and place the mouse pointer on it until you see the box outline and down arrow appear.

Then, click the down arrow and press **Modify**. The Modify Style dialog box appears as shown in Figure 10.2.

Figure 10.2 The Modify Style dialog box allows you to edit the name of a style and modify all the attributes found in the style.

3. To modify the style, select the **Format** button. A menu appears, allowing you to modify the following attributes in the style:

- Font
- Paragraph
- Tabs
- Borders
- Language
- Frame
- Numbering

4. Select one of the choices provided in the Format box. The appropriate dialog box appears, allowing you to edit the settings for the chosen attributes. For example, if you want to modify the font attributes for the style, click the **Format** arrow and select **Font** from the list provided. The Font dialog box appears.

5. When you have finished modifying the Font attributes for the style (or for whichever style type you chose to modify), click **OK**. You are returned to the **Modify Style** dialog box.

6. Modify other attributes of the style as needed by making the appropriate choices from the menus.

7. When you have completed your style modifications, click **OK** in the Modify Style dialog box and you return to the task pane with the changes made.

> **TIP** **You Can Delete Unwanted Styles** You can delete styles that you've created that you no longer need. Open the **Styles and Formatting** task pane and place the mouse pointer on the style in the **Pick Formatting to Apply** list. Wait for the box outline and down arrow to appear, and then click the **Delete** button under the down arrow. The style is removed from the Style list.

Using the Style Organizer

Word also has the capability to copy styles from other documents and templates into your current document. This provides you with an easy way to add already existing styles to a document (rather than reinventing the wheel or style).

To copy styles from another document or template, follow these steps:

1. Select the **Tools** command, and then choose **Templates and Add-Ins**.

2. In the Templates and Add-Ins dialog box, click the **Organizer** button. The Organizer dialog box appears as shown in Figure 10.3.

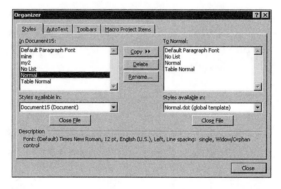

Figure 10.3 The Organizer dialog box makes it easy for you to copy a style or styles from one document to another.

3. The styles in the current document appear on the left side of the Organizer dialog box. Styles in the template that your current document was based on are shown on the right side of the Organizer dialog box (all documents are based on a template, even if it is just the Word Normal template). To close the template file on the right side of the dialog box, click the **Close File** button (in Figure 10.3, click **Close File** under the Normal.dot template on the right of the dialog box).

4. Now you can open a new template or document and copy the styles that it contains to the current document (shown on the left of the dialog box). Click **Open File** on the right side of the Organizer dialog box. Locate the document or template from which you want to copy the styles. Double-click the file in the Open dialog box to open the file.

5. You are returned to the Organizer dialog box, and the styles for the recently opened template or document are listed on the right side of the dialog box. To copy a style or styles, select the style and click the **Copy** button. The style is copied to the styles in your current document.

TIP **Copy More Than One Style at a Time** To select several styles to copy to your document simultaneously, click the first style you want to copy and then hold down the **Shift** key and click the last style you want to copy. All the styles in between these two are also selected. To select styles that are not in a series, click the first style you want to copy, and then hold down the **Ctrl** key and click any other styles you want to select.

6. When you have finished copying styles (styles can be copied from either of the documents in the Organizer dialog box), click **Close** to close the Organizer dialog box.

As you can see, the Organizer makes it very easy for you to share the styles that you create between your documents. Remember, styles that you create reside only in the document where you create them. The only way to copy those styles to another document is to use the Style Organizer.

Using AutoFormatting to Change Text Attributes

In this lesson, you learn how to quickly change the look of your text with AutoFormat and apply text attributes automatically as you type.

Understanding AutoFormatting

AutoFormat is a great feature that helps you create professional-looking documents. AutoFormatting actually examines the text elements that you have placed in your document (such as headings, tables, lists, regular body text, and other items) and then automatically formats these elements using an appropriate Word style. Even though this formatting is automatic, you can accept or reject the changes AutoFormatting makes. You can also make additional changes to the document as you see fit by using other styles or font and paragraph formatting attributes (for more about styles, see Lesson 10, "Working with Styles").

You will also find that AutoFormat does more than just apply styles to your document elements. It can remove extra line breaks between paragraphs and apply the hyperlink styles to e-mail addresses or Web addresses that you place in your documents.

You can use AutoFormat in two ways. You can turn on AutoFormatting so that items are formatted as you type, or you can create a new document and then use AutoFormat to format the entire document at once.

Formatting As You Type

You can have your document elements formatted as you type. However, this feature requires that you supply Word with certain cues so that the correct formatting is applied to the text. For example, if you turn on AutoFormat As You Type and want to create a bulleted list that is automatically formatted by the AutoFormat feature, you must begin the bulleted line with a dash, an asterisk, or a lowercase "o" so that Word knows to apply the bulleted list formatting.

Many AutoFormat As You Type features are enabled by default, although others are not. To customize the AutoFormat As You Type feature, follow these steps:

1. Select **Tools**, **AutoCorrect Options**. The AutoCorrect dialog box appears.

2. Select the **AutoFormat As You Type** tab on the dialog box (see Figure 11.1).

Figure 11.1 The AutoFormat As You Type tab of the AutoCorrect Options dialog box allows you to select which document elements will be formatted automatically as you type.

3. A series of check boxes on the AutoFormat As You Type tab allows you to select which document elements will be formatted as you type. Again, you need to type certain characters for a particular element so that the AutoFormat feature recognizes and then formats the text.

- **Built-In Heading Styles**—Select this check box to have all headings that you apply to an outline or a legal document be automatically assigned the appropriate built-in heading style (using Headings 1–9).

- **Border Lines**—Select this check box to have borders automatically placed between paragraphs. You must type three dashes (-) for a thin border, three underscores (_) for a bold line, or three equal signs (=) for a double-line border.

- **Tables**—Select this check box to automatically create tables. You must type a series of plus symbols (+) and dashes (-) to signify the number of columns (+) and the distance between the columns (-).

- **Automatic Bulleted Lists**—Select this check box to create bulleted lists automatically. Start each line in the list with an asterisk (*), a dash (-), or a lowercase "o."

- **Automatic Numbered Lists**—Select this check box to create numbered lists. Start a line with a letter or number and it is turned into a numbered list item. Paragraphs following the first numbered line are numbered sequentially if the Format Beginning of List Item Like the One Before It check box is selected.

Other AutoFormatting check boxes include features that format your quotation marks, ordinals (1st), and fractions ($\frac{1}{2}$). Select (or deselect) the various AutoFormat As You Type options and then click **OK** to close the dialog box.

 TIP **Create Styles As You Type** If you select the Define Styles Based on Your Formatting check box, Word automatically takes your character and paragraph formatting attributes and turns them into styles. You can then use the created styles to format other paragraphs.

Although formatting as you type might seem like a real timesaver, you must remember which special characters to use to automatically begin a particular formatting type.

Applying AutoFormat to a Document

The alternative to autoformatting as you type is to create the document and then format it after the fact with AutoFormat. Waiting to format a document until after its completion allows you to concentrate on the document content as you type. You then can concentrate on the look and feel of the document by selecting from the various AutoFormatting options. Heads, numbered or bulleted lists, and other items you have designated throughout the text are identified and formatted.

To AutoFormat a document, follow these steps:

1. Make sure that you are in the Print Layout view (select View, then Print Layout, this allows you to see the various formatting tags applied to the document when you review the autoformat changes). Select **Format, AutoFormat**. The AutoFormat dialog box appears (see Figure 11.2).

2. You can increase the accuracy of the formatting process by choosing a particular document type. Click the General Document type drop-down arrow and select from the document types listed on the drop-down list (the default setting is **General Document**; you can also select **Letter** or **Memo** as the document type from the list).

Figure 11.2   The AutoFormat dialog box allows you to immediately format the document or review each of the suggested formatting changes.

3. Now you can AutoFormat the document. If you want to AutoFormat the current document without reviewing the formatting changes, click the **AutoFormat Now** option button and then click **OK**. The document is automatically formatted.

4. If you want to review the AutoFormatting process after the changes are made, click the **AutoFormat and Review Each Change** option button. Then click **OK**.

5. The document is formatted, and then the AutoFormat/Review Changes dialog box appears. If you already know whether you are happy with the results, choose to **Accept All** or **Reject All** using the appropriate button in the dialog box. You can also click **Review Changes** to review the changes to your document so that you can decide whether you're happy with the results on a change-by-change basis. The Review AutoFormat Changes dialog box appears (see Figure 11.3).

Figure 11.3   This dialog box enables you to review each of the formatting changes made in the document.

6. Click the **Find** (forward) button (this button has a right-pointing arrow) to begin the review process. Notice that all the changes that AutoFormat has made to the document are tagged with a red line and a description box in the document.

7. When you are asked to review a particular change (the change appears in the Changes box), either select **Reject** to reject the change or click the **Find** button to skip to the next formatting change in the document. You can also choose to **Accept All** or **Reject All** using the appropriate button in the dialog box.

8. When you reach the bottom of the document, Word notifies you that it can start searching for changes at the top of the document. If you had the insertion point at the top of the document when you began the review process, click **Cancel**. Then, click **Cancel** to close the two subsequent dialog boxes as well.

To safeguard any automatic formatting changes that have been made, be sure to immediately save your document.

Changing AutoFormat Options

You can customize certain options related to the AutoFormat feature. This dialog box can be reached by selecting the **Tools** menu and then **AutoCorrect**. Make sure that the **AutoFormat** tab is selected.

The options that you have control over on the AutoFormat tab are similar to those found on the AutoFormat As You Type tab. You can choose check boxes that automatically format headings, lists, and so on (see Figure 11.4).

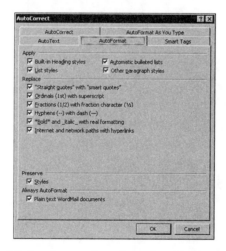

Figure 11.4   You can set the various options for automatic formatting on the AutoFormat tab of the AutoCorrect dialog box.

You can also choose to have Word retain the style that you have already placed in the document (prior to running AutoFormat). Select the **Styles** check box to do so.

TIP   **AutoFormat Text-Only E-Mail Automatically**   If you use Word as your e-mail editor for Outlook (see Part II of this book for information on using Outlook), you can have any text-only e-mail messages that you receive automatically formatted so they look better when you read them. Select the **Plain Text Wordmail Document** check box at the bottom of the AutoFormat tab.

After you select the options you want to set for AutoFormat, select **OK**. You can now run AutoFormat, and your options will be in force as your document is formatted.

Adding Document Text with AutoText and Using Special Characters

In this lesson, you learn how to quickly add repeating text elements to your documents using the AutoText feature. You also learn how to add special characters to your document, such as the copyright symbol.

Understanding AutoText

AutoText provides you with a way to build a library of words and text phrases that you use often in your documents. An AutoText entry can consist of a company name, your name, or an entire paragraph that you commonly place in your documents.

AutoText makes it easy for you to quickly insert items from your AutoText list into any document. Creating AutoText entries is also very straightforward.

Creating AutoText Entries

You can create an AutoText entry using text from an existing document, or you can type the text that you want to add to the AutoText list in a blank document. It's then just a matter of copying the text to your AutoText list.

To create an AutoText entry, follow these steps:

1. Type the text you want to use for the AutoText entry or open the document containing the text that will serve as the AutoText entry.
2. Select the text.
3. Select the **Insert** menu, point at **AutoText**, and then select **New** from the cascading menu. The Create AutoText dialog box appears as shown in Figure 12.1.

TIP **AutoText Isn't on My Insert Menu** Remember that Word uses a personalized menu system that places your most recently used commands on the various menus. If you click a menu and don't see a particular command, rest your pointer in the menu for a moment; the menu will expand and provide a list of all the commands available on that particular menu.

Figure 12.1 Type a name for your new AutoText entry into the Create AutoText dialog box.

4. Type the name that you want to use to retrieve this AutoText entry in the text box provided (for one-word text entries, the selected text can also serve as the entry name).

5. After providing the name for the AutoText entry, click **OK**.

Your selected text is added to the AutoText list. You can repeat this procedure and add as many text items to the AutoText list as you want.

Inserting AutoText Entries

After you add an AutoText entry or entries to the list, you can insert them into any Word document. One method of inserting an AutoText entry into the current document is to pull the entry directly from the AutoText list.

To insert an AutoText entry into a document, follow these steps:

1. Place the insertion point in the document where you want to insert the AutoText entry.

2. Select the **Insert** menu, point at **AutoText**, and then select **AutoText**. The AutoCorrect dialog box appears as shown in Figure 12.2.

3. The AutoText tab of the AutoCorrect dialog box displays an alphabetical list (as well as various default entries that Word provides) of the AutoText entries that you have added to the AutoText list. Select the entry you want to insert and click **Insert**. Or double-click any entry on the list to insert it into the document.

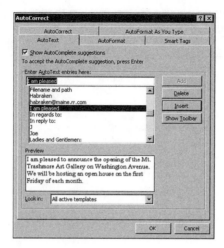

Figure 12.2 Insert your AutoText entries from the AutoCorrect dialog box.

An alternative to manually inserting AutoText into the document is using the AutoComplete feature to automatically insert an entry into your document. For example, if you have an entry in your AutoText list that reads "I am pleased to announce," you can automatically insert this entry into your document by beginning to type the entry. As you type the first few letters in the AutoText entry, an AutoComplete box appears, containing the complete AutoText entry, as shown in Figure 12.3.

To insert the entry into the document, press the **Enter** key. AutoComplete also helps you enter items that are not included on your AutoText list into your document. These items include the current date, days of the week, and names of months. For example, as you begin to type the name of a month, the AutoComplete box message appears, telling you to press **Enter** to insert the complete word.

TIP **Use the AutoText Toolbar to Quickly Insert AutoText Entries** Right-click any toolbar, and then select **AutoText** from the menu. To add an entry into the current document, click the **All Entries** button on the AutoText toolbar and select your AutoText from the list.

Figure 12.3 AutoComplete automatically places entries from your AutoText list into your documents.

Deleting AutoText Entries

You can easily delete items on the AutoText list when you no longer need them. This is done on the AutoText tab of the AutoCorrect dialog box.

To delete an AutoText entry, follow these steps:

1. Select the **Insert** menu, point at **AutoText**, and then select **AutoText** from the cascading menu. The AutoCorrect dialog box appears.

2. Select any of the entries in the AutoText list.

3. Click **Delete** to remove the entry from the list.

After you have completed your deletion of AutoText entries, click **OK** to close the AutoText dialog box.

Using Special Characters and Symbols

Special characters and symbols are characters that can't be found on your keyboard and that are not part of what is considered to be the standard character set. Characters such as the German "u" with an umlaut (Ü) are special characters, and an item such as the trademark is an example of a symbol.

Many special characters and symbols exist. Table 12.1 lists some of the commonly used special characters and symbols.

Table 12.1   Common Special Characters and Symbols

Special Character or Symbol	Use
Copyright symbol ©	Used in a copyright notice in a document.
Trademark symbol ™	Placed to the right of official trademarks placed in a document.
Em dash —	Used to bracket asides or sudden changes in emphasis in a sentence—rather than using a comma. It appears as a long dash.
En dash –	Slightly shorter than an em dash, this dash is commonly used to separate numbers from capital letters, such as Figure B–1.
Wingdings	A group of special icons that can be used in your documents for emphasis or as bullets.
Foreign language font (é)	Characters that include special accents.

The basic special characters and symbols are held in three groups:

- **Symbol**—This group contains mathematical symbols, arrows, trademark and copyright symbols, and letters from the Greek alphabet.
- **Normal Text**—This group provides you with special characters containing accents and other special marks.
- **Wingdings**—Special icons and symbols for many purposes.

Additional special character sets might be available to you, depending on which fonts have been installed on your computer (you can purchase software with unique fonts and symbols, as well).

 TIP   **Shortcut to Making an Em Dash**   As you are typing along, you may quickly insert an em dash into the text by pressing **Ctrl+Alt+the minus sign** on the number pad. The em dash appears.

You can easily insert special characters and symbols into your documents using the Insert Symbol feature. To insert a special character or symbol, follow these steps:

1. Place the insertion point in your document where you want to insert the special character or symbol. Select **Insert, Symbol**. The Symbol dialog box appears as shown in Figure 12.4.

Figure 12.4 The Symbol dialog box gives you access to symbols and special characters that you can insert into your document.

2. To insert a symbol, make sure the Symbol tab is selected on the Insert dialog box (if you want to insert a special character, go to step 5). Use the Font drop-down box to select the symbol set from which you want to choose your symbol. The symbol set that you choose dictates which symbols are available, so select a symbol set that provides the symbol you want to insert. You will find that the normal text symbol set provides most of the commonly used symbols, such as copyright and trademark.

3. After you select the symbol set (such as normal text, Symbol, Wingdings, or another font family), click to select the symbol you want to insert.

4. After selecting the symbol, click the **Insert** button.

5. If you want to insert a special character, such as the copyright symbol or an em dash, click the **Special Characters** tab on the Symbol dialog box.

6. Select the special character and then click **Insert**.

7. When you have finished inserting your symbol or special character, click the **Close** button on the Symbol dialog box.

CAUTION

My Key Combination Turns into a Symbol—The Word AutoCorrect feature is set up to replace several character combinations with special characters. You can override these changes made by the AutoCorrect feature by immediately pressing the **Backspace** key. For more on AutoCorrect, see Lesson 4, "Using Proofreading Tools."

After you've inserted the symbol or special character into the document, you can continue typing or editing your text. Symbols and special characters give your document a finished, typeset look.

Adding Headers, Footers, and Page Numbers

In this lesson, you learn how to add headers, footers, and page numbers to your documents.

Understanding Headers and Footers

Another aspect of creating a document is using headers and footers to insert information that you want repeated on every page of the document or in the pages of a particular document section.

 Header   The header resides inside the top margin on the page; it holds information such as the date or draft number that appears at the top of every page of the document. Every section of a document could potentially have a separate header.

 Footer   The footer resides inside the bottom margin of the page; it holds information such as the page number or other information that appears at the bottom of every page of the document. Every section of a document could potentially have a separate footer.

Headers and footers provide you with a way to include a document title, the current date, or the current page number on the top or bottom of each page in the document. Headers can include text, graphics, or other items.

Adding Headers and Footers

You can add a header or footer to a document in any view. To add a header or footer, follow these steps:

1. Select **View**, **Header and Footer**. You are temporarily switched to the Print Layout mode and placed in the header area of the document (see Figure 13.1). The regular text area is dimmed and unavailable while you work in the header or footer box.

2. Type your text into the header area. If you want to create a footer, click the **Switch Between Header and Footer** button on the Header and Footer toolbar, which is also available in the document window.

Figure 13.1 The header area of the page is where you type your header text. The Header and Footer toolbar provides you with tools to insert page numbers, the date, and to switch between your headers and footers.

3. You can add a page number, the current date, the current time, and other elements using the appropriate buttons on the Header and Footer toolbar (see Table 13.1).

4. In cases where you need to align or format the text, use the appropriate buttons on the Word Formatting toolbar (while in the header/footer areas) as you would for text on the document page.

5. When you have finished entering your header and footer text, click the **Close** button on the Header and Footer toolbar.

You are returned to your document text. In the Normal view, you are not able to see your header or footer. In the Print Layout view, however, header and footer text appears dimmed.

You can edit your headers and footers by selecting **View, Header and Footer**. Move to the appropriate header or footer using the navigation buttons on the Header and Footer toolbar shown in Table 13.1. To quickly enter a header or footer box, in the Print Layout view double-click the header or footer text.

Table 13.1   The Header and Footer Toolbar Buttons

Button	Purpose
	Inserts the page number
	Inserts the page count or number of total pages
	Edits the format of the page number
	Inserts the current date
	Inserts the current time
	Opens the Page Setup dialog box to the Layout tab, where you can change the header and footer settings
	Hides the document text while you work on your header and footer
	Sets up the next header the same as the current header (or footer)
	Switches between your header and footer
	Moves to the previous header or footer in the document
	Moves to the next header or footer in the document

Several toolbar choices, such as Same As Previous and Move to Previous or Next (header or footer) relate to documents that have several sections and so have different headers or footers within the same document. You can also have more than one header or footer in the document if you choose to have different headers or footers for odd- and even-numbered pages.

Using Odd- and Even-Numbered Page Headers and Footers

By default, the header and footer layout settings in Word assume that one header or footer appears on all the pages of a document (except in cases where the document is divided into more than one section; each section can have different headers and footers). You can change the header and footer settings so that different headers and/or footers appear on the odd- and even-numbered pages of your document (or the odd- and even-numbered pages of a document section).

To change the layout settings for Word Headers and Footers, follow these steps:

1. After activating the Header and Footer view (so that the Header and Footer toolbar appears), click the **Page Setup** button.

   TIP **Changing Header and Footer Layout When You Aren't in the Header or Footer** To get to the header and footer layout options when you don't have the header or footer displayed, select **File, Page Setup**. The Page Setup dialog box appears. If it is not already selected, click the **Layout** tab.

2. In the Page Setup dialog box, click the **Different Odd and Even** check box to enable odd and even headers and/or footers in the current document (or document section).

3. If you want to have a header or footer (or none) on the first page of your document that is different from subsequent pages in the document, click the **Different First Page** check box (see Figure 13.2).

   TIP **Headers and Footer Can Be Applied to Document Sections** The only way to specify where a header or footer begins in a document (other than the first page of the document) is to break the document into sections. Creating sections is discussed in Lesson 20, "Working with Larger Documents."

4. Click **OK** to close the Page Setup dialog box. If you are returned to your document, select **View, Header and Footer** to add the odd- or even-numbered page headers to the document. If you were already in the Header and Footer view when you exited the Page Setup dialog box, you are returned to the current header and footer.

5. If you want to specify how close the header or footer is to the margin edge of the top or bottom of the document, respectively, use the Header or Footer spin boxes to set the distance.

6. When you have finished adding your odd- and even-numbered page headers and/or footers or your first page and subsequent page headers, click the **Close** button on the Header and Footer toolbar.

Odd- and even-numbered page headers and footers are set up exactly the way you would typically set up a header or footer in the document. Use the **Show Next** or **Show Previous** button to move between the odd- and even-numbered page headers or footers and enter the text you want to appear on them.

Figure 13.2 On the Layout tab of the Page Setup dialog box, you can select whether to have different odd- and even-numbered page headers/footers or a different header/footer on the first page of the document.

Adding Page Numbering to a Document

Headers and footers enable you to place repeating information in your documents, including the date, other important text, and most important—page numbers. When you want to place only page numbers on your document pages, you can forgo the Header and Footer command and quickly add page numbers using the Insert menu.

To place page numbers in your document, follow these steps:

1. Select **Insert**, **Page Numbers**. The Page Numbers dialog box appears (see Figure 13.3).

Figure 13.3 Use the Page Numbers dialog box to select the position and alignment of page numbers in your document.

2. To select the position for your page numbers, select the **Position** drop-down arrow and select **Top of Page (Header)** or **Bottom of Page (Footer)**.

3. You can select the alignment for the page numbers using the **Alignment** drop-down box. Select **Center**, **Left**, or **Right** to position the page numbers. When you are using mirror margins on a document that will be printed on both sides of the paper, select **Inside** or **Outside** (relative to a central binding, like that of a book) to position your page numbers.

4. To select the format for your page numbers, click the **Format** button. The Format dialog box appears.

5. Use the **Page Number Format** drop-down box (shown in Figure 13.4) to choose the format for your page numbers (Arabic numerals—1, 2, 3—is the default). When you have selected your number format, click **OK** to return to the Format dialog box.

6. To have the page numbering start on a specific page in the document, click the **Start at** option button and then use the spinner box to specify the page number.

Figure 13.4   Use the Page Number Format drop-down box to choose the format for your page numbers.

7. Click **OK** to close the Page Number Format dialog box.

The page numbers are placed in the header or footer of your document according to your positioning and formatting choices. You can edit the page numbers and add text if you want by selecting **View**, **Header and Footer**.

Printing Documents

In this lesson, you learn how to preview your documents and then print them.

Sending Your Document to the Printer

 When you have finished a particular document and are ready to generate a hard copy, Word makes it easy for you to get your document to the printer. In fact, you have three choices. You can send the document directly to the printer (no questions asked) by clicking the **Print** button on the Standard toolbar. You can open the Print dialog box (select **File, Print**) and set any print options that you want, such as printing a particular range of pages or printing multiple copies of the same document. You also have the option of previewing your hard copy before printing. This enables you to view your document exactly as it will appear on the printed page.

 To preview your document before printing, click the **Print Preview** button on the Word Standard toolbar. The Print Preview window opens for the current document (see Figure 14.1).

You will find that the Print Preview window provides several viewing tools that you can use to examine your document before printing.

 • **Zoom In or Out**—In the Print Preview window, the mouse pointer appears as a magnifying glass. Click once on your document to zoom in, and then click a second time to zoom out. To turn this feature off (or on again), click the **Magnifier** button.

 • **Zoom by Percentage**—You can change to different zoom levels on the current document by using the **Zoom** drop-down arrow.

• **View Multiple Pages**—You can also zoom out and view several pages at once in the Preview window. Click **Multiple Pages**, and then drag to select the number of pages to be shown at once.

• **Shrink to Fit**—In cases where you have a two-page document and only a small amount of text appears on the second page, you can condense all the text to fit on the first page only; click the **Shrink to Fit** button.

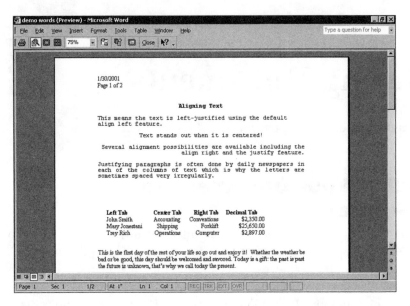

Figure 14.1   The Print Preview mode enables you to view your document the way it will print.

When you have completed viewing your document in the Print Preview mode, you can click the **Print** button to print the document, or if you want to edit the document before printing, click the **Close** button on the toolbar.

Changing Print Settings

In some situations, you might want to print only the current page or a certain range of pages. These options are controlled in the Print dialog box. The Print dialog box supplies you with several options, including the printer to which you send the print job, the number of copies, and the page range to be printed.

To open the Print dialog box, select **File**, then **Print**. The Print dialog box is shown in Figure 14.2.

Depending on your home or office situation, you might have your computer connected to more than one printer (especially if you are on a network). The Print dialog box has a drop-down box that lists all the printers to which you have access. To select a printer other than the current printer, click the drop-down arrow in the **Name** box and choose your printer from the list.

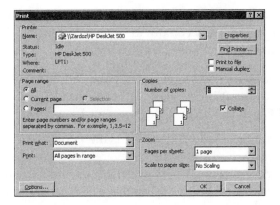

Figure 14.2   The Print dialog box gives you control over the various print options for your document.

The Print dialog box also enables you to select the range to be printed. This range can consist of a page, a group of specific pages in a sequence, or all the pages in the document.

- **All Pages**—To print all the pages in the document, make sure the **All** option button is selected.

- **Current Page**—To print a single page, click the **Current Page** option button (this prints the page that the insertion point is parked on).

- **Page Range**—To designate a range of pages, click the **Pages** option button and type the page numbers into the Pages box.

TIP   **Specifying Page Ranges**   To print a continuous range of pages, use the 1–5 format (where 1 is the start and 5 is the end of the range). For pages not in a continuous range, use the 5,9,11 format (where each distinct page number to be printed is separated by a comma). You can also mix the two formats. For example, you could specify 1–5,9,11.

- **Number of Copies**—In the Copies area of the Print dialog box, use the increment buttons in the Number of Copies box to select the number of copies you want to print. You can also double-click inside the Number of Copies box and type in a particular value for the number of copies you want.

- **Collate**—In addition to specifying the number of copies, you can select whether to collate your document by checking the Collate box in the copies area. *Collate* means that the document is printed in the proper order for stapling or binding. For example, a 10-page document would be printed from page 1 through 10 and then the subsequent copies would also print in this "collated" arrangement. If you do not choose to collage, all the copies of page 1 will be printed, then page 2, and so on.

You can also choose to print all the pages in a chosen range or print only the odd or even pages. Click the **Print** drop-down box (near the bottom left of the dialog box) and select **All Pages in Range**, **Odd Pages**, or **Even Pages,** as required.

Another print option worth mentioning is the Zoom print option in the Print dialog box. This feature enables you to place several document pages on one sheet of paper. To use Zoom print, click the **Pages per Sheet** drop-down box in the **Zoom** area of the Print dialog box and select the number of document pages you want to place on a sheet of paper. To select a scale for the print job (the scale is the relative size of the mini-pages on the printout page, such as 8.5 by 11 inches or legal size), click the **Scale to Paper Size** drop-down box.

After you select these two options, proceed with your print job. Be advised, however, that the more pages you place on a single sheet, the smaller the text appears.

Finally, you can print special items that you have placed in your document, such as comments, styles, and AutoText entries. When you choose to print one of these items, you are supplied with a page or pages separate from the main document that list the comments, styles, or other items you've selected.

Select the **Print What** drop-down arrow and select from the list of items (**Document**, **Document Properties**, **Document Showing Markup**, **List of Markup**, **Styles**, **AutoText Entries**, or **Key Assignments**). If you want to print more than one of these optional items with the document printout, you must select them in the Print Options dialog box.

Selecting Paper Trays, Draft Quality, and Other Options

Several additional print options are also available from the Print dialog box. To access these options, click the **Options** button on the bottom left of the Print dialog box (see Figure 14.3).

The Print options dialog box, using a series of check boxes, gives you control over the output of the print job as well as other options. You can also select the paper tray in your printer that you want to use for the print job (this is very useful in cases where you have a specific tray for letterhead, envelopes, and so on). Several of these options are described in Table 14.1.

Figure 14.3 In the Print options dialog box, you can select or deselect certain options associated with your print job.

Table 14.1 Print Options on the Print Dialog Box

Option	Purpose
Draft Output	Prints the document faster with less resolution
Reverse Print Order	Prints pages last to first, collating your document on printers that output documents face up
Background Printing	Prints the document quickly to a memory buffer so that you can work while the output is actually sent out to the printer
Document Properties	Prints the document properties

When you have finished selecting the various options for the printing of your document, click the **OK** button. You are returned to the Print dialog box. When you are ready to print the document, click **OK**.

Creating Numbered and Bulleted Lists

In this lesson, you learn how to create and edit numbered and bulleted lists.

Understanding Numbered and Bulleted Lists

You can add emphasis to a list of points or delineate a list of items in a document by adding numbers or bullets to the items in the list. Numbered lists are great for steps or points that should be read in order. Bulleted lists work best when you want to separate and highlight different items or points in a list, but the items do not have to appear in any particular order.

The style and look of the numbers or bullets that you apply to a list can easily be edited, and you can even change the starting number for a numbered list. The list then renumbers itself automatically. Also, as you add new lines to numbered or bulleted lists, the items are automatically set up with the same numbering style (with the proper number in the list sequence) or bullet style.

Creating a Numbered or a Bulleted List

You can create numbered or bulleted lists from scratch or add numbers or bullets to an existing list.

To create a new numbered list, follow these steps:

1. Place the insertion point where you want to begin the numbered list in your document.

2. Select **Format**, **Bullets and Numbering**. The Bullets and Numbering dialog box appears.

3. For a numbered list, select the **Numbered** tab (see Figure 15.1).

Figure 15.1 Use the Numbered tab on the Bullets and Numbering dialog box to select a number style for your numbered list.

TIP **Quickly Start a Numbered or Bulleted List Using the Formatting Toolbar** To start a numbered or bulleted list using the default number or bullet style, click the Numbering or Bullets button on the Formatting toolbar. To turn off the numbers or bullets, click the appropriate button on the toolbar.

4. On the **Numbered** tab, click the style box for the particular style that you want to use for the numbers in the list. If you want to customize any of the default styles offered, select the style box and then click the **Customize** button. The Customize Numbered List dialog box appears (see Figure 15.2).

Figure 15.2 The Customize Numbered List dialog box enables you to set the number style, format, and start number for the list.

5. Use this dialog box to change the number style, the format, the start number, the font for the numbers, or the number position. A preview of your changes appears at the bottom of the dialog box.

6. When you have selected your options for the number style for your list, click **OK**. You are returned to the Bullets and Numbering dialog box. Click **OK** to return to the document.

You can also easily create a bulleted list using the Bullets and Numbering dialog box; follow these steps:

1. To start a bulleted list, open the Bullets and Numbering dialog box, as previously discussed (select **Format**, **Bullets and Numbering**). Click the **Bulleted** tab.

2. Select the bullet style you want to use by clicking the appropriate box. If you need to customize your bullet style, click the **Customize** button (see Figure 15.3).

Figure 15.3 Use the Customize Bulleted List dialog box to select the bullet style or shape for your bulleted list.

3. The Customize dialog box enables you to select any symbol available in the various font symbol sets or create your button from a graphic available in the Office clip art library. Use the **Font** and **Character** buttons to select your bullet style from the various symbol sets (as discussed in Lesson 12, "Adding Document Text with AutoText and Using Special Characters"). If you want to use a graphic as the bullet, click the **Picture** button. Use the Picture Bullet dialog box that appears to select the bullet graphic you want to use, and then click **OK** (see Figure 15.4).

Figure 15.4 You can select from several bullet graphics using the Picture Bullet dialog box.

4. Your new bullet style (either selected from a symbol set or from the Picture Bullet dialog box) will appear in the Customize Bulleted List dialog box. Click **OK** to return to the Bullets and Numbering dialog box.

5. When you are ready to begin the bulleted list, click **OK** to close the Bullets and Numbering dialog box. The first bullet for the list will appear in your document.

Adding Items to the List

After you've turned on numbering or bulleting, you will notice that a number or a bullet appears at the beginning of the line that holds the insertion point. Type the text for this numbered or bulleted item.

Press the **Enter** key to begin a new line. The numbering (sequentially) or bulleting continues with each subsequent line. Just add the needed text and press **Enter** whenever you are ready to move to the next new item in the list.

You can turn off the numbering or bulleting when you have finished creating your list. Click the **Numbering** button or the **Bullets** button, respectively, on the Formatting toolbar.

Creating a Numbered or a Bulleted List from Existing Text

You can also add numbers or bullets to existing text. Select the text list, as shown in Figure 15.5, and then select **Format, Bullets and Numbering**. Select the appropriate tab on the Bullets and Numbering dialog box and select the style of bullets or numbers you want to use.

When you have completed making your selection, click **OK**. The numbers or bullets appear on the text list.

 TIP **Add Numbers or Bullets with a Click** You can quickly add numbers or bullets to an existing list. Select the list of items and click the Numbering or Bullets buttons, respectively, on the Formatting toolbar.

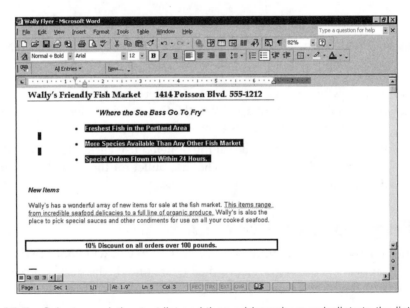

Figure 15.5 Select an existing text list and then add numbers or bullets to the list.

Creating Multilevel Lists

You can also create multilevel lists by using the numbering and bullet feature. Multilevel lists contain two or more levels within a particular list. For example, a multilevel list might number primary items in the list, but secondary items (which fall under a particular primary item) in the list are denoted by sequential letters of the alphabet. Figure 15.6 shows a numbered, multilevel list.

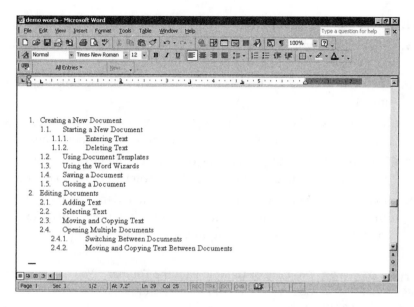

Figure 15.6   A multilevel numbered list uses several levels of numbering, as an outline does.

To create a multilevel list, follow these steps:

1. Place the insertion point where you want to begin the list, or select text in an already existing list.

2. Select **Format**, **Bullets and Numbering**. The Bullets and Numbering dialog box opens.

3. Click the **Outline Numbered** tab to view the multilevel options (see Figure 15.7).

Figure 15.7   Use the Outline Numbered tab to select the outline style for your multilevel list.

4. Select the style of multilevel list you want to use in your document.

5. After customizing the list options in the Customize Outline Numbered list, click **OK** to return to the Outline Numbered tab.

6. Click **OK** to close the Bullets and Numbering dialog box and return to the document.

7. To enter first-level items in the list, type the item (it will be automatically numbered as is appropriate). Press **Enter** to move to the next line.

8. To demote the next line to the next sublevel (the next level of numbering), press the **Tab** key. Then, type your text. Press **Enter** to move to the next line.

9. If you decide to promote a line that you have demoted using the **Tab**, make sure the insertion point is on the line, and then press **Shift+Tab**. When you have finished with the current line, press **Enter** to continue.

 Promote or Demote with the Toolbar You can also promote or demote items using Decrease Indent and Increase Indent on the Formatting toolbar.

 When you have completed your list, you can turn off the numbering by clicking the **Numbering** button on the Formatting toolbar (this deactivates numbering).

Using Word Tables

In this lesson, you learn how to create and format tables in your Word document. You also learn how to place math formulas in a table.

Understanding Tables and Cells

A Word table is made up of vertical columns and horizontal rows—a tabular format. The intersection of a row and a column in a table is called a *cell*. A tabular format gives you flexibility to arrange text and graphics in an organized fashion. Tables enable you to enter and work with information in a self-contained grid.

 Cell   A table cell is the intersection of a column and row.

Word makes it easy for you to create a table of any size with any number of columns and rows in your document and then easily edit it. In addition to editing text or graphics in a table, you have access to several formatting options related to the table itself, such as row and column attributes and the capability to easily add or delete rows and columns from the table.

Word also offers you several approaches for actually placing the table into the document. You can insert the table into the document or draw the table using the Draw Table command.

Inserting a Table

One option for placing a table into your document is inserting the table. Inserting a table enables you to select the number of rows and columns in the table. The height and the width of the rows and columns are set to the default (one line space [based on the current font height] for the row height and 1.23 inches for the column width). Using the Insert command for a new table is the simplest way to select the number of rows and columns for the table. Also, to place the table, you need only to place the insertion point at the position where the new table is to be inserted. The insertion point marks the top-left starting point of the table.

Inserted tables are static; you can move them to a new location in a document only by selecting the entire table and then using cut and paste. If you want to have better control over the placement of the table, you might want to draw a table (as described in the next section). This type of table can be dragged to any location in the document because it is created inside a portable frame.

To insert a table into your document, follow these steps:

1. Place the insertion point in the document where you want to place the table; select **Table**, and then point to **Insert**. Select **Table** from the cascading menu. The Insert Table dialog box appears (see Figure 16.1).

Figure 16.1   The Insert Table dialog box enables you to specify the number of columns and rows for your new table.

2. Use the click arrows in the **Number of Columns** text box to set the number of columns. Use the click arrows in the **Number of Rows** text box to set the number of rows.

3. If you want to set the number of columns and rows as the default for subsequent tables, click the **Set As Default for New Tables** check box.

4. To set the table so that it automatically adjusts the column widths to accommodate the text that you type in the column, select the **AutoFit to Contents** option button. If you are going to save the Word document containing the table as a Web document (and use it on a Web site), select the **AutoFit to Window** option button. This allows the table to automatically adjust within a Web browser window so that it can be viewed when the browser window is sized.

5. When you have completed your settings for the table, click **OK**.

The table is inserted into your document.

TIP   **Use the Toolbar to Insert a Table**   Click the **Insert Table** button on the Standard toolbar, and then drag down and to the right to select the number of rows and columns (a column and row counter shows you the number selected). Release the mouse to insert the table (or click cancel if you change your mind).

Drawing a Table

An alternative to inserting a table into your document is to draw the table. This method creates a table that resides inside a table cell. (This cell is not the same thing as the intersection of a column and a row, but a movable box that the table lives inside—much like a frame. It can be dragged to any position in the document.) You actually draw the table with a drawing tool and use the tool to add rows and columns to the table.

When you draw the table, you will find that it is created without any rows or columns. You then must manually insert the rows and columns using the Table Drawing tool. Although you can build a highly customized table using this method, it is not as fast as inserting a table with a prescribed number of rows and columns, as described in the previous section.

To draw a table in your document, follow these steps:

1. Select **Table, Draw Table**. The mouse pointer becomes a "pencil" drawing tool. The Tables and Borders toolbar also appears in the document window.

2. Click and drag to create the table's outside borders (its box shape). Release the mouse when you have the outside perimeter of the table completed.

3. To add rows and columns to the table, use the pencil to draw (hold down the left mouse button and drag the mouse) the row and column lines (see Figure 16.2).

4. When you have completed your table, click the **Tables and Borders** button on the standard toolbar to deactivate the Draw Tables feature.

TIP   **Use the Tables and Borders Button to Show Draw Tables Tools**   Click the **Tables and Borders** button on the Standard toolbar, and the Draw Table pencil pointer (and other tools necessary for creating your custom table) appears on your screen. Click the button again when you are finished drawing.

347

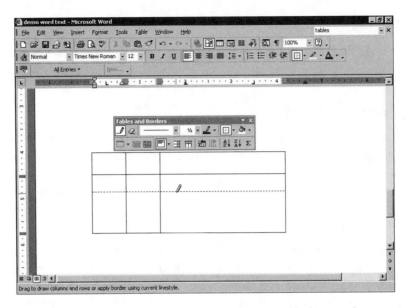

Figure 16.2 With the table drawing tool, you can draw a table in your document, and then draw in the row and column lines. The borders all snap to right-angled lines on an unseen grid so your table will always have straight lines.

The Tables and Borders toolbar provides you with buttons that enable you to edit the attributes of the table. Several of the buttons on the Tables and Borders toolbar are useful for customizing your table:

- **Distribute Rows Evenly**—This button makes the row heights in the table all the same.

- **Distribute Columns Evenly**—This button makes all the column widths consistent.

- **Eraser**—This button enables you to turn on the eraser; drag it across any row or column line in the table to erase it.

- **Line Style**—This drop-down box enables you to change the weight and style of the row or column lines you create.

You can also move the table anywhere on the document page (it's not anchored in one place like tables that are placed on the page using the Insert Table command). Place the mouse on the upper-left edge of the table and a Move icon (a four-headed arrow) appears. Drag the icon to a new location on the page. When you release the mouse, the table is placed in the new location.

CAUTION

When I Insert or Draw a Table, My Screen View Changes For you to be able to see the table formatting as it occurs, Word automatically sets your document view to Print Layout. If you had previously been in the Normal view, your screen will look different because it is now showing all layout instructions. To switch back, select your desired page view under the **View** menu.

Entering Text and Navigating in a Table

Entering text into the table is very straightforward. Click in the first cell of the table (the open box where the first column and first row of the table meet) and enter the appropriate text. To move to the next cell (horizontally, then vertically), press the **Tab** key. You can continue to move through the cells in the tables by pressing **Tab** and entering your text. If you want to back up a cell, press **Shift+Tab**. This moves you to the cell to the left of the current cell and selects any text entered in that cell.

Several other keyboard combinations are useful as you work in your table:

- **Alt+Home**—Takes you to the first cell in the current row
- **Alt+Page Up**—Takes you to the top cell in the current column
- **Alt+End**—Takes you to the last cell in the current row
- **Alt+Page Down**—Takes you to the last cell in the current column

Of course, you can use the mouse to click any cell of the table at any time.

Deleting text in the table is really no different from deleting text in your document. Select text in the table and press **Delete** to remove it. If you want to delete text in an entire row, but you want to keep the row in the table, place the mouse pointer at the left edge of the particular row. The mouse arrow pointer appears in the selection area. Click to select the entire row. When you press Delete, all the text in the cells in that particular row is deleted. You can also use a column pointer (a solid black arrow; place the mouse at the top of any column) to select an entire column and delete text using the Delete key.

Inserting and Deleting Rows and Columns

You also have complete control over the number of rows and columns in your table. You can delete empty or filled rows and columns depending on your particular need.

To insert a row or column into the table, place the insertion point in a cell that is in the row or column next to where you want to place a new row or column. Select **Table** and then point to **Insert** to see the available options. Options can be selected from a cascading menu:

- **Rows Above**—Insert a new row above the selected row.
- **Rows Below**—Insert a new row below the selected row.
- **Columns to the Left**—Insert a new column to the left of the selected column.
- **Columns to the Right**—Insert a new column to the right of the selected column.

You can also easily delete columns or rows from your table. Select the rows or columns, and then select the **Table** menu. Point at **Delete**, and then select **Columns** or **Rows** from the cascading menu, as appropriate. The columns or rows selected are removed from the table.

 TIP   **Quick Select Multiple Columns**   To select several cells, drag the mouse across them. You can also click the first cell in the series and then hold down the **Shift** key as you click the last cell you want to select.

Formatting a Table

Formatting a table can involve several things: You can change the width of a column or the height of a row, and you can also format the various table borders with different line weights or colors. Some of the table attributes can be modified directly on the table, but other attributes are best handled by modifying settings in the Table Properties dialog box or by using the AutoFormat dialog box.

Modifying Cell Size

An important aspect of working with your rows and columns is adjusting column widths and row heights to fit the needs of the information that you place inside the table cells. Both of these formatting tasks are mouse work. However, in cases where you want to enter an actual value for all the column widths or row heights, you can use the Table Properties dialog box discussed in this section.

Place the mouse pointer on the border between any columns in your table. A sizing tool appears (see Figure 16.3). Drag the sizing tool to adjust the width of the column.

 TIP   **Use the Ruler As Your Guide**   You can also use the column border markers on the ruler to adjust the width of a column or columns in your table. This provides a method of sizing columns using the ruler as a measurement guide. Drag the marker on the ruler to the appropriate width. To view the ruler, select **View, Ruler**.

Figure 16.3 Use the column sizing tool to adjust the width of a column.

Be Careful When Sizing Columns If a Cell Is Selected If a cell is selected anywhere in a column and you attempt to drag the sizing tool to change the column width, only the width of the row holding the selected cell is changed. Make sure no cells are selected if you want to size the entire column.

CAUTION

You can also adjust the column widths and the row heights in the table using the Table Properties dialog box. If you want to adjust the row or column attributes for just one row or column, make sure the insertion point is in that row or column. If you want to adjust the values for the entire table, click anywhere in the table, choose the **Table** menu, point at **Select**, and then choose **Table**. This selects the entire table.

Follow these steps to open the dialog box and adjust the various properties associated with the current table:

1. Select **Table, Table Properties**. The Table Properties dialog box appears.
2. To adjust column widths using the dialog box, select the **Column** tab.
3. Make sure the **Specify Width** check box is selected, and then use the width click arrows to adjust the width (see Figure 16.4).

Figure 16.4   Adjust your column widths using the Column tab of the Table Properties dialog box.

4. If you want to change the width of the next column, click the **Next Column** button. The **Previous Column** button enables you to adjust the width of the previous column.

5. When you have completed adjusting column widths, click the **OK** button.

You can adjust row heights in a like manner. Use the **Row** tab of the Table Properties dialog box. You can use the Specify Height box to specify the row height and Previous Row and Next Row buttons to specify the row for which you want to adjust the height.

TIP   **Working with Drawn Tables**   If you've created your table using the Draw Table command and then inserted your rows and columns with the Drawing tool, you might find it faster to align any irregularly sized elements (such as rows or columns) with the mouse rather than using the Table Properties dialog box.

Formatting Table Borders

Formatting your table borders is a matter of selecting the cells (or the entire table) and then selecting the formatting parameters. After you've selected the appropriate cells, select the **Format** menu, and then select **Borders and Shading**.

TIP   **Select the Entire Table**   A fast way to select the entire table is to place the insertion point in the table and then select **Table**, point at **Select**, and then select **Table**.

The Borders and Shading dialog box appears. Select the style of border that you want to place on the selected area of the table.

To select the border style, choose from one of the following:

- **Box**—This places a box around the outside of the table.
- **All**—This places a box around the table, gridlines inside the table, and also applies any shadow and color parameters that have been set in Word.
- **Grid**—This places a border around the table and places a border (grid) on the row and column lines.
- **Custom**—When you select **Custom**, you must then specify on the Preview table the border lines you want to format. To change the style, color, and width of your border lines, use the **Style**, **Color**, and **Width** drop-down boxes to select the options for your border lines. When you have completed your selections, click **OK** to return to the table.

The border options that you selected are used to format the cells that you selected in the table.

Automatically Formatting the Table

You can also format your table in a more automatic fashion using the Table AutoFormat feature. This feature enables you to select from a list of predetermined table formats that configure the borders and provide text and background colors in the cells; you can even select a particular font for the text contained in the cells.

To AutoFormat your table, click any cell of the table and then follow these steps:

1. Select **Table**, **AutoFormat**. The Table AutoFormat dialog box appears (see Figure 16.5).
2. To preview the various formats provided, click a format in the **Formats** scroll box. A preview of the format is shown.
3. When you have found the format that you want to use, select the format and then click **Apply**.

 TIP   **Select the Table Items You Want to Format with AutoFormat**   The AutoFormat dialog box provides several check boxes (Borders, Shading, Font, Color, and so on) that can be deselected if you don't want your AutoFormat selection to format these particular items in your table (otherwise, the entire table will be formatted).

Figure 16.5 The Table AutoFormat dialog box enables you to select and apply a format style for your entire table.

Creating Columns in a Document

In this lesson, you learn how to create and edit column settings in your document.

Understanding Word Columns

Word makes it very easy for you to insert and format columns for newsletters, brochures, and other special documents. It gives you complete control over the number of columns, column widths, and the space between the columns. You can insert columns for the entire page run of a document or place columns only in a particular document section.

The columns that you work with in Word are called newspaper or "snaking columns." This means that if you have two columns on a page and fill the first column, the text snakes over into the second column and continues there. This format is typical of your daily newspaper's columns.

 TIP **For Side-by-Side Columns, Use a Table** If you want to create columns that allow you to place paragraphs of information side by side in a document, place the text in a table that is not formatted with a visible border. This gives you great control over the individual text blocks in the separate columns that you create (see Lesson 16, "Using Word Tables").

Creating Columns

You can format a new document for columns, or you can select text and then apply column settings to that specific text. When you apply column settings to any selected text, Word automatically places the text (now in the number of columns you selected) into its own document section with a section break above and below the text. This allows you to switch from text in regular paragraphs (which are basically one column that covers all the space between the left and right margins) to text placed in multiple columns. You can also turn off the columns and return to text in paragraphs with very little effort on your part. Figure 17.1 shows a document that contains a section of text in paragraphs followed by text in columns, followed by text in paragraphs (three sections in the same document). Sections are covered in Lesson 20, "Working with Larger Documents."

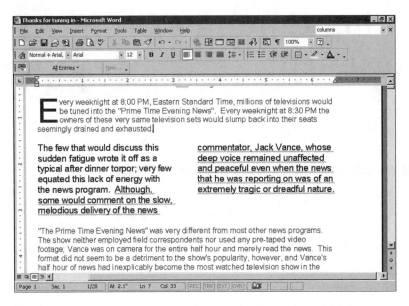

Figure 17.1 Documents can contain text in paragraphs and text in columns, as needed.

To place additional columns into a document, follow these steps:

1. Place the insertion point where you want the columns to begin or select the text that you want to format with the columns.

2. Select **Format**, **Columns**, and the Columns dialog box appears (see Figure 17.2).

Figure 17.2 The Columns dialog box enables you to set the number of columns and column options for the columns that you place into your document.

3. To select the number of columns you want to place in the document, you can choose from several preset options or specify a number of custom columns. To use the Presets select one of the following (all presets create columns separated by half-inch space):

- **One**—The default setting, this removes columns from the document and places all text in the normal one-column configuration.
- **Two**—Creates two equal columns.
- **Three**—Creates three equal columns.
- **Left**—Creates two columns where the left column is half as wide as the right column.
- **Right**—Creates two columns where the right column is half as wide as the left column.

4. If you want to select a custom number of columns (rather than using the Presets), use the **Number of Columns** spinner box (or type a number in the box). Use the Width and Spacing box, located beneath the Number of Columns spinner box, to specify the width for each column and the distance between each of the columns.

5. If you want to place a vertical line between the columns, select the **Line Between** check box.

6. You can apply these new columns to the entire document (if you've selected text, it applies only to that particular text) or click the **Apply To** drop-down box and select **Whole Document** or **This Point Forward**. If you choose This Point Forward, the columns are placed in the document from the insertion point to the end of the document (in their own section).

7. When you have finished selecting your column options, click **OK**.

 TIP **Create Columns with a Click of the Mouse** You can also create columns for currently selected text or insert columns into the text using the Columns button on the Standard toolbar. Click the **Columns** button and then select 1, 2, 3, or 4 columns from the drop-down box (you can choose **Cancel** if you change your mind). If you choose to create multiple columns using this method, columns of equal width are created.

Editing Column Settings

If you want to edit any of the column settings in your document, such as column number or column width, you can return to the Column dialog box to change any of the options.

1. Make sure that you click in the document section that contains the columns you want to modify.

2. Select **Format**, **Columns**. The Column dialog box appears.

3. Edit the various settings, described in the "Creating Columns" section, as needed. When you have completed your selections, click **OK**.

Inserting a Column Break

Because you are working with continuous, newspaper-type column settings, at times you might want to force a column break in a column. This allows you to balance the text between columns or end the text in a column at a particular point and force the rest of the text into the next column. To force a column break, follow these steps:

1. Place the insertion point in the column text where you want to force the break.

2. Select **Insert**, **Break**. The Break dialog box appears.

3. Select the **Column Break** option button.

4. Click **OK** to place the break in the column.

 TIP   **Use the Keyboard to Insert a Column Break**   You can also quickly place a column break in a column by pressing **Ctrl+Shift+Enter**.

The text at the break is moved into the next column in the document. Column breaks in the Print Layout view appear the way they will print, and you'll notice that all the column borders show in this view. In the Normal view, multiple columns are displayed as a single continuous column. The column break appears as a dotted horizontal line labeled Column Break.

Removing Column Breaks

Removing column breaks is very straightforward. Methods do vary, however, depending on the view that you are currently in.

In Print Layout mode, place the insertion point at the beginning of the text just after the break, click **Columns**, and then drag to select one column. This removes the break from the document.

 TIP   ¶   **Use the Show/Hide Button to Reveal Column Breaks**   You can also quickly show all your column breaks by clicking the **Show/Hide Button.** After you see the column breaks, just delete them.

In the Normal view, you can actually see the Column Break line (it appears as a dashed line). Select the break line with the mouse and then press **Delete**.

Adding Graphics to Documents

In this lesson, you learn how to insert graphics, such as clip art, into your document and how to use the Word drawing tools to create your own graphics.

Inserting a Graphic

Adding a graphic to your document is really just a matter of identifying the place in the document where you want to place the picture and then selecting a specific graphic file. Word provides you with a large clip-art gallery of ready-made graphics (in the metafile format .wmf), and you can also place images into your document that you find on the World Wide Web, that you receive attached to e-mail messages, that are imported from a scanner or digital camera, and more.

Word also embraces several graphic file formats, including the following file types:

- CompuServe GIF (.gif)
- Encapsulated PostScript (.eps)
- Various paint programs (.pcx)
- Tagged Image File format (.tif)
- Windows bitmap (.bmp)
- JPEG file interchange format (.jpg)
- WordPerfect graphics (.wpg)

To add a graphic file (a picture other than one of the Word clip-art files), you insert the image using the Insert menu.

Follow these steps to add a graphic to your document:

1. Place the insertion point where you want to place the graphic in the document.
2. Select **Insert**, **Picture**, and then select **From File** on the cascading menu. The Insert Picture dialog box appears.
3. Use the **Look In** box to locate the drive and folder that contains the picture file. After you locate the picture, click the file to view a preview (see Figure 18.1).

The Views drop-down arrow enables you to choose
to see a list, preview, or thumbnails, among others.

Figure 18.1   You can preview your graphical images before inserting them into your
document.

4. After you select the picture you want to insert into the document, click **Insert**
in the lower-right corner of the Insert Picture dialog box.

The picture is placed in your document, and the Picture toolbar appears in the document window. The Picture toolbar provides several tools you can use to modify and
edit the graphics in your document. See the "Modifying Graphics" section in this
lesson.

Probably the first thing you will want to do to any graphic or picture that you insert
into a document is size the image so it fits better on the page in relation to your text.
Most inserted graphics, even those from the Office clip-art library, tend to be inserted into a document in a fairly large size.

To size a graphic, click it to select it. Sizing handles (small boxes) appear on the border of the graphic. Place the mouse on any of these sizing handles. The mouse pointer becomes a sizing tool with arrows pointing in the directions in which you can
change the size; drag to size the graphic. To maintain the height/width ratio of the
image (so you don't stretch or distort the image), use the sizing handles on the corners of the image and drag diagonally.

 TIP   **Add a Graphic with Copy and Paste**   You can copy a graphic to the Windows
Clipboard from any Windows graphic program that you are running and then paste
it into your Word document.

Using the Word Clip Art

If you don't have a collection of your own pictures and graphics to place in your document, don't worry; Word provides a large collection of clip-art images you can use to liven up your documents. The clip-art library is organized by theme. For example, if you want to peruse the animal clip art that Word provides, you can select the **Animal** theme.

To insert Word clip art into your document, follow these steps:

1. Place the insertion point where you want to place the graphic in the document.

2. Select **Insert**, **Picture**, and then select **Clip Art** on the cascading menu. The Insert Clip Art task pane appears (see Figure 18.2).

Figure 18.2   The Insert Clip Art task pane gives you access to the Word clip art gallery.

3. Type in a clip-art theme, such as **Animals**, into the **Search Text** area.

4. (Optional) By default, the search will be conducted on all your media collections, including the Office Collections. If you want to preclude certain collections from the search (to speed up the search process), click the **All Collections** drop-down arrow and clear the check mark from any of the locations listed.

5. (Optional) If you want to preclude certain file types from the search (to speed up the search process), select the **All Media File Types** drop-down box and deselect any of the file types (ClipArt, Photographs, and so on) as required.

TIP   **Sound and Action Imagery Available, Too**   You can insert sound or movie clips into your document from the Clip Art task pane. By default, they are included in the results for any search you conduct.

6. Click the **Search** button and various clip-art images that fit your search criteria appear.

7. When you have located the clip art you want to place in the document, click the image. An image drop-down box appears. Select **Insert** to place the image in your document (see Figure 18.3).

Figure 18.3 Click a particular clip-art category to view the clip-art images.

If used appropriately, pictures and clip art can definitely improve the look and feel of your documents, particularly special documents such as flyers, newsletters, and brochures. If you find the clip-art library provided doesn't have what you need, click the **Media Gallery Online** link under the **See Also** section near the bottom of the task pane. Your Web browser opens and you go to Microsoft's online clip-art library, which offers additional clip-art images for your use.

CAUTION

Images and Copyright   Clip-art images, such as those that ship with Microsoft Word, are considered "free" images and can be used in any of your Word documents. Other images that you find on the World Wide Web might be copyrighted. You are responsible for determining whether you have the right to use an image before copying it. Sometimes you can pay a fee for one-time use or make another agreement.

Modifying Graphics

You can modify the images you place into your documents. An invaluable tool for modifying images is the Picture toolbar. It provides buttons that enable you to modify several picture parameters. You can also easily crop and resize your graphics.

When you click a picture (a picture file or Word clip art) in the document, the Picture toolbar automatically appears. You can use the toolbar to adjust the brightness or contrast of the image. You can also add a border to the graphic or adjust other picture properties. Word's Picture toolbar offers a large number of possibilities. Table 18.1 provides a listing and a description of the most commonly used buttons on the Picture toolbar.

Table 18.1   The Picture Toolbar Buttons and Their Purpose

Button	Click To
	Insert a new picture at the current picture position.
	Change the image to grayscale or black and white.
	Crop the image (after selecting, you must drag the image border to a new cropping position).
	Select a line style for the image border (you must first use the Borders and Shading command to add a border to the image).
	Control how text wraps around the image (square, tight, behind image, and so on).
	Open the Format Picture dialog box.
	Reset the image to its original formatting values.

You can select from several formatting options for your picture when you select the **Format Picture** button; this opens the Format Picture dialog box (see Figure 18.4).

The Format Picture dialog box provides several tabs that can be used to control various formatting attributes related to the picture. These tabs are

- **Colors and Lines**—This tab enables you to change the fill color (or background color) for the picture. This tab also provides settings for line weight and color and the style of arrows used on lines. Line options are available only if you have created the image using the tools on the Drawing toolbar.

Figure 18.4   The Format Picture dialog box offers several ways to modify your picture.

- **Size**—This tab enables you to specify the height and width of the image in inches. It also enables you to specify the height and width scale (in percentages) for the image.

- **Layout**—This tab enables you to specify how text should wrap around the image (see Figure 18.5). Other options enable you to place the image behind or in front of the text.

Figure 18.5   The Layout tab of the Format Picture dialog box enables you to select how text near the image is wrapped.

- **Picture**—This tab enables you to crop the picture (refer to Figure 18.4). It also provides an Image control area that lets you control the brightness and contrast of the image. You also can change the color of the image from the default (Automatic) to Grayscale, Black and White, and Washout using the Color drop-down box.

- **Web**—This tab enables you to include message text for the image that will appear as the image is loaded on a Web page. You need to use this option only if the Word document containing the image is going to be saved as a Web page and used on a Web site.

CAUTION

Why Is the Text Box Tab Unavailable? The Text box tab is available only when you are using the dialog box to change the format options on a text box that you have created using the Text Box tool on the Drawing toolbar.

After making formatting changes to the picture using the Format Picture dialog box, click **OK** to return to your document.

TIP **Formatting Drawings You Create** If you create your own image in a Word document using the tools on the Drawing toolbar, you can format the drawing using the Format Drawing Canvas dialog box that contains the same tabs as those found on the Format Picture dialog box. To open the Format Drawing Canvas dialog box, select the drawing you have created, and select **Format**, **Drawing Canvas**.

TIP **Resize or Crop with the Mouse** Select the picture, and then drag the resizing handles (the black boxes on the picture borders) to increase or decrease the size of your picture. If you want to crop the picture, hold down the **Shift** key as you drag any of the resizing handles.

You can delete a picture you no longer want in the document by clicking the picture and then pressing the **Delete** key on the keyboard. You can also move or copy the picture to another place in the current document—or to another document—using the **Cut**, **Copy**, and **Paste** commands (for general information about moving, copying, and pasting items in Word, see Lesson 3, "Editing Documents").

Using the Word Drawing Toolbar

You can also create your own graphics in your documents using the drawing tools provided on the Word Drawing toolbar. This toolbar provides several tools, including line, arrow, rectangle, oval, and text box tools. You can also use the appropriate tools to change the fill color on a box or circle, change the line color on your drawing object, or change the arrow style on arrows you have placed on the page.

To display the Drawing toolbar, select **View**, point at **Toolbar**, and then select **Drawing** from the toolbar list.

TIP **Quickly Access Toolbars** You can also right-click any toolbar in the Word window to access the toolbar list; then select **Drawing**.

The Drawing toolbar appears at the bottom of the document window just above the Word status bar. Figure 18.6 shows the Drawing toolbar and the tools available on it.

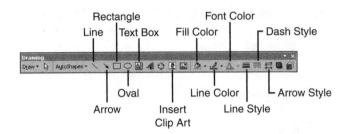

Figure 18.6 The Drawing toolbar makes it easy for you to create your own graphics in your documents.

Word provides you with an add-on program called WordArt that enables you to create special text effects in your document. You can create text that wraps around a circle, as well as a number of other special text "looks." In Word, click the **WordArt** button on the Drawing toolbar to start the WordArt program. WordArt can also be used in other Office programs, such as PowerPoint, to create visually exciting text items.

Creating a New Object

To draw a particular object, click the appropriate button on the toolbar. Then, drag the mouse to create the object in your document. To draw a square or circle, click the **Rectangle** tool or the **Oval** tool and hold down the **Shift** key as you draw the object with the mouse. If you find that you aren't very good at actually drawing graphical objects, click the **AutoShapes** drop-down arrow (near the left side of the drawing toolbar) and select a particular object shape from the list provided.

Modifying Drawn Objects

You can also control the various attributes for a particular object that you've drawn. You must first select the object using the selection pointer (click the **Select Objects** tool, and then click the object). You can manipulate the object's line style, fill color, and line color. Just choose the appropriate tool on the toolbar, and make your selection from the list of possibilities.

You can also size and move objects that you draw. Select an object, and use the sizing handles to increase or decrease the size of the particular object. If you want to move the object to a new position, place the mouse pointer in the middle of the selected object and drag it to a new position.

If you draw several related objects, you can select all the objects at once and drag them together to a new location. Select the first object and then hold down the **Shift** key and select subsequent objects, as needed. When you drag any of the objects to a new location, all the selected objects move together.

At times you will want to delete a particular object from your document. Simply select the object and then press **Delete** to remove it.

You will find that the Drawing toolbar provides you with all the tools (except natural artistic ability) you need to create fairly sophisticated custom images. A little practice with the various tools goes a long way in helping you create objects that add interest to your documents.

Inserting Images from Scanners and Other Sources

You can also place images into your Word documents that do not currently exist as a picture or clip-art file. You can actually attach to a particular *input device*, such as a scanner or digital camera, and then have it scan an image or take a picture that is then inserted into your document.

Input Device   Any device, such as a scanner or a digital camera, that can be attached to your computer to be used to acquire a picture.

Word enables you to acquire images from an attached scanner, a digital camera, or other device such as a video camera. All you have to do is set up the device so that it works on your computer (consult your device's documentation), and Word can use it to capture any image that device provides.

To insert an image from an attached device, follow these steps:

1. Place the insertion point in the document where you want to insert the image.
2. Select the **Insert** menu, point at **Picture**, and then click **From Scanner or Camera**. The Insert Picture from Camera or Scanner dialog box appears.
3. Click the **Device** drop-down box and select the device you want to capture the picture from (this is necessary only if you have more than one device attached).
4. Click the **Insert** button. The device scans the image or, in the case of a camera, downloads a particular image and places the image in your document.

Creating Personalized Mass Mailings

In this lesson, you learn how to create form letters, envelopes, and mailing labels for mass mailings using the Word merge feature.

Understanding the Mail Merge Feature

Word makes it easy for you to take a list of names and addresses and merge them with a form letter, an envelope template, or mailing labels. This enables you to quickly create items for mass mailings that appear to others to be customized for each person on the mailing list.

Although the Mail Merge Wizard walks you through the merge process, the entire procedure can be somewhat confusing. Two different documents are produced during the merge process: a main document and a data source. The main document is your form letter or mailing label template, and the data source is a Word document that provides the list of names and addresses that are inserted into the main document during the merge.

The information in the data source is inserted into the form letter or mailing label using placeholder codes called *merge fields*. Each merge field in the main document relates to a piece of information in the data source document, such as first name or street address, and the merge field gets its name from that particular field in the data source.

 Merge Fields Codes that serve as placeholders in your main document; for example, {FirstName} is an example of a merge field code that serves as a placeholder for the first name information that is pulled from the data source.

 Data Source The file of information, such as a list of names and addresses, to be merged into the main document (such as form letters, envelopes, or mailing labels). Data sources in Word typically take the form of a table, with each row in the table containing the name and address of a different individual.

The best way to understand how the various elements of the merge process—the main document, the data source, and field codes—relate is to actually perform a merge. Working through a merge that creates form letters for the entire list of people in a data source is a good place to start because creating other merge documents, such as labels and envelopes, is a similar process.

Because the merge process really consists of four different actions—creating the main document, creating the data source, completing the main document and inserting the merge fields, and running the merge—this lesson breaks down each of these actions in their own section. We begin with starting the Mail Merge Wizard and creating the main document.

Specifying the Main Document

The first step in the merge process is to specify a main document for the merge. The main document can be the currently open document in the Word workspace, or you can open a preexisting document during the merge process. To begin the merge process and designate a main document for the merge, follow these steps:

1. Open a new, blank document in the Word window, and click the **New Blank Document** icon on the Standard toolbar.

2. Select **Tools**, point at the **Letters and Mailing** arrow, and then select **Mail Merge Wizard**. The Mail Merge task pane opens, as shown in Figure 19.1.

Figure 19.1 The Mail Merge task pane walks you through the steps of merging a main document with a data source.

3. Under **Select Document Type** on the Mail Merge task pane, choose the type of main document you want to create using one of the following option buttons: Letters, E-Mail Messages, Envelopes, Labels, or a Directory. A directory, in this case, is a list of names and addresses that the wizard creates. It does not create a separate item for each person in the data source as the other options do.

4. After selecting the appropriate option button (for this example, **Letters** has been selected), click the **Next: Starting Document** link at the bottom of the task pane.

5. The next wizard step provided in the task pane provides three different option buttons; select one of the following:

   - **Use the Current Document**—This option enables you to build your main document using the new, blank document that was opened in step 1 (and it will be the approach that we use in the steps that follow in this section).

   - **Start from a Template**—When this option button is selected, a Select template link appears in the Mail Merge task pane. Click **Select Template**, and the Select Template dialog box appears. This dialog box enables you to base your main document on any of Word's document templates. After selecting a particular template on one of the dialog box tabs, click **OK** to return to the Mail Merge task pane.

   - **Start from Existing Document**—If you select this option button, a Start from Existing File box appears in the task pane. Click the **Open** button at the bottom of the box. The Open dialog box appears. Use it to select the existing Word document that will serve as the main merge document. Click **OK** to close the Open dialog box and return to the task pane.

6. After selecting one of the options (as discussed in step 4), click the **Next: Select Recipients** link at the bottom of the task pane. This allows you to either create or specify the document that contains the names and addresses (the data source) that we will use for the merge. We discuss the data source document in the next section.

A few things should be said about the options available in step 4. When you select one of these options, you are only setting the stage for how the main document will look when it is completed (meaning when the merge fields and any text that the document will include have been inserted).

If you use a blank document, you will have to add any special formatting or document layout features that you want to include in the document (as well as all the text that the document will contain). If you use an existing document, it can already contain the body text for the form letter and various formatting attributes. Using the document template option enables you to use one of Word's templates to determine the overall look of the document. Templates also often insert placeholder text in a document, allowing you to quickly replace it with text of your own.

No matter how you create the main document (as discussed in this section), field codes will need to be inserted. The actual field codes used will be determined by the data source document, which we discuss in the next section.

Creating or Obtaining the Data Source

The next step in the process is to open or create a data source document. This document not only provides the names and addresses that will be merged into your form letter, but it also dictates the merge fields that are placed in the main document (as placeholders for the actual data that will be placed in the form letters during the merge).

Creating a data source during the Mail Merge process is very straightforward because the Mail Merge Wizard provides you with a form that you use to enter people's names, addresses, and other information. When you enter the information for a particular person, you are creating a record. Each record pertains to one person.

However, you also can use existing data sources for the merge. For example, you can use Access database tables (see Part V, "Access," for information on creating databases in Access), your Outlook Contacts list, or any Word data source document that you created for a previous merge.

To provide you with a complete, from-scratch look at the merge process, we will create a new data source document in this section of the lesson. The following steps pick up from the previous section, where we specified the main document for the merge.

Record Information in the data source that contains information about a particular person (or place or thing).

Merge Field A code that tells Word to automatically insert information into your main document during the merge. For example, the Last Name field inserts your letter recipient's last name.

Using Your Outlook Contacts As a Data Source The Word Mail Merge Wizard also enables you to use information from your Outlook Contacts list as the data source for a mail merge. For more about the Outlook Contacts list, see Lesson 11, "Creating a Contacts List," in Part II of this book.

1. In the Mail Merge task pane (which currently shows Step 3 of 6, as shown in Figure 19.2), choose one of the following options to specify the data source for the merge:

   - **Use an Existing List**—This option is selected by default. If you have a Word document that contains a table or an Access table that contains the name and address information you want to use for the merge, select the **Browse** button in the task pane. This opens the Select Data Source dialog box. Locate your data source file, select it, and then click **Open** to return to the Word window and the Mail Merge task pane. The Mail Merge Recipients dialog box appears in the Word window providing a data source list based on the source file (it will appear the same as the Mail Merge Recipients dialog box shown later in Figure 19.4).

Figure 19.2   You can use an existing document or your Outlook Contacts list as the data source, or you can create a new data source from scratch.

   - **Select from Outlook Contacts List**—This option enables you to select the names and addresses for the merge from your Outlook Contacts. When this option is selected, a Choose Contacts Folder link appears in the task pane. Click the link and specify the location of your Contacts folder in the Select Contact List Folder dialog box that opens (in almost all cases it finds your Contacts folder for you). Click **OK** to return to Word and the task pane. The Mail Merge Recipients dialog box appears containing a list of your contacts (it is the same as the dialog box shown later in Figure 19.4).

- **Type a New List**—This option enables you to create a new data source (you will use this option to explore how you create a new data source). After selecting this option, click the **Create** button in the task pane to open the New Address List dialog box (you explore this dialog box in step 2).

2. After selecting one of the options listed in step 1 and clicking the **Create** link, either the Mail Merge Recipients dialog box appears (when you select either the existing list or Outlook Contacts list options; we discuss the Mail Merge Recipients dialog box in step 5) or, in the case of the **Type a New List** option, the New Address List dialog box appears (see Figure 19.3).

Figure 19.3 Use the New Address List dialog box to create the new data source for the merge.

3. Enter the name, address, and other information that you want to place in the record for the first recipient. When you have finished entering the data, click the **New Entry** button on the New Address List dialog box to enter the next record.

4. Enter additional records as needed. When you have finished entering your records, click the **Close** button on the New Address List dialog box. The Save Address List dialog box opens (see Figure 19.4).

5. Enter a name for the file and specify a location (if necessary—by default, the address list is saved in a special My Data Sources folder that was created when you installed Office). Click **Save** to save the data source file.

6. The Mail Merge Recipients list appears (see Figure 19.5). If you used your Outlook Contacts list or an existing data source, this dialog box appears after you completed step 1 in this section.

Figure 19.4 Specify a location and filename for the new data source address list.

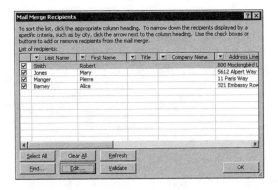

Figure 19.5 Use the Mail Merge Recipients dialog box to sort or select the recipients of the form letter.

7. If you want to deselect any of the recipients in the Mail Merge Recipients dialog box, clear the check box to the left of their records. If you want to sort the list by a particular field (such as last name), click that column's heading.

TIP   **Editing Recipient Information**   If you want to edit one of the records in the Mail Merge Recipients dialog box, select the record and click the **Edit** button. To add a new record, open an existing record using the **Edit** button and click **New Entry**.

8. After selecting recipients or sorting the recipient list, click **OK** to close the Mail Merge Recipients dialog box.

After creating your recipient list as discussed in this section, you are ready to complete the main document and enter the merge fields. These topics are discussed in the next section.

Completing the Main Document and Inserting the Merge Fields

Now that you have specified the recipients for the merge, text, such as the body of the letter, can be added to the main document. The merge fields that pull information from the data source can also be inserted.

Inserting merge fields is a very straightforward process. You can insert individual merge fields for information, such as first name and last name, or you can allow Word to automatically insert several fields into the letter. For example, you can click the Address Block icon that the Mail Merge task pane provides. This inserts the merge fields for the recipient's name and the appropriate address merge fields.

Follow these steps:

1. After specifying or creating a data source (as detailed in the last section), click the **Next: Write Your Letter** link at the bottom of the task pane.

2. The Write Your Letter (Step 4 of 6) part of the merge process appears in the Mail Merge task pane (see Figure 19.6).

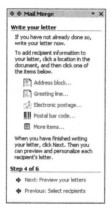

Figure 19.6 You can insert merge fields into the form letter using the icons in the task pane.

3. A good practice is to go ahead and click in the blank main document and type your letter text, such as the body of the letter. You can also add the closing of the letter or any other information.

4. You can insert the merge fields after typing the text for the letter. Place the insertion point in the main document where you want to place the first merge field. For example, to place recipients' addresses in a form letter, place the

insertion point four lines above the greeting. Click the **Address Block** icon in the task pane. The Insert Address Block dialog box appears.

5. The Insert Address Block dialog box provides you with different formats for inserting the recipient's name and their address information. Choose one of the formats listed (see Figure 19.7).

Figure 19.7   You can insert merge fields into the form letter using the icons in the task pane.

TIP   **Matching Fields**   Insertion commands such as Address Block or Greeting Line are configured to use the default field names that Word creates for its data source documents. If you created your data source in another application, such as Microsoft Access, you must specify the field names that you used for merge fields that specify information such as the recipient's name or address. Click the **Match Fields** button on the Address Block or Greeting Line dialog box and use the drop-down lists to select the field name that you used for fields such as Last Name, First Name, and Address. Then, click **OK** to return to the Address Block or Greeting Line dialog box.

6. Option buttons related to the inclusion of the country/region field in the address block are also included. Select the appropriate option button, and click **OK** to close the dialog box. Word inserts the Address Block code into the letter.

Now that you've inserted an Address field, move the insertion point to the position where you want to place the next set of merge fields—for example, the Greeting line.

To insert a Greeting line, click the **Greeting Line** icon on the task pane. The Greeting Line dialog box appears. Use the drop-down lists to select the format for your letter's greeting line, including the punctuation used at the end of the line, such as a comma or a colon, and to insert the appropriate merge fields, such as Last Name, that would be included on the greeting line. Then, click **OK**.

You can insert any other merge fields, as needed, into the document. If you want to insert individual merge fields into the letter, click the **More Items** icon on the task pane. The Insert Merge Field dialog box appears. Select a merge field, and then click **Insert**. When you have finished inserting any needed merge fields, click **Close**.

Finally, you might want to insert a date at the top of your form letter (the main document). Press **Ctrl+Home** to go to the top of the document, and then select **Insert**, **Date and Time**. Select your date format in the Date and Time dialog box, and then click **OK** to insert the date.

Figure 19.8 shows a main document that has been completed. Note that it contains merge fields for the address block and greeting line.

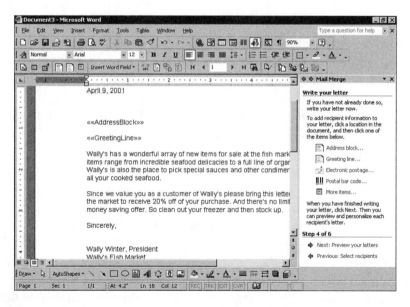

Figure 19.8 Your finished main document will include merge fields, a date, and the body text for the letter.

After you've finished your form letter (including the insertion of the appropriate merge fields), you are ready to complete the merge. The next section discusses the completion of the merge and the viewing of your finished form letters.

Merging the Documents

The next step in the merge process is to have Word create the merged documents so that you can preview the letters that are created. This enables you to be sure that the merge worked correctly (based on the merge fields you placed in the main document). It also enables you to edit any of the form letters created before you print them. Although the Mail Merge task pane allows you to preview each letter separately, the merge process actually creates a single document that places each form letter on a separate page.

Follow these steps:

1. Click the **Next: Preview Your Letters** link at the bottom of the task pane (refer to Figure 19.6; this is Step 4 of 6 and picks up where the previous section left off).

2. The first form letter appears in the Word window (see Figure 19.9). Check to be sure that the merge fields have placed the appropriate information into the form letter. To view the next recipient's letter, click the **Next** button (>>) at the top of the task pane.

3. Continue to view the form letters that were created during the merge (using the **Next** button; if you want to go back to a previous letter, click the **Previous** button, <<). If you come across a letter to a recipient that you do not want to keep as part of the merge, click the **Exclude This Recipient** button. The form letter is deleted and the form letter for the next recipient appears in the Word window.

4. When you have finished viewing the form letters created by the merge and are ready to complete the merge process, click the **Next: Complete the Merge** link at the bottom of the task pane.

5. To send the form letters to your printer, click the **Print** icon on the task pane. Word sends the letters to your printer.

6. If you want to save the form letters so that you can print in the future (or save them for later reference), click the **Save** button on the Standard toolbar. Provide a name and location for the document in the Save As dialog box. Then, click **Save** to save the document.

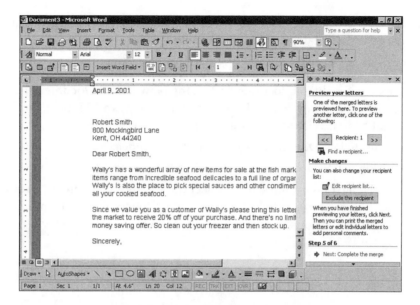

Figure 19.9   You can view each form letter created by the merge.

 TIP   **I Have a Lot of Records in My Data Source**   Because the merge can create a very large document (especially if you have a lot of records in your data source), you might want to close other applications you are running so all your computer's memory is available for the new file that is created. After the merge document has been created, make sure you save the file immediately. You can then view it at your leisure and print out all or some of the pages as needed.

After you print the form letters or save the merged document, the merge process is complete. At this point, you can close the task pane, if you want to. Click its **Close** (**X**) button.

Creating Envelopes and Mailing Labels

The procedure for using the merge feature discussed in this lesson assumes that you are using a form letter as your main document and creating copies of the letter for each person listed in the data source. You can also use the merge feature to create other document types, such as envelopes and labels.

The procedure for creating envelopes, mailing labels, or letters is almost the same. In each case, you use the Mail Merge Wizard to specify the type of document that you are creating, and then you are walked through the entire merge process. The steps that follow discuss how to create envelopes using the Mail Merge Wizard, but you can just as easily create mailing labels using this process.

To create envelopes using the Mail Merge Wizard, follow these steps:

1. Open a new blank document (click the **New Blank Document** icon on the Standard toolbar). Select **Tools**, point at **Letters and Mailing**, and then select **Mail Merge Wizard**. The Mail Merge task pane opens.

2. Under **Select Document Type**, select **Envelopes**.

3. Click **Next: Starting Document** at the bottom of the task pane.

4. On the next task pane screen, select the **Change Document Layout** option button (if necessary). To select the envelope type to use for the merge, click the **Envelope Options** icon. The Envelope Options dialog box will appear (see Figure 19.10).

Figure 19.10 Choose the type of envelope you need in the Envelope Options dialog box.

5. Select the envelope type you want to use for the merge using the **Envelope Size** drop-down list. If you want to edit any of the fonts for the envelope, use the appropriate **Font** button on the dialog box. When you have finished setting your envelope options, click **OK**.

6. To proceed to the next step in the merge, click **Next: Select Recipients** at the bottom of the task pane.

7. You will need to open or create a data source document. After opening or creating a new data source (as discussed earlier in this lesson), the Mail Merge Recipients dialog box appears. Click **OK** to close this dialog box.

8. To proceed to the next step in the merge process and place the merge fields on the envelope, click **Next: Arrange Your Envelope**.

9. Insert the merge fields on the envelope using the **Address Block** or **More Items** icons provided in the Mail Merge task pane. To center the recipient address on the envelope, press **Enter** as required and then click the **Center** icon on the Formatting toolbar.

10. After placing the merge fields on the envelope, click **Next: Preview Your Envelopes**. Use the **Next** (>>) or **Previous** (<<) buttons as needed to view all the envelopes. Remove any envelopes that you do not want to create by clicking the **Exclude This Recipient** button on the task pane.

11. To complete the merge, click **Next: Complete the Merge** at the bottom of the task pane.

At this point, you can click the **Print** icon on the task pane to send the envelopes to your printer. You also can save the envelope document created (each recipient's envelope is placed on a separate page in the merged document) and then print individual pages as needed (click the **Save** button on the Standard toolbar).

Working with Larger Documents

In this lesson, you learn how to work with larger documents, including inserting section breaks and building a table of contents.

Adding Sections to Documents

When you work with larger documents, you might have several parts in the document, such as a cover page, a table of contents, and then the body of the document. In most cases, these different parts of the document require different formatting and layout attributes. To divide a document into different parts that have different layouts, you use sections. A *section* is a defined portion of the document that can contain its own set of formatting options. You can divide a document into as many sections as you need.

Section A portion of a document (defined with marks that you insert) that can then be formatted differently from the rest of the document or other distinct sections of the document.

When you first begin a new document, the document consists of one section with consistent page formatting throughout the document. If you look at the status bar in a new document, you find that it reads "Sec 1," which means that the insertion point is currently in Section 1 of the document (which would be the entire document, in this case).

Sections are defined in your document as section breaks (which mean a certain position in the document serves as the break between the existing section and the new section you insert). To place additional section breaks in a document, follow these steps:

1. Place the insertion point where you would like to insert the new section break.
2. Select **Insert**, **Break**. The Break dialog box appears. In the lower half of the Break dialog box, several section break types are available (see Figure 20.1).

Figure 20.1 Select your type of section break in the Break dialog box.

- **Next Page**—A page break is placed in the document, and the new section begins on this new page.
- **Continuous**—The new section starts at the insertion point and continues for the rest of the document (or until it comes to the next defined section).
- **Even Page**—The new section starts on the next even-numbered page.
- **Odd Page**—The new section starts on the next odd-numbered page.

3. Select the option button for the type of section break you want to place in the document.

4. Click **OK** to insert the new section into the document.

Your new section break appears in the document. In the Normal view, the section break appears as a double horizontal line marked with the text "Section Break" followed by the type of section you selected. If you are working in the Print Layout view, the only way to see which section you're in is to look at the number displayed on the status bar (see Figure 20.2).

After you have the new section in the document, you can apply page formatting to it as needed.

If you want to delete a section break, place the mouse pointer in the selection area and select the section break the same as you would any other line of text (this won't work in the Print Layout view). After the section break is selected, press the **Delete** key to remove it.

Section breaks are visible in the Normal View.

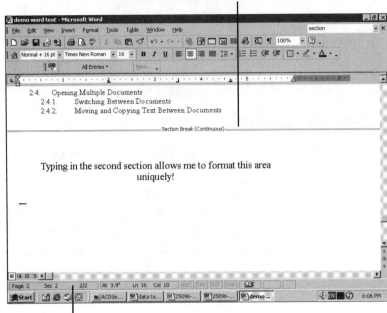

The status bar lists which section your pointer is in.

Figure 20.2 You can easily find out which section of a document you are in by reading the status bar or switching the document to Normal View.

Creating a Table of Contents

If you want to make it easy for the reader of a large document to find specific sections or parts of the document, you must include a table of contents. Creating a table of contents in Word relies heavily on using specific text styles to format and organize your document. As long as you do this, creating a table of contents is actually very straightforward.

For example, you can use either Word's built-in heading styles (Heading 1, Heading 2, Heading 3, and so forth) to format the different levels of headings in the document, or you can create your own styles to do so. Using these headings requires you to use some methodology to break down the contents of your document, such as using section levels or chapter levels. The important thing is that you use them consistently to format the various headings that you use in the document.

A good example is a document that is divided into parts and then further subdivided into chapters (each part contains several chapters). If you use Word's heading styles to format the different division levels in the document, you would use Heading 1 for the parts (Part I, Part II, and so forth) and Heading 2 for the chapter titles. By assigning these built-in styles (or your own) to your different headings, you can generate a table of contents that shows two levels: parts and chapters. This process works because Word can pinpoint a particular heading level by the style that you've assigned to it (for more about working with and creating styles, see Lesson 10, "Working with Styles").

After you've placed your various headings for parts, chapters, or other divisions into your document and have assigned a particular style to each group of headings, you are ready to use the Word Table of Contents feature to generate the actual table of contents.

To create a table of contents using the Word heading styles—or unique styles that you have created—follow these steps:

1. Create a blank page at the beginning of your document for your table of contents (or create a new section in which to place your table of contents) and place your insertion point in it.

2. On the **Insert** menu, choose **Reference, Index and Tables**.

3. When the Index and Tables dialog box appears, select the **Table of Contents** tab (see Figure 20.3).

Figure 20.3   The Table of Contents tab on the Index and Tables dialog box is where you specify the options for your new table of contents. You see both a Print Preview and a Web Preview.

4. The Table of Contents tab provides you with a preview of the table of contents (TOC) hierarchy for Word's built-in heading styles. If you used the Word heading styles to format and specify the various division levels in your document, you can skip down to step 7. If you made your own unique heading or section styles, click the **Options** button.

5. The Table of Contents Options dialog box appears. This is where you specify the styles you used to format the various TOC levels in your document. Scroll down through the **Available Styles** list. To specify a style as a TOC hierarchical level, type the level number (1, 2, 3, and so on) into the appropriate style's TOC level box.

6. When you have selected the styles that serve as your various TOC levels, click **OK** to return to the Table of Contents tab.

7. To select a style for the TOC, click the **Formats** drop-down list. You can choose from several styles, such as Classic, Distinctive, and Fancy. After you select a format, a preview is provided in the Print Preview and Web Preview areas of the dialog box.

TIP **Open the Outlining Toolbar for Quick Access of TOC Features** If you will be editing headings in the document that will affect the TOC after you generate it, you might want to click the **Show Outlining Toolbar** button on the Table of Contents tab. This opens the Outlining toolbar. After generating the TOC and doing any editing in the document, you can use the Update TOC button on the Outlining toolbar to quickly regenerate the TOC. The toolbar also provides a Go to TOC button that can be used to quickly move from anywhere in the document back to the TOC.

8. Use the various check boxes on the tab to select or deselect options for formatting the table of contents. After you've specified options such as right align, page numbers, and the tab leader style, you are ready to generate the table of contents; click **OK**.

Your new table of contents appears in the document (see Figure 20.4). You can add a title to the table of contents (such as Table of Contents) and format the text as needed. If you want to remove the table of contents from the document, place the mouse pointer in the selection area to the left of the table of contents. Click to select the TOC. Press the **Delete** key to remove it from the document.

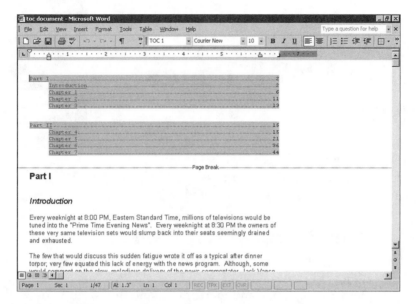

Figure 20.4   The table of contents is generated at the insertion point in your document. You can add your own title.

TIP   **Use the TOC to Quickly Move to a Particular Chapter**   A real slick feature associated with a table of contents in your document is that you can use it to quickly jump to a particular part of your document. For example, if you wanted to move to the beginning of Chapter 3 in the document, from the TOC, press **Ctrl+click** on the Chapter 3 notation in the table of contents. You are linked directly to the beginning of Chapter 3.

Creating Web Pages in Word

In this lesson, you learn how to work with Word's capability to build World Wide Web pages, and you learn how to add hyperlinks to your documents that quickly take you to a particular Web page.

What Is the World Wide Web?

The Internet is a global network of interconnected computer systems that provides several ways for users to communicate with each other, such as electronic mail (e-mail), Internet Relay Chat, and more important, the World Wide Web (WWW). The Web is the newest onramp to the Internet, and it enables you to move quickly from computer to computer (no matter the distance between the computers) by hopping from Web page to Web page using a Web browser (such as Microsoft Internet Explorer).

The sites that you view on the Web are made up of linked documents created in the *HTML (Hypertext Markup Language)* programming language. Your Web browser is able to translate HTML into a format that is viewable (and usable) on your home or office computer.

 TERM   **HTML**   Hypertext Markup Language is the coding system used to create Web pages for the World Wide Web. Basically, all documents must be translated into this universal language before being published to the WWW.

In the Web's infancy, the creation of a Web site required a pretty good understanding of the HTML language so that the various elements of the Web pages included on the Web site were coded with the appropriate HTML tag. In very basic terms, tagging Web page headings, pictures, or other elements with HTML codes is not unlike using a Word style to format a particular line of text or paragraph.

Word makes it very easy for you to create Web pages for the WWW; you can create your own personal Web site or create Web pages for use on your corporate Web site. Word even provides a wizard that walks you through the steps of Web page creation.

Saving a Word Document As a Web Page

One way to create an HTML file from a Word document is to create the document in Word (as a typical document) and then save it in the HTML file format. This strategy enables you to use all of Word's familiar layout features to create a document that looks good when it is viewed online using a Web browser.

Even if you save the document in the HTML file format, you can still open it in Word and edit the document when needed. To save a Word document as an HTML file, follow these steps:

1. Create the document the same as you would any other Word document. You can include graphics, links to objects, and so on.
2. Select **File**, **Save As Web Page**. The Save As dialog box appears.
3. Using the **Save In** drop-down box, select the location where you would like to save the HTML file. Also type a name for your HTML document into the **File Name** box (the format of the HTML document has already been selected for you in the Save As Type box).

   If you are on a corporate network that has an Internet Web server (a computer that hosts the company's Web site), or if you are supplied with Web space on your Internet service provider's Web server, you can save your HTML document directly to the server itself. All you need to know is the FTP address of the server (something like ftp.webserver.com). In the **Save In** drop-down box, select **Add/Modify FTP Locations**. The Add/Modify FTP Locations dialog box appears. Type in the name of the FTP site and provide your username and password. When you click **OK**, the FTP site is added to the list of folders in the Save In drop-down box. Select the FTP site as the location to which you save the file. Then click **OK** to save the file.

 FTP   FTP, or File Transport Protocol, is an Internet service used to send and receive files. An FTP server is a computer on the Internet that enables you to save and retrieve files using the File Transport Protocol, which is supported by all the Office applications.

 Saving Files Directly to a Web Server   If you save to the Web server of an Internet service provider, be sure that you are connected to the Internet through your dial-in service before you attempt to save the HTML file directly to the FTP location.

4. Click **Save** to save the HTML document to the specified location.

Even though your file is now in the HTML format, you can still open the document in Word and edit the document as needed. Figure 21.1 shows a document in the HTML format open in the Word window.

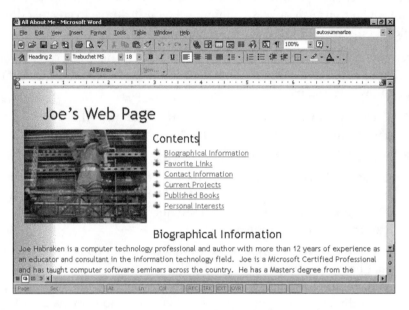

Figure 21.1 Use Word's various desktop publishing features to design a document, and then save it as a Web page for use on your Web site.

Creating a Web Site with a Wizard

If you would like more assistance in formulating and laying out a complete Web site that looks good and works well on the WWW, you can take advantage of the Word Web Page Wizard. The wizard walks you through the Web site creation process and helps you choose various themes and layouts for your new Web page or pages.

To create a Web page using the wizard, follow these steps:

1. Select **File**, **New**. In the New Document task pane, click the **General Templates** link to bring up the Templates dialog box (see Figure 21.2).

2. Several types of Web page templates reside on the Web Pages tab. To start the Web Page Wizard, double-click the **Web Page Wizard** icon.

3. The Web Page Wizard dialog box appears in the Word document window. To begin, click **Next**.

Figure 21.2 Double-click the Web Page Wizard icon on the Web Pages tab to begin the process of creating a Web page.

4. This wizard screen asks that you enter a name for your Web site and select a Web site location (the computer or server to which you want to save the file). If you are saving the file directly to a Web server, use the appropriate FTP address. Otherwise, save it to an appropriate folder on your computer (see Figure 21.3). Then click **Next** to continue.

Figure 21.3 Specify a name and a location for your new Web site.

5. On the next screen, select the navigational setup for your page. You can choose to have a frame on the left side of the Web page by selecting the **Vertical Frame** option button or on the top of the Web page by selecting **Horizontal Frame**. If you don't want a navigational frame on your main Web page, select the **Separate Page** option button. After making your selection, click **Next** to continue.

TERM   **Frame**   A separate area or pane in the Web page window that typically contains navigational links. When you click a particular link in the frame, the Web page referenced appears in the main part of the Web page window.

6. On the next page, you can determine how many pages you would like in your new Web site (see Figure 21.4). The default is a Personal Web page (the main page for the site) and two blank pages. To add additional blank pages, click **Add New Blank Page**. You can also add existing files to your Web site by clicking **Add Existing File** and then selecting the appropriate file in the Add Existing File dialog box. Click **OK** to return to the wizard. When you have selected the number of pages or files you want to have in your Web site, click **Next** to continue.

Figure 21.4   Specify the number of pages you would like in your new Web site.

 TIP   **Determining the Number of Pages in Your Web Site**   When you are trying to figure out the number of pages for your Web site, remember that a Web browser, such as Internet Explorer, only really shows one screen of information at a time. You are better off breaking up the information that you want to present on your Web site into several pages (where you only use the top half of the page for information). Having several one-screen pages is preferable to having one very long Web page that would require a viewer to scroll through a lot of information. Think of your Web site as a collection of index cards that are linked rather than full pages of information.

7. On the next wizard screen, you can arrange your link pages in the order you want them to appear on the Web site. Select a particular page in the list, and then use the **Move Up** or **Move Down** buttons to change the position of the page. When you have organized your pages. You should arrange the pages as you would have them appear on your Web site. The introductory Web page should be first, and subsequent pages should be listed as you would access them on the Web site. (Think of this wizard screen as providing you with a way to create a visual index of how your pages should appear on the site.) When you have arranged the pages, click **Next** to continue.

8. On the next wizard screen, you can select a theme for your new Web site. Themes provide colors and design elements for your new Web pages. To look at the list of themes available, click the **Browse Themes** button. Click a particular theme to see a preview. When you have selected the theme you want to use, click **OK** to return to the wizard. Then click **Next** to continue.

Theme A predetermined set of colors and design elements that you can use for your Web pages. Word provides several themes for your use.

9. The final screen of the Web Page Wizard appears. Click **Finish** to end the process and view your new Web page in the Word window.

Your new Web page consists of premade links, design elements, and various topic areas that contain placeholder text (see Figure 21.5). You must fill in the various information areas to personalize the Web pages created for your use.

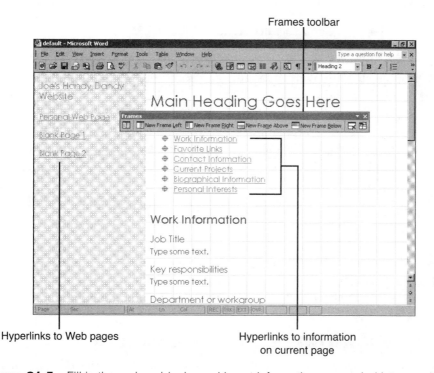

Figure 21.5 Fill in the various blanks and insert information as needed into your Web page's placeholder text.

When the new Web page opens, the Frames toolbar also appears. This toolbar enables you to place new frames anywhere on a Web page. A frame becomes an independent area on the Web page. It can be used to place text or graphics (by default, your Web pages are created with two frames).

To add a new frame, place the insertion point on the current page where you want to place the new frame. Then, click the appropriate button on the Frame toolbar. You can place the new frame to the left, right, above, or below the frame that currently holds the insertion point.

You can also change the theme for your Web site if you want. Select **Format, Themes**, and then select a new theme from the list. Click **OK** to return to your Web page.

Creating a Web Page from Scratch

You can also create your Web pages from scratch, which means you have to add the various elements (pictures, hyperlinks, and so on) that make up the page. This is also a requirement for blank pages that you have included in a Web site that the Web Page Wizard generates.

To create a Web page from scratch, follow these steps:

1. Select **File, New**. In the New dialog box, click the **General** tab if necessary.

2. Double-click the **Web Page** template. Your new Web document opens in the Web Layout view.

3. Add the various elements (text and graphics) to your document as required, the same as you would a normal Word document. For headings on your Web page, use the heading styles provided in the **Style** drop-down box on the Word Formatting toolbar (or create your own styles or modify the styles available, if you want).

4. After adding the text and other elements to the new Web document, save the file. It is automatically saved in the Web document (HTML) format.

 TIP **Where Is the Frames Toolbar?** You can use the Frames toolbar when working on a Web page created using the Web Page template. Right-click on any toolbar and select **Frames** from the list that appears.

Adding Hyperlinks to a Document

An important aspect of creating Web pages is being able to insert a *hyperlink* into a particular document. Hyperlinks provide the main navigational tool for the Web.

If you've spent any time on the Web at all, you know that you move from site to site using hyperlinks.

You can also designate graphics that you create and pictures that you place on your Web pages as hyperlinks. Rather than clicking a text link, you click a picture, and it takes you to the referenced Web site.

Hyperlink   A hyperlink references another Web page or site. Hyperlinks can appear as text or graphics on a Web page. When the hyperlink is clicked, you are taken to that page or site.

Hyperlinks Can Reference Regular Documents and Files   Hyperlinks don't have to reference Web pages or Web sites. They can be used to link typical Word documents. For example, you can use a hyperlink to open another Word file on your hard drive.

When you create Web pages using the Web Page Wizard, hyperlinks are automatically created in your Web documents. They appear as underlined text elements. They also appear in a particular color. After you use a hyperlink, it appears in a different color when you return to the page containing it. This lets you know that you've used that particular link before.

To place a hyperlink into a Word document, follow these steps:

1. Select the text or other items that will serve as the hyperlink.

2. Select **Insert**, **Hyperlink**. The Insert Hyperlink dialog box appears (see Figure 21.6).

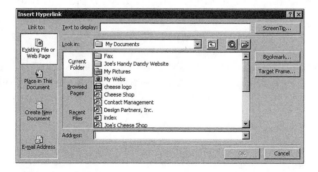

Figure 21.6   Enter the Web site address or the local filename for the new hyperlink into the Insert Hyperlink dialog box.

3. Enter the Web site address (URL—Uniform Resource Locator name—such as www.mcp.com) into the **Address** box.

4. To have text other than the actual hyperlink address appear as the hyperlink, type the text into the Text to Display box.

5. Click **OK**. You return to your document. The hyperlink is underscored and appears in a different color, denoting it as a hyperlink.

6. Repeat steps 2–4 as necessary to create all the hyperlinks for your document.

You can also create nontext hyperlinks. To make a picture, button, or other design element a hyperlink, right-click the object and select **Hyperlink** from the shortcut menu. Enter the address for the Web site into the **Web Page Name** box of the Insert Hyperlink dialog box. Click **OK**. Now when you click the picture hyperlink, you are taken to the referenced Web address.

Previewing Your Web Pages

You can preview your Web pages in the Internet Explorer Web browser as you work on them. This enables you to get a Web-based view of how your pages are turning out. In the Internet Explorer window, you can also check out any hyperlinks that you've placed on your Web page.

To preview your Web page in Internet Explorer, follow these steps:

1. Select **File**, **Web Page Preview**. Microsoft Internet Explorer opens with your Web page in its window.

2. Test your hyperlinks and other command elements as needed.

3. When you have finished viewing your Web page in Internet Explorer, click the **Close** (**X**) button on the upper-right corner of the window. You return to the Word window and your document.

Creating Web pages in Word can be quite easy (and very satisfying) because you are working in an environment that you use to create a variety of other, more "typical," documents.

Excel

Creating a New Workbook

In this lesson, you learn how to start and exit Excel and you become familiar with the Excel window. You also learn how to create new workbooks and open existing workbook files.

Starting Excel

Excel is a spreadsheet program that can help you create worksheets and invoices and do simple and sophisticated number crunching; it is designed to help you calculate the results to formulas and help you analyze numerical data.

To start Excel from the Windows desktop, follow these steps:

1. Click the **Start** button, and the Start menu appears.
2. Choose **Programs**, and the Programs menu appears.
3. Choose **Microsoft Excel** to start the program.

Understanding the Excel Window

When you click the Microsoft Excel icon, the Excel application window appears, displaying a blank workbook labeled Book1 (see Figure 1.1). On the right side of the Excel window is the New Workbook task pane. This task pane enables you to open existing Excel workbooks or create new blank workbooks or workbooks based on various Excel templates (which is discussed later in the lesson).

TIP **Close the Task Pane** If you would like a little more room in the Excel window to work on the current workbook sheet, click the **Close (X)** button on the task pane.

When you work in Excel, you use workbook files to hold your numerical data, formulas, and other objects, such as Excel charts. Each Excel workbook can consist of several sheets; each sheet is called a worksheet.

Workbook An Excel file is called a workbook. Each workbook consists of several worksheets made up of rows and columns of information.

You enter your numbers and formulas on one of the workbook's worksheets. Each worksheet consists of 256 columns. The columns begin with column A and proceed through the alphabet. The 27th column is AA, followed by AB, AC, and this convention for naming subsequent columns continues through the entire alphabet until you end up with the last column (column 256), which is designated IV.

Each worksheet also consists of 65,536 rows. The intersection of a column and a row on the worksheet is called a cell. Each cell has an address that consists of the column and row that intersect to make the cell. For example, the very first cell on a worksheet is in column A and row 1, so the cell's address is A1.

 Worksheet   One sheet in an Excel workbook. Each worksheet consists of 256 columns and 65,536 rows (plenty of space to create even the most enormous spreadsheets).

 Cell   Where a row and column intersect, each cell has an address that consists of the column letter and row number (A1, B3, C4, and so on). You enter data and formulas in the cells to create your worksheets.

Figure 1.1 shows cell A1 highlighted in worksheet 1 (designated as Sheet1 on its tab) of Workbook 1 (designated in the title bar as Book1; this will change to a particular filename after you name the workbook using the Save function).

The Excel window shown here includes many of the various elements available in other Office applications, such as Word or PowerPoint. These elements include a menu bar (from which you select commands), a status bar (which displays the status of the current activity), and toolbars (which contain buttons and drop-down lists that provide quick access to various commands and features).

In addition, the window contains several elements that are unique to Excel, as shown in Table 1.1.

Table 1.1   Elements of the Excel Window

Element	Description
Formula bar	When you enter information into a cell, it appears in the Formula bar. You can use the Formula bar to edit the data later. The cell's location also appears in the Formula bar.
Column headings	The letters across the top of the worksheet, which identify the columns in the worksheet.
Row headings	The numbers down the side of the worksheet, which identify the rows in the worksheet.

Table 1.1 Continued

Element	Description
Cell selector	The dark outline that indicates the active cell. (It highlights the cell you are currently working in.)
Worksheet tabs	These tabs help you move from worksheet to worksheet within the workbook.

Figure 1.1 Excel provides a new workbook and the menus and toolbars necessary for doing some serious number crunching.

Starting a New Workbook

As you've already seen, when you start Excel, it opens a new blank workbook. It is ready to accept data entry, which is discussed in Lesson 2, "Entering Data into the Worksheet."

The empty workbook that appears when you start Excel is pretty much a blank canvas, but Excel also enables you to create new workbooks based on a template. A *template* is a predesigned workbook that you can modify to suit your needs. Excel contains templates for creating invoices, expense reports, and other common business accounting forms.

To create a new workbook, follow these steps:

1. Open the **File** menu and select **New**. The New Workbook task pane appears on the right side of the Excel window (if you did not close it as outlined earlier, it should already be open).

2. The New Workbook task pane enables you to create new blank workbooks or create workbooks based on a template (see Figure 1.2).

Figure 1.2 The New Workbook task pane provides quick access to commands for creating new Excel workbooks.

3. To create a blank workbook, click the **Blank Workbook** icon. A new blank workbook opens in the Excel window.

  TIP **Instant Workbook** You can also quickly start a new blank workbook by clicking the **New** button on the Standard toolbar.

Blank templates are fine when you have a design in mind for the overall look of the workbook. However, for some help with workbook layout and formatting, you can base your new workbook on an Excel template. To use an Excel template, follow these steps:

1. Click the **General Templates** icon in the New from Template menu of the New Workbook task pane. The Templates dialog box appears.

2. Click the **Spreadsheet Solutions** tab on the Templates dialog box. The various workbook template icons appear (see Figure 1.3).

Figure 1.3   The Spreadsheet Solutions tab provides the different Excel templates.

3. Select a template by clicking its icon, and then click **OK** or press **Enter**. A new workbook opens onscreen with a default name based on the template you chose. For example, if you chose the Timecard template, the new workbook is named Timecard1, as shown at the top of Figure 1.4.

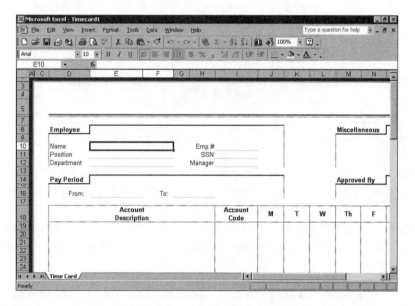

Figure 1.4   A new workbook based on a template provides a basic layout for a particular business form.

Saving and Naming a Workbook

Whether you build your workbook from a blank template or use one of the Excel templates, after you enter some data into the workbook, you should save the file (you learn about data entry in Lesson 2, "Entering Data into the Worksheet"). Also, because changes that you make to the workbook are not automatically saved, you should occasionally save the edited version of your work.

The first time you save a workbook, you must name it and specify a location where it should be saved. Follow these steps to save your workbook:

 1. Open the **File** menu and select **Save**, or click the **Save** button on the Standard toolbar. The Save As dialog box appears (see Figure 1.5).

Figure 1.5   Specify the name and location for your new workbook in the Save As dialog box.

2. Type the name you want to give the workbook in the **File Name** text box. You can use up to 218 characters, including any combination of letters, numbers, and spaces.

3. Normally, Excel saves your workbooks in the My Documents folder. To save the file to a different folder or drive (such as a network drive), select a new location using the **Save In** list.

CAUTION   **The Folder I Want to Save In Doesn't Exist!**   You can create a new folder from the Save As dialog box: click the **Create New Folder** button on the toolbar of the Save As dialog box, type a name for the new folder, and then press **Enter**.

4. Click **Save** to save your workbook and close the Save As dialog box.

To save changes that you make to a workbook that you have previously saved, just click the **Save** button on the Standard toolbar. You can also press the short-cut key combination of **Ctrl+S** to save changes to your workbook.

Saving a Workbook Under a New Name or Location

There might be an occasion when you want to save a copy of a particular workbook under a different name or in a different location. Excel makes it easy for you to make duplicates of a workbook. Follow these steps:

1. Select the **File** menu and select **Save As**. The Save As dialog box opens, just as if you were saving the workbook for the first time.

2. To save the workbook under a new name, type the new filename over the exist-ing name in the **File Name** text box.

3. To save the new file on a different drive or in a different folder, select the drive letter or the folder from the **Save In** list.

4. To save the new file in a different format (such as Lotus 1-2-3 or Quattro Pro), click the **Save As Type** drop-down arrow and select the desired format.

5. Click the **Save** button or press **Enter**.

 TIP **Saving Excel Workbooks in Other File Formats** Occasionally, you might share Excel workbook data with co-workers or colleagues who don't use Excel. Being able to save Excel workbooks in other file formats, such as Lotus 1-2-3 (as discussed in step 4), enables you to provide another user a file that they can open in their spreadsheet program.

Opening an Existing Workbook

If you have a workbook you've previously saved that you would like to work on, you must open the file first, before you can make any changes. Follow these steps to open an existing workbook:

1. Open the **File** menu and select **Open**, or click the **Open** button on the Standard toolbar. The Open dialog box shown in Figure 1.6 appears.

2. If the file is not located in the current folder, open the **Look In** drop-down list box and select the correct drive and folder.

3. Select the file you want to open in the files and folders list.

Figure 1.6 Use the Open dialog box to locate and open an existing Excel workbook.

4. To see a preview of the workbook before you open it, click the **Views** button and select **Preview**. Excel displays the contents of the workbook in a window to the right of the dialog box.

5. Click **Open** to open the currently selected workbook.

TIP **Recently Used Workbooks** If the workbook you want to open is one of your four most recently used workbooks, you'll find it listed at the bottom of the File menu. It will also be listed at the top of the New Workbook task pane (if the task pane is active).

Closing Workbooks

When you have finished with a particular workbook and want to continue working in Excel, you can easily close the current workbook. Click the **Close** (x) button in the upper-right corner of the workbook. (There are two Close buttons: The one on top closes Excel; the one below it closes the current workbook window.) You can also close the current workbook by selecting **File, Close**. If you have changed the workbook since the last time you saved it, you will be prompted to save any changes.

TIP **It's Closing Time!** If you have more than one workbook open, you can close all of them at once by holding down the **Shift** key, selecting the **File** menu, and then selecting **Close All**.

Exiting Excel

When you have finished working with Excel, you need to exit the application. This closes all workbooks that are currently open. To exit Excel, select the **File** menu and select **Exit**. Or you can click the **Close** (**x**) button at the upper-right corner of the Excel window.

If you have changed any of the workbooks that you were working with, you are prompted to save changes to these workbook files before exiting Excel.

Entering Data into the Worksheet

In this lesson, you learn how to enter different date types into an Excel worksheet.

Understanding Excel Data Types

When you work in Excel, you enter different types of information, such as text, numbers, dates, times, formulas, and functions (which is a special built-in formula provided by Excel). Excel data basically comes in two varieties: labels and values.

A label is a text entry; it is called a label because it typically provides descriptive information such as the name of a person, place, or thing. A label has no numerical significance in Excel; it's just there to describe accompanying values.

 Label Any text entry made on an Excel worksheet.

A value is data that has numerical significance. This includes numbers, dates, and times that you enter on your worksheet. Values can be acted on by formulas and functions. Formulas are discussed in Lesson 3, "Performing Simple Calculations," and Excel functions in Lesson 5, "Performing Calculations with Functions."

 Values Entries, such as numbers and dates, that have numerical significance and can be acted upon by formulas or functions.

Entering Text

Text is any combination of letters, numbers, and spaces. By default, text is automatically left-aligned in a cell, whereas numerical data is right-aligned.

To enter text into a cell, follow these steps:

1. Use your mouse or the keyboard arrows to select the cell in which you want to enter text.

2. Type the text. As you type, your text appears in the cell and in the Formula bar, as shown in Figure 2.1.

Figure 2.1   Data that you enter into a cell also appears in the Formula bar as you type it.

3. Press **Enter**. Your text appears in the cell, left-aligned. The cell selector moves down one cell. You can also press **Tab** or an arrow key to enter the text and move to the next cell to the right (or in the direction of the arrow).

CAUTION

But My Entry Doesn't Fit!   When text does not fit into a cell (because of the column width set for that column), Excel displays the information in one of two ways: If the next cell is empty, the text overflows into that cell, allowing you to see your entire entry. If the cell to the right of your entry is not empty, you will be able to see only the portion of your entry that fits within the confines of the cell. This can easily be remedied by changing the column width. You learn about changing column widths in Lesson 12, "Inserting and Removing Cells, Rows, and Columns."

TIP

Entering Numbers As Text   To enter a number that you want treated as text (such as a ZIP code), precede the entry with a single quotation mark ('), as in '46220. The single quotation mark is an alignment prefix that tells Excel to treat the following characters as text and left-align them in the cell. You do not have to do this to "text" numerical entries, but it ensures that they will not be mistakenly acted upon by formulas or functions.

Tips on Entering Column and Row Labels

Column and row labels identify your data. Column labels appear across the top of the worksheet beneath the worksheet title (if any). Row labels are entered on the left side of the worksheet.

Column labels describe what the numbers in a column represent. Typically, column labels specify time intervals such as years, months, days, quarters, and so on. Row labels describe what the numbers in each row represent. Typically, row labels specify data categories, such as product names, employee names, or income and expense items in a budget.

When entering your column labels, enter the first label and press the **Tab** key instead of pressing Enter. This moves you to the next cell on the right so that you can enter another column label. When entering row labels, use the down-arrow key instead of the Tab key. Figure 2.2 shows the various labels for a quarterly sales summary.

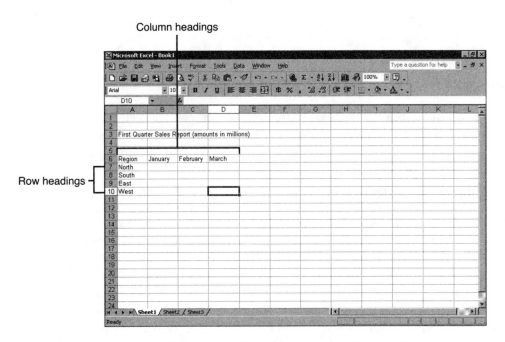

Figure 2.2   Column and row headings serve as labels for the data you enter on the worksheet.

If you need to enter similar data (such as a series of months or years) as column or row labels, you can enter them quickly as a series; this technique is discussed later in this lesson.

Adding Comments to Cells

Although not really considered cell content (such as labels and values), you can add comments to particular cells. These comments allow you to associate information with a cell—information that does not appear (by default) with the worksheet when sent to the printer.

Comments are similar to placing a Post-it note on a cell, reminding you that an outstanding issue is related to that cell. For example, if you need to check the value that you've placed in a particular cell to make sure that it's accurate, you can place a comment in the cell (see Figure 2.3). Cells containing comments are marked with a red triangle in the upper-right corner of the cell. To view a comment, place the mouse pointer on the comment triangle.

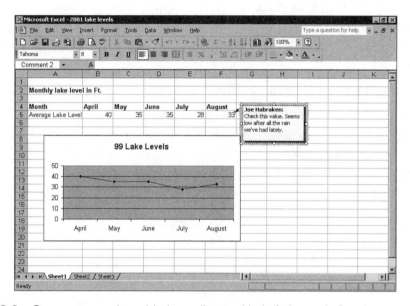

Figure 2.3   Comments can be added to cells as a kind of electronic Post-it note.

To insert a comment into a cell, follow these steps:

1. Click the cell in which you want to place the comment.
2. Select **Insert**, **Comment**. A comment box appears next to the cell.
3. Type your information into the comment box.
4. Click anywhere else in the worksheet to close the comment box.

You can also easily remove comments from cells. Select the cell, and then select **Edit** and point at **Clear**. On the cascading menu, select **Comments** to remove the comment.

Entering Numbers

Data that serves as the values in your workbooks can include the numeric characters 0–9. Because formulas are also considered values (you learn about simple calculations in Lesson 3, "Performing Simple Calculations"), other valid value characters include symbols such as +, −, /, and *. You can also use characters such as a comma (,), a percent sign (%), or a dollar sign ($) in your values. You will find, however, that you can save yourself a few data-entry keystrokes and add these characters using different Excel formatting options (you learn about Excel formatting in Lesson 9, "Changing How Numbers and Text Look").

For example, you could enter the dollar amount $700.00 including the dollar sign and the decimal point. However, it's probably faster to enter the 700 into the cell and then format all the cells that contain dollar amounts after you have entered all the data.

To enter a value, follow these steps:

1. Click in the cell where you want to enter the value.

2. Type the value. To enter a negative number, precede it with a minus sign or surround it with parentheses.

3. Press **Enter** or the **Tab** key; the value appears in the cell right-aligned. Figure 2.4 shows various values entered into a simple worksheet.

	A	B	C	D	E	F
1						
2						
3	First Quarter Sales Report (amounts in millions)					
4						
5						
6	Region	January	February	March		
7	North	70	35	90		
8	South	100	56	66		
9	East	54	84	55		
10	West	66	33	70		
11						
12						
13						
14						

Figure 2.4 Values are right-aligned in a cell.

 TIP **What Are All Those Pound Signs?** If you enter a number and it appears in the cell as all pound signs (######) or in scientific notation (such as 7.78E+06), the cell just isn't wide enough to display the entire number. To fix it, double-click the right border of the column's heading. The column expands to fit the largest entry in that column. See Lesson 12, "Inserting and Removing Cells, Rows, and Columns," for more information on working with column widths.

Entering Dates and Times

Dates that you enter into an Excel workbook have numerical significance. Excel converts the date into a number that reflects the number of days that have elapsed since

January 1, 1900. Even though you won't see this number (Excel displays your entry as a normal date), the number is used whenever you use this date in a calculation. Times are also considered values. Excel sees them as the number of seconds that have passed since 12 a.m.

Follow these steps to enter a date or time:

1. Click in the cell where you want to enter a date or a time.

2. To enter a date, use the format MM/DD/YY or the format MM-DD-YY, as in 5/9/01 or 5-9-01.

   To enter a time, be sure to specify a.m. or p.m., as in 7:21 p or 8:22 a.

 TIP   A.M. or P.M.?   Unless you type am or pm after your time entry, Excel assumes that you are using a 24-hour international clock. Therefore, 8:20 is assumed to be a.m., not p.m. (20:20 would be p.m.: 8 plus 12 hours). Therefore, if you mean p.m., type the entry as 8:20 pm (or 8:20 p). Note that you must type a space between the time and the am or pm notation.

3. Press **Enter**. As long as Excel recognizes the entry as a date or a time, it appears right-aligned in the cell. If Excel doesn't recognize it, it's treated as text and left-aligned.

After you enter your date or time, you can format the cells to display the date or time exactly as you want it to appear, such as September 16, 1998, or 16:50 (international time). If you're entering a column of dates or times, you can format the entire column in one easy step. To format a column, click the column header to select the column. Then open the **Format** menu and select **Cells**. On the **Numbers** tab, select the date or time format you want to use (you learn more about formatting text and numbers in Lesson 9).

Copying (Filling) the Same Data to Other Cells

Another way to enter labels or values onto a sheet is to use the Fill feature. You can copy (fill) an entry into surrounding cells. For example, suppose you have a list of salespeople on a worksheet, and they will each get a $100 bonus. You can enter the 100 once and then use the Fill feature to insert multiple copies of 100 into nearby cells. To use the Fill feature for copying, follow these steps:

1. Click the fill handle of the cell (the small block in the lower-right corner of the cell) that holds the data that you want to copy (see Figure 2.5).

2. Drag the fill handle down or to the right to copy the data to adjacent cells. A data tag appears to let you know exactly what data is being copied into the cells.

	A	B	C	D	E	F
1						
2						
3						
4	Sales Force Data (First Quarter Totals)					
5						
6	First Name	Last Name	Total	Bonus		
7	Bob	Smith	800	100		
8	Alice	Turney	500			
9	Alfred	Juarez	789			
10	Katie	Jones	680			
11	John	Roberts	780			
12					100	
13						
14						
15						

Figure 2.5   Drag the fill handle to copy the contents of a cell into neighboring cells.

3. Release the mouse button. The data is "filled" into the selected cells.

When you release the mouse, a shortcut box for Fill options appears at the end of the cells that you filled. Copy Cells is the default option for the Fill feature, so you can ignore the shortcut box for the moment. It does come into play when you enter a series in the next section.

Watch That Fill!   The data you're copying replaces any existing data in the adjacent cells that you fill.

CAUTION

Entering a Series of Numbers, Dates, and Other Data

Entering a value *series* (such as January, February, and March or 1, 2, 3, 4, and so on) is accomplished using the Fill feature discussed in the preceding section. When you use the Fill feature, Excel looks at the cell holding the data and tries to determine whether you want to just copy that information into the adjacent cells or use it as the starting point for a particular series of data. For example, with Monday entered in the first cell of the series, Excel automatically inserts Tuesday, Wednesday, and so on into the adjacent cells when you use the Fill feature.

Sometimes Excel isn't quite sure whether you want to copy the data when you use Fill or create a series. This is where the Fill options shortcut box comes in. It enables you to select how the Fill feature should treat the data that you have "filled" into the adjacent cells. Figure 2.6 shows the creation of a day series using Fill.

Figure 2.6   Fill can also be used to create a series of data in adjacent cells.

When you create a series using Fill, the series progresses by one increment. For example, a series starting with 1 would proceed to 2, 3, 4, and so on. If you want to create a series that uses some increment other than 1, you must create a custom series, which is discussed in the next section.

Entering a Custom Series

If you want to create a series such as 10, 20, 30, where the series uses a custom increment between the values, you need to create a custom series. Excel provides two ways to create a custom series. To create a custom series using Fill, follow these steps:

1. Enter the first value in the series into a cell.

2. Enter the second value in the series into the next cell. For example, you might enter **10** into the first cell and then **20** into the second cell. This lets Excel know that the increment for the series is 10.

3. Select both cells by clicking the first cell and dragging over the second cell.

4. Drag the fill handle of the second cell to the other cells that will be part of the series. Excel analyzes the two cells, sees the incremental pattern, and re-creates it in subsequent cells.

You can also create a custom series using the Series dialog box. This enables you to specify the increment or step value for the series and even specify a stop value for the series.

1. Enter the first value in the series into a cell.

2. Select the cells that you want included in the series.

3. Select the **Edit** menu, point at **Fill**, and then select **Series**. The Series dialog box opens (see Figure 2.7).

Figure 2.7   The Series dialog box enables you to create a custom series.

4. Enter the Step Value for the series. You can also enter a Stop Value for the series if you did not select the cells used for the series in step 2. For example, if you want to add a series to a column of cells and have clicked in the first cell that will receive a value, using a Stop Value (such as 100 for a series that will go from 1 to 100) will "stop" entering values in the cells when it reaches 100—the Stop Value.

5. Click **OK** to create the series.

TIP   **Different Series Types**   Not only can you create a linear series using the Series dialog box (as discussed in the steps in this section), but you can also create growth and date series. In a growth series, the data you're copying replaces any existing data in the adjacent cells that you fill.

Taking Advantage of AutoComplete

Another useful feature that Excel provides to help take some of the drudgery out of entering information into a workbook is the AutoComplete feature. Excel keeps a list of all the labels that you enter on a worksheet by column. For example, suppose you have a worksheet tracking sales in Europe and you are entering country names, such as Germany, Italy, and so on, multiple times into a particular column in the worksheet. After you enter Germany the first time, it becomes part of the AutoComplete list for that column. The next time you enter the letter G into a cell in that column, Excel completes the entry as "Germany."

You can also select an entry from the AutoComplete list. This allows you to see the entire list of available entries. Follow these steps:

1. Enter your text and value data as needed onto the worksheet.

2. If you want to select a text entry from the AutoComplete list, to fill an empty cell, right-click that cell. A shortcut menu appears.

3. Select **Pick from List** from the shortcut menu. A list of text entries (in alphabetical order) appears below the current cell.

4. Click a word in the list to insert it into the current, empty cell.

 TIP   **Adding Data to Excel Using Voice Recognition**   The Office Speech Recognition feature can also be used to enter data into an Excel worksheet and to perform voice commands. If you have a computer that is set up with a sound card and microphone, you can use this feature. See Lesson 4, "Using the Office Speech Feature," in Part 1 of this book to learn how to get the voice feature up and running and to use it to enter information into Office applications such as Excel.

Performing Simple Calculations

In this lesson, you learn how to use formulas to calculate results in your worksheets.

Understanding Excel Formulas

One way to add calculations to an Excel workbook is to create your own formulas. Formulas are typically used to perform calculations such as addition, subtraction, multiplication, and division. More complex calculations are better left to Excel Functions, which is a built-in set of formulas that provide financial, mathematical, and statistical calculations. You learn more about functions in Lesson 5, "Performing Calculations with Functions."

Formulas that you create typically include cell addresses that reference cells on which you want to perform a calculation. Formulas also consist of mathematical operators, such as + (addition) or * (multiplication). For example, if you wanted to multiply two cells, such as C3 and D3, and then divide the product by 3, you would design a formula that looks like this:

`=(C3*D3)/3`

Notice that the formula begins with the equal sign (=). This lets Excel know that the information that you are placing in the cell is meant to do a calculation. The parentheses are used to let Excel know that you want C3 multiplied by D3 before the result is divided by 3. Creating appropriate formulas requires an understanding of the order of mathematical operations, or what is often called the rules of precedence. The natural order of math operations is covered in the next section.

As previously mentioned, you can create formulas that add, subtract, and multiply cells in the worksheet. Table 3.1 lists some of the operators that you can use and how you would use them in a simple formula.

Table 3.1 Excel's Mathematical Operators

Operator	Performs	Sample Formula	Result
^	Exponentiation	=A1^3	Enters the result of raising the value in cell A1 to the third power
+	Addition	=A1+A2	Enters the total of the values in cells A1 and A2
–	Subtraction	=A1–A2	Subtracts the value in cell A2 from the value in cell A1
*	Multiplication	=A2*A3	Multiplies the value in cell A2 by cell A3
/	Division	=A1/B1	Divides the value in cell A1 by the value in cell B1

Figure 3.1 shows some formulas that have been created for an Excel worksheet. So that you can see how I wrote the formulas, I've configured Excel so that it shows the formula that has been placed in a cell rather than the results of the formula (which is what you would normally see).

Figure 3.1 You can create formulas to do simple calculations in your worksheets.

Order of Operations

The order of operations, or *operator precedence*, simply means that some operations take precedence over other operations in a formula. For example, in the formula =C2+D2*E2, the multiplication of D2 times E2 takes precedence, so D2 is multiplied by E2 and then the value in cell C2 is added to the result.

You can force the precedence of an operation by using parentheses. For example, if you want C2 and D2 added before they are multiplied by E2, the formula would have to be written =(C2+D2)*E2.

The natural order of math operators follows:

1st	Exponent (^) and calculations within parentheses
2nd	Multiplication (*) and division (/)
3rd	Addition (+) and subtraction (–)

In the case of operations such as multiplication and division, which operate at the same level in the natural order, a formula containing the multiplication operator followed by the division operator will execute these operators in the order they appear in the formula from left to right. If you don't take this order into consideration, you could run into problems when entering your formulas. For example, if you want to determine the average of the values in cells A1, B1, and C1, and you enter =A1+B1+C1/3, you'll get the wrong answer. The value in C1 will be divided by 3, and that result will be added to A1+B1. To determine the total of A1 through C1 first, you must enclose that group of values in parentheses: =(A1+B1+C1)/3.

Entering Formulas

You can enter formulas in one of two ways: by typing the entire formula, including the cell addresses, or by typing the formula operators and selecting the cell references. Take a look at both ways.

To type a formula, perform the following steps:

1. Select the cell where you will place the formula.
2. Type an equal sign (=) into the cell to begin the formula.
3. Enter the appropriate cell references and operators for the formula. Figure 3.2 shows a simple multiplication formula. The formula also appears in the Formula bar as you type it. The cells that you specify in the formula are highlighted with a colored border.

SUM	▾ X ✓ ƒ	=D7*E7							
	A	B	C	D	E	F	G	H	
1									
2									
3	**Customer**								
4	**Orders**								
5									
6	First Name	Last Name	Product Ordered	Cost/Item	Amount	Total	Discount Coupon	Adjusted Total	
7	Pierre	Manger	hard drive	100	2	=D7*E7	10		
8	Bob	Jones	RAM 128 MB DIMM	80	4		5		
9	Alice	Barney	modem	90	1		0		
10	Kim	Reech	RAM 128 MB DIMM	80	3		5		
11	Larry	Curly-Moe	sound card	60	2		15		
12	Edward	Reech	keyboard	50	5		0		
13									
14									
15									

Figure 3.2   The formula appears in the cell and in the Formula bar as you type it.

4. Press **Enter** when you have finished the formula, and Excel calculates the result.

 TIP   **Unwanted Formula**   If you start to enter a formula and then decide you don't want to use it, you can skip entering the formula by pressing **Esc**.

To enter a formula by selecting cell addresses, follow these steps:

1. Click in the cell where you will place the formula.

2. Type the equal sign (=) to begin the formula.

3. Click the cell whose address you want to appear first in the formula. You can also click a cell in a different worksheet or workbook. The cell address appears in the cell and in the Formula bar.

4. Type a mathematical operator after the value to indicate the next operation you want to perform. The operator appears in the cell and in the Formula bar.

5. Continue clicking cells and typing operators until the formula is complete.

6. Press **Enter** to accept the formula and have Excel place its results into the cell.

 CAUTION   **Error!**   If ERR appears in a cell, you've likely made a mistake somewhere in the formula. Be sure you did not commit one of these common errors: dividing by zero, using a blank cell as a divisor, referring to a blank cell, deleting a cell used in a formula, or including a reference to the same cell in which the formula appears.

 TIP   **Natural Language Formulas**   Excel also enables you to create what are called Natural Language formulas. You can refer to a cell by its column heading name and the corresponding row label. For example, if you had a column labeled Total and a column labeled Discount for each customer, you can write a formula such as =Smith Total–Smith Discount. You are referring to cells by the labels that you have placed in the worksheet rather than the actual cell addresses.

Using the Status Bar AutoCalculate Feature

Using a feature that Excel calls AutoCalculate, you can view the sum of a column of cells simply by selecting the cells and looking at the status bar. The values in the selected cells are added. You can also right-click the AutoCalculate area of the status bar and choose different formulas, such as average, minimum, maximum, and count.

This feature is useful if you want to quickly check the total for a group of cells or compute the average. It also allows you to "try out" an Excel function (discussed in Lesson 5) before actually entering it into a cell. You can also view the average, minimum, maximum, and count of a range of cells. To display something other than the sum, highlight the group of cells you want the operation performed on, right-click the status bar, and select the option you want from the shortcut menu that appears (see Figure 3.3).

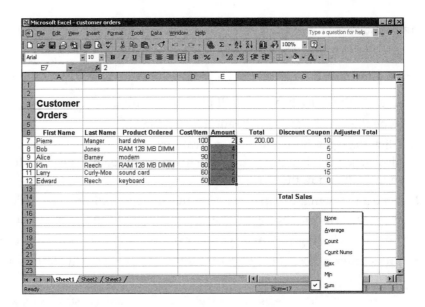

Figure 3.3   You can view the results of different built-in formulas in the status bar.

 TIP   **Where's the Status Bar?**   If the status bar is not visible on your screen, you can display it by selecting the **View** menu and then selecting **Status Bar**.

Displaying Formulas

Normally, Excel does not display the formula in a cell. Instead, it displays the result of the calculation. You can view the formula by selecting the cell and looking in the Formula bar. However, if you're trying to review all the formulas in a large worksheet, it would be easier if you could see them all at once (and even print them). If you want to view formulas in a worksheet, follow these steps:

1. Open the **Tools** menu and choose **Options**.

2. Click the **View** tab.

3. In the Window options area of the View tab (near the bottom of the tab), click to select the **Formulas** check box.

4. Click **OK**.

Editing Formulas

Editing a formula is the same as editing any entry in Excel. The following steps show how you do it:

1. Select the cell that contains the formula you want to edit.

2. Click in the Formula bar to place the insertion point in the formula, or press **F2** to enter Edit mode (the insertion point is placed at the end of the entry in that cell).

 TIP   **In-Cell Editing**   To quickly edit the contents of a cell, double-click the cell. The insertion point appears inside the cell, and you can make any necessary changes.

3. Press the left-arrow key or the right-arrow key to move the insertion point within the formula. Then, use the **Backspace** key to delete characters to the left, or use the **Delete** key to delete characters to the right. Type any additional characters.

4. When you finish editing the data, click the **Enter** button on the Formula bar or press **Enter** to accept your changes.

Manipulating Formulas and Understanding Cell References

In this lesson, you learn how to copy formulas, use relative and absolute cell references, and change calculation settings.

Copying Formulas

Copying labels and values in Excel is no big deal. You can use the Copy and Paste commands (discussed in Lesson 8, "Editing Worksheets") or you can use some of the Fill features discussed in Lesson 2, "Entering Data into the Worksheet." Copying or moving formulas, however, is a little trickier.

Suppose that you create the formula =D7*E7 and place it into cell F7, as shown in Figure 4.1. You have designed the formula to reference cells D7 and E7. However, Excel looks at these cell references a little differently. Excel sees cell D7 as the entry that is located two cells to the left of F7 (where the formula has been placed, in this example). It sees cell E7 as being the location that is one cell to the left of F7.

Excel's method of referencing cells is called *relative referencing*. The great thing about this method of referencing cells is that when you copy a formula to a new location, it adjusts to the relative cell references around it and provides you with the correct calculation.

For example, you could copy the formula in cell F7 to cell F8, and Excel would use relative referencing to change the cell addresses in the formula. The original formula =D7*E7 would appear as D8*D7 when copied to cell F8.

Relative referencing is very useful in most situations where you copy a formula to several cells in the same column. However, it can get you into trouble when you cut and paste a formula to a new location or copy the formula to a location where it can no longer reference the appropriate cells to provide you with the correct calculation. In these situations, you must use absolute referencing so that the formula references only specified cells and does not change the cell references in the formula when pasted to the new location. Absolute referencing is discussed in the next section.

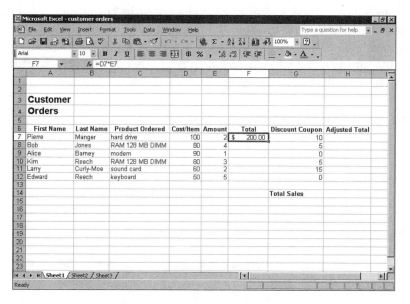

Figure 4.1 Formulas you place in Excel use relative referencing for calculations.

You can copy formulas using the Copy and Paste commands (see Lesson 8); however, when you need to copy a formula to multiple locations, you can also use the Fill feature discussed in Lesson 2.

Because Excel uses relative referencing by default, the formula adjusts to each of its new locations. An alternative way to "copy" a formula to multiple adjacent cells is to select all cells that will contain the formula before you actually write the formula in the first cell. Follow these steps:

1. Select all the cells that will contain the formula (dragging so that the cell that you will write the formula in is the first of the selected group of cells).

2. Enter the formula into the first cell.

3. Press **Ctrl+Enter** and the formula is placed in all the selected cells.

Get an Error?   If you get an error message in a cell after copying a formula, verify the cell references in the copied formula. For more information on sorting out cell referencing, see the next section in this lesson.

CAUTION

Using Relative and Absolute Cell Addresses

As mentioned at the beginning of this lesson, when you copy a formula from one place in the worksheet to another, Excel adjusts the cell references in the formulas relative to their new positions in the worksheet. There might be occasions when you don't want Excel to change the reference related to a particular cell that appears in a formula (or in an Excel function, which is discussed in Lesson 5, "Performing Calculations with Functions").

TIP   **Absolute Versus Relative**   An *absolute reference* is a cell reference in a formula that does not change when copied to a new location. A *relative reference* is a cell reference in a formula that is adjusted when the formula is copied.

For example, suppose you have a worksheet that computes the commission made on sales by each of your salespeople. Sales have been so good that you've decided to give each person on the sales team a $200 bonus. Figure 4.2 shows the worksheet that you've created.

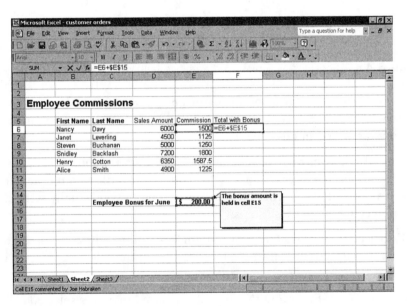

Figure 4.2   Some formulas require absolute references.

Notice that the bonus amount is contained in only one cell on the worksheet (cell E15). Therefore, when you create the formula that will be used in F6 and then copied to cells F7 through F11, you need to make sure that the bonus amount in cell E15 is always referenced by the formula. This is a case where you must "absolutely" reference the bonus amount in cell E15.

To make a cell reference in a formula absolute, add a $ (dollar sign) before the column letter and before the row number that make up the cell address. For example, in Figure 4.2, the formula in F6 must read as follows:

=E6+E15

The address, E15, refers to cell E15, meaning that cell E15 is absolutely referenced by the formula. This cell reference remains "locked" even when you copy the formula to the other cells in the E column.

To create an absolute reference in a formula (or a function, which is discussed in Lesson 5), create your formula as you normally would (as detailed in Lesson 3, "Performing Simple Calculations"). After typing or pointing out a cell address in a formula that needs to be an absolute reference, press **F4**. A dollar sign ($) is placed before the cell and row designation for that cell.

Some formulas might contain cell addresses where you will make the column designation absolute, but not the row (or vice versa). For example, you could have a formula $A2/2. You are telling Excel that the values will always be contained in column A (it is absolute), but the row reference (2) can change when the formula is copied. Having a cell address in a formula that contains an absolute designation and a relative reference is called a *mixed reference*.

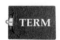

Mixed References   A reference that is only partially absolute, such as A$2 or $A2. When a formula that uses a mixed reference is copied to another cell, only part of the cell reference (the relative part) is adjusted.

Absolute referencing and mixed references are also required by some of Excel's built-in functions. You work with functions in the next lesson.

Recalculating the Worksheet

Excel automatically recalculates the results in your worksheet every time you enter a new value or edit a value or formula. This is fine for most workbooks. However, if you have a computer with limited memory and processing power, you might find that having Excel recalculate all the results in a very large worksheet every time you make a change means that you are sitting and waiting for Excel to complete the recalculation.

You can turn off the automatic recalculation. However, this won't be necessary except in situations where you are working with huge workbooks that contain a very large number of formulas, functions, and data. Turning off the automatic calculation feature also means that you must remember to manually recalculate the values

427

in the worksheet before you print. To change the recalculation setting, take the following steps:

1. Open the **Tools** menu and choose **Options**.

2. Click the **Calculation** tab to display the options shown in Figure 4.3.

Figure 4.3   You can turn off the automatic recalculation feature.

3. Select one of the following Calculation options:

   - **Automatic**—This is the default setting. It recalculates the entire workbook each time you edit or enter a formula.

   - **Automatic Except Tables**—This automatically recalculates everything except formulas in a data table.

   - **Manual**—This option tells Excel to recalculate only when you say so. To recalculate manually, press the **F9** key. When this option is selected, you can turn the Recalculate Before Save option off or on.

4. Click **OK.**

Performing Calculations with Functions

In this lesson, you learn how to perform calculations with functions and how to use the Insert Function feature to quickly insert functions into your worksheets.

What Are Functions?

You already learned in Lesson 3, "Performing Simple Calculations," how to create your own formulas in Excel. When you work with more complex calculations, you are better off using Excel's built-in formulas—functions.

Functions are ready-made formulas that perform a series of operations on a specified range of values. For example, to determine the sum of a series of numbers in cells A1 through H1, you can enter the function =SUM(A1:H1). Excel functions can do all kinds of calculations for all kinds of purposes, including financial and statistical calculations.

Every function consists of the following three elements:

- The = sign, which indicates that what follows is a function (formula).
- The function name, such as SUM, that indicates which operation that will be performed.
- A list of cell addresses, such as (A1:H1), which are to be acted upon by the function. Some functions can include more than one set of cell addresses, which are separated by commas (such as A1,B1,H1).

You can enter functions into the worksheet by typing the function and cell references (as you did with your own formulas), or you can use the Insert Function feature, which walks you through the process of creating a function in a worksheet (you will work with the Insert Function feature in a moment). Table 5.1 lists some of the Excel functions that you will probably use most often in your worksheets.

Table 5.1 Commonly Used Excel Functions

Function	Example	Description
AVERAGE	=AVERAGE(B4:B9)	Calculates the mean or average of a group of cell values.
COUNT	=COUNT(A3:A7)	Counts the number of cells that hold values in the selected range or group of cells. This can also be used to tell you how many cells are in a particular column, which tells you how many rows are in your spreadsheet.
IF	=IF(A3>=1000,"BONUS", "NO BONUS")	Allows you to place a conditional function in a cell. In this example, if A3 is greater than or equal to 1000, the true value, BONUS, is used. If A3 is less than 1000, the false value, NO BONUS, is placed in the cell.
MAX	=MAX(B4:B10)	Returns the maximum value in a range of cells.
MIN	=MIN(B4:B10)	Returns the minimum value in a range of cells.
PMT	=PMT(.0825/12,360, 180000)	Calculates the monthly payment on a 30-year loan (360 monthly payments) at 8.25% a year (.0825/12 a month) for $180,000.
SUM	=SUM(A1:A10)	Calculates the total in a range of cells.

TIP **Specify Text with Quotation Marks** When entering text into a function, the text must be enclosed within quotation marks. For example, in the function =IF(A5>2000,"BONUS","NO BONUS"), if the condition is met (the cell value is greater than 2000), the word BONUS will be returned by the function. If the condition is not met, the phrase NO BONUS will be returned in the cell by the function.

Excel provides a large number of functions listed by category. There are Financial functions, Date and Time functions, Statistical functions, and Logical functions (such as the IF function described in Table 5.1). The group of functions that you use most often depends on the type of worksheets you typically build. For example, if you do a lot of accounting work, you will find that the Financial functions offer functions for computing monthly payments, figuring out the growth on an investment, and even computing the depreciation on capital equipment.

Although some commonly used functions have been defined in Table 5.1, as you become more adept at using Excel you might want to explore some of the other functions available. Select **Help, Microsoft Excel Help**. On the Contents tab of the Help window, open the **Function Reference** topic. Several subtopics related to Excel functions and their use are provided.

Using AutoSum

Adding a group of cells is probably one of the most often-used calculations in an Excel worksheet. Because of this fact, Excel makes it very easy for you to place the SUM function into a cell. Excel provides the AutoSum button on the Standard toolbar. AutoSum looks at a column or row of cell values and tries to select the cells that should be included in the SUM function.

To use AutoSum, follow these steps:

1. Select the cell where you want to place the SUM function. Typically, you will choose a cell that is at the bottom of a column of values or at the end of a row of data. This makes it easy for AutoSum to figure out the range of cells that it should include in the SUM function.

2. Click the **AutoSum** button on the Standard toolbar. AutoSum inserts =SUM and the cell addresses that it thinks should be included in the function (see Figure 5.1).

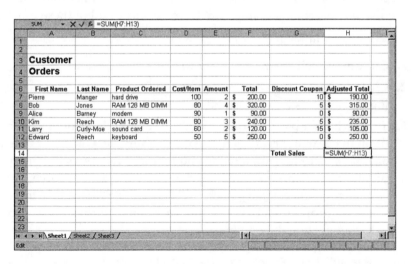

Figure 5.1 AutoSum inserts the SUM function and selects the cells that will be totaled by the function.

3. If the range of cell addresses that AutoSum selected is incorrect, use the mouse to drag and select the appropriate group of cells.

4. Press the **Enter** key. AutoSum calculates the total for the selected range of cells.

 TIP **Quick AutoSum**   To bypass the step where Excel displays the SUM formula and its arguments in the cell, select the cell in which you want the sum inserted and double-click the **AutoSum** button on the Standard toolbar.

Using the Insert Function Feature

After you become familiar with a function or a group of functions, you place a particular function in an Excel worksheet by typing the function name and the cells to be referenced by the function (the same as you have done for formulas that you create as outlined in Lesson 3). However, when you are first starting out with functions, you will find it much easier to create them using the Insert Function feature. The Insert Function feature leads you through the process of inserting a function and specifying the appropriate cell addresses in the function.

For example, suppose you want to compute the average, maximum, and minimum of a group of cells that contain the weekly commissions for your sales force. Figure 5.2 shows how these three functions would look on a worksheet (the display has been changed in Excel to show you the functions rather than their results). You could use the Insert Function feature to create any or all of these functions.

To use the Insert Function feature, follow these steps:

1. Click in the cell where you want to place the function.

 2. Click the **Insert Function** button on the Formula bar. The Insert Function dialog box appears (see Figure 5.3).

3. To search for a particular function, type a brief description of what you want to do in the Search for a Function box (for example, you could type `monthly payment` and Excel would show you financial functions that help you calculate monthly payments), and then click **Go** to conduct the search. You also can select a function category, such as Financial or Statistical, using the Select a Category drop-down box. In either case, a list of functions is provided in the Select a Function dialog box.

 TIP **Recently Used Functions**   The Insert Function dialog box by default lists the functions that you have used most recently.

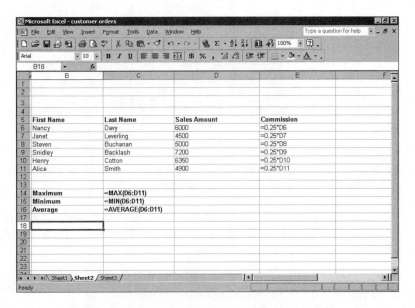

Figure 5.2 Functions can be placed into a worksheet using the Insert Function feature.

Figure 5.3 The Insert Function dialog box helps you select the function you want to use.

4. From the Functions list, select the function you want to insert. Then click **OK**. The Function Arguments dialog box appears. This dialog box allows you to specify the range of cells (some functions require multiple ranges of cells) that the function acts upon (see Figure 5.4).

5. Next, you must enter the range of cells that will be acted upon by the function. Click the **Collapse** button on the far right of the Number1 text box in the Function Arguments dialog box. This returns you to the worksheet.

Figure 5.4 The Function Arguments dialog box is where you specify the cells that will be acted upon by the function. The argument specified in this case is for the Maximum function.

6. Use the mouse to select the cells that you want to place in the function (see Figure 5.5). Then click the **Expand** button on the right of the Function Arguments dialog box.

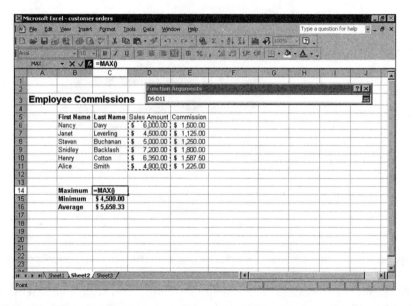

Figure 5.5 The Function Arguments collapses and allows you to select the cells that will be acted upon by the function.

7. Click **OK**. Excel inserts the function and cell addresses for the function into the selected cell and displays the result.

 If you find that you would like to edit the list of cells acted upon by a particular function, select the cell that holds the function and click the **Insert Function**

button on the Formula bar. The Function Arguments dialog box for the function appears. Select a new range of cells for the function, as discussed in steps 4 and 5.

 TIP   **What's This Function?**   If you'd like to know more about a particular function, click the **Help on This Function** link at the bottom of the Function Arguments dialog box. The Help window will open with help on this specific function.

Getting Around in Excel

In this lesson, you learn the basics of moving around in a worksheet and within a workbook.

Moving from Worksheet to Worksheet

Now that you've taken a look at how to enter labels, values, formulas, and functions, you should take a look at how to navigate the space provided by Excel workbooks and worksheets. By default, each workbook starts off with three worksheets. You can add or delete worksheets from the workbook as needed. Because each workbook consists of one or more worksheets, you need a way of moving easily from worksheet to worksheet. Use one of the following methods:

- Click the tab of the worksheet you want to go to (see Figure 6.1). If the tab is not shown, use the tab scroll buttons to bring the tab into view, and then click the tab.
- Press **Ctrl+PgDn** to move to the next worksheet or **Ctrl+PgUp** to move to the previous one.

Switching Between Workbooks

Switching between the different workbooks that you have open on the Windows desktop is very straightforward. By default, each workbook has its own button on the Windows taskbar and opens in its own Excel application window (refer to Figure 6.1). To switch between workbooks, click the button for the workbook you want.

If you don't want to have a separate taskbar entry for each open Excel workbook, you can turn this feature off using the Windows in Taskbar option on the View tab of the Options dialog box (click **Tools**, **Options**). Keep in mind, however, that disabling this feature means that you will have to use the Window menu to switch between Excel workbooks. To do so, select the Window menu, and then select the name of the workbook you want to make the current workbook in the Excel application window.

Display last worksheet
Display next worksheet
Display previous worksheet
Display first worksheet

Figure 6.1 Use the tabs to move from worksheet to worksheet.

Moving Within a Worksheet

To enter your worksheet data, you need some way of moving to the various cells within the worksheet. Keep in mind that the part of the worksheet displayed onscreen is only a small piece of the actual worksheet.

Using the Keyboard

To move around the worksheet with your keyboard, use the key combinations listed in Table 6.1.

Table 6.1 Moving Around a Worksheet with the Keyboard

To Move	Press This
Up one cell	Up-arrow key
Down one cell	Down-arrow key
Right one cell	Right-arrow key
Left one cell	Left-arrow key
Up one screen	Page Up

Table 6.1 Continued

To Move	Press This
Down one screen	Page Down
Leftmost cell in a row (column A)	Home
Lower-right corner of the data area	Ctrl+End
Cell A1	Ctrl+Home
Last occupied cell to the right of a row	End+right-arrow key

You can also quickly go to a specific cell address in a worksheet using the Go To feature. Press **Ctrl+G** (or select **Edit, Go To**). Type the cell address you want to go to into the Reference box, and then click the **OK** button (see Figure 6.2).

Figure 6.2 The Go To feature can be used to move to a specific cell address on the worksheet.

The Go To feature keeps a list of cells that you have recently moved to using the Go To feature. To quickly move to a particular cell in the Go To list, double-click that cell address.

TIP **Even Faster Than Go To** To move quickly to a specific cell on a worksheet, type the cell's address (the column letter and row number; for example, **C25**) into the Name box at the left end of the Formula bar and press **Enter**.

Using a Mouse

To scroll through a worksheet with a mouse, follow the techniques listed in Table 6.2.

Table 6.2 Moving Around a Worksheet with the Mouse

To Move	Click This
Move the selector to a particular cell.	Any cell.
View one more row, up or down.	Up or down arrows on the vertical scrollbar.

Table 6.2 Continued

To Move	Click This
View one more column, left or right.	Left or right arrows on the horizontal scrollbar.
Move through a worksheet quickly.	The vertical or horizontal scrollbar; drag it up or down or right and left, respectively. As you drag, a ScreenTip displays the current row/column number.

TIP **Watch the Scroll Box** The size of the scroll box changes to represent the amount of the total worksheet that is currently visible. If the scroll box is large, you know you're seeing almost all of the current worksheet in the window. If the scroll box is small, most of the worksheet is currently hidden from view.

Using a Wheel-Enabled Mouse

If you use the Microsoft IntelliMouse or any wheel-enabled mouse, you can move through a worksheet even faster than you can using the scrollbars and a conventional mouse. Here's how:

To:	Do This:
Scroll a few rows (scroll up and down)	Rotate the wheel in the middle of the mouse forward or backward.
Scroll faster (pan)	Click and hold the wheel button, and then drag the mouse in the direction in which you want to pan. The farther away from the origin mark (the four-headed arrow) you drag the mouse, the faster the panning action. To slow the pan, drag the mouse back toward the origin mark.
Pan without holding the wheel	Click the wheel once, and then move the mouse in the direction in which you want to pan. (You'll continue to pan when you move the mouse until you turn panning off by clicking the wheel again.)
Zoom in and out	Press the **Ctrl** key as you rotate the middle wheel. If you zoom out, you can click any cell you want to jump to. You can then zoom back in so you can see your data.

Different Ways to View Your Worksheet

In this lesson, you learn about the various ways in which you can view your worksheets.

Changing the Worksheet View

There are many ways to change how your worksheet appears within the Excel window. Changing the view has no effect on how your worksheets look when printed (unless you choose to hide data onscreen). However, changing the view and getting a different perspective helps you to see the overall layout of the worksheet and allows you to view worksheet cells that might not appear in the default screen view. For example, you can enlarge or reduce the size of the worksheet so that you can view more or less of it at one time.

To enlarge or reduce your view of the current worksheet, use the Zoom feature. Simply click the **Zoom** button on the Standard toolbar and select the zoom percentage you want to use from the following: 25%, 50%, 75%, 100% or 200%. If you want to zoom by a number that's not listed, just type the number into the Zoom box and press **Enter**.

You can also have Excel zoom in on a particular portion of a worksheet. This is particularly useful when you have created very large worksheets. Select the area of the worksheet you want to zoom in on, and then click the **Zoom** button list and click **Selection**. You can then select different zoom values on the Zoom list to zoom in or out on that particular portion of the worksheet. Keep in mind that Excel zooms in on the entire worksheet, not just the selected cells. (It just makes sure that you can see the selected cells when you change the zoom values.)

> **TIP** **Fast Zoom with a Wheel Mouse** If you use the Microsoft IntelliMouse or another compatible wheel mouse, you can zoom in and out quickly by holding down the **Ctrl** key as you move the wheel forward or back.

You also can display your worksheet so that it takes up the full screen. This eliminates all the other items in the Excel window, such as the toolbars, the Formula bar, the status bar, and so on. Figure 7.1 shows a worksheet in the Full Screen view.

To use this view, select the **View** menu and select **Full Screen**. To return to Normal view, click **Close Full Screen**.

Figure 7.1 View your worksheet on the entire screen.

Freezing Column and Row Labels

When you work with very large worksheets, it can be very annoying as you scroll to the right or down through the worksheet when you can no longer see your row headings or column headings, respectively. For example, you might be entering customer data where the customer's name is in the first column of the worksheet, and when you scroll to the extreme right to enter data, you can no longer see the customer names.

You can freeze your column and row labels so that you can view them no matter how far you scroll down or to the right in your worksheet. For example, Figure 7.2 shows frozen row headings that allow you to see the customer names no matter how far you move to the right of the worksheet.

To freeze row or column headings (or both), follow these steps:

1. Click the cell to the right of the row labels and/or below any column labels you want to freeze. This highlights the cell.

2. Select the **Window** menu, and then select **Freeze Panes**.

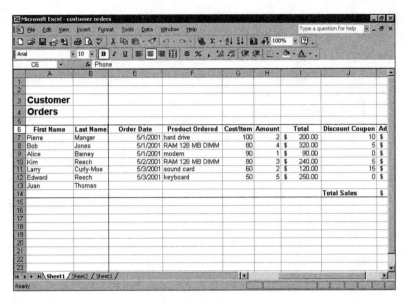

Figure 7.2 You can freeze row and column headings so that they remain onscreen as you scroll.

You might want to experiment on a large worksheet. Freeze the column and row headings, and then use the keyboard or the mouse to move around in the worksheet. As you do, the row and/or column headings remain locked in their positions. This enables you to view data in other parts of the worksheet without losing track of what that data represents.

When you have finished working with the frozen column and row headings, you can easily unfreeze them. Select the **Window** menu again and select **Unfreeze Panes**.

Splitting Worksheets

When you work with very large worksheets, you might actually want to split the worksheet into multiple windows. This enables you to view the same worksheet in different windows. You can then scroll through the multiple copies of the same worksheet and compare data in cells that are normally far apart in the worksheet.

Figure 7.3 shows a worksheet that has been split into multiple panes. Each "copy" of the worksheet will have its own set of vertical and horizontal scrollbars.

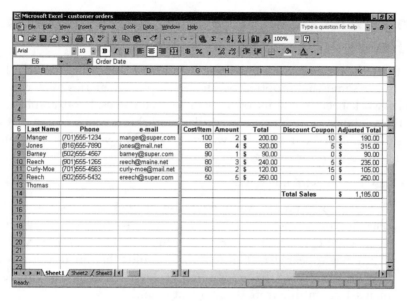

Figure 7.3   You can split a worksheet into two windows, making it easy to compare data in the worksheet.

To split a worksheet, follow these steps:

1. Click in the cell where you want to create the split. A split appears to the left of the selected cell and above the selected cell.

2. You can adjust the vertical or horizontal split bars using the mouse. Place the mouse on the split bar and drag it to a new location.

3. You can use the scrollbars in the different split panes to view data in the worksheet (different data can be viewed in each pane).

To remove the split, select the **Window** menu and select **Remove Split**.

TIP   **Create Splits with the Split Boxes**   You can also create a vertical or horizontal split in a worksheet by using the split boxes. A horizontal split box rests just above the vertical scrollbar, and a vertical split box rests on the far right of the horizontal scrollbar. Place your mouse on either of these split boxes and drag them onto the worksheet to create a split bar.

Hiding Workbooks, Worksheets, Columns, and Rows

For those times when you're working on top-secret information (or at least information that is somewhat proprietary, such as employee salaries), you can hide workbooks, worksheets, columns, or rows from prying eyes. For example, if you have confidential data stored in one particular worksheet, you can hide that worksheet, yet still be able to view the other worksheets in that workbook. You can also hide particular columns or rows within a worksheet.

Use these methods to hide data:

- To hide a row or a column in a worksheet, click a row or column heading to select it (you can select adjacent columns or rows by dragging across them). Then, right-click within the row or column and select **Hide** from the shortcut menu that appears (see Figure 7.4). To unhide the row or column, right-click the border between the hidden item and rows or columns that are visible, and then select **Unhide** from the shortcut menu.

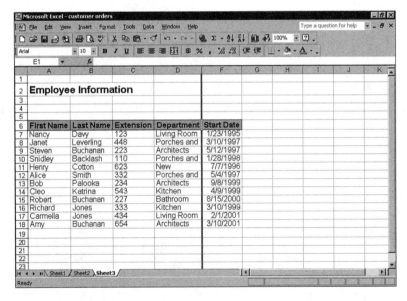

Figure 7.4   Column E, which contains employee salaries, has been hidden on a worksheet.

- To hide a worksheet, click its tab to select it. Then, open the **Format** menu and select **Sheet**, **Hide**. To unhide the worksheet, select **Format**, **Sheet**, and then **Unhide**. Select the worksheet to unhide in the Unhide dialog box that appears, and then click **OK**.

- To hide an entire workbook, open the **Window** menu and select **Hide**. This removes the workbook from the Excel window, even though the workbook is open. To unhide the workbook, select **Window**, **Unhide**.

Locking Cells in a Worksheet

In some situations, you might create a worksheet or worksheets and someone else will enter the data. In these situations, you might want to lock cells that contain formulas and functions so that the person doing the data entry does not accidentally overwrite or delete the worksheet formulas or functions. Locking cells in a worksheet is a two-step process. You must first select and lock the cells. Then, you must turn on protection on the entire worksheet for the "lock" to go into effect.

Follow these steps to lock cells on a worksheet:

1. Select the cells in the worksheet that you want to lock. These are typically the cells that contain formulas or functions.

2. Select **Format** and then **Cells**. The Format Cells dialog box appears. Click the **Protection** tab on the dialog box (see Figure 7.5).

Figure 7.5   Cells can be locked using the Protection tab of the Format Cells dialog box.

3. Be sure the Locked check box is selected on the Protection tab. Then click **OK**.

4. Now you must protect the entire worksheet to have the lock feature protect the cells that you selected. Select the **Tools** menu, point at **Protections**, and then select **Protect Sheet**. The Protect Sheet dialog box appears (see Figure 7.6).

Figure 7.6 The worksheet must be protected if you want to lock cells containing formulas or functions.

5. Enter a password if you want to require a password for "unprotecting" the worksheet. Then click **OK**.

The cells that you locked in steps 1, 2, and 3 will no longer accept data entry. Every time someone tries to enter data into one of those cells, Excel displays a message stating that data will not be accepted. The cells are now protected and you can pass the workbook on to the person who handles the data entry.

Editing Worksheets

In this lesson, you learn how to change data and how to undo those changes if necessary. You also learn how to search for data and replace it with other data, how to spell check your work, and how to copy, move, and delete data.

Correcting Data

You've taken a look at entering text, values, formulas, and functions. There will definitely be occasions when you need to edit information in a cell. One way to change an entry in a cell is to replace it by selecting the cell and then entering new data. Just press **Enter** after entering the information. If you just want to modify the existing cell content, you can also edit data within a cell.

To edit information in a cell, follow these steps:

1. Select the cell in which you want to edit data.

2. To begin editing, click in the Formula bar to place the insertion point into the cell entry. To edit within the cell itself, press **F2** or double-click the cell. This puts you in Edit mode; the word Edit appears in the status bar.

3. Press the right- or left-arrow key to move the insertion point within the entry. Press the **Backspace** key to delete characters to the left of the insertion point; press the **Delete** key to delete characters to the right. Then, type any characters you want to add.

4. Press the **Enter** key when you have finished making your changes.

   If you change your mind and you no longer want to edit your entry, click the **Cancel** button on the Formula bar or press **Esc**.

 TIP   **Moving to the Beginning or End of a Cell Entry**   In Edit mode, you can quickly move to the beginning or end of a cell's contents. Press **Home** to move to the beginning of the entry; press **End** to move to the end of the entry.

Undoing an Action

Although editing a worksheet is supposed to improve it, you might find that you've done something to a cell or range of cells that you had not intended. This is where the Undo feature comes in.

You can undo just about any action while working in Excel, including any changes you make to a cell's data. To undo a change, click the **Undo** button on the Standard toolbar (or select **Edit, Undo**).

 You can also undo an undo. Just click the **Redo** button on the Standard toolbar.

TIP **Undoing/Redoing More Than One Thing** The Undo button undoes only the most recent action. To undo several previous actions, click the **Undo** button multiple times or click the drop-down arrow on the undo button and select the number of actions you want undone.

Using the Replace Feature

Suppose you've entered a particular label or value into the worksheet and find that you have consistently entered it incorrectly. A great way to change multiple occurrences of a label or value is using Excel's Replace feature; you can locate data in the worksheet and replace it with new data. To find and replace data, follow these steps:

1. Select the **Edit** menu, and then select **Replace**. The Find and Replace dialog box appears, as shown in Figure 8.1.

Figure 8.1 Find and replace data with the Find and Replace dialog box.

2. Type the text or value that you want to find into the **Find What** text box.

3. Click in the **Replace With** text box and type the text you want to use as replacement text.

4. To expand the options available to you in the dialog box, click the **Options** button (Figure 8.1 shows the dialog box in its expanded form).

5. If you want to match the exact case of your entry so that Excel factors in capitalization, click the **Match Case** check box. If you want to locate cells that contain exactly what you entered into the Find What text box (and no additional data), click the **Match Entire Cell Contents** check box.

6. To search for entries with particular formatting, click the **Format** button to the right of the Find What box. The Find Format dialog box appears (see Figure 8.2). You can search for entries that have been assigned number, alignment, font, border, patterns, and protection using the appropriate tab on the Find Format dialog box. After making your selection, click the **OK** button.

Figure 8.2   The Find Format dialog box enables you to search for entries that have been assigned a particular formatting.

7. You can also replace your entries with a particular formatting. Click the **Format** button to the right of the Replace With box. The Replace Format dialog box appears. It is the same as the Find Format dialog box. Simply select any formats you want to assign to your replacement, and then click **OK**.

8. Click **Find Next** to find the first occurrence of your specified entry.

9. When an occurrence is found, it is highlighted. Click **Replace** to replace only this occurrence and then click **Find Next** to find the next occurrence.

10. If you want to find all the occurrences, click **Find All;** you can also replace all the occurrences of the entry with **Replace All**.

11. When you have finished working with the Find and Replace dialog box, click **Close**.

TIP   **Search an Entire Workbook**   If you want to search an entire workbook for a particular entry, click the **Within** drop-down list in the Find and Replace dialog box and select **Workbook**.

If you don't need to replace an entry but would like to find it in the worksheet, you can use the Find feature. Select **Edit**, **Find**, and then type the data you want to locate into the Find What text box and click **Find Next**.

Checking Your Spelling

Because worksheets also include text entries, you might want to make sure that you check for any misspellings in a worksheet before printing the data. Excel offers a spell-checking feature that finds and corrects misspellings in a worksheet.

To run the Spelling Checker, follow these steps:

1. Click the **Spelling** button on the Standard toolbar (or select **Tools**, **Spelling**). The Spelling dialog box appears. Excel finds the first misspelled word and displays it at the top of the Spelling dialog box. A suggested correction appears in the Suggestions box (see Figure 8.3).

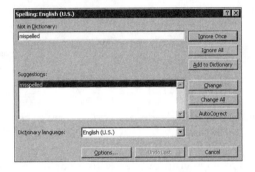

Figure 8.3   Correct spelling mistakes with the options in the Spelling dialog box.

2. To accept the suggestion in the Suggestions box, click **Change**, or click **Change All** to change all occurrences of the misspelled word.

3. If the suggestion in the Suggestions box is not correct, you can do any of the following:

- Select a different suggestion from the Suggestions box, and then click **Change** or **Change All**.
- Type your own correction into the Change To box, and then click **Change** or **Change All**.
- Click **Ignore Once** to leave the word unchanged.
- Click **Ignore All** to leave all occurrences of the word unchanged.
- Click **Add to Dictionary** to add the word to the dictionary so that Excel won't flag it as misspelled again.

- Click **AutoCorrect** to add a correctly spelled word to the AutoCorrect list so that Excel can correct it automatically as you type.

- If you make a mistake related to a particular entry, click the **Undo Last** button to undo the last change that you made.

4. You might see a message asking whether you want to continue checking spelling at the beginning of the sheet. If so, click **Yes** to continue. When the Spelling Checker can't find any more misspelled words, it displays a prompt telling you that the spelling check is complete. Click **OK** to confirm that the spelling check is finished.

TIP **Setting Spelling Options**   If you want to set options related to the Spelling feature, such as ignoring words in uppercase and words with numbers, click the **Options** button in the Spelling dialog box. This takes you to the Options dialog box for the Speller. Set options as needed and then click **OK** to return to the Spelling dialog box.

Copying and Moving Data

In Lesson 2, you learned how to use the Fill feature to copy a particular entry to multiple cells. In this section, you take a closer look at the Copy feature. When you copy or cut data in a cell, that data is held in a temporary storage area (a part of the computer's memory) called the Clipboard.

Excel 2002 (and all the Office XP applications) makes it easy for you to work with the Clipboard because it can be viewed in the Office Clipboard task pane (you look at the Clipboard later in this lesson). This enables you to keep track of items that you have copied or cut to the Clipboard. The Clipboard not only enables you to copy or move data with Excel, but it enables you to place Excel data directly into another application (see Lesson 7, "Sharing Information Among Office Applications," in Part I of this book).

TERM **Clipboard**   The Clipboard is an area of memory that is accessible to all Windows programs. The Clipboard is used to copy or move data from place to place within a program or between programs.

When you copy data, you create a duplicate of data in a cell or range of cells. Follow these steps to copy data:

1. Select the cell(s) that you want to copy. You can select any range or several ranges if you want. (See Lesson 11, "Working with Ranges," for more information).

2. Click the **Copy** button on the Standard toolbar. The contents of the selected cell(s) are copied to the Clipboard.

3. Select the first cell in the area where you would like to place the copy. (To copy the data to another worksheet or workbook, change to that worksheet or workbook first.)

4. Click the **Paste** button. Excel inserts the contents of the Clipboard at the location of the insertion point.

Watch Out!   When copying or moving data, be careful not to paste the data over existing data (unless, of course, you intend to).

CAUTION

You can copy the same data to several places by repeating the **Paste** command. Items remain on the Clipboard until you remove them.

Using Drag and Drop

The fastest way to copy something is to drag and drop it. Select the cells you want to copy, hold down the **Ctrl** key, and drag the border of the range you selected (see Figure 8.4). When you release the mouse button, the contents are copied to the new location. To insert the data between existing cells, press **Ctrl+Shift** as you drag.

	A	B	C	D	E	F	G	H	I	J
3		**Employee Commissions Week of 03/19/01**								
4										
5		First Name	Last Name	Sales Amount	Commission					
6		Nancy	Davy	$ 6,000.00	$ 1,500.00					
7		Janet	Leverling	$ 4,500.00	$ 1,125.00					
8		Steven	Buchanan	$ 5,000.00	$ 1,250.00					
9		Snidley	Backlash	$ 7,200.00	$ 1,800.00					
10		Henry	Cotton	$ 6,350.00	$ 1,587.50					
11		Alice	Smith	$ 4,900.00	$ 1,225.00					
12										
13										
14		**Employee Commissions Week of 03/19/01**								
15										
16										
17										
18										
19										
20										
21										
22										
23				B16:C22						
24										
25										

Sheet1 \ Sheet2 / Sheet3 /

Drag to copy cell contents, use Alt key to switch sheets

Figure 8.4   Dragging is the fastest way to copy data.

To drag a copy to a different sheet, press **Ctrl+Alt** as you drag the selection to the sheet's tab. Excel switches you to that sheet, where you can drop your selection into the appropriate location.

Moving Data

Moving data is similar to copying except that the data is removed from its original place and placed into the new location.

To move data, follow these steps:

1. Select the cells you want to move.

 2. Click the **Cut** button.

3. Select the first cell in the area where you want to place the data. To move the data to another worksheet, change to that worksheet.

 4. Click **Paste**.

Using Drag and Drop to Move Data

You can also move data using drag and drop. Select the data to be moved, and then drag the border of the selected cells to its new location. To insert the data between existing cells, press **Shift** while you drag. To move the data to a different worksheet, press the **Alt** key and drag the selection to the worksheet's tab. You're switched to that sheet, where you can drop your selection at the appropriate point.

Using the Office Clipboard

You can use the Office Clipboard to store multiple items that you cut or copy from an Excel worksheet (or workbook). You can then paste or move these items within Excel or to other Office applications. The Office Clipboard can hold up to 24 items.

What a Drag! You can't use the Drag-and-Drop feature to copy or move data to the Office Clipboard.

CAUTION

The Office Clipboard is viewed in the Clipboard task Pane. Follow these steps to open the Office Clipboard:

1. Select the **Edit** menu, and then select **Office Clipboard**. The Clipboard task pane appears. Any items that you have cut or copied appear on the Clipboard (see Figure 8.5).

2. To paste an item that appears on the Clipboard, click in a cell on the worksheet, and then click the item on the Clipboard. It is then pasted into the selected cell.

You can remove any of the items from the Clipboard. Place the mouse pointer on an item listed on the Clipboard and click the drop-down arrow that appears. Click **Delete** on the shortcut menu that appears.

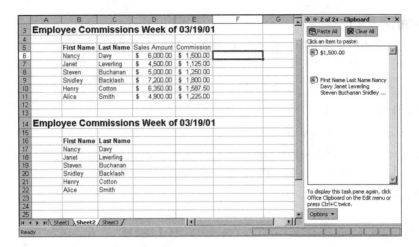

Figure 8.5 The Clipboard provides a list of items that you have cut or copied.

You can also clear all the items from the Clipboard. Click the **Clear All** button at the top of the Clipboard task pane.

TIP **Open the Clipboard from the System Tray** You can quickly open the Office Clipboard in any Office application by double-clicking the Clipboard icon in the Windows System Tray (at the far right of the Windows taskbar).

Deleting Data

To delete the data in a cell or range of cells, select them and press **Delete**. Excel also offers some additional options for deleting cells and their contents:

- With the **Edit**, **Clear** command, you can delete only the formatting of a cell (or an attached comment) without deleting its contents. The formatting of a cell includes the cell's color, border style, numeric format, font size, and so on. You'll learn more about this option in a moment.

- With the **Edit**, **Delete** command, you can remove cells and then shift surrounding cells over to take their place (this option is described in more detail in Lesson 12, "Inserting and Removing Cells, Rows, and Columns").

To use the Clear command to remove the formatting of a cell or a note, follow these steps:

1. Select the cells you want to clear.

2. Open the **Edit** menu and point at **Clear**. The Clear submenu appears.

3. Select the desired Clear option: **All** (which clears the cells of all contents, formatting, and notes), **Formats**, **Contents**, or **Comments**.

Changing How Numbers and Text Look

In this lesson, you learn how to customize the appearance of numbers in your worksheet and how to customize your text formatting to achieve the look you want.

Formatting Text and Numbers

When you work in Excel, you work with two types of formatting: value formatting and font formatting. Value formatting is where you assign a particular number style to a cell (or cells) that holds numeric data. You can assign a currency style, a percent style, and several other numeric styles to values.

Another formatting option available to you in Excel relates to different font attributes. For example, you can add bold or italic to the contents of a cell or cells. You can also change the font used for a range of cells or increase the font size.

Next, you take a look at numeric formatting, and then you look at how different font attributes are controlled in Excel.

Using the Style Buttons to Format Numbers

The Formatting toolbar (just below the Standard toolbar) contains several buttons for applying a format to your numbers, including the following:

Button	Name	Example/Description
$	Currency Style	$1,200.90
%	Percent Style	20.90%
,	Comma Style	1,200.90
+.0 .00	Increase Decimal	Adds one decimal place
.00 +.0	Decrease Decimal	Deletes one decimal place

To use one of these buttons, select the cell or cells you want to format, and then click the desired button. If you would like more formatting options for numeric values, read on; they are covered in the next section.

Numeric Formatting Options

The numeric values that you place in your Excel cells are more than just numbers; they often represent dollar amounts, a date, or a percentage. If the various numeric style buttons on the Formatting toolbar (discussed in the previous section) do not offer the exact format you want for your numbers, don't worry. Excel's Format Cells dialog box offers a wide range of number formats and even allows you to create custom formats.

To use the Format Cells dialog box to assign numeric formatting to cells in a worksheet, follow these steps:

1. Select the cell or range that contains the values you want to format.

2. Select the **Format** menu and select **Cells**. The Format Cells dialog box appears.

3. Click the **Number** tab. The different categories of numeric formats are displayed in a Category list (see Figure 9.1).

Figure 9.1   Apply a numeric format in the Number tab of the Format Cells dialog box.

4. In the Category list, select the numeric format category you want to use. The sample box displays the default format for that category.

5. Click **OK** to assign the numeric format to the selected cells.

As you can see from the Number tab on the Format Cells dialog box, Excel offers several numeric formatting styles. Table 9.1 provides a list of these different number formats.

Table 9.1 Excel's Number Formats

Number Format	Examples	Description
General	10.6 $456,908.00	Excel displays your value as you enter it. In other words, this format displays currency or percent signs only if you enter them yourself.
Number	3400.50 Ð120.39	The default Number format has two decimal places. Negative numbers are preceded by a minus sign, but they can also appear in red and/or parentheses.
Currency	$3,400.50 Ð$3,400.50	The default Currency format has two decimal places and a dollar sign. Negative numbers appear with a minus sign, but they can also appear in red and/or parentheses.
Accounting	$3,400.00 $978.21	Use this format to align dollar signs and decimal points in a column. The default Accounting format has two decimal places and a dollar sign.
Date	11/7	The default Date format is the month and day separated by a slash; however, you can select from numerous other formats.
Time	10:00	The default Time format is the hour and minutes separated by a colon; however, you can opt to display seconds, a.m., or p.m.
Percentage	99.50%	The default Percentage format has two decimal places. Excel multiplies the value in a cell by 100 and displays the result with a percent sign.
Fraction	1/2	The default Fraction format is up to one digit on each side of the slash. Use this format to display the number of digits you want on each side of the slash and the fraction type (such as halves, quarters, eighths, and so on).
Scientific	3.40E+03	The default Scientific format has two decimal places. Use this format to display numbers in scientific notation.
Text	135RV90	Use Text format to display both text and numbers in a cell as text. Excel displays the entry exactly as you type it.

Table 9.1 Continued

Number Format	Examples	Description
Special	02110	This format is specifically designed to display ZIP codes, phone numbers, and Social Security numbers correctly so that you don't have to enter any special characters, such as hyphens.
Custom	00.0%	Use Custom format to create your own number format. You can use any of the format codes in the Type list and then make changes to those codes. The # symbol represents a number placeholder, and 0 represents a zero placeholder.

You can also open the Format Cell dialog box using a shortcut menu. Select the cell or cells that you want to assign a numeric format to, and then right-click those cells. On the shortcut menu that appears, select **Format Cells**. Then, select the **Number** tab to select your numeric format.

That's Not the Date I Entered!   If you enter a date into a cell that is already formatted with the Number format, the date appears as a value that represents the number of days between January 1, 1900 and that date. Change the cell's formatting from a Number format to a Date format and select a date type. The entry in the cell then appears as an actual date.

CAUTION

TIP **How Do I Get Rid of a Numeric Format?**   To remove a number format from a cell (and return it to General format), select the cell whose formatting you want to remove, open the **Edit** menu, select **Clear**, and select **Formats**.

How You Can Make Text Look Different

When you type text into a cell, Excel automatically formats it in the Arial font with a text size of 10 points. The 12-point font size is considered typical for business documents (the higher the point size, the bigger the text is; there are approximately 72 points in an inch). You can select from several fonts (such as Baskerville, Modern, or Rockwell) and change the size of any font characters in a cell. You can also apply special font attributes, such as bold, italic, and underline.

Font   A font is a set of characters that have the same typeface, which means they are of a single design (such as Times New Roman).

Before you take a look at applying different font attributes to the cells in a worksheet, take a look at how you change the default font for all your Excel workbooks. This enables you to select a different font and font size for your worksheets.

To change the default font, follow these steps:

1. Select **Tools** and then click **Options** to open the Options dialog box.

2. Click the **General** tab (see Figure 9.2).

3. In the Standard Font area, use the drop-down list to select a new font. Use the Size drop-down list to select a new default font size.

Figure 9.2   You can set a new default font and font size for your Excel workbooks.

4. When you click the **OK** button, Excel makes your preference the default font and size.

Changing Text Attributes with Toolbar Buttons

When you are working on your various Excel worksheets, you will probably apply a variety of formatting options to the different cells in a particular worksheet. A fast way to assign text attributes, such as bold and italic, is to use the various font attribute buttons on the Excel Formatting toolbar.

To use the Formatting toolbar to change text attributes, follow these steps:

1. Select the cell or range that contains the text whose look you want to change.

2. To change the font, click the **Font** drop-down list, and select a new font name. To change the font size, click the **Font Size** drop-down list and select the size you want to use. You can also type the point size into the Font Size box and then press **Enter**.

B
I **U**

3. To add an attribute such as bold, italic, or underlining to the selected cells, click the appropriate button: **Bold**, **Italic**, or **Underline**, respectively.

> **TIP** **Font Keyboard Shortcuts**   You can apply certain attributes quickly by using keyboard shortcuts. First select the cell(s), and then press **Ctrl+B** for bold, **Ctrl+I** for italic, **Ctrl+U** for single underline, or **Ctrl+5** for strikethrough.

You can also change the color of the font in a cell or cells. Select the cell or cells and click the **Font Color** drop-down arrow on the Formatting toolbar. Select a font color from the Color palette that appears.

Accessing Different Font Attributes

If you would like to access a greater number of font format options for a cell or range of cells, you can use the Font tab of the Format Cells dialog box. It provides access to different fonts, font styles, font sizes, font colors, and other text attributes, such as strikethrough and superscript/subscript. To format cells using the Font tab of the Format Cells dialog box, follow these steps:

1. Select the cell or range that contains the text you want to format.

2. Select the **Format** menu and select **Cells**, or press **Ctrl+1**. (You can also right-click the selected cells and choose **Format Cells** from the shortcut menu.)

3. Click the **Font** tab. The Font tab provides drop-down lists and check boxes for selecting the various font attributes (see Figure 9.3).

Figure 9.3   The Font tab provides access to all the font attributes.

4. Select the options you want.

5. Click **OK** to close the dialog box and return to your worksheet.

Aligning Text in Cells

When you enter data into a cell, that data is aligned automatically. Text is aligned on the left, and numbers are aligned on the right (values resulting from a formula or function are also right-aligned). Both text and numbers are initially set at the bottom of the cells. However, you can change both the vertical and the horizontal alignment of data in your cells.

Follow these steps to change the alignment:

1. Select the cell or range you want to align.

2. Select the **Format** menu and then select **Cells**. The Format Cells dialog box appears.

3. Click the **Alignment** tab (see Figure 9.4).

Figure 9.4 Select from the Alignment options on the Alignment tab of the Format Cells dialog box.

4. Choose from the following options to set the alignment:

- **Horizontal**—Lets you specify a left/right alignment in the cells. (The **Center Across** selection centers a title or other text within a range of cells, which is discussed in a moment.)

- **Vertical**—Lets you specify how you want the text aligned in relation to the top and bottom of the cells.

- **Orientation**—Lets you flip the text sideways or print it from top to bottom instead of left to right.

- **Wrap Text**—Tells Excel to wrap long lines of text within a cell without changing the width of the cell. (Normally, Excel displays all text in a cell on one line.)

- **Shrink to Fit**—Shrinks the text to fit within the cell's current width. If the cell's width is adjusted, the text increases or decreases in size accordingly.

- **Merge Cells**—Combines several cells into a single cell. All data is overlaid, except for the cell in the upper-left corner of the selected cells.

5. Click **OK** when you have finished making your selections.

 TIP **Changing Text Orientation** The Alignment tab also provides an Orientation box that enables you to rotate text within a cell or a group of merged cells. Drag the degree dial on the Alignment tab or use the Degree box to specify the amount of rotation for the text.

Aligning Text from the Toolbar

Like the font attributes such as bold and italic, you can also select certain alignment options directly from the Formatting toolbar. The following buttons enable you to align the text:

Button	Name	Description
≣	Align Left	Places data at left edge of cell
≣	Align Right	Places data at right edge of cell
≣	Center	Centers data in cell
⊞	Merge and Center	Centers data in selected cell range

Excel also enables you to indent your text within a cell. If you're typing a paragraph's worth of information into a single cell, for example, you can indent that paragraph by selecting **Left Alignment** from the Horizontal list box in the Format Cells dialog box (as explained earlier). After selecting Left Alignment, set the amount of indent you want with the Indent spin box in the Format Cells dialog box.

In addition, you can add an indent quickly by clicking the following buttons on the Formatting toolbar:

Button	Name	Description
⊏≣	Decrease Indent	Removes an indent or creates a negative indent
⊐≣	Increase Indent	Adds an indent

Combining Cells and Wrapping Text

 You can also center text across a range of cells or merge several cells to hold a sheet title or other text information. If you want to center a title or other text over a range of cells, select the entire range of blank cells in which you want the text centered. This should include the cell that contains the text you want to center (which should be in the cell on the far left of the cell range). Then, click the **Merge and Center** button on the Formatting toolbar.

Combining a group of cells also allows you to place a special heading or other text into the cells (this works well in cases where you use a large font size for the text). Select the cells that you want to combine. Then, select **Format, Cells** and select the **Alignment** tab of the Format Cells dialog box.

Click the **Merge Cells** check box and then click **OK**. The cells are then merged.

If you have a cell or a group of merged cells that holds a large amount of text (such as an explanation), you might want to wrap the text within the cell or merged cells. Click the cell that holds the text entry, and then select **Format, Cells**. Select the **Alignment** tab of the Format Cells dialog box.

Click the **Wrap Text** check box. Then, click **OK**.

Copying Formats with Format Painter

After applying a numeric format or various font attributes to a cell or cell range, you can easily copy those formatting options to other cells. This works whether you're copying numeric or text formatting or shading or borders, as you'll learn in upcoming lessons. To copy a format from one cell to another, follow these steps:

1. Select the cells that contain the formatting you want to copy.

2. Click the **Format Painter** button on the Standard toolbar. Excel copies the formatting. The mouse pointer changes into a paintbrush with a plus sign next to it.

3. Click one cell or drag over several cells to which you want to apply the copied formatting.

4. Release the mouse button, and Excel copies the formatting and applies it to the selected cells.

TIP   **Painting Several Cells**   To paint several areas with the same formatting at one time, double-click the **Format Painter** button to toggle it on. When you're through, press **Esc** or click the **Format Painter** button again to return to a normal mouse pointer.

Adding Cell Borders and Shading

In this lesson, you learn how to add borders and shading to your worksheets.

Adding Borders to Cells

As you work with your worksheet onscreen, you'll notice that each cell is identified by gridlines that surround the cell. By default, these gridlines do not print; even if you choose to print them, they don't look very good on the printed page. To create well-defined lines on the printout (and onscreen, for that matter), you can add borders to selected cells or entire cell ranges. A border can appear on all four sides of a cell or only on selected sides; it's up to you.

 TIP **Printing the Gridlines** It's true that gridlines do not print by default. But if you want to try printing your worksheet with gridlines, just to see what it looks like, open the **File** menu, select **Page Setup**, click the **Sheet** tab, check the **Gridlines** box, and click **OK**.

To add borders to a cell or range, perform the following steps:

1. Select the cell(s) around which you want a border to appear.
2. Open the **Format** menu and choose **Cells**. The Format Cells dialog box appears.
3. Click the **Border** tab to see the Border options shown in Figure 10.1.
4. Select the desired position, style (thickness), and color for the border. The position of the border is selected using the buttons along the left of the Border box. You can also click inside the **Border** box itself to place the border.
5. Click **OK** or press **Enter**.

When adding borders to a worksheet, hiding the gridlines onscreen gives you a preview of how the borders will look when printed. To hide gridlines, select the **Tools** menu, select **Options** (this opens the Options dialog box), and then select the **View** tab. Remove the check mark from the Gridlines check box, and then click **OK** to return to the worksheet. Selecting this option has no effect on whether the gridlines actually print, only on whether they are displayed onscreen.

Figure 10.1 Choose Border options from the Format Cells dialog box.

 TIP **Add Borders from the Toolbar** You can use the Borders button on the Formatting toolbar to add a border to cells or cell ranges. Select the cells, and then click the **Borders** drop-down arrow on the Formatting toolbar to select a border type.

Adding Shading to Cells

Another way to offset certain cells in a worksheet is to add shading to those cells. With shading, you can add a color or gray shading to the background of a cell. You can add shading that consists of a solid color, or you can select a pattern as part of the shading options, such as a repeating diagonal line.

Follow these steps to add shading to a cell or range. As you make your selections, keep in mind that if you plan to print your worksheet with a black-and-white printer, the colors you select might not provide enough contrast on the printout to provide any differentiation between ranges of cells. You can always use the Print Preview command (as explained in Lesson 14, "Printing Your Workbook") to view your results in black and white before you print.

1. Select the cell(s) you want to shade.
2. Open the **Format** menu and choose **Cells**.
3. Click the **Patterns** tab. Excel displays the shading options (see Figure 10.2).
4. Click the **Pattern** drop-down arrow to see a grid that contains colors and patterns.

Figure 10.2 Choose colors and patterns from the Patterns tab of the Format Cells dialog box.

5. Select the shading color and pattern you want to use. The Color options let you choose a color for the overall shading. The Pattern options let you select a black or colored pattern that is placed on top of the cell-shading color you selected. A preview of the results appears in the Sample box.

6. When you have finished making your selections, click **OK**.

TIP **Add Cell Shading with the Toolbar** Select the cells you want to shade. Click the **Fill Color** drop-down arrow on the Formatting toolbar and then select the fill color from the Color palette that appears.

Using AutoFormat

If you don't want to take the time to test different border types and shading styles, you can let Excel help you with the task of adding some emphasis and interest to the cells of your worksheet. You can take advantage of AutoFormat, which provides various predesigned table formats that you can apply to a worksheet.

To use predesigned formats, perform the following steps:

1. Select the cell(s) that contain the data you want to format. This could be the entire worksheet.

2. Select the **Format** menu, and then select **AutoFormat**. The AutoFormat dialog box appears (see Figure 10.3).

Figure 10.3 Select a format from the AutoFormat dialog box.

3. Scroll through the list to view the various AutoFormat styles provided. When you find a format that you want to use, click it to select it.

4. To prevent AutoFormat from overwriting certain existing formatting (such as numbers, alignment, or fonts), click the **Options** button and deselect the appropriate check boxes.

5. Click **OK**, and your worksheet is formatted.

 TIP **Yuck! I Chose That?** If you don't like what AutoFormat did to your worksheet, click the **Undo** button (or press **Ctrl+Z**).

Applying Conditional Formatting

Another useful formatting feature that Excel provides is conditional formatting. Conditional formatting allows you to specify that certain results in the worksheet be formatted so that they stand out from the other entries in the worksheet. For example, if you wanted to track all the monthly sales figures that are below a certain amount, you can use conditional formatting to format them in red. Conditional formatting formats only cells that meet a certain condition.

To apply conditional formatting, follow these steps:

1. Select the cells to which you want to apply the conditional formatting.

2. Select the **Format** menu and select **Conditional Formatting**. The Conditional Formatting dialog box appears, as shown in Figure 10.4.

3. Be sure that **Cell Value Is** is selected in the Condition 1 drop-down box on the left of the dialog box.

Figure 10.4   Apply formats conditionally to highlight certain values.

4. In the next drop-down box to the right, you select the condition. The default is Between. Other conditions include Equal To, Greater Than, Less Than, and other possibilities. Use the drop-down box to select the appropriate condition.

5. After selecting the condition, you must specify a cell or cells in the worksheet that Excel can use as a reference for the conditional formatting. For example, if you select Less Than as the condition, you must specify a cell in the worksheet that contains a value that can be used for comparison with the cells that you are applying the conditional formatting to. Click the **Shrink** button on the Conditional Formatting dialog box. You are returned to the worksheet. Select the reference cell for the condition.

6. Click the **Expand** button on the Conditional Formatting dialog box to expand the dialog box.

7. Now you can set the formatting that will be applied to cells that meet your condition. Click the **Format** button in the Conditional Formatting dialog box and select the formatting options for your condition in the Format Cells dialog box. Then click **OK**. Figure 10.5 shows a conditional format that applies bold and italic to values that are less than the value contained in cell D6.

Figure 10.5   Set the various options for your conditional formatting.

8. After setting the conditions to be met for conditional formatting (you can click **Add** to set more than one condition), click **OK**.

You are returned to the worksheet. Cells that meet the condition you set up for conditional formatting will be formatted with the options you specified. Figure 10.6 shows cells that the settings used in Figure 10.5 conditionally formatted.

	A	B	C	D	E	F	G	H	I	J	
1											
2											
3		**Employee Commissions Week of 03/19/01**									
4											
5		First Name	Last Name	Sales Amount	Commission						
6		Nancy	Davy	$ 6,000.00	$ 1,500.00						
7		Janet	Leverling	$ 4,500.00	*$ 1,125.00*						
8		Steven	Buchanan	$ 5,000.00	*$ 1,250.00*						
9		Snidley	Backlash	$ 7,200.00	$ 1,800.00						
10		Henry	Cotton	$ 6,350.00	$ 1,587.50						
11		Alice	Smith	$ 4,900.00	*$ 1,225.00*						
12											
13											
14											
15											
16											
17											
18											
19											
20											
21											
22											
23											

Sheet1 \ Sheet2 / Sheet3 /

Figure 10.6 Conditional formatting formats only the cells that meet your conditions.

TIP **Conditional Formatting Applied to Formulas**   You can also set up conditional formatting to highlight cells that contain a particular formula or function. Select **Formula Is** for Condition 1 in the Conditional Formatting dialog box and then type the formula or function in the box to the right.

Working with Ranges

In this lesson, you learn how to select and name ranges.

What Is a Range?

When you select a group of cells (which you have done numerous times in the various Excel lessons), you are in fact selecting a range. A cell range may consist of one cell or any group of contiguous cells.

Ranges are referred to by their anchor points (the upper-left corner and the lower-right corner). For example, a range that begins with cell C10 and ends with I14 is referred to as C10:I14.

TERM
Range   A group of contiguous cells on an Excel worksheet.

Although selecting ranges is certainly not rocket science (however, a few tricks for selecting cell ranges are discussed in the next section), you can do a number of things with a selected range of cells. For example, you can select a range of cells and print them (rather than printing the entire worksheet). You can also name ranges, which makes it much easier to include the cell range in a formula or function (you learn about range names and using range names in formulas later in the lesson).

Selecting a Range

To select a range using the mouse, follow these steps:

1. Move the mouse pointer to the upper-left corner of a range.

2. Click and hold the left mouse button.

3. Drag the mouse to the lower-right corner of the range and release the mouse button. The cells are highlighted on the worksheet (see Figure 11.1).

Techniques that you can use to quickly select a row, a column, an entire worksheet, or several ranges are shown in Table 11.1.

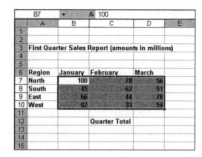

Figure 11.1 A range is any combination of cells that forms a rectangle or a square.

Table 11.1 Selection Techniques

To Select This	Do This
Several ranges	Select the first range, hold down the **Ctrl** key, and select the next range. Continue holding down the **Ctrl** key while you select additional ranges.
Row	Click the row heading number at the left edge of the worksheet. You also can press **Shift+Spacebar**. To select several adjacent rows, drag over their headers. To select nonadjacent rows, press **Ctrl** as you click each row's header.
Column	Click the column heading letter at the top edge of the worksheet. You also can press **Ctrl+Spacebar**.
Entire worksheet	Click the **Select All** button (the blank rectangle in the upper-left corner of the worksheet, above row 1 and left of column A). You also can press **Ctrl+A**.
The same range on several sheets	Press and hold **Ctrl** as you click the worksheets you want to use, and then select the range in the usual way.
Range that is out of view	Press **Ctrl+G** (**Go To**) or click in the **Name** box on the Formula bar and type the address of the range you want to select. For example, to select the range R100 to T250, type **R100:T250** and press **Enter**.

 TIP **Deselecting a Range** To deselect a range, click any cell in the worksheet.

Selected cells are not highlighted in reverse video, as in previous versions of Excel, but in a slightly grayed tone, so you can still read your data.

Naming Ranges

Up to this point, when you have created formulas or functions or formatted cells in a worksheet, you have specified cells and cell ranges using the cell addresses. You can also name a cell or range of cells. For example, you could select a range of values and assign that range a name. You also could select a range of cells that includes your expenses and name that range EXPENSES. You can then name a range of cells that includes your income and name that range INCOME. It would be very simple to then create a formula that subtracts your expenses from your income using the range names that you created. The formulas would be written as follows:

```
=INCOME-EXPENSES
```

Using range names in formulas and functions can definitely make your life easier. Range names are very useful when you create formulas or functions that pull information from more than one worksheet in a workbook or different workbooks. You can even use a range name to create a chart (you learn about charts in Lesson 15, "Creating Charts").

Follow these steps to name a range:

1. Select the range you want to name (the cells must be located on the same worksheet). If you want to name a single cell, simply select that cell.

2. Select the **Insert** menu, point at **Name**, and then select **Define**. The Define Name dialog box appears (see Figure 11.2).

Figure 11.2 Use the Define Name dialog box to name a cell range.

3. Type the name for the range in the box at the top of the dialog box. You can use up to 255 characters, and valid range names can include letters, numbers, periods, and underlines, but no spaces.

4. Click the **Add** button to name the range. The name is added to the list of range names.

5. Click **OK**.

TIP **Selecting a Different Range** You can change the selected range from the Define Name dialog box. Click the **Shrink** button at the bottom of the dialog box, and then select the range on the worksheet. To return to the dialog box, click the **Expand** button on the Define Name dialog box.

You can also use the Define Name dialog box to delete any unwanted range names. Select **Insert**, point at **Name**, and then select **Define**. Select an unwanted range name from the list and click the **Delete** button. To close the dialog box, click **OK**.

 TIP **Quickly Create a Range Name** You can also create a range name by typing it into the Name box on the Formula bar. Select the cell range, click in the Name box, and type the name for the range. Then press **Enter**.

Creating Range Names from Worksheet Labels

You can also create range names using the column and row labels that you have created for your worksheet. The row labels are used to create a range name for each row of cells, and the column labels are used to create a range name for each column of cells. Follow these steps:

1. Select the worksheet, including the column and row labels.

2. Select the **Insert** menu, point at **Name**, and then select **Create**. The Create Names dialog box appears (see Figure 11.3).

3. Click in the check boxes that define the position of the row and column labels in the worksheet.

Figure 11.3 Use the Create Names dialog box to create range names for the cells in the worksheet.

4. After specifying the location of the row and column labels, click **OK**.

You can check the range names (and their range of cells) that were created using the Create Name feature in the Define Name dialog box. Select **Insert**, point at **Name**, and then select **Define**. All the range names that you created appear in the Names in Workbook list.

Inserting a Range Name to a Formula or Function

As previously discussed in this lesson, range names make it easy for you to specify a range of cells in a formula or function. To insert a range name into a formula or function, follow these steps:

1. Click in the cell where you want to place the formula or function.

2. Type the formula or function (begin the formula or function with the equal sign).

3. When you are ready to insert the range name into the formula or function, select the **Insert** menu, point at **Name**, and then select **Paste**. The Paste Name dialog box appears (see Figure 11.4).

Figure 11.4 Use the Paste Name dialog box to insert a range name into a formula or function.

4. Select the range name you want to place in the formula or function, and then click **OK**.

5. Finish typing the formula or function (including the appropriate operators).

6. Press **Enter** to place the formula or function into the cell and return the calculated value.

Inserting and Removing Cells, Rows, and Columns

In this lesson, you learn how to rearrange the data in your worksheet by adding and removing cells, rows, and columns. You also learn how to adjust the width of your columns and the height of your rows to make the best use of the worksheet space.

Inserting Rows and Columns

As you edit and enhance your worksheets, you might need to add rows or columns within the worksheet. Inserting entire rows and columns into your worksheet is very straightforward. Follow these steps:

1. To insert a single row or column, select a cell to the right of where you want to insert a column or below where you want to insert a row.

   To insert multiple columns or rows, select the number of columns or rows you want to insert. To insert columns, drag over the column letters at the top of the worksheet. To insert rows, drag over the row numbers. For example, select three column letters or row numbers to insert three rows or columns.

2. Select the **Insert** menu, and then select **Rows** or **Columns**. Excel inserts rows above your selection and columns to the left of your selection. The inserted rows or columns contain the same formatting as the cells (or rows and columns) you selected in step 1. Figure 12.1 shows a worksheet where additional columns have been added to a worksheet.

As you can see, when you insert rows or columns, the Insert Options shortcut icon appears to the right of the inserted columns or below inserted rows. Use the Insert Options menu to specify from where the column or row should copy its formatting. For example, in the case of inserted columns, you can choose to copy the formatting from the column to the right or left of the inserted column or columns, or you can choose to clear the formatting in the inserted columns.

Figure 12.1 Columns can easily be inserted into an Excel worksheet.

TIP **Fast Insert** To quickly insert rows or columns, select one or more rows or columns, right-click one of them, and choose **Insert** from the shortcut menu.

Removing Rows and Columns

When you delete a row in your worksheet, the rows below the deleted row move up to fill the space. When you delete a column, the columns to the right shift left.

Follow these steps to delete a row or column:

1. Click the row number or column letter of the row or column you want to delete. You can select more than one row or column by dragging over the row numbers or column letters.

2. Select the **Edit** menu and then select **Delete**. Excel deletes the rows or columns and renumbers the remaining rows and columns sequentially. All cell references in formulas and functions are updated appropriately.

Inserting Cells

Although inserting rows and columns makes it easy to dramatically change the layout of a worksheet, on occasion you might need to insert only a cell or cells into a worksheet. Inserting cells causes the data in existing cells to shift down a row or over a column to create a space for the new cells.

Watch Your Formulas and Functions   Inserting cells into a worksheet can throw off the cell references in formulas and functions. Double-check your formulas and functions after inserting cells to make sure that the calculations are acting upon the appropriate cell addresses.

CAUTION

To insert a single cell or a group of cells, follow these steps:

1. Select the area where you want the new cells inserted. Excel inserts the same number of cells as you select.

2. Select the **Insert** menu and then select **Cells**. The Insert dialog box appears (see Figure 12.2).

Figure 12.2   You can insert cells into a worksheet using the Insert dialog box.

3. Select **Shift Cells Right** or **Shift Cells Down** (or you can choose to have an entire row or column inserted).

4. Click **OK**. Excel inserts the cells and shifts the adjacent cells in the direction you specify.

You will find that inserting cells is useful if you have entered rows of information and have mismatched data, such as a customer's name with someone else's order information. Inserting a couple of cells enables you to quickly edit the data without having to delete data or insert a new row.

TIP   **Drag Insert Cells**   A quick way to insert cells is to select the number of cells you want, hold down the **Shift** key, and then drag the fill handle up, down, left, or right to set the position of the new cells.

Removing Cells

You already learned about deleting the data in cells back in Lesson 8, "Editing Worksheets," and you learned that you could also delete cells from a worksheet. Eliminating cells from the worksheet rather than just clearing their contents means that the cells surrounding the deleted cells in the worksheet are moved to fill the gap that is created. Remove cells only if you want the other cells in the worksheet to shift to new positions. Otherwise, just delete the data in the cells or type new data into the cells.

If you want to remove cells from a worksheet, use the following steps:

1. Select the cell or range of cells you want to remove.

2. Open the **Edit** menu and choose **Delete**. The Delete dialog box appears (see Figure 12.3).

Figure 12.3 Use the Delete dialog box to specify how the gap left by the deleted cells should be filled.

3. Select **Shift Cells Left** or **Shift Cells Up** to specify how the remaining cells in the worksheet should move to fill the gap left by the deleted cells.

4. Click **OK**. Surrounding cells are shifted to fill the gap left by the deleted cells.

As with inserting cells, you should check the cell references in your formulas and functions after removing cells from the worksheet. Be sure that your calculations are referencing the appropriate cells on the worksheet.

Adjusting Column Width and Row Height with a Mouse

It doesn't take very long when you are working in Excel to realize that the default column width of 8.43 characters doesn't accommodate long text entries or values that have been formatted as currency or other numeric formats. You can adjust the width of a column quickly using the mouse.

You can also adjust row heights, if you want, using the mouse. However, your row heights will adjust to any font size changes that you make to data held in a particular row. Row heights also adjust if you wrap text entries within them. You will probably find that you need to adjust column widths in your worksheets far more often than row heights.

What Is ########? When you format a value in a cell with a numeric formatting and Excel cannot display the result in the cell because of the column width, Excel places ######## in the cell. This lets you know that you need to adjust the column width so that it can accommodate the entry and its formatting.

CAUTION

To adjust a column width with the mouse, place the mouse pointer on the right border of the column. A sizing tool appears, as shown in Figure 12.4. Drag the column border to the desired width. You can also adjust the column width to automatically accommodate the widest entry within a column; just double-click the sizing tool. This is called AutoFit, and the column adjusts according to the widest entry.

Figure 12.4 Use the column width sizing tool to adjust the width of a column.

If you want to adjust several columns at once, select the columns. Place the mouse on any of the column borders and drag to increase or decrease the width. Each selected column is adjusted to the width you select.

Changing row heights is similar to adjusting column widths. Place the mouse on the lower border of a row and drag the sizing tool to increase or decrease the row height. To change the height of multiple rows, select the rows and then drag the border of any of the selected rows to the desired height.

Using the Format Menu for Precise Control

If you want to precisely specify the width of a column or columns or the height of a row or rows, you can enter specific sizes using a dialog box. This provides you with a little more control than just dragging a row height or column width.

To specify a column width, follow these steps:

1. Select the columns you want to change.

2. Select the **Format** menu, point at **Column**, and then select **Width**. The Column Width dialog box appears (see Figure 12.5).

Figure 12.5   Column widths can also be specified in the Column Width dialog box.

3. Type the column width into the dialog box (the width is measured in number of characters).

4. Click **OK**. Your column(s) width is adjusted accordingly.

Adjusting row heights is similar to adjusting column widths. Select the row or rows, and then select the **Format** menu, point at **Rows**, and select **Height**. In the Row Height dialog box that appears, type in the row height and then click **OK**.

Managing Your Worksheets

In this lesson, you learn how to add and delete worksheets within workbooks. You also learn how to copy, move, and rename worksheets.

Selecting Worksheets

By default, each workbook consists of three worksheets whose names appear on tabs at the bottom of the Excel window. You can add or delete worksheets as desired. One advantage of having multiple worksheets within a workbook is that it enables you to organize your data into logical chunks. Another advantage of having separate worksheets for your data is that you can easily reorganize the worksheets (and the associated data) in a workbook.

Before you learn about the details of inserting, deleting, and copying worksheets, you should know how to select one or more worksheets. Selecting a single worksheet is a method of moving from worksheet to worksheet in a workbook.

Selecting multiple worksheets in a workbook, however, is another story. Selecting multiple workbooks enables you to apply the same autoformatting or cell formatting to more than one worksheet at a time. This is particularly useful in cases where you might have several worksheets in a workbook that will end up looking very much the same. For example, you might have a workbook that contains four worksheets—each of the worksheets serving as a quarterly summary. Because the design of these worksheets is similar, applying formatting to more than one sheet at a time enables you to keep the sheets consistent in appearance.

To select a worksheet or worksheets, perform one of the following actions:

- To select a single worksheet, click its tab. The tab becomes highlighted to show that the worksheet is selected.
- To select several neighboring or adjacent worksheets, click the tab of the first worksheet in the group and then hold down the **Shift** key and click the tab of the last worksheet in the group. Each worksheet tab will be highlighted (but only the first sheet selected will be visible).
- To select several nonadjacent worksheets, hold down the **Ctrl** key and click each worksheet's tab.

If you select two or more worksheets, they remain selected as a group until you ungroup them. To ungroup worksheets, do one of the following:

- Right-click one of the selected worksheets and choose **Ungroup Sheets**.
- Hold down the **Shift** key and click the tab of the active worksheet.
- Click any worksheet tab to deselect all the other worksheets.

Inserting Worksheets

When you create a new workbook, it contains three worksheets. You can easily add additional worksheets to a workbook.

Follow these steps to add a worksheet to a workbook:

1. Select the worksheet that you want to be to the right of the inserted worksheet. For example, if you select the quarter3 sheet shown in Figure 13.1, the new sheet will be inserted to the left of quarter3.

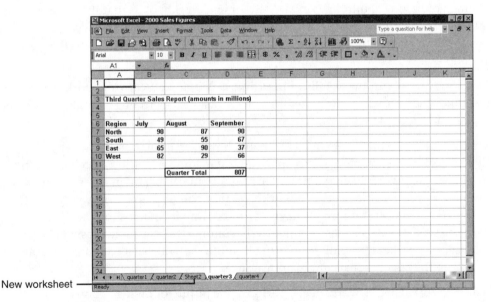

New worksheet

Figure 13.1 Excel inserts the new worksheet to the left of the active worksheet.

2. Select the **Insert** menu.

3. Select **Worksheet**. Excel inserts the new worksheet to the right of the previously selected worksheet.

TIP   **Use the Shortcut Menu**   A faster way to work with worksheets is to right-click the worksheet tab. This brings up a shortcut menu that lets you insert, delete, rename, move, copy, or select all worksheets.

TIP   **Start with More Sheets**   You can change the default number of worksheets Excel places in a new workbook by opening the **Tools** menu, selecting **Options**, clicking the **General** tab, and then changing the number in the **Sheets in New Workbook** option. Click **OK** to save your changes. The maximum value for the number of sheets in a workbook is determined by the amount of memory on your computer. You might find that using more than 20 sheets in a workbook that are full of data start to slow down Excel's overall performance.

Deleting Worksheets

If you find that you have a worksheet you no longer need, or if you plan to use only one worksheet of the three that Excel puts into each workbook by default, you can remove the unwanted worksheets. Here's how you remove a worksheet:

1. Select the worksheet(s) you want to delete.

2. Select the **Edit** menu and then select **Delete Sheet**.

3. If the sheet contains data, a dialog box appears, asking you to confirm the deletion. Click **Delete** to delete the sheet. You will lose any data that the sheet contained.

You can delete multiple sheets if you want. Use the techniques discussed earlier in this lesson to select multiple sheets, and then use steps 2 and 3 in this section to delete the sheets.

Moving and Copying Worksheets

You can move or copy worksheets within a workbook or from one workbook to another. Copying a worksheet enables you to copy the formatting of the sheet and other items, such as the column labels and the row labels. Follow these steps:

1. Select the worksheet or worksheets you want to move or copy. If you want to move or copy worksheets from one workbook to another, be sure the target workbook is open.

2. Select the **Edit** menu and choose **Move or Copy Sheet**. The Move or Copy dialog box appears, as shown in Figure 13.2.

Figure 13.2   The Move or Copy dialog box asks where you want to copy or move a worksheet.

3. To move the worksheets to a different workbook, be sure that workbook is open, and then select that workbook's name from the To Book drop-down list. If you want to move or copy the worksheets to a new workbook, select **(New Book)** in the To Book drop-down list. Excel creates a new workbook and then copies or moves the worksheets to it.

4. In the Before Sheet list box, choose the worksheet you want to follow the selected worksheets.

5. To move the selected worksheet, skip to step 6. To copy the selected worksheets instead of moving them, select the **Create a Copy** option.

6. Select **OK**. The selected worksheets are copied or moved as specified.

Moving a Worksheet Within a Workbook with Drag and Drop

A fast way to copy or move worksheets within a workbook is to use drag and drop. First, select the tab of the worksheet(s) you want to copy or move.

Move the mouse pointer over one of the selected tabs, click and hold the mouse button, and drag the tab where you want it moved. To copy the worksheet, hold down the **Ctrl** key while dragging. When you release the mouse button, the worksheet is copied or moved.

Moving or Copying a Worksheet Between Workbooks with Drag and Drop

You can also use the Drag-and-Drop feature to quickly copy or move worksheets between workbooks.

1. Open the workbooks you want to use for the copy or move.

2. Select **Window** and select **Arrange**. The Arrange dialog box opens.

3. You can arrange the different workbook windows horizontally, vertically, tiled, or cascaded in the Excel application window. For more than two open workbooks, your best selection is probably the **Tiled** option (see Figure 13.3).

Figure 13.3   You can arrange multiple workbooks in the Excel window and then move or copy worksheets.

4. After making your selection, click **OK** to arrange the workbook windows within the Excel application window.

5. Select the tab of the worksheet(s) you want to copy or move.

6. Move the mouse pointer over one of the selected tabs, click and hold the mouse button, and drag the tab where you want it moved. To copy the worksheet, hold down the **Ctrl** key while dragging.

7. When you release the mouse button, the worksheet is copied or moved.

Changing Worksheet Tab Names

By default, all worksheets are named SheetX, where X is a number starting with the number 1. So that you'll have a better idea of the information each sheet contains, you should change the names that appear on the tabs. Here's how to do it:

1. Double-click the tab of the worksheet you want to rename. The current name is highlighted.

2. Type a new name for the worksheet and press **Enter**. Excel replaces the default name with the name you type.

Printing Your Workbook

In this lesson, you learn how to preview your print jobs, repeat row and column headings on pages, and add headers and footers to your worksheets. You also learn how to print an entire workbook and large worksheets.

Previewing a Print Job

After you've finished a particular worksheet and want to send it to the printer, you might want to take a quick look at how the worksheet will look on the printed page. You will find that worksheets don't always print the way that they look on the screen.

To preview a print job, select the **File** menu and then select **Print Preview**, or click the **Print Preview** button on the Standard toolbar. Your workbook appears in the same format that it will be in when sent to the printer (see Figure 14.1).

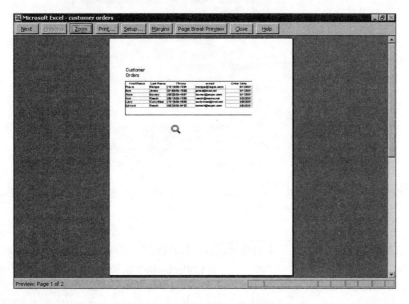

Figure 14.1 By previewing the worksheet, you can determine which page layout attributes need adjusting.

> **TIP**   **A Close-Up View**   Zoom in on any area of the preview by clicking it with the mouse pointer (which looks like a magnifying glass). Or use the **Zoom** button on the Print Preview toolbar.

When you have finished previewing your worksheet, you can print the worksheet by clicking the **Print** button, or you can return to the worksheet by clicking **Close**.

Changing the Page Setup

After you preview your worksheet, you might want to adjust page attributes or change the way the page is set up for printing. For example, you might want to print the column and row labels on every page of the printout. This is particularly useful for large worksheets that span several pages; then you don't have to keep looking back to the first page of the printout to determine what the column headings are.

Printing column and row labels and other worksheet page attributes, such as scaling a worksheet to print out on a single page or adding headers or footers to a worksheet printout, are handled in the Page Setup dialog box. To access this dialog box, select the **File** menu and then select **Page Setup** (see Figure 14.2).

The following sections provide information on some of the most common page setup attributes that you will work with before printing your Excel worksheets.

Figure 14.2   Access the Page Setup dialog box to make sure your worksheet page is set to print correctly.

Printing Column and Row Labels on Every Page

Excel provides a way for you to select labels and titles that are located on the top edge and left side of a large worksheet and to print them on every page of the printout. This option is useful when a worksheet is too wide to print on a single page.

If you don't use this option, the extra columns or rows are printed on subsequent pages without any descriptive labels.

Follow these steps to print column or row labels on every page:

1. Select the **File** menu and then select **Page Setup**. The Page Setup dialog box appears.

2. Click the **Sheet** tab to display the Sheet options (see Figure 14.3).

Figure 14.3 Use the Sheet tab to specify headings you want to repeat in the printout.

3. To repeat column labels and a worksheet title, click the **Shrink** button to the right of the Rows to Repeat at Top text box.

4. Drag over the rows that you want to print on every page. A dashed line border surrounds the selected area, and absolute cell references with dollar signs ($) appear in the Rows to Repeat at Top text box.

5. Click the **Expand** button on the collapsed dialog box to expand the Page Setup dialog box.

6. To repeat row labels that appear on the left of the worksheet, click the **Shrink** button to the right of the Columns to Repeat at Left text box. Excel reduces the Page Setup dialog box.

7. Select the columns that contain the row labels you want to repeat.

8. Click the **Expand** button to return again to the Page Setup dialog box.

9. To print your worksheet, click **Print** to display the Print dialog box. Then click **OK**.

TIP   Select Your Print Area Carefully   If you select rows or columns to repeat, and those rows or columns are part of your print area, the selected rows or columns might print twice. To fix this, select your print area again, leaving out the rows or columns you're repeating.

TIP   Access Print Preview from Other Dialog Boxes   Page Setup and Print dialog boxes also include a Preview button, so you can check any last-minute changes you made in either dialog box without having to close the box first.

Scaling a Worksheet to Fit on a Page

If your worksheet is too large to print on one page even after you change the orientation and margins, consider using the **Fit To** option. This option shrinks the worksheet to make it fit on the specified number of pages. You can specify the document's width and height.

Follow these steps to scale a worksheet to fit on a page:

1. Select the **File** menu and then select **Page Setup**. The Page Setup dialog box appears.

2. Click the **Page** tab to display the Page options.

3. In the Fit to XX Page(s) Wide by XX Tall text boxes, enter the number of pages into which you want Excel to fit your data.

4. Click **OK** to close the Page Setup dialog box and return to your worksheet, or click the **Print** button in the Page Setup dialog box to display the Print dialog box, and then click **OK** to print your worksheet.

TIP   Change the Page Orientation   The Page tab of the Page Setup dialog box also enables you to change the orientation of the worksheet from Portrait to Landscape. Landscape orientation is useful if you have a worksheet with a large number of columns.

Adding Headers and Footers

Excel enables you to add headers and footers to your worksheets that will appear at the top and bottom of every page of the printout (respectively). The information can include any text, as well as page numbers, the current date and time, the workbook filename, and the worksheet tab name.

You can choose the headers and footers suggested by Excel, or you can include any text plus special commands to control the appearance of the header or footer. For example, you can apply bold, italic, or underline to the header or footer text. You can also left-align, center, or right-align your text in a header or footer (see Lesson 9, "Changing How Numbers and Text Look," for more information).

To add headers and footers, follow these steps:

1. Select the **File** menu and then select **Page Setup**. The Page Setup dialog box appears. Click the **Header/Footer** tab on the dialog box (see Figure 14.4).

Figure 14.4 Add headers and footers with Header/Footer options.

2. To select a header, click the **Header** drop-down arrow. Excel displays a list of suggested header information. Scroll through the list and click a header you want. The sample header appears at the top of the Header/Footer tab.

TIP **Don't See One You Like?** If none of the suggested headers or footers suit you, click the **Custom Header** or **Custom Footer** button and enter your own information.

3. To select a footer, click the **Footer** drop-down arrow. Excel displays a list of suggested footer information. Scroll through the list and click a footer you want. The sample footer appears at the bottom of the Header/Footer tab.

4. Click **OK** to close the Page Setup dialog box and return to your worksheet, or click the **Print** button to display the Print dialog box and click **OK** to print your worksheet.

TIP **Don't Want Headers or Footers Anymore?** To remove the header and/or footer, choose **(None)** in the **Header** and/or **Footer** lists.

Printing Your Workbook

After adjusting the page settings for the worksheet and previewing your data, it is time to print. You can print selected data, selected sheets, or the entire workbook.

To print your workbook, follow these steps:

1. If you want to print a portion of the worksheet, select the range of cells you want to print. To print only a chart, click it (you learn about creating charts in Lesson 15, "Creating Charts"). If you want to print one or more worksheets within the workbook, select the sheet tabs (see Lesson 13, "Managing Your Worksheets"). To print the entire workbook, skip this step.

2. Select the **File** menu and then select **Print** (or press **Ctrl+P**). The Print dialog box appears, as shown in Figure 14.5.

Figure 14.5   In the Print dialog box, select your printer and a page range to print.

TIP   **Print Using the Default Settings**   If you click the **Print** button (instead of using the **File** menu and clicking **Print**), Excel prints your current worksheet without letting you make any selections.

3. Select the options you would like to use:

- **Print Range**—Lets you print one or more pages. For example, if the selected print area contains 15 pages and you want to print only pages 5–10, select **Page(s)** and then type the numbers of the first and last page you want to print into the **From** and **To** boxes.

- **Print What**—Enables you to print the currently selected cells, the selected worksheets, or the entire workbook.

- **Copies**—Enables you to print more than one copy of the selection, worksheet, or workbook.

- **Collate**—Enables you to print a complete copy of the selection, worksheet, or workbook before the first page of the next copy is printed. This option is available when you print multiple copies.

4. Click **OK** to print your selection, worksheet, or workbook.

While your job is printing, you can continue working in Excel. If the printer is working on another job that you (or someone else, in the case of a network printer) sent, Windows holds the job until the printer is ready for it.

Sometimes you might want to delete a job while it is printing or before it prints. For example, suppose you think of other numbers to add to the worksheet or realize that you forgot to format some text; you'll want to fix these things before you print the file. To display the print queue and delete a print job, follow these steps:

1. Double-click the **Printer** icon in the Windows system tray (at the far right of the taskbar), and the print queue appears.
2. Click the job you want to delete.
3. Select the **Document** menu and then select **Cancel Printing**, or just press **Delete**.

    To delete all the files from the print queue, open the **Printer** menu and select **Purge Print Documents**. This cancels the print jobs but doesn't delete the files from your computer.

Selecting a Large Worksheet Print Area

You do not have to always print an entire worksheet; instead, you can easily tell Excel what part of the worksheet you want to print by selecting the print area yourself. If the area you select is too large to fit on one page, no problem; Excel breaks it into multiple pages. When you do not select a print area yourself, Excel prints either the entire worksheet or the entire workbook, depending on the options set in the Print dialog box.

To select a print area, follow these steps:

1. Click the upper-left cell of the range you want to print.
2. Drag downward and to the right until the range you want is selected.
3. Select the **File** menu, point at **Print Area**, and then select **Set Print Area**.

To remove the print area so you can print the entire worksheet again, select the **File** menu, select **Print Area**, and select **Clear Print Area**.

Adjusting Page Breaks

When you print a workbook, Excel determines the page breaks based on the paper size, the margins, and the selected print area. To make the pages look better and to break information in logical places, you might want to override the automatic page breaks with your own breaks. However, before you add page breaks, try these options:

- Adjust the widths of individual columns to make the best use of space.
- Consider printing the workbook using the Landscape orientation.
- Change the left, right, top, and bottom margins to smaller values.

After trying these options, if you still want to insert page breaks, Excel offers you an option of previewing exactly where the page breaks appear and then adjusting them. Follow these steps:

1. Select the **View** menu and select **Page Break Preview**.

2. If a message appears telling you how to adjust page breaks, click **OK**. Your worksheet is displayed with page breaks, as shown in Figure 14.6.

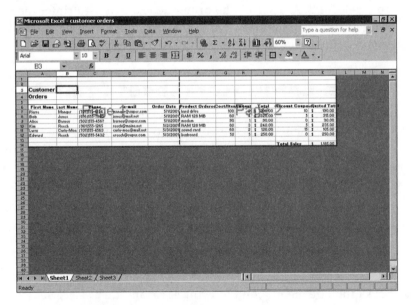

Figure 14.6   Check your page breaks before printing your worksheet.

3. To move a page break, drag the blue line to the desired location.

To delete a page break, drag it off the screen.

To insert a page break, move to the first cell in the column to the right of where you want the page break inserted, or move to the row below where you want the break inserted. For example, to insert a page break between columns G and H, move to cell H1. To insert a page break between rows 24 and 25, move to cell A25. Then, open the **Insert** menu and select **Page Break**. A dashed line appears to the left of the selected column or above the selected row.

4. To exit Page Break Preview and return to your normal worksheet view, open the **View** menu and select **Normal**.

Creating Charts

In this lesson, you learn how to create graphical representations (charts) of workbook data.

Understanding Charting Terminology

Charts enable you to create a graphical representation of data in a worksheet. You can use charts to make data more understandable to people who view your printed worksheets. Before you start creating charts, you should familiarize yourself with the following terminology:

- **Data Series**—The bars, pie wedges, lines, or other elements that represent plotted values in a chart. For example, a chart might show a set of similar bars that reflects a series of values for the same item. The bars in the same data series would all have the same pattern. If you have more than one pattern of bars, each pattern would represent a separate data series. For example, charting the sales for Territory 1 versus Territory 2 would require two data series—one for each territory. Often, data series correspond to rows of data in your worksheet (although they can correspond to columns of data if that is how you have arranged the information in your worksheet).

- **Categories**—Categories reflect the number of elements in a series. You might have two data series that compare the sales of two territories and four categories that compare these sales over four quarters. Some charts have only one category, and others have several. Categories normally correspond to the columns in your worksheet, with the category labels coming from the column headings.

- **Axis**—One side of a chart. A two-dimensional chart has an x-axis (horizontal) and a y-axis (vertical). The x-axis contains the data series and categories in the chart. If you have more than one category, the x-axis often contains labels that define what each category represents. The y-axis reflects the values of the bars, lines, or plot points. In a three-dimensional chart, the z-axis represents the vertical plane, and the x-axis (distance) and y-axis (width) represent the two sides on the floor of the chart.

- **Legend**—Defines the separate series of a chart. For example, the legend for a pie chart shows what each piece of the pie represents.

- **Gridlines**—Typically, gridlines appear along the y-axis of the chart. The y-axis is where your values are displayed, although they can emanate from the x-axis as well (the x-axis is where label information normally appears on the chart). Gridlines help you determine a point's exact value.

Working with Different Chart Types

With Excel, you can create many types of charts. Some common chart types are shown in Figure 15.1. The chart type you choose depends on the kind of data you're trying to chart and on how you want to present that data. The following are the major chart types and their purposes:

- **Pie**—Use this chart type to show the relationship among parts of a whole.

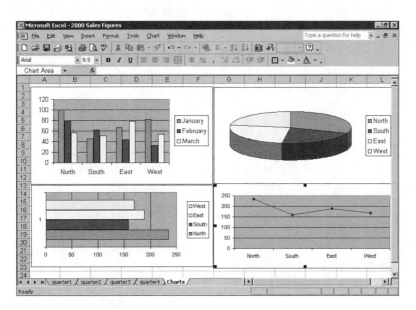

Figure 15.1   Excel chart types enable you to analyze and present your data.

- **Bar**—Use this chart type to compare values at a given point in time.

- **Column**—Similar to the bar chart; use this chart type to emphasize the difference between items.

- **Line**—Use this chart type to emphasize trends and the change of values over time.

- **Scatter**—Similar to a line chart; use this chart type to emphasize the difference between two sets of values.

- **Area**—Similar to the line chart; use this chart type to emphasize the amount of change in values over time.

Most of these basic chart types also come in three-dimensional varieties. In addition to looking more professional than the standard flat charts, 3D charts can often help your audience distinguish between different sets of data.

Creating and Saving a Chart

You can place your new chart on the same worksheet that contains the chart data (an embedded chart) or on a separate worksheet (a chart sheet). If you create an embedded chart, it is typically printed side by side with your worksheet data. Embedded charts are useful for showing the actual data and its graphical representation side by side. If you create a chart on a separate worksheet, however, you can print it independently. Both types of charts are linked to the worksheet data that they represent, so when you change the data, the chart is automatically updated.

The **Chart Wizard** button on the Standard toolbar enables you to quickly create a chart. To use the Chart Wizard, follow these steps:

1. Select the data you want to chart. If you typed column or row labels (such as Qtr 1, Qtr 2, and so on) that you want included in the chart, be sure you select those, too.

2. Click the **Chart Wizard** button on the Standard toolbar.

3. The **Chart Wizard - Step 1 of 4** dialog box appears (see Figure 15.2). Select a **Chart Type** and a **Chart Sub-Type** (a variation on the selected chart type). Click **Next**.

4. Next, Excel asks whether the selected range is correct. You can correct the range by typing a new range or by clicking the **Shrink** button (located at the right end of the **Data Range** text box) and selecting the range you want to use.

5. By default, Excel assumes that your different data series are stored in rows. You can change this to columns if necessary by clicking the **Series in Columns** option. When you're ready for the next step, click **Next**.

6. Click the various tabs to change options for your chart (see Figure 15.3). For example, you can delete the legend by clicking the **Legend** tab and deselecting **Show Legend**. You can add a chart title on the **Titles** tab. Add data labels (labels that display the actual value being represented by each bar, line, and so on) by clicking the **Data Labels** tab. When you finish making changes, click **Next**.

Figure 15.2 Choose the chart type using the Chart Wizard.

Figure 15.3 Select from various chart appearance options.

7. Finally, Excel asks whether you want to embed the chart (as an object) in the current worksheet (or any other existing worksheet in the workbook) or if you want to create a new worksheet for it. Make your selection and click the **Finish** button. Your completed chart appears.

TIP **Create a Chart Fast!** To create a chart quickly, select the data you want to use and press **F11**. Excel creates a column chart (the default chart type) on its own sheet. You can then customize the chart as needed.

The charts you create are part of the current workbook. To save a chart, simply save the workbook that contains the chart.

Moving and Resizing a Chart

To move an embedded chart, click anywhere in the chart area and drag it to the new location. To change the size of a chart, select the chart and then drag one of its handles (the black squares that border the chart). Drag a corner handle to change the height and width, or drag a side handle to change only one dimension. (Note that you can't really resize a chart that is on a sheet by itself.)

Printing a Chart

If a chart is an embedded chart, it will print when you print the worksheet that contains the chart. If you want to print just the embedded chart, click it to select it, and then open the **File** menu and select **Print**. Be sure the **Selected Chart** option is turned on. Then, click **OK** to print the chart.

If you created a chart on a separate worksheet, you can print the chart separately by printing only that worksheet. For more information about printing, refer to Lesson 14, "Printing Your Workbook."

Access

Working in Access

In this lesson, you learn what a database is and how to plan one.
You also learn how to start Microsoft Access, become familiar
with its toolbars, and then exit the software.

Understanding Access Databases

Strictly speaking, a *database* is any collection of information. Your local telephone
book, for example, is a database, as is your Contacts folder in Outlook. Microsoft
Access makes creating databases very straightforward and relatively simple. The
electronic container that Access provides for holding your data is called a *table* (see
Figure 1.1).

Fields

	Employee ID	First Name	Last Name	Extension	Department	Start Date
	2	Janet	Leverling	448	Porches and Decks	3/10/1997
	3	Steven	Buchanan	223	Architects	5/12/1997
	4	Snidley	Backlash	110	Porches and Decks	1/28/1998
	5	Henry	Cotton	623	New Construction	7/7/1996
	6	Alice	Smith	332	Porches and Decks	5/4/1997
	7	Bob	Palooka	234	Architects	9/8/1999
	8	Cleo	Katrina	543	Kitchen Design	4/9/1999
	9	Robert	Buchanan	227	Bathroom Design	8/15/2000
	10	Richard	Jones	333	Kitchen Design	3/10/1999
	11	Carmella	Jones	434	Living Room Design	2/1/2001
	12	Amy	Buchanan	654	Architects	3/10/2001

Record: 4 of 12

Records

Figure 1.1   A table serves as the container for your database information.

A table consists of rows and columns. Access stores each database entry (for example, each employee or each inventory item) in its own row; this is a *record*. Each
record contains specific information related to one person, place, or thing.

Table   A container for your database information consisting of columns and rows.

Each record is broken up into discrete pieces of information, called fields. Each *field* consists of a separate column in the table. Each field contains a different piece of information that taken all together makes up a particular record. For example, Last Name is a field. All the last names in the entire table (all in the same column) are collectively known as the Last Name field.

Record   A row in a table that contains information about a particular person, place, or thing.

Field   A discrete piece of information making up a record. Each column in the Access table is a different field.

Access is a special kind of database called a *relational database*. A relational database divides information into discrete subsets. Each subset groups information by a particular theme, such as customer information, sales orders, or product information. In Access, these subsets of data reside in individual tables like the one described previously.

Access enables you to build relationships between tables. These relationships are based on a field that is common to two tables. Each table must have a field called the primary key (you learn how to specify a field as the primary key in Access Lessons 3 and 4). The primary key must uniquely identify each record in the table. So, the primary key field is typically a field that assigns a unique number (no duplicates within that table) to each record.

For example, a Customers table might contain a Customer Identification field (shown as CustomerID in Figure 1.2) that identifies each customer by a unique number (such as your Social Security number). You might also have a table that holds all your sales orders. To link the Sales table to the Customers table, you include the Customer Identification field in the Sales table. This identifies each sale by customer and links the Sales table data to the Customers table data.

Relational Database   A collection of individual tables holding discrete subsets of information that are linked by common data fields.

You will find that even a simple database consists of several tables that are related. Figure 1.2 shows a database and the different table relationships. Access Lesson 9, "Creating Relationships Between Tables," provides information on creating table relationships.

Figure 1.2   A relational database contains related tables.

Introducing Access Objects

The table is just one type of object found in Access. You can also work with forms, queries, and reports.

- A *form* is used to enter, edit, and view data in a table, one record at a time.

- A *query* enables you to ask your database questions. The answer to the query can be used to manipulate data in a table, such as deleting records or viewing the data in a table that meets only certain criteria.

- A *report* enables you to summarize database information in a format that is suitable for printing.

In essence, each of these different database objects allows you a different way of viewing and manipulating the data found in your tables. Each of these objects (including the table) should also be considered as you plan a new database.

Planning a Database

When you do create a new database, you want to make sure that the database is designed not only to meet your data entry needs, but also to meet your needs for viewing and reporting the data that is held in the various tables that make up the database. Taking a little time to plan your database before you create it can save you from headaches down the road. The sections that follow provide some tips on planning a database.

Determining Your Tables

Technically, you need only one table to make a database. However, because Access is a relational database program, it's meant to handle many tables and create relationships among them. For example, in a database that keeps track of customer orders, you might have the following tables:

- Customers
- Orders
- Products
- Salespeople
- Shipping Methods

Using many tables that hold subsets of the database information can help you avoid making redundant data entries. For example, suppose you want to keep contact information on your customers along with a record of each transaction they make. If you kept it all in one table, you would have to repeat the customer's full name, address, and phone number each time you entered a new transaction. It would also be a nightmare if the customer's address changed; you would have to change the address in every transaction record for that customer.

A better way is to assign each customer an ID number. Include that ID number in a table that contains names and addresses, and then use the same ID number as a link to a separate transactions table. Basically, then, each table in your database should have a particular theme—for example, Employee Contact Information or Customer Transactions. Don't try to have more than one theme per table.

A table design requirement is to be sure that every table that you create uses the first field (the first column of the table) as a way to uniquely identify each record in the table. This field can then serve as the table's primary key. For example, customers can be assigned a customer number, or sales transactions can be assigned a transaction number. The primary key is the only way that you can then link the table to another table in the database.

It's a good idea to do some work on paper and jot down a list of tables that will be contained in the database and the fields that they will contain. Restructuring tables because of poor planning isn't impossible, but it isn't much fun, either.

Determining Your Forms

As already mentioned, forms are used for data entry. They allow you to enter data one record at a time (see Figure 1.3). Complex forms can also be constructed that actually allow you to enter data into more than one table at a time (this is because fields can be pulled from several tables in the same database into one form).

Figure 1.3 A form allows you to enter data one record at a time.

Planning the forms that you use for data entry is not as crucial as planning the tables that make up the database. Forms should be designed to make data entry easier. They are great in that they allow you to concentrate on the entry or editing of data one record at a time. You might want to have a form for each table in the database, or you might want to create composite forms that allow you to enter data into the form that is actually deposited into more than one table.

The great thing about forms is that they don't have to contain all the fields that are in a particular table. For example, if you have someone else enter the data that you keep in an employee database, but you don't want that data entry person to see the employee salaries, you can design a form that does not contain the salary field.

Determining Your Queries

Queries enable you to manipulate the data in your database tables. A query can contain criteria that allow you to delete old customer records, or it can provide you with a list of employees who have worked at the company for more than 10 years.

Deciding the queries that you will use before all the data is entered can be difficult. However, if you are running a store—a cheese shop, for example—and know that it is important for you to keep close tabs on your cheese inventory, you will probably want to build some queries to track sales and inventory.

Queries are an excellent way for you to determine the status of your particular endeavor. For example, you could create a query to give you total sales for a particular month. Queries are, in effect, questions. Use queries to get the answers that you need from your database information.

Determining Your Reports

A report is used to publish the data in the database. It places the data on the page (or pages) in a highly readable format. Reports are meant to be printed (unlike tables and forms, which are usually used onscreen). For example, you might run a club and want a report of all people who haven't paid their membership dues or who owe more than $1,000 on their account.

A report is usually for the benefit of other people who aren't sitting with you at your computer. For example, you might print a report to hand out to your board of directors to encourage them to keep you on as CEO. A report can pull data from many tables at once, perform calculations on the data (such as summing or averaging), and present you with neatly formatted results. Figure 1.4 shows a database report.

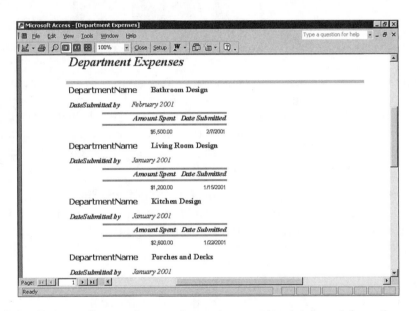

Figure 1.4   Reports allow you to organize and summarize database information.

You can create new reports at any time; you don't have to plan them before you create your database. However, if you know you will want a certain report, you might design your tables in the format that will be most effective for that report's use.

Designing good databases is an acquired skill. The more databases that you work with, the better each will be. Now that you've gotten your feet wet with database planning, take a look at how to start Access.

Starting Access

You can start Access in several ways, depending on how you've installed it. One way is to use the Start menu button. Follow these steps:

1. Click the **Start** button. A menu appears.

2. Highlight or point to **Programs**. A list of programs installed on your computer appears.

3. Click **Microsoft Access** in the list of applications. Access starts.

TIP   **Moving Programs Around on the Start Menu**   If you prefer to have Access in a different program group, open the **Start** menu and drag the Access item to another location of your choice.

Other Ways to Start Access

Some other ways to start Access require more knowledge of Windows and Microsoft Office. If you're confused by them, stick with the primary method explained in the preceding section.

- You can create a shortcut icon for Access that sits on your desktop; you can then start Access by double-clicking the icon. To create the shortcut icon, drag the Access item from the **Start** menu to the desktop.

- When you're browsing files in Windows Explorer, you can double-click any Access data file to start Access and open that data file. Access data files have an .mdb extension and a little icon next to them that resembles the icon next to Microsoft Access on the Programs menu.

- If you can't find Access, you can search for it. Click the **Start** button and select **Find**, select **Files or Folders**, and then type **msaccess.exe** into the Named text box. Open the **Look In** list and select **My Computer**. Then click **Find Now**. When the file appears on the list at the bottom of the Find window, double-click it to start Access, or right-click and drag it to the desktop to create an Access shortcut.

Parts of the Access Screen

Access is much like any other Windows program: It contains menus, toolbars, a status bar, the Ask a Question box, and so on. Figure 1.5 provides a look at these different areas of the Access window. This view assumes that you have either created a new database or opened an existing database in the Access workspace. Creating a new database and opening an existing database are discussed in Lesson 2, "Creating a New Database."

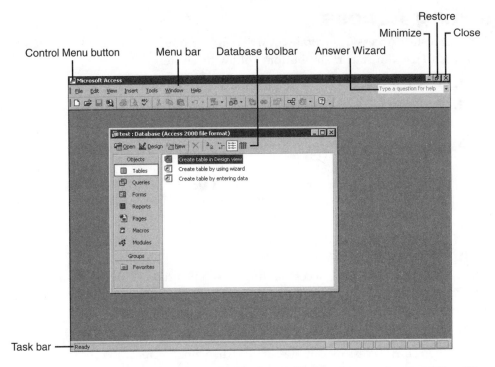

Control Menu button   Menu bar   Database toolbar   Answer Wizard

Restore
Minimize ┐ ┌ Close

Task bar

Figure 1.5   Access provides the typical tools provided by the members of Office XP.

You probably have noticed that most of the buttons on the toolbar are unavailable. That's because you haven't created any objects, such as tables or forms, for the new database. The toolbar currently displayed in the Access window is the Database toolbar. Access differs from the other Office applications in that it has a different toolbar for each database object. In some cases, multiple toolbars exist for an object, depending on whether you are entering data into the object or changing the design parameters of the object.

For example, Access tables have two toolbars. The Table Datasheet toolbar provides you with tools that help you enter and manipulate the data in the table when you work with it in the Datasheet view. If you switch to the Design view of the table, a Table Design toolbar helps you manipulate the design settings for the table.

Because you will be working with each Access object type, you will also become familiar with each object toolbar. As you work with the various buttons on the toolbars, remember that you can place the mouse pointer on any toolbar button to receive a ToolTip. The ToolTip provides the name of the button, which usually is indicative of what the particular tool is used for.

One other thing that should be mentioned related to the Access window is that only one database at a time can be open in the Access window. It doesn't enable you to work on multiple databases at the same time, as you could work with multiple documents, or workbooks in Word or Excel.

TIP   **Choose Your Toolbars**   As you work in Access on the various objects, right-click any toolbar to view a shortcut menu that provides a list of available toolbars. Typically, you are limited to the toolbar specific to the object that you are working on.

Exiting Access

Although you have only barely gotten your feet wet with Access, take a look at how you exit the application. You can exit Access in several ways:

- Select **File**, and then select **Exit**.
- Click the Access window's **Close (x)** button on the upper right of the Access window.
- Press **Alt+F4**.

Creating a New Database

*In this lesson, you learn how to create a blank database. You also
learn how to create a new database using a database template
and the Database Wizard. You also learn how to close your database, open it, and how to find a
misplaced database file.*

Choosing How to Create Your Database

Before you can create your database tables and actually enter data, you must create a
database file. The database is really just a container file that holds all the database
objects, such as the tables, forms, and reports. You also have two options for creating
a new database: You can create a blank database from scratch or create a new database based on a database template.

Creating a new database based on a template means that you take advantage of the
Database Wizard, which not only creates your new database file but also helps you
quickly create tables, forms, and other objects for the database.

 TIP **Database Wizard** Access provides several templates for creating new database
files, and the Database Wizard walks you through the process of creating objects,
such as tables, for the new database.

Whether you create your new database from scratch or use one of the database templates depends on how closely one of the Access templates meets your database
needs. If one of the templates provides you with the type of tables and other objects
necessary for your project, it makes sense to use a template. For example, if you want
to create a database that helps you manage your company's inventory, you can take
advantage of the Inventory Control template that Access provides. This template provides you with the basic tables and other objects to start the process of getting a handle on your inventory database.

In some cases, the templates might not meet your needs. For example, if you want to
create a complex database that allows you to track sales, customers, and employee
performance, it might be easier to create a blank database and then create each table
for the database from scratch. Let's start the overview of database creation with creating a blank database.

Selecting a Database File Type

One thing to discuss before you look at creating a new database is the database file format. By default, new databases created in Access 2002 are created in the Access 2000 file format. This makes your database files compatible with earlier versions of Access, such as Access 2000 and Access 97.

Saving the database in the Access 2000 file format does not negate you from using any of the tools or features available in Access 2002. If you use your database files only in Access 2002 and share the databases with co-workers who also use Access 2002, you can set the default file format for new databases to Access 2002. Select the **Tools** menu, and then select **Options**. The Options dialog box opens.

Select the **Advanced** tab on the Options dialog box. Click the **Default File Format** drop-down box and select **Access 2002**. Now take a look at creating new databases.

Creating a Blank Database

Creating a blank database is very straightforward. As mentioned previously, you are just creating the container file that holds all the objects that actually make up the database. To create a blank database, follow these steps:

1. Open the Access window (click **Start**, **Programs**, **Access**).

2. Select **Blank Database** in the task pane or click the **New** button on the Database toolbar. The File New Database dialog box appears (see Figure 2.1).

Figure 2.1   Provide a location and a name for the new database file.

3. Use the Save In drop-down box to locate the folder in which you want to save the new database. Type a name for the new file into the **File Name** text box.

4. When you are ready to create the database file, click **Create**. The new database window appears in the Access workspace (see Figure 2.2).

Object icons   Object pane

Figure 2.2   A new database window opens in Access.

The database window provides you with a set of icons that allows you to select a particular object type. For example, the Tables icon is selected by default after you create the new database (which makes sense, because you need to create at least one table before you can create any of the other object types such as a form or a report).

Shortcuts for different methods of creating tables are provided at the top of the Object pane on the right side of the database window. After you create a new table for the database, it is listed in this pane. In Lesson 3, "Creating a Table with the Table Wizard," and Lesson 4, "Creating a Table from Scratch," you take a look at creating tables.

The database window enables you to view the different objects that you've created for a particular database (or those that have been created when you use the Database Wizard). When you want to switch the database window's focus to a different Access object, all you have to do is click the appropriate icon in the Objects list.

TIP   **Different Ways to View the Database Windows**   The toolbar on the database window provides buttons for opening or creating a particular database object, such as a table or a form. The toolbar also provides buttons that can be used to change the view in the Object pane: **Large Icons**, **Small Icons**, **List** (the default view) and **Details** (which provides information such as when the object was last modified).

Closing a Database

When you finish working with a database, you might want to close it so that you can concentrate on creating a new database (such as you do in the next section). However, because Access allows you to have only one database open at a time, as soon as you begin creating a new database the currently open database closes. Opening an existing database also closes the current database (which is something you do later in this lesson).

If you want to close a database, there are a couple of possibilities: you can click the **Close** (**X**) button on the database window, or you can select **File**, **Close**. In either case, the database window closes, clearing the Access workspace.

Creating a Database from a Template

Another option for creating a new database is using one of the Access database templates. Templates are available for asset tracking, contact management, inventory control, and other database types. Another perk of using an Access template to create a new database is that a Database Wizard creates tables and other objects, such as forms and reports, for the new database. The wizard also sets up the relationships between the various tables (making your database relational).

Your interaction with the Database Wizard is somewhat limited; the wizard allows you to select the fields that will be used in the tables that it creates for the database. However, you don't have a say about which tables are initially created (tables can always be deleted later if you don't need them). You are, however, given the opportunity to select the format for screen displays (for forms and reports) and select the format for printed reports.

To create a database from a template, follow these steps:

1. In the Access window, click **General Templates** on the task pane. If the task pane is not currently in the Access window, select **File**, **New** to open it.

 TIP   **Opening the Task Pane**   When you are working on a particular database and want to open the task pane, select the **View** menu, point at **Toolbars**, and then select **Task Pane**.

2. The Templates dialog box appears. If necessary, click the Databases tab on the dialog box to view the database templates (see Figure 2.3).

3. Click the database template you want to use (for example, the Contact Management template) and then click **OK**. The File New Database dialog box appears.

Figure 2.3   Access provides several database templates.

4. Specify a location for the database using the Save In drop-down list, type a name for the database, and then click **Create** to continue. A new database file is created, and then the Database Wizard associated with the template starts. For example, if you chose the Contact Management template, the wizard appears and explains the type of information that the database holds.

5. To move past the wizard's opening screen, click **Next**. On the next screen, a list of the tables that will be created appears (see Figure 2.4). The tables in the database are listed on the left of the screen and the selected table's fields appear on the right.

Figure 2.4   You can examine and deselect (or select) the fields that will be contained in each table.

6. Select a table to examine its fields. If you do not want to include a field in the table, clear the check box next to the field name. Optional fields are also listed for each field and are shown in italic. To include an optional field, click it to

place a check mark next to it. When you have finished viewing the tables and their fields, click **Next** to continue.

CAUTION

Be Careful Deselecting Fields! Because you are stuck with the tables that the Database Wizard creates, you must be very careful removing fields from the tables. This is especially true of fields that uniquely identify the records in a table, such as Contact ID. These fields are often used to relate the tables in the database. You might want to leave all the fields alone initially when you use the wizard.

7. The next screen asks you to select the screen display style you want to use. This affects how forms appear on the screen. Click a display style in the list to preview the style; after selecting the style you want to use, click **Next**.

8. On the next screen, the wizard asks you for a style for your printed reports. Click a report style and examine the preview of it. When you decide on a style, click it, and then click **Next**.

TIP

Report Background The colored backgrounds used for some report styles look nice onscreen, but they don't print well on a black-and-white printer. Unless you have access to a color printer, stick to plain backgrounds for the best report print-outs.

9. On the next wizard screen, you are asked to provide a title for the database. This title appears on reports and can be different from the filename. Enter a title as shown in Figure 2.5.

Figure 2.5 Enter a title for the database, and as an option, choose a graphic to use for a logo.

10. (Optional) To include a picture on your forms and reports (for example, your company's logo), click the **Yes, I'd Like to Include a Picture** check box. Then, click the **Picture** button, choose a picture file from your hard drive (or other source), and click **OK** to return to the wizard.

11. Click **Next** to continue. You are taken to the last wizard screen; click **Finish** to open the new database. The wizard goes to work creating your database and its database objects.

When the wizard has finished creating the database, the database's Main Switchboard window appears (see Figure 2.6). The Main Switchboard opens automatically whenever you open the database.

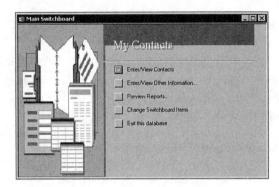

Figure 2.6   The Switchboard window is a database navigation tool provided by the Database Wizard.

All the databases created using one of the Access templates (other than the Blank Database template) include a Main Switchboard. The Switchboard is nothing more than a fancy form with some programming built in to it. It enables you to perform common tasks related to database management by clicking a button. It is very useful when a person is unfamiliar with how to manipulate the various objects in a database.

Using the Main Switchboard is pretty much self-explanatory. After you become familiar with Access, you probably won't even use it. To close the Switchboard, click its **Close** (**X**) button.

TIP   **I Hate That Switchboard!**   To prevent the Switchboard from opening when you open the database, choose **Tools, Startup**. In the Startup dialog box, select the **Display Form/Page** drop-down list and select **[None]**. Click **OK**.

After you close the Switchboard window, you will find that the database window has been minimized in the Access workspace. Just double-click its title bar (at the bottom-left corner of the screen) to open it. To see the tables that the wizard created, click the **Tables** object type. Click the other object types (such as forms) to see the other objects that were created by the wizard.

The tables that the wizard creates are, of course, empty. After you fill them with data (either inputting the data directly into the table or using a form), you will be able to run queries and create reports.

Opening a Database

You have already taken a look at how to close a database; next, you walk through the process of opening a database file. The next time you start Access or after you finish working with another database, you need to know how to open your other database files.

One of the easiest ways to open a database you've recently used is to select it from the File menu. Follow these steps:

1. Open the **File** menu. You'll see up to four databases that you've recently used listed at the bottom of the menu.

2. If the database you need is listed there, click it.

 TIP   **Want to See More Files?**   To increase the number of files displayed in this list, open the **Tools** menu and select **Options**. Then, from the **General** tab of the Options dialog box, select a number from 1 to 9 (the default is 4) in the **Recently Used Files** drop-down list.

A list of recently used databases also appears on the tip of the Access task pane. You can open any of the files by clicking the filename (to open the task pane, select **View, Toolbars, Task Pane**).

If a file you want to open is not listed either on the File menu or the task pane, you can open it using the Open command. Follow these steps:

 1. Select **File, Open,** or click the toolbar's **Open** button. The Open dialog box appears (see Figure 2.7).

2. If the file isn't in the currently displayed folder, use the Look In drop-down list to access the correct drive, and then double-click folders displayed in the dialog box to locate the file.

3. When you have located the database file, double-click the file to open it.

Figure 2.7   Use the Open dialog box to locate a database file you want to open.

Creating a Table with the Table Wizard

In this lesson, you learn how to create a table by using the Table Wizard.

Tables Are Essential

As discussed in Lesson 1, your tables really provide the essential framework for your database. Tables not only hold the data that you enter into the database, but they are designed so that relationships can be established between the various tables in the database. Tables can be created from scratch, as discussed in the next lesson, or they can be created using the Table Wizard.

Working with the Table Wizard

The Table Wizard can save you a lot of time by supplying you with all the needed fields and field formats for entering your database information. Access provides a large number of different kinds of tables that you can create with the wizard. The wizard is also fairly flexible, allowing you to select the fields the table will contain and the way in which they will be arranged. You can also change the name of a field during the process. If the wizard doesn't provide a particular field, you can always add it to the table later, as discussed in Lesson 5, "Editing a Table's Structure."

To create a table using the Table Wizard, follow these steps:

1. In the database window, click the **Tables** object icon, and then double-click **Create Table by Using Wizard**. The Table Wizard opens.

TIP **Alternative Routes** You can also start the Table Wizard by clicking the **New** button in the database window or choosing **Insert**, **Table**. In both cases, the New Table dialog box opens. Then, choose **Table Wizard** and click **OK**.

2. On the first Table Wizard screen, you can select from two categories of table types: **Business** or **Personal**. Your choice determines the list of sample tables that appears (see Figure 3.1).

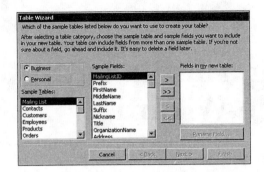

Figure 3.1 Select either the Business or Personal category to view a list of tables.

3. Select a table in the Sample Tables list; its fields appear in the Sample Fields list.

4. To include a field from the Sample Fields list in the table, select the field and click the **Add (>)** button to move it to the **Fields in My New Table** list. You can include all the fields in Sample Fields list by clicking the **Add All (>>)** button.

5. If you want to rename a field that you have added, click the **Rename Field** button, type a new name into the Rename field box, and then click **OK**.

TIP **Remove Unwanted Fields**   If you add a field that you don't want in the table, select the field in the **Fields in My New Table** list and click the **Remove (<)** button. To remove all the fields and start over, click **Remove All (<<)**.

6. Repeat steps 3 and 4 as needed to select more fields for the table. You can select fields from more than one of the sample tables for the table that you are creating (remember that you want fields in the table related only to a particular theme, such as customer information). When you're finished adding fields, click **Next** to continue.

7. The next screen asks you to provide a name for the table (see Figure 3.2). Type a more descriptive name if necessary to replace the default name.

8. This dialog box also asks whether you want the wizard to create a primary key for the table or allow you to select the primary key yourself. The *primary key* is the field that uniquely identifies each of the records in the table. For example, CustomerID is an excellent primary key because each customer is assigned a different ID number. In this case, click **Yes, Set a Primary Key for Me** to have the wizard choose your primary key field. You can learn to set your own primary keys in Lesson 4, "Creating a Table from Scratch."

Figure 3.2   Provide a name for the table and allow the wizard to select a primary key for the table.

Primary Key   The field that uniquely identifies each record in the table. Every table must have a primary key. This is usually an ID number because most other fields could conceivably hold the same data for more than one record (for example, you might have several people with the last name of Smith).

9. Click **Next** to continue. Because you're allowing the wizard to select the primary key, you are taken to the last wizard screen. On the last wizard screen, you have the options of modifying the table's design, entering data directly into the new table, or having the wizard create a data entry form for you. To see the table the wizard created, go with the default: Enter Data Directly into the Table (see Figure 3.3).

Figure 3.3   After completing the table, you can have the wizard open it so that you can enter data.

10. Click **Finish**.

The new table appears in the Access workspace (see Figure 3.4). From here you can enter data into the table, the specifics of which are discussed in Lesson 6, "Entering Data into a Table." When you close the table, it appears in the Object pane of the database window (you must also select the Tables object icon).

Figure 3.4 Your new table appears in the Access workspace when you close the Table Wizard.

Creating a Table from Scratch

In this lesson, you learn how to create a table in Table Design view.

Creating Tables Without the Wizard

Although the Table Wizard provides an easy method for quickly creating tables, it does not provide you with complete control over all the aspects of creating the table. It does allow you to select the fields used in the table from a set list, but it restricts you to only those predefined fields (there are also several types of fields, each used for a different data type). Creating tables from scratch in the Design view allows you to build the table from the bottom up and gives you complete control over all aspects of the table's design.

Design View   This view allows you to enter field names, select the data type that a field will hold, and customize each field's properties. A Design view is available for all the Access objects, including tables, forms, queries, and reports.

The Design view isn't the only way to create a table from scratch in Access. You can also create a table in the Datasheet view by labeling your field columns directly on the table's datasheet, which is similar to creating a worksheet in Excel. Take a look at both methods for creating a new table.

Datasheet View   This view places each record in a separate row and each field in a separate column (column headings are provided by the field names). This view is used to enter data directly into the table. You will use the Datasheet view whenever you want to view the records in the table or add or edit records.

Creating a Table in Table Design View

When you create a table in the Design view, you are creating the structure for the table; you create a list of the fields that will be in the table. You also select the data type for each field. (Fields can hold text, numbers, even graphics—you learn the types of fields that can be created later in this lesson.) You also have the option of entering a description for each field. Field descriptions are useful in that they pro-vide a quick summary of the type of data that goes into the field.

Another issue that relates to creating a table in the Design view (or editing a table's structure in the Design view) is that any changes you make must be saved before closing the table. If you have worked in other applications, such as Word or Excel, you might think that saving your work is just common sense. However, when you actually start working on entering data into a table or a form, Access automatically saves your records as you enter them. Therefore, in Access, you need to remember to save only the changes that you make to the structure of a table, form, query, or report. You learn more about this in Lesson 5, "Editing a Table's Structure."

 TIP   **Field Naming Rules**   Field names in Access can be up to 64 characters long and can contain spaces and both alphanumeric and numeric characters. You can't use periods or exclamation points in your field names. Also, avoid special characters (such as $, %, or #) in field names because some of these characters have special meanings in Access code.

To create a table in Table Design view, follow these steps:

1. In the database window (of a particular database) click the **Tables** icon if necessary, and then double-click **Create Table in Design View**. The Table Design view opens (see Figure 4.1).

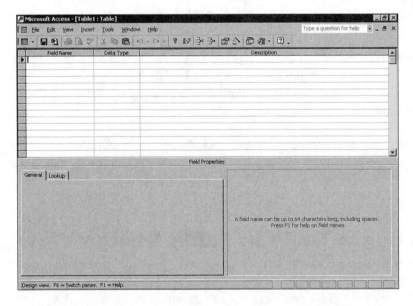

Figure 4.1   The Table Design view allows you to create the structure for your table.

2. Be sure that the insertion point is in the first row of the Field Name column. Type the field name for the first field in your table. Then, press **Tab** or **Enter** to move to the Data Type column.

3. When you move to the Data Type column, an arrow appears for a drop-down list. The default data type setting is Text; several other data types are available, such as AutoNumber, which automatically numbers each of your records. This field type is excellent for customer number fields or employee ID fields. Click the **Data Type** drop-down list and select a field type. The different data types are discussed in later in this lesson, in the section "Understanding Data Types and Formats."

4. After selecting the data type, press **Enter** to move to the Description column; type a description for the field. (This is optional; the table will work fine without it.)

TIP   **Deleting a Field**   If you enter a field and decide that you don't want it in the table's structure, select the field (its entire row) and press the **Delete** key.

5. Enter other fields and their field types (descriptions are optional) as needed. Figure 4.2 shows the structure for a table that will be used to enter product information.

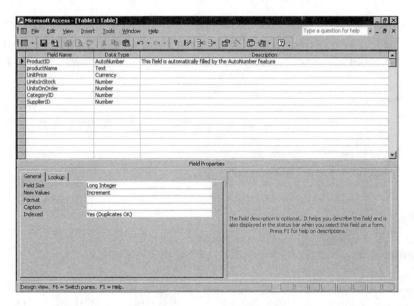

Figure 4.2   A table's structure consists of several fields; fields may differ by field type.

Setting the Primary Key

An important aspect of table structure design is that each table must have a field that is used to uniquely identify the records in the table. This field is called the *primary key*. Setting an appropriate key is trickier than it appears because no two records can have the same key value. In a table of customers, for example, you might think the Last Name field would be a good key, but this theory falls flat as soon as you find that you have more than one customer with the same last name. A more appropriate primary key for your customers is a Social Security number (although people don't like to give these out) because it uniquely identifies each customer.

A good general rule is to create an identification field, such as a customer number, that allows you to assign a sequential number to each customer as you add them to your database table. Access can even help you out with the assigning of numbers to the customers because you can make the field type for the Customer Number field AutoNumber. An AutoNumber field type assigns a number to each record starting with the number 1.

TIP   **Creating the Primary Key**   Typically, the first field in the table serves as the primary key.

To set a primary key, follow these steps:

1. In Table Design view, select the field that you want for the primary key.

2. Select **Edit**, **Primary Key**, or click the **Primary Key** button on the toolbar. A key symbol appears to the left of the field name, as shown in Figure 4.3.

Primary Key

Field Name	Data Type	Description
ProductID	AutoNumber	This field is automatically filled by the AutoNumber feature
productName	Text	
UnitPrice	Currency	
UnitsInStock	Number	
UnitsOnOrder	Number	
CategoryID	Number	
SupplierID	Number	

Figure 4.3   The primary key field is marked by a key symbol.

3. After you select the primary key and have finished entering your table fields, you should save the table. Click the **Save** button on the Table Design toolbar to open the Save As dialog box.

4. Enter a name for the table, and then click **OK**.

5. After saving the table, you can either switch to the Datasheet view (to enter data) by clicking the **View** button on the toolbar, or you can choose to close the table by clicking the table's **Close (x)** button.

> **TIP**   **No Primary Key!**   If you attempt to close your new table in the Design view without specifying a primary key (even if you have saved the table), a message appears, letting you know that no primary key has been assigned. Click **Yes** on the message box to have Access assign a primary key to the table. If have set up your table to contain an AutoNumber field, Access will make this field the primary key. Otherwise, Access creates a new AutoNumber field in the table and specifies it as the primary key. You can change the name of this new field as needed.

Understanding Data Types and Formats

To assign appropriate data types to the fields you create in a table, it is necessary for you to know what differentiates the different data types available for use with your table fields. When you create a field, you want to assign it a data type so that Access knows how to handle its contents. The following are the different data types you can choose:

- **Text**—Text and numbers up to 255 characters (numbers that are not going to be used in calculations).
- **Memo**—Lengthy text.
- **Number**—Numbers used in mathematical calculations.
- **Date/Time**—Date and time values.
- **Currency**—Numbers formatted for currency.
- **AutoNumber**—Sequentially numbers each new record. Only one AutoNumber field can be placed in a table. This field type is typically used for the primary key field.
- **Yes/No**—Lets you set up fields with a true/false data type.
- **OLE (Object Linking and Embedding)**—A picture, spreadsheet, or other item from another software program.
- **Hyperlink**—A link to another file or a location on a Web page. This field type lets you jump from the current field to information in another file.
- **Lookup Wizard**—This field type chooses its values from another table.

In addition to a field type, each field has other formatting options you can set. They appear in the bottom half of the dialog box, in the Field Properties area. The formatting options change depending on the field type; there are too many to list here, but Table 4.1 shows some of the most important ones you'll encounter.

Table 4.1   Formatting Options for Data Types

Formatting Option	Description
Field Size	The maximum number of characters a user can input in that field (applies only to text fields).
Format	A drop-down list of the available formats for that field type. You can also create custom formats.
Decimal Places	For number fields, you can set the default number of decimal places that a number shows.
Default Value	If a field is usually going to contain a certain value (for example, a certain ZIP code for almost everyone), you can set that as the Default Value option. It always appears in a new record, but you can type over it in the rare instances when it doesn't apply.
Required	Choose **Yes** if a particular field is required to be filled in each record.

The best general rule for setting the data type for the field is to take a moment to consider what kind of data will go into that field. For example, if you are working with the monetary value of a product, you will probably want to use currency.

The different formatting options provided for a field in the Field Properties box are often used to help make sure that data is entered correctly. For example, the Field Size option can be used to limit a Number data type field to only a single or double digit. In the case of the default value, you can actually save data entry time because you use this option when a particular field almost always has a certain value or text entry.

Creating a Table in the Datasheet View

After you feel comfortable creating new tables in the Design view, you might want to dive right in and create tables in the Datasheet view. Creating tables this way immediately creates a table with 20 field columns and 30 record rows. This method still requires, however, that you enter the Table Design view to specify the key field, the field data types, field descriptions, and any field property changes.

Creating tables in the Datasheet view is really useful only if you feel the need to quickly enter some data into the table before setting up the table's properties. To create a table in the Datasheet view, follow these steps:

1. In the database window (with the Table icon selected), double-click **Create Table by Entering Data**. A new table in Datasheet view appears in the Access workspace (see Figure 4.4).

Figure 4.4   Tables can be created in the Datasheet view.

2. To enter the field names, double-click any field column heading (Field1, Field2, and so on). Then, type in the field name.

3. After you have placed the field names, you can begin entering data.

Creating a table in the Datasheet view might be fine for quickly entering data, but you will still probably need to switch to the Table Design view at some point and set up the various field data types and properties.

You can switch to the Design view from the Datasheet view by clicking the **View** icon on the Table Datasheet toolbar. Remember to save any changes to the table's design that you make in the Design view.

Editing a Table's Structure

In this lesson, you learn how to change your table structure by adding and removing fields and hiding columns.

Editing Fields and Their Properties

After you've created a table with the Table Wizard or from scratch, you might find that you want to fine-tune the table's structure. This requires that you edit your fields and their properties.

You can delete fields, add new fields, or change the order of fields in the table. You also can change a field's data type. Because the table's structure is discussed here and not the data, you need to work in the Table Design view.

 Get the Table's Structure Down Before Entering Data   You should try to finalize the table's field structure and properties before you enter data. Changing data types or other field properties can actually delete data that you've already entered into the **CAUTION** table.

You can open an existing table in the Table Design view in several ways:

- In the database window, click the **Table** object icon, select the table you want to work with in the right pane of the database window, and then click the **Design** button on the database window's toolbar.

- Right-click the table in the database window and select **Design View** from the shortcut menu that appears.

 - If you are in the table's Datasheet view, click the **View** button on the Table Datasheet view toolbar.

Changing Field Names and Data Types

When you are in the Design view (see Figure 5.1), you can enhance or rework your table's structure. For example, you can change a field's name. Just double-click the field's current name and type in a new one.

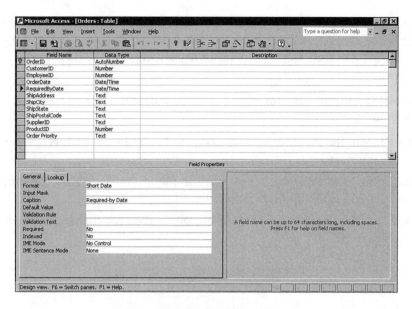

Figure 5.1 A table's existing structure can be edited in the Design view.

You can also change the data type for an existing field. Click the field's Data Type box and select a new data type from the drop-down list. Remember that when you change a field name or a field's data type, you must save the changes that you've made to the table's structure.

Setting Field Properties

Field properties can also be edited for each field using the various Properties boxes found in the Field Properties pane. Lesson 4, "Creating a Table from Scratch," provides a quick overview of some of the properties that are available.

Another very useful field property, particularly for fields that use text entries (remember that text entries can include numbers) is an *input mask*. An input mask is used to format that data as you enter it into a field. For example, you might want to enter a date in a particular format, such as the format xx/xx/xx. The input mask can be used so that when you enter the data into the date field, all you need to enter is the two-digit input for the month, day, and year. Access automatically places the slashes in the field for you.

Input Mask A field property that limits the number of characters that can be entered in a field.

Input masks are also very useful for entering ZIP codes. The input mask limits the number of characters that can be entered (such as those in a ZIP code), and if you use the 5-4 ZIP code format, the input mask can place the dash into the ZIP code for you.

To create an input mask for a field (such as a date field or a Design view field), follow these steps:

1. Click in the Field Name box to select the field for which you want to create the input mask.

2. In the Field Properties pane, click in the Input Mask box. The Input Mask Wizard button appears in the box.

3. Click the **Input Mask Wizard** button to open the dialog box shown in Figure 5.2.

Figure 5.2 The Input Mask Wizard helps you create an input mask for a field.

4. The Input Mask Wizard offers a list of possible masks for the field based on the field's data type. For example, Figure 5.2 shows the Input Mask Wizard used for a field with the Date data type. Select one of the mask formats listed, and then click **Next**.

5. The next wizard screen shows you the input mask you have chosen and gives you the opportunity to change the format. You can also test the input mask format by typing some data into the Try It box. Edit the input mask format if necessary and then click **Next** to continue.

6. You are taken to the last wizard screen. Click **Finish** to create the input mask. The input mask appears in the Input Mask box in the Field Properties pane (see Figure 5.3).

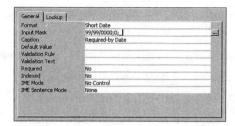

Figure 5.3   The input mask appears in the Input Mask box.

7. Click the **Save** button to save changes that you have made to the table structure.

Adding, Deleting, and Moving Fields

You can also add additional fields to your table's structure. All you have to do is add a new row to the field list and then enter the new field name and data type. Follow these steps:

1. Click the record selector (the gray square to the left of the field name) to select the field that will follow the new field that you create (in the field list).

2. Select **Insert, Row**. A blank row appears in the Field Name list.

3. Enter a name, a data type, a description, and so on for the new field.

You can also delete any unwanted fields. Click the record selector for the field and then press the **Delete** key on the keyboard. A message box appears that requires you to confirm the field's deletion. Click **Yes** to delete the field.

CAUTION

Don't Remove Important Fields!   Be very careful about deleting fields after you start entering records into your table. When you delete a field, all the information stored for each record in that field is gone, too. The best time to experiment with deleting fields is before you enter any data into the table.

You can also rearrange the fields in the table. Click the record selector for the field to select the field. Then, use the mouse to drag the field to a new position in the field list. Remember to save any changes that you have made to the table's structure.

Deleting a Table

No matter how hard you work on a table's design, you might find as you design the other tables for your database that you just don't need a particular table. It's easy to delete a table (although it might not be easy to forget the time that you spent creating the table); simply follow these steps:

1. In the database window, click the **Tables** object type.
2. In the right pane of the database window, select the table you want to delete.
3. Select **Edit, Delete**, or press the **Delete** key on your keyboard.
4. A message appears asking whether you're sure you want to do this. Click **Yes**.

Entering Data into a Table

In this lesson, you learn how to add records to a table, print the table, and close it.

Entering a Record

After you've created the table and fine-tuned its structure, you are ready to enter data into the table. This means that you should have access to all the data that you need to enter. Then, all you have to do is open the table and input the data records.

TIP **Using Forms to Enter Data** Access doesn't limit you to entering data directly into the table. You can also enter data using a form. Form creation and data entry using a form are covered in Lesson 11, "Modifying a Form."

First, from the database window, double-click the table in which you want to enter the records. The table opens in the Datasheet view (see Figure 6.1). If this is the first time you have entered data into the table, only one empty record appears in the table. As you complete each record, a new blank record (a new row) appears.

Customer ID	FirstName	LastName	Address	City	State/Province	Postal Code	Phone Number

Figure 6.1 A table's existing structure can be edited in the Design view.

To enter records into the table, follow these steps:

1. Click in the first field of the first blank record (if necessary). If the first field is an identification field, such as Customer ID, and you selected the AutoNumber data type for the field, press **Tab** to advance to the next field (the AutoNumber field is automatically filled in for you).

2. Type the value for that field.

3. Press **Tab** to move to the next field and enter that field's data.

4. Continue pressing **Tab** and entering data until you complete the last field in the record. When you press **Tab** in the last field, a new record (a new row) appears, and the insertion point moves to the first field in the new record.

5. Continue entering records as required.

TIP **Data Entry Tricks** Access offers some hotkey combinations for entering dates and data found in the same field in a previous record. To insert the current date, press **Ctrl+;** (semicolon). To insert the current time, press **Ctrl+:** (colon). To repeat the value from the same field in the previous record, press **Ctrl+'** (apostrophe).

You should be aware that, as you enter each field's data and move onto the next field, Access automatically saves your table data. This is very different from other Office applications, such as Word or Excel, where you must save your data after entering it.

TIP **Voice Data Entry** Access and the other Office XP applications can now accept data that is entered by voice. See Lesson 4, "Using the Office Speech Feature," in the "Office XP Introduction and Shared Features," section of this book.

Moving Around in a Table

So far, you've used the Tab key only to move from field to field in the table. You might have also used the mouse to move the insertion point from a field in one record to another field in that record, or to a field in a different record. Because you do your data entry from the keyboard, Access provides several keystrokes that can be used to navigate the various fields in the table. For example, you can back up one field in a record by pressing **Shift+Tab**. Table 6.1 summarizes the various keyboard shortcuts for moving around in a table.

Table 6.1 Table Movement Keys

To Move To	Press
Next field	Tab
Previous field	Shift+Tab
Last field in the record	End
First field in the record	Home
Same field in the next record	Down-arrow key
Same field in the previous record	Up-arrow key
Same field in the last record	Ctrl+down-arrow key

Table 6.1   Continued

To Move To	Press
Same field in the first record	Ctrl+up-arrow key
Last field in the last record	Ctrl+End
First field in the first record	Ctrl+Home

Hiding a Field

When you are entering data into the table, you might find that you have not actually collected the data that you need to enter into a particular field. This means that you must skip this field in all the records as you enter your data (until you come up with the data).

You can hide a field or fields in the table datasheet. This doesn't delete the field column or disrupt any of the field properties that you set for that particular field. It just hides the field from your view as you enter your data. To hide a field, follow these steps:

1. In the Datasheet view, select the field or fields that you want to hide (click a field's column heading, as shown in Figure 6.2). To select multiple contiguous fields, click the first field, and then hold down the **Shift** key and click the last field.

Figure 6.2   You can select a column and then hide it.

2. Select **Format** and then **Hide Columns**, or right-click the column and select **Hide Columns**. The column or columns disappear.

3. Enter your data records into your table; the hidden column is skipped as you move from column to column.

4. When you have finished entering data into the other fields in the table, you can unhide the column. Select **Format**, **Unhide Columns**. The Unhide Columns dialog box appears (see Figure 6.3). Fields with a check mark next to them are unhidden; fields without a check mark are hidden.

Figure 6.3 The Unhide Columns dialog box shows you which columns are currently hidden.

5. Click the check box of any hidden field to "unhide" the field.

6. Click **Close**. The hidden column (or columns) reappear in the table.

Freezing a Column

Another useful manipulation of the field columns in an Access table that can make data entry easier is freezing a column. For example, if a table has a large number of fields, as you move to the right in the table during data entry, fields in the beginning of the table scroll off the screen. This can be very annoying if you lose your place, because you might not remember which customer you were entering data for.

You can freeze columns so that they remain on the screen even when you scroll to the far right of a table record. Follow these steps:

1. Click the column heading of the field column you want to freeze. This selects the entire column of data.

2. Click the **Format** menu; then click **Freeze Columns**.

3. The frozen field column moves over to the first field position in the table. Click anywhere in the table to deselect the field column.

4. When you move through the fields in a record toward the far right of the table, the frozen field column remains on the screen. This allows you to see important data such as the customer's name as you attempt to enter other data into a particular record.

You can freeze multiple columns if you want, such as the Last Name field and the First Name field. When you want to unfreeze the column or columns in the table, select the **Format** menu, and then select **Unfreeze All Columns**.

Using the Spelling Feature

To ensure your data entry accuracy, you can quickly check the spelling of the data that you have input into your table. This should help you clear up any typos that might have happened during your entry of the table records.

The Spelling feature, obviously, won't be able to check the numerical information that you input or help you enter proper names, but it can help you avoid embarrassing misspellings. To check the spelling in a table, follow these steps:

1. Click the **Spelling** button on the Table Datasheet toolbar, or you can select **Tools**, **Spelling** to open the Spelling dialog box (see Figure 6.4).

Figure 6.4   The Spelling feature enables you to quickly check for typos and misspellings in your Access table.

2. Words flagged as misspelled appear in the dialog box. A list of suggestions also appears from which you can choose a correct spelling. You can either correct the misspellings manually or click one of the suggestions. When you're ready, click **Change** to correct the spelling. The Speller then moves to the next misspelled word.

3. If you want to add the flagged word to the dictionary, click the **Add** button. If a flagged word is correctly spelled, click the **Ignore** button to ignore the word and continue with the spell check.

4. If the field containing the flagged word is a field that typically holds proper names or other values that the Spelling feature will always flag as misspelled, click the **Ignore "Field Name"** button.

Closing a Table

After you have finished entering data into a particular table and checking the spelling, you should close that table. Because the table is just like any other window, click the table's **Close** (**x**) button to close the table. You are then returned to the database window.

Editing Data in a Table

In this lesson, you learn how to edit information in a field, select records, and insert and delete records.

Changing a Field's Content

After you enter the records in a table, you will probably find that you need to make some changes; sometimes data is entered incorrectly or the data for a particular record might actually change. Editing a field's content is easy. You can replace the old field content entirely or edit it.

Replacing a Field's Content

If the data in a field must be updated or has been entered incorrectly, the easiest way to replace this data is to enter the new data from scratch. To replace the old content in a field, follow these steps:

1. You can use the **Tab** key to move to the field you want to edit (the contents of the field will be selected), or select the contents of a field with the mouse. To use your mouse, place the mouse pointer on the upper left or right edge of the field. The mouse pointer becomes a plus sign (+) as shown in Figure 7.1. Click the field to select its content.

Field selection pointer

	Customer ID	First Name	Last Name	Phone	Street	City	State	
	1	Pierre	Manger	(216) 555-1234	111 Eiffel Blvd	Paris	PA	55330-
	3	Bob	Jones	(216) 555-5436	1340 America Dr.	Crystal	PA	35012-
	4	Alice	Barney	(216) 555-7777	1420 Mineshaft Street	Big City	PA	65437-
	5	Kim	Reech	(512) 555-3643	55 Platinum St.	Los Angeles	OH	44240-
	6	Larry	Curly-Moe	(216) 555-8444	3 Stooges Lane	Hollywood	OH	44240-
	7	Edward	Reech	(345) 555-7776	456 Rural Lane	Friendly Heights	VA	64544-

Figure 7.1 To select a field's entire content, make sure that the mouse pointer is a plus sign when you click.

2. Type the new data, which replaces the old data.

3. You can the use the **Tab** key or the mouse to move to the next field you need to edit.

Editing a Field's Content with a Mouse

Replacing the entire contents of a field is kind of a heavy-handed way to edit a field if you need to correct the entry of only one or two characters. You can also fine-tune your entries by editing a portion of the data in the field. Follow these steps:

1. Place the mouse pointer over the position in the field where you want to correct data. The mouse pointer should become an I-beam.

2. Click once to place the insertion point at that position in the field (see Figure 7.2). Now you can edit the content of the field.

Insertion point

Figure 7.2 Place the insertion point into a field to edit its content.

3. Press **Backspace** to remove the character to the left of the insertion point or **Delete** to remove the character to the right of the insertion point.

4. Enter new text into the field as needed. New entries in the field are inserted, meaning they displace the current entry but do not overwrite it.

Moving Around a Field with a Keyboard

Although the mouse provides a quick way to place the insertion point into a field, you might want to be able to navigate inside a field using the keyboard, especially when you are editing a fairly long field entry. Access provides several keyboard possibilities for moving inside a cell. Table 7.1 lists these keyboard-movement keys.

Table 7.1 Moving Within a Field

To Move	Press
One character to the right	Right-arrow key
One character to the left	Left-arrow key
One word to the right	Ctrl+right-arrow key
One word to the left	Ctrl+left-arrow key
To the end of the line	End
To the beginning of the line	Home

Moving and Copying Data

As in any Office application, you can use the Cut, Copy, and Paste commands to copy and move data in your table fields. This is particularly useful if you want to quickly copy a ZIP code that is the same for more than one customer, or you want to cut data that you put in the wrong field, so that you can paste it into the appropriate field. To use copy, cut, and paste, follow these steps:

1. Select the entire field or the portion of a field's content that you want to cut or copy.

2. Select **Edit**, and then **Cut** (to move) or **Copy** (to copy). Or press **Ctrl+X** to cut or **Ctrl+C** to copy.

3. Position the insertion point where you want to insert the cut or copied material.

4. Select **Edit**, **Paste,** or press **Ctrl+V** to paste.

  TIP **Toolbar Shortcuts**   You can also use the Cut, Copy, and Paste buttons on the Table Datasheet toolbar to manipulate text in the table fields.

Inserting and Deleting Fields

You can also insert and delete fields in the Table Datasheet view. This allows you to quickly enter the data into a new field or delete an unneeded field. It is preferable, however, to insert new fields into the table in the Design view and then enter data. This is because you will eventually have to switch to Table Design view to specify the data type or other properties of the new field.

To insert a field, follow these steps:

1. Select the existing field column in which you want to insert the new field. The new field column is inserted to the left of the currently selected field column.

2. Select **Insert, Column**. The new column appears in the table (see Figure 7.3).

Figure 7.3 New field columns can be added to the table in the Datasheet view.

3. To name the new field, double-click the field heading (such as Field1) and type the new name for the field.

4. Enter data into the new field as needed.

Deleting a field or fields is also very straightforward. Remember, however, that deleting a field also deletes any data that you have entered into that field. Select the field that you want to delete and then select **Edit, Delete Column**. You are asked to verify the deletion of the field. If you're sure, click **Yes**.

Inserting New Records

As your customer base increases or other new data becomes available for your database, you will definitely be adding records to the various tables in the database. New records are inserted automatically. As soon as you begin to enter data into a record, a new blank record appears at the bottom of the table (see Figure 7.4).

New record

Figure 7.4 New records are automatically inserted at the bottom of the table.

This process is re-created every time you complete a record and then start a new record. Inserting information into the first field of the new record inserts another new record below the one you are working on.

You can't insert new records between existing ones or at the top of the table. New records are always entered at the bottom of the table, below the last completed record.

TIP **What If I Want the Records in a Different Order?** Although you can enter new records only at the bottom of the table, you can rearrange the order of your records if you want. This can be done using the sorting feature discussed in Lesson 15, "Creating a Simple Query."

Deleting Records

You will probably find that certain records in the table become outdated or no longer pertinent to the database (such as an employee who has left your company but still has a record in the Employee table). You can delete a record or several records at a time.

To delete a record or records, follow these steps:

1. To select the record that you want to delete, click the record selector button (the small gray box to the left of the record, as shown in Figure 7.5). If you want to select multiple records, click and drag the record selector buttons of the contiguous records.

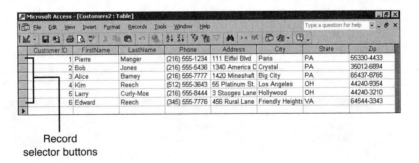

Record
selector buttons

Figure 7.5   Select the record or records you want to delete.

2. To delete the record or records, perform any of the following:

- Click the **Delete Record** button on the toolbar.
- Press the **Delete** key on the keyboard.
- Select the **Edit, Delete Record.**

3. A dialog box appears, letting you know that you are deleting a record and will not be able to undo this action. To delete the record or records, click **Yes**.

CAUTION

Deleting Records Affects the AutoNumber Sequence   When you delete records in the table that were assigned an identification number using the AutoNumber data type, that number (or numbers) will be lost from the sequence. For example, if you delete a customer with the AutoNumber customer ID of 3, the number 3 is removed from the sequence. When listing your customers, the customer numbers would then appear as 1, 2, 4, 5, and so on.

Formatting Access Tables

In this lesson, you learn how to improve the look of a table by adjusting the row and column sizes, changing the font, and choosing text alignment options.

Changing the Look of Your Table

Most people don't spend a lot of time formatting Access tables because they don't always use the table for data entry; instead, they use a form. Most people also don't typically print their tables. They use data-entry forms to see the records onscreen and reports to print their records. The tables are merely holding tanks for the raw data.

However, creating forms and reports might be more work than you want to tackle right now. And formatting a table so that data entry is a little less tedious (and less hard on the eyes) or so you can quickly print a copy of a table (covered in Lesson 20, "Printing Access Objects") is certainly no crime. Making a table more readable onscreen is certainly nice for the person using the table to enter data.

Changing Column Width and Row Height

One common problem with a table is that you can't see the complete contents of the fields. Fields often hold more data than will fit across a column's width. This causes the data in your table to appear to be cut off.

You can fix this problem in two ways: make the column wider so it can display more data, or make the row taller so it can display more than one line of data.

Changing Column Width

Access offers many ways to adjust column width in a table; you can choose the method you like best. One of the easiest ways to adjust the column width is to drag the column headings. Follow these steps:

1. Position the mouse pointer between two field names (column headings) so that the pointer turns into a vertical line with left- and right-pointing arrows; this is the sizing tool (see Figure 8.1). You'll be adjusting the column on the left; the column on the right will move to accommodate it.

Figure 8.1 Position the mouse pointer between two column headings.

2. Click and hold the mouse button and drag the edge of the column to the right or left to increase or decrease the width.

3. Release the mouse button when the column is the desired width.

Alternatively, you can double-click the column's vertical border when the sizing tool is showing, which automatically adjusts the width of the column on the left so that it accommodates the largest amount of data entered in that particular field.

Another, more precise, way to adjust column width is to use the Column Width dialog box. Follow these steps:

1. Select the column(s) for which you want to adjust the width.

2. From the **Format** menu, choose **Column Width**, or right-click and choose **Column Width** from the shortcut menu. The Column Width dialog box appears (see Figure 8.2).

Figure 8.2 Adjust the column width precisely in the Column Width dialog box.

3. Do one of the following to set the column width:

- Adjust the column to exactly the width needed for the longest entry in it by clicking **Best Fit**.
- Set the width to a precise number of field characters by typing a value in the **Column Width** text box.
- Reset the column width to its default value by selecting the **Standard Width** check box.

4. Click **OK** to apply the changes.

Because changing the width of a field column in the table is actually changing the field's length (which you designated in the Design view when you created the table), you do need to save these changes. Click the **Save** button on the Table Datasheet toolbar.

Changing Row Height

You can also change the height of the rows or records in the table. This allows you to see more text in a field that contains a large amount of data, such as a memo field.

Adjusting One Row Height Adjusts Them All   If you change the height of one row, it changes the height of all the rows or records in the table. Edit the row height only in cases where it allows you to see more data in a particular field for each **CAUTION**   record.

One way to make rows taller (or shorter) is to drag a particular row's border, enlarging the record's row. Position the mouse pointer between two rows in the row selection area, and then drag up or down. Remember that this changes the height of all the rows in the table (meaning all the records).

Another way is to use the Row Height dialog box. It works the same as the Column Width dialog box, except that no Best Fit option is available. Select the **Format** menu and then choose **Row Height**. The Row Height dialog box appears.

Enter the height for the table's rows into the dialog box (or click **Standard Height** to return the rows to the default height) and click **OK**.

Changing the Font and Font Size

Unlike other Access views (such as Report and Form), you can't format individual fields or portions of the data that are entered in a particular view. You can format the font style only for the entire table. Font changes are automatically applied to all data in the table, including the field column headings.

Font changes that you make in Datasheet view won't affect the way your data looks in other Access objects, such as your reports, queries, or forms. They affect only the table itself.

There are some good reasons for changing the font style in a table. For example, you might want to increase the font size so that the field contents are easier to read. Or you might bold the data in the table so that you get a nice, crisp printout when you print the table (refer to Lesson 20).

Changing the Default Font Style

If the default style used in Access for tables has been bugging you from the beginning, you can change the default font used in Datasheet view for all the tables you create in Access.

Select **Tools**, and then **Options**. Select the **Datasheet** tab of the Options dialog box (see Figure 8.3).

Figure 8.3 You can change the default Datasheet font properties in the Options dialog box.

Use the different drop-down menus in the Default Font box of the Datasheet tab to select the font name, font weight, or font size. When you have finished making your changes, click **OK**.

Changing the Font Style for a Table

Font changes that you make to a specific table override the default font settings. To choose a different font for a currently open table datasheet, follow these steps:

1. From the **Format** menu, choose **Font**. The Font dialog box appears (see Figure 8.4).
2. Select a font from the **Font** list box.
3. Select a style from the **Font Style** list box.
4. Select a size from the **Size** list box.
5. Select a color from the **Color** drop-down list.
6. (Optional) Click the **Underline** check box if you want underlined text.
7. You can see a sample of your changes in the Sample area. When you're happy with the look of the sample text, click **OK**.

Figure 8.4   Select the different font options in the Font dialog box.

Another way you can change the look of your table is with the Datasheet Formatting dialog box (choose **Format**, **Datasheet**). You can change the cell special effects, background color, the color of the grid lines between each row and column, and whether the lines show.

Creating Relationships Between Tables

In this lesson, you learn how to link two or more tables using a common field and create a relational database.

Understanding Table Relationships

You've already learned in Lesson 1, "Working in Access," that the best way to design a database is to create tables that hold discrete types of information. For example, one table can contain customer information, and another table can hold order information. By creating relationships between tables, you enable forms, queries, and reports to combine information from the tables to produce meaningful results.

Suppose that you have two tables in your database. One table, Customers, contains names and addresses; the other, Orders, contains orders the customers have placed. The two tables both contain a common field: Customer ID. All records in the Orders table correspond to a record in the Customers table. (This is called a one-to-many relationship because one customer could have many orders.)

The secret to creating relationships revolves around the primary keys for your tables. For example, in a Customers table, the primary key is the Customer ID. It uniquely identifies each customer record. Then, when you design an Orders table, you make sure that you include the Customer ID field. In the Orders table, the Customer ID is not the primary key (it is actually called the foreign key), a field such as Order Number would be the primary key field. You include the Customer ID field in the Orders table so that order information can be linked to customer information in the Customers table.

Foreign Key   A primary key field in a table that is duplicated in a second table (where it is not the primary key) and used to link the tables together.

Creating a Relationship Between Tables

To create a relationship between tables, open the Relationships window. Before you can create relationships between tables, you must first add the tables to the Relationships window. Follow these steps:

1. In the database, select **Tools**, **Relationships**, or click the **Relationships** button on the toolbar to open the Relationships window.

2. If you haven't selected any tables yet, the Show Table dialog box appears automatically (see Figure 9.1). If it doesn't appear, choose **Relationships**, **Show Table**.

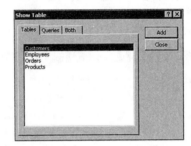

Figure 9.1   Add tables to your Relationships window with the Show Table dialog box.

3. Click a table that you want to include in the Relationships window, and then click the **Add** button.

 TIP   **Well-Designed Databases and Relationships**   In a well-designed database, every table in the database is related to at least one other table in the database. So, you might want to add all your tables to the Relationships window.

4. Repeat step 3 to select all the tables you require in the Relationships window, and then click **Close**. Each table appears in its own box in the Relationships window, as shown in Figure 9.2. Each table box lists all the fields in that table.

 TIP   **Enlarge the Table Box**   If you can't see all the fields in a table's box, drag the table border to make it large enough to see all the fields.

5. After you have the tables available in the relationships window, you can create the relationships between the table. Remember that you must link the tables using a common field. For example, you can link the Customers table to the Orders table using the Customer ID field, as shown in Figure 9.2. Select the

common field in the table where it is the primary key (in this case, the Customer table). Drag the field and drop it on its counterpart (the same field name) in the other table (in this case, Orders). The Edit Relationships window opens (see Figure 9.3).

Figure 9.2 Tables in the Relationships window.

Field Type Matters The fields to be linked must be of the same data type (date, number, text, and so on). The only exception is that you can link a field with an AutoNumber format to another field with a number format; AutoNumber fields are considered long-integer number fields.

CAUTION

Figure 9.3 The Edit Relationships dialog box asks you to define the relationship you're creating.

6. The Edit Relationships dialog box shows the fields that will be related. It also allows you to enforce referential integrity, which you learn about in the next section. For now, click **Create**. A relationship is created, and you'll see a join line between the two fields in the Relationships window (see Figure 9.4).

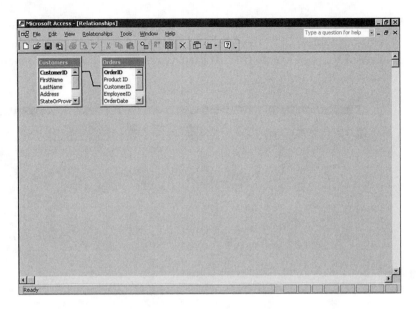

Figure 9.4   The join line represents a relationship between the two fields.

 When you create relationships between tables, it's important that you save them. Click the **Save** button on the Relationships toolbar to save the current relationships (and the list of tables available in the Relationships window).

Enforcing Referential Integrity

In the Edit Relationships box is a check box called Enforce Referential Integrity. What does this mean? *Referential integrity* means that data entered in a field that is used to link two tables must match from one table to another. Actually, the data entered in the table where the field does not serve as the primary key must match the entries that are in the table where the field serves as the primary key.

TERM   **Referential Integrity**   The data contained in a primary key field used in a table relationship must be matched in that same field in the secondary table. Otherwise, Access returns an error message.

For example, you could link a Customers table that has a Customer ID field as its primary key to an Orders table that also holds the Customer ID field, where it does not serve as the primary key (the Customer ID is providing the link for the relationship). If you enforce referential integrity, values entered into the Order table's Customer ID field must match values already entered into the Customers table's Customer ID field. Enforcing referential integrity is a way to make sure that data is entered correctly into the secondary table.

When referential integrity is breached during data entry, (meaning a value is entered into the secondary table in the relationship that was not in the linking field of the primary table), an error message appears (see Figure 9.5). This error message lets you know that the field value you have entered in the linking field is not contained in a record in the other table in the relationship (where the field is the primary key).

Figure 9.5   Enforcing referential integrity means that values entered in the linking field must be contained in the field in the table where it serves as the primary key.

Two other options are possible when data entered into a field violates referential integrity. Figure 9.6 shows the Edit Relationships with the Enforce Referential Integrity box selected. The two additional options provided are

- **Cascade Update Related Fields**—If this check box is selected, any data changes that you make to the linking field in the primary table (Customers, in this example) are updated to the secondary table. For example, if you had a customer in the Customers table listed with Customer ID 5 and you changed that to Customer ID 6, any references to Customer ID 5 would be updated to Customer ID 6 in the Orders table.

- **Cascade Delete Related Fields**—If this check box is marked and you change the linking field's data in the primary table so that it no longer matches in the secondary table, the field information is deleted from the secondary table. Therefore, if you changed a Customer ID number in the Customers table, the field data in Customer ID field in the Orders table would be deleted.

Figure 9.6   The Edit Relationships dialog box is used to change the options related to a particular relationship.

You should probably set up your relationships and enforce referential integrity before you do any data entry in the related tables. You should also typically enter the data first into the table where the linking field is the primary key. For example, you should fill in as much of your Customers table information as possible before you try to fill the data fields in the related Orders table.

Editing a Relationship

You can edit any of the relationships that you create between your tables. Just double-click the relationship line and the Edit Relationships dialog box appears (refer to Figure 9.6). For example, you might want to enforce referential integrity on an existing relationship or change other options related to the relationship as discussed in the previous section.

When you have finished editing the relationship, click **OK** to close the Edit Relationships box. This returns you to the Relationships window.

Removing a Relationship

To delete a relationship, just click it in the Relationships window (the line between the tables turns bold to indicate that it is selected), and then press **Delete**. Access asks for confirmation; click **Yes**, and the relationship disappears.

If you delete relationships between tables, you are affecting how information in the tables can be combined in a query, form, or report. It is a good practice to design your tables so that they can be related. Remember that each table is supposed to hold a subset of the database information. If each table is set up correctly, it should have at least one other table in the database that it can be related to.

Creating a Simple Form

In this lesson, you learn how to create a form using the AutoForm, the Form Wizard, and from scratch.

Creating Forms

As discussed in Lesson 6, "Entering Data into a Table," entering data directly into a table has its downside. It can become difficult to concentrate on one record at a time, and if you are working with a large number of fields, information is constantly scrolling on and off the screen.

An alternative to entering data into the table is to use a form. With a form, you can allot as much space as you need for each field, you get to concentrate on one record at a time, and you can create forms that simultaneously enter data into more than one table. You can create a form in three ways:

- AutoForms provide very quick, generic forms that contain all the fields in a single table.

- The Form Wizard helps you create a form by providing a series of screens in which you can choose the fields and style for the form.

- Creating a form from scratch means that you work in the Form Design view and select the fields from the appropriate table or tables. This is the most difficult way to create a new form (at first), but it also provides the most control.

Creating a Form with AutoForm

The easiest way to create a form is with AutoForm. AutoForm takes the fields from a specified table and creates a form; it's not very flexible, but it is very convenient. To use the AutoForm feature, follow these steps:

1. From the database window, click the **Forms** object type.

2. Click the **New** button on the database window toolbar. The New Form dialog box appears (see Figure 10.1).

Figure 10.1 Choose how you want to create your form.

3. You can click several types of forms, including
   - **AutoForm:Columnar**—A columnar form (the most popular kind). This creates a form that contains your fields in a single column, from top to bottom.
   - **AutoForm:Tabular**—A form that resembles a table.
   - **AutoForm:Datasheet**—A form that resembles a datasheet.

4. Open the drop-down list at the bottom of the dialog box and choose the table or query you want to use as the source of the form's fields.

5. Click **OK**. The form appears, ready for data entry (see Figure 10.2).

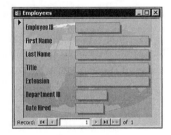

Figure 10.2 AutoForm creates a form based on a single table.

Forms created with AutoForm can be edited using the Form Design view, which is discussed later in this lesson. When you attempt to close the AutoForm, you are asked whether you want to save it. If you do, click **Yes**. Then, enter a name for the form into the Save As box and click **OK**.

 TIP **Create an AutoForm in the Table Datasheet View** You can also create an AutoForm while you are working on a table in the Datasheet view. Click the **AutoForm** button on the Table Datasheet toolbar. A new form appears, based on the table's fields.

Creating a Form with the Form Wizard

The Form Wizard offers a good compromise between the automation of AutoForm and the control of creating a form from scratch. The wizard allows you to select the fields for the form and select the layout and look for the form. Follow these steps to use the Form Wizard:

1. From the database window, click the **Forms** object type.

2. Double-click **Create Form by Using Wizard** to open the Form Wizard (see Figure 10.3).

Figure 10.3   The Form Wizard enables you to choose which fields you want to include from as many different tables in the database as you like.

3. From the Tables/Queries drop-down list, choose a table or query from which to select fields. (By default, the first table in alphabetical order is selected, which probably isn't what you want.)

4. Click a field in the Available Fields list that you want to include on the form, and then click the **Add** (>) button to move it to the Selected Fields list.

5. Repeat step 4 until you've selected all the fields you want to include from that table. If you want to include fields from another table or query, go back to step 3 and choose another table.

TIP   **Selecting All Fields**   You can quickly move all the fields from the Available Fields list to the Selected Fields list by clicking the **Add All** (>>) button. If you make a mistake, you can remove a field from the Selected Fields list by clicking it and then clicking either the **Remove** (<) button or the **Remove All** (<<) button.

6. Click **Next** to continue. You're asked to choose a layout: **Columnar**, **Tabular**, **Datasheet**, or **Justified**. Click each button to see a preview of that type (Columnar is the most common). Select the layout you want to use, and then click **Next**.

7. The next screen asks you to select a style for your form (see Figure 10.4). Click each style listed to see a preview of it; click **Next** when you've selected a style.

Figure 10.4   You can select from several form styles.

8. On the last screen, enter a title for the form into the text box at the top of the dialog box (if you want a title other than the default).

9. Click the **Finish** button. The form appears, ready for data entry (see Figure 10.5).

Figure 10.5   The Form Wizard creates a usable form using the fields, format, and style that you selected.

If your form's field labels are cut off or need some additional layout work, you can fix them in the Form Design view. You learn about modifying a form in Lesson 11, "Modifying a Form."

Creating a Form from Scratch

You can also create a form from scratch in the Form Design view. This method might seem difficult at first, but Access provides tools, such as the Field list and the Toolbox, to help you create your form. The most powerful and difficult way to create a form is with Form Design view. In this view, you decide exactly where to place each field and how to format it.

To open the Form Design view and create a new form, follow these steps:

1. From the database window, click the **Forms** object type.
2. Click the **New** button. The New Form dialog box appears.
3. Click **Design View**.
4. Select a table or query from the drop-down list at the bottom of the dialog box. This table provides a Field list that makes it easy to place fields on the form.
5. Click **OK**. A Form Design window appears (see Figure 10.6). You're ready to create your form.

Field list

Toolbox

Figure 10.6   Form Design view presents a blank canvas for your new form.

Notice that a Field list and Toolbox appear in the Form Design view. You work with creating form controls (the equivalent of a field in a table) using these tools in the next section.

You can also start the process of building a form in the Design view by double-clicking the **Create Form in Design View** link in the database window. Because you are not specifying a table for the Field list to use (as you did in the steps outlined in this section), however, that Field list won't be available. Instead, you must specify a table for the Field list.

 To do this, click the **Properties** button on the Form Design toolbar. The form's properties dialog box appears (see Figure 10.7).

Figure 10.7   The properties dialog box enables you to set a number of properties for the form.

In the properties dialog box, be sure that the **All** tab is selected. Click in the Record Source box, and then use the drop-down arrow that appears to specify the table that will serve as the field source for the form. The Field list appears. Close the properties dialog box.

 TIP   **Don't See the Toolbox or Field List?**   You need to use the Form Design toolbox and the Field list to help in the design of your form. If they're not visible, click the **Toolbox** button or the **Field List** button in the toolbar.

Adding Controls to a Form

The basic idea of the Form Design window is simple: It's similar to a light table or a paste-up board where you place the elements of your form. The fields you add to a form appear in the form's Detail area. The Detail area is the only area visible at first; you'll learn how to add other areas in the next lesson.

 TIP   **Controls and Fields**   When you are working with a table, you work directly with fields of data. On forms and reports, you work with controls, which are elements that display data from a field, hold informative text (such as titles and labels), or are purely decorative (such as lines and rectangles).

To add a control displaying a field to the form, follow these steps:

1. Display the Field list if it's not showing. Choose the **Field List** from the **View** menu to do so.

2. Drag a field from the Field list onto the Detail area of the form. The mouse pointer changes to show that a field is being placed.

3. Repeat step 2 to add as many fields as you like to the form (see Figure 10.8).

Figure 10.8   Drag fields from the Field list to the form grid.

When you drag a field to a form from the Field list, it becomes a control that displays data from that table field on the form. It is basically a link between the table field and the control on the form. You can drag more than one field to the form at once using the steps described earlier. However, in step 2, rather than clicking and dragging a single field, do one of the following before dragging:

- To select a block of adjacent fields, click the first one you want and hold down the **Shift** key while you click the last one.

- To select nonadjacent fields, hold down the **Ctrl** key as you click each one you want.

- To select all the fields on the list, double-click the **Field List** title bar.

You can move objects around on a form after you initially place them; you'll learn how to do this in the next lesson. Don't worry if your form doesn't look very professional at this point; in the next several lessons, you see how to modify and improve your form.

> **TIP** **Using Snap to Grid** If you find it hard to align the fields neatly, choose **Snap to Grid** from the **Format** menu to place a check mark next to that command. This forces the borders of the fields included on your form to "snap" to the grid that appears in the Design view. If you want to align the fields on your own, select **Snap to Grid** again to turn it off.

 After you have placed all the controls on the form that relate to the fields in a particular table or tables, you are ready to do some data entry. First, however, you must save the form's structure. Click the **Save** button on the Form Design toolbar. Type a name for the form into the Save As dialog box. Then click **OK**.

Entering Data into a Form

The point of creating a form is so that you can enter data more easily into your tables. The form acts as an attractive mask that shields you from the stark reality of the table's Datasheet view. To enter data into a form, follow these steps:

1. Open the form. In the database window, click the **Form** tab, and then double-click the form's name.

2. Click in the field you want to begin with and type your data.

3. Press **Tab** to move to the next field. If you need to go back, you can press **Shift+Tab** to move to the previous field. When you reach the last field, pressing **Tab** moves you to the first field in a new, blank record.

   To move to the next record before you reach the bottom field or to move back to previous records, click the right- and left-arrow buttons on the left end of the navigation bar at the bottom of the window.

4. Repeat steps 2 and 3 to enter all the records you like. They're saved automatically as you enter them.

Modifying a Form

In this lesson, you learn how to modify a form's design.

Cleaning Up Your Form: An Overview

After you've created a form, you might find that it doesn't quite look as good as you like. Controls might need realignment, or you might want to resize the label for a particular control or controls. You also might want to expand the form grid areas so that you can rearrange the form controls or add additional controls to the form.

All these actions can be accomplished in the Form Design view. Using this view, you can edit the structure of any form that you create, regardless of whether you created the form using AutoForm, the Form Wizard, or the Design view.

Moving Field Controls

The most common change to a form is to reposition a control. For example, you might want to move several controls down so you can insert a new control, or you might want to rearrange how the controls appear on the grid.

If you placed controls on the form to begin with (rather than using AutoForm or the Form Wizard), you have probably noticed that the control consists of two parts: a label and the actual control. You can manipulate various aspects of the label and the control independently (such as their sizes or the distance between them). You work with label and control sizing later in this lesson.

 TIP   **More Space**   If you want to create extra space at the bottom of the controls so that you have more room to move them around, drag the Form Footer pane down so that more of the Detail area is visible. You can also drag the right side of the grid to make the form wider. If you need more space at the top of the form, highlight all the controls and move them down as a group.

Follow these steps:

1. From the database window, select a form in the Form list, and then click the **Design** button on the database window toolbar. The form is opened in Design view.

2. Click a control's label to select it. Selection handles appear around the label (a displacement handle also appears on the control, but you don't want to touch that right now). You can select several controls by holding down **Shift** as you click each control's label.

3. Position the mouse pointer on the edge of the control's label so that the pointer becomes a hand (see Figure 11.1). If you're moving more than one selected control, you can position the mouse pointer on any selected control's label.

Figure 11.1   To move a control, first select it. Then, drag it by its label using the hand pointer.

4. Drag the control's label and the control to a new location.

5. Release the mouse button when the control is at the desired new location.

CAUTION

The Label Moved Without the Control Attached!   When you position the mouse pointer over the control to be moved, be sure the pointer changes to an open hand, as shown in Figure 11.1. If you see a pointing finger, you are on the control's displacement box. The pointing finger is used to move controls and labels independently, as you'll learn in the next section.

Moving Controls and Field Labels Independently

Depending on how you are laying out the controls in your form, you might want to separate the control label from the control. For example, you might want to arrange the form in a tabular format where the control names are positioned over the controls. Separating controls and labels also allows you to move the control so that the field label isn't cut off. Then you can resize the label.

TIP   **Field Controls: The Most Commonly Used Controls**   Controls related to fields in a table and their attached labels are discussed in this lesson, but the same methods can be used with other controls that have attached labels, such as combo boxes and list boxes (which are discussed in Lesson 12, "Adding Special Controls to Forms").

To move a control or its attached label by itself, follow these steps:

1. Click the control that you want to separate from its label.

2. Position the mouse pointer over the displacement handle at the top left of the label or the control (the large box handle on the top left of the label or the control). The mouse pointer becomes a pointing finger (see Figure 11.2).

Figure 11.2   Drag the displacement handle to move the control or label independently.

3. Drag the label or the control to a new position.

 TIP   **Deleting Labels**   If a certain control is self-explanatory (such as a picture), you might want to delete its attached label. To do so, select the label and press **Delete**.

Separating the label from a control allows you to arrange your controls in all kinds of tabular and columnar arrangements on the form grid. Just make sure that you keep the correct label in close proximity to the appropriate control.

Changing Label and Control Sizes

You can also change the width or height of a label or control. Separating a label from its control, as discussed in the previous section, provides you with the room to resize the label or the control independently. To change a label's or control's width (length)

1. Click the label or the control to select it. If you are going to resize the control itself, be sure you click the control. Selection handles (small boxes) appear around it.

2. Position the mouse pointer on either the right or left of the label or control until the mouse pointer becomes a sizing tool (a horizontal double-headed arrow, as shown in Figure 11.3).

Figure 11.3   You can change the size of a label or control by dragging a sizing box.

3. Drag the label's or control's sizing handle to increase or decrease the length as needed. Then release the mouse button.

Viewing Headers and Footers

So far, you have been working in the main part of the form grid called the Detail area. The Detail area is where you place the various field controls for the form (and additional controls, such as those discussed in the next lesson).

There are other areas of a form. For example, a form header can be used to include a title for the form (header information appears at the top of the form). The other form areas are

- **Form Header**—An area at the top of the form that can be used for repeating information, such as a form title.

- **Form Footer**—An area at the bottom of the form that can be used for repeating information, such as the current date or explanatory information related to the form.

- **Page Header**—Forms that are built to add data to multiple tables can consist of multiple pages. You can also include a Page Header area on a form that enables you to include information that you want to repeat on each page of the form when it is printed out, such as your name or company information.

- **Page Footer**—This area enables you to place information, such as page numbering, that appears on every page when the form is printed.

These different areas of the form grid aren't displayed by default; to display these areas, such as the Form Header/Footer, use the View menu. To show the Form Header/Footer, for example, select **View, Form Header/Footer**.

When you create a form with the Form Wizard, the Form Header and Form Footer areas appear in Design view, but nothing is in them. To make some room to work in the Form Header, click the **Detail Header** bar to select it, position the mouse pointer between the bars, and drag downward (see Figure 11.4).

Figure 11.4   Drag the Detail Header bar down to create space to add text in the Form header.

The Detail section contains controls whose data changes with every record. As already mentioned, the Form Header contains text you want repeated on each onscreen form. This makes the Form Header a great place to add a label that contains a title for the form.

Adding Labels

You can add a label to any of the areas in the form. Adding labels to the form enables you to place titles, subtitles, or explanatory text on the form. Because you will want these types of labels to repeat at the top or bottom of the form, the best place to add them is to the form's header or footer. To add titles and other general information to a header or a footer or to add information specific to particular controls to the Detail area, follow these steps:

1. If the toolbox isn't displayed, choose **Toolbox** from the **View** menu, or click the **Toolbox** button on the toolbar.

2. Click the **Label** tool in the toolbox (the one with the italicized letters *Aa* on it). The mouse pointer changes to a capital A with a plus sign next to it.

3. Place the Label pointer on an area of the form grid, such as the Form Header area. Drag to create a box or rectangle for text entry (see Figure 11.5).

Figure 11.5   Select the Label tool in the toolbox.

4. When you release the mouse button, a new label box appears with an insertion point inside it. Type the text you want the label box to contain.

> **TIP**   **You Must Type the Text Now**   If you don't type anything before you go on to step 5, the box disappears as soon as you click away from it.

5. Click anywhere outside the control's area to finish, or press **Enter**.

Don't worry about positioning the label as you create it; you can move a label control in the same way that you move other controls. Just click it, position the mouse pointer so that the hand appears, and then drag it to where you want it to go.

Formatting Text on a Form

After you place all your information on the form (that is, the controls you want to include and labels to display any titles or explanatory text), the next step is to make the form look more appealing.

All the formatting tools you need are on the Formatting toolbar (the top toolbar in the Form Design view). Table 11.1 describes several of the formatting tools. To format a control or label, select it, and then click the appropriate formatting tool to apply the format to the control or label.

Table 11.1 Tools on the Formatting Toolbar

Tool	Purpose
B	Toggles bold on/off
I	Toggles italic on/off
U	Toggles underline on/off
	Left-aligns text
	Centers text
	Right-aligns text
	Fills the selected box with the selected color
A	Colors the text in the selected box
	Colors the outline of the selected box
	Adds a border to the selected box
	Adds a special effect to the selected box

Some tools, such as the Font and Size tools, are drop-down lists. You click the down arrow next to the tool and then select from the list. Other tools are simple buttons for turning bold and italic on or off. Still other tools, such as the Color and Border tools, combine a button and a drop-down list. If you click the button, it applies the current value. You can click the down arrow next to the button to change the value.

You can change the color of the form background, too. Just click the header for the section you want to change (for example, **Detail**) to select the entire section. Then right-click and choose **Fill/Back** color to change the color.

 TIP   **AutoFormat**   You can use a shortcut for formatting your form. Choose **Format**, **AutoFormat**. You can choose from among several premade color and formatting schemes. If you don't like the formatting after you apply it, press **Ctrl+Z** to undo.

Changing Tab Order

When you enter data on a form, press **Tab** to move from control to control in the order they're shown in the form. The progression from control to control on the form is the *tab order*. When you first create a form, the tab order runs from top to bottom.

When you move and rearrange controls, the tab order doesn't change automatically. For example, suppose you had 10 controls arranged in a column and you rearranged them so that the tenth one was at the beginning. It would still require 10 presses of the **Tab** key to move the insertion point to that control, even though it's now at the top of the form. This makes it more difficult to fill in the form, so you'll want to adjust the tab order to reflect the new structure of the form.

 TIP   **Tab Order Improvements**   To make data entry easier, you might want to change the tab order to be different from the obvious top-to-bottom structure. For example, if 90% of the records you enter skip several controls, you might want to put those controls last in the tab order so that you can skip over them easily.

Follow these steps to adjust the tab order:

1. Choose **View, Tab Order,** The Tab Order dialog box appears (see Figure 11.6).

Figure 11.6   Use the Tab Order dialog box to decide what tab order to use on your form.

2. Choose the section for which you want to set tab order. The default is Detail.

3. The controls appear in their tab order. To change the order, click a control and then drag it up or down in the list.

4. To quickly set the tab order based on the controls' current positions in the form (top to bottom), click the **Auto Order** button.

5. Click **OK**.

When you have finished making different enhancements to your form, you must save the changes. Click the **Save** button on the Form Design toolbar.

Adding Special Controls to Forms

In this lesson, you learn about some special controls you can include on your forms.

Using Special Form Controls

So far, you've taken a look at adding controls to a form that directly relate to fields on a table or tables. This means that unless the control is linked to a field in a table that uses the AutoNumber data type, you are going to have to type absolutely all the data that you enter into the form (exactly as you would in the table).

Fortunately, Access offers some special form controls that can be used to help you enter data. For example, a list box can contain a list of entries for a control. All you have to do is select the appropriate entry from the list. Other special controls also exist that can make it easier to get your data into the form. These controls are

- **List Box**—Presents a list from which you choose an item.
- **Combo Group**—Like a list box, but you can type in other entries in addition to those on the list.
- **Option Group**—Provides you with different types of input buttons (you can select only one type of button when you create an Option group). You can use option buttons, toggle buttons, or check boxes.
- **Command Button**—Performs some function when you click it, such as starting another program, printing a report, saving the record, or anything else you specify.

Figure 12.1 shows some special controls in the Form view. In this lesson, you create each of these control types.

All these special controls can be created using the buttons on the Toolbox. Wizards are also available that walk you through the steps of creating each of these special control types. To use the wizard for a particular special control, make sure that the Control Wizards button is activated on the Toolbox. Figure 12.2 shows the Toolbox and the buttons that you are working with in this lesson.

Command button

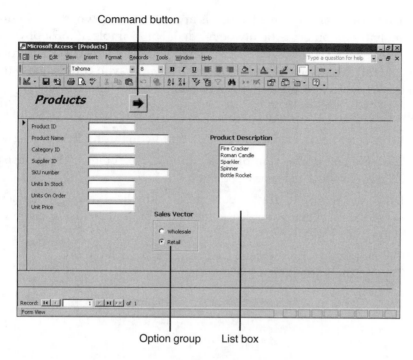

Option group   List box

Figure 12.1   Special controls can make data entry easier.

Control Wizards

Option Group button

Control Box

List Box

Command Button

Combo Box

Figure 12.2   To use wizards, make sure that the Control Wizards button is selected.

Creating a List Box or a Combo Box

A *list box* or a *combo box* can come in handy if you find yourself repeatedly typing
certain values into a field. For example, if you have to enter the name of one of your
12 branch offices each time you use a form, you might find it easier to create a list
box containing the branch office names, and then you can click to select a particular
name from the list. With a list box, the person doing the data entry is limited to the
choices that display on the list.

A combo box is useful when a list box is appropriate, but when it's possible that a different entry might occasionally be needed. For example, if most of your customers come from one of six states, but occasionally you get a new customer from another state, you might use a combo box. During data entry, you could choose the state from the list when appropriate and type a new state when it's not.

Follow these steps to create a list box or combo box from Form Design view:

1. Make sure that the **Control Wizards** button on the Toolbox is selected.

2. Click the **List Box** or **Combo Box** button in the Toolbox. The mouse pointer changes to show the type of box you selected.

3. Drag your mouse to draw a box on the grid where you want the new element to be placed. When you release the mouse button, the list or combo box wizard starts.

4. On the wizard's first screen (see Figure 12.3), click the option button **I Will Type In the Values That I Want**. Then click **Next**.

Figure 12.3 The wizard walks you through the steps of creating a list box or a combo box.

 TIP **Another Way to Enter Values**   List boxes and combo boxes can also be set up so that they pull their list of values from an existing table in the database (or a query that you've created). Select **I Want the List Box to Look Up the Values in a Table or Query** on the first wizard screen, and then specify the table or query that should supply the values for the list.

5. On the next screen, a column of boxes (only one box shows before you enter your values) is provided that you use to enter the values that you want to appear in the list. Type them in (as shown in Figure 12.4), pressing the **Tab** key after each one. Then click **Next**.

Figure 12.4   Type the values for the list or combo box.

6. On the next screen, you choose the option of Access either remembering the values in the list for later use (such as in a calculation) or entering a value selected from the list in a particular field. Because you are using this box for data entry, select **Store That Value in This Field**, and then choose a field from the drop-down list that is supplied. For example, if you want this list to provide data from your Product Description field, select it in the drop-down list. Click **Next** to continue.

TIP   **Tying a List or Combo Box to a Field**   The best way to approach list and combo boxes is to create a form that includes all the fields from a particular table. Then, you can delete the controls for fields in the Form Design view that you want to "re-create" as list or combo boxes. You then store the values from the list or combo box in one of the fields that you removed from the form.

7. On the next screen, type the label text for the new list or combo box control.

8. Click **Finish**. Your new list or combo box appears on your form (see Figure 12.5).

Where Are My Values?   Don't be alarmed that the values you entered for the control don't appear in the box in the Design view. The values will be available when you switch to the Form view and do data entry on the form.

CAUTION

TIP   **I Picked the Wrong Box Type!**   You can easily switch between a list box and a combo box, even after you create it. In Form Design view, right-click the control, click **Change To** from the shortcut menu that appears, and select a new control type.

Figure 12.5 Your list or combo box appears on the form grid.

Creating an Option Group

Another useful special control is the *option group*. An option group provides different types of buttons or input boxes that can be used to quickly input information into a form. An option group can use one of the following types of buttons:

- **Option buttons**—A separate option button is provided for each choice you supply on the form. To make a particular choice, click the appropriate option button.

- **Check boxes**—A separate check box is provided for each item you place in the option group. To select a particular item, click the appropriate check box.

- **Toggle buttons**—A button is provided for the response required, which can be toggled on and off by clicking the button.

Option groups work best when a fairly limited number of choices is available, and when you create your option group, you should select the type of button or box that best suits your need. If you have several responses where only one response is valid, use option buttons. If you have a situation in which more than one response is possible, use check boxes. Toggle buttons are used when only one response is possible, and it responds to a yes or no type question. The option button is then turned on or off with a click of the mouse.

TIP **Other Options** You can create a series of option buttons or check boxes using the Option Group button, or you can opt to directly create option buttons or check boxes by clicking the required button (the **Option** button or the **Check Box** button, respectively) on the Toolbox.

To create an Option Group control (you will create a control that uses option buttons), follow these steps:

1. Make sure that the **Control Wizards** button in the Toolbox is selected.

2. Click the **Option Group** button on the Toolbox. Your mouse pointer changes to show the Option Group icon.

3. Drag your mouse pointer on your form to draw a box where you want the option group to appear. When you release the mouse button, the wizard starts.

4. The wizard prompts you to enter the labels you want for each button (or check box or toggle button), as shown in Figure 12.6. You will need a label for each button that will appear in the group. These labels should be the same as the type of data you would normally insert into the field you are building the option group for (which is specified in step 7). Enter the labels needed, pressing **Tab** after each one; then click **Next**.

Figure 12.6 Enter the labels you want for each option here.

5. On the next screen, you can select one of the labels that you input in step 4 as the default choice for the option group. Specify the label, and then click **Yes, the Default Choice Is**. Or click **No, I Don't Want a Default As the Other Possibility**. Then click **Next**.

6. On the next screen, the wizard asks what value you want to assign to each option (such as 1, 2, and so on). These values provide a numerical equivalent for each label you listed in step 4 and are used by Access to store the response provided by a particular option button or check box. You should use the default values that Access provides. Click **Next** to continue.

7. On the next screen, you decide whether the value that you assigned to each of your option labels is stored in a particular field or saved by Access for later use. Because you are using the option group to input data into a particular field, be sure the **Store the Value in This Field** option button is selected. This stores the data that the option group provides in a particular field. Select the field from the drop-down list provided. Then, click **Next** to continue.

8. On the next screen, select the type of control (option button, check box, or toggle button—see Figure 12.7) you want to use and a style for the controls; then click **Next**.

Figure 12.7 You can choose different input controls for your Option group.

9. On the last screen, type a label for the new control. Then click **Finish**.

Your new Option control appears on the grid area of the form. All the different option values that you entered appear in the control. When you switch to the Form view to enter data, you can use the various option buttons or check boxes to select an actual value for that particular field.

Adding Command Buttons

Another special control type that you can add to your form is a command button. Command buttons are used to perform a particular action. For example, you could put a command button on a form that enables you to move to the next record or to print the form. Access offers different command button types that you can place on your forms:

- **Record Navigation**—You can add command buttons that allow you to move to the next, previous, first, or last record.
- **Record Operations**—You can make buttons that delete, duplicate, print, save, or undo a record.

- **Form Operations**—Command buttons can print a form, open a page (on a multiple-page form), or close the form.

- **Application**—Command buttons can exit Access or run some other application.

- **Miscellaneous**—Command buttons can print a table, run a macro, run a query, or use the AutoDialer to dial a phone number specified on a form.

 TIP **Placing Command Button** Form headers or footers make a great place to put any command buttons that you create. Placing them in the header makes it easy for you to go to the top of the form and click a particular command button.

To place a command button on a form, follow these steps:

1. Be sure that the **Control Wizards** button in the Toolbox is selected.

2. Click the **Command Button** in the Toolbox. Your mouse pointer changes to show the Command Button icon.

3. Click your form where you want the command button to appear (such as the header of the form). The Command Button Wizard opens.

4. On the first wizard screen, select an action category in the Categories list, and then in the Actions box (see Figure 12.8), select the action that the button should perform. Then click **Next**.

Figure 12.8 Choose what action you want the command button to execute.

5. On the next screen, you can select to have either text or a picture appear on the command button. For text, choose **Text** and then enter the text into the appropriate box. To place a picture on the button, select **Picture** and then select a picture from the list provided (you can use your own bitmap pictures on the buttons if they are available; use the **Browse** button to locate them). Then click **Next**.

583

6. On the next screen, type a name for your new button. Then click **Finish**. The button appears on your form. You can move it around like any other control.

Searching for Information in Your Database

In this lesson, you learn how to search for data in a database using the Find feature and how to find and replace data using the Replace feature.

Using the Find Feature

Whether you are viewing the records in the table using the Datasheet view or a form, the Find feature is useful for locating a particular record in a table. For example, if you keep a database of customers, you might want to find a particular customer's record quickly by searching using the customer's last name. You can search the table using a specific field, or you can search the entire table (all the fields) for a certain text string.

Although the Find feature is designed to find information in a table, you can use the Find feature in both the Table Datasheet view and the Form view. The results of a particular search display only the first match of the parameters, but you can repeat the search to find additional records (one at a time).

 TIP   **Finding More Than One Record**   If you need to find several records at once, Find is not the best tool because it locates only one record at a time. A better tool for locating multiple records is a filter, discussed in the next lesson.

To find a particular record, follow these steps:

1. Open your table in the Datasheet view or open a form that is used to enter data in the table that you want to search.
2. Click in the field that contains the data you want to search for.
3. Select **Edit**, **Find**, or press **Ctrl+F**. The Find and Replace dialog box appears (see Figure 13.1) with the Find tab on top.

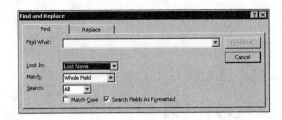

Figure 13.1 Use the Find and Replace dialog box to find data in a record.

4. Type the data string that you want to find into the **Find What** text box.

5. The default value for Look In is the field you selected in step 2. If you want to search the entire table, click the **Look In** list drop-down box and select the table's name.

6. From the **Match** drop-down list, select one of the following:

   - **Whole Field**—Select this to find fields where the specified text is the only thing in that field. For example, "Smith" would not find "Smithsonian."

   - **Start of Field**—Select this to find fields that begin with the specified text. For example, "Smith" would find "Smith" and "Smithsonian," but not "Joe Smith."

   - **Any Part of Field**—Select this to find fields that contain the specified text in any way. "Smith" would find "Smith," "Smithsonian," and "Joe Smith."

7. To limit the match to entries that are the same case (uppercase or lowercase) as the search string, select the **Match Case** check box.

8. To find only fields with the same formatting as the text you type, select **Search Fields As Formatted** (this option can slow down the search on a large table, so don't use it unless you think it will affect the search results).

9. When you are ready to run the search, click **Find Next**.

10. If needed, move the Find and Replace dialog box out of the way by dragging its title bar so that you can see the record it found. If Access finds a field matching your search, it highlights the field entry containing the found text (see Figure 13.2).

11. To find the next occurrence, click **Find Next**. If Access can't find any more occurrences, it tells you the search item was not found. Click **OK** to clear that message.

12. When you finish finding your data, click the Find and Replace dialog box **Close (x)** button.

Figure 13.2   Access finds records, one record at a time, that contain the search text.

Using the Replace Feature

The Replace feature is similar to the Find feature, except that you can stipulate that a value, which you specify, replace the data found during the search. For example, if you found that you misspelled a brand name or other value in a table, you could replace the word with the correct spelling. This is useful for correcting proper names because the Spelling Checker doesn't help correct those types of spelling errors.

To find and replace data, follow these steps:

1. Select **Edit**, **Replace**, or press **Ctrl+H**. The Find and Replace dialog box appears with the Replace tab displayed (see Figure 13.3).

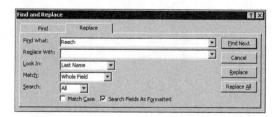

Figure 13.3   You can find specific text in a table and then replace it using the Replace feature.

2. Type the text you want to find into the **Find What** text box.

3. Type the text you want to replace it with into the **Replace With** text box.

4. Select any options you want using the Match drop-down list or the check boxes on the Search tab. They work the same as the options discussed on the Find tab (in the previous section).

5. To start the search, click **Find Next**. Access finds the first occurrence of the search string.

6. Click the **Replace** button to replace the text.

7. Click **Find Next** to find other occurrences, if desired, and replace them by clicking the **Replace** button.

8. If you decide that you would like to replace all occurrences of the search string in the table, click the **Replace All** button.

9. When you have found the last occurrence of the search string (Access lets you know that the string can no longer be located, which means you are at the end of the table), click the **Close** (**X**) button on the Find and Replace dialog box.

The Find and Replace feature works well when you want to work with data in a particular field, but it is limited because you can work with only one record at a time. Other, more sophisticated ways exist to locate records that contain a particular parameter. For example, you can filter records (discussed in the next lesson) using a particular field's content as the filter criteria. This provides you with a subset of the current table, showing you only the records that include the filter criteria.

Queries also provide you with a method for creating a subset of records found in a database table. Queries are discussed in Lesson 15, "Creating a Simple Query," and Lesson 16, "Creating Queries from Scratch."

Sorting, Filtering, and Indexing Data

In this lesson, you learn how to find data by sorting and filtering and how to speed up searches with indexing.

Finding and Organizing Your Data

You've already had a chance to work with the Find and Replace features (in the previous lesson). Find and Replace are great features when you're working with individual instances of a particular value and want to search for it in a particular field. This lesson takes a look at other ways to organize the data in the table, including the Sort and Filter features.

Sorting Data

Although you probably entered your records into the table in some kind of logical order, perhaps by employee number or employee start date, being able to change the order of the records in the table based on a particular field parameter can be extremely useful. This is where the Sort feature comes in.

Using Sort, you can rearrange the records in the table based on any field in the table (more complex sorts can also be created that allow you to sort by more than one field, such as Last Name and then First Name). You can sort in either ascending (A to Z, 1 to 10) or descending (Z to A, 10 to 1) order.

TIP **Which View?** You can sort either in Form view or Datasheet view, but the Datasheet view is better because it shows you all the records in the table in their new sort order.

The fastest way to sort is to use either the **Sort Ascending** or **Sort Descending** button on the Table toolbar. However, this easy road to sorting limits you to sorting by one field or adjacent fields.

Follow these steps to sort records:

1. Place the insertion point in the field by which you want to sort the table (if you want to sort by more than one adjacent field, select the field columns by clicking and dragging the Field Column names). Figure 14.1 shows a Customers table where the insertion point has been placed in the Country field.

Figure 14.1 Place the insertion point in the field you want to sort that table by.

2. To sort the records in the table by that field in ascending order (alphabetically from A to Z), click the **Sort Ascending** button. Figure 14.2 shows the results of an ascending sort by Country field on the table that was shown in Figure 14.1.

3. To sort the records in descending order, click the **Sort Descending** button.

4. To place the records back in their presorted order, select the **Records** menu, and then select **Remove Filter/Sort**.

As already mentioned, you can sort a table by adjacent fields using the sort buttons. All you have to do is select the field headings for those particular field columns, and then click the correct sort button. For example, if you wanted to sort a customer table by last name and then first name, the last name would have to be in the column that is directly to the left of the First Name field.

Address	City	Region	Postal Code	Country	Phone	
Cerrito 333	Buenos Aires		1010	Argentina	(1) 135-5555	(1)
Ing. Gustavo Moncada 8585	Buenos Aires		1010	Argentina	(1) 135-5333	(1)
Av. del Libertador 900	Buenos Aires		1010	Argentina	(1) 123-5555	(1)
Geisweg 14	Salzburg		5020	Austria	6562-9722	656
Kirchgasse 6	Graz		8010	Austria	7675-3425	762
Rue Joseph-Bens 532	Bruxelles		B-1180	Belgium	(02) 201 24 67	(02
Boulevard Tirou, 255	Charleroi		B-6000	Belgium	(071) 23 67 22 2	(07
Alameda dos Canários, 891	São Paulo	SP	05487-020	Brazil	(11) 555-1189	
Av. dos Lusíadas, 23	São Paulo	SP	05432-043	Brazil	(11) 555-7647	
Rua do Paço, 67	Rio de Janeiro	RJ	05454-876	Brazil	(21) 555-0091	(21
Av. Brasil, 442	Campinas	SP	04876-786	Brazil	(11) 555-9482	
Rua da Panificadora, 12	Rio de Janeiro	RJ	02389-673	Brazil	(21) 555-4252	(21
Av. Copacabana, 267	Rio de Janeiro	RJ	02389-890	Brazil	(21) 555-3412	
Rua Orós, 92	São Paulo	SP	05442-030	Brazil	(11) 555-9857	
Av. Inês de Castro, 414	São Paulo	SP	05634-030	Brazil	(11) 555-2167	(11
Rua do Mercado, 12	Resende	SP	08737-363	Brazil	(14) 555-8122	
43 rue St. Laurent	Montréal	Québec	H1J 1C3	Canada	(514) 555-8054	(51
1900 Oak St.	Vancouver	BC	V3F 2K1	Canada	(604) 555-3392	(60
23 Tsawassen Blvd.	Tsawassen	BC	T2F 8M4	Canada	(604) 555-4729	(60
Vinbæltet 34	København		1734	Denmark	31 12 34 56	31
Smagsløget 45	Århus		8200	Denmark	86 21 32 43	86
Keskuskatu 45	Helsinki		21240	Finland	90-224 8858	90-
Torikatu 38	Oulu		90110	Finland	981-443655	981
54, rue Royale	Nantes		44000	France	40.32.21.21	40.
12 rue des Bouchers	Marseille		13008	France	91 24 45 40	91

Record: |◄| ◄ | 1 | ►| ►| |►★| of 92

Datasheet View

Figure 14.2   The table records are sorted based on the field that you selected.

Filtering Data

Although sorting rearranges the records in the table, you might need to see a subset of the records in a table based on a particular criterion. Filtering is used for this purpose. The Filter feature temporarily hides records from the table that do not meet the filter criteria.

For example, you might want to view the records in an employee table where the employees have exceeded their sales goal for the year. Or in an order table, you might want to find orders that were placed on a particular date. Filters can help you temporarily narrow down the records shown in the table based on your criteria.

You can apply a filter in three ways: Filter by Selection (or Filter Excluding Selection), Filter by Form, and Advanced Filter/Sort. The first two methods are very easy ways to quickly filter the records in a table.

The Advanced Filter/Sort feature uses a Design view that is almost the same as the Query Design view (covered in Lesson 16). If you learn how to create queries (which are really nothing more than advanced filters/sorts), you will be able to work with the Advanced Filter/Sort feature.

This section covers Filter by Selection and Filter by Form. Next, take a look at how you filter by selection.

Filter by Selection

Filtering by selection is the easiest method of filtering, but before you can use it, you must locate a field that contains the value that you want to use to filter the table. For example, if you want to filter a customer table by a country, such as Germany, you must locate a field in a record that contains the text "Germany."

To filter by selection, follow these steps:

1. Locate a field in a record that contains the value you want to use to filter the table. For example, if you want to see all the customers in Germany, you would find a field in the Country field column that contains "Germany."

2. Select the data in the field.

3. Click the **Filter by Selection** button on the toolbar, or select **Records**, point at **Filter**, and then choose **Filter by Selection**. The records that match the criteria you selected appear as shown in Figure 14.3.

TIP   **Fine-Tuning Filter by Selection**   You can also filter the table by selecting only a portion of an entry in a field. For example, if you want to filter the records by last names beginning with the letter S, select the S in a last name that appears in the Last Name field in a record.

Address	City	Region	Postal Code	Country	Phone	
Obere Str. 57	Berlin		12209	Germany	030-0074321	030-0
Forsterstr. 57	Mannheim		68306	Germany	0621-08460	0621-
Walserweg 21	Aachen		52066	Germany	0241-039123	0241-
Berliner Platz 43	München		80805	Germany	089-0877310	089-0
Maubelstr. 90	Brandenburg		14776	Germany	0555-09876	
Magazinweg 7	Frankfurt a.M.		60528	Germany	069-0245984	069-0
Heerstr. 22	Leipzig		04179	Germany	0342-023176	
Mehrheimerstr. 369	Köln		50739	Germany	0221-0644327	0221-
Taucherstraße 10	Cunewalde		01307	Germany	0372-035188	
Luisenstr. 48	Münster		44087	Germany	0251-031259	0251-
Adenauerallee 900	Stuttgart		70563	Germany	0711-020361	0711-

Figure 14.3   The table will be filtered by the field data you selected.

With Filter by Selection, you can filter by only one criterion at a time. However, you can apply successive filters after the first one to further narrow the list of matching records.

You can also filter for records that don't contain the selected value. Follow the same steps as outlined in this section, but choose **Records**, point at **Filter**, and choose **Filter Excluding Selection** in step 3.

After you have finished viewing the records that match your filter criteria, you will want to bring all the table records back on screen. Select **Records, Remove Filter/Sort**.

Filter by Form

Filtering by form is a more powerful filtering method than filtering by selection. With Filter by Form, you can filter by more than one criterion at a time. To filter by form, follow these steps:

1. With the table open in the Datasheet view, click the **Filter by Form** button on the toolbar, or select **Records**, point at **Filter**, and then select **Filter by Form**. A blank form appears, resembling an empty datasheet with a single record line.

2. Click in the field for which you want to set a criterion. A down arrow appears for a drop-down list. Click the arrow and select the value you want from the list (see Figure 14.4). You also can type the value directly into the field if you prefer.

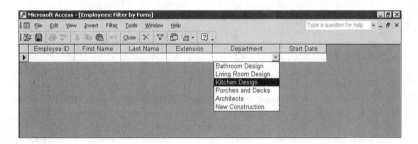

Figure 14.4   Set the criteria for the filter using the drop-down list in each field.

3. Enter additional criteria for the filter as needed using the drop-down lists provided by the other fields in the table.

4. After you enter your criteria, click the **Apply Filter** button on the toolbar. Your filtered data appears in the Table window.

As in Filter by Selection, you can remove a filter by clicking the **Remove Filter** button or by selecting **Records, Remove Filter/Sort**.

Saving Your Filter As a Query

If you design a filter that you would like to keep, you can save it as a query. After it is saved as a query, it resides on the Query list in the database window. You will work with queries in Lessons 15 and 16.

To save a filter as a query, follow these steps:

1. Display the filter in Filter by Form view.

2. Select **File**, **Save As Query**. Access asks for the name of the new query.

3. Type a name and click **OK**. Access saves the filter as a query.

Indexing Data

Although not a method of manipulating data like a sort or a filter, indexes provide a method for speeding up searches, sorts, and filters by cataloging the contents of a particular field. The primary key field in a table is automatically indexed. If you have a large database table and frequently search, sort, or filter by a field other than the primary key field, you might want to create an index for that field.

Can't Be Indexed   You can't index a field whose data type is Memo, Hyperlink, or OLE Object. There is no way for Access to verify the content of fields containing these types of entries, making it impossible to create an index.

CAUTION

To index a field, follow these steps:

1. Open the table in Design view.

2. Select the field that you want to index.

3. In the Field Properties pane on the General tab, click in the **Indexed** box.

4. From the Indexed field's drop-down list, select either **Yes (Duplicates OK)** or **Yes (No Duplicates)**, depending on whether that field's content should be unique for each record (see Figure 14.5). For example, in the case of indexing a last name field, you would want to allow duplicates (Duplicates OK), but in the case of a Social Security number field where you know each entry is unique, you would not want to allow duplicates (No Duplicates).

Figure 14.5   To index a field, set its Indexed value to one of the Yes choices.

5. Save your changes to the table's structure by clicking the **Save** button on the Design toolbar.

6. Close the Design view of the table.

Indexes aren't glamorous. They work behind the scenes to speed up your searches and filters. They don't really have any independent functions of their own.

Creating a Simple Query

In this lesson, you create a simple query.

Understanding Queries

As you learned in the previous lesson, Access offers many ways to help you narrow down the information you're looking at, including sorting and filtering. The most flexible way to sort and filter data, however, is using a query.

A *query* is a question that you pose to a database table or tables. For example, you might want to know which of your customers live in a specific state or how many of your salespeople have reached a particular sales goal. The great thing about queries is that you can save queries and use them to create tables, delete records, or copy records to another table.

Queries enable you to specify

- The table fields that appear in the query
- The order of the fields in the query
- Filter and sort criteria for each field in the query

 Query A query enables you to "question" your database using different criteria that can sort, filter, and summarize table data.

Queries are a powerful tool for analyzing and summarizing database information. In this lesson, you take a look at the queries you can create using a wizard. Creating queries in the Design view is covered in Lesson 16, "Creating Queries from Scratch."

Using the Simple Query Wizard

The easiest way to create a query is with the Simple Query Wizard, which enables you to select the table fields you want to include in the query. A simple query is useful when you want to weed out extraneous fields but still want to see every record in the database table. The Simple Query Wizard helps you create a *select query*.

Select Query The select query is used to select certain data from a table or tables. It not only filters the data, but it can also sort the data. It can even perform simple calculations on the results (such as counting and averaging).

To create a select query with the Simple Query Wizard, follow these steps:

1. In the Access window, open the database you want to work with and select the **Queries** icon in the database window.

2. Double-click **Create Query by Using Wizard**. The first dialog box of the Simple Query Wizard appears (see Figure 15.1).

Figure 15.1 The Simple Query Wizard first asks what fields you want to include in the query.

3. Choose the table from which you want to select fields from the Tables/Queries drop-down list.

4. Click a field name in the Available Fields list; then click the **Add >** button to move the field name to the Selected Fields list. Add fields as needed, or move them all at once with the **Add All >>** button.

5. (Optional) Select another table or query from the Tables/Queries list and add some of its fields to the Selected Fields list (this enables you to pull data from more than one table into the query. When you have finished adding fields, click **Next**.

CAUTION **Relationships Required** If you're going to use two or more tables in your query, they must be joined by a relationship. See Lesson 9, "Creating Relationships Between Tables," for more information.

6. On the next screen, enter a title for the query. Then, click **Finish** to view the query results. Figure 15.2 shows the results of a simple query.

First Name	Last Name	DepartmentName	Amount Spent	Date Submitted
Nancy	Davy	Customer Service	$1,200.00	1/15/2001
Janet	Leverling	Design	$300.00	1/18/2001
Richard	Jones	Design	$2,600.00	1/22/2001
Steven	Buchanan	Design	$1,800.00	1/23/2001
Henry	Cotton	Warehouse	$920.00	1/24/2001
Snidley	Backlash	Warehouse	$1,560.00	2/3/2001
Alice	Smith	Design	$2,200.00	2/5/2001
Robert	Buchanan	Warehouse	$5,500.00	2/7/2001
Bob	Palooka	Customer Service	$1,400.00	2/8/2001

Figure 15.2 Queries created using the Simple Query Wizard list the data from the fields you selected.

The problem with queries created using the Simple Query Wizard is that you aren't supplied with the option of setting sort parameters for the records or the capability to filter them by particular criteria. Simple queries just allow you to select the fields. For this query to provide a little more manipulation of the table data, you would have to edit this Query Design view, which is discussed in the next lesson. Building queries from scratch provides you with a lot more control over how the data is filtered, sorted, and summarized.

Saving a Query

When you create a query, Access saves it automatically. You don't need to do anything special to save it. When you are finished viewing the results of the query, click its **Close (x)** button. The new query is then listed in the Query list that the database window provides.

Rerunning a Query

At any time, you can rerun your query. If the data has changed in the table fields that you included in a query, rerunning the query provides you with an updated set of results.

To rerun a query, follow these steps:

1. Open the database containing the query.
2. Select the **Queries** icon in the database window.
3. In the Query list, double-click the query you want to run, or click it once and then click the **Open** button.

 TIP   **Queries Look Like Tables**   Queries can be manipulated in the Datasheet view just like a table. You can use the Sort and Filter features on a query, or you can delete records from the query.

Using Other Query Wizards

Access's different query features are quite powerful; they can do amazingly compli-cated calculations and comparisons on data from several tables. Queries also can do calculations to summarize data or arrange the query data in a special format called a crosstab. Creating more advanced queries means that your database tables must be joined by the appropriate relationships; otherwise, the query cannot pull the data from multiple tables.

You can create very complex queries from the Query Design view, which you learn about in the next lesson. However, Access also provides some wizards that can be used to create some of the more complex query types. These wizards include the fol-lowing:

- **Crosstab Query Wizard**—This wizard displays summarized values, such as sums, counts, and averages, from a field. One field is used on the left side of the Query datasheet to cross-reference other field columns in the Query datasheet. For example, Figure 15.3 shows a Crosstab table that shows the dif-ferent products that a customer has ordered, sorted on the customer's first name.

Figure 15.3 Crosstab Queries allow you to cross-tabulate information between table fields.

- **Find Duplicates Query Wizard**—This query is used to compare two tables and find duplicate records.
- **Find Unmatched Query Wizard**—This wizard compares two tables and finds all records that don't appear in both tables (based on comparing certain fields).

You can access any of these query wizards from the database window. With the Query icon selected, click the **New** button on the database window toolbar. The New Query dialog box appears, as shown in Figure 15.4.

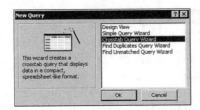

Figure 15.4   The other query wizards can be accessed from the New Query dialog box.

Select the wizard that you want to use for your query and click **OK**. Work with the wizard as it walks you through the steps for creating your new query.

Understanding Access Query Types

Before this lesson ends, you should spend a little time learning about the different types of queries that Access offers. In this lesson, you created a select query that "selects" data from a table or tables based on your query criteria. You can also build other types of queries. The different query types are

- **Make Table Query**—This type of query is similar to a select query, but it takes the data pulled together by the criteria and creates a new table for the database.

- **Update Query**—This query updates field information in a record. For example, you might have placed a certain credit limit for customers and want to update it in all the records. You would use an Update query.

- **Append Query**—This type of query is used to copy records from one table and place them (append them) into another table. For example, you might want to append employee records from an Active Employee table to a Former Employee table.

- **Delete Query**—This type of query is used to delete records from a table. For example, you might want to delete old records from a table based on particular criteria.

Now, you might be thinking that all these query types are a little too much to handle. However, you create different query types just as you would a select query.

As a matter of fact, you actually design each of these different query types as a select table (using a wizard, Query Design view, or a combination of both), and then you change the query type in the Query Design view. It's just a matter of selecting the query type from the Query menu.

Creating Queries from Scratch

16

In this lesson, you learn how to open a query in Design view, how to select fields to include in it, and how to specify criteria for filtering the records.

Introducing Query Design View

In Lesson 15, "Creating a Simple Query," you created a simple query using the Simple Query Wizard. This wizard allowed you to select the fields from a particular table and then create a standard select query. Although the Simple Query Wizard makes it easy to create a query based on one table, you will find that building more sophisticated queries is best done in the Query Design view.

The Query Design view provides two distinct areas as you work. A Table pane shows you the tables currently being used for the query. The bottom pane, the Query Design grid (see Figure 16.1) enables you to list the fields in the query and select how these fields will be sorted or the information in them filtered when you run the query.

Opening a Query in Query Design View

One thing that you can do in the Query Design view is edit existing queries, such as the simple query that you created in the previous lesson. You can change the fields used in the query and change the action that takes place on that field (or fields) when you run the query. To open an existing query in Query Design view, follow these steps:

1. Open the database that contains the query you want to edit (select **File, Open**).

2. In the database window, click the **Queries** icon.

3. In the Query list, select the query you want to edit.

4. Click the **Design** button on the database window toolbar.

The query opens in the Query Design window.

Table pane   Query Design grid

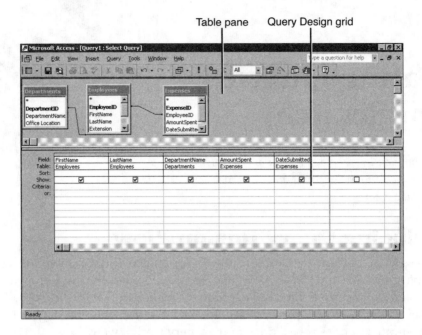

Figure 16.1   The Query Design view is divided into a Table pane and a Query Design grid.

Starting a New Query in Query Design View

Creating a new query from scratch in the Query Design view allows you to select both the tables and the fields that you use to build the query. To begin a new query in Query Design view, follow these steps:

1. Open the database that holds the table or tables that you will use to build the query.

2. Click the **Queries** icon in the database window.

3. In the Query list, double-click **Create Query in Design View**. The Show Table dialog box appears, listing all the tables in the database (see Figure 16.2).

4. Click a table that contains fields you want to use in the query, and then click the **Add** button. Repeat for each table you want to add.

5. Click **Close** when you finish adding tables. The Query Design view window opens.

The tables chosen for the query appear in the top pane of the Query Design view. Field names do not appear in the Query Design grid until you add them. Adding fields to the query is covered in the next section.

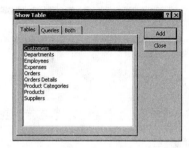

Figure 16.2 Choose which tables you want to include in the query.

 TIP **Create Table Relationships** When you create queries from multiple tables, these tables must be related. See Lesson 9, "Creating Relationships Between Tables," for more information.

Adding Fields to a Query

Whether you create your query from scratch or modify an existing query, the Query Design view provides the capability to add the table fields that will be contained in the query. Be sure that the tables that contain the fields for the query are present in the design window.

 TIP **Adding More Tables** You can add tables to your query at any time. Click the **Show Table** button on the toolbar, or select **Query**, **Show Table**. Then, select the tables you want and click **Add**. Click **Close** to return to your query design.

To add a field to the query, follow these steps:

1. In the first field column of the query grid, click in the **Field** box. A drop-down arrow list appears.

2. Click the drop-down list and select a field (see Figure 16.3). Because all the fields available in the tables you selected for the query are listed, you might have to scroll down through the list to find the field you want to use.

3. Click in the next field column and repeat the procedure. Add the other fields that you want to include in the query as needed.

As you add the fields to the query from left to right, be advised that this will be the order in which the fields appear in the query when you run it. If you need to change the field that you've placed in a particular field column, use the Field drop-down list in the column to select a different field.

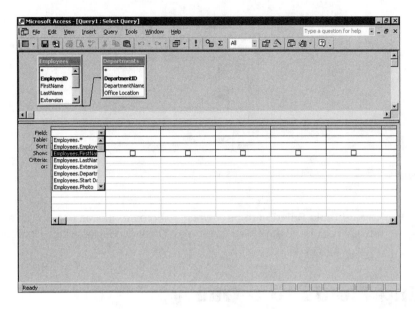

Figure 16.3 Scroll through the Field list to locate the field you want to place in the query.

 TIP **Quickly Add Fields to the Query** You can also add fields to the query directly from the tables that appear in the Table pane of the Query Design view. In one of the tables, locate the field that you want to place in the first field column and double-click the field name (in the table itself). The field appears in the Field box in the first field column of the query grid. To add the next field, locate it in a table, and then double-click it. This method enables you to select the fields from specific tables rather than scrolling through a long, continuous list of field names.

Deleting a Field

If you place a field that you don't want into a field column, you can replace it using the drop-down list in the Field box (of that column) to select a different field. If you don't want a field in that field column at all, you can delete the field from the query. Deleting the field deletes the entire field column from the query. You can use two methods for deleting a field column from the query:

- Click anywhere in the column and select **Edit, Delete Columns**.
- Position the mouse pointer directly above the column so that the pointer turns into a downward-pointing black arrow. Then click to select the entire column. To delete the selected field column, press **Delete**.

After you have the fields selected that you will use in the table, you are ready to set the criteria for the query.

Adding Criteria

The criteria that you set for your query determines how the field information found in the selected fields appears in the completed query. You set criteria in the query to filter the field data. The criteria that you set in a query are similar to the criteria that you worked with when you used the filtering features in Lesson 14, "Sorting, Filtering, and Indexing Data."

For example, suppose you have a query where you have selected fields from an Employee table and a Department table (which are related tables in your company database). The query lists the employees and their departments. You would also like to list only employees that were hired before March 1999. This means that you would set a criteria for your Start Date field of <03/01/99. Using the less-than sign (<) simply tells Access that you want the query to filter out employee records where the start date is before (less than) March 1, 1999.

To set criteria for a field in your query, follow these steps:

1. In Query Design view, click the **Criteria** row in the desired field's column.

2. Type the criteria you want to use (see Figure 16.4).

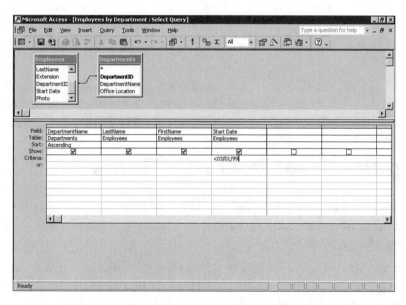

Figure 16.4 Enter your criteria into the Criteria row of the appropriate field's column.

3. Queries can contain multiple criteria. Repeat steps 1 and 2 as needed to add additional criteria to field columns in the query.

Query criteria can act both on alphanumeric field data (text) and numeric data (dates are seen by Access as numerical information). For example, suppose you have a Customer table that lists customers in two states: Ohio (OH) and Pennsylvania (PA). Criteria used to filter the customer data in a query so that only customers in PA are shown in the query results would be PA. It's that simple.

When you work with criteria, symbols are used (such as the less-than sign that appears in the criteria in Figure 16.4) to specify how the query should react to the data string that you place in the Criteria box. Table 16.1 provides a list of some of these symbols and what you use them for.

Table 16.1 Sample Criteria for Queries

Symbol	Used For
< (less than)	Matching values must be less than (or before in the case of dates) the specified numerical string.
> (greater than)	Matching values must be greater than (or after in the case of dates) the specified numerical string.
<= (less than or equal to)	Matching values must be equal to or less than the value used in the criteria.
>= (greater than or equal to)	Matching values must be equal to or greater than the value used in the criteria.
= (equal to)	Matching values must be equal to the criteria string. This symbol can be used both with text and numeric entries.
Not	Values matching the criteria string will not be included in the results. For example, Not PA filters out all the records in which PA is in the state field.

Using the Total Row in a Query

You can also do calculations in a query, such as totaling numeric information in a particular field or taking the average of numeric information found in a particular field in the query. To add calculations to a query, you must add the Total row to the Query Design grid.

After the Total row is available in the query grid, different calculations can be chosen from a drop-down list in any of the fields that you have chosen for the query. For example, you can sum (total) the numeric information in a field, calculate the average, and even do more intense statistical analysis with formulas such as minimum, maximum, and standard deviation.

To add a calculation to a field in the query grid, follow these steps:

1. In Query Design view, click the **Totals** button on the Query Design toolbar. The Total row is added to the Query Design grid (just below the Table row).

2. Click in the Total row for a field in the Query Design grid that contains numerical information. A drop-down arrow appears.

3. Click the drop-down arrow (see Figure 16.5) to select the formula you want to place in the field's Total box. The following are some of the more commonly used formula expressions:

- **Sum**—Totals the values found in the field.
- **Avg**—Calculates the average for the values found in the field.
- **Min**—Displays the lowest value (the minimum) found in the field.
- **Max**—Displays the highest value (the maximum) found in the field.
- **Count**—Calculates the number of entries in the field; it actually "counts" the entries.
- **StDev**—Calculates the standard deviation for the values in the field. The standard deviation calculates how widely values in the field differ from the field's average value.

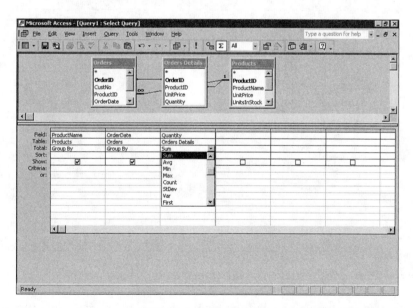

Figure 16.5 Calculations added to the Total row are chosen from a drop-down list.

4. Repeat steps 2 and 3 to place formulas into other field columns.

When you use the Total row, you can summarize the information in a particular field mathematically when you run the query. For example, you might want to total the number of orders for a particular product, so you would use the sum formula provided by the Total drop-down list.

Viewing Query Results

After you have selected the fields for the query and have set your field criteria, you are ready to run the query. As with tables created in the Design view and forms created in the Design view, you should save the query after you have finished designing it.

Just click the **Save** button on the Query Design toolbar. Supply a name for the query and then click **Yes**.

Now, you are ready to run the query. Click the **Run** button on the Query Design toolbar, or choose **Query**, **Run**. The query results appear in a datasheet that looks like an Access table (see Figure 16.6).

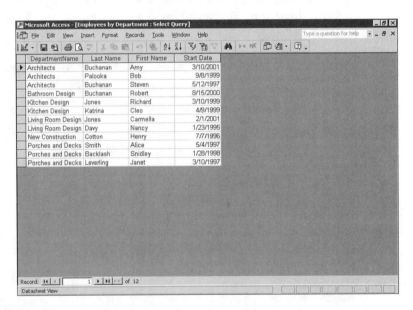

Figure 16.6 The results of the query appear as a table datasheet.

After you have reviewed the results of your query, you can quickly return to the Query Design view to edit the query fields or criteria. Just click the **Design View** button on the toolbar.

Creating a Simple Report

*In this lesson, you learn how to create reports in Access by
using the AutoReport feature and the Report Wizard.*

Understanding Reports

So far, the discussion of Access objects has centered on objects that are used either to
input data or manipulate data that has already been entered into a table. Tables and
forms provide different ways of entering records into the database, and queries
enable you to sort and filter the data in the database.

Now you are going to turn your attention to a database object that is designed to
summarize data and provide a printout of your database information—an Access
report. Reports are designed specifically to be printed and shared with other people.

You can create a report in several ways, ranging from easy to difficult. An
AutoReport, the simplest possibility, takes all the records in a table and provides a
summary that is ready to print. The Report Wizard, an intermediate possibility, is
still simple to use but requires more decisions on your part to select the fields and
the structure of the report. Finally, the most difficult method of creating a report is
building a report from scratch in the Report Design view. You learn about the Report
Design view in the next lesson.

Using AutoReport to Create a Report

The fastest way to take data in a table and get it into a format that is appropriate for
printing is AutoReport. The AutoReport feature can create a report in a tabular or
columnar format. A tabular report resembles a datasheet in that it arranges the data
from left to right on the page. A columnar report resembles a form in that it displays
each record in the table from top to bottom. The downside of AutoReport is that it
can create a report from only one table or query.

To use the AutoReport feature to create a simple report, follow these steps:

   1. Open the database containing the table or query that you will use to create the
   report.

2. Click the **Reports** icon in the left pane of the database window.

3. Click the **New** button on the database toolbar. The New Report dialog box appears (see Figure 17.1).

Figure 17.1 Choose one of the AutoReport formats in the New Report dialog box.

4. Select **AutoReport:Columnar** or **AutoReport:Tabular**.

5. In the drop-down list at the bottom of the dialog box, select the table or query on which you want to base the report.

6. Click **OK**. The report appears in Print Preview. The Print Preview mode allows you to examine your report before printing. You learn more about Print Preview later in this lesson.

TIP **Create an AutoReport from an Open Table** You can also create an AutoReport directly from an open table. With the table open in the Access window, click the **New Object** drop-down list on the Table Datasheet toolbar and select AutoReport. This creates a simple columnar report.

AutoReport produces fairly simple-looking reports. To have more control over the report format and layout, you can create a report using the Report Wizard.

Creating a Report with the Report Wizard

The Report Wizard offers a good compromise between ease-of-use and control over the report that is created. With the Report Wizard, you can build a report that uses multiple tables or queries. You can also choose a layout and format for the report. Follow these steps to create a report with Report Wizard:

1. Open the database containing the table or query on which you want to report.

2. Click the **Reports** icon in the database window.

3. In the Reports pane of the database window, double-click **Create Report by Using Wizard** to start the Report Wizard (see Figure 17.2). The first wizard screen enables you to choose the fields to include in the report.

Figure 17.2 The first Report Wizard screen enables you to select the fields for the report.

4. From the Tables/Queries drop-down list, select a table or query from which you want to include fields.

5. Click a field in the Available Fields list, and then click the **Add >** button to move it to the Selected Fields list. Repeat this step to select all the fields you want, or click **Add All >>** to move all the fields over at once.

6. For a report using fields from multiple tables, select another table or query from the Tables/Queries list and repeat step 5. To build the report from more than one table, you must create a relationship between the tables. When you finish selecting fields, click **Next** to continue.

7. On the next wizard screen, Access gives you the option of viewing the data by a particular category of information. The wizard provides this option only when you build a report from multiple tables. For example, if you have a report that includes fields from a Customer table, a Products table, and an Orders table, the information in the report can be organized either by customer, product, or order information (see Figure 17.3). Select the viewpoint for the data from the list on the left of the wizard screen; then select **Next** to continue.

8. On the next wizard screen, you can further group records in the report by a particular field. To group by a field, click the field and then click the **>** button. You can select several grouping levels in the order you want them. Then click **Next** to move on.

Figure 17.3 Data in the report can be arranged from a particular viewpoint based on the tables used to create the report.

 TIP **Grouping?** By default, the field data in the report are not grouped. By selecting different group levels, you can group information by department, product, or any field that you select. Grouping the data enables you to create a report that has been divided into logical subsections.

9. The wizard asks whether you would like to sort the records in the report (see Figure 17.4). If you want to sort the records by a particular field or fields (you can sort by more than one field, such as by last name and then first name), open the top drop-down list and select a field by which to sort. From the drop-down lists, select up to four fields to sort by, and then click **Next**.

Figure 17.4 Set the sort order for your records.

10. On the next wizard screen, choose a layout option from the Layout section. When you click an option button for a particular layout, the sample in the box changes to show your selection.

TIP **Where Are All the Layouts?** If you don't choose any groupings in your report, you are limited to three layout choices: Columnar, Tabular, and Justified. More layouts are available when you have set grouping options for the report.

11. In the next wizard dialog box, choose a report style. Several are listed; click one to see a sample of it, and then click **Next** when you're satisfied with your choice.

12. On the last wizard screen, you're asked for a report title. Enter one into the Report text box, and click **Finish** to see your report in Print Preview.

Viewing and Printing Reports in Print Preview

When you create a report with either AutoReport or the Report Wizard, the report appears in Print Preview (as shown in Figure 17.5). From there, you can print the report if you're happy with it or go to Report Design view to make changes. (You'll learn more about the Report Design view in Lesson 18, "Customizing a Report.")

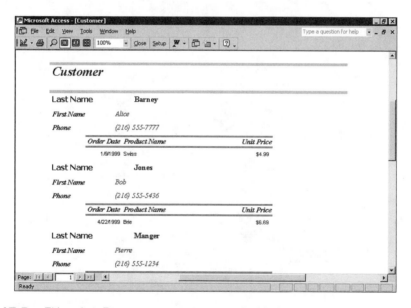

Figure 17.5 Either AutoReports or reports created with the wizard automatically open in Print Preview.

In the Print Preview mode, you can zoom in and out on the report using the **Zoom** tool (click once to zoom in and click again to zoom out). Using the appropriate button on the Print Preview toolbar, you can also display the report as one page, two pages, or multiple pages.

If you want to print the report and specify any print options (such as the number of copies), choose **File, Print**. If you want a quick hard copy, click the toolbar's **Print** button.

If you click the **Close** (**X**) button on the Print Preview toolbar, you are taken directly to the Report Design view. You learn about the Report Design view in the next lesson.

Customizing a Report

In this lesson, you learn how to use Report Design view to make your reports more attractive.

Entering Report Design View

You've already seen that you can create reports using AutoReport and the Report Wizard. After you've created a report using either of these methods, you can edit or enhance the report in the Report Design view. You can also create Reports from scratch in the Report Design view.

The Report Design view is similar to the Form Design view that you worked with in Access Lesson 11, "Modifying a Form," and Lesson 12, "Adding Special Controls to Forms." Like forms, reports are made up of controls that are bound to fields in a table or tables in the database.

To edit an existing report in the Design view, follow these steps:

1. Click the **Reports** icon in the database window.
2. In the list of reports provided, select the report you want to modify.
3. Click the **Design** button on the database toolbar. The report appears in Design view, as shown in Figure 18.1.

As you can see in Figure 18.1, the report's underlying structure contains several areas. The Detail area contains the actual controls that relate to the table fields included in the report. Above the Detail area is the Page Header, which contains the labels that are associated with the controls in the Detail area. At the very top of the report is the Report Header. It contains a text box that displays the name of the report.

At the bottom of the report are two footers. The Page Footer contains formulas that display the current date and print the page number of the report. At the very bottom of the report is the Report Footer. The Report Footer is blank in Figure 18.1. It can be used, however, to insert a summary formula or other calculation that works with the data that appears in the Detail area (you will add a calculation to a report later in the lesson).

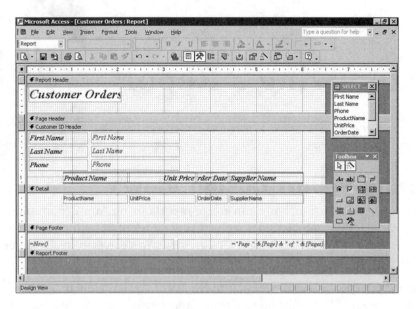

Figure 18.1 The report is divided into several areas in the Design view.

As already mentioned, the Report Design view is similar to Form Design view. The Report Design view also supplies the Toolbox, which is used to add text boxes and special controls to the report. The Field list allows you to add field controls to the report.

Using Special Controls on a Report Access enables you to place any type of control on a report, even command buttons or combo boxes. These won't do you much good on a report, however. It's better to stick to text boxes, labels, and graphics on reports—items that enhance the overall look of the report when it is printed.

CAUTION

Working with Controls on Your Report

Working with report controls in Report Design view is the same as working with controls in Form Design view. You might want to turn back to Lesson 11 to review how you manipulate controls and their labels. The following is a brief review:

- **Selecting Controls**—Click the control to select it. Selection handles appear around the control.
- **Moving Objects**—To move a control, first select it. Next, position the mouse pointer over a border so that the pointer turns into an open hand. Then, click and drag the control to a new location.

TIP   **Moving Between Report Areas**   You can't drag a control from one section of the report to another, but if you do need to move it, you can use cut and paste. Select the control (or label) and press **Ctrl+X** to cut it. Then, click the title of the section where you want to move it and press **Ctrl+V** to paste it into the newly selected section.

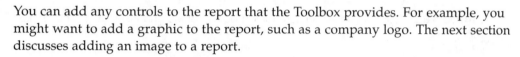

- **Resizing Objects**—First, select the object. Then, position the mouse pointer over a selection handle and drag it to resize the object.

- **Formatting Text Objects**—Use the **Font** and **Font Size** drop-down lists on the toolbar to choose fonts; then use the **Bold**, **Italic**, and **Underline** toolbar buttons to set special attributes.

You can add any controls to the report that the Toolbox provides. For example, you might want to add a graphic to the report, such as a company logo. The next section discusses adding an image to a report.

Adding an Image to a Report

You can add graphics, clip art, or even images from a digital camera to your Access reports. For example, if you want to add a company logo to a report, all you need is access to the logo image file on your computer (or a company's network). If you want to include an image, such as a company logo, on the very first page of the report, you will want to add it to the Report Header. Any information or graphics placed in the Report Header will appear at the very top of the report. Images that you want to use to illustrate information in the report should go in the Details area.

To add an image to a report, follow these steps:

1. Expand the area of the report (such as the Report Header) in which you want to place the image. For example, to expand the Report Header, drag the Page Header's title bar downward using the mouse (the mouse becomes a sizing tool when you place it on an area's border).

2. Click the **Image** button on the Toolbox. The mouse pointer becomes an image drawing tool.

3. Drag to create a box or rectangle that will contain the image in the appropriate area of the report. When you release the mouse, the Insert Picture dialog box appears (see Figure 18.2).

4. Use the Look In drop-down list to locate the drive that contains the image file, and then open the appropriate folder by double-clicking.

Figure 18.2 Use the Insert Picture dialog box to locate and insert your picture into the report.

5. When you locate your image, click the filename to select it, and then click **OK**. The image is inserted into the report.

You might find that the image file is larger than the image control that you have created. To make the image fit into the control, right-click the Image control and select **Properties** from the shortcut menu that appears. In the Properties dialog box, select the **Format** tab. Then, click in the Size Mode box and select **Zoom** from the drop-down list. This automatically sizes the graphic to fit into the control (which means that it typically shrinks the image to fit into the control). You can then close the Properties box.

 TIP **Check Your Report Design in Print Preview**   As you work on the structure of your report in the Design view, you can check to see how things will look by switching to the Print Preview mode. Click the **Print Preview** button on the Report Design toolbar.

Arranging and Removing Controls

As already mentioned, you can move or resize the controls on the report. This also goes for any new controls that you add from the Toolbox or by using the Field list. You can also remove unwanted controls from the report.

To delete a control, select it by clicking it, and then press **Delete**. Deleting a control from the report doesn't delete the field from the associated table.

Adding Text Labels

You can also add descriptive labels to your report. For example, you might want to add a text box containing descriptive text to the Report Header.

 Click the **Label** button on the Toolbox. The mouse pointer becomes a label drawing tool. Drag with the mouse to create a text box in any of the areas on the report. When you release the mouse, you can begin typing the text that will be contained in the text label.

Placing a Calculation in the Report

Controls (also called text boxes in a report) most commonly display data from fields, as you've seen in the reports that you have created. However, text boxes can also hold calculations based on values in different fields.

Creating a text box is a bit complicated: First, you must create an unbound control/text box (that is, one that's not associated with any particular field), and then you must type the calculation into the text box. Follow these steps:

1. Click the **Text Box** tool in the Toolbox, and then click and drag on the report to create a text box.

2. Change the label to reflect what's going in the text box. For example, if it's sales tax or the total of your orders multiplied by the price of your various products, change the label accordingly. Position the label where you want it.

3. Click in the text box and type the formula that you want calculated. (See the following list for guidance.)

4. Click anywhere outside the text box when you finish.

Figure 18.3 shows a control that provides the total value of the orders for each item. This control multiplies the Quantity control (which is tied to a field that supplies the number of orders for each item) by the UnitPrice control (which provides the price of each item).

The formulas you enter into your calculated text box use standard mathematical symbols:

+	Add
-	Subtract
*	Multiply
/	Divide

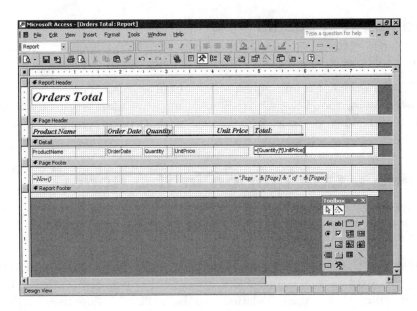

Figure 18.3   You can add controls to the report that do math.

All formulas begin with an equal sign (=), and all field names are in parentheses.
The following are some examples:

- To calculate a total price where a control called Quantity contains the number
  of items and a control called Price holds the price of each item, you would multiply these data in these two controls. The formula would look like this:
  =[Quantity]*[Price].

- To calculate a 25% discount off the value in the field, such as a field called Cost,
  you would type the formula **=[Cost]*.075**.

- To add the total of the values in three fields, enter **[Field1]+[Field2]+[Field3]**
  (where Field# is the name of the field).

 TIP   **More Room**   If you run out of room in the text box when typing your formula, press
Shift+F2 to open a Zoom box, which gives you more room.

Taking Advantage of Database Relationships

In this lesson, you learn how to view related table data and use related tables in forms and reports.

Reviewing Table Relationships

When we first discussed creating a database in the Access section of this book, we made a case for creating tables that held discrete subsets of the data that would make up the database. We then discussed the importance of creating relationships between these tables, as discussed in Lesson 9, "Creating Relationships Between Tables." In this lesson, you take a look at how you can take advantage of related tables when creating other Access objects, such as forms, queries, and reports.

As previously discussed in Lessons 1 and 9, tables are related by a field that is common to each table. The common field serves as the primary key in one of the tables and as the foreign key in the other table. (The foreign key is the same field, but it is held in a table where it does not serve as the primary key.)

For example, in Figure 19.1, an Employees table is linked to two other tables: Expenses and Departments. The Employees table and the Expenses table are related because of the EmployeeID field. The Employees table and the Departments table are related by the DepartmentID field.

The more complex your database, the more tables and table relationships the database contains. For example, Figure 19.2 shows a complex company database that contains several related tables.

More important to the discussion in this lesson is how you take advantage of related tables to create complex forms and reports. First, take a look at how related table data can be viewed in the Table Datasheet view.

Figure 19.1 Related tables share a common field.

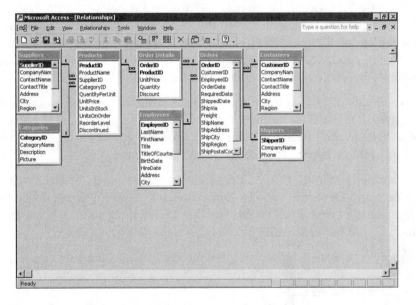

Figure 19.2 Complex databases contain many related tables.

Viewing Related Records in the Datasheet View

When working with a table in the Datasheet view, you can view data held in a related table. The information that can be viewed is contained in any table that is subordinate to the table you currently have open in the Datasheet view. Tables subordinate to a particular table hold the foreign key (which is the primary key in the top-level table in the relationship).

For example, suppose you are viewing the Departments table that was included in the table relationships shown in Figure 19.1. A plus sign appears to the left of each record in the table (see Figure 19.3). To view related data for each record, click the plus sign. A table appears that contains the related data for that record. In this example, the Employees table provides the related data (which, if you look back at Figure 19.1, was related subordinately to the Departments table).

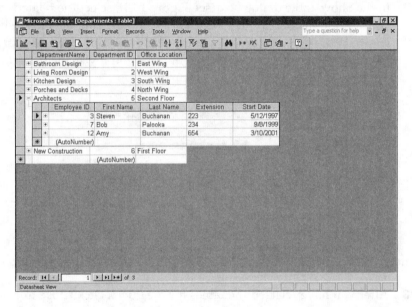

Figure 19.3 Display related records in the linked table by clicking a plus sign next to a record.

When related records are displayed, the plus sign turns into a minus sign. Click that minus sign to hide the related records again.

As you can see in Figure 19.3, even the related records can have linked information. For example, clicking any of the plus signs next to the records containing employee information shows data pulled from the Expenses table (which, again referring to Figure 19.1, is related to the Employees table).

Creating Multi-Table Queries

The real power of relational databases is to use the related tables to create other Access objects, such as queries. Multi-table queries enable you to pull information from several related tables. You can then use this query to create a report or a form.

The easiest way to create a multi-table query is in the Query Design view. Follow these steps:

1. From the database window (with the Query icon selected), double-click **Create Query in Design View**. The Show Table dialog box appears.

2. In the Show Table dialog box (see Figure 19.4), select the related tables that you want to include in the query. For example, using the tables shown in Figure 19.4, you could create a query using the Employees, Departments, and Expenses tables that would show you each employee, the department, and any expenses that the employee has incurred.

Figure 19.4   Select the tables that will be used to create the multi-table query.

3. After you have selected the tables for the query, click **Close** to close the Show Table dialog box. The tables and their relationships appear at the top of the Query Design window.

4. Add the fields to the Query grid that make up the query. The fields can come from any of the tables that you have included in the query. Figure 19.5 shows a multi-table query that includes fields from the Employees, Departments, and Expenses tables.

5. When you have finished designing the multi-table query, you can run it. Click the **Run** button on the toolbar.

The query results appear in the Datasheet view. Combining data from related tables into one query allows you to create other objects from that query, such as forms or reports.

Figure 19.5   Multi-table queries enable you to pull data from fields on more than one table.

Creating Multi-Table Forms

Forms can be created from more than one table using the Form Wizard or the Form Design view. Creating a form from fields that reside in more than one table allows you to enter data into more than one table using just the single form.

A very simple way to create a multi-table form is to add a *subform* to an existing form. For example, you might have a form that is based on a Customers table. If you would also like to be able to view and enter order information when you work with the Customers form, you can add an Orders subform to it. It is important that the tables used to create the two forms (the main form and the subform) are related tables.

Subform   A form control that actually consists of an entire form based on another table or tables.

The easiest way to create a subform is to actually drag an existing form onto another form in the Design view. The following steps describe how you do it:

1. Use the AutoForm feature, the Form Wizard, or the Form Design view to create two forms: the form that serves as the main form and the form that serves as the subform. These forms should be based on tables that are related.

2. In the Form Design view, open the form that will serve as the main form.

3. Size the Form Design window so that you can also see the database window in the Access workspace (see Figure 19.6).

Figure 19.6   The subform is dragged from the database window onto the Design view of the main form.

4. In the database window, be sure that the Forms list is showing. Then, drag the form that will serve as the subform onto the main form that is open in the Design view. When the mouse pointer enters the Design view, it becomes a control pointer. Release the mouse button when you are in the general area where you want to place the subform. The subform control appears on the main form.

5. Maximize the Form Design window. Reposition or size the subform in the Design view until you are happy with its location (see Figure 19.7).

6. Save the changes that you have made to the main form (specifically, the addition of the subform).

7. To change to the Form view to view or add data to the composite form, click the **View** button on the Form Design toolbar.

Figure 19.8 shows the main form and the subform in the Form view. The form can be used to view or enter data into two tables at once.

Figure 19.7 The subform becomes another control on the main form.

Figure 19.8 The composite form can be used to view and enter data into more than one table.

Creating Multi-Table Reports

You can also create reports that include information from more than one table or query. The process is the same as the procedure that you used in Lesson 17, "Creating a Simple Report," when you used the Report Wizard to create a report. All you have to do is select fields from related tables during the report creation process. This allows the report to pull information from the related tables.

An alternative to creating reports that contain fields from more than one table is to create a report that contains a *subreport*. The procedure is similar to the procedure discussed in the previous section, when you created a main form that held a sub-form.

 TERM   **Subreport**   A report control that consists of an entire report based on another table or tables.

To create a report that contains a subreport, follow these steps:

1. Use the AutoReport feature, the Report Wizard, or the Report Design view to create two reports: the report that serves as the main report and the report that serves as the subreport. These reports should be based on tables that are related.

2. In the Report Design view, open the report that will serve as the main report. Size the area in which you will place the subreport. For example, you might want to place the subreport in the Report Header area so that it can be viewed on any page of the printed report.

3. Size the Report Design window so that you can also see the database window in the Access workspace.

4. In the database window, be sure that the Reports list is showing. Then, drag the report that will serve as the subreport onto the main report in the Design view window. Don't release the mouse until you have positioned the mouse pointer in the area (such as the Report Header) where you want to place the subreport.

5. Size or move the subreport control as needed and then save any changes that you have made to the main report.

When you view the composite report in the Print Preview mode, the subreport appears as part of the main report. Figure 19.9 shows the composite report in the Print Preview mode. Placing subreports on a main report enables you to include summary data that can be referenced while data on the main report is viewed either on the screen or on the printed page.

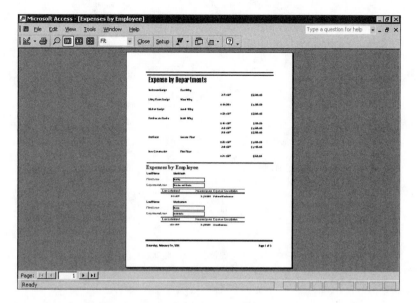

Figure 19.9   Composite reports enable you to report the data in different ways on the same report.

Printing Access Objects

In this lesson, you learn how to print Access tables, forms, queries, and reports.

Access Objects and the Printed Page

You have probably gotten a feel for the fact that tables, forms, and queries are used mainly to view and manipulate database information on your computer's screen, whereas the report is designed to be printed. This doesn't mean that you can't print a table or a form; it's just that the report provides the greatest amount of control in placing information on the printed page.

First, this lesson discusses printing Access objects with the report. Then, you look at printing some of the other Access objects, such as a table or form.

Printing Reports

As you learned earlier in this section of the book, the Access report is the ideal format for presenting database information on the printed page. Using reports, you can add page numbering controls and other header or footer information that repeat on each page of the report.

Whether you create a report using AutoReport or the Report Wizard, the completed report appears in the Print Preview mode, as shown in Figure 20.1.

You can immediately send the report to the default printer by clicking the **Print** button on the Print Preview toolbar. If you find that you would like to change the margins on the report or change how the report is oriented on the page, click the **Setup** button on the Print Preview toolbar. The Page Setup dialog box appears (see Figure 20.2).

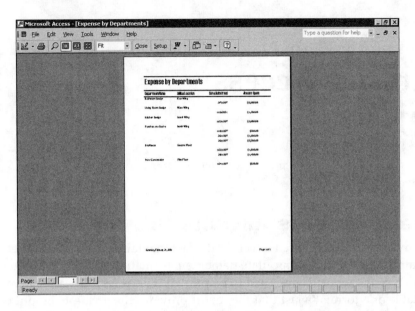

Figure 20.1 Reports created using AutoReport or the Report Wizard open in the Print Preview mode.

Figure 20.2 The Page Setup dialog box enables you to control the margins and page orientation of the printed report.

Three tabs are on the Page Setup dialog box:

- **Margins**—This tab enables you to set the top, bottom, left, and right margins. To change one of the default settings (1 inch), type the new setting in the appropriate margin box.

- **Page**—This tab enables you to change the orientation of the report on the printed page. Portrait, which is the default setting, orients the report text from top to bottom on a regular 8 1/2-inch by 11-inch page. Landscape turns the page 180 degrees, making it an 11-inch by 8 1/2-inch page. Landscape orientation works well for reports that contain a large number of fields placed from left to right on the report. This tab also enables you to select the type of paper that you are going to use for the printout (such as letter, legal, and so on).

- **Columns**—This tab enables you to change the number of columns in the report and the distance between the columns. Because the columns for the report are determined when you create the report using AutoReport or the Report Wizard, you probably won't want to tamper with the column settings. It's easier to change the distance between field controls in the Report Design view.

 TIP **Use the Report Design View to Make Design Changes**   If you find that the report needs some major structural changes, click the **View** button to go to the Design view.

After you have finished making your choices in the Page Setup dialog box, click **OK** to close the dialog box. You can now print the report.

Printing Other Database Objects

The fastest way to print a database object, such as a table, form, or query, is to select the object in the database window. Just select the appropriate object icon in the database window and select an object in the object list, such as a table.

After the object is selected, click the **Print** button on the database toolbar. Your database object is sent to the printer.

If you would like to preview the printout of a table, form, or query, either select the particular object in the database window or open the particular object and then click the **Print Preview** button. The object is then displayed in the Print Preview mode, such as the table shown in Figure 20.3.

When you print tables, forms, or queries, the name of the object and the current date are placed at the top of the printout. Page numbering is automatically placed at the bottom of the printout. You can control the margins and the page layout (portrait or landscape) for the table printout (or other object) using the Page Setup dialog box (discussed earlier in this lesson).

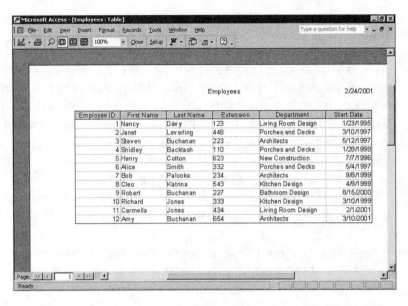

Figure 20.3   Any database object, such as a table, can be viewed in Print Preview.

Using the Print Dialog Box

So far, this discussion of printing in Access has assumed that you want to print to your default printer. You can also print a report or other database object to a different printer and control the range of pages that are printed or the actual records that are printed. These settings are controlled in the Print dialog box.

From the Print Preview mode or with a particular object open in the Access window, select **File**, **Print**. The Print dialog box appears (see Figure 20.4).

Figure 20.4   The Print dialog box enables you to select a different printer or specify a print range.

To select a different printer (one other than the default), click the **Name** drop-down list and select a printer by name. If you want to select a range of pages to print (such as a range of pages in a report), click the **Pages** option button and then type the page range into the page boxes.

In the case of tables and queries, you can also print selected records. Before you open the Print dialog box, select the records in the table or query. Then, when you open the Print dialog box, click the **Selected Record(s)** option button.

When you have finished changing the default printer or specifying a page range or the printing of select records, you are ready to print the object. Click the **OK** button. This closes the Print dialog box and sends the object to the printer.

PowerPoint

Working in PowerPoint

In this lesson, you learn how to start and exit PowerPoint. You also learn about the PowerPoint presentation window.

Starting PowerPoint

PowerPoint is a powerful presentation application that enables you to create presentations that can be viewed on a computer. Using PowerPoint, you can print handouts or create film slides for a presentation. PowerPoint also enables you to add animation and sound to your presentations, which makes it the perfect presentation tool for business presentations or classroom lectures.

To start PowerPoint, follow these steps:

1. Click the **Start** button.
2. Move your mouse pointer to **Programs**. A menu of programs appears.
3. Move your mouse pointer to the **Microsoft PowerPoint** icon and click it. The PowerPoint application window opens, as shown in Figure 1.1.

The first thing you see when you open PowerPoint is that the application window is divided into different areas. The default view for PowerPoint is the Normal view (you learn about the different PowerPoint views in Lesson 3, "Working with Slides in Different Views"). On the left of the screen is a pane that can be used to switch between an Outline and Slides view of the current presentation. In the center of the PowerPoint application window is the Slide pane; this is where you work individually on each slide in the presentation.

Below the Slide pane is the Notes pane, which enables you to add notes to the presentation for each slide. On the far right of the application window is the New Presentation task pane. The task pane provides different commands and features depending on what you are currently doing in PowerPoint.

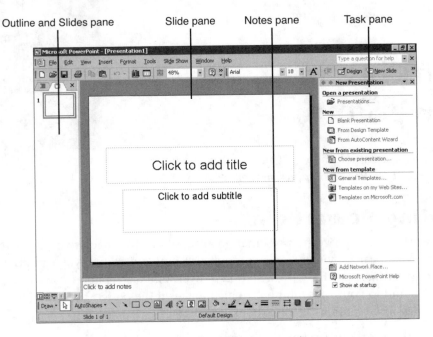

Figure 1.1   The PowerPoint window is divided into several panes.

Getting Comfortable with the PowerPoint Window

Although PowerPoint looks a little different from the other Office applications, such as Word and Excel, all the standard Office application components, such as the menu bar and various toolbars, are available to you as you design your presentations. The basic element of a presentation is a slide, to which you add text and other objects, such as images, using the Slide pane (which is discussed in the next lesson). PowerPoint provides several slide layouts; each layout provides the necessary text boxes or clip-art boxes for creating a particular type of slide.

Adding text to a slide is very straightforward. Each slide that you add to a presentation (Lesson 5, "Inserting, Deleting, and Copying Slides," discusses inserting slides into a presentation) contains placeholder text that tells you what to type into a particular text box on the slide. For example, Figure 1.2 shows a title slide. Note that the top text box on the slide says Click to Add Title.

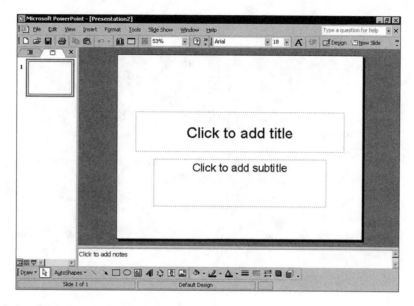

Figure 1.2   Click the placeholder text to input text into a slide.

To replace the placeholder text with your own text, just click the placeholder text. Then, you can type your entry into that text box.

Because a presentation consists of several slides, PowerPoint provides a thumbnail view of each slide in the presentation to the left of the Slides pane. Figure 1.3 shows an example of a complete presentation with a series of these thumbnail slides. This view can be used to keep track of your slides as you add them to the presentation and can even be used to rearrange slides in the presentation.

Because presentations require a certain logical arrangement of information, you can view the slides in the presentation as an outline. This enables you to make sure that you have the facts presented by each slide in the proper order for the presentation. The Outline pane also enables you to move topics within the presentation and even move information from slide to slide. Figure 1.4 shows the Outline pane for a presentation that contains several slides.

You learn about using the Slides and Outline pane in Lesson 3, "Working with Slides in Different Views."

Lesson 3 shows you how you can edit the presentation's text in either the Outline or the Slide pane. Changes in one pane are reflected in the other pane. When you want to place a nontext object on a slide (such as a graphic), you do so in the Slide pane.

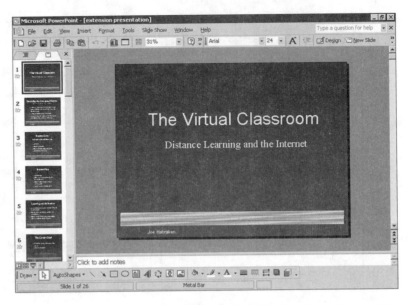

Figure 1.3   The Slides pane enables you to view thumbnails of the slides in the presentation.

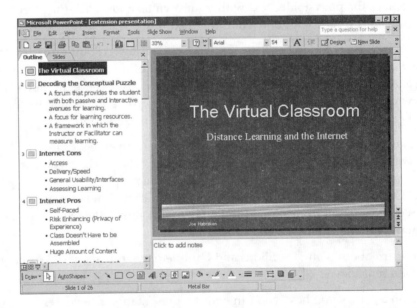

Figure 1.4   The Outline pane enables you to view the topic of each slide and each piece of text information included in a slide.

Exiting PowerPoint

When you finish using PowerPoint, you can exit the application. This closes any open presentations (PowerPoint might prompt you to save changes to those presentations).

To exit PowerPoint, perform one of the following:

- Click the PowerPoint window's **Close (x)** button.
- Double-click the **Control Menu** icon in the left corner of the title bar, or click it once to open the **Control** menu and then select **Close**.
- Open the **File** menu and select **Exit**.
- Press **Alt+F4**.

Creating a New Presentation

2

In this lesson, you learn several ways to create a presentation. You also learn how to save, close, and open an existing presentation.

Three Choices for Starting a New Presentation

PowerPoint offers several ways to create a new presentation. Before you begin, decide which method is right for you:

- The AutoContent Wizard offers the highest degree of help. It walks you through each step of creating the new presentation. When you're finished, you have a standardized group of slides, all with a similar look and feel, for a particular situation. Each slide created includes dummy text that you can replace with your own text.

- A design template provides a professionally designed color, background, and font scheme that applies to the slides you create yourself. It does not provide sample slides.

- You can start from scratch and create a totally blank presentation. The means that you build the presentation from the ground up and create each slide in the presentation (beginners might want to use the wizard or templates until they get a feel for the overall design approach used to create a cohesive slide presentation).

 Design Template A design template is a preformatted presentation file (without any slides in it). When you select a template, PowerPoint applies the color scheme and general layout of the template to each slide you create for the presentation.

Creating a New Presentation with the AutoContent Wizard

With the AutoContent Wizard, you select the type of presentation you want to create (such as corporate, sales, or various projects), and PowerPoint creates an outline for the presentation.

The following steps describe how you use the AutoContent Wizard:

1. Select the **File** menu and select **New**. The New Presentation task pane appears on the right of the PowerPoint window, as shown in Figure 2.1 (if the Presentation task pane was already open in the window, you can skip to step 2).

Figure 2.1   Start the AutoContent Wizard from the task pane.

2. Click the **From AutoContent Wizard** link on the task pane.

3. The AutoContent Wizard starts. The opening wizard screen summarizes the process you should follow to create a new presentation. Click **Next** to continue.

4. The wizard provides you with category buttons for different categories of presentations: General, Corporate, Projects, Sales/Marketing, and Carnegie Coach. Select a category by selecting the appropriate button (see Figure 2.2). To see all the presentations available, click the **All** button.

Figure 2.2   Select a category button to view a list of presentation types.

TIP **What Is the Carnegie Coach?** The Carnegie Coach provides presentations that can be used to sell your ideas or motivate a team; they are named after Dale Carnegie, the motivational speaker and author.

5. After selecting a particular category of presentations, select a presentation type in the list provided and then click **Next** to continue.

6. On the next screen, you select how you will give the presentation. Select one of the following options:

- **Onscreen Presentation**—Choose this if you plan to use a computer and your PowerPoint file to present the show.

- **Web Presentation**—Choose this if you are planning to distribute the presentation as a self-running or user-interactive show.

- **Black-and-White Overheads**—Choose this if you plan to make black-and-white transparencies for your show.

- **Color Overheads**—Choose this if you plan to make color transparencies for your show.

- **35mm Slides**—Choose this if you plan to send your PowerPoint presentation to a service bureau to have 35mm slides made. (You probably don't have such expensive and specialized equipment in your own company.)

7. After selecting how you will give the presentation, click **Next** to continue.

8. On the next screen, type the presentation title into the text box provided (see Figure 2.3). If you want to add a footer (such as your name or other) that will appear at the bottom of each slide of the presentation, click in the Footer box and type the appropriate text. If you do not want a date and/or slide number on each slide, deselect the **Date Last Updated** and/or **Slide Number** check boxes.

Figure 2.3 Provide a title for the presentation.

9. After supplying the presentation title and any optional information, click **Next** to continue.

10. PowerPoint takes you to the last wizard screen, where you should simply click **Finish**.

The title slide of your new presentation appears in the Slide pane. The entire presentation, including the dummy text placed on each slide, appears in the Outline pane on the left of the PowerPoint window (see Figure 2.4).

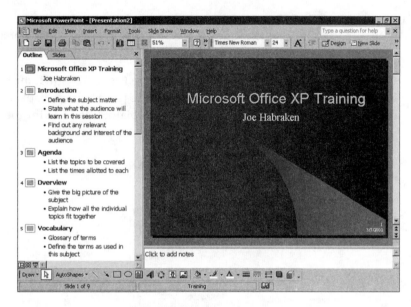

Figure 2.4   Your new presentation appears in the PowerPoint window.

You can start working on your presentation right away by replacing the dummy text on the slides with your own text. Just select the existing text in a text box and type right over it. You learn about editing text in slide text boxes in Lesson 7, "Adding and Modifying Slide Text."

Creating a New Presentation with a Design Template

A template is the middle ground between maximum hand-holding (the AutoContent Wizard) and no help at all (Blank Presentation). Two kinds of templates are available: presentation templates and design templates.

When you use the AutoContent Wizard, you use a presentation template. It contains not only formatting, but also sample slides that contain placeholder text. The other kind of template is a design template. It contains the overall formatting for the slides of the presentation but does not actually create any slides. If you want to use a presentation template, use the AutoContent Wizard, as explained in the preceding section.

To start a new presentation using a design template, follow these steps:

1. Select the **File** menu and select **New**. The New Presentation task pane appears on the right of the PowerPoint window.

 TIP **Select Your Task Pane** If the task pane is already open for another PowerPoint feature, click the drop-down arrow on its title bar and select **New Presentation** from the list that appears.

2. On the New Presentation task pane, click the **From Design Template** link. PowerPoint switches to the Slide Design side pane, which displays a list of design templates, as shown in Figure 2.5. A blank title slide for the presentation appears in the Slide pane.

Figure 2.5 Design templates are listed in the task pane.

3. Click a template from the Available for Use section of the task pane. PowerPoint then formats the title slide in the Slide pane using the selected template.

You can select different templates to determine the best look for your presentation. When you have found the design template that you want to use, you can immediately start working on the slides for the presentation.

> **TIP**   **The Next Step?**   Add more slides by clicking the **New Slide** button on the toolbar. Inserting slides into a presentation is covered in Lesson 5, "Inserting, Deleting, and Copying Slides."

Creating a Blank Presentation

Your third option for creating a new presentation is to create a blank presentation. This means that you have to create all the slides from scratch. A design for the slides can then be selected using the Slide Design task pane. You open this task pane by selecting **Format**, **Slide Design**. In the Slide Design task pane, be sure that the **Design Templates** icon is selected.

Creating a new, blank presentation takes only a click: Click the **New** button on the Standard toolbar or click the **Blank Presentation** link on the New Presentation task pane. The new presentation appears in the PowerPoint window. A blank title slide is ready for you to edit.

Saving a Presentation

After you create a new presentation, it makes sense to save it. To save a presentation for the first time, follow these steps:

1. Select **File**, **Save**, or just click the **Save** button on the Standard toolbar. The Save As dialog box appears (see Figure 2.6).

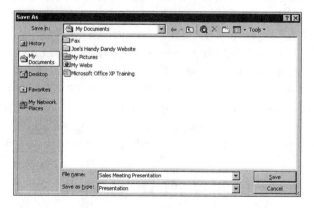

Figure 2.6   Type a name for your presentation into the Save As dialog box.

2. In the **File Name** text box, type the name you want to assign to the presentation. Your filenames can be as long as 255 characters and can include spaces.

3. The Save In box shows in which folder the file will be saved. The default is My Documents. To select a different drive location for the file, click the Save In drop-down arrow and select one from the list that appears. To save to a specific folder in the drive location you've selected, double-click the folder in which you want to store the file.

4. Click **Save**.

 Now that you have named the file and saved it to a disk, you can save any changes you make simply by pressing **Ctrl+S** or clicking the **Save** button on the Standard toolbar. Your data is saved under the filename you assigned the presentation in the Save As dialog box.

To create a copy of a presentation under a different filename or location, select **File**, **Save As**. The Save As dialog box reappears; follow steps 2 to 4 as discussed in this section to give the file a new name or location.

Closing a Presentation

You can close a presentation at any time. Note that although this closes the presentation window, it does not exit PowerPoint as with the methods discussed in Lesson 1. To close a presentation, follow these steps:

1. If more than one presentation is open, click a presentation's button on the Windows taskbar to make it the active presentation, or you can select the **Window** menu and select the presentation from the list provided.

2. Select **File** and then select **Close,** or click the presentation's **Close (x)** button. (It's the lower of the two Close buttons; the upper one is for the PowerPoint window.) If you haven't saved the presentation or if you haven't saved since you last made changes, a dialog box appears, asking whether you want to save.

3. To save your changes, click **Yes**. If this is a new presentation that has never been saved, refer to the steps in the preceding section for saving a presentation. If you have saved the file previously, the presentation window closes.

Opening a Presentation

Because a presentation, like Rome, is not built in a day, you will probably fine-tune a presentation over time. To open a saved presentation file that you want to work on, follow these steps:

1. Select **File, Open**, or click the **Open** button on the Standard toolbar. The Open dialog box appears (see Figure 2.7).

Figure 2.7   Select the presentation you want to open.

2. If the file isn't in the currently displayed folder, select the **Look In** drop-down arrow to choose from a list of other drives and/or folders.

3. Browse to the location containing the file and double-click it to open it in PowerPoint.

Finding a Presentation File

If you're having trouble locating your file, PowerPoint can help you look. Follow these steps to find a file:

1. Select the **File** menu and then select **Open** (if the Open dialog box is not already open).

2. Click the **Tools** drop-down button in the Open dialog box and select **Search**. The Find dialog box appears (see Figure 2.8).

3. In the **Search Text** box, type text that is contained in the presentation's file-name. Use the Search In box to specify where you want the search to be conducted. In the Results Should Be box, specify the file types you want to be included in the search.

4. When you are ready to conduct the search, click the **Search** button.

5. Files that meet the search criteria are listed in the Results box (if you see your file in the Results box and the search is continuing, click the **Stop** button).

6. To open a file in the Results box, double-click the filename.

7. You are returned to the Open dialog box with the file listed in the File Name box. Click **OK** to open the file. A PowerPoint presentation then opens in the PowerPoint window.

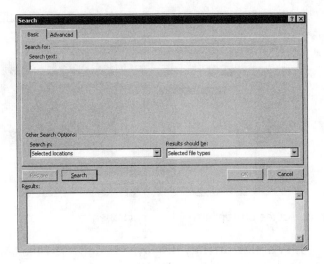

Figure 2.8   Use the Search dialog box to find a presentation on your computer.

Working with Slides in Different Views

In this lesson, you learn how to display a presentation in different views and how to edit slides in the Outline and Slide views.

Understanding PowerPoint's Different Views

PowerPoint can display your presentation in different views. Each of these views is designed for you to perform certain tasks as you create and edit a presentation. For example, Normal view has the Outline/Slides, Slide, and Notes panes; it provides an ideal environment for creating your presentation slides and to quickly view the organization of the slides or the information in the presentation (using the Outline or the Slides tabs). Another view, the Slide Sorter view, enables you to quickly rearrange the slides in the presentation (and is similar to the Slides view that shares the pane with the Outline tab when you are in the Normal view).

To change views, open the **View** menu and choose the desired view: **Normal**, **Slide Sorter**, **Slide Show**, or **Notes Page**.

- **Normal**—The default, three-pane view (which is discussed in Lesson 1, "Working in PowerPoint").

- **Slide Sorter**—This view shows all the slides as thumbnails so that you can easily rearrange them by dragging slides to new positions in the presentation (Figure 3.1 shows the Slide Sorter).

- **Slide Show**—A specialized view that enables you to preview and present your show onscreen. It enables you to test the presentation as you add slides, and it is used later when your presentation is complete.

- **Notes Page**—This view provides a large pane for creating notes for your speech. You can also type these notes in Normal view, but Notes Page view gives you more room and allows you to concentrate on your note text.

Figure 3.1 The Slide Sorter view is used to rearrange the slides in a presentation.

An even faster way to switch to certain views is to use the view buttons that are provided along the lower-left corner of the PowerPoint window. These buttons, from left to right, are Normal View, Slide Sorter View, and Slide Show (from current slide) button. A button is not provided for the Notes view.

Moving from Slide to Slide

PowerPoint provides several ways to move from slide to slide in the presentation. The particular view you are in somewhat controls the procedure for moving to a specific slide.

In the Normal view, you can move from slide to slide using these techniques:

- Click the **Outline** tab on the far left of the window. To go to a particular slide in the outline, click the slide icon next to the slide number (see Figure 3.2). The slide opens in the Slide pane.

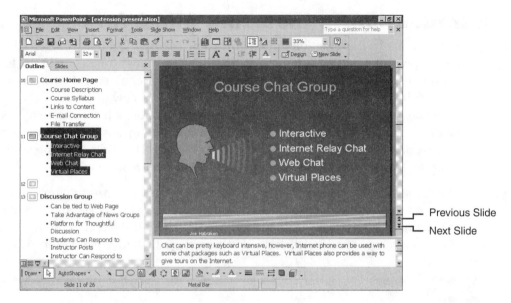

Figure 3.2 The Outline view can be used to quickly move to a particular slide.

- Press the **Page Up** or **Page Down** keys to move to the previous or next slide, respectively.

- Click the **Previous Slide** or **Next Slide** button just below the vertical scrollbar (refer to Figure 3.2), or drag the scroll box inside the vertical scrollbar until the desired slide number is displayed.

- Click the **Slides** tab on the far left of the PowerPoint window. This enables you to move from slide to slide in the Normal view by selecting a particular slide's thumbnail. When you click the thumbnail, the slide appears in the Slide pane.

You can also move from slide to slide in other views, such as the Slide Sorter view or the Slide Show view. In the Slide Sorter view (refer to Figure 3.1), just click a slide's thumbnail to move to that slide. You then can use any of the tools that PowerPoint provides to format the selected slide (or delete it). If you want to actually open a slide when you are working in the Slide Sorter view, so that you can edit the text it contains, double-click the slide. You are returned to the Normal view.

When you are actually showing a presentation in the Slide Show view, you can use the **Page Up** or **Page Down** keys to move from slide to slide (unless you have set up timers to change slides). You can also click a slide with the mouse to move to the next slide. You learn more about the Slide Show view in Lesson 12, "Presenting an Onscreen Slide Show."

Introduction to Inserting Slide Text

If you created a presentation in Lesson 2 using the AutoContent Wizard, you already have a presentation that contains several slides, but they won't contain the text you want to use. Slides created by the wizard contain placeholder text that you must replace. If you created a blank presentation or based a new presentation on a design template, you have only a title slide in that presentation, which, of course, needs to be personalized for your particular presentation. This means that additional slides will need to be added to the presentation. Lesson 5, "Inserting, Deleting, and Copying Slides," covers the creation of new slides for a presentation.

The sections that follow in this lesson look at the basics of inserting text into the text boxes provided on slides. You will look at adding new text boxes and formatting text in text boxes in Lesson 7, "Adding and Modifying Slide Text." Upcoming lessons also discuss how to add pictures and other objects to your PowerPoint slides.

Object   An object is any item on a slide, including text, graphics, and charts.

Editing Text in the Slide Pane

The text on your slides resides within boxes (all objects appear on a slide in their own boxes for easy manipulation). As shown in Figure 3.3, to edit text on a slide, click the text box to select it and then click where you want the insertion point moved, or select the text you want to replace.

When you work with the Slide pane, you might want to close the Outline/Slides pane. Just click the pane's **Close** button (**X**) to provide the Slide pane with the entire PowerPoint window (refer to Figure 3.3). In Lesson 7, "Adding and Modifying Slide Text," you'll learn more about adding text to a slide, including creating your own text boxes on a slide.

TIP   **Opening the Outline Pane**   If you close the Outline pane to concentrate on the Slide pane, click **View**, **Normal (Restore Panes)** to restore it to the application window.

Editing Text in the Outline Pane

The Outline pane provides another way to edit text in a slide. To switch to the Outline view on the Outline/Slides pane, click the **Outline** tab. You simply click to move the insertion point where you want it (or select the range of text you want to replace) in the outline, and then type your text (see Figure 3.4). If you've placed the insertion point in the slide text (without selecting a range), press the **Del** key to delete characters to the right of the insertion point or press the **Backspace** key to delete characters to the left. If you've selected a range of text, either of these keys deletes the text. If you want to move the highlighted text, simply drag it to where you want it moved.

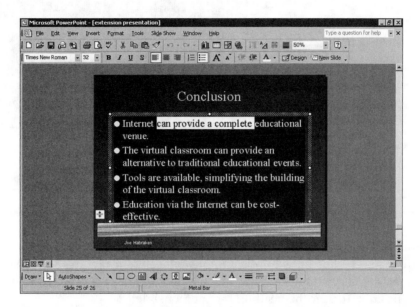

Figure 3.3   You can edit your text directly on the slide in the Slide pane.

TIP   **Larger Outline**   You might want to enlarge the Outline pane by dragging its divider to the right in the Normal view.

TIP   **Auto Word Select**   When you select text, PowerPoint selects whole words. If you want to select individual characters, open the **Tools** menu, select **Options**, click the **Edit** tab, and click the **When Selecting, Automatically Select Entire Word** check box to turn it off. Click **OK**.

Moving Text in the Outline Pane

As you work in the Normal view, you can also view your presentation slides as an outline using the Outline pane. This provides you with a quick way to move text items around on a slide or move them from slide to slide. Just select the text and drag it to a new position.

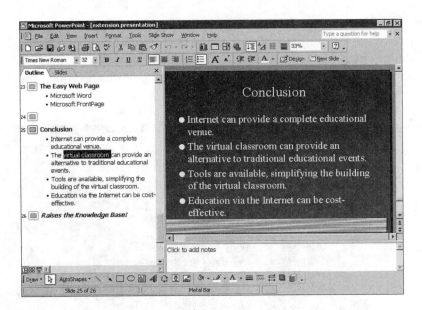

Figure 3.4   You can edit your text in Outline view.

As already mentioned, you can also drag text from one slide to another. All you have to do is select a line of text in the Outline pane and drag it to another slide. You can also move a slide in the Outline pane. Drag the slide's icon in the Outline pane to a new position (under the heading for another slide).

If you aren't that confident with your dragging skills, PowerPoint provides you with help in the form of the Outlining toolbar. It provides buttons that make it easy to move text up or down on a slide (with respect to other text on the slide) or to move a slide up or down in the presentation.

To turn on the Outlining toolbar, right-click one of the PowerPoint toolbars and select **Outlining**. Figure 3.5 shows the Outlining toolbar on the left side of the Outline pane (the Outline pane has also been expanded to take up more of the PowerPoint window).

- To move a paragraph or text line up in a slide, select it and click the **Move Up** button.
- To move a paragraph or text down in a slide, select it and click the **Move Down** button.

You can also use the **Move Up** and **Move Down** buttons to move entire slides up or down in the presentation. Click the slide's icon and then use the appropriate button (it might take several clicks to move a slide up or down with respect to another slide).

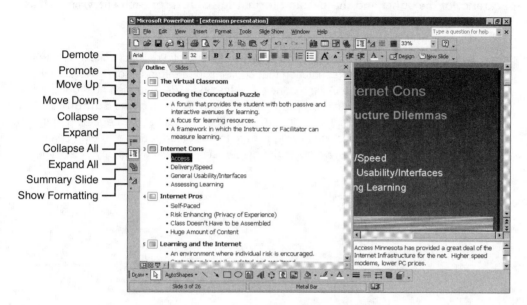

Figure 3.5   You can use the Outlining toolbar to move text and slides in the presentation.

If you want to see how the text is actually formatted on the slides that you are viewing in the Outline pane, click the **Show Formatting** button on the Outlining toolbar. Viewing the text as it is formatted can help you determine where the text should appear on a slide as you move the text (or whether you will have to reformat the text later).

Rearranging Text in the Outline Pane

As you can see from Figure 3.5, your presentation is organized in a multilevel outline format. The slides are at the top level of the outline, and each slide's contents are subordinate under that slide. Some slides have multiple levels of subordination (for example, a bulleted list within a bulleted list).

You can easily change an object's level in Outline view with the Tab key or the Outlining toolbar:

- To demote a paragraph in the outline, click the text, and then press the **Tab** key or click the **Demote** button on the Outlining toolbar.
- To promote a paragraph in the outline, click the text, and then press **Shift+Tab** or click the **Promote** button on the Outlining toolbar.

In most cases, subordinate items on a slide appear as items in a bulleted list. In Lesson 8, "Creating Columns, Tables, and Lists," you learn how to change the appearance of the bullet and the size and formatting of text for each entry, as well as how much the text is indented for each level.

 TIP   **Create Summary Slides in the Outline Pane**   If you would like to create a summary slide for your presentation that contains the headings from several slides, select those slides in the Outline pane (click the first slide, and then hold down the Shift key and click the last slide you want to select). Then, click the **Summary Slide** button on the Outlining toolbar. A new slide appears at the beginning of the selected slides containing the headings from the selected slides. You then can position the Summary slide anywhere in the presentation as you would any other slide.

Changing a Presentation's Look

In this lesson, you learn various ways to give your presentation a professional and consistent look.

Giving Your Slides a Professional Look

PowerPoint comes with dozens of professionally created designs and color schemes that you can apply to your presentations. These designs include background patterns, color choices, font choices, and more. When you apply a design template to your presentation, it applies its formatting to a special slide called the Slide Master.

The Slide Master is not really a slide, but it looks like one. It is a master design grid that you make changes to; these changes affect every slide in the presentation. When you apply a template, you are actually applying the template to the Slide Master, which in turn applies it to each slide in the presentation.

 Master Slide A slide that contains the master layout and color scheme for the slides in a presentation.

You don't have to work with the Slide Master itself when you apply template or color scheme changes to your presentations. Just be aware that you can open the Slide Master (select **View**, point at **Master**, and then select **Slide Master**) and change the style and fonts used by the text boxes in a presentation (see Figure 4.1). You can also select a custom background color for the slides in the presentation. Any changes that you make to the Slide Master affect all the slides in the presentation.

You will probably find that PowerPoint provides enough template and color scheme options that you won't need to format the Slide Master itself very often. Edit its properties only if you have a very strict formatting need for the presentation that isn't covered in the templates and color schemes provided. For example, one good reason to edit the Slide Master would be a situation in which you want a graphic to appear on every slide (such as a company logo); you can place the image on the Slide Master instead of pasting it onto each slide individually.

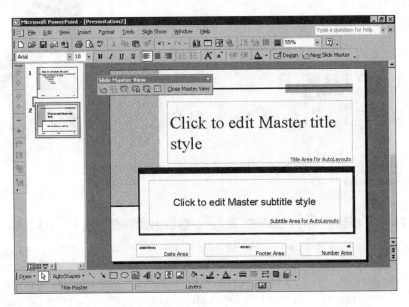

Figure 4.1 The Slide Master holds the default design and color options for the entire presentation.

 TIP **Close the Slide Master** If you open the Slide Master, you can close it by clicking **Close Master View** on the Master View toolbar.

Applying a Different Design Template

You can apply a different template to your presentation at any time, no matter how you originally created the presentation. To change the design template, follow these steps:

1. Select **Format**, **Slide Design** to open the Slide Design task pane. Then, if necessary, click the **Design Templates** icon at the top of the task pane. This provides a listing of PowerPoint's many design templates (see Figure 4.2).

2. Click the template that you want to use in the list. The template is immediately applied to the slide in the Slide pane.

 3. When you have decided on a particular template (you can click on any number of templates to see how they affect your slides), save the presentation (click the **Save** button on the toolbar).

Figure 4.2   Choose a different template from the Design Templates task pane.

CAUTION

The Design Template Changes Custom Formatting   If you spent time bolding text items on a slide or changing font colors, these changes are affected (lost) when you select a new design template. For example, if you have customized bold items in black in your original design template and switch to another template that uses white text, you lose your customizations. You should choose your design template early in the process of creating your presentation. Then, you can do any customized formatting at the end of the process so that it is not affected by a design template change.

When you work with design templates, you can apply them to all the slides in the presentation (as discussed in the steps provided in this section), or you can apply the template to selected slides in the presentation. Follow these steps to apply a template to a selected group of slides in a presentation:

1. Switch to the Slide Sorter view (select **View, Slide Sorter**).
2. Open the Slide Design task pane as outlined in the previous steps.
3. Now you must select the slide (or slides) to which you want to apply the template. Click the first slide you want to select, and then hold down the **Ctrl** key as you click other slides you want to select.
4. Point at the design template you want to use in the Slide Design task pane; a drop-down arrow appears.
5. Click the template's drop-down arrow and select **Apply to Selected Slides** (see Figure 4.3).

Figure 4.3 Design templates can be assigned to selected slides in a presentation.

The template's design is then applied to the selected slides.

TIP **View a Larger Design Sample** To expand the view of the design templates, click the drop-down arrow on the template and select **Show Large Previews**.

Using Color Schemes

Design templates enable you to change the overall design and color scheme applied to the slides in the presentation (or selected slides in the presentation, as discussed in the previous section). If you like the overall design of the slides in the presentation but would like to explore some other color options, you can select a different color scheme for the particular template that you are using.

The number of color schemes available for a particular design template depends on the template itself. Some templates provide only three or four color schemes, whereas other templates provide more. As with design templates, you can assign a new color scheme to all the slides in the presentation or to selected slides.

To change the color scheme for the presentation or selected slides, follow these steps:

1. In the Normal or Slide Sorter view (use the Slide Sorter view if you want to change the color scheme for selected slides), open the task pane by selecting **View**, **Task Pane** (if the task pane is already open, skip to the next step).

2. Select the task pane's drop-down arrow and then select **Slide Design-Color Schemes**. This switches to the Color Schemes section of the Slide Design task pane. The color schemes available for the design template that you are using appear in the Apply a Color Scheme section (see Figure 4.4).

Figure 4.4   You can choose from a list of color schemes for the presentation or selected slides.

3. (Optional) If you are in the Slide Sorter view and want to assign a new color scheme only to selected slides, select those slides (click the first slide and then hold down **Ctrl** and click additional slides).

4. To assign the new color scheme to all the slides in the presentation, click a scheme in the Slide Design task pane. If you are assigning the color scheme only to selected slides, point at the color scheme and click its drop-down arrow. Select **Apply to Selected Slides**.

The new color scheme is applied to the slides in the presentation (or selected slides in the presentation). If you decide you don't like the color scheme, select another scheme from the task pane.

Changing the Background Fill

You can also fine-tune the color scheme that you add to a slide or slides by changing the background fill. This works best in cases where the design template and color scheme that you selected don't provide a background color for the slide or slides. You must be careful, however, because you don't want to pick a background color that obscures the texts and graphics that you place on the slide or slides.

To change the background fill on a slide or slides, follow these steps:

1. Switch to the Slide Sorter view (select **View, Slide Sorter**).

2. (Optional) If you are going to change the background fill for selected slides, select those slides in the Slide Sorter window.

3. Select the **Format** menu and then select **Background**. The Background dialog box appears (see Figure 4.5).

Figure 4.5   Use the Background dialog box to add a fill color to a slide or slides.

4. Click the drop-down arrow at the bottom of the dialog box and choose a fill color from the color palette that appears.

5. To assign the fill color to all the slides in the presentation, click **Apply to All**. To assign the fill color to selected slides (if you selected slides in step 2), click **Apply**.

Inserting, Deleting, and Copying Slides

In this lesson, you learn how to insert new slides, delete slides, and copy slides in a presentation.

Inserting a New Slide

You can insert a slide into a presentation at any time and at any position in the presentation. To insert a new slide, follow these steps:

1. On the Outline or Slides panes, select the slide that appears just before the place where you want to insert the new slide (you can also insert a new slide in the Slide Sorter view, if you want).

2. Choose the **Insert** menu and then **New Slide**, or click the **New Slide** button on the PowerPoint toolbar. A new blank slide appears in the PowerPoint window, along with the Slide Layout task pane (see Figure 5.1).

New Slide button

Figure 5.1   Your new slide appears in the PowerPoint window.

3. In the Slide Layout task pane, select the slide layout that you want to use for the new slide. Several text slide layouts and layouts for slides that contain graphics are provided.

4. Follow the directions indicated on the slide in the Slide pane to add text or other objects. For text boxes, you click an area to select it and then type in your text. For other object placeholders, you double-click the placeholder.

TIP   **Cloning a Slide**   To create an exact replica of an existing slide (in any view), select the slide you want to duplicate. Click **Insert** and then select **Duplicate Slide**. The new slide is inserted after the original slide. You can then choose a different layout for the slide if you want.

Inserting Slides from Another Presentation

If you want to insert some or all of the slides from another presentation into the current presentation, perform these steps:

1. Open the presentation into which you want to insert the slides.

2. Select the slide located before the position where you want to insert the slides.

3. Select the **Insert** menu and select **Slides from Files**. The Slide Finder dialog box appears (see Figure 5.2).

Figure 5.2   Use the Slide Finder dialog box to insert slides from another presentation.

4. Click the **Browse** button to display the Browse dialog box. In the Browse dialog box, locate the presentation that contains the slides that you want to insert into the current presentation (use the **Look In** drop-down arrow to switch drives, if necessary).

5. When you locate the presentation, double-click it.

6. The slides in the presentation appear in the Slide Finder's Select Slides box. To select the slides that you want to insert into the current presentation, click the first slide and then hold down **Ctrl** and click any subsequent slides.

7. When you have selected all the slides you want to insert, click **Insert** (if you want to insert all the slides, click **Insert All**).

8. PowerPoint inserts the slides into the presentation at the point you originally selected. Click **OK** to close the Slide Finder dialog box.

Creating Slides from a Document Outline

If you have created a document in Word that includes outline-style headings and numbered or bulleted lists (see Lesson 8, "Examining Your Documents in Different Views," in the Word section of this book for more information), PowerPoint can pull the headings and the text from the document and create slides. To create slides from a document outline, follow these steps:

1. Choose the **Insert** menu, and then choose **Slides from Outline**. The Insert Outline dialog box appears (it is similar to the Open dialog box used to open a presentation or other file).

2. Use the Insert Outline dialog box to locate the document file you want to use.

3. Double-click the name of the document file.

PowerPoint then uses all the first-level headings to create slides for your presentation. Any text in the document below a first-level outline heading is added to the slide in an additional text box.

Selecting Slides

In the following sections, you learn how to delete, copy, and move slides. However, before you can do anything with a slide, you must select it. To select slides, follow these directions:

- To select a single slide, click it.
- To select two or more contiguous slides in the Outline pane, click the first slide, and then hold down the **Shift** key while you click the last slide in the group.
- To select two or more contiguous slides in the Slides pane or the Slide Sorter view, place the mouse pointer in front of the first slide you want to select (not on it), and drag to select additional slides.

CAUTION

Don't Drag the Slide If you are trying to select multiple, contiguous slides by dragging with the mouse, drag from in front of the first slide. Don't start dragging while pointing directly at the first slide because it will move the slide rather than highlight the remaining slides that you want to select.

- To select multiple noncontiguous slides in Slide Sorter view, click the first slide and hold down the **Ctrl** key while clicking subsequent slides in the group.

Deleting Slides

You can delete a slide from any view. To delete a slide, perform the following steps:

1. Select the slide you want to delete. You can delete multiple slides by selecting more than one slide (on the Outline or Slides pane or in the Slide Sorter view).

2. Choose the **Edit** menu, and then choose **Delete Slide**. The slide is removed from the presentation.

TIP **Use the Delete Key** You can quickly delete slides by selecting the slide or slides and then pressing the **Delete** key on the keyboard.

CAUTION

Oops! If you deleted a slide by mistake, you can get it back. Select **Edit**, **Undo**, or press **Ctrl+Z**. This works only if you do it immediately. You cannot undo the change if you exit PowerPoint and restart the application.

Cutting, Copying, and Pasting Slides

In Lesson 6, "Rearranging Slides in a Presentation," you learn how to rearrange slides using the Slide Sorter and the Outline/Slides pane. Although dragging slides to new positions in the Slide Sorter is probably the easiest way to move slides, you can use the Cut, Copy, and Paste commands to move or copy slides in the presentation. Follow these steps:

1. Change to Slide Sorter view, or display Normal view and work with the Outline or Slides panes.

2. Select the slide(s) you want to copy or cut.

3. Open the **Edit** menu and select **Cut** or **Copy** to either move or copy the slide(s), respectively, or you can use the **Cut** or **Copy** toolbar buttons.

TIP **Quick Cut or Copy** From the keyboard, press **Ctrl+C** to copy or **Ctrl+X** to cut.

4. In Slide Sorter view, select the slide after which you want to place the cut or copied slide(s), or on the Outline pane, move the insertion point to the end of the text in the slide after which you want to insert the cut or copied slide(s).

 5. Choose the **Edit** menu and choose **Paste**, or click the **Paste** toolbar button. PowerPoint inserts the cut or copied slides.

 TIP   **Keyboard Shortcut**   You can also press **Ctrl+V** to paste an item that you cut or copied.

Rearranging Slides in a Presentation

In this lesson, you learn how to rearrange your slides using the Slide Sorter view and the Outline/Slides pane.

Rearranging Slides in Slide Sorter View

Slide Sorter view shows thumbnails of the slides in your presentation. This enables you to view many if not all slides in the presentation at one time. Slide Sorter view provides the ideal environment for arranging slides in the appropriate order for your presentation. To rearrange slides in Slide Sorter view, perform the following steps:

1. If necessary, switch to Slide Sorter view by selecting **View** and then choosing **Slide Sorter**.

2. Place the mouse pointer on the slide you want to move.

3. Hold down the left mouse button and drag the slide to a new position in the presentation. The mouse pointer becomes a small slide box.

4. To position the slide, place the mouse before or after another slide in the presentation. A vertical line appears before or after the slide (see Figure 6.1).

CAUTION

Destination Not in View?   If you have more than just a few slides in your presentation, you might not be able to see the slide's final destination in the Slide Sorter. Don't worry; just drag the slide in the direction of the destination, and the Slide Sorter pane scrolls in that direction.

5. Release the mouse button. PowerPoint places the slide into its new position and shifts the surrounding slides to make room for the inserted slide.

You can also copy a slide in Slide Sorter view as easily as you can move a slide. Simply hold down the **Ctrl** key while you drag the slide. When you release the mouse, PowerPoint inserts a copy of the selected slide into the presentation.

Although the Slides pane on the left side of the Normal view window does not provide as much workspace as the Slide Sorter, you can use the techniques discussed in this section to move or copy a slide. The Slides pane probably works best when you have only a few slides in the presentation. When you have a large number of slides, you might want to switch from the Normal view to the Slide Sorter view.

Figure 6.1 Drag a slide in the presentation to a new position.

Rearranging Slides in the Outline Pane

In the Outline pane of the Normal view, you see the presentation as an outline that numbers each slide and shows its title and slide text. This provides you with a pretty good picture of the content and overall organization of your presentation. To rearrange the slides in your presentation using the Outline pane, follow these steps:

1. Switch to the Normal view by selecting **View**, **Normal**, or by clicking the **Normal** button on the bottom left of the PowerPoint window.

2. Click the slide number you want to move. This highlights the contents of the entire slide.

3. Place the mouse on the slide icon for that particular slide and drag the slide up or down within the presentation; then release the mouse.

TIP   **Use the Up or Down Buttons**   You can also move a slide in the outline by selecting the slide and then using the **Move Up** or **Move Down** buttons on the Outlining toolbar.

Hiding Slides

Before you give a presentation, you should try to anticipate any questions that your audience might have and be prepared to answer those questions. You might even want to create slides to support your answers to these questions and then keep the slides hidden until you need them. To hide one or more slides, perform the following steps:

1. In the Slide Sorter view or the Slides pane of the Normal view, select the slides you want to hide.

2. Select the **Slide Show** menu and then select **Hide Slide**. In the Slide Sorter view and in the Slides pane, the hidden slide's number appears in a box with a line through it (see Figure 6.2).

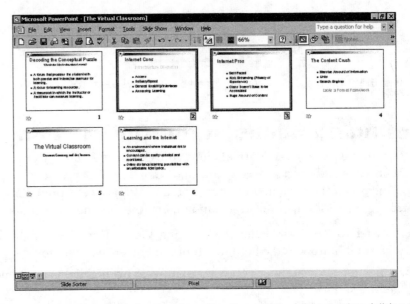

Figure 6.2 Hidden slides are denoted by a line through the slide number (slides 2 and 3 in this figure).

3. To unhide the slides, display or select the hidden slides, choose the **Slide Show** menu, and then select **Hide Slide**.

TIP **Right-Click Shortcut** To quickly hide a slide, you can right-click it and select **Hide Slide** from the shortcut menu that appears. To unhide the slide, right-click it again and select **Hide Slide** again.

Adding and Modifying Slide Text

In this lesson, you learn how to add text boxes to a slide and change the text alignment and line spacing.

Creating a Text Box

As you learned in Lesson 3, "Working with Slides in Different Views," the text on slides resides in various text boxes. To edit the text in a text box, click in the box to place the insertion point, and then enter or edit the text within the box. If you want to add additional text to a slide that will not be contained in one of the text boxes already on the slide, you must create a new text box.

TERM   **Text Box**   A text box acts as a receptacle for the text. Text boxes often contain bulleted lists, notes, and labels (used to point to important parts of illustrations).

To create a text box, perform the following steps:

1. If necessary, switch to the Normal view (select **View**, **Normal**). Use the Slides or Outline tab on the left of the workspace to select the slide that you want to work on. The slide appears in the Slide pane.

2. Click the **Text Box** button on the Drawing toolbar (if the Drawing toolbar isn't visible, right-click any toolbar and select **Drawing**).

3. Click the slide where you want the text box to appear. A small text box appears (see Figure 7.1). (It will expand as you type in it.)

4. Type the text that you want to appear in the text box. Press **Enter** to start a new paragraph. Don't worry if the text box becomes too wide; you can resize it after you are done typing.

5. When you are finished, click anywhere outside the text box to see how the text appears on the finished slide.

6. If you want, drag the text box's selection handles to resize it. If you make the box narrower, text within a paragraph might wrap to the next line.

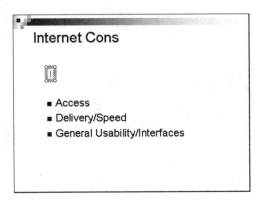

Figure 7.1   Text boxes can be inserted from the Drawing toolbar.

If the text does not align correctly in the text box, see the section "Changing the Text Alignment and Line Spacing" later in this lesson to learn how to change it.

   TIP   **Rotate a Text Box**   You can rotate a text box using the green rotation handle that appears at the top center of a selected text box. Place the mouse pointer on the handle, and the rotation icon appears. Use the mouse to drag the rotation handle to the desired position to rotate the box.

Changing Font Attributes

You can enhance your text by using the Font dialog box or by using various tools on the Formatting toolbar. Use the Font dialog box if you want to add several enhancements to your text at one time. Use the Formatting toolbar to add one font enhancement at a time.

   Fonts, Styles, and Effects   In PowerPoint, a font is a family of text that has the same design or typeface (for example, Arial or Courier). A style is a standard enhancement, such as bold or italic. An effect is a special enhancement, such as shadow or underline.

Using the Font Dialog Box

The font dialog box offers you control over all the attributes you can apply to text. Attributes such as strikethrough, superscript, subscript, and shadow are available as check boxes in this dialog box.

You can change the font of existing text or of text you are about to type by performing the following steps:

1. To change the font of existing text, select text by clicking and dragging the I-beam pointer over the text in a particular text box. If you want to change font attributes for all the text in a text box, select the text box (do not place the insertion point within the text box).

2. Choose the **Format** menu and then choose **Font**. The Font dialog box appears, as shown in Figure 7.2.

Figure 7.2 The Font dialog box enables you to change all the text attributes for selected text.

 TIP **Right-Click Quick**   You can right-click the text and select **Font** from the shortcut menu to open the Font dialog box.

3. From the **Font** list, select the font you want to use.

4. From the Font Style list, select any style you want to apply to the text, such as **Bold** or **Italic**. (To remove styles from text, select **Regular**.)

5. From the Size list, select any size in the list, or type a size directly into the box. (With TrueType fonts—the fonts marked with the TT logo—you can type any point size, even sizes that do not appear on the list.)

6. In the Effects box, select any special effects you want to add to the text, such as **Underline**, **Shadow**, or **Emboss**. You can also choose **Superscript** or **Subscript**, although these are less common.

7. To change the color of your text, click the arrow button to the right of the Color list and click the desired color. (For more colors, click the **More Colors** option at the bottom of the Color drop-down list; to select a color, use the dialog box that appears.)

8. Click **OK** to apply the new look to your selected text.

TIP **Title and Object Area Text** If you change a font on an individual slide, the font change applies only to that slide. To change the font for all the slides in the presentation, you need to change the font on the Slide Master. Select **View**, point at **Master**, and then select **Slide Master**. Select a text area and perform the preceding steps to change the look of the text on all slides. Be careful, however, because these changes override any font styles that are supplied by the design template assigned to the presentation.

Formatting Text with the Formatting Toolbar

The Formatting toolbar provides several buttons that enable you to change font attributes for the text on your slides. It makes it easy for you to quickly bold selected text or to change the color of text in a text box.

To use the different Formatting toolbar font tools, follow these steps:

1. To change the look of existing text, select the text, or select a particular text box to change the look of all the text within that box.

2. To change fonts, open the **Font** drop-down list and click the desired font.

3. To change font size, open the **Font Size** drop-down list, click the desired size or type a size directly into the box, and then press **Enter**.

 TIP **Incrementing the Type Size** To increase or decrease the text size to the next size up or down, click the **Increase Font Size** or **Decrease Font Size** buttons on the Formatting toolbar.

4. To add a style or effect to the text (bold, italic, underline, and/or shadow), click the appropriate button(s):

Bold

Italic

Underline

Shadow

As you have already seen, you can change the font color through the Font dialog box. You can also change it with the **Font Color** button on the Formatting toolbar. Just do the following:

1. Select the text for which you want to change the color.

2. Click the down-pointing arrow next to the **Font Color** button on the Formatting toolbar. A color palette appears (see Figure 7.3).

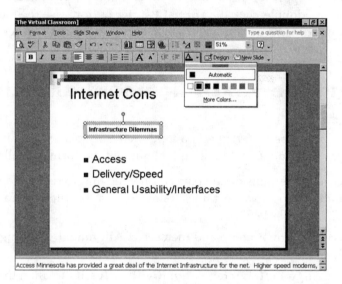

Figure 7.3   When you click the arrow next to the Font Colors button, a color palette appears.

3. Do one of the following:

   • Click a color on the palette to change the color of the selected text or the text box (the colors available are based on the design template and color scheme you have selected for the presentation).

   • Click the **More Font Colors** option to display a Colors dialog box. Click a color on the Standard tab or use the Custom tab to create your own color. Then click **OK**. The color is applied to the text.

Copying Text Formats

If your presentation contains text with a format you want to use, you can copy that text's format and apply it to other text on the slide (or other slides). To copy text formats, perform the following steps:

1. Highlight the text with the format you want to use.

2. Click the **Format Painter** button on the toolbar. PowerPoint copies the format.

3. Drag the mouse pointer (which now looks like the Format Painter icon) across the text to which you want to apply the format.

If you want to apply a format to different text lines or even different text boxes on a slide or slides, double-click the **Format Painter** button. Use the mouse to apply styles to as many text items as you want. Then, click the **Format Painter** button again to turn off the feature.

Changing the Text Alignment and Line Spacing

When you first type text, PowerPoint automatically places it against the left edge of the text box. To change the paragraph alignment, perform the following steps:

1. Click anywhere inside the paragraph you want to realign (a paragraph is any text line or wrapped text lines followed by a line break—created when you press the **Enter** key).

2. Select the **Format** menu and then select **Alignment**. The Alignment submenu appears (see Figure 7.4).

3. Select **Align Left**, **Center**, **Align Right**, or **Justify** to align the paragraph as required.

Figure 7.4   You can align each text line or paragraph in a text box.

TIP   **Some Alignment Shortcuts**   To quickly set left alignment, press **Ctrl+L** or click the **Align Left** button on the Formatting toolbar. For centered alignment, press **Ctrl+C** or click the **Center** button. For right alignment, press **Ctrl+R** or click the **Align Right** button.

If you want to align all the text in a text box in the same way (rather than aligning the text line by line), select the entire text box (click the box border) and then use the Alignment menu selection or the alignment buttons on the Formatting toolbar.

You can also change the spacing between text lines (remember, PowerPoint considers these to be paragraphs) in a text box. The default setting for line spacing is single space. To change the line spacing in a paragraph, perform these steps:

1. Click inside the paragraph you want to change, or select all the paragraphs you want to change by selecting the entire text box.

2. Select **Format, Line Spacing**. The Line Spacing dialog box appears, as shown in Figure 7.5.

Figure 7.5   Select **Format, Line Spacing** to open the Line Spacing dialog box.

3. Click the arrow buttons to the right of any of the following text boxes to change the spacing for the following:

- **Line Spacing**—This setting controls the space between the lines in a paragraph.
- **Before Paragraph**—This setting controls the space between this paragraph and the paragraph that comes before it.
- **After Paragraph**—This setting controls the space between this paragraph and the paragraph that comes after it.

4. After you make your selections, click **OK**.

TIP   **Lines or Points?**   The drop-down list box that appears to the right of each setting enables you to set the line spacing in lines or points. A line is the current line height (based on the current text size). A point is a unit commonly used to measure text. One point is 1/72 of an inch.

Selecting, Deleting, and Moving a Text Box

If you go back and click anywhere inside the text box, a selection box appears around it. If you click the selection box border, handles appear around the text box. You can drag the box's border to move the box or drag a handle to resize it. PowerPoint wraps the text automatically as needed to fit inside the box.

To delete a text box, select it (so that handles appear around it and no insertion point appears inside it), and then press the **Delete** key.

Adding a WordArt Object

PowerPoint comes with an add-on program called WordArt (which is also available in other Office applications, such as Word and Excel) that can help you create graphical text effects. You can create text wrapped in a circle and text that has 3D effects and other special alignment options. To insert a WordArt object onto a slide, perform the following steps:

1. In the Slide view, display the slide on which you want to place the WordArt object.
2. Click the **Insert** menu, point at **Picture**, and then select **WordArt**. The WordArt Gallery dialog box appears, showing many samples of WordArt types.
3. Click the sample that best represents the WordArt type you want and click **OK**. The Edit WordArt Text dialog box appears (see Figure 7.6).

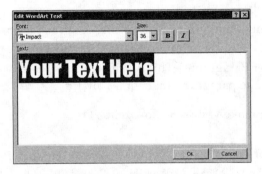

Figure 7.6   Enter the text, size, and font to be used into the Edit WordArt Text dialog box.

4. Choose a font and size from the respective drop-down lists.
5. Type the text you want to use into the Text box.
6. Click **OK**. PowerPoint creates the WordArt text on your slide, as shown in Figure 7.7.

Figure 7.7 The WordArt toolbar is available when your WordArt object is selected.

After you have created WordArt, you have access to the WordArt toolbar, shown in Figure 7.7. You can use it to modify your WordArt. Table 7.1 summarizes the toolbar's buttons.

Table 7.1 Buttons on the WordArt Toolbar

To Do This	Click This
Insert a new WordArt object	🔲
Edit the text, size, and font of the selected WordArt object	Edit Text...
Change the style of the current WordArt object in the WordArt Gallery	🔲
Open a Format WordArt dialog box	🔲
Change the shape of the WordArt	Abc
Make all the letters the same height	Aa
Toggle between vertical and horizontal text orientation	ᵇ
Change the text alignment	☰
Change the spacing between letters	AV

You can rotate a WordArt object by dragging the rotation handle on the WordArt box. To edit the WordArt object, double-click it to display the WordArt toolbar and text entry box. Enter your changes and then click outside the WordArt object. You can move the object by dragging its border or resize it by dragging a handle.

Creating Columns, Tables, and Lists

In this lesson, you learn how to use tabs to create columns of text, bulleted lists, numbered lists, and other types of lists.

Working in Multiple Columns

Depending on the type of slide that you are creating, you might find the occasion to arrange text on a slide in multiple columns. PowerPoint provides three options for placing text into columns on a slide:

- You can use the Title and 2 Column slide layout to create a slide with side-by-side text columns.
- You can place tab stops in a single text box and press Tab to create columns for your text.
- You can use a table to create a two- or multiple-column text grid.

In this lesson, you learn about all these methods.

Creating Columns with a Slide Layout

The easiest way to create columns of text is to change a slide's layout so that it provides side-by-side text boxes. Because the default layout for slides is a slide with a title box and a single text box, you will probably need to use the Slide Layout task pane to change its format to include two text columns. Follow these steps:

1. Create a new slide or select a slide that you want to format with the two-column layout (using the Outline or Slides pane).
2. Open the task pane (select **View**, **Task Pane**).
3. Select the task pane drop-down arrow and select **Slide Layout**.
4. Click the **Title and 2 Column** slide layout from the Text Layouts section of the Slide Layout task pane to format the slide (see Figure 8.1).

Figure 8.1 A two-column slide layout provides two panes in which to enter text.

You can then type the text that you want to appear in the two text boxes provided on the slide.

TIP **Place the Mouse on a Slide Layout to See Its Description** If you place the mouse on any of the slide layouts in the Slide Layout task pane, a tip appears, describing the layout.

Using Tabs to Create Columns

You can also create multiple columns in a text box using tab stops. To set the tabs for a multicolumn list, perform the following steps:

1. Open the presentation and select the slide you want to work with in Slide view.

2. Create a text box for the text if one does not already exist (use the **Text Box** icon on the Drawing toolbar to create the text box).

Disappearing Text Box If you are creating a brand-new text box in step 2, type a few characters in it to anchor it to the slide. Otherwise, it disappears when you click outside it, meaning it no longer exists and you will have to insert it all over again.

CAUTION

3. Click anywhere inside the text box. After the insertion point is in the text box, you can set the tabs.

4. If you already typed text inside the text box, select the text.

5. If the ruler is not onscreen, select the **View** menu and then select **Ruler** to display the ruler.

6. Click the **Tab** button at the left end of the ruler until it represents the type of tab you want to set (see Table 8.1 for more information on the type of tabs available).

7. Click in various positions on the ruler to place a tab stop using the type of tab you currently have selected. Figure 8.2 shows several tab stops that have been placed in a text box.

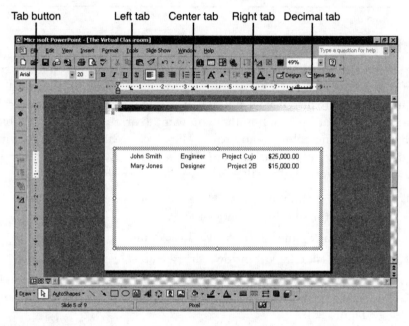

Figure 8.2 The ruler enables you to create tab stops for a text box.

8. Repeat steps 6 and 7 if you want to set different types of tab stops at different positions.

9. To change the position of an existing tab stop setting, drag it on the ruler to the desired position. To delete an existing tab stop setting, drag it off the ruler.

10. (Optional) To hide the ruler, select the **View** menu and then select **Ruler**.

Table 8.1 Tab Button Stop Types

Button Appearance	Tab Stop Type
L	Aligns the left end of the line against the tab stop.
⊥	Centers the text on the tab stop.
⌐	Aligns the right end of the line against the tab stop.
⊥	Aligns the tab stop on a period. This is called a decimal tab and is useful for aligning a column of numbers that uses decimal points.

Creating a Table

Tables can also be used to place text in side-by-side columns. You can create tables that provide two columns, three columns, or any number of columns that you require. Tables are also very useful when you want to display numerical information in a grid layout or information that you want to arrange in rows. A table is a collection of intersecting columns and rows. The block created when a column and a row intersects is often referred to as a *cell*. The easiest way to create a table on a slide is to use the Table layout. Follow these steps:

1. Create a new slide or select a slide that you want to format with the Table layout (using the Outline or Slides pane).

2. Open the task pane (select **View**, **Task Pane**).

3. Select the task pane drop-down arrow and select **Slide Layout**.

4. Scroll down through the slide layouts in the task pane, and then click the **Title and Table** layout. This assigns the Title and Table layout to the current slide (see Figure 8.3).

5. After you assign the Title and Table layout to the slide, you can set the number of columns and rows for the table. Double-click the Table icon on the slide. The Insert dialog box appears.

6. Specify the number of columns and rows that you want in the table and then click **OK**. The table is placed on the slide.

Figure 8.3 The Table layout enables you to place a table on a slide.

You can also insert a table onto an existing slide. This allows you to include a table on a slide where you don't want to change the slide's layout as discussed in the preceding steps. Follow these steps:

1. Display the slide on which you want to place the table.

2. Select the **Insert** menu and then choose **Table**. The Insert Table dialog box appears.

3. Enter the number of columns and rows that you want to have in the table.

4. Click **OK**. The table appears on the slide.

When the table appears on the slide, the Tables and Borders toolbar also appears in the PowerPoint window (we will use this toolbar in a moment). After you have a table on a slide, you can work with it like this:

• Click inside a table cell and enter your text. You can move from cell to cell by pressing **Tab** to go forward or **Shift+Tab** to go back. Enter text as needed.

• If you need to resize the table, drag a selection handle, the same as you would any object.

• To adjust the row height or column width, position the mouse pointer on a line between two rows or columns and drag. The mouse pointer becomes a sizing tool when you place it on any column or row border.

• If you want to change the style of the borders around certain cells on the table (or the entire table), select the cells (drag the mouse across the cells to select them). You can then use the buttons on the Tables and Borders toolbar to change the border attributes (see Figure 8.4). Use the Border Style button and the Border Width button to change the border style and border line weight, respectively. If you want to change the border color, use the Border Color button. The buttons on the Tables and Borders toolbar to adjust the thickness and style of the table gridlines.

Figure 8.4 Border attributes for the table can be changed using the buttons on the Tables and Borders toolbar.

To make a table appear to be multiple columns of text without the table borders, turn off all the gridlines in the table. To do so, select all the cells in the table; then right-click and choose **Borders and Fill**. In the Format Table dialog box that appears (see Figure 8.5), click each of the border buttons provided on the table diagram to turn the border off for each side of each cell in the table. Click **OK** to return to the table.

Figure 8.5 The Format Table dialog box can be used to control border lines and other table attributes.

Making a Bulleted List

When you enter new slides into a presentation, the default layout provides a title box and a text box that is set up as a simple bulleted list. Therefore, just creating a new slide creates a bulleted list.

You can turn off the bullets in front of any paragraphs by selecting the paragraphs and clicking the **Bullets** button on the Formatting toolbar to toggle the bullets off. If you want to remove the bullets from all the paragraphs (remember a text line followed by the Enter key is a paragraph), select the entire text box and click the **Bullets** button.

When you insert your own text boxes using the Text Box button on the Drawing toolbar, the text does not have bullets by default. You can add your own bullets by following these steps:

1. Click the text line (paragraph) that you want to format for bullets. If you want to add bullets to all the text lines in a text box, select the text box.

2. Select the **Format** menu, and then select **Bullets and Numbering**. The Bullets and Numbering dialog box appears (see Figure 8.6).

Figure 8.6 The Bullets and Numbering dialog box enables you to select the bullets for your bulleted items.

TIP **Quick Bullets** To bypass the dialog box, click the **Bullets** button on the Formatting toolbar to insert a bullet, or right-click and select **Bullet** from the shortcut menu. You can click the **Bullets** button again to remove the bullet.

3. Select the bullet style you want to use from the list PowerPoint provides.

4. Click **OK**. PowerPoint formats the selected text into a bulleted list. (If you press **Enter** at the end of a bulleted paragraph, the next paragraph starts with a bullet.)

TIP   **Create Your Own Bullets**   You can select from a number of pictures and symbols for the bullets that you apply to text in PowerPoint. In the Bullets and Numbering dialog box, select **Picture** to choose from several bullet pictures. Select **Customize** to select from several bullet symbols.

Working with Numbered Lists

Numbered lists are like bulleted lists, except they have sequential numbers instead of symbols. You can convert any paragraphs to a numbered list by selecting them and clicking the **Numbering** button on the Formatting toolbar. Select the paragraphs again and click the **Numbering** button again to toggle the numbering off.

You can also create numbered lists with the Bullets and Numbering dialog box, the same as you did with bullets. Follow these steps:

1. Select the paragraphs that you want to convert to a numbered list.

2. Choose **Format**, and then select **Bullets and Numbering**.

3. Click the **Numbered** tab on the dialog box. The numbered list styles appear (see Figure 8.7).

Figure 8.7   Choose the numbering style you want or turn numbering off by choosing **None**.

4. Click the number style you want for your list.

5. (Optional) Change the Size and/or Color of the numbers.

6. (Optional) If you want the list to start at a number other than 1, enter it into the **Start At** text box.

7. Click **OK**.

Adding Graphics to a Slide

In this lesson, you learn how to add PowerPoint clip art to your presentations and how to add images from other sources.

Introducing the Insert Clip Art Task Pane

With the introduction of the task pane in Office XP, accessing clip art and other graphics for use on your PowerPoint slides has changed dramatically from earlier versions of Office. The Insert Clip Art task pane provides you with a search engine that you can use to search for clip art, photographs, movies, and sounds that are stored on your computer. You can also search for clip art and other items using Microsoft's online clip library. (You must be connected to the Internet when using PowerPoint to access the Microsoft online library.)

Figure 9.1 shows the Insert Clip Art task pane. You can use this task pane to search for and insert images onto your slides, or you can take advantage of slides that use a layout that contains a placeholder for images and clip art.

You learn about using the Clip Art task pane and slide layouts that provide image placeholders in this lesson. In Lesson 10, "Adding Sounds and Movies to a Slide," you take a look at using the Clip Art task pane to add movies and slides to your PowerPoint slides.

 Clip Art   A collection of previously created images or pictures that you can place on a slide. Microsoft Office provides clip art and other media types, such as movies and sounds.

You can open the Clip Art task pane in any of these ways:

- Click the **Insert Clip Art** button on the Drawing toolbar.
- Select the **Insert** menu, point at **Picture**, and then choose **Clip Art**.
- Open the task pane, click the task pane drop-down arrow, and then select **Insert Clip Art** to switch to the Insert Clip Art task pane.

Figure 9.1 The Insert Clip Art task pane manages pictures, motion clips, and sounds—all in one convenient place.

When you use the Insert Clip Art task pane, you search for images by keywords. In the following sections, you take a look at inserting clip art from the task pane and learn how you can insert clip art using some of the slide layouts (that provide a clip art placeholder on the slide).

 TIP   **Clip Organizer Scan**   The first time you open the Insert Clip Art task pane, PowerPoint prompts you to allow the Clip Organizer (which is discussed later in the lesson) to search your hard drive. Clip Organizer then creates category folders and image indexes from the clip art and images that it finds there. Click **Yes** to allow this process to take place.

Inserting an Image from the Task Pane

As previously mentioned, the Insert Clip Art task pane allows you to search for clip art files using keywords. If you wanted to search for clip art of cats, you would search for the word "cats." To insert a piece of the clip art using the task pane, follow these steps:

1. Select the slide on which you want to place the image so that it appears in the Slide pane.

2. Select **Insert**, point at **Picture**, and then select **Clip Art**. The Insert Clip Art task pane appears.

3. Type keywords into the Search Text box in the task pane that will be used to find your clip art images.

4. Click the **Search** button. Images that match your search criteria appear in the task pane as thumbnails.

5. In the Results list, locate the image that you want to place on the slide. Then click the image, and the clip art is placed on the slide (see Figure 9.2).

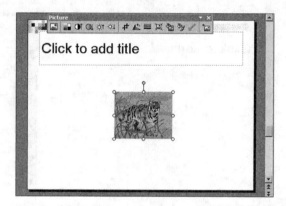

Figure 9.2 Click the clip art thumbnail to place the image onto the current slide.

You can use the sizing handles on the image to size the clip art box. Or you can drag the clip art box to a new location on the slide.

Inserting an Image from an Image Box

Another way that you can add clip art images to a slide in your presentation is to create the slide using a slide format that supplies a clip art placeholder box on the slide. These slide layout types are called content layouts because they make it easy to insert objects such as clip art, charts, and other items onto a slide. You can then use the object placeholder on the slide to access the clip art library and insert a particular image onto the slide.

Follow these steps:

1. Create a new slide or select the slide you want to assign a layout to that contains a clip art placeholder box.

2. Open the task pane (**View, Task Pane**) and then click the task pane drop-down menu and select **Slide Layout** (the Slide Layout task pane automatically opens if you've just created a new slide).

3. Scroll down through the layouts provided until you locate either the Content layout or the Text and Content layout. Both of these layout categories provide slide layouts that contain object placeholders or object placeholders and text boxes, respectively.

4. Select the layout that best suits the purpose of your slide (see Figure 9.3).

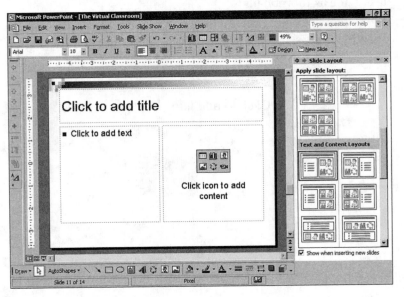

Figure 9.3 Select a slide layout that contains an object placeholder.

5. The slide layout you choose provides you with a placeholder box that contains icons for tables, charts, clip art, and other objects. Click the **Insert Clip Art** icon in the placeholder box. The Select Picture dialog box appears (see Figure 9.4).

6. Scroll down through the list of clip art and other images to find a particular image (the list will be lengthy because it includes all the Office Clip Art and any other images that were located on your computer when the Clip Organizer cataloged the images on your computer).

7. If you want, you can search for particular images by keyword. Type the search criteria into the Search Text box and then click **Search**. Images that match the search criteria appear in the Select Picture dialog box.

8. Click the picture thumbnail that you want to place on the slide. Then click **OK**.

PowerPoint places the image on the slide in the object placeholder box. You can size the box or move it on the slide.

Figure 9.4 The Select Picture dialog box enables you to scroll through or search through the entire clip art and image library on your computer.

Inserting a Clip from a File

If you have an image stored on your computer that you would like to place on a slide, you can insert the picture directly from the file. This means that you don't have to use the Insert Clip Art task pane to search for and then insert the image.

To place a graphical image on a slide directly from a file, follow these steps:

1. Select the slide on which the image will be placed.
2. Select the **Insert** menu, point at **Picture**, and then select **From File**. The Insert Picture dialog box appears (see Figure 9.5).

Figure 9.5 Use the Insert Picture dialog box to place images on a slide.

3. Select the picture you want to use. You can view all the picture files in a particular location as thumbnails. Select the **Views** button, and then select **Thumbnails** on the menu that appears.

4. Click **Insert** to place the image on the slide.

If the picture is too big or too small, you can drag the selection handles (the small squares) around the edge of the image to resize it. Hold down the **Shift** key to proportionally resize the image (this maintains the height/width ratio of the image so that you cannot stretch or distort it). See Lesson 11, "Working with PowerPoint Objects," for more details about resizing and cropping images and other objects on a slide.

 TIP **Link It Up**   You can link a graphic to the presentation so that whenever the original changes, the version in the presentation changes, too. Just open the drop-down list on the **Insert** button in the Insert Picture dialog box (refer to Figure 9.5) and choose **Link to File**.

Managing Images in the Clip Organizer

Occasionally, you might want to add or delete clip art images from folders on your computer. Managing images is accomplished using the Clip Organizer. When you install Microsoft Office XP (using the default installation), a fairly large library of clip art is placed on your hard drive in different category folders. You can manage these clip art images and other images on your computer, such as scanned images or pictures from a digital camera. To open the Clip Organizer, follow these steps:

1. With the Insert Clip Art task pane open in the PowerPoint window, click the **Clip Organizer** link near the bottom of the task pane to open the Clip Organizer.

2. To view the clip art categories Microsoft Office has provided, click the plus sign (+) to the left of the Office Collections folder in the Collection list (this folder is located on the left side of the Clip Organizer window). Category folders such as Academic, Agriculture, and so on will appear in the Collection list.

3. Click one of the category folders to view the clip art that it holds (for example, click **Food**). The clip art in that category folder appears in the Clip Organizer window (see Figure 9.6).

Figure 9.6   Use the Clip Organizer to manage your clip art and image files.

Not only does the Clip Organizer allow you to browse the various clip art and other images on your computer, it allows you to copy, delete, or move images. For example, if you find an image you no longer want to store on your computer, select the image in the Clip Organizer window and press **Delete**. A dialog box appears, letting you know that this image will be removed from all collections on the computer. Click **OK** to delete the image.

You can also use the Clip Organizer to copy or move clip art images from a location on your hard drive to one of the clip art collections. Locate the images you want to move or copy to a particular collection and then select them.

To move the images to a collection, Select the **Edit** menu, and then **Move to Collection**. The Move to Collection dialog box appears (see Figure 9.7). Select a location in the dialog box and click **OK** to move the selected image or images.

Figure 9.7   You can move images from one location to another using the Clip Organizer.

You can also copy images to a new location using the Copy to Collection command. Select the images in a particular folder on your computer using the Clip Organizer window. Select the **Edit** menu and then **Copy to Collection**. Select a location in the Copy to Collection dialog box where you would like to place copies of the images, and then click **OK**.

Adding Sounds and Movies to a Slide

In this lesson, you learn how to add sound and video clips to a PowerPoint presentation.

Working with Sounds and Movies

A great way to add some interest to your PowerPoint presentations is to add sounds and movies to your slides. Sounds enable you to emphasize certain slides, and movie animations can add humor and style to your presentations. Next, you take a look at adding sounds and then adding movie animations to your slides.

Including Sounds in a Presentation

Sounds can be used to add emphasis to information on slides or to add some auditory interest to your presentation. You can place sound files on your slides in two different ways:

- You can insert a sound clip as an icon on a slide. When you click the icon, the sound plays.
- You can assign a sound to another object on a slide so that when you click the object, the sound plays. For example, you could assign a sound to an image. When you click the image, the sound plays (sounds added to PowerPoint animations play when the animation plays).

Inserting a Sound onto a Slide

To insert a sound clip as an object onto a slide, you can either use the Insert Clip Art task pane or insert the sound as a file. The Clip Art task pane can provide you only with sound files that have been included in the Office clip art library or sound files that you have added to your collection using the Clip Organizer (which is discussed in the previous lesson). Any sound file that you have recorded or otherwise acquired can be inserted as a file.

To insert a sound clip from the Clip Art task pane, follow these steps:

1. Select the slide on which you will place the sound, so that it appears in the Slide pane.

2. Select **Insert**, point at **Movies and Sounds**, and then select **Sound from Media Gallery**. The Insert Clip Art task pane appears with a list of sound files.

3. To preview a particular sound file, point at the file and click the menu arrow that appears. Select **Preview/Properties** from the menu. The Preview/Properties dialog box for that sound file appears (see Figure 10.1).

Figure 10.1 Preview a sound clip before placing it onto a slide.

4. To play the sound, click the **Play** button on the left side of the dialog box. When you have finished previewing a sound file, click **Close** to close the Preview/Properties dialog box.

5. When you are ready to insert a sound file onto the slide, click the sound file on the task pane.

6. A dialog box opens, asking you whether you want the sound to play automatically when you run the slide show. Click **Yes** to have the sound played automatically. Click **No** to set up the sound so that you will have to click it during the slide show to play the sound.

Regardless of whether you choose to have PowerPoint play the sound automatically, it appears as a sound icon on the slide.

If you have recorded a sound file or have acquired a sound file that you want to use on a slide without using the Insert Clip Art task pane, you can insert it as a file. To insert a sound clip from a file, follow these steps:

1. Choose the **Insert** menu, point at **Movies and Sounds,** and then choose **Sound from File**.

2. In the Insert Sound dialog box, navigate to the drive and folder containing the sound you want to use (see Figure 10.2).

Figure 10.2 Choose the sound clip you want to include on your slide.

3. Select the sound clip and then click **OK**.

4. A dialog box opens, asking you whether you want the sound to play automatically when you run the slide show. As with the earlier steps, you can click **Yes** to have the sound played automatically or **No** to set up the sound so that you will have to click it during the slide show to play the sound.

Like before, the sound file appears on the slide as a sound icon. If you want to play the sound file on the slide, right-click the sound icon and select **Play Sound** from the shortcut menu.

Associating a Sound with Another Object on the Slide

If you want to avoid having a sound icon on your slide, you can associate the sound with some other object already on the slide, such as a graphic. To do so, follow these steps:

1. Right-click the object (such as a clip art image) to which you want to assign the sound.

2. Choose **Action Settings** from the shortcut menu. The Actions Settings dialog box appears.

3. If you want the sound to play when the object is pointed at, click the **Mouse Over** tab. Otherwise, click the **Mouse Click** tab. The Mouse Click option requires that the sound icon be clicked on for the sound to play.

4. Click the **Play Sound** check box. A drop-down list of sounds becomes available (see Figure 10.3).

Figure 10.3   Choose a sound to be associated with the object.

5. Open the **Play Sound** drop-down list and choose the sound you want.

If the sound you want is not on the list, choose **Other Sound** and locate the sound using the Add Sound dialog box that appears. Select the sound from there and click **OK**.

6. When you have chosen the sound you want, click **OK** to close the Action Settings dialog box.

Now, when you are giving the presentation, you can play the sound by either clicking or pointing at the object (depending on how you configured the sound to play). To test this, jump to the Slide Show view (Select the **View** menu and then click **Slide Show**) and try it out. Press **Esc** to return to the Normal view when you are finished testing the sound file.

Placing a Movie onto a Slide

The procedure for placing a movie onto a slide is very much the same as that for a sound. You can place a movie using the Insert Clip Art task pane or from a file. You will find that the task pane Clip Gallery provides several movies that can be used to add interest to your slides. To insert a movie onto a slide, follow these steps:

1. Choose the **Insert** menu, point at **Movies and Sounds**, and then select **Movies from Clip Gallery**.

2. Scroll through the movies listed on the Insert Clip Art task pane.

3. Point at a movie clip you want to preview. Click the menu arrow that appears and select **Preview/Properties**. The Preview Properties dialog box for the movie appears.

4. PowerPoint previews the movie on the left side of the dialog box (see Figure 10.4). If you want to place a caption onto the movie clip, click in the **Caption** box below the Preview pane and type a caption.

Figure 10.4   Preview a movie in the Preview/Properties dialog box.

5. Click **Close** to close the Preview/Properties dialog box. To insert the movie into your slide, click the movie in the task pane.

After the movie icon is in place on your slide, you can size the movie box using the usual sizing handles or move it to another position on the slide. If you want to test view the movie on the slide, jump to the Slide Show view (select the **View** menu and then click **Slide Show**) and try it out. Press **Esc** to return to the Normal view when you are finished testing the movie.

TIP   **Clip Gallery Movies Really Aren't Movies**   The clip gallery movies provided by Microsoft Office are really just animations. They are designed to play automatically when the slide containing the image is opened during a slide show.

You can also place actual videos on a slide as a file. This enables you to place video captures that you have created or video files from other sources.

Follow these steps:

1. Choose the **Insert** menu, point at **Movies and Sounds**, and then choose **Movie from File**.

2. In the Insert Sound dialog box that appears, navigate to the drive and folder containing the movie file you want to use.

3. Select the file and click **OK** to place it on the slide.

4. A dialog box appears (see Figure 10.5) that allows you to have the movie play when the slide appears in the slide show. Click **Yes**. To require that you click the movie's icon to make it play during the slide show, click **No**.

Figure 10.5 You can choose how the movie will be handled during the slide show.

After you make your selection in step 4, PowerPoint places the movie onto the slide. To preview the video file on the slide, right-click the video icon and then select **Play Movie**.

Working with PowerPoint Objects

In this lesson, you learn how to manipulate objects on your slides, such as clip art and other items, to create impressive presentations.

Selecting Objects

In the previous two lessons, you learned about inserting clip art, image files, sound files, and movie files onto the slides of your PowerPoint presentation. Any type of special content that you place on a slide is called an object. In addition to the object types just listed, objects could also be items from other Office applications. For example, you could create an object on a slide that is actually an Excel worksheet or chart (for more about sharing information between Office applications see Lesson 7, "Sharing Information Among Office Applications," in the "Office XP Introduction and Shared Features" section of this book.

After you select an object, you can do all kinds of things to it, such as copying, moving, deleting, or resizing it. The following is a review of ways you can select objects on a PowerPoint slide:

- To select a single object, click it. (If you click text, a frame appears around the text. Click the frame to select the text object.)

- To select more than one object, hold down the **Ctrl** or **Shift** key while clicking each object. Handles appear around the selected objects, as shown in Figure 11.1 (this temporarily groups the objects so that you can move them all simultaneously on the slide).

- To deselect selected objects, click anywhere outside the selected object or objects.

TIP   **Select Objects Tool**   Use the Select Objects tool on the Drawing toolbar to drag a selection box around several objects you want to select. When you release the mouse button, PowerPoint selects all the objects inside the box.

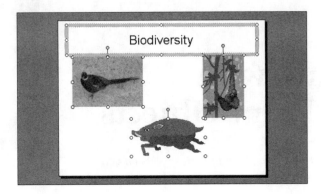

Figure 11.1   You can select multiple objects on a slide.

Working with Layers of Objects

As you place objects onscreen, they might start to overlap, creating layers of objects where the lower layers are often difficult or impossible to select. To move objects in layers, perform the following steps:

1. Click the object you want to move up or down in the stack. If the Drawing toolbar is not available in the PowerPoint window, right-click on any toolbar and select **Drawing** from the menu that appears.

2. Click the **Draw** button on the Drawing toolbar to open the Draw menu, and select **Order**, as shown in Figure 11.2.

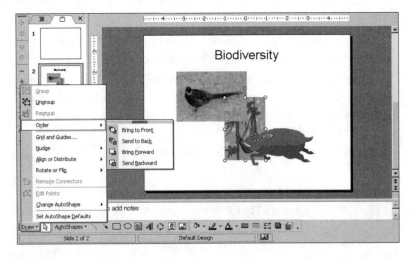

Figure 11.2   Use the Draw menu on the Drawing toolbar to change the layer on which a graphic appears on your slide.

3. Select one of the following options:

- **Bring to Front**—Brings the object to the top of the stack.
- **Send to Back**—Sends the object to the bottom of the stack.
- **Bring Forward**—Brings the object up one layer.
- **Send Backward**—Sends the object back one layer.

Grouping and Ungrouping Objects

Each object on a slide, including text boxes, is an individual object. However, some-times you want two or more objects to act as a group. For example, you might want to make the lines of several objects the same thickness or group several objects so that they can easily be moved together on the slide. If you want to treat two or more objects as a group, perform the following steps:

1. Select the objects you want to group. Remember, to select more than one object, hold down the **Shift** or **Ctrl** key as you click each one.

2. Click the **Draw** button on the Drawing toolbar to open the Draw menu, and then select **Group**.

3. To ungroup the objects, select any object in the group and select **Draw**, and then choose **Ungroup**.

Cutting, Copying, and Pasting Objects

You can cut, copy, and paste objects onto a slide (or onto another slide) the same as you would normal text. When you cut an object, PowerPoint removes the object from the slide and places it in a temporary holding area called the Office Clipboard. When you copy or cut an object, a copy of the object, or the object itself when you use Cut, is placed on the Office Clipboard. You can place multiple objects onto the Clipboard and paste them as needed onto a slide or slides in your presentation.

To view the Office Clipboard, select **View**, **Task Pane**. Then, on the task pane drop-down menu, select **Clipboard**. Figure 11.3 shows the Clipboard task pane.

To cut or copy an object, perform the following steps:

1. Select the object(s) you want to cut, copy, or move.

2. Select the **Edit** menu and then choose **Cut** or **Copy**, or click the **Cut** or **Copy** buttons on the Standard toolbar.

Figure 11.3 Use the Clipboard to keep track of objects that you have cut or copied.

 TIP **Right-Click Shortcut** Right-click a selection to choose **Cut** or **Copy** from the shortcut menu.

3. Display the slide on which you want to paste the cut or copied objects.

 4. Select **Edit** and then choose **Paste**, or click the **Paste** button on the Standard toolbar. PowerPoint pastes the objects onto the slide.

 TIP **Keyboard Shortcuts** Instead of using the toolbar buttons or the menu, you can press **Ctrl+X** to cut, **Ctrl+C** to copy, and **Ctrl+V** to paste.

To remove an object without placing it on the Clipboard, select the object and press the **Delete** key.

Rotating an Object

When you select an object on a slide, a handle with a green end on it appears at the top center of the object. This is the rotation handle, and it can be used to rotate any object on a slide. The rotation handle enables you to revolve an object around a center point.

To rotate an object, do the following:

1. Click the object you want to rotate.

2. Place the mouse pointer on the object's **Rotation** handle (the green dot) until the Rotation icon appears.

3. Hold down the mouse button and drag the **Rotation** handle until the object is in the position you want.

4. Release the mouse button.

The Draw menu (on the Drawing toolbar) also enables you to rotate or flip an object. You can flip an object horizontally left or right or flip the object vertically from top to bottom. To flip an object, click the **Draw** button on the Drawing toolbar and then point at **Rotate and Flip**. Select either **Flip Horizontal** or **Flip Vertical** from the menu that appears.

 TIP   **Can't Find the Drawing Toolbar?**   If the Drawing toolbar does not appear at the bottom of the PowerPoint application window, right-click any visible toolbar and select **Drawing**.

Resizing Objects

You will find that objects such as pictures and clip art are not always inserted onto a slide in the correct size. You can resize the object by performing these steps:

1. Select the object to resize. Selection handles appear.

2. Drag one of the following handles (the squares that surround the object) until the object is the desired size:

- Drag a corner handle to change both the height and width of an object. PowerPoint retains the object's height-to-width ratio.

- Drag a side, top, or bottom handle to change the height or width alone.

- To keep the original center of the object stationary while sizing, hold down the **Ctrl** key while dragging a sizing handle.

3. Release the mouse button when you have completed resizing the object.

Cropping a Picture

Besides resizing a picture, you can crop it; that is, you can trim a side or a corner off the picture to remove an element from the picture or cut off some whitespace. This enables you to clean up the picture within the object box.

To crop a picture, perform the following steps:

1. Click the picture you want to crop.

2. To crop the picture, you need the Picture toolbar. Right-click any toolbar currently showing in the PowerPoint window and select **Picture**. The Picture toolbar appears.

3. Click the **Crop** button on the Picture toolbar. Cropping handles appear around the picture (see Figure 11.4).

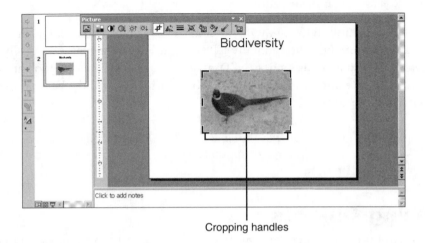

Cropping handles

Figure 11.4   Use the cropping handles on the figure to crop portions of the picture.

4. Move the mouse pointer over one of the cropping handles. The mouse pointer becomes the same shape as the cropping handle. (Use a corner handle to crop two sides at once. Use a side, top, or bottom handle to crop only one side.)

5. Hold down the mouse button and drag the pointer until the crop lines are where you want them.

6. Release the mouse button. PowerPoint crops the image.

7. After cropping that image, move or resize the picture as needed.

Stop That Crop!   To undo the cropping of a picture immediately after you crop it, select **Edit** and then choose **Undo Crop Picture**.

CAUTION

Presenting an Onscreen Slide Show

In this lesson, you learn how to view a slide show onscreen, how to make basic movements within a presentation, and how to set show options. You also learn how to create a self-running show with timings and how to work with slide transitions.

Viewing an Onscreen Slide Show

Before you show your presentation to an audience, you should run through it several times on your own computer, checking that all the slides are in the right order and that the timings and transitions between the slides work correctly. This also enables you to fine-tune any monologue you might have to give as you show the slides so that what you are saying at any point in the presentation is synchronized with the slide that is being shown at that moment.

You can preview a slide show at any time; follow these steps:

1. Open the presentation you want to view.

2. Choose the **Slide Show** menu and choose **View Show**. The first slide in the presentation appears full screen (see Figure 12.1).

3. To display the next or the previous slide, do one of the following:

- To display the next slide, click the left mouse button, press the **Page Down** key, or press the right-arrow or down-arrow key.

- To display the previous slide, click the right mouse button, press the **Page Up** key, or press the left-arrow or up-arrow key.

4. When you have finished running the slide show, press the **Esc** key.

TIP **Start the Show!** You can also start a slide show by clicking the **Slide Show** button in the bottom-left corner of the presentation window or by pressing **F5**.

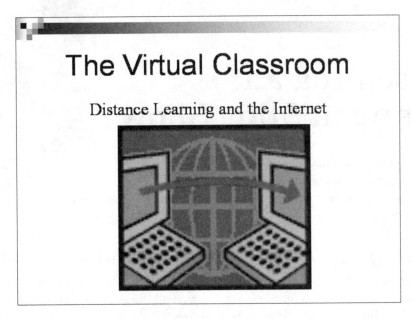

Figure 12.1 When you run your slide show, the entire screen is used to display the sides.

Setting Slide Animation Schemes

After running the slide show a few times, you might find that the presentation doesn't really provide the visual impact that you had hoped. Even though you have designed your slides well and created slides that include images and movies, you are still looking for something with a more "artsy" feel. A great way to add visual impact to the presentation is to assign an animation scheme to a slide or slides in the presentation.

An animation scheme controls how the text in the text boxes on the slide appear or materialize on the slide during the presentation. For example, you can select a slide animation scheme called Bounce, where the various text on the slide "bounces" onto the slide when it appears onscreen during the slide show.

 Animation Scheme A scheme that controls how objects materialize onto the slide during the slide show.

PowerPoint provides three categories of animation schemes that you can assign to a slide: Subtle, Moderate, and Exciting. Each of these categories provides a number of animation schemes. The great thing about the animation schemes is that you can assign them to a slide or slides and then try them out in the Normal view. If you don't like the animation scheme, you can select another.

To assign an animation scheme to a slide in the presentation, follow these steps:

1. Select the slide to which you will assign the animation scheme so that it appears in the Slide pane in the Normal view.

2. Select the **Slide Show** menu and select **Animation Schemes**. The Animation Schemes list appears in the Slide Design task pane on the right side of the PowerPoint window (see Figure 12.2).

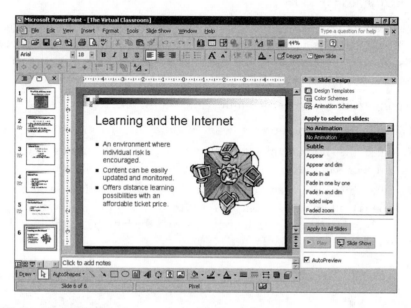

Figure 12.2 The task pane houses the animation schemes that you can assign to the slides in your presentation.

3. Scroll through the list of animation schemes. When you find a scheme that you want to try, select the scheme in the list box.

4. To try the scheme, click the **Play** button in the task pane.

5. If you don't like the scheme, select another.

6. If you find a scheme that you would like to apply to all the slides in the presentation, click the **Apply to All Slides** button.

TIP **Assign Animation Schemes to Selected Slides** You can select several slides in the Slide Sorter view and then use the Slide Design task pane to assign the same animation scheme to all the selected slides.

Setting Up a Self-Running Show

In a self-running show, the slide show runs itself. Each slide advances after a specified period of time. This allows you to concentrate on the narrative aspects of the presentation as you use the slide show for a speech or classroom presentation. For a self-running show, you must set timings. You can set the same timing for all slides (for example, a 20-second delay between each slide), or you can set a separate timing for each slide individually.

When you set up a self-running show, you can also select different slide transitions. A slide transition is a special effect that is executed when the slide appears during the slide show. For example, you can have a slide dissolve onto the screen, or you can have the slide appear on the screen using a checkerboard effect.

To configure the show to use timings and transitions, follow these steps:

1. Open the presentation you want to view.

2. Select the slide to which you would like to apply a timing or transition so that it appears in the Slides pane in the Normal view.

3. Select **Slide Show** and click **Slide Transition**. The Slide Transition task pane opens containing controls for the type of transition you want to use, the speed with which that transition executes, and the length of time the slide should remain onscreen (see Figure 12.3).

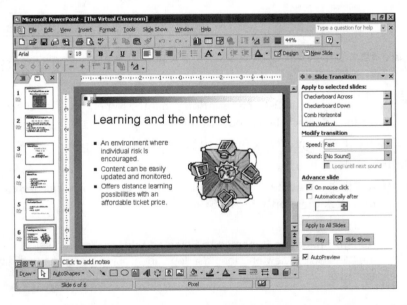

Figure 12.3   The Slide Transition task pane houses the controls necessary for tailoring the way a slide transitions onto the screen during a presentation.

4. To select a transition for the slide, select one of the transitions supplied in the Apply to Selected Slides box.

5. To test the transition, click the **Play** button.

6. If you want to change the speed of the transition, click the Speed drop-down list and select **Slow, Medium,** or **Fast** (Fast is the default).

7. (Optional) If you want to select a sound to accompany the slide transition (such as Applause, Drum Roll, or Laser), click the Sound drop-down list and select one of the supplied sounds.

8. To set the timing for the slide in the Advance Slide section of the task pane, click the **Automatically After** check box. Use the click box below the check box to enter the number of seconds for the slide's automatic timing.

9. If you want to apply the selected transition and the timing to all the slides in the presentation, click the **Apply to All Slides** button.

My Slides Don't Advance Using the Timings   If you find when you run the slide show that the slides don't advance using the timings that you have set, select **Slide Show, Set Up Show**. In the Set Up Show dialog box, be sure that the **Using Timings, If Present** option button is selected. Then click **OK**.

CAUTION

When you run the slide show, the slides advance according to the timings that you have set. The slides also use any transitions that you have selected for them. Take the time to run the slide show several times so that you can gauge whether the transitions and timings work well. Remember that the slide must be onscreen long enough for your audience to read and understand the text on the slide.

TIP   **Assign Transitions and Timings to Selected Slides**   You can select several slides in the Slide Sorter view and then use the Slide Transition task pane to assign the same transition and/or timing to the selected slides.

Don't Get Too Fancy!   If you are going to use slide transitions and animation schemes on each and every slide, you might find that your slide show is becoming "too exciting," like a film with too many explosions, car chases, and other special effects. Viewers of the slide show will likely have trouble concentrating on the text on the slides if too many things are going on at once. Remember, everything in moderation.

CAUTION

Using the Slide Show Menu Tools

PowerPoint also provides some other features that you will find very useful when you are running your slide show. For example, you can turn the mouse pointer into a pen that enables you to draw on a particular slide, enabling you to quickly emphasize a particular point visually. A Meeting Minder feature enables you to take notes during the actual presentation, which is a great way to record audience questions or comments concerning the presentation as you actually show it.

These tools are found on a menu that you can access during a slide show by right-clicking the screen. Figure 12.4 shows the menu. Three of the most useful tools are discussed in the following sections of this lesson.

Figure 12.4   You can access the pen and other tools, such as your Speaker Notes, from the menu on the Slide Show screen.

Drawing with the Pen

An extremely useful tool is the pen, which enables you to draw on a particular slide. This is great for highlighting information on a slide to emphasize a particular point.

To use the pen during the slide show, follow these steps:

1. With the slide show running, right-click anywhere on the screen. The Slide Show menu appears.

2. Point at **Pointer Options** on the menu and then choose **Pen**. The mouse pointer becomes a pen.

3. Press the left mouse button and draw on the slide as needed (see Figure 12.5).

4. After you've finished working with the pen, you can return to the arrow pointer. Right-click on the screen, point at **Pointer Options** on the menu, and then select **Arrow**. You can now use the mouse to advance to the next slide.

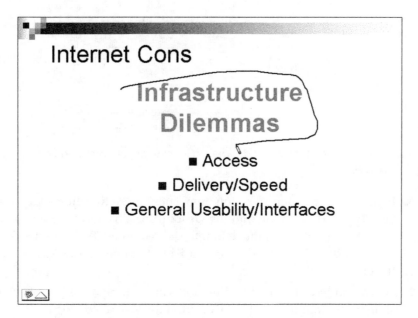

Figure 12.5   The pen provides you with an easy way to highlight a particular item on a slide.

You can also choose the pen color that you use to draw on the slides. This option is available on the Slide Show menu (point at **Pointer Options**, point at **Pen Color**, and then select the pen color you want to use from the cascading menu).

Taking Notes with the Meeting Minder

Another useful tool that you can take advantage of while showing your slide presentation is the Meeting Minder. The Meeting Minder enables you to quickly take notes or create action related to the discussion or to audience comments made during your presentation.

To use the Meeting Minder, follow these steps:

1. With the slide show running, right-click anywhere on the screen. The Slide Show menu appears.

2. Click **Meeting Minder**. The Meeting Minder dialog box opens (see Figure 12.6).

3. Type your notes onto the **Meeting Minutes** tab of the dialog box.

Figure 12.6 The Meeting Minder makes it easy for you to record notes or a task related to your presentation.

4. If you want to create an action item, click the **Action Items** tab on the dialog box. Type a description into the **Description** box and type the name of the person who will work on the item into the **Assigned To** box. After filling in this information, click the **Add** button to add the item to the Action Items list on the tab.

5. When you have finished adding notes or creating action items related to the slide presentation, click the **OK** button to close the dialog box.

Finding a Particular Slide During the Show

As you reach the end of a presentation, you might be asked to reshow a particular slide or subset of slides that you included in your slide show. The easiest way to go to a particular slide when you are in the Slide Show view is the Slide Navigator. The Slide Navigator lists all the slides in the current slide show.

To use the Slide Navigator, follow these steps:

1. With the slide show running, right-click anywhere on the screen. The Slide Show menu appears.

2. Point at **Go** and then click **Slide Navigator**. The Slide Navigator dialog box opens.

3. To move to a particular slide, click the slide's title in the Slide Navigator's slide list and then click **Go To**. PowerPoint takes you to the selected slide.

Adding Action Buttons to User-Interactive Shows

You may create slide show presentations that will be played on a computer where your audience actually interacts with the slide show (for example, a computer at a trade show that tells potential customers about your company). This means that you need to give the audience some means of controlling the show. You can simply provide access to a keyboard and/or mouse and let the user control the show in the same way you learned earlier in this lesson, or you can provide action buttons onscreen that make it easy to jump to specific slides.

Action buttons are like controls on an audio CD player; they enable you to jump to any slide quickly, to go backward, to go forward, or even to stop the presentation.

TIP **The Same Controls on All Slides?** If you want to add the same action buttons to all slides in the presentation, add the action buttons to the Slide Master. To display the Slide Master, select **View**, point at **Master**, and then choose **Slide Master**.

To add an action button to a slide, follow these steps:

1. Display the slide in Normal view.

2. Select **Slide Show**, point at **Action Buttons**, and pick a button from the palette that appears. For example, if you want to create a button that advances to the next slide, you might choose the button with the arrow pointing to the right.

TIP **Which Button Should I Choose?** Consider the action that you want the button to perform, and then pick a button picture that matches it well. To change the button picture, you must delete the button and create a new one.

3. Your mouse pointer turns into a crosshair. Drag to draw a box on the slide where you want the button to appear. (You can resize it later if you want.) PowerPoint draws the button on the slide and opens the Action Settings dialog box (see Figure 12.7).

Figure 12.7 Set the action for your button in the Action Settings dialog box.

4. Select either **Mouse Click** or **Mouse Over** to set the action for the button (Mouse Click options require a click; Mouse Over requires only that the mouse pointer be placed on the button).

5. Choose the type of action you want to happen when the user clicks the button. Click the **Hyperlink To** drop-down list and select an action such as **Next Slide**.

6. (Optional) If you want a sound to play when the user clicks the button, select the **Play Sound** check box and choose a sound from the drop-down list.

7. Click **OK**. Your button appears on the slide.

8. View the presentation (as you learned at the beginning of this lesson) to try out the button.

If you do use buttons on your slides so that users can run the slide show, be sure you use the same style of button on each of your slides for a particular action. This kind of consistency gives the viewer of the presentation a feeling of comfort and control.

 TIP   **Buttons Can Do Many Things**   You can also create action buttons that run a program or fire off a macro that has been created using the Visual Basic for Applications programming language. Although these are very advanced features not covered in this book, keep in mind as you learn more about PowerPoint that many possibilities exist for making very creative and complex slide show presentations.

Setting Slide Show Options

Depending on the type of show you're presenting, you might find it useful to make some adjustments to the way the show runs, such as making it run in a window (the default is full screen) or showing only certain slides. You'll find these controls and more in the Set Up Show dialog box, which you can open by clicking the **Slide Show** menu and selecting **Set Up Show** (see Figure 12.8).

In this dialog box, you can choose from several options, including the following:

- Choose the medium for showing the presentation. Your choices are **Presented by a Speaker (Full Screen)**, **Browsed by an Individual (Window)**, and **Browsed at a Kiosk (Full Screen)**.
- Choose whether to loop the slide show continuously or to show it only once. You might want to loop it continuously so that it operates unaided at a kiosk at a trade show, for example.

Figure 12.8 Use the Set Up Show dialog box to give PowerPoint some basic instructions about how to present your slide show.

- Show all the slides or a range of them (enter the range into the **From** and **To** boxes).
- Choose whether to advance slides manually or to use timings you set up.
- Choose a pen color. Use the Pen Color drop-down box to select a color.

Printing Presentations, Notes, and Handouts

In this lesson, you learn how to select a size and orientation for the slides in your presentation and how to print the slides, notes, and handouts you create.

Using PowerPoint Notes and Handouts

Although PowerPoint presentations are designed to be shown on a computer screen, you might want to print some items related to the presentation. For example, as you design your presentation, you can enter notes related to each slide that you create in the Notes pane. These notes can then be printed out and used during the presentation.

Using speaker notes helps you keep on track during the presentation and provides you with the information that you want to present related to each slide in the presentation. When you print your notes, each slide is printed on a separate page with the notes printed below the slide.

If you want to make it easier for your presentation audience to follow the presentation and perhaps take notes of their own, you can print out handouts. Handouts provide a hard copy of each slide. The number of slides printed on each page of the handout can range from 1 to 9 slides. If you choose to print three slides per page (this is set up in the Print dialog box, which is discussed later in this lesson), PowerPoint automatically places note lines on the printout pages to the right of each slide (which makes it even easier for your audience to take notes related to the slides in the presentation).

This lesson covers the options related to printing hard copies of your slides, notes, and handouts. Let's start with a look at printing out presentation slides.

Quick Printing with No Options

You can quickly print all the slides in the presentation. You don't get to make any decisions about your output, but you do get your printout without delay.

To print a quick copy of each slide in the presentation, choose one of these methods:

- Click the **Print** button on the Standard toolbar.
- Choose the **File** menu, choose **Print**, and click **OK**.
- Press **Ctrl+P** and click **OK**.

The downside of printing the presentation in this way is that you will get a printout of only one slide per page in the landscape orientation. It doesn't matter what view you are in—you just get the slides. This uses up a lot of printer ink or toner, and if you want to print the presentation as an outline or print the presentation so that you can see the presentation notes that you've made, you need to access printing options that provide more control over the printout.

One way to fine-tune some of the settings that control how pages will be printed is the Page Setup dialog box.

Changing the Page Setup

The Page Setup dialog box enables you to select how slides, notes, and handouts should be oriented on the page (Portrait or Landscape) and the type of page that the slides should be formatted for, such as On-Screen Show, overhead sheets or regular 8 1/2-inch by 11-inch paper.

To customize the Page Setup settings, follow these steps:

1. Select the **File** menu and select **Page Setup**. The Page Setup dialog box appears as shown in Figure 13.1.

Figure 13.1 The Page Setup dialog box enables you to set the paper type and the orientation of slides and notes on the page.

2. Perform one of the following procedures to set the slide size:

- To use a standard size, select a size from the **Slides Sized For** drop-down list. For example, you can have slides sized for regular 8 1/2-inch by 11-inch paper, overheads, or 35mm slides (if you have a special printer that can create slides).

- To create a custom size, enter the dimensions into the **Width** and **Height** text boxes.

TIP   **Spin Boxes**   The arrows to the right of the Width and Height text boxes enable you to adjust the settings in those boxes. Click the up arrow to increase the setting by .1 inch or the down arrow to decrease it by .1 inch.

3. In the **Number Slides From** text box, type the number with which you want to start numbering slides. (This is usually **1**, but you might want to start with a different number if the presentation is a continuation of another.)

4. Under the Slides heading, choose **Portrait** or **Landscape** orientation for your slides.

5. In the Notes, Handouts and Outline section, choose **Portrait** or **Landscape** for those items.

6. Click **OK**. If you changed the orientation of your slides, you might have to wait a moment while PowerPoint repositions the slides.

Choosing What and How to Print

To really control your printouts related to a particular presentation, use the various options supplied in the Print dialog box. The Print dialog box enables you to specify what to print, such as handouts or the presentation as an outline; it also enables you to specify the printer to use for the printout. For example, you might want to use a color printer for overhead transparencies and a black-and-white printer for your handouts. To set your print options, follow these steps:

1. Select the **File** menu and select **Print**. The Print dialog box appears with the name of the currently selected printer in the Name box (see Figure 13.2).

2. If you want to use a different printer, open the Name drop-down list and select the printer you want.

TIP   **Printer Properties**   The Properties button enables you to adjust graphics quality, select paper size, and choose which paper tray to use, among other things.

3. Choose what to print in the Print Range section:

- Choose **All** to print all the slides in the presentation.
- Choose **Current Slide** to print only the currently displayed slide.
- Enter a range of slide numbers into the **Slides** text box; for example, enter 2–4 to print slides 2, 3, and 4.

Figure 13.2   The Print dialog box enables you to control the printer and the printouts.

4. Open the **Print What** drop-down list and choose what you want to print. You can print slides, handouts, notes, or outlines.

5. If you want more than one copy, enter the number of copies you want into the **Number of Copies** box.

6. Use the Color/Grayscale drop-down box to specify whether the printout should be in color, grayscale, or black and white.

7. If you are printing handouts, use the Handouts box on the dialog box to specify the number of slides that should be printed per page and the orientation used for the printed page (Portrait or Landscape).

8. Select or deselect any of these check boxes in the dialog box, as required:

- **Print to File**—Select this option to send the output to a file rather than to your printer.

- **Collate**—If you are printing more than one copy, select this check box to collate (1, 2, 3, 1, 2, 3) each printed copy instead of printing all the copies of each page at once (1, 1, 2, 2, 3, 3).

- **Scale to Fit Paper**—If the slide (or whatever you're printing) is too large to fit on the page, select this check box to decrease the size of the slide to make it fit on the page. Now you won't have to paste two pieces of paper together to see the whole slide.

- **Frame Slides**—Select this check box if you want to print a border around each slide.

- **Print Hidden Slides**—If you have any hidden slides, you can choose whether to print them. If you don't have any hidden slides, this check box will be unavailable.

- **Include Animations**—If you have any animated elements on the slide, mark this check box and PowerPoint will do its best to approximate them in still form.

- **Include Comment Pages**—Prints all the comments on the slides of the presentation on a separate comments page.

 TIP   **Preview Your Printout Selection**   After specifying the various options in the Print dialog box, you might want to preview the printout before you send it to the printer. Click the **Preview** button. You are taken to the Print Preview screen. If things look good on the Print Preview screen, click **Print** to send the printout to the printer.

9. Click **OK** to print.

FrontPage

Getting Familiar with FrontPage

In this lesson, you learn how to start Microsoft FrontPage and navigate the FrontPage window. You also learn about some of the special tools that FrontPage provides for designing Web sites.

Starting FrontPage

Microsoft FrontPage is a full-featured Web design application that provides you with all the tools you need to create your own Web page or Web site and get it onto the Web. Wizards and templates are provided that make it easy for you to create simple, personal Web sites or complex Web sites for your business. FrontPage not only makes it easy for you to create your own Web pages and sites, it also enables you to test and troubleshoot the site before publishing it to the World Wide Web.

Web pages and sites must be created in the HTML (Hypertext Markup Language) programming language for them to function when viewed in a Web browser such as Microsoft Internet Explorer (for more about Internet Explorer, see Part VIII of this book). FrontPage helps you create sophisticated Web pages and sites without having to learn HTML.

 Web Page   A single page containing text and graphics that has been labeled with the appropriate HTML coding for the Web.

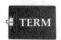 **Web Site**   A collection of linked Web pages containing various content that can easily be navigated using a Web browser.

Before you can take advantage of FrontPage's capabilities, you must open its application window. To start the FrontPage program, follow these steps:

1. From the Windows desktop, click **Start** and select **Programs**. The Programs menu appears.

2. To start FrontPage, click the **FrontPage** icon. The FrontPage application window opens.

Understanding the FrontPage Environment

When you start FrontPage, the FrontPage application window opens (see Figure 1.1). The overall geography of the FrontPage window is similar to that of other Microsoft Office applications, such as Excel and Word. In fact, you will find that when you create and edit Web pages and Web sites in the FrontPage window, you use many of the techniques and tools you use in a word processing application such as Microsoft Word.

Toolbars   Title bar   Menu bar

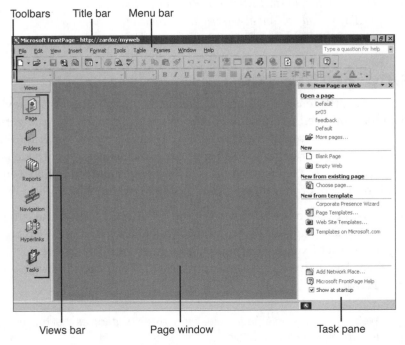

Views bar   Page window   Task pane

Figure 1.1 The FrontPage window is where you create your Web pages and Web sites.

FrontPage does have an area of its window that is distinct from other Office applications. The Views bar on the left side of the FrontPage window enables you to quickly switch between different views associated with the currently open Web site. For example, the Page view enables you to view and edit the current Web page (see Figure 1.2). Another view, the Navigation view, enables you to view all the pages in the current Web site and see how they are linked to form a complete site (for more about the views available on the Views bar, see Lesson 2, "Creating a New Web Site").

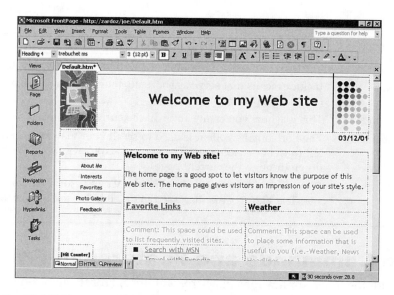

Figure 1.2 The Views pane enables you to quickly switch to a different view of a Web site, such as the Page view.

CAUTION

Don't Confuse the Views Bar with the View Tabs FrontPage uses the term *view* in two contexts. The Views bar enables you to change your view of your Web site by changing the entire View pane to a Page view, a Navigation view, and so on. Within Page view, the View tabs enable you to change the view for the current Web page to a regular view, an HTML code view, and a preview (for more about the View tabs, see Lesson 3, "Working with Web Pages and Themes").

You might notice that the largest area of the window is currently blank; a new, blank Web page (serving the same function as a blank document window in Word) appears in the FrontPage window when you start the application. You can use this blank page to build a new Web page from scratch, or you can use one of the templates that FrontPage offers (for more about creating individual Web pages and the use of templates, see Lesson 3).

Table 1.1 describes the elements you see in the FrontPage application window.

Table 1.1 Elements of the FrontPage Window

Element	Description
Title bar	Includes the name of the application (FrontPage) and the Minimize, Maximize, and Close buttons.
Task pane	The task pane is used for many FrontPage features, such as creating a new Web page and adding graphics to a Web. Lesson 3 provides an introduction to the task pane.

Table 1.1 Continued

Element	Description
Menu bar	Contains menus of commands you can use to perform tasks in the program.
Toolbar	Includes icons that serve as shortcuts for common commands, such as Save, Print, and Spelling.
Page window	This is where you create and edit the current Web page.
Scrollbars	The horizontal scrollbar is used to scroll your view of the current page from left to right or vice versa. The vertical scrollbar is used to scroll up and down through the current page.
Views bar	Provides quick access to the different views associated with the current Web site. The Views bar is discussed in detail in Lesson 2, "Creating a New Web Site."

Using Commands and Features in FrontPage

As with the other applications in Microsoft Office, FrontPage provides several ways to access the commands and features used to create your Web pages. You can access these commands using the menus on the menu bar and the buttons on the various toolbars that FrontPage supplies.

You can also access many FrontPage commands using shortcut menus. These menus are accessed by right-clicking a particular page element. The shortcut menu appears with a list of commands related to the item that you are currently working on, such as text or a picture. Lesson 2, "Using Common Office Features," in Part I of this book provides a primer on common Office features, such as menus, toolbars, and dialog boxes.

Exiting FrontPage

When you work in FrontPage, you will find that a Web site consists of multiple, linked Web pages (although a simple Web site can consist of one Web page). The lessons that follow in this section of the book walk you through the creation of a simple Web site from beginning to Web publication.

When you have finished your initial survey of the FrontPage application window or whenever you have finished your work in the program, you will want to exit the software. You can exit FrontPage by selecting **File**, **Exit**, or you can close FrontPage with one click of the mouse by clicking the FrontPage **Close** (**X**) button in the upper-right corner of the application window.

When you close FrontPage, you are prompted to save any work that you have done in the application window. If you were just experimenting as you read through this lesson, you can click **No**. The current Web page is not saved, and the FrontPage application window closes. All the ins and outs of actually saving your Web pages and the structure of your Web site are covered in Lesson 2.

Creating a New Web Site

2

In this lesson, you learn how to create a new Web site using the FrontPage Web Wizards. You also become familiar with the different Web views provided on the FrontPage Views bar.

Using the Web Site Wizards

FrontPage provides several wizards you can use to create your own Web site (in FrontPage, a Web site is called a *web*). These wizards can create different kinds of sites ranging from the personal to the professional, or they can help you add certain types of functions to your current Web site (such as a discussion page or a page for project management).

Table 2.1 lists the Web Wizards that are available and the type of web they help you create.

Table 2.1 Selecting a Web Wizard for Your New Web Site

Web Wizard	Site Created
One Page Web	A web consisting of a single blank page (the home page).
Corporate Presence	A multipage web with pages for products and services and links for e-mail messages to the company.
Customer Support	A web that provides a FAQ (frequently asked questions) page, a suggestion page, a download page, and a search page to help support customers using the site.
Discussion Web	A web consisting of a discussion page that allows visitors to your site to post and read discussion messages.
Database Interface	A web that connects to a database and allows you to view and update records.
Empty Web	A web consisting of no pages.
Import Web	A web based on imported files from a Web site created in another program or directly from the World Wide Web.
Personal Web	A multipage web consisting of interests, photos, and links pages.
Project Web	A multipage web used to manage a particular project. A schedule page, a discussion page, and other project management pages are created. This type of site would typically be used on an intranet (a corporation's private web).

When you work with the various wizards, you will find that they provide you with blank pages, partially completed pages, or pages containing text, links, and picture placeholders. In all cases, you must add and edit material in the site to complete your web before you can publish it to the World Wide Web where Web users can access it.

Remember that when you provide a name for the web you are going to create using the wizard, you are actually creating a folder on your computer where the web will reside. Webs do not consist of a single file like an Excel worksheet or Word document does. Webs consist of several page files, picture files, and other elements. When you specify the name for the web, you are making a place for FrontPage to store all the files that make your web look the way it does. A complex web can contain many files, so be sure you have plenty of space on the drive that you use to store the web.

Creating a New Web

The various Web Wizards that you can use to walk you through web creation determine the level of sophistication of your new web. Although the wizards act in similar ways, the more complex the site, the more questions you have to answer and the more steps you have to complete before the site is created. For example, the Personal Web Wizard provides a fast and easy avenue to a simple Web site for your own use, whereas the Corporate Web Wizard helps you create a complex web that contains a great deal of information (that you provide) about the company that the site is for.

CAUTION

Close the Open Blank Page Before Creating a New Web   When you start FrontPage, it automatically opens a new blank web page for you and displays it in the Page view (discussed later in this lesson). When you create your new web using a wizard, this page does not become part of the actual web, but it still takes the theme and attributes of the web you create. You might want to close this blank page (click the **Close** button in the upper-right corner of the page) before you build your site. This can prevent confusion caused by a page that appears in the Page view but is not really part of the web you have created.

To create a site using one of the wizards, follow these steps:

1. With the FrontPage application running on the Windows desktop, select the **File** menu and point at **New**. This opens the New page or Web task pane. Select Web Site Templates from the **New from Templates** section. The Web Site Templates dialog box opens showing the Web Site Wizards (see Figure 2.1).

2. Select one of the wizard icons in the dialog box, such as **Corporate Presence Wizard**.

Figure 2.1 The Web Site Templates dialog box is where you select the wizard you want to use to build your new web.

3. In the **Specify the Location of the New Web** text box in the **Options** section, specify a name and location for the new web. The default main folder for FrontPage webs is My Webs; however, you can use the **Browse** button to select a new location.

4. Click **OK** to begin the web creation process.

5. Depending on the wizard you selected, your next action begins either with editing and enhancing the Web pages that the wizard creates or answering some questions that the wizard poses before it creates the pages. For example, in the case of the Corporate Presence Web (and other business-related webs such as the Customer Support site), a wizard screen appears, describing the purpose of the wizard. Click **Next** to continue.

6. Answer the questions on each wizard screen and click **Next** to continue. Figure 2.2 shows a screen from the Corporate Presence Web Wizard in which it asks you to determine the topic areas that should appear on the new web's home page.

7. Depending on the wizard that you chose to create your new web, you might be asked to select a theme for your new site. FrontPage themes provide design elements and color schemes that can really help you create eye-catching webs. Themes are discussed in Lesson 6, "Inserting Special FrontPage Components." After you have completed all the wizard's questions, the final wizard screen provides a Finish button. Click **Finish** to end the web creation process.

Figure 2.2   The wizard screens let you determine the pages in the web as well as topic areas and items found on individual pages.

Understanding the Web Views

When you complete your new web, you are taken to the Navigation view of the web, which shows all the pages that were created for your new site and their relationship to other pages in the site. The site consists of a home page and several other pages that branch from the home page (and are subordinate to it). Figure 2.3 shows the Navigation view of a web created using the Personal Web Wizard. Each wizard creates a different number of pages for the site and arranges them in a manner that depends on the purpose of the web.

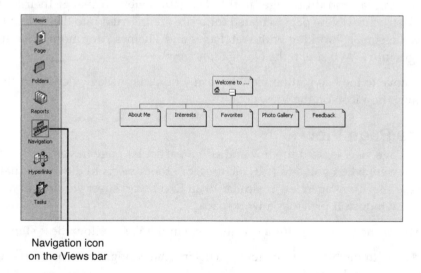

Navigation icon
on the Views bar

Figure 2.3   The various wizards end the creation process by showing your new web pages and their configuration in the Navigation view.

Some Wizards Dump You into the Task View The Corporate Presence Wizard provides an option on the second-to-last wizard screen to take you to the Task view rather than to the Navigation view. If you do not deselect the check box for Task view, you will end up there on completion of the web. The different views available to you in FrontPage are covered in the remainder of this lesson.

The key to completing a web that has been created using a web wizard is understanding how the various views on the FrontPage Views bar are used as you edit and enhance the new web. Each view provides a different information set that shows you how the overall construction of the web is progressing. These views are defined in the sections that follow. You also use these views in the subsequent lessons that discuss FrontPage.

The Navigation View

The Navigation view (refer to Figure 2.3) enables you to see all the pages in the web in a flowchart format, which gives you the hierarchy for the site. (This view is usually the default view for a site created using one of the wizards.) The home page for the site is at the top of the hierarchy, and all pages that branch from the home page are shown below the home page with a connecting line. FrontPage calls the pages that are below the home page in the web *child pages*.

Child pages are not limited to the home page, however, and any page in the Web site can have child pages. A page that has child pages is called a *parent page*.

You can drag and drop pages in the Navigation view to change their location in the web structure. New pages created for a site are inserted into the web in this manner (see Lesson 3, "Working with Web Pages and Themes," for more about inserting new pages into a Web site in the Navigation view).

To move to the Navigation view from any other FrontPage view, click the **Navigation** icon on the Views bar.

The Page View

The Page view is used to view and edit a particular page in your web. You use the Page view when you add text, pictures, or other objects to the individual Web pages in the site. The Page view is similar to an Excel worksheet window or a Word document window. It provides a workspace.

To enter the Page view for a specific page in the Web, follow these steps:

1. Go to the Navigation view by clicking the **Navigation** icon on the Views bar (refer to Figure 2.3).

2. Double-click a particular page in the Navigation view. The page opens in the Page view (as shown in Figure 2.4). The look of the page depends on the theme that you chose.

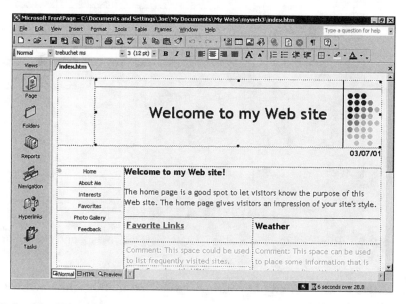

Figure 2.4   The Page view is where you focus on a particular page in the web and edit and enhance it.

When you are in the Page view, you can edit the current page as needed (see details in Lesson 3).

 TIP   **Quickly Return to the Previously Opened Page**   If you open a particular page in the Page view by double-clicking it in the Navigation view (or Folders view) and then move to a different view (such as returning to the Navigation view), you can quickly return to the previously opened page by clicking the **Page View** icon on the Views bar.

The Folders View

The Folders view shows the folders and files in the current web. When you create a web using one of the wizards, several folders and files are created (the files created depend on the wizard that you used).

Click the **Folders** icon in the Views bar to view the folders and files in the web. Figure 2.5 shows the folders and files that are created when you use the Personal Web Wizard to create a new web.

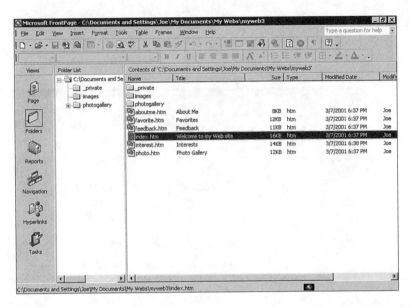

Figure 2.5 The Folders view enables you to view the folders and files contained in the current web.

The folders created for any of your new webs (no matter which wizard you use) consist of the following:

- **Web Folder**—This is designated by the name that you provided for the web's location in the Specify the Location of the New Web box in the New dialog box.
- **Private Folder**—This folder is created to hold any data that is input into special forms or other data input objects that you place on a page or pages in your Web site. Because the folder is private, a visitor to your Web site cannot gain access to the information that it holds.
- **Images Folder**—This folder provides a place to save pictures and clip art that are part of the Web site. Any images placed in the web by the wizard are contained in this folder.

Files that are contained in the web can also be seen in the Folders view. Each web typically contains an index.htm file that serves as the home page for the web; the other pages in the web depend on the wizard that was used (each with the .htm extension, which means the page is an HTML document).

You can delete files from the web in the Folders view (select the file and press **Delete**). You can also open pages in the Folders view by double-clicking them. They open in the Page view.

The Reports View

The Reports view enables you to view statistics and other information related to your web. These statistical reports are created automatically when you create the web, and they are updated as you work on the web. To view the statistics for your site, click the **Reports View** icon on the Views bar.

Figure 2.6 shows the Reports view for a personal web. Statistics such as the number of files and pictures in the web are reported as *mini-reports*. Other data provided include unverified links in the web (these usually consist of links to other Web sites on the World Wide Web that have not yet been verified by going online with your web).

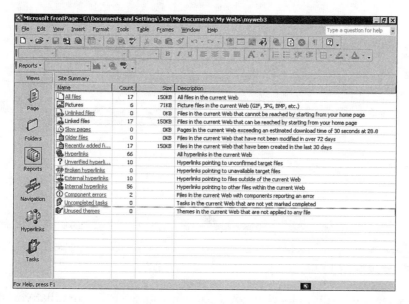

Figure 2.6   The Reports view provides you with important statistics related to your web.

The Reporting toolbar enables you to change the statistics displayed in the Reports window (it appears directly below the other FrontPage toolbars). The default list for the Reports view is the Site Summary (refer to Figure 2.6), which shows all the statistics. If you want to view a certain statistic, such as unlinked files (in the web), click the drop-down box on the Reports toolbar and select the statistic—in this example, **Unlinked Files**—from the **Problems** list. These files are listed. Any views found in the Site Summary view can be viewed alone by selecting the appropriate report title from the toolbar drop-down list.

The Hyperlinks View

The Hyperlinks view enables you to view the hyperlinks from a particular page in the site to other pages in the site and to other Web sites on the World Wide Web. Figure 2.7 shows the Hyperlinks view for the Favorites page in a Personal Web site. The page has internal links to the other pages in the web (so that you can quickly go to those pages). It also contains external links that enable you to jump to other sites found on the World Wide Web.

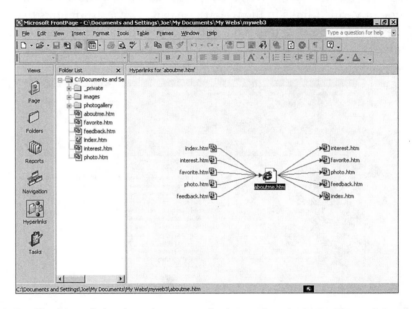

Figure 2.7   The Hyperlinks view shows you the internal and external hyperlinks on a specific page in your web.

To go to the Hyperlinks view for a page in your web, be sure that you first select the page in the Folders view or the Navigation view. Then click the **Hyperlinks View** icon on the Views bar. The page and its hyperlinks are displayed. Creating and managing hyperlinks is discussed in Lesson 7, "Working with Hyperlinks."

The Tasks View

The Tasks view enables you to see tasks that are used to help you complete various aspects of your Web site. You can create tasks related to specific pages in the web or items on a Web page, such as a picture or other item. When you start a task that appears on your Tasks list, the task automatically opens the page or goes to the item on the page for which the task was created. Some of the wizards, such as the Corporate Presence Wizard, automatically create a list of tasks that is used to make sure all aspects of the new web are addressed before the web is placed on the World Wide Web for viewing. Tasks are covered in more detail in Lesson 8, "Completing and Publishing Your Web Site."

To go to the Tasks view, click the **Tasks View** icon on the Views bar. Figure 2.8 shows the tasks that were created when the Corporate Presence Wizard was used to create a new web.

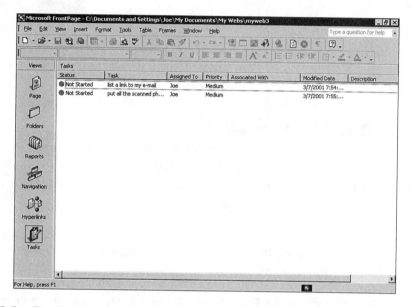

Figure 2.8   The Tasks view enables you to create and monitor tasks that are related to the completion of your web.

You might find that you use different views provided by the Views bar as you create or fine-tune your webs. These views are visited and revisited in the other lessons found in this part of the book.

Working with Web Pages and Themes

In this lesson, you learn how to create new Web pages using the FrontPage templates and how to delete pages and import pages created in other applications. You also learn how to enhance the look of your Web pages with FrontPage themes.

Creating a New Web Page

FrontPage makes it easy for you to create new Web pages and place them into your web. You can create blank pages or pages that use a FrontPage template. These templates provide you with pages that can add functionality to your Web site.

To create a new page in a web, follow these steps:

1. To open the web where you want to place the new page, select the **File** menu and point at **Recent Webs**; from the cascading menu that appears, select the web you want to open.

CAUTION

My Web Isn't on the Recent Webs Menu! If you have created more than four webs using FrontPage, there is a good chance your most infrequently used webs will no longer appear on the Recent Webs menu, which shows only the last four webs). To open webs not listed, select **File**, **Open Web**. Use the Open Web dialog box to specify the location for the web. When you have located the web, select it and then click **Open**.

2. With the appropriate web open, you can now create a new page for the web. First, click the **Page View** icon in the View bar to go to the Page view.

3. Select the **File** menu, point at **New,** and the New Page or Web task pane opens. Under **New from Template**, select **Page Templates**, which opens the Page Templates dialog box (see Figure 3.1).

4. The new page templates are available on the General tab of the Page Templates dialog box. Click the template that you want to use for your new page. Then, click **OK** to create the new page.

Figure 3.1 The General tab of the Page Templates dialog box is where you select the template for your new page.

The new page appears in the FrontPage Page view. Figure 3.2 shows a two-column page that was created using the Two-Column Body template. The templates create pages that contain placeholder text and other items that you can modify. (Working with text on your pages is covered in Lesson 4, "Working with Text in FrontPage.")

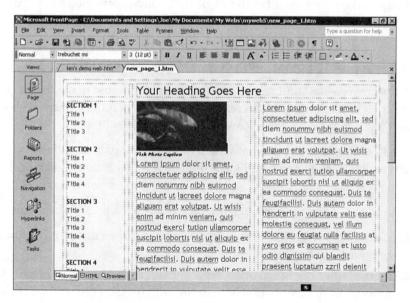

Figure 3.2 The new page appears in the FrontPage editing window in the Page view.

You will also find that the new page (even though it's not included in the navigational structure of your web yet) embraces the theme that you assigned to the current web. (FrontPage themes are covered later in this lesson.)

Now that you have the new page, you need to save it. Follow these steps:

1. Click the **Save** button on the FrontPage toolbar. The Save As dialog box opens.

2. Type a filename for your new page into the **File Name** box.

3. You also should change the page title for the new page. This title appears in the Web browser when you view the particular page on the World Wide Web. To change the page title, click the **Change** button. The Set Page Title dialog box opens (see Figure 3.3).

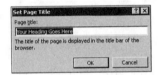

Figure 3.3   Type the page title that you want to appear in the Web browser when the page is viewed on the World Wide Web.

4. Type the new page title and click **OK**. You are returned to the Save As dialog box. Click **Save** to complete the process.

Inserting a New Page into the Web

After you've created and saved the new page, you must make the page part of the current web. You might think creating the page when the current web is open in FrontPage should have taken care of that, but it doesn't.

You add the page to the current web by linking the page to either your site's home page (which in most cases will have the name index.htm) or to any other subordinate page in the web.

To add the new page to the navigational structure of your web, follow these steps:

1. Click the **Navigation** icon on the Views bar. The current navigational structure of your page appears.

2. To the left of the Navigation view, a Folder List should appear. If you don't see a list of all the pages available in the web (in the Folder List), click the **Folder List** button on the toolbar.

3. To add the new page to the structure of the web, locate the file in the Folder List, and then drag the file onto the Navigation view, placing the box that represents the file underneath your home page. Figure 3.4 shows a page named "all about whales.htm" being added to the web structure.

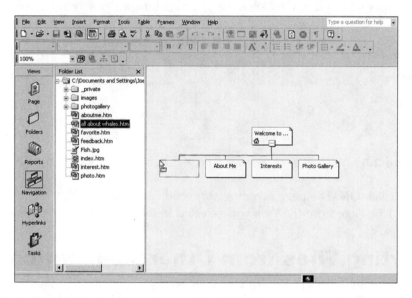

Figure 3.4   The Navigation view makes it easy for you to add new pages to your web.

After the page has been added to the web structure, it appears as a page box, as the other pages in the web appear when you are using the Navigation view. If you want to view the page itself, double-click its page box in the Navigation view and it will open in Page view.

Deleting a Page from the Web

Deleting a page from the web is best done in the Navigation view. This not only allows you to quickly delete the page from the navigational structure of the web, but it also removes the appropriate HTML document from the Folder List at the same time.

To delete a page from your web, follow these steps:

1. Click the **Navigation** icon on the Views bar to go to the Navigation view.

2. Click the page that you want to remove from the web (in the Navigation window).

3. Press the **Delete** key on the keyboard. The Delete Page dialog box appears.

4. You have the choice of removing the page from the navigational structure of the web (this does not delete the page file) or deleting the page from the web (this removes it from the structure and deletes the file). Select the appropriate option button in the Delete Page dialog box, as shown in Figure 3.5.

Figure 3.5   You can easily remove a page from the web in the Navigation view.

5. Click **OK**. The page is removed from the structure. (The file is deleted if Delete This Page from the Web was selected in the dialog box.)

Importing Files from Other Applications

You can also import page files into your web that you create in other applications. For example, suppose you designed a Web page in Microsoft Word and saved the document as an HTML file. You can easily import that particular file into the current web (for more about using Word to create Web pages, see Lesson 21, "Creating Web Pages in Word," in Part III of this book.

To import a file into the current web, follow these steps:

1. Select the **File** menu and select **Import**. The Import dialog box appears.

2. Click the **Add File** button. The Add File to Import List dialog box appears.

3. Use the **Look In** drop-down box to locate the drive that holds the file you want to import, and then navigate the folders in the main window until you reach the file's exact location. After selecting the file, click the **OK** button.

4. The filename appears in the Import dialog box (see Figure 3.6). Repeat steps 2 and 3 if you want to add more files to the Import list.

5. When you have added all the files to the Import list that you want to import into the current web, click the **OK** button.

Figure 3.6   You can import one or several files into the current web.

The file (or files) is imported into the current web. You can find the files listed in the Folder List of your web. The files then must be made part of the web's navigational structure. Go to the Navigation view and drag the file or files from the Folder List and add them to the Navigation window as discussed earlier in this lesson.

Using the FrontPage Themes

Whereas the page templates available in FrontPage for creating new pages control the overall functional layout of the page, the FrontPage themes control things such as the look, the design, and the color scheme of the pages. When you create a new web using some of the wizards (such as the Corporate Presence Wizard), you are asked to choose a theme during the web creation process. However, you can select a theme for the pages that are inserted into an empty web or created with one of the wizards (such as the Personal Web Wizard) that use the default theme (Straight Edge theme) for the newly created web.

To choose a theme for your Web pages, follow these steps:

1. Go to the Page view by clicking the **Page** icon on the Views bar.
2. Select the **Format** menu and select **Theme**. The Themes dialog box appears (see Figure 3.7).
3. You can apply the theme to the currently open Web page (the page that was shown in the Page view) or apply the theme to all the pages in the web. Click either the **Selected Page(s)** or the **All Pages** option button, respectively.
4. To choose your theme, scroll down through the themes in the **Theme** scroll box. Select a particular theme to see a preview of the theme in the Sample of Theme box in the dialog box.

Figure 3.7 The Themes dialog box gives you access to all the FrontPage themes.

5. When you have found the theme you want to use for your page or pages, select it and then click the **OK** button.

The theme is applied to the page (or pages) in your Web. Figure 3.8 shows a page to which the Spiral theme has been applied.

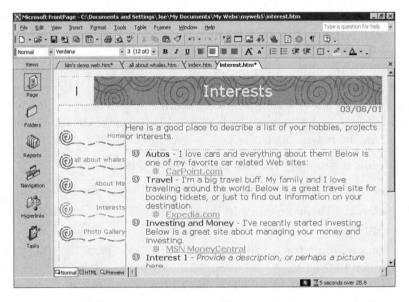

Figure 3.8 Each theme embraces a unique color scheme and related design elements.

Themes can help set the tone for a Web site and can also add a great deal of visual interest to a web. You will find that you do have control over some aspects of the theme's design.

When you are in the Themes dialog box, click the **Modify** button located near the bottom center of the dialog box. Three buttons appear just above the Modify button: Color, Graphics, and Text. Click the **Color** button to select a new color scheme for the theme. To change the background graphic used in the theme, click the **Graphics** button and then use the drop-down box to select a new graphic file. To modify the font used in the theme, click the **Text** button and make a font selection using the **Font** scroll box that appears.

Working with Text in FrontPage

In this lesson, you learn how to add, edit, and format text on your Web pages, including the creation of your own styles. You also learn how to change the page names for pages in your web.

Inserting and Modifying Text

Working with text in FrontPage is similar to working with text in any word processor, particularly Microsoft Word. Many of the text commands and features that you find in Word are also available in FrontPage (for more about working with text in Word, see Lesson 3, "Editing Documents," in the Word part of this book).

If you create your Web pages using a wizard, or if you create a new page using a template, you will see placeholder text on the pages or page. A great deal of the text work you do in FrontPage is replacing placeholder text with your own text. When you replace placeholder text with your own text, the formatting (font, text size, color, and so on) that was present on the placeholder text is also applied to the text you enter.

If you create a blank page, any text that is inserted onto the page must be formatted with an appropriate font, color, or other text attribute. Like Word, FrontPage also provides you with the capability to align text.

Replacing Placeholder Text

Replacing the placeholder text that the wizards and templates place on your text pages is just a matter of selecting the text and then typing your new text.

To replace placeholder text, follow these steps:

1. Open the page you want to edit in the Page view.
2. Select the placeholder text you want to replace on the page (see Figure 4.1).
3. Type the text that replaces the placeholder text.
4. After you change the text on a particular page, be sure you save the changes; click the **Save** button on the toolbar.

Selected placeholder text

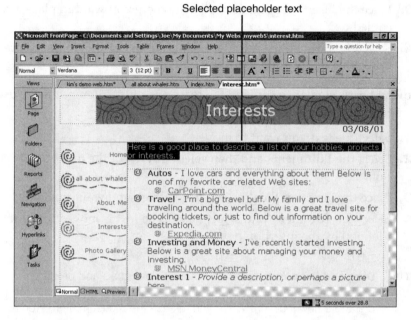

Figure 4.1 Select the placeholder text and then type your own text to replace it.

Inserting New Text

Inserting new text is a matter of positioning the insertion point (the mouse I-beam) on the page and then typing your new text. When you add new text to the page, the text is formatted using the default text attributes for the page (determined by the theme assigned to that page). This includes text formatting such as the font, size, and color of the text.

If you insert text onto a new page that does not have a theme assigned to it, the text is inserted in a Times New Roman default font. You can then modify the look of the text as needed.

Copying, Moving, and Deleting Text

You can copy or cut text and then paste it to another location on the current page or switch to another page in the web and paste the text there. Follow these steps to copy and paste text:

1. Select the text you want to copy.

2. Select the **Edit** menu and select **Copy**.

3. Place the insertion point on the page where you want to place a copy of the copied text.

4. Select the **Edit** menu and select **Paste**. A copy of the text is inserted at the insertion point.

Moving text is similar to copying the text—the only difference is the use of the Cut command rather than Copy:

1. Select the text you want to move.

2. Select the **Edit** menu, and then select **Cut** to cut the text from its current position.

3. Place the insertion point on the page where you want to move the text.

4. Select the **Edit** menu and select **Paste**. The text is moved to the new location (defined by the insertion point).

 TIP   **Drag and Drop Your Text**   You can also use drag and drop to move text on a Web page. Select the text and, without releasing the mouse button, drag the insertion point to a new location. When you release the mouse button, FrontPage moves your text to the insertion point's new location.

To delete placeholder text or text that you've placed on a page, select the text and press the **Delete** key on the keyboard.

Changing How the Text Looks

You have complete control over the formatting attributes of the text on the pages of your web. You can format text using the various buttons on the FrontPage Formatting toolbar, or you can take advantage of the text styles that are provided by the theme or template that you assign to your Web page or pages.

Using the Formatting Toolbar

B **I** **U**   The Formatting toolbar enables you to change the font, text size, text attributes (such as bold and italic), and color of the font. In most cases, it's a matter of selecting the text and then clicking the appropriate attribute button on the Formatting toolbar to change the look of the text. Bold, italic, and underline work in this manner.

Other attributes, such as the font, font size, or font color, require that you select the text and then select your formatting change from a list or palette. For example, to change the font, select the text and then select a new font using the Font drop-down box on the Formatting toolbar. Font size is also controlled by a drop-down box on the Formatting toolbar. Changing the color of selected text requires that you choose a new color from a color palette.

To change the color of the text on a page, follow these steps:

1. Select the word or other text that you want to change the color of.

 2. Click the **Font Color** drop-down button on the Formatting toolbar. The color palette appears (see Figure 4.2).

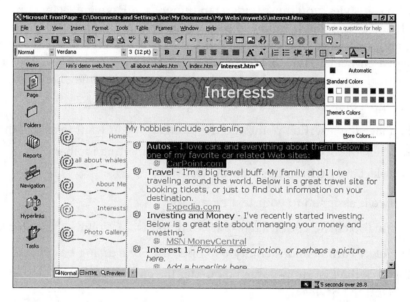

Figure 4.2   Changing text attributes such as color requires that you select the text and then choose the new attribute on the Formatting toolbar.

3. Choose a font color from the palette. The text color changes.

4. Click anywhere on the page to deselect the text.

CAUTION

Text Attribute Changes Override Theme Styles   FrontPage relies heavily on styles to format the text on the pages in your web, especially if you've chosen a theme for your pages. When you select text and change the formatting using the buttons on the Formatting toolbar, these changes override the current style. In fact, even if you change the style of this modified text, the attributes provided by the new style also are overridden by your former formatting changes.

Using FrontPage Styles

A style is a grouping of formatting attributes identified by a style name. A style might include text-formatting attributes such as bold text, a particular font color, and a particular font size. Styles can also contain text alignment attributes such as center or right-align.

FrontPage provides several built-in styles from which you can choose. There are a series of heading styles, styles for bulleted and numbered lists, and a number of others. To use styles, you must understand how FrontPage views text on a Web page. Each line of text that is followed by a paragraph mark (placed at the end of the line or paragraph when you press the Enter key) is considered a separate paragraph. To assign a particular style to a text paragraph (whether it's a single line or several lines of text), all you have to do is place the insertion point somewhere in the text block.

To assign a built-in style to text on a page, follow these steps:

1. Place the insertion point into the paragraph you want to assign the style to.
2. Click the **Style** drop-down box on the Formatting toolbar.
3. Select a style from the drop-down list.

The style is assigned to your text paragraph.

You can also create your own text styles if you want. Follow these steps:

1. Select **Format** and then **Style** to open the Style dialog box (see Figure 4.3).
2. Click the **List** drop-down box under the currently listed styles and select **User-Defined Styles**.

Figure 4.3   The Style dialog box is the starting place for creating, editing, and managing the styles for your pages.

3. To create the new style, click the **New** button. The New Style dialog box appears.

4. Type a name for your new style into the **Name** box.

5. Click the **Format** button on the bottom left of the New Style dialog box. Select **Font** to change the font attributes for style (the Font dialog box appears).

6. After completing your font attribute selections, click **OK** to return to the New Style dialog box. To include other attributes in the style, click the **Format** button again and select **Paragraph**, **Border**, or other style attributes as required.

7. When you have finished the formatting choices for the style, click **OK** to close the New Style dialog box and return to the Style dialog box. Your new style appears in the style list.

8. Click **OK** again to return to your page.

You can assign your new style to text on the page the same as you can any of the premade styles. Place the insertion point on the text and click the **Style** drop-down box on the Formatting toolbar. Select your style (which appears at the end of the style list).

> **Styles Are Not Shared by Different Pages**   When you create a FrontPage style for a particular page, it is good only on that page. You can't use it on any other pages—not even pages in the same web. You must re-create it for each page on which you want to use it.

Aligning Text

Another aspect of formatting text is aligning it on the page. The default alignment for new text on a Web page is left-justified. This means it aligns directly against the left margin of a page or against any shared borders that have been placed on the left side of a page. (Shared borders are discussed in Lesson 6, "Inserting Special FrontPage Components.")

The simplest way to align text on a page is using the alignment buttons on the Formatting toolbar. First, place the insertion point in the text and then select one of the following alignment possibilities:

- **Left Justified**—The default justification for normal text, aligned on the left. Click the **Align Left** button on the Formatting toolbar.

- **Right Justified**—Text is aligned at the right margin. A ragged-left edge is present on text that is right-aligned. Click the **Align Right** button on the Formatting toolbar.

- **Center**—The text is centered between the left and right margins of the page. Click the **Center** button on the Formatting toolbar.

Changing Page Names

When you create pages using the Web Wizards, default page names are assigned to the pages in the web. Often, you want to customize these page names to suit your own needs. Unfortunately, when you click one of the premade page banners placed at the top of the page, you will find that you cannot edit the text as you would regular text on the page. The banner does not allow you to select the text or place the insertion point on the banner.

For example, if you create a new web using the Personal Web Wizard, four pages are created for you: Home Page, Interests, Photo Album, and Favorites. The wizard automatically places page banners at the top of each page (more about page banners is covered in Lesson 6). If you want to change the text in the banner, you must change the page name itself. For example, if you want to change the Interests page's banner to read Hobbies, you must change the page's name.

To change the page name for a page in your web, follow these steps:

1. Click the **Navigation** icon on the Views bar to go to the Navigation view.
2. Right-click the page you want to rename and select **Rename** from the shortcut menu that appears (see Figure 4.4).

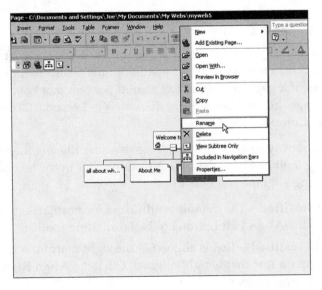

Figure 4.4 Change the page name of a page in the Navigation view.

3. Type the new name for the page.

4. Click any other page in the web to deselect the **Name** box for the page that was edited.

Working with Graphics in FrontPage

In this lesson, you learn how to insert pictures, clip art, and motion clips onto your Web pages and save the graphical files as part of your web. You also learn how to preview pages in the web.

Inserting Pictures

FrontPage makes it easy for you to insert images, clip art, and special animated images into your Web pages. You can insert pictures that you download from the World Wide Web, scan with a scanner, or capture with a digital camera. You can also insert clip art and motion clips from the Clip Art Gallery.

You will find that FrontPage enables you to insert several picture file formats into your Web pages:

- CompuServe GIF (.gif)
- Encapsulated PostScript (.eps)
- Various paint programs (.pcx)
- Tagged Image File format (.tif)
- Windows bitmap (.bmp)
- JPEG File Interchange format (.jpg)

Inserting a picture onto a Web page is really just a matter of placing the insertion point at the appropriate position and then locating the picture file that you want to insert.

To insert a picture file, follow these steps:

1. Open the page (double-click it in the Navigation view) where you want to place the picture. You are in the Page view.

2. Place the insertion point where you want to place the graphic.

3. Select **Insert**, point at **Picture**, and select **From File** on the cascading menu. The Picture dialog box appears (see Figure 5.1).

Figure 5.1 The Picture dialog box allows you to insert picture files into your Web pages.

4. Use the **Look In** drop-down list (near the top left of the dialog box) to locate the drive that contains the picture file, and double-click to open the folder that holds the file. After you locate the picture, click the file to select it.

5. Click **OK**, and the image is placed on your page (see Figure 5.2).

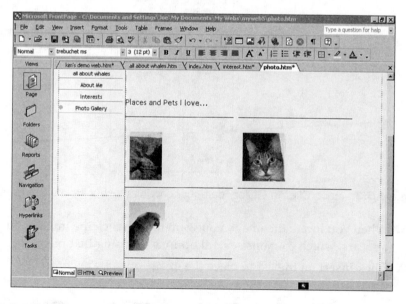

Figure 5.2 Pictures can add visual interest to your Web pages.

Inserting Clip Art

You can also insert any number of images from the Clip Art Gallery. Drawings of animals, computers, and even cartoons are available for you to use on your Web pages.

To insert clip art images, follow these steps:

1. Open the page (double-click it in the Navigation view) where you want to place the picture. You are in the Page view.

2. Place the insertion point where you want to place the clip art.

3. Select the **Insert** menu and point at **Picture**. Select **Clip Art** from the cascading menu. The Insert Clip Art task pane opens.

4. Type a subject or category (such as Animals) into the Search text box to view a set of images (see Figure 5.3).

Figure 5.3   Each Clip Art Gallery category provides a set of related images.

5. When you locate the image you want to use, click the image. A drop-down list appears, which contains several options for using that piece of clip art.

6. Click **Insert** on the list to place the image on your page.

Inserting Clip Art Gallery Motion Clips

The Clip Art Gallery also provides several motion clips that you can place on your Web pages. These motion clips are actually animated clip art. These animated images are activated when someone visits a page on your web that contains the animation.

Motion clips can add interest and excitement to your site. To insert a motion clip, follow these steps:

1. Open the page (double-click it in the Navigation view) where you want to place the picture. You are in the Page view.
2. Place the insertion point where you want to place the clip art.
3. Select the **Insert** menu and then point at **Picture**. Select **Clip Art** from the cascading menu. The Clip Art task pane opens.
4. Type in a subject (such as Clocks) under **Search Text**.
5. Check the **Movies** box under the **Results Should Be** pull-down menu. Then, click the **Search** button.

Not All the Clip Categories Provide Motion Clips   When you are looking for motion clips in the various Clip Art Gallery categories, you might find that a particular category does not provide any motion clips at all.

CAUTION

6. To preview a motion clip, click the clip's pop-up menu and click **Preview/Properties**. A Preview/Properties box appears, and the animation starts playing (see Figure 5.4).

Figure 5.4   Motion clips can be previewed by clicking **Preview/Properties** before you insert the clips onto your Web pages.

7. When you have finished previewing the motion clip, click the **Close** button in the preview's lower-right corner.
8. To insert a motion clip, click the image and then click **Insert** on the pop-up menu to place the image onto your page.

The motion clip appears as a static image on your Web page. You must preview the page to see the motion clip in action (see the section "Previewing Your Images" in this lesson for more information).

Saving the Image to Your Web

You might think that inserting a picture file, clip-art image, or motion clip onto a particular page makes that image part of your web—it is, after all, on one of the web's pages. Unfortunately, like inserting a new page into the Web (as covered in Lesson 3, "Working with Web Pages and Themes"), that's not the case. When you save the page where you inserted the image, you also have to save the image itself as a separate file that is placed with the other files held in the current Web folder. A Save Embedded Files dialog box appears after your save the page. Use this dialog box to save the images that you have placed on the page as separate Web files.

Web pages can't have graphics that are embedded on the pages. So, when you insert a graphic onto a FrontPage Web page, you are actually setting up a link between the page and the graphic that you inserted. When you view Web pages on the World Wide Web using your Web browser, the pictures you see are linked to the page that you open in your browser.

Another thing you should be aware of is that when the inserted image (picture, clip art, and so on) is saved to the web, it is saved in a file format that is best for viewing on Web pages. Files in any format other than .gif or .jpg are converted to .gif files when you save them to the web. Web pages typically contain .gif and .jpg files because these two file formats provide good resolution and color in a fairly compact file size.

To save a page image as part of the web, follow these steps:

1. With the page open in the Page view, click the **Save** button on the toolbar. The Save Embedded Files dialog box appears (see Figure 5.5).

Figure 5.5   Embedded graphics must be saved as separate files in the Web folder.

2. A new name for the file is provided (based on the original filename of the image) and the image is saved as a .gif file by default (if it's not already a .jpg). Click **OK** to save the file.

The image file is now part of the web. The new file created in step 2 is placed in your Web folder.

TIP   **Save Photos As .jpg Files**—The Save Embedded Files dialog box saves all inserted images that are not .jpg files as .gif files by default. In the case of scanned photos or photos taken with a digital camera that are not .jpg files when you insert them, you might want to force FrontPage to save them as .jpg files rather than .gif files. Photos look better on the Web when saved as .jpg. In the Save Embedded Files dialog box, select the photo's filename, and then click the **Picture Options** button. In the Picture Options dialog box that appears, click the **JPEG** option button, and then click OK. Now when you save the file it is saved in the .jpg format.

CAUTION   **The Save As Dialog Box Appears If the Page Hasn't Been Saved**   When you click the **Save** button to save an embedded image on a page, the Save As dialog box appears if the page itself hasn't been saved before. Provide a name and save the page. Then, the Save Embedded Files dialog box appears, and you can save the image file to the web.

Sizing the Image

You can size any image you place on a page. As you size an image, you will find that it affects the text below the image. The larger you make the picture, the more the text is moved down the page.

To size an image, follow these steps:

1. Click the image to select it.

2. Place the mouse pointer on any of the sizing handles that appear around the image. The mouse pointer becomes a two-headed arrow.

3. Drag to increase or decrease the size of the image (see Figure 5.6). Release the mouse when you have finished sizing the image.

Mouse pointer

Figure 5.6   Use the sizing handles to increase or decrease the size of your image.

TIP   Maintain the Image's Height/Width Ratio   Use the sizing handles on the corners of the image and drag diagonally to maintain the image's height/width ratio. This keeps the image from looking distorted.

Aligning the Image

You can also align your images on the page. The simplest way to align a graphic is using the alignment buttons on the Formatting toolbar. For example, to place an image on the center of the page, click the **Center** button on the toolbar.

When you use the Formatting toolbar buttons, however, you are changing only the position of the image; you are not changing how text on the page wraps around the image. The default setting for how text relates to a picture is for text not to wrap around the image.

To change the position of an image in relation to surrounding text, you must use settings found in the Picture Properties dialog box.

To change image alignment and how text wraps around the image, follow these steps:

1. Right-click the image and select **Picture Properties** from the shortcut menu. The Picture Properties dialog box appears.

2. Click the **Appearance** tab on the Picture Properties dialog box. Picture alignment and text wrapping are controlled by the Alignment drop-down box and the Wrapping Style boxes (see Figure 5.7).

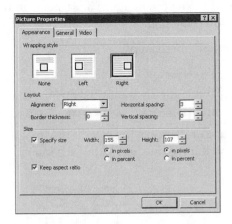

Figure 5.7   Use the Alignment box and the Wrapping Style boxes on the Appearance tab to control the alignment of a picture and how text wraps around it.

3. The first time you go to the Appearance tab, the setting in the Alignment box is Default. Default means that the picture is aligned where you inserted it (normally on the left side of the page) and text does not wrap around the picture.

4. To change the position of the picture and how text wraps around the picture, click one of the Wrapping Style boxes to make one of the following selections:

   - **Left**—This aligns the picture on the left of the page and allows text to wrap around the image on the right.

   - **None**—This enables you to place text on both the left and right side of the image. (It does not center the image relative to the page, but places the image in the center of the text.)

   - **Right**—This places the image on the right of the page and allows text to wrap around the left side of the picture.

5. After you make your alignment selection, click **OK** to close the Picture Properties dialog box.

You are returned to your page. You can now insert text on the page so that it wraps around the picture (depending on which of the alignment options you chose).

If you want to place a border around a particular picture, open the Picture Properties dialog box for that picture and click the **Appearance** tab. Use the **Border Thickness** box to set a thickness for a border around the picture. Click **OK** to close the dialog box after you've set the border thickness.

Previewing Your Images

When you work with pictures and graphics on a page, it's nice to be able to take a quick look at how they appear when your pages are viewed on the World Wide Web. This is particularly useful if you've placed motion clips on your pages and want to see how they look when the animations are playing.

When you are in Page view, you can quickly preview a particular page and the elements you have placed on that page. Click the **Preview** tab at the bottom of the page window. The page as it appears in a Web browser displays in the Preview mode (see Figure 5.8).

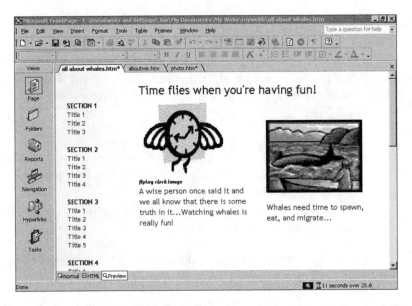

Figure 5.8 Previewing your pages enables you to see how graphics (especially motion clips) look on the World Wide Web.

To return to your page so that you can edit it, click the **Normal** tab.

The Preview mode provides a quick view of how things will appear on the World Wide Web. The test, however, is to view pages in a Web browser, which gives you a true picture of how the site will look. Keep in mind, however, that Web pages will look decidedly different in different Web browsers. FrontPage is set up to produce webs that work well when viewed with Microsoft Internet Explorer. If your audience is going to use other Web browsers (and they will if your audience is everyone on the Internet), you should test your site using other browsers, such as Netscape Navigator.

Inserting Special FrontPage Components

In this lesson, you learn how to insert special FrontPage components such as navigation bars, page banners, shared borders, and hit counters.

Understanding Special Components

FrontPage provides several special elements, called *components*, that you can place on your Web pages. These components are designed to take the place of sophisticated elements such as navigation bars and hit counters that you would normally have to create using the HTML coding language.

Many special components are available in FrontPage. Table 6.1 defines some of the commonly used components.

Table 6.1 FrontPage Special Components

Component	Purpose
Shared borders	A shared border is an area that is common to the pages in your web. Any item placed in a shared border appears on all the pages of the web.
Page banner	Displays the page name at the top of the page. Page banners use the text attributes and pictures of a theme assigned to that page. Page banners placed in shared borders display the page name of every page in the web.
Navigation bar	A set of text or graphics that provides hyperlinks to the other pages in a Web site. A navigation bar placed in a shared border is displayed on all the pages in the web.
Hit counters	A page component that appears as a numbered counter and keeps count of the number of visits (called *hits*) to your Web site.

Normally, the creation of items such as those mentioned in Table 6.1 requires a good understanding of HTML programming and is usually the sign of a fairly sophisticated Web site. However, FrontPage enables you to place very complex components (complex in a programming sense) on your Web pages by taking advantage of the options available on the Insert menu.

CAUTION

The FrontPage Extensions Must Be Installed on the Web Server If You Use Special Components The FrontPage special components require that FrontPage extensions be installed on the Web server that hosts your web. You should talk to your Internet service provider before publishing your web to their web server. If they do not use the FrontPage extensions, you should forgo the use of special components in your web if you want it to function correctly on the server.

Using Shared Borders

Shared borders enable you to create an area on the top, bottom, left, or right of a page that can be shared by all the pages in the Web site. Shared borders are similar to headers and footers used in Microsoft Word where you want information of some type to appear on all the pages of a document. In FrontPage, this enables you to put items such as navigation bars or page banners in the shared border area so that they appear on all the pages. This means that you have to insert the component (such as a navigation bar) into the shared border area on only one of the pages in the web, and the component appears on all the pages in the web (in the shared border area).

If you've used any of the Web Wizards to create your web, you've already seen the application of shared borders. For example, webs created using the Personal Web Wizard automatically place shared borders on the left and top of the pages in the web.

To insert shared borders on your Web pages or to modify the current shared borders, follow these steps:

1. Open one of the pages in your web (double-click it in the Navigation view).

2. Select the **Format** menu and then select **Shared Borders**. The Shared Borders dialog box appears (see Figure 6.1).

Figure 6.1 Set shared border parameters in the Shared Borders dialog box.

3. Option buttons at the top of the dialog box enable you to place the shared borders on **All Pages** or **Current Page**. For a web with consistent design, select the **All Pages** option button.

4. Click the appropriate check box for the location of the shared borders you want to place on the pages: **Top, Left, Right, Bottom**. You can check more than one box.

5. If you select Top or Left, you can also choose to have navigation buttons for the web automatically placed in the shared border area. Click the **Include Navigation Buttons** check box as needed to include navigation buttons.

6. When you have finished your selections, click **OK**.

Your shared borders appear on the page or pages of your web (depending on the selections you made in the Shared Borders dialog box). The shared border areas are excellent places to insert other special components, such as page banners, navigation bars, or even company logos or pictures. Any items you want to repeat on your Web pages can be placed in a shared border area. Figure 6.2 shows a Web page that has shared borders at the top and left of the page.

Figure 6.2   Shared borders enable you to place repeating elements on all the pages in your web.

Creating Page Banners

Page banners provide a colorful heading for your pages that is consistent across the pages in a web. Page banners can consist of text that uses the font and colors of the theme selected for the web (if a theme was selected). Page banners can also consist of a graphical image with text that uses graphical elements, fonts, and colors from the current theme.

Page banners can be placed anywhere on the page (but are most useful at the top of the page as the main heading for that page). When a page banner is placed in a shared border area, it displays the appropriate page name for the current page and also appears on the other pages in the web. (The page name is the name assigned to the page in the Navigation view.)

To insert a page banner, follow these steps:

1. Open the page (double-click it in the Navigation view) where you want to place the page banner. If you plan on placing the banner in a shared border area, you can open any page in the web (displaying the shared border).

2. Place the insertion point where you want to place the banner. To place it in a shared border area, click within the shared border (placeholder text in the border area is selected).

3. Select **Insert**, **Page Banner**. The Page Banner Properties dialog box appears (see Figure 6.3).

Figure 6.3   The Page Banner Properties dialog box enables you to insert a text or a graphical banner on your Web page.

4. Select the **Picture** or **Text** option button to determine the type of banner you create. If you select Picture, the banner will consist of a graphic containing the page's name. The banner format is based on the theme that has been selected for the web. If you use the Text option, the banner is inserted as regular text and can be formatted or aligned on the page as any other text element.

5. If you want to change the page banner text, select the text in the Page Banner Text box and type the new banner heading.

6. Click **OK** and the banner is placed on your page (see Figure 6.4).

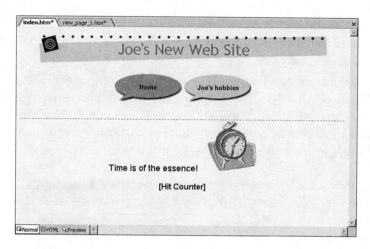

Figure 6.4   The new page banner appears on your Web page.

If you chose to place the page banner in a shared border, the new banner appears on each page in the web. If you want to modify a page banner, double-click the banner to open the Page Banner dialog box. You can remove a banner by selecting it and pressing the **Delete** key on the keyboard.

Changing the Banner Text Changes the Page Name   If you decide to change the text for the banner in the Page Banner dialog box, this also changes the name of that particular page when you go to the Navigation view for the web.

CAUTION

Inserting Navigation Bars

Making it easy for visitors to your Web site to move between the pages in your web is a necessity (or they might not stay and view your site). Navigation links must be available on each page. Fortunately, FrontPage provides a way to quickly (and easily) place navigation links on your page in the form of navigation bars. Navigation bars—preprogrammed components that can be placed in the shared border area of your Web pages—provide direction-finding buttons that take you to the other pages in your web.

To insert a navigation bar into your web, follow these steps:

1. Open the page (double-click it in the Navigation view) where you want to place the navigation bar. If you plan on placing the navigation bar in a shared border area, you can open any page in the web (displaying the shared border).

2. Place the insertion point where you want to place the banner. To place it in a shared border area, click within the shared border (placeholder text in the border area is selected).

3. Select **Insert**, **Navigation**. The Insert Web Component dialog box appears (see Figure 6.5). Under Choose a Bar Type, you can select from several navigational bars (a description appears below each one as you click it). Choose a bar type and then an orientation (horizontal or vertical) for your links buttons. Press **Finish** when your selections are completed.

Figure 6.5 The Insert Web Component dialog box allows you to determine the type of navigation bar that is created on the pages.

4. After you press **Finish**, a Link Bar Properties box appears (see Figure 6.6). Option buttons are provided for you to choose the type of links (set up for you as hyperlinks) that can appear on the navigation bar. Select one of the buttons, depending on the navigation links you want to create:

   - **Parent Level**—Provides a button or text link that takes you to the parent page of the current page.
   - **Same Level**—Provides links to other pages in the web that are at the same level as the current page (when viewed in the Navigation view).
   - **Back and Next**—Provides links to take you to the previous page and the next page.
   - **Child Level**—Provides links to any child pages of the current page (pages shown below the current page in the Navigation view).
   - **Top Level**—Provides links to any pages (including the home page) that are on the home page's level in the navigational structure of the web.
   - **Child Pages Under Home**—Provides links to pages under Home. This is useful if you've divided your web into sections using section pages under Home in the navigational structure of the web.

Figure 6.6   The Link Bar Properties box is where you choose the type of navigational structure you want on each page.

5. You can also choose to have links to your home page or parent page of the current page by selecting either the **Home Page** or **Parent Page** check box on the right of the dialog box. These links appear on the navigation bar in addition to the other links that you chose in step 4.

6. After making all your selections, click **OK**.

The navigation bar appears on the current page. Figure 6.7 shows a navigation bar that uses the colors and design elements of the current theme for the web (the Blocks theme). Buttons are chosen to show links to the home page of the web (the current page shown) and child pages of the current page (the other pages currently in the web).

Figure 6.7   A navigation bar provides links to the other pages in your web.

If you want to edit the navigation bar, double-click it to open the Navigation Bar dialog box. If you want to delete the navigation bar, select it and press the **Delete** key.

Inserting Hit Counters

Another useful component that you might want to place on the home page of your web is a hit counter. Hit counters show you and the visitors to your Web site how many hits (or visits) have been made to your site. It's fun for visitors to see that their visit counts, literally, and it's also important to see what kind of traffic your Web site is experiencing. Creating a hit counter normally requires pretty good knowledge of HTML coding. Fortunately, FrontPage provides a number of ready-made hit counters that you can insert as components.

To insert a FrontPage hit counter, follow these steps:

1. Open the home page for your site in the Page view. (The hit counter is typically placed on the main page for your site.)

2. Place the insertion point where you want to place the hit counter. Most sites place them directly below any text or graphics found on the home page of the Web site.

3. Select **Insert**, point at **Web Component**, and the Insert Web Component box appears (see Figure 6.8).

Figure 6.8 The Insert Web Component dialog box provides you with several hit counter styles.

4. Under Component Type choose **Hit Counter**. To the right, you see the Choose a Counter Style box. Select one of the hit counter styles from the dialog box.

5. Click **Finish**, and the Hit Counter Properties dialog box appears with your selection. Press **OK** to insert the selected hit counter onto your page.

The hit counter appears on your page as text (Hit Counter) enclosed in brackets. You cannot view the hit counter until you save the current web and publish it to a Web server that contains the Office server extension files. (Discuss the server extensions with your Internet service provider; the extension files must be on the ISP's Web server for special components such as the hit counter to work.)

Working with Hyperlinks

In this lesson, you learn how to insert and manage hyperlinks on your Web pages.

Understanding Hyperlinks

An important aspect of creating Web pages is being able to insert hyperlinks onto the pages of your Web site. A *hyperlink* references another Web page on your site or another Web site on the World Wide Web. Hyperlinks are the main tool for navigating the World Wide Web.

For example, the navigation bars that you place on your Web pages so that visitors can navigate your Web site really consist of a list of ready-made hyperlinks to the pages on your site. (For more about navigation bars, see Lesson 6, "Inserting Special FrontPage Components.") You can also insert hyperlinks into your site that enable you to access other Web sites on the Web or send e-mail to a specific person.

Because FrontPage provides navigation bars that automatically provide hyperlinks to the pages in your web, you might wonder why you would ever create your own hyperlinks. First, if you want to create links to other Web sites on the Web, you must use hyperlinks. Also, if you place your Web pages on a Web server that does not recognize the Office Web server extensions, special FrontPage components such as the navigation bars do not function correctly; therefore, you must insert your own hyperlinks for the navigation of the pages in your site. You can then build a working site and post it to any Web server.

Hyperlinks can take the form of text or graphics. For example, a text line referencing a particular Web site can easily be turned into a hyperlink that takes you to that site. If you would rather link to another site using a graphic (such as a company logo), it can also be set up as a hyperlink. As with other Web page elements such as graphics, you should limit the number of hyperlinks that you place on the page. Avoiding cluttering up the page makes it easier for someone to use the hyperlinks to jump to other content on your Web.

FrontPage makes it easy for you to create hyperlinks to the pages in your own Web site using bookmarks. Bookmarks are discussed later in this lesson in "Using Bookmarks."

Creating Text Hyperlinks

Text hyperlinks are great for listing your favorite Web sites. You can create a list of text entries that describe the site to which the hyperlink connects. The descriptive text can be selected and then turned into a hyperlink for the described destination.

Another advantage of using text for hyperlinks is that the text appears in one color when viewed on the Web (blue, for example, is the default in FrontPage). When the link has been used (to go to the destination of the hyperlink) and the text is viewed again, it appears in a different color (violet is the default color for previously viewed hyperlinks in FrontPage). This makes it easy to keep track of the hyperlinks that have been used and those that have not.

To place a text hyperlink on a Web page, follow these steps:

1. Open the page (double-click it in the Navigation view) on which you want to place the hyperlink.
2. Type the text that will serve as the hyperlink. It can be the name of the site or any descriptive text you want.
3. Select the text you want to use as the hyperlink.
4. Select **Insert** and then select **Hyperlink**. The Insert Hyperlink dialog box appears (see Figure 7.1).

Figure 7.1   The Insert Hyperlink dialog box enables you to create hyperlinks on your Web pages.

5. To create a link to a Web site, type the address of the site into the Address box. This address typically takes the form www.*nameofsite*.com. You can also select the address for the link by using your Web browser. If you are connecting to the Internet, you can click the **Browse the Web** button (to the right of the Look In box). Your Web browser opens. Go to the page you want to link to and click its address. Then return to FrontPage. The page address appears in the Address box.

6. After you have the address in the Address box, click **OK**.

7. Click anywhere on the page to deselect the hyperlink text.

The text that was selected for the hyperlink is now underlined on your Web page (see Figure 7.2).

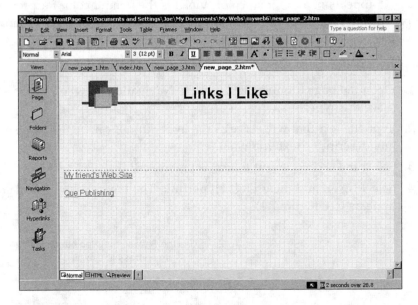

Figure 7.2   Your text hyperlink is underlined on the Web page.

TIP   **How to Test External Hyperlinks**   If you want to test a hyperlink you've created that points to another Web site, open the page that contains the hyperlink. Be sure you are connected to the Internet, and then click the **Preview in Browser** button. This opens the current page in your Web browser. Click the hyperlink, and you should be taken to the site to which the hyperlink points.

Creating Graphical Hyperlinks

You can also make a graphic, such as a picture or clip art, a hyperlink to a page in your Web site or to a page in another Web site. The process of creating image hyperlinks is very straightforward and similar to the process of creating text hyperlinks.

To place a graphical hyperlink on a Web page, follow these steps:

1. Open the page (double-click it in the Navigation view) on which you want to place the hyperlink.

2. Insert the picture or clip art you want to use as the hyperlink.

3. Select the graphic you want to use as the hyperlink.

4. Select **Insert**, **Hyperlink**. The Insert Hyperlink dialog box appears.

5. Type the address for the Web site you want to link to into the **Address** box. You can also select the address for the link by using your Web browser. If you are connecting to the Internet, you can click the **Browse the Web** button. Locate the page you want to link to and click its address. Then return to FrontPage. The page address appears in the Address box.

6. Click **OK** to return to the Web page.

The graphic is now a hyperlink to the address you provided in the Insert Hyperlink dialog box. Save the page and use your Web browser to test the link.

Using Bookmarks

If you want to create hyperlinks between pages on your own Web site or create links that jump to a particular position on a page (useful for very long pages that must be scrolled through), you might want to take advantage of bookmarks. A bookmark is a particular place or text on a page that you have marked—that is, you have made that spot on the page a bookmark. You can then use the bookmark to create a hyperlink that takes you to that bookmark.

To place a bookmark on a page, follow these steps:

1. In Page view, position the insertion point where you want to create a bookmark, or select the text or a graphic to which you want to assign the bookmark.

2. Select the **Insert** menu and then select **Bookmark**. The Bookmark dialog box opens (see Figure 7.3).

3. In the **Bookmark Name** box, type the name of the bookmark. If you selected text to serve as the bookmark, the selected text appears in the Bookmark Name box.

4. When you have finished naming your bookmark, click **OK**.

Figure 7.3 The Bookmark dialog box is where you name the new bookmark.

Selected text that has been designated as a bookmark has a dashed line under it. If you designate a particular place on a page as a bookmark by inserting the insertion point, a small flag appears at that point on the page.

Now that you've got a bookmark, you can create a hyperlink using it. Follow these steps:

1. Go to the page where you want to place the hyperlink and select the text or graphic you want to use as the hyperlink.
2. Select **Insert**, **Hyperlink**. The Insert Hyperlink dialog box appears.
3. Click the **Bookmark** button and select the bookmark that will serve as the destination for the hyperlink.
4. Click **OK** to return to the Web page.

Now when you test the hyperlink, you should find that it takes you to the page in your web where you placed the bookmark.

To delete a bookmark that you no longer want or need, follow these steps:

1. Select the **Insert** menu and then select **Bookmark**.
2. In the Bookmark dialog box, select the bookmark you want to remove and click the **Clear** button.
3. Click **OK** to close the dialog box.

Editing or Deleting Hyperlinks

You can also edit or delete the hyperlinks you place on your pages. You might think that by deleting a graphic or text that has been assigned a hyperlink, you also delete the hyperlink; in fact, you do. But in most cases, you probably want to keep the text or graphic on your Web page and change the hyperlink URL address or remove just the hyperlink attached to the text or graphic. Both of these tasks are handled in the Hyperlink dialog box.

Follow these steps to edit or remove a hyperlink:

1. Right-click the graphic or text that has been assigned the hyperlink. A shortcut menu appears.

2. Select **Hyperlink Properties** on the shortcut menu. The Edit Hyperlink dialog box opens.

3. To edit the hyperlink, select the address in the **Address** box and type a new address.

4. To delete the hyperlink, click the **Remove Link** button next to the address box. The address currently showing will have its link disconnected.

5. Click the **OK** button.

You will find that if the link was a text entry and you remove its hyperlinking capability, the text is no longer underlined. Edited hyperlinks can be tested by previewing the page in your Web browser.

Completing and Publishing Your Web Site

In this lesson, you learn how to complete a web using tasks and how to publish your web to the World Wide Web.

Using Tasks to Complete a Web

As you create and fine-tune a web you want to place on the World Wide Web, you will find that you must complete many individual tasks before the site is ready to be published. You have to make sure that graphics or other images have been placed in the appropriate places and that hyperlinks correctly point to their particular destinations. Even the simplest of sites requires you to make changes and improvements to pages in the web, even if you created the web with a wizard.

FrontPage offers a tool for helping you to stay organized as you create and complete a web. FrontPage tasks provide a way to keep a running list of your web duties as you work on the site. This Tasks list can be viewed any time in the Tasks view.

You will find that tasks are automatically created by some of the FrontPage wizards, such as the Corporate Presence Wizard. Figure 8.1 shows a list of tasks associated with a new web created using the Corporate Presence Wizard.

Creating a New Task

You can create tasks and link them to an entire web page or to items on that page, such as pictures or other objects. The easiest way to create a new task that is linked to a particular page is to create the task with the page in the Page view. For example, suppose you have a page that will contain hyperlinks to your favorite sites. You can create a task for this page to make sure you've placed all the appropriate hyperlinks (to your favorite sites) on the page before you publish the web.

Figure 8.1 Tasks are automatically created by some of FrontPage's web wizards.

Follow these steps to create a new task:

1. Open the page (double-click it in the Navigation view) for which you want to create a task.

2. Select the **File** menu, point at **New**, and then select **Task** (or select **Edit**, **Task**, and **Add Task**). The New Task dialog box opens (see Figure 8.2).

Figure 8.2 The New Task dialog box is where you name, set the priority for, and describe your new task.

3. Type a task name into the Task Name box. To assign a priority to the task (other than the default, which is Medium), click the appropriate option button in the Priority area.

4. Type a description for the task into the Description box.

5. Click **OK** to create the new task.

The new task is created and linked to the current page. To view the new task, click the **Tasks** button on the Views bar.

 TIP   **Create Your Task List Up Front**   To help you plan the work flow on a new Web site, create the tasks for that web as soon as you (or a wizard) create the pages for that web. Staying organized ensures that your site is complete before you place it on the World Wide Web.

Starting a Task

After you create the task (or several tasks), you can view the task in the Tasks view. This view is also where you start a task, mark a task as complete, or delete an unwanted task.

To start a particular task, follow these steps:

1. In the Tasks view, double-click the task you want to start. The Task Details dialog box opens (see Figure 8.3).

Figure 8.3   Start your task using the Task Details dialog box.

2. Click the **Start Task** button.

FrontPage takes you to the page or other object to which the task was linked. For example, if your task is to create hyperlinks on a particular page, you are taken to that page where you can begin creating the needed hyperlinks.

Completing a Task

After you finish a particular task, you can mark that task as completed. Saving the page that the task was assigned to does this. Follow these steps:

1. Click the **Save** button on the toolbar. A message box appears, letting you know that this page was opened from the Tasks view.

2. To mark the task as completed, click **Yes** (if you haven't completed the task but want to save your changes, click **No**, and you can complete the task at a later time).

When you return to the Tasks view (click the **Tasks** icon on the Views bar), the task is marked as completed. You can also mark tasks as completed directly in the Tasks view. Right-click the task and select **Mark Complete** on the shortcut menu that appears.

If you find that you end up with redundant tasks or create a task that doesn't end up fitting into your web plan—for example, you might want to delete the page associated with the task—you can easily delete any task on the list. Right-click the task and select **Delete** on the shortcut menu. FrontPage asks whether you want to delete the current task. Click **Yes** to delete the task.

Check the Web Reports   Even if you use tasks to make sure that you cover all the details related to your web, check the Reports view before publishing the site. Reports concerning unverified or broken hyperlinks or unlinked graphics (these reports are generated automatically by FrontPage) can help you avoid the embarrassment of publishing a Web site that doesn't work the way you intended it to.

CAUTION

Publishing Your Web

After you have finished your site (check the Tasks view to decide whether you are truly finished), you are ready to publish the web. Publishing the web means that you place all the folders and files in the web onto a Web server. The Web server then serves up your site to visitors on the World Wide Web.

You can take two routes to get your web onto your Web server: You can use HTTP (Hypertext Transfer Protocol) to upload your web to the server, or you can use FTP (File Transfer Protocol) to move the files.

If you use HTTP, the server you send your web files to must have the FrontPage server extensions installed on it. You should check with your Internet service provider before you upload a FrontPage web to the server to be sure the extensions are available.

If the server is not enabled with the FrontPage extensions, you can still upload to your Web server by using FTP. Be advised, however, that Web servers that do not support the FrontPage extensions preclude you from using special components on your Web pages—for example, FrontPage hit counters and themes might not work correctly.

Specifying whether you are publishing your site using HTTP or FTP is determined by how you enter the address for the Web server into the FrontPage Publish Web dialog box (covered in detail in the steps that follow). For example, suppose your Web server on the World Wide Web is called joe.com. If you are using HTTP to upload your web files, this server's address is specified as http://www.joe.com. If you are using FTP to upload the files, the address for this site is ftp.joe.com.

To publish your web, follow these steps:

1. Connect to the Internet using your dial-up connection to your Internet service provider.

2. In FrontPage, select the **File** menu and then select **Publish Web**. The Publish Destination dialog box appears (see Figure 8.4).

Figure 8.4   Enter your Web site's address into the Publish Destination dialog box.

3. Enter the address of the server that you will upload your web to in the **Enter Publish Destination** box (using either an HTTP or FTP address, as discussed earlier in this section). Click **OK**.

4. The Publish Web dialog box appears (see Figure 8.5). This box displays all the files in your web. If the web has been published previously to the address you specified in step 3, you can see the files currently stored on the Web server by clicking the **Show** button. This opens a second pane in the Publish Web dialog box showing the destination server and the web files it contains.

5. (optional) If you are publishing this web to update a Web site that has been published previously, you can choose to update only pages that have changed (since the last time you published the web). Click the **Options** button on the Publish Web dialog box. The Options dialog box appears.

Figure 8.5   The Publish Web dialog box is where you select publishing options.

6. (optional) In the Options dialog box, click the **Changed Pages Only** option button, and then click **OK** to return to the Publish Web dialog box.

7. If the current web contains hyperlinks to other webs that you have created but not published (called subwebs), select the **Include Subwebs** check box to publish these along with the current web.

8. Click the **Publish** button.

You are kept apprised of the progress of the publishing of your web while you wait. When the process has completed, click the **Done** button to close the notification box.

Your web is now available on the World Wide Web. You can use your Web browser to visit your Web site and be sure it is functioning correctly. If you need to modify pages or update the Web site, modify the original web in FrontPage and then publish the web to the server again, making sure that you check the option for changed pages to replace pages already on the server.

Internet Explorer

Using Internet Explorer

1

In this lesson, you learn how to update to the most current version of Internet Explorer and set up an Internet connection.

Installing Internet Explorer

Microsoft Office XP provides several features that are closely tied to resources on the World Wide Web. For example, Microsoft provides an online gallery of clip art and templates for use in Office applications such as Word.

To access and take advantage of information and resources on the World Wide Web, you need a Web browser. Internet Explorer provides a full-featured tool that enables you to access Web sites, download files from the Internet, and view and listen to multimedia content on the Web.

Each version of Windows (Windows 98, Windows Me, Windows 2000, and Windows XP) comes with a version of the Internet Explorer Web browser. The easiest way to get the most up-to-date version of Internet Explorer is to use the Windows Update Web site for your particular version of Windows. (If you haven't used the current version of your Internet Explorer Web browser before, you will need to run the Connection Wizard described in the next section before updating your version of Internet Explorer.)

 TIP **How Do I Check the Version of My Current Internet Explorer?** To check what version of Internet Explorer is currently installed on your computer, open Internet Explorer (double-click the icon on the desktop). Click the **Help** menu, and then select **About Internet Explorer**. The current version number is displayed in the dialog box that appears. Click **OK** to close the dialog box.

Follow these steps to upgrade your version of Internet Explorer:

1. Connect to the Internet, select the **Start** button, and then click **Windows Update**.

2. The Internet Explorer window opens and displays the update page for your version of Windows. Click the **Product Updates** link on the left of this Web page.

3. Windows Update checks your Windows configuration for installed components (this can take a few moments) and the Products Update page appears (see Figure 1.1).

Figure 1.1   Use the Windows Update page to install the most current version of Internet Explorer.

4. Scroll through the available updates and determine whether a more current version of Internet Explorer is available. If you see one, click the check box next to the newer version of Internet Explorer, and then click the **Download** button at the top of the Update page.

5. Follow the prompts provided to install the new version of Internet Explorer. You might have to restart your system to complete the installation.

Occasionally, Microsoft offers beta versions of Internet Explorer on the various Windows Update sites. Because this software is considered a work in progress, you should be advised that beta software can often cause problems on your computer. This is particularly true of Internet Explorer because it is so tightly integrated with Microsoft Windows. Install beta versions of Internet Explorer at your own risk.

CAUTION

My Company's Firewall Is Blocking Access to the Windows Update Site Many companies and small businesses use firewalls to block attacks on their internal networks from the Internet. Depending on how the firewall is configured, it can block some secured sites like the Windows Update Web sites. Consult your network administrator to provide you with the most up-to-date version of Internet Explorer that your company sanctions. If you use personal firewall software on your computer, consult the manual so that you can configure the firewall to allow interaction with secure Web sites.

Assembling Your Account Information

If you haven't already taken advantage of Internet Explorer and the other tools that it provides, such as the Outlook Express e-mail client (if you don't have Outlook installed on your system, you can use Outlook Express to send and receive Internet e-mail), you need to provide Windows with information that allows it to set up an e-mail account for you and actually connect to the Internet. The Windows Internet Connection Wizard handles this setup. The following list provides the information you must have available when you run the Connection Wizard: If you don't have some of this information, contact your Internet service provider (ISP) and ask.

- **E-Mail Account and Password**—For example, habraken@provider.com
- **Local Phone Number to Dial**—For example, 555-3948
- **Name of Incoming Mail Server**—For example, pop.provider.com
- **Name of Outgoing Mail Server**—For example, smtp.provider.com
- **Name of News Server**—For example, news.provider.com (optional if you don't intend to browse the Usenet newsgroups)

If you don't already have an account, the Internet Connection Wizard can help you sign up for an account from a service such as the Microsoft Network (MSN). The next section discusses the different options available when you run the Internet Connection Wizard.

Running the Connection Wizard

The Connection Wizard creates a Dial-Up Networking connection that dials your ISP and sends the correct settings that enable you to connect to the Internet (or allows you to configure a connection to the Web over your corporate network). It also configures Outlook Express, the program that manages your e-mail and newsgroups, and Internet Explorer, the program that enables you to browse the Web.

Follow these steps:

1. Select the **Start** button and then point at **Programs** on the Start menu that appears. On the Programs menu, point at **Accessories**, point at **Communications**, and then select **Internet Connection Wizard**. The Connection Wizard starts.

2. Click the **Next** button to begin.

3. On the first screen of the Connection Wizard (see Figure 1.2), choose one of the three options presented:

   - **I Want to Sign Up for a New Internet Account**—Choose this if you are starting from scratch, with no account.

   - **I Want to Transfer My Existing Internet Account to This Computer**— Use this if you have an account but have not used it from this computer.

   - **I Want to Set Up My Internet Connection Manually, or I Want to Connect Through a Local Area Network (LAN)**—Use this if you already have connected to your account with this computer and want to change certain settings. Also use this choice in cases where your computer is connected to the Internet by a DSL or cable-modem connection.

Figure 1.2 Use the Internet Connection Wizard to set up your computer to connect to the Internet.

4. After making your selection, click **Next**.

Depending on which of these options you choose, the wizard takes different paths at this point. If you choose the first option, it dials a phone number for an ISP referral service that helps you choose an Internet service provider from a list. It then walks you through the steps of choosing and connecting to the ISP. The list that is generated by the referral service is based on your area code.

CAUTION

Not the Only Providers   The companies shown by the Microsoft Internet Referral Service (the MIRS, not the IRS) have paid a fee to be listed. A good, economical service provider that is not listed there might be in your area. It might pay to shop around before selecting one of these providers.

If you choose the second option in step 3, you are prompted for information about how you plan to connect (phone line or LAN), and it walks you through creating the appropriate dial-up connection, if needed. Just follow the prompts, entering any information that it requests.

If you choose the third option in step 3, the Connection Wizard checks to make sure that the existing connection has all the right stuff, and then it quickly ushers you out of the program.

Using the Internet Explorer Web Browser

To open the Internet Explorer, double-click the **Internet Explorer** icon on the Windows desktop, or you can click the **Internet Explorer** icon on the Quick Start toolbar that resides on the Windows taskbar.

To actually use Internet Explorer to browse the Internet, you must be connected to your ISP. In other words, your dial-up modem, DSL modem, cable modem, or LAN must be connected to the Internet. (Usually, with a DSL modem, cable modem, or LAN, you are always connected, so you don't need to worry about establishing the connection.)

After you are connected and the Internet Explorer window opens, the browser's default Web site appears. If you're using a new installation of Internet Explorer or have not changed your home page since installing it, your home page is the MSN home page shown in Figure 1.3.

Now that you are connected to the Internet and have Internet Explorer up and running, you are ready to explore other Web sites on the World Wide Web. The next two sections discuss some of the basics of navigating Web pages.

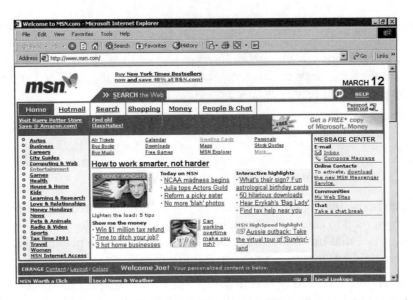

Figure 1.3 When you open the Internet Explorer, the MSN home page is opened.

Browsing with Hyperlinks

On most Web pages, one or more pictures or bits of underlined text are hyperlinks. This means you can click them to jump to other pages. For example, in Figure 1.3, on the MSN home page, almost everything you see is a hyperlink. Text and graphics both can serve as hyperlinks. The mouse pointer turns into a hand when it's over a hyperlink.

Text hyperlinks usually provide a description of the page that the hyperlink opens when you click it. Just place the mouse on a hyperlink and then click the left mouse button to use the hyperlink to jump to that page. If you would like to see the Web address (also called a URL) that the hyperlink opens before actually clicking it, place the mouse pointer on the hyperlink. The URL appears on the Internet Explorer status bar at the bottom of the window.

Going to a Specific Site

Another way to go to a specific site on the Web is to use a Web site address. For example, if someone gives you a Web address (a URL, or uniform resource locator) to investigate, you can type it directly into the Address box located at the top of the screen. In Figure 1.3, for example, you would click and drag to select the current address (`http://www.msn.com/`) and then type a new address in its place. Try `http://www.quepublishing.com` if you don't have another address handy, and then press **Enter**. In fact, because Microsoft Internet Explorer is pretty smart, you don't have to type the http:// prefix to go to a particular site. Typing www.quepublishing. com and pressing **Enter** takes you to the Que Publishing home page, as shown in Figure 1.4.

Figure 1.4   You can jump to Web sites by typing their URLs into the Address box.

Using Back and Forward

Internet Explorer makes it easy for you to move backward and forward when you are visiting Web sites. You can use the **Back** button to return to the previous site or the **Forward** button to move forward one site (which would be the site you visited before clicking the **Back** button). Both of these buttons are found on the left side of the Internet Explorer toolbar.

When you first open Internet Explorer, neither the Back nor Forward button is available. As soon as you click a hyperlink on the current Web site and move to another site, the Back button becomes active. This means that you can return to the original Web site by clicking **Back**.

If you do click **Back**, Internet Explorer remembers the site address that you just left, and the Forward button becomes available. Click **Forward** to jump back to this second site that you visited.

As soon as you click another hyperlink on either of the pages, the Forward button will again become inactive. Only going back to the page that contained the hyperlink (that got you where you are now) reactivates the Forward button.

Notice that the Back and Forward buttons both have down-pointing arrows. Click one of these arrows to open a drop-down list of all the places you have been during this session, and click the one you want. For example, to return to a site you visited recently, click the **Back** drop-down arrow and select a site from the list.

 TIP **Getting Back Home** You can quickly return to your home page by clicking the **Home** button on the Internet Explorer toolbar.

Specifying Your Home Page

If you have a Web site that you frequently visit or your own home page, you can make it the home page for Internet Explorer. Then, whenever you start a new Internet Explorer session or click the **Home** button on the toolbar, you are taken to that site.

To set your own home page in Internet Explorer, follow these steps:

1. Use Internet Explorer to go to the Web site that you want to make your new home page.

2. In the Internet Explorer window, select the **Tools** menu and then select **Internet Options**.

3. Click the **General** tab of the Internet Options dialog box (see Figure 1.5). The address of the default home page currently appears in the Address box. To make the site that you have open in the browser window your home page, click the **Use Current** button.

Figure 1.5 You can make any Web site your home page.

4. When you have finished making your selection, click **OK** to close the Internet Options dialog box.

Exiting Internet Explorer

When you have finished working in Internet Explorer (which is discussed in the lessons that follow in this section of the book), you will want to close the Internet Explorer window. Select **File**, **Close**, or click the **Close** (**x**) button on the upper-right corner of the Internet Explorer window.

Creating and Managing Internet Explorer Favorites

In this lesson, you learn to add, manage, and remove your favorite Web sites from the Internet Explorer Favorites list.

Adding Internet Explorer Favorites

Microsoft Internet Explorer makes it easy for you to return to your favorite Web sites. It's just a matter of going to the site and then adding it to the Internet Explorer Favorites list. You can then access this list and quickly go to a site of your choice.

To add a Web site to your Favorites list, follow these steps:

1. Open the Internet Explorer window and go to a Web site you want to add to the Favorites list. You can type the site's address into the **Address** box, use a link to go to the site, or use **Search** to locate the site (searching the Web is discussed in Lesson 5, "Searching the World Wide Web").

2. Select the **Favorites** menu, and then select **Add to Favorites**. The Add Favorite dialog box appears (see Figure 2.1). The Add Favorite dialog box offers options related to adding the current site to your Favorites list:

   - **Make Available Offline**—Click this check box if you want to have the content on this site downloaded to your computer periodically so that you can view the site offline.

   - **Name**—Type a name for the site (if you want to change the default listing) into this box.

   - **Create In**—If you want to place the Favorite listing into an existing folder, click the **Create In** button (you can also create a new folder to hold the item). The Add Favorite dialog box expands and shows the existing folders available. Double-click the folder you want to place the listing in.

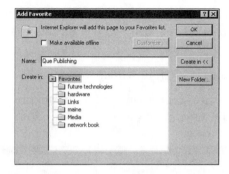

Figure 2.1 Use the Add Favorite dialog box to add a Web site to your Favorites list.

3. Select the options you want to use, as discussed earlier, and then click **OK** to add the site to the Favorites list (if you don't select any options, the Web site is placed on the main Favorites list).

TIP **Create a Folder for the Web Site Address** If you want to create a folder to hold the listing, click the **New Folder** button in the expanded Add Favorite dialog box. The Create New Folder dialog box appears. Type a name for the folder and then click **OK**.

Using the Favorites List

After you've added a site or sites to the Favorites list, you can quickly access them at any time. You will find that Internet Explorer also provides a default list of favorites that provides links to different Microsoft sites and media sites, such as CNBC. Internet Explorer provides two ways to view your Favorites list and select the site you want to go to.

To access your favorites from the Favorites menu, follow these steps:

1. Select the **Favorites** menu.

2. Select the site you want to go to from the list that appears.

TIP **Access a Folder Holding an Address** If you placed the site address into a folder on the Favorites list, point at the folder and select the site you want to go to.

After you select the site from the list, the site's address appears in the Internet Explorer Address box. You then are taken to the site.

You can also open a Favorites pane on the left side of the Internet Explorer window. This enables you to easily view your favorites and then select from the list as needed.

To open the Favorites pane, follow these steps:

1. Click the **Favorites** button on the Internet Explorer toolbar. The Favorites pane appears on the left side of the Explorer window (see Figure 2.2).

Figure 2.2 The Favorites pane enables you to view all your favorites and the folders that you have created.

2. Select the site you want to go to from the list (or point at a folder to view the site address that it contains).

When you have finished working with the Favorites pane, click the **Close** (**x**) button in its upper-left corner to close the pane.

TIP   **Add a Web Site Address from the Favorites Pane**   If you have the Favorites pane open, you can add your current Web site to the list. Click the **Add** button at the top of the pane, and the Add Favorites dialog box appears.

Organizing Your Favorites

You might find that over time you end up with a fairly large Favorites list. In fact, if you accumulate enough Web addresses, when you click the Favorites menu, the list is so large that you have to scroll through the possibilities to find the site you want to access.

You can organize your favorites into folders that make it easier for you to view the sites in the Favorites list. For example, you might want to take all the sites related to comedy or humor and place them in a Comedy folder. You also might want to delete sites from your Favorites list that you don't visit anymore or that are no longer available.

To organize the sites in your Favorites list, follow these steps:

1. Select the **Favorites** menu and then select **Organize Favorites**. The Organize Favorites dialog box appears (see Figure 2.3). This dialog box offers you several options for managing the sites on your Favorites list:

   - **Create Folder**—Click this button to create a new folder to hold a site (or sites). The Create New Folder dialog box appears. Type a name for the folder and then click **OK**. The folder appears on the Favorites list.

   - **Rename**—Select a site on the list, and then click **Rename**. Type a new name for the selected site.

   - **Move to Folder**—Select a site, and then click the **Move to Folder** button. The Browse for Folder dialog box appears. Select the folder you want to place the site address in, and then click **OK**.

   - **Delete**—Select a site, and then click the **Delete** button to remove the site from your Favorites list. You are asked to confirm the deletion; click **Yes**.

Figure 2.3 The Organize Favorites dialog box enables you to manage the sites you placed on your Favorites list.

2. When you have completed organizing your Favorites list, click **Close** to close the Organize Favorites dialog box.

 TIP **Organize Your Favorites from the Favorites Pane** If you have the Favorites pane open, you can access the Organize Favorites dialog box; click the **Organize** button at the top of the pane.

Downloading Files Using Internet Explorer

In this lesson, you learn how to download software files from the Web using Internet Explorer.

Getting Software on the Web

As you explore the Web with Internet Explorer, you might find that the World Wide Web not only is a huge collection of informational Web sites, but it also enables you to download files from software libraries and then use these software applications on your computer. These software products come in two flavors: shareware and freeware.

Shareware   Typically, a fully operational program that asks you to send the programmer of the product a certain fee. Sometimes shareware products operate only for a limited time (a month or so) so that you can use the software and then decide whether you want to keep using it by paying the programmer. Some shareware is called "nag-ware" because it will constantly remind you that you need to pay the author of the program if you want to keep using it.

Freeware   Programs you can download and use free. These are usually add-on programs or other specialty programs written by someone who needed a particular application. They then share it with anyone who would like to use the program.

The software applications available on the Web range from Web browser add-ons such as Macromedia Shockwave and Adobe Acrobat Reader (both discussed in Lesson 4, "Using Internet Explorer Add-Ons," in this section of the book) to full-blown applications. Other types of programs you're likely to come across include home finance programs, drawing programs, and computer games. You name it—it's probably available for downloading from the Web.

Locating the Best Sites

Quite a few sites exist on the Web that you can download files from. These sites range from catchall sites that contain a variety of types of software, to sites that contain specific categories of software, such as Internet-related applications.

You can start your own search for software sites using the Search feature in Internet Explorer (see Lesson 5, "Searching the World Wide Web"). You can search for sites that contain software downloads by searching for keywords such as **freeware** or **shareware**. Some Web sites that are considered the best sites to find and download software from are listed in Table 3.1.

Table 3.1   Web Sites Containing Freeware and Shareware

Web Site	Type of Software	URL Address
Shareware.com	A large collection of shareware and freeware in nearly all categories. Shareware.com has its own search engine for locating files.	`www.shareware.com`
TUCOWS	The Ultimate Collection of Winsock Software (thus the name TUCOWS) contains Internet-related shareware and freeware. TUCOWS rates each software product.	`www.tucows.com`
Microsoft	Microsoft provides updates and patches for all its products (such as Windows and the Office applications), and freeware tools and trial software applications for downloading.	`www.microsoft.com`
CNET	CNET provides a download page that links you to sites where you can download games, shareware, and freeware software, and even MP3 and other audio files.	`download.cnet.com`

TIP   **Be Careful Downloading from Obscure or Unfamiliar Sites**   Most of the sites that offer shareware and freeware (particularly those listed in Table 3.1) make sure that the files they offer are virus free. Not all sites, however, spend the time and effort necessary to make sure that the files they contain are virus and error free. You download at your own risk, so try to use sites that claim to provide virus-free files.

Downloading Files

Downloading files is really a matter of locating the specific file on a site, clicking its hyperlink, and then letting Internet Explorer take over. Selecting a particular hyperlink either begins the download process or takes you to a Web page where links are provided for the actual download. When it begins the download process, Internet Explorer simply pulls a copy of the file off the site hosting it and places it on your computer.

To download a file from a Web site, follow these steps:

1. Go to the Web site from which you want to download a file (such as TUCOWS).

2. Select the type of software or the operating system you use to see a list of files available (in the case of TUCOWS, software is listed according to the operating system it is designed for, such as Windows 2000).

3. Most sites provide a list of software categories for you to choose from (see Figure 3.1). For example, if you want to download an add-on for your Internet Explorer browser, click the **Browser Add-Ons** link.

4. Scroll down through the list of files provided. Many of the applications available on the major software download sites (such as TUCOWS) are rated, and reviews are available. When you find the application you want to download, click the download link for that application.

5. After you click the download link, the File Download dialog box appears (see Figure 3.2). Click **OK** to begin the download.

6. The Save As dialog box appears. Choose the folder and drive on your computer that you want to have the file saved on. Then click **Save**.

A download dialog box appears that keeps you apprised of the download of the selected file. The time that it takes to download the file depends on the speed of your Internet connection and the size of the file. The File Download dialog box tells you when the download is complete. Click **Close** to close the dialog box.

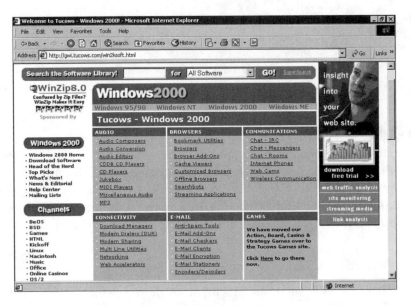

Figure 3.1   Most sites provide categories of software applications for you to choose from.

Figure 3.2   The File Download dialog box allows you to save the file to your computer.

Installing a Downloaded Application

After the file has been downloaded to your computer, you can install the software. Because most software you download from the Web has been compressed to speed up download times, you must have WinZip (see the WinZip tip in this section) or some file compression/decompression utility installed on your computer that you can use to decompress the installation files.

TIP   **WinZip**   WinZip is a tool that is used to "zip" (compress) and "unzip" (decompress) files that you download from the Web. Files that you download are typically zipped so that they don't take up a lot of space on the Web server that stores them and so that you can download them faster. You can download WinZip from Shareware.com and the WinZip site at `www.winzip.com`. If you are using Microsoft Windows Me or Microsoft Windows 2000 (or even Windows XP), a Zip-compatible tool is built into Windows Explorer, which makes it easy for you to open compressed files without installing WinZip or another zip program.

Unzipping a Downloaded File

Unzipping downloaded files from the Web is usually a very straightforward process that can be done using Windows Explorer and a zip utility such as WinZip to unzip the files. The file you downloaded is actually a group of files called an *archive*. This archive contains all the files you need to install the application you downloaded. Zip archives appear as a single file icon in Windows Explorer.

To unzip an application you've downloaded from the Web, follow these steps:

1. Right-click the **My Computer** icon on your Windows desktop and choose **Explorer** from the shortcut menu that appears (Windows Explorer opens).

2. In the left pane of the Internet Explorer window, click the drive that the down-loaded file resides on.

3. In the right pane of Internet Explorer, double-click the folder that holds the file.

4. Locate the downloaded file and double-click it.

5. If you have a WinZip-compatible compression program installed on your sys-tem, Windows opens that program and displays the contents of the compressed file (see Figure 3.3). If you're using WinZip, you can extract the compressed files by clicking the **Extract** button on the WinZip toolbar.

6. Specify a folder in the Extract dialog box that you want WinZip to place the extracted files into (such as your Windows Temporary folder).

7. Click **Extract** to extract the files to the specified folder.

TIP   **Some Downloaded Files Are Zipped and Some Are Not**   Some applications you download from the Web aren't zipped, but they are contained in autoexecutable compressed files. Just double-click their icons in the folders that they were down-loaded to. This begins the installation process. If you are using a version of Windows that supports compressed folders (the Microsoft version of Zip), you can even double-click zipped files and copy their contents to a new location in the Windows Explorer window.

Figure 3.3   WinZip opens the compressed file archive you downloaded.

Installing the Unzipped Application

After you've unzipped the file archive to a particular folder, you can then use the Windows Run dialog box to install the software. The installation process for the software you downloaded is the same or very similar to software that you bought on disk or on a CD.

After the application is installed on your computer, you can start it by clicking the **Start** button, pointing at **Programs**, and then clicking the icon for that particular application. Some applications also install a shortcut icon on the desktop that you can use to start the application. You can now use the software the same as you would any other software application.

Remember that you might be bound to certain restrictions when you are using shareware products. For example, you might be limited to a 30-day trial period. If you have any questions regarding the software, the best place to start is the help system provided with the particular application.

Using Internet Explorer Add-Ons

In this lesson, you learn how to use Internet Explorer add-ons such as Windows Media Player, Macromedia Shockwave, and the Adobe Acrobat Reader.

Understanding Internet Explorer Add-Ons

Internet Explorer provides a robust, full-featured Web browser; it's great for surfing the World Wide Web, searching for your favorite Web sites, and downloading files and software. Believe it or not, you can extend and enhance the capabilities of Explorer with browser add-ons—applications that work with Internet Explorer to allow you to view special Web content.

 Browser Add-On A miniprogram that runs in conjunction with the browser and that supplies you with additional Web tools, such as a viewer for special content such as Macromedia Shockwave.

Add-ons enhance your Web interactions in a variety of ways. For example, Windows Media Player enables you to play sound and video files on the Web. Other add-ons, such as Macromedia Shockwave, enable you to view interactive multimedia content that has been placed on a Web page.

Playing Video and Sound Files with Windows Media Player

Many sites on the Web provide video and sound files you can play. To play these files, click the appropriate link, and Windows Media Player (or whichever software application that you have made your default media player) opens. The video or audio file is played within the Media Player window. Although not an add-on for

Internet Explorer, Media Player is actually an add-on to the Windows operating system itself. And because Internet Explorer is tightly integrated with your Windows operating system, it takes advantage of this media utility to play any special media files it finds on the Web.

Media Player supports most of the sound and video formats found on the Web. You can play video files such as .avi, .mov, and others. A number of sound formats, including .wav, are also supported.

Media Player can also be used to play real-time video and audio feeds from the Web. For example, many sites, such as CNN (www.cnn.com) and MSNBC News (www.msnbc.com), provide live video and audio feeds you can view or listen to by using Media Player.

 TIP **Download the Latest Version of the Windows Media Player**   You can download and install the latest version of the Windows Media Player from the Windows Update Web site. Follow the steps provided in Lesson 1, "Using Internet Explorer," to obtain the latest version of the Media Player.

To use Windows Media Player, follow these steps:

1. Go to any site that provides links to audio or video content using Internet Explorer (try www.cnn.com). Many sites offer live news broadcasts and other media content you can view using Media Player. The Media Player itself also provides links to movie trailers and a number of sites that provide sound and video links.

2. Click a link to the video (or audio) content. In some cases, you click a **Play** button on a video box showing a frame of the video that plays (in some cases, you might also have to select Media Player as the player for the content available on a site).

3. The Media Player window opens (see Figure 4.1). You might have to wait a moment for the video to begin playing. After the video (or audio) has finished playing, click the **Close** (**x**) button in the upper-right corner of the Media Player window to close it.

Figure 4.1   You will find a large number of sites on the Web that provide video and audio content.

Using Shockwave

You already know that you can play and view audio, video, and animation files on the Web using Windows Media Player. Going to the next step and adding interactivity to special content on the Web greatly increases the possibilities for learning and fun on the Web.

Macromedia, the company that developed interactive multimedia authoring tools such as Macromedia Director and AuthorWare, has developed a way to get interactive multimedia onto the Web: a product called Shockwave.

When you have the Shockwave add-on for Internet Explorer installed on your computer, you can interact with multimedia content on Web sites. This content is regular interactive multimedia (developed in Director or AuthorWare) that has been *shocked* for the Web. Shocked content can be used to provide interactive games, educational content, and more—all on the Web.

Shocked   Multimedia content that has been converted to Web content using Shockwave.

You can download the latest version of Shockwave from the Macromedia Web site at www.shockwave.com. After you've installed this add-on, you're ready to take advantage of shocked content on the Web (for more about downloading and installing applications from the Web, see Lesson 3, "Downloading Files Using Internet Explorer").

To view shocked content on the Web, follow these steps:

1. Use the Internet Explorer to go to a Web site that contains Shockwave content. A good place to start is Macromedia's Shockwave site at www.shockwave.com. It provides links to games, animations, and all kinds of interactive Shockwave content.

2. Click a link, such as **Shows**, on this page.

3. You are taken to a page that provides links to Shockwave animations. Click any of the links to play one of the animations.

 TIP **Patience** On a normal dial-up Internet connection, some shocked content can take a long time to load into your Web browser window; at times, this requires you to be very patient.

Although you might find some of the shocked content on the Web frivolous and even idiotic, sites exist that are attempting to use shocked content for educational and informational purposes. Use your favorite search engine to see what kind of shocked content you can find.

 TIP **Install Shockwave Flash** Many Web sites also use Shockwave Flash content for short animations and other multimedia events on their Web pages. You might also want to download and install Flash when you visit the Macromedia Web site.

Using Adobe Acrobat Reader

Another extremely useful Web browser add-on is the Adobe Acrobat Reader. Adobe Acrobat is a tool that is used to convert manuals, books, and other content that has been desktop published to Web content. This allows you to view content in the Adobe Acrobat Reader that looks very much like material that you would see in a printed book.

The Adobe Acrobat Reader is freeware, which means that you can download and use it without a fee. You can download and install the latest version of the Adobe Acrobat Reader from the Adobe Acrobat Reader Web site at www.adobe.com/products/acrobat/main.html. Because it is freeware, you are restricted to using it only for reading documents that use its .pdf file format.

CAUTION

The Adobe Acrobat Reader Does Not Create Acrobat Files The freeware Adobe Acrobat Reader is used to view existing .pdf files; it does not enable you to create Acrobat files. If you want to create your own Acrobat .pdf files, you must purchase the full-featured Adobe Acrobat program from Adobe. The Adobe site referenced in this section also supplies information about the Adobe Acrobat software.

After the Acrobat Reader is installed (you download and install it as discussed in Lesson 3, "Downloading Files Using Internet Explorer"), you can access Acrobat content provided on any Web site. All you have to do is click a link to an Adobe Acrobat document that is provided by a particular Web site.

When you click the link, Adobe Acrobat Reader loads automatically. The Acrobat content appears in an Internet Explorer window, as shown in Figure 4.2.

Adobe Acrobat Reader toolbar

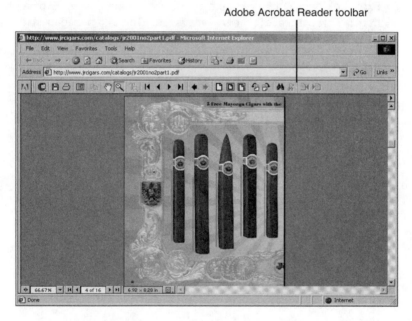

Figure 4.2 Adobe Acrobat content opens in the Internet Explorer window.

When you view Adobe Acrobat content in the Internet Explorer window, a special Acrobat toolbar is added to the Internet Explorer window (refer to Figure 4.2). It provides Previous Page and Next Page buttons that can be used to move through the pages of the Acrobat document. A Zoom button enables you to change the mouse into a Zoom tool that can be used to zoom in and out on the pages of the Acrobat document.

Some Adobe Acrobat documents can even be saved to your hard drive so that you can consult them later without having to access the Web site that provided the link to the document. Click the **Save** button on the Acrobat toolbar, and then specify a location for the Acrobat file on your computer in the Save As dialog box. Click **Save** when you are ready to save the file. You can open the file later by accessing it in Windows Explorer and then double-clicking the filename to start the Adobe Acrobat Reader.

When you are finished viewing the Adobe Acrobat content, you can close the Internet Explorer window that contains it. Click the **Close (x)** button in the upper-right corner of the window.

 TIP   **Other Add-Ons of Note**   Microsoft also supplies other add-ons for Internet Explorer. Check out some of the possibilities at the Internet Explorer home page: `http://www.microsoft.com/Windows/IE/`. This site provides links to add-ons such as special Internet Explorer navigation bars that can be added to the Explorer window. One Internet Explorer bar especially designed for children, called Surf Monkey, can be used to block access to inappropriate sites and sites using inappropriate language as kids browse the Web.

Searching the World Wide Web

In this lesson, you learn how to search the World Wide Web using Internet Explorer.

Setting Up a Simple Search

Internet Explorer enables you to search for Web pages, people's e-mail addresses, and even for maps and information about businesses contained in online yellow pages. Internet Explorer also gives you easy access to many search engines, such as MSN, Lycos, and Yahoo!.

TIP **How Search Engines Work** Search engines are basically giant databases that collect information from the Web sites on the World Wide Web. They build their databases based on keywords that are found on the sites themselves. That's why you often get mixed results when you do a search by a particular keyword. Searching the Web using the word "cheese" gets you plenty of matches that supply information on cheese, but you also get matches such as the Cheesiest Web Sites on the Web.

The absolute easiest way to conduct a simple search for a Web site on the World Wide Web is to type a keyword related to the site into the Address box of Internet Explorer. You can conduct this type of simple search no matter what Web site you are currently visiting.

For example, suppose you want to find the Comedy Central Web site but you're not sure of its actual address. Type **comedy** into the Address box at the top left of the Internet Explorer window and then press **Enter**.

A list of Web addresses found by searching for the "comedy" keyword appears in the browser window. Notice in Figure 5.1 that one of the listed sites is for Comedy Central.

When you run a simple search like the one described here, Internet Explorer uses the default search engine to do the search. By default, Internet Explorer uses the MSN search engine.

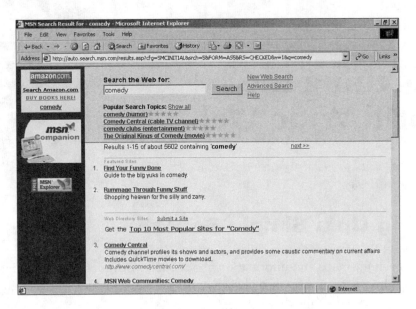

Figure 5.1 You can run a simple search right from the Address box.

After you are taken to the MSN search page (shown in Figure 5.1), you can use the Search box at the top of the page to do a new search, or you can supply more keywords and repeat your current search. Just type keywords into the search box provided and then click the **Search** button.

TIP **Searching from the MSN Home Page** If you use MSN as your home page, you can also do quick, simple searches using the Search box provided at the top right of the MSN home page. Just enter your search terms and then click **Go**.

Using the Search Pane

If you prefer to have a little more control over your search and would also like to have Internet Explorer remain on the current Web page that you are browsing, you can conduct a search from the Search pane. Not only does the Search pane enable you to search for Web sites, e-mail addresses, and other information, but you can also customize the Search pane to use different search engines when you search.

Click the **Search** button on the Explorer toolbar. A Search pane appears, as shown in Figure 5.2.

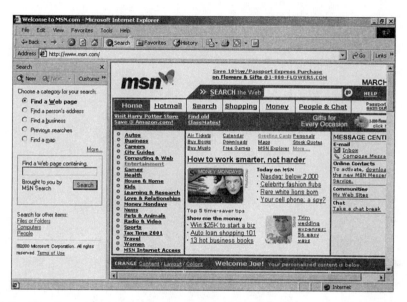

Figure 5.2   The Search pane provides you with more control over your search parameters.

Several option buttons appear at the top of the Search pane and enable you to select the type of item you are looking for, such as a particular Web site, a person's address, information on a company, and so on. Click the appropriate option button. After selecting the type of item you want to search for, you must enter the actual search parameters. Next, take a look at using some of these options.

Searching for Web Pages

The first search type found in the Search pane is Find a Web Page. It is certainly one of the most common searches that you will run when using the Search feature. Like your simple search performed earlier in the lesson, type your search parameters into the Search box, and then click the **Search** button.

The results of your search are listed in the Search pane (the Internet Explorer window remains on the current Web site). Because only a subset of the results can be listed in the Search pane, you can view more results by scrolling to the bottom of the Search pane and clicking **Next**; more results are displayed (to go back to the previous list of results at any time, click **Previous**).

If you find that your search didn't really provide the results that you wanted, you can run an advanced search. Click the **Use Advanced Search** button near the top of the Search pane to bring up the controls for an advanced search (see Figure 5.3). The Advanced Search button appears only after you have run a simple search as described previously.

Figure 5.3 The Advanced Search commands enable you to refine your search parameters.

To refine your search using the Advanced Search feature, you can do the following:

- Use the Find drop-down box to specify how multiple search terms should be handled. Select **All the Words**, **Any of the Words**, **Exact Phrase**, or other parameters provided to change how Search uses your keywords.

- Use the Language box to specify the language that should be used for the search. All is the default, but you can also choose to search in a specific language, such as German, English, Spanish, and many other languages.

- Use the Within Domain box to specify a particular Internet domain for your search. For example, specifying Microsoft.com would limit the search to Microsoft Web pages.

- The Modified Between boxes can be used to enter a range of dates that specify when the Web site you are searching for was last modified.

- Use the Results Must Contain check boxes to specify that sites matching the search criteria contain images, video, audio, and so on (this search parameter is useful if you are searching for a particular media type, such as MP3 audio files).

After specifying your advanced search parameters, click the **Search** button. The results of your search appear in the Search pane.

 TIP **Rerun Previous Searches** If you want to rerun a previous search that you conducted, click the **Previous Searches** option button in the Search pane. Searches (the last 10) that you have run appear in a list. Just click a previous search to run it.

Searching for People

The Internet Explorer Search pane can also be used to search for information about people. For example, it can be used to try to find an e-mail address for a specific person (you can also use it to find a person's mailing address).

Follow these steps:

1. If required, click the **New** button at the top of the Search pane to clear any previous search information.
2. Click the **Find a Person's Address** option button at the top of the Search pane.
3. In the Search For drop-down box, select **E-Mail Address**.
4. Type the person's name into the First Name and Last Name boxes (see Figure 5.4).

Figure 5.4   You can search for a person's e-mail address.

5. If you know the city and the state for the person, type the information into the appropriate boxes.
6. When you complete entering your information, click the **Search** button.

The results of your search appear in the Search pane. You can actually send an e-mail message to the person using an e-mail address that appears in the search results. Click the e-mail address and a new e-mail message window appears, using your default e-mail client (such as Outlook or Outlook Express). Type your e-mail message and then click **Send**.

Searches for E-Mail Addresses Can Provide Out-of-Date Information   In the case of e-mail addresses and other information that you search for related to people (such as addresses), the information can often be out of date. Just run a search for your own e-mail address and you might find that old e-mail addresses you have used are returned by the search rather than your current e-mail address.

CAUTION

Finding a Map

The Internet Explorer Search pane also enables you to find a map of an address or a particular landmark. Start a new search by clicking the **New** button at the top of the Search pane. Then select the **Find a Map** option button. Enter an address (or land-mark), a city, a state/province, and/or a ZIP code into the appropriate boxes.

When you are ready to search for a map of the address or place that you have speci-fied, click the **Search** button. A map of the destination appears in the Internet Explorer window, as shown in Figure 5.5.

Figure 5.5   You can find a map of an address.

Customizing the Search Feature

You can control the search engines that the Internet Explorer Search feature uses for the various types of searches that it provides. You can also determine the order in which the different Web search engines are used when you conduct your search.

To view the Search pane's Customize Search Settings dialog box, click the **Customize** button. The Customize Search Settings page opens (see Figure 5.6).

Figure 5.6   You can customize the Search feature by selecting the search engines it uses for the various types of searches you conduct.

The page is broken down into 12 parts, each part controlling a different type of search, such as Find a Web Page, Find a Person's Address, Find a Company, Find a Map, and so on (the last section of the Customize page enables you to set the number of previous searches shown in the Search pane). Scroll down to the search type you want to customize.

For example, in the Find a Web Page section, you can select among eight search engines to conduct this type of search by selecting some or all of the check boxes provided for the various search engines. You can also select a particular search engine already appearing in the list and use the Move Up or Move Down buttons (directly below the search engine box) to change the position of the search engine in the list (the position in the list is used to determine the order in which the search engines run when a particular search is conducted).

After you have customized your search options, click the **OK** button to accept the changes that you have made and return to the Search pane. You can now run a new search based on the settings you placed in the Customize window.

When you have finished working with the Search pane, you can close it. Click the **Close (x)** button at the top right of the Search pane.

Setting Internet Explorer Options

In this lesson, you learn how to set the various Internet Explorer options.

Deleting Temporary Files and the History

Internet Explorer enables you to control many configuration settings that are related to how Internet Explorer actually operates. All these configuration settings are handled in the Internet Options dialog box, which is the subject of this lesson.

When you work with Internet Explorer, you will find that it accumulates temporary files and offline content that take up space on your computer's hard drive. Internet Explorer also keeps a history of the sites that you visit. The history can be used to access Web sites that you've recently visited (see the "Using the History to Access Visited Web Sites" tip).

 TIP **Using the History to Access Visited Web Sites** To view your History file and use it to access visited Web sites, click the **History** button on the Internet Explorer toolbar. A History pane opens that lets you use the different folders it contains (such as the Today folder) to access a list of visited sites. When you find a site you want to visit, click the link in the History pane.

You can delete the temporary files that Internet Explorer has accumulated and control how long the History file should store accumulated Web site addresses before it deletes them. To perform these tasks, follow these steps:

1. In the Internet Explorer window, select the **Tools** menu, and then select **Internet Options**. The Internet Options dialog box appears. Be sure the General tab is selected (see Figure 6.1).

2. To delete temporary files, click the **Delete Files** button; the Delete Files dialog box appears.

3. If you want to also delete offline content (accumulated for sites you included in your Favorites list that you have set to view offline), click the **Delete All Offline Content**.

4. To delete the temporary files and the offline content (if selected), click **OK**.

Figure 6.1 The General tab of the Internet Options dialog box enables you to delete temporary and history files.

After the files are deleted, you are returned to the General tab of the Internet Options dialog box. To change the days to keep pages in history, use the spinner box provided. You can delete accumulated history files by clicking the **Clear History** button. You are asked whether you want to delete the history file; click **Yes**.

When you have finished clearing the temporary files and the history file (remember, this is only an option; you don't have to clear either), you can close the Internet Options dialog box. Click **OK** to return to the Internet Explorer window.

Setting Security Options

Although Internet Explorer is configured to enable you to easily interact with Web sites on the World Wide Web and freely download files and add-ons for your browser, you can control some of these parameters using the Internet Options dialog box. You can add sites to a trusted list and sites to restricted list. When sites in the restricted list are accessed using Internet Explorer, certain features, such as the capability to download files for the site, are disabled.

Probably the best way to approach using the security options is to create a list of restricted sites. This assumes that any other sites on the Web are trusted (which is the default setting for any and all Web sites on the Web). As you come across sites that you do not feel comfortable with, you can add them to the restricted list. This feature doesn't actually block content, just the capability of a particular site to damage your computer by automatically downloading a virus or other destructive program.

To take advantage of the security options related to Internet Explorer, follow these steps:

1. Open the Internet Options dialog box (select **Tools, Internet Options**). Select the **Security** tab (see Figure 6.2).

Figure 6.2 The Security tab of the Internet Options dialog box allows you to disable certain Internet Explorer features for restricted sites.

2. As mentioned previously, if you want to use this feature, your best bet is just to add sites you don't trust or those to which you want to restrict certain features (such as file downloads) to the restricted list. Click the **Restricted Sites** icon at the top of the dialog box, and then click the **Sites** button. The Restricted Sites dialog box appears (see Figure 6.3).

Figure 6.3 Add restricted sites to the Restricted Sites dialog box.

830

3. Type the Web address of the site in the Add This Web Site to the Zone box. Then click the **Add** button. Add as many sites as you want, but remember that access to these sites will be restricted.

4. When you have finished adding sites to the list, click **OK**.

5. To view the restrictions that are placed on restricted sites, click the **Custom Level** button on the Security tab (be sure the Restricted Sites icon is selected). The Custom Level dialog box opens.

6. Scroll through the list of restrictions. Notice that features such as the downloading of ActiveX controls (which are often used to view special content on a site) and the capability to download files from restricted sites have been disabled. Because the whole purpose of the security feature is to disable the restricted site's capability to damage your computer, you will probably want to leave these settings as they are. Click **OK** to close the dialog box.

If you have finished working with the Internet Options dialog box, click **OK** to close the dialog box. Use the Security options only if you feel that you need this level of protection from certain sites on the Web (and in cases where you share your computer with other users, particularly children).

Using the Content Advisor

You can use the Internet Explorer Content Advisor to block access to sites that contain inappropriate language, nudity, and violence. Although this feature will not block objectionable sites as well as special software packages such as Net Nanny do, you can use it to help corral some of the sites that can be accessed by children who use Internet Explorer on your computer.

Follow these steps:

1. Open the Internet Options dialog box (select **Tools, Internet Options**). Select the **Content** tab.

2. To turn this feature on and determine the level of control, click the **Enable** button at the top of the Content tab. The Content Advisor opens (see Figure 6.4).

3. On the Ratings tab, select one of the content areas such as **Language** to set the restriction level. Having the slider set to 0 is the most restrictive. In the case of language, it allows only sites that contain inoffensive slang.

4. Set the restriction level for each of the items (such as Language or Nudity) using the Ratings tab.

Figure 6.4   Use the Content Advisor to set content restrictions.

5. To password protect the Content Advisor settings (so that a password is required to change the settings or to access content that these settings have restricted), click the **General** tab. Be sure that the Supervisor Can Type a Password check box is selected. Then click the **Change Password** dialog box.

6. Enter a new password into the Change Supervisor Password dialog box and confirm the password. Then click **OK**.

7. When you have finished working with the Content Advisor, click **OK**. Then click **OK** to close the Internet Options dialog box.

CAUTION

Understand the Content Advisor Before Using It   Be sure that you read this section carefully and also read the help section that Internet Explorer provides regarding the Content Advisor (see Lesson 5, "Getting Help in Microsoft Office," in the first section of this book for general information on using Help). This feature can be very useful to limit access to objectionable content, but only if you configure it correctly.

Setting Associated Programs

When you are browsing the Web using Internet Explorer, you will come across hyperlinks that lead to destinations, such as e-mail addresses and Internet newsgroups, that Internet Explorer is not equipped to deal with. You can make sure that the appropriate helper application opens when you access these special content links using the Programs tab of the Internet Options dialog box.

Follow these steps:

1. Open the Internet Options dialog box (select **Tools, Internet Options**). Select the **Programs** tab (see Figure 6.5).

Figure 6.5   Use the Programs tab to specify which helper applications are used by Internet Explorer.

2. Use the drop-down boxes to select the application that you want Internet Explorer to use when executing an operation in each category. For example, to have Internet Explorer open an e-mail application if you click an e-mail hyper-link, select the E-Mail drop-down list and select an e-mail client. Generally, your options include Microsoft Outlook, Outlook Express, and Hotmail (if you have a Hotmail account).

3. When you have finished making your selections, click **OK** to close the dialog box.

Most of the time, Internet Explorer already has the programs you use for these func-tions set as the default. Therefore, change these settings only if you know that your setup uses one of the alternative applications that are listed on the various drop-down lists.

Using the Internet Explorer Radio Toolbar

In this lesson, you learn how to use the Internet Explorer Radio toolbar.

Opening the Radio Toolbar

If your computer is outfitted with a sound card and speakers, you can listen to the radio as you browse the Web using Internet Explorer. The World Wide Web offers a large number of Web radio stations that provide a variety of music and talk radio. The easiest way to access this Web audio content is using the Internet Explorer Radio toolbar.

To open the Radio toolbar, select the **View** menu, point at **Toolbars**, and then select **Radio**. The Radio toolbar appears in the Internet Explorer window (see Figure 7.1).

Radio toolbar

Figure 7.1 The Radio toolbar makes it easy to access Web audio content.

The Radio toolbar enables you to select from many preset radio stations and also to select your own list of radio stations by searching the Web for radio content. Next, take a look at the different possibilities.

Using Radio Presets

One way to access music and talk-radio Web content is to use the preset stations that the Radio toolbar provides. Click the **Radio Station** button on the Radio toolbar, and then select **Radio Station Guide**. The Radio Station Guide appears in the Internet Explorer window (see Figure 7.2).

Figure 7.2   The Radio Station Guide provides a list of preset stations that you can access.

To listen to one of the preset stations, double-click the station in the Presets list. It might take a moment for the station to load, but you will then hear the broadcast. You can now browse the Web using Internet Explorer as you normally do. The radio station you selected continues to play, even when you leave the Radio Station Guide Web page.

Finding Specific Radio Content

The Preset list provides only a small subset of the Web radio content that is available. You can search for radio content on the Web using keyword searches. After you locate Web radio stations that provide the type of content that you like, you can add these stations to your own list of presets for easy access in the future.

To search for Web radio content, follow these steps:

1. Open the Radio toolbar if necessary (click **View**, **Toolbars**, **Radio**). Click the **Radio Station** button on the Radio toolbar, and then select **Radio Station Guide**.

2. In the Radio Station Guide window, click the **Station Finder** drop-down list and select the type of search you want to conduct. You can search by Format (such as Alternative Rock or Big Band), Language, and even keyword.

3. For example, if you select Keyword, a search box appears to the right of the Station Finder drop-down list. Type a keyword into the box and then click **Find**.

4. Web radio stations that match your search parameters appear in pthe Station Finder list (see Figure 7.3).

Figure 7.3 You can search for Web radio stations using the Station Finder feature.

5. To listen to one of the stations that you found, select the station in the Station Finder list, and then click the **Play** button at the bottom of the Radio Station Guide (or double-click the listing).

Creating Your Own Presets

When you find Web radio stations that you would like to access easily in the future, you can add them to your own list of presets. To create your own presets, follow these steps:

1. In the Radio Station Guide window, click the **Presets** drop-down list and select **My Presets**. If this is the first time you've used this feature, no presets are listed.

2. Select a radio station in the Station Finder pane that you want to add to your presets (you can run a new search before adding a station, as discussed in the previous section).

3. Click the **Add Station** button to place the radio station in your preset list (see Figure 7.4).

Figure 7.4   Add Web stations to your own list of presets.

4. Add other stations as you like (you can run other searches and then add stations to your preset list).

5. To play a radio station that you have added to your preset list, double-click the radio station.

Now you can access your own presets when you want to listen to a particular radio station. Just click the **Radio Station** button on the Radio toolbar and select **Radio Station Guide**. Click the **Presets** drop-down list and select **My Presets** to access your preset list. Double-click the radio station you want to listen to.

Accessing Mail and Newsgroups from Internet Explorer

In this lesson, you learn how to access and send e-mail from Internet Explorer and use the Outlook Express Newsreader.

Sending Web Pages As a Link

As you use Internet Explorer to browse the Web, you might find that you locate Web pages that you would like to share with colleagues or friends. You can send Web pages to others as a link that is placed in an e-mail message. Then, when the recipient of the e-mail message opens the message, the recipient can quickly access the Web page by clicking the link that you have provided.

To send a Web page as an e-mail link, follow these steps:

1. In the Internet Explorer window, access the Web page that you want to send as an e-mail link.

2. Click the **Mail** button on the Internet Explorer toolbar and select **Send a Link**.

3. A new e-mail message appears in your e-mail client, such as Outlook. Add the address of a recipient for the e-mail message and add a subject and any message text that you want.

4. Click the **Send** button to send the e-mail message containing the link.

 TIP **Accessing and Sending E-Mail from Internet Explorer**   You can also quickly open your e-mail client, such as Microsoft Outlook, directly from the Internet Explorer window. Click the **Mail** icon on the Internet Explorer toolbar and select **Read Mail**. If you want to send a new e-mail message, click the **Mail** icon and then select **New Message**. A new message window opens.

Sending Web Pages As an Attachment

You can also send Web pages as attachments to an e-mail message. This enables recipients of the message to view the attached Web page in their e-mail client, such as Outlook.

1. Access the Web page you want to send as an attachment, and then click the **Mail** button on the Internet Explorer toolbar and select **Send Page**.

2. A new e-mail message appears in your e-mail client, and the Web page appears in the message body.

3. Click **Send** to send the message.

When the recipient opens the message, the Web page appears in the body of the message. The recipient can click any of the links on the page to further explore the attached page.

CAUTION

Some E-Mail Clients Will Not Provide a View of the Web Page   If you send a Web page as an attachment to an e-mail message, some recipients might not be able to directly view the Web page when they open the e-mail message. They will have to open the attachment using their Web browser to view the page.

TIP

Using Outlook for E-Mail   For more information about using Outlook as an e-mail client, see Lessons 4, 5, and 6 in the Outlook section of this book.

Using Newsgroups

When you install Internet Explorer on a computer, Microsoft Outlook Express, an e-mail client and a newsreader, is also installed. And even though you probably use Microsoft Outlook as your e-mail program, Outlook Express can still be used to access newsgroups on the Internet (which Outlook cannot do). Newsgroups are a large collection of discussion groups held on news servers around the world. A particular newsgroup is much like a bulletin board; you can read messages posted there and post your own. Newsgroups cover information from current events to software, hobbies, pets, and other personal interests.

TERM

Newsgroup   An Internet online bulletin board that allows users to post and read messages. Newsgroups are part of Usenet, which is a consortium of Internet news servers that enable users (such as you) to download and post messages.

CAUTION

Don't Confuse Outlook Express with Outlook Outlook Express is a basic e-mail client and newsreader that is one of the Internet Explorer tools. It is not the same as the Outlook personal information manager that is discussed in Part II of this book.

Setting Up the Newsreader

You can access newsgroups from the Internet Explorer window by starting the Outlook Express Newsreader (it is one of the components that is installed when you download and install Internet Explorer). To use Outlook Express as a newsreader, follow these steps:

1. In the Internet Explorer window, click the **Mail** menu, and then click **Read News**. The Outlook Express Newsreader opens.

2. The first time you use the Outlook Express Newsreader, you are asked to subscribe to newsgroups that are supplied by your Internet service provider. Click **Yes** to view a list of available newsgroups.

TIP **Configuring Your Newsgroup Account** The first time you use Internet Explorer (as discussed in Lesson 1, "Using Internet Explorer," of this part of the book), the Internet Connection Wizard is run to configure your Internet connection. During this process you specify your newsgroup account information that your ISP must supply. If you didn't configure the newsgroup account information, rerun the Internet Connection Wizard (see Lesson 1) and configure the news server settings.

3. The Newsgroup Subscriptions dialog box appears (see Figure 8.1). This dialog box contains a very long list of newsgroups (depending on the speed of your Internet connection, this can take a while). To see a subset of the list, based on keywords, type a keyword into the Display Newsgroups Which Contain box.

Figure 8.1 Use the Newsgroup Subscriptions dialog box to subscribe to newsgroups that you want to use.

4. When you find a newsgroup that you might want to frequent, select the newsgroup in the Newsgroup list and then click **Subscribe**.

5. You can repeat step 4 as necessary to subscribe to other newsgroups.

6. After subscribing to the newsgroups you want to read, click **OK**.

 TIP **Check Out Newsgroups Before Subscribing** If you want to view the posts in a newsgroup before subscribing, select a newsgroup in the list and click **Go To**. This opens the newsgroup without subscribing.

You are returned to the Outlook Express window (see Figure 8.2). A list of the groups you subscribed to appears in the Newsgroup window on the right side of the Outlook Express window.

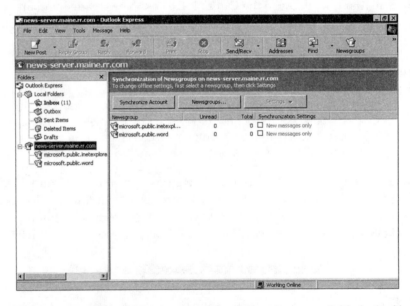

Figure 8.2 The newsgroups that you subscribe to are always available in the Newsgroup list on the left side of the Outlook Express window.

Reading Newsgroup Postings

After you have subscribed to a newsgroup or newsgroups, you are ready to read and post messages. If you have just subscribed to your newsgroups for the first time and have closed the Newsgroup Subscriptions dialog box, just click any of your subscribed groups to read the postings.

To read a particular message that appears when you open a group, select that message in the message list at the top of the Outlook Express window. The text in the post appears in the Preview pane at the bottom of the Outlook Express window (see Figure 8.3).

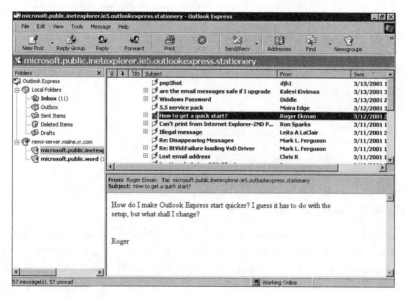

Figure 8.3 Just click a post to read it.

If you want to open a particular post in a separate window, double-click that post in the message list.

Posting to Newsgroups

You can also post your own messages to the newsgroups. These posts can be new posts or they can be replies or comments on posts that already exist in the newsgroups.

To send a post that is based on a current post (such as a reply or comment on the post) in the newsgroup, select the post message and click the **Reply Group** button on the Outlook Express toolbar. A new message box appears (see Figure 8.4). The subject of the post will be based on the post that you are replying to. Enter your post's text into the message box.

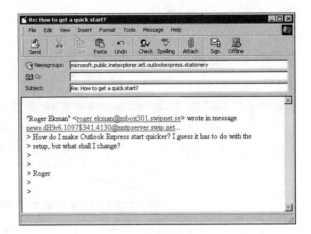

Figure 8.4   Type your reply post into the message box.

After you have finished typing the message, you can post it to the group. Click the **Send** button in the message window.

You can also post new messages to the newsgroup. Click the **New Post** button on the Outlook Express toolbar. A new message window opens. Type a subject for the message into the **Subject** box. Type the message itself into the Message pane of the new message window. After you've completed your message, click the **Send** button.

After you click the **Send** button, a message window appears, telling you that your new message has been posted but may not immediately appear with the messages already in the newsgroup.

When you have finished reading and sending newsgroup messages, you can switch to another newsgroup or you can close the Outlook Express Newsreader. Click the Outlook Express **Close** (**x**) button to close the Newsreader window. You are returned to the Internet Explorer, which was originally used to launch the newsreader.

Installing Microsoft Office XP

In this appendix, you learn how to install Microsoft Office XP on your computer.

Office XP Hardware Requirements

Before you install Microsoft Office XP, you should be sure that your computer meets the minimum hardware requirements needed to run the software correctly. The hardware needed to run Office XP is related to the version of the Windows operating system you are running on your computer. Different memory or RAM configurations are required by the different Windows operating systems, as follows:

- **Windows 98**—32MB of RAM (64MB of RAM is recommended).
- **Windows Me**—40MB of RAM (64MB of RAM is recommended).
- **Windows NT 4.0**—Service Pack 6 must be installed on the computer. RAM requirements are 40MB of RAM (with 64MB recommended).
- **Windows 2000**—72MB of RAM (128MB recommended).

No matter which Windows version you are using, you will also need 165MB of free hard-drive space (only 115MB of hard-drive space is required if you are installing Office XP on a computer that is already running Office 2000). Office XP also requires a Super VGA monitor and at least a Pentium class (or Pentium clone) processor that runs in excess of 133MHz.

Installing Microsoft Office from the CD-ROM

Installing Microsoft Office from its CD-ROM is very straightforward, especially because the CD autostarts when you place it into your CD-ROM drive. To begin a new installation of Office XP, place your CD-ROM into your CD-ROM drive. The CD autostarts, opening the Office Installation window.

TIP   **My Office CD-ROM Did Not Autostart**   You can load the installation software manually. Click the Windows **Start** button, and then click **Run**. In the Run box, type **D:\setup.exe**. Be sure that you designate the drive letter of your CD-ROM in the place of the "D" shown. Then click **OK** to load the Office installation program.

The Installation window welcomes you to the Office XP installation and asks you to provide your name, initials, organization, and the CD Product Key for your Office CD (see Figure A.1). The key is usually found on the back of the jewel case (on yellow sticker) that the Office CD came in.

Figure A.1   Provide your name and CD Product Key to begin the Office installation.

After you've provided this information (only a name and the CD Product Key are actually required), click **Next** to continue with the installation.

The next screen in the installation process asks you to read the license agreement for the Office software that you have purchased. After you have read the agreement, click the **I Accept the Terms in the License Agreement** option button and click **Next** to continue. If you don't agree with the license agreement, Office XP will not install.

The next screen is the installation type window and it provides three installation possibilities (see Figure A.2). You can select **Install Now**, which installs the most commonly used Office XP components.

If you want, you can choose to install absolutely all the Office XP files by selecting the **Complete** option button. The third installation possibility is to select the **Custom** option button; you will then have to specify the Office applications that you want to install on your computer.

This screen also enables you to choose a custom location for the installation files. If you don't want to install Office XP to the default location, select the **Browse** button, locate a new location in the Browse window, and then select it. Click **OK** to return to the Installation screen.

Figure A.2   You are provided with the option of a quick installation or you can do a complete or a custom installation.

Click **Next** after making your selection of the installation type. The sections that follow discuss what happens when you select the different installation types.

 TIP   **Previous Versions of Office Are Removed**   If you have a previous version of Office on your computer, the installation process removes it unless you specify otherwise. In any case, the Office XP applications replace any current versions of Office that you have on your computer.

Understanding the Typical and Complete Installations

When you select **Install Now**, you are basically leaving the installation up to the Office CD, which installs the applications and tools that are considered the common Office components (this includes all the Office core applications: Word, Excel, Access, PowerPoint, Outlook, and FrontPage).

The Install Now option requires no further input from you, and you will not be prompted again until after the typical Office components are installed on your C: drive. At the completion of the installation, a dialog box appears, letting you know that the installation was completed.

If you selected **Complete** on the installation type screen and then clicked **Next**, the CD again takes over and installs all the different Office components onto your computer. This installation takes longer than the typical installation discussed, but it does provide you with absolutely all the features that Office XP provides. It is a good installation choice if you have plenty of hard-drive space.

Selecting the Custom Installation

An alternative to the typical and complete installations is the Custom installation, which provides you with much more control over which Office components are installed.

When you select the **Custom** installation and then click **Next**, you are taken to a screen that enables you to select the Office components that should be installed (see Figure A.3). To deselect any of the Office applications from the installation, click the check box next to the application to clear it.

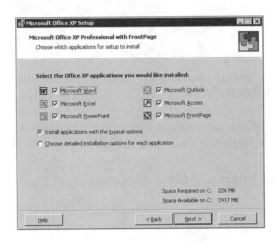

Figure A.3   In the Custom installation, you can specify the components that are to be installed.

You can further customize which components of each Office XP application are installed by clicking the **Choose Detailed Installation Options for Each Application** option button (recommended only if you are very familiar with each of these components and their functions). For the purposes of this book, we're going to stick with selecting the **Install Applications with the Typical Options** option button. After you deselect applications from the installation, click the **Next** button. The installation proceeds as discussed in the previous section.

Adding and Removing Office Components

No matter what type of installation you do (the typical, complete, or custom installation), after you start using your software, you might find that you would like to add components that were not installed during your initial run-through with the software. This doesn't pose a problem. Just insert the CD-ROM back into the CD-ROM drive. A window automatically opens. Click the **Add or Remove Features** button, and then select components that you want to install (or remove) in the Select Features interface window.

CAUTION   **My CD-ROM Doesn't Autorun**   If nothing happens when you insert the CD-ROM, you will have to start the Office installation manually. Click the Windows **Start** button, and then click **Run**. In the **Run** box, type `D:\setup.exe`. Be sure to designate the drive letter of your CD-ROM in the place of the "D" shown. Then click **OK** to load the Office installation program.

To add a component to your computer, you need to change it from its current Installed on First Use status or Not Available status. Click the particular component (remember, to view the components under a particular application such as Word or Excel, click the plus (+) symbol next to that application) and select **Run from My Computer** on the menu that appears.

To remove a component from your computer, click that component in the Features list and select **Not Available** on the menu.

After you've selected items to install (or remove from your computer), click the **Update Now** button in the Update Features window. The component is added (or removed). When the installation is complete, a notification box appears. Click **OK** to close it.

TIP   **What Is the Office Product Activation?**   The first time you start one of the Office applications, you will have to activate your copy of the Office software either by the Internet or over the phone. This is a new process devised by Microsoft to cut down the illegal copying of the Office software. Product Activation is discussed in more detail in Lesson 1, "What's New in Office XP?," in Part I of this book.

Index

Datasheet command (Access Format menu), 552

Datasheet Formatting dialog box (Access), 552

Datasheet tab (Access Options dialog box)
default font, 551
messages, 45

Datasheet view (Access), 525
creating tables, 530-531

Date/Time data type
Access tables, 529

dates (Excel worksheets)
entering, 412-415
formatting, 413, 457-458

Day/Week/Month view (Outlook), 96

Decrease Decimal button (Excel Formatting toolbar), 455

Decrease Font Size button (PowerPoint Formatting toolbar), 678

Decrease Indent button
Excel Formatting toolbar, 462
Word Formatting toolbar, 289, 344

Define command (Excel Insert, Name menu), 472-474

Define Name dialog box (Excel), 472

Define Views command (Outlook View menu), 96

Delete button (Outlook Inbox toolbar), 118-119

Delete Column command (Access Edit menu), 545

Delete Columns command (Access Edit menu), 604

Delete command
Access Edit menu, 536
Excel Edit menu, 454, 476-478
Outlook Edit menu, 118-119
Word Table menu, 350

Delete dialog box (Excel), 478

Delete key, 258

Delete Page dialog box (FrontPage), 750

Delete Query (Access), 600. *See also* queries

Delete Record command (Access Edit menu), 546

Delete Sheet command (Excel Edit menu), 483

Delete Slide command (PowerPoint Edit menu), 670

deleting
archive files (Outlook), 221-222
AutoText entries (Word), 324
cell comments (Excel), 411
column breaks (Word), 358
columns/rows (Word tables), 350
controls, Access reports, 618
e-mail accounts, 86-88
Excel data, 454
field contents (Access tables), 543
fields (Access tables), 535, 545
Design view, 527
graphics (Word), 367
hyperlinks
FrontPage Web pages, 784-785
Internet Explorer history/temporary files, 828-829
labels (Access forms), 569

naviagtion bars (FrontPage), 778
Office components, 848-849
Outlook folders, 123
page banners (FrontPage), 775
print jobs, 493
records (Access), 546-547
section breaks (Word documents), 383
slides (PowerPoint), 670
table relationships (Access), 558
table rows/columns (Word), 350
tables (Access), 535-536
tables of contents (Word), 386
tabs (Word), 287-288
tasks (FrontPage), 789
tasks (Outlook), 189
text
FrontPage Web pages, 756
Word, 258
Word tables, 349
text boxes (PowerPoint), 682
Web pages (FrontPage), 749-750
Folders view, 742
Navigation view, 750
worksheets (Excel), 483
cells, 478
rows/columns, 476

deleting e-mail, 118-120
undeleting, 118-119

delivery options, e-mail, 144-145

demoting/promoting text (PowerPoint slides), 659-660

design templates (PowerPoint). *See* templates, PowerPoint

V

values (Excel), 408

aligning, 461-463

entering, 411-412

custom series, 415-416

series, 414-415

formatting, 455-458

clearing formats, 458

Format Cells dialog box

Numbers tab, 456-458

style buttons (Formatting

toolbar), 455-456

**vertical text alignment (Excel),
461-462**

video

playing with Shockwave,
817-818

playing with Windows

Media Player, 815-817

PowerPoint presentations,
704-706

View button, Access

Form Design toolbar, 626

Table Datasheet toolbar,
531-532

Table Design toolbar, 529

View menu commands

Access

Form Header/Footer,
571

Toolbars, Task Pane, 515,
519

Toolbox, 572

Excel

Full Screen, 441

Page Break Preview, 494

Status Bar, 422

Office Task Pane, 20

Outlook

Current View, Customize
Current View, 147

Current View, Define
Views, 96

Folder List, 75

Options, 141

Outlook Bar, 75

Preview Pane, 75

Status Bar, 75

Toolbars, 75

PowerPoint, 653

Master, Slide Master, 661

Ruler, 687

Slide Sorter, 663, 666

Task Pane, 664, 685

Word

Document Map, 299

Full Screen, 297

Header and Footer,
327-332

Normal, 293

Outline, 296

Print Layout, 295

Ruler, 235, 287

Web Layout, 293

Zoom, 298

**View Show command
(PowerPoint Slide Show
menu), 713**

View tab

Excel Options dialog box,
423

PowerPoint Options dialog
box, 44

Word Options dialog box,
244

View toolbar (Word)

Normal button, 293

Outline button, 296

Print Layout button, 295

Web Layout button, 295

viewing

contacts (Outlook)

contact activities,
162-163. *See also* Journal
(Outlook)

Contacts list, 161-162

formulas (Excel), 423

FrontPage Web sites, 733,
739-745

Folders view, 741-742

Hyperlinks view, 744

Navigation view,
739-740, 749-750

Page view, 740-741, 747

Reports view, 743, 789

Tasks view, 744-745

Journal entries (Outlook),
192, 197-198

notes (Outlook), 201-202

page breaks (Excel), 494

query results (Access), 608

related records (Access),
622-623

reports (Access), 613-614

sent e-mail, 130-131

slides (PowerPoint), 653-654

Outline view, 655

slide shows, 713-714

Slide Sorter view, 654

switching views, 653-654

task panes, 20-21

Access, 515

tasks (Outlook), 187-188

Word documents, 292. *See
also* views, Word

split windows, 300-301

zooming, 298-299, 333

worksheets (Excel), 440-441

views

Access

Datasheet. *See* Datasheet
view (Access)

Design. *See* Design view
(Access)

Outlook

changing, 94-95

creating custom views,
96-97

Word

Document Map, 299-300

Full Screen, 297

Header and Footer, 327

Normal view, 293-294

X-Y-Z

Hey, you've got enough worries.

Don't let IT training be one of them.

Get on the fast track to IT training at InformIT,
your total Information Technology training network.

 │ **www.informit.com** │

- Hundreds of timely articles on dozens of topics ■ Discounts on IT books from all our publishing partners, including Que Publishing ■ Free, unabridged books from the InformIT Free Library ■ "Expert Q&A"—our live, online chat with IT experts ■ Faster, easier certification and training from our Web- or classroom-based training programs ■ Current IT news ■ Software downloads
- Career-enhancing resources